THIRD EDITION

Counseling Children

Charles L. Thompson
University of Tennessee at Knoxville

Linda B. Rudolph
Austin Peay State University

Brooks/Cole Publishing Company
Pacific Grove, California

Dedicated to our families

Harriet
Charles, Cynthia, Marcia

Bill
John, Steve, Andy

 A CLAIREMONT BOOK

Brooks/Cole Publishing Company
A Division of Wadsworth, Inc.

Printed in the United States of America
10   9   8   7   6   5   4   3

Library of Congress Cataloging in Publication Data
Thompson, Charles L.
    Counseling children / Charles L. Thompson, Linda B. Rudolph—3rd ed.
        p.   cm.
    Includes bibliographical references and index.
    ISBN 0-534-17196-6
1. Child psychotherapy.   2. Children—Counseling of.   I. Rudolph, Linda B., [date].
II. Title.
RJ504.T49 1992
618.92'8914—dc20   91-24926
                                                                              CIP

Sponsoring Editor: *Claire Verduin*
Marketing Representative: *Mark Francisco*
Editorial Associate: *Gay C. Bond*
Production Editor: *Kay Mikel*
Manuscript Editor: *Laurie Vaughn*
Permissions Editor: *Mary Kay Hancharick*
Interior Design: *Sharon L. Kinghan*
Cover Design: *Katherine Minerva*
Art Coordinator: *Cloyce J. Wall*
Photo Editor: *Ruth Minerva*
Typesetting: *Graphic World Inc.*
Cover Printing: *Lehigh Press Lithographers/Autoscreen*
Printing and Binding: *Arcata Graphics/Fairfield*

PHOTO CREDITS: **1.** Gale Zucker; **59.** Elizabeth Crews; and **319.** Karen Preuss/The Image Works.

About the Authors

Charles L. Thompson is a professor of educational and counseling psychology in the College of Education at The University of Tennessee at Knoxville. He received his bachelor's and master's degrees in science education and educational psychology from the University of Tennessee and his Ph.D. degree in counselor education and developmental and counseling psychology at The Ohio State University where he held NDEA and Delta Theta Tau fellowships. Charles is a former teacher and counselor in grades 7–12. Charles holds memberships in the American Association of Counseling and Development and the American Psychological Association. He is a licensed psychologist and certified school counselor. His research interests are in counselor education and individual counseling. He has published articles in *The Journal of Counseling & Development, The Elementary School Guidance & Counseling Journal, The School Counselor, Counselor Education and Supervision,* and *The Journal of Counseling Psychology,* and has coauthored five books on counseling. Charles had been editor of the IDEA Exchange in the *Elementary School Guidance & Counseling Journal* since 1979.

Linda Rudolph is a professor of psychology at Austin Peay State University, Clarksville, Tennessee. She earned undergraduate and master's degrees in psychology and holds a doctorate in counselor education with a cognate area in psychology. She has taught psychology for more than 15 years and has concentrated in the counseling field for over 10 years. She is a licensed educational psychologist and certified professional counselor in the State of Tennessee and has served as both vice president and president for the state licensing Board for Professional Counselors and Marital and Family Therapists. Linda holds membership in the American Association for Counseling and Development as well as state and regional affiliations. Active for many years in the counselor licensure and accreditation movements, she presently serves on the ACES Committee for Review of CACREP Standards. Linda has been active in state, regional, and national counseling associations, presenting workshops on counseling with children as well as the results of her research on women's career choices. Her research interests have focused primarily on children of divorce, assessment, and the effects of women's backgrounds, values, and choices on their professional advancement. She has published numerous articles in professional journals and coauthored a chapter on women's career development in a textbook on counseling with women.

Preface

Counseling Children was written to fill the need for a contemporary textbook designed to put theory into practice for counseling children. *Counseling Children* is for people preparing themselves for careers in working with children as well as for professionals already established in their careers. Counselors, psychologists, teachers, social workers, and parents should find the book useful in developing approaches for teaching children how to find better ways to meet their needs. The book brings together ideas from research and practice. We have attempted to present practical, up-to-date methods for helping children with specific developmental, social, or behavioral problems. Also included are specific suggestions for counseling children who are "exceptional" or who may be experiencing special concerns that result from societal problems—divorce, death, abuse, homelessness, alcoholism—or children who are victims of AIDS or satanic cults.

The primary rationale for revising a textbook is to update each chapter's theory and practice sections by surveying and summarizing the current research and theoretical literature on all topics presented. We made the literature search our first priority and have added 306 new references to the third edition. Next, we evaluated our book in light of current trends in counseling children, and our evaluation has resulted in the following modifications.

Part One of the third edition begins with an explanation of what causes children's problems. Exploring the commonalities shared by effective counselors, we take the point of view that counseling can be remedial, preventive, or developmental. Chapter 1 includes a short section that discusses the influence of gender in development as it relates to counseling. Counselor preparation, career choices, and credentialing are also discussed in this chapter. Chapter 2, "The Counseling Process," addresses such practical questions as: How do counseling and psychotherapy differ? What steps and stages do effective counselors follow in counseling interviews? How do giving advice and giving information differ? and What can the counselor do with the silent client? In addition, Chapter 2 has been expanded to include more detail on developmental stages of children and adolescents, with implications for counseling clients in each stage.

Part Two presents nine counseling theories and the techniques used in counseling sessions with children. These nine theories range from Sigmund Freud's psychodynamic theory to a behavioral-counseling method developed from B. F. Skinner's behavioral technology. Part Two also presents cognitive behavioral approaches that incorporate the ideas of Albert Ellis and behaviorism. Carl Roger's person-centered method represents a third approach to counseling. Other theories addressed include William Glasser's reality therapy, Fritz Perls's Gestalt therapy, and Eric Berne's transactional analysis. Chapter 11, "Family Therapy," features the work of Virginia Satir, with short summaries of contributions to family therapy by Salvador Minuchin, Milton Erickson, Jay Haley, and Cloe Madanes. Additions to the chapter include methods for incorporating eclectic counseling into family therapy and ways to integrate feminist therapy concepts into family systems.

Other additions to Part Two include cross-cultural applications of counseling methods, applications of each theory to educational and community settings, information on building self-esteem through individual and group counseling, steps in conducting a behavior analysis, and increased emphasis on using the expressive arts and play therapy in counseling. Presentation of each theory includes a biographical sketch of the theorist, a philosophical statement concerning the nature of people, a discussion of the theory and of methods used in practice, case histories that demonstrate application of these methods, and an updated summary of research on and reactions to the theory.

Part Three of the book, "Counseling with Children: Special Topics," includes revised and updated chapters that address a number of important issues. Chapter 12 describes consulting models for school and mental health settings. Chapter 13, "Group Counseling with Children," has been revised and reorganized and includes a new section on group crisis intervention.

Chapters 14 and 15 focus on children with special concerns such as abuse, divorce and stepfamilies, alcoholism, facing death and dying, differing cultures, and exceptional children. New information and the latest research findings have been added to each section. Children now face new societal problems; therefore, this edition contains sections on counseling latchkey children, children in homeless families, suicidal children, children in satanic cults, and children with AIDS. The section that addresses counseling with children of other cultures has been expanded to address the specific needs of certain cultural groups: African American, Asian American, Hispanic American, and Native American children.

Chapter 15 also includes updated research and literature on six "exceptional" conditions. The previous edition discussed the gifted, learning-disabled, mentally retarded, those with behavior disorders, and the physically handicapped. Information on attention-deficit hyperactivity disorder (ADHD) has been added because in recent years ADHD has been diagnosed so frequently.

The annotated bibliographies of children's literature in Chapters 14 and 15 have been updated and cover a variety of special concerns and exceptionalities.

The last chapter of Part Three addresses the legal and ethical issues involved in counseling children. Twenty new situations that address ethical or legal issues or both have been posed for the reader's review, with references to the appropriate AACD, APA, or NASW ethical codes. The principle or standard that responds to each situation is cited, and the authors explain fully why they believe the behavior is ethical or unethical.

In the previous edition, the chapters that suggested interventions for conflicts with self and others had been placed in a separate section. Because these suggested interventions were not actually "chapters," they have been moved and now constitute Appendixes A and B. A notation at the beginning of the appendixes advises the reader that these two sections are for reference in designing interventions and treatment plans. Categories for classifying clients according to the DSM-III-R have been suggested for counselors in private practice or working in community agencies.

We realize that the efficacy of any strategy for changing children's behavior depends on many variables—the severity of the problem, the resistance or cooperation of the child and significant adults, and the orientation of the counselor. This book is our way of sharing with readers the ideas and methods we have found useful for changing children's ineffective behavior and helping them to become responsible, fully functioning persons.

We would like to acknowledge the encouraging support of our work from the following people: from the University of Tennessee at Knoxville, former chairpersons Lawrence M. DeRidder, Michael J. Patton, Siegfried C. Dietz, and current chair R. Steve McCallum of the Department of Educational and Counseling Psychology, and Dean Richard Wisniewski; and from Austin Peay State University, Oscar C. Page, President, and John L. Butler, Vice President for Academic Affairs. A special note of thanks is extended to Alicia Barber for her hard work updating the bibliographic sections in Chapter 13 and 14. Appreciation is also extended to our reviewers for their helpful comments: Susan A. Anzivino, University of Maine at Farmington; and Bea Wehrly, Western Illinois University. They were invaluable in guiding us through this revision. We also thank Claire Verduin, Gay C. Bond, Kay Mikel, and the excellent staff of Brooks/Cole Publishing Company for their support, encouragement, and remembrances over the past few years. Kay has a special way of giving expert advice and criticism while allowing us to maintain our sense of self-esteem. Very special appreciation goes to Claire Verduin, who has guided and motivated us with expertise and warm encouragement through three editions. We especially thank our students who assisted with the research and contributed reactions, ideas, and counseling cases to this work. Appreciation and recognition go also to our secretaries, Judy Dooley and Martha Woodall, for their valuable assistance in preparing the manuscript. Very special thanks is given to Naomi Jones Thompson for her editorial assistance. And thanks to Larry Marks for his thorough proofreading of the manuscript.

Finally, to our spouses, Harriet and Bill, we give our love and appreciation for your patience, support, understanding, and encouragement. To our children, now adults of whom we are very proud, thank you for teaching us about children, parenting, and unconditional love.

Charles L. Thompson
Linda B. Rudolph

Contents

PART TWO

CHAPTER 6

Rational-Emotive Therapy and Cognitive-Behavior Therapy   132

CHAPTER 7

Behavioral Counseling   157

CHAPTER 8

Psychodynamic Counseling   185

CHAPTER 9

Transactional Analysis   214

CHAPTER 10

Individual Psychology   247

CHAPTER 11

Family Therapy   281

CHAPTER 15

Counseling with Exceptional Children   427

CHAPTER 16

Legal and Ethical
Considerations for Counselors   460

APPENDIXES   481

APPENDIX A

Children's Conflicts with Others: Alternatives for Intervention   483

APPENDIX B

Children's Conflicts with Self: Alternatives for Intervention   509

APPENDIX C

Ethical Standards: American Association for Counseling and development   532

APPENDIX D

Ethical Principles of Psychologists: American Psychological Association   545

APPENDIX E

Code of Ethics: National Association of Social Workers   557

PART ONE

INTRODUCTION TO COUNSELING CHILDREN

CHAPTER 1

Introduction

The United States prides itself on being a child-oriented nation. Laws have been passed to prevent children from being misused in the workplace, to punish adults who physically or psychologically harm children, to provide means for all children to obtain an education regardless of their mental or physical condition, and to support programs for medical care, food, and clothing for children in need. Politicians debate "save our children" issues such as educational reform, sex and violence on television, an adolescent girl's right to an abortion without parental consent, family-leave policies in the workplace, burdening our children and grandchildren with an increasing national debt, and ways of providing a more environmentally safe world for our children's future.

In sharp contrast to the foregoing, Tuma (1989) reports that "the latest epidemiologic data available indicate that from 15 percent (9.5 million) to 19 percent of the nation's approximately 63 million children and youth suffer from emotional or other problems that warrant mental health treatment" (p. 188). According to Tuma, commissions and panels appointed by those at the highest government levels and charged to study issues of mental health treatment for children continue to point out that children receive inadequate and inappropriate services.

Teachers, counselors, psychologists, social workers, and other professionals who work with children increasingly express strong concerns about the children growing up in today's society. Recent statistics* indicate the following:

1. In 1987, 2,025,200 cases of child neglect and abuse were reported.
2. In 1988, 28,200 males under 18 years of age were arrested for serious crimes such as murder, forcible rape, robbery, and assault. Another 14,200 were arrested for less serious crimes (fraud, forgery, vandalism, and others).

---

*Statistics for items 1 through 4 were reported in *Statistical Abstract of the United States: 1990* (110th ed.), U.S. Department of Commerce, Bureau of the Census, Washington, DC, 1990.

3. In 1988, the number of high school dropouts equaled 10.9 percent of the total school population, or 4,300,000 students.
4. In 1986, the suicide rate for children 10–14 years old was 1.5 per 100,000 population, an increase from 0.8 in 1980. For 15- to 19-year-olds, the suicide rate climbed from 8.5 per 100,000 in 1980 to 10.2 in 1986. More males than females in these age ranges commit suicide.

The Children's Defense Fund (Glosoff & Koprowicz, 1990) cites the following statistics:

- Every day, 2989 American children see their parents divorced.
- Every 26 seconds, a child runs away from home.
- Every 47 seconds, a child is abused or neglected.
- Every seven minutes, a child is killed or injured by guns.
- Every 53 minutes, a child dies because of poverty.
- Every day, 100,000 children are homeless.
- Every school day, 135,000 children bring guns to school.
- Every eight seconds of the school day, a child drops out of school.
- Every day, six teenagers commit suicide.

What is happening in the lives of our children? What is happening in American homes and society to cause approximately 9 million children to experience problems that will require the help of a mental health professional?

The problems of children are increasing with serious rapidity, giving cause for grave concern. Intense consideration must be given to the factors that contribute to these statistics, and methods for individuals and society to help these children must be found.

Tuma (1989) contends that professionals need special skills and training to work effectively with children. According to her data, approximately 10 percent of psychiatrists and less than 1 percent of psychologists work primarily with children, as do about 7000 child or family social workers and 1000 child- and family-oriented nurses. Tuma does not include figures indicating how many counselors provide services for children.

Obviously, some children are born into warm and loving homes that provide excellent environments for growth and development. Many children pass successfully through the developmental stages of childhood and adolescence and become fully functioning or self-actualizing adults. However, a growing number of children have emotional, behavior, social, and other problems that warrant mental health treatment. Therefore, serious attention must be paid to the factors that contribute to these problems and to ways in which individuals and society as a whole can help such children.

Resources for counselors and others who work with children are increasing; however, clinical, agency, and school professionals have felt frustrated because information suggesting specific counseling procedures for the unique developmental, learning, and behavioral problems has been limited and difficult to obtain. This book attempts to provide counselors in the clinic, agency, school, and other counseling situations with a source of suggestions for counseling children with specific learning or behavioral problems.

THE CHILDREN'S RIGHTS MOVEMENT

Children's rights has been a world focus since 1979, when the United Nations designated the International Year of the Child and developed a list of children's rights. Among the rights suggested are the right to love and understanding, adequate food and health care, free education, play, an identity, and special attention if handicapped, regardless of race, color, sex, religion, and national or social origin (Caldwell, 1989). It is fashionable and politically wise to be a child advocate. No one objects to protecting children and providing for their needs. However, the underlying motivation and strength of the nation's commitment to children can be questioned when one considers certain statistics and actions.

Most of us agree with the rights enumerated in these UN articles because they seem to provide the necessary conditions for children to grow and develop into effective and productive adults. We fail to recognize that many of our country's young people are not among those who enjoy a loving, supportive home, the right to be treated with dignity, good food, adequate physical and mental health care, freedom from others' prejudices, and the other conditions children need to become useful members of society.

The United Nations Convention on the Rights of the Child grew out of the 1979 celebration of the International Year of the Child. Strong emphasis is placed on the rights of the child as a human being separate from the family (Cohen & Naimark, 1991). According to Cohen and Naimark, the articles "demand that the State refrain from interference with the child's right to an opinion, to freedom of expression, to freedom of assembly, and to freedom of religion" (p. 61). These articles even require "the State to protect the child's right to *privacy*" and the child's "assertion of these rights by linking them to the child's evolving capacities" (p. 61). Cohen and Naimark believe that the articles also address protection of a child's mental health as a part of his or her rights and that meeting only basic survival and physical needs is not enough. The child also needs psychological care to foster development as a productive and healthy adult (Cohen & Naimark, 1991). Hart (1991) describes the history and evolution of children's rights, asserting that they have moved over the years "from property to person status."

WHAT CAUSES OUR
CHILDREN'S PROBLEMS?

Janice is a sixth-grader who complains of headaches, stomach pains, sleeplessness, and other symptoms of general anxiety. Janice has always been an outstanding student academically, usually earning straight "A's" on her report cards. Additionally, she is very popular and takes dance and piano lessons, plays on the school tennis team, and works with young children in her church.

Jason is the eldest of three children living with their recently widowed father. He is a typical "latchkey child" and is responsible for his two younger brothers after school until about 6:00 P.M. each weekday. According to his teacher, he has recently been "acting out," showing unusual anger and striking out verbally at people for minor causes. The teacher is also troubled by the strange stories Jason tells her. She believes they are either exaggerations or totally imagined events.

Tanya is 9 years old, the sixth child of a never-married woman who has had numerous "uncles" or live-in "friends." When the school social worker visited the home, she reported that pornographic pictures, magazines, and tapes were openly present and accessible to Tanya. The teacher has complained about Tanya's language and sexually suggestive behavior. Tanya is very knowledgeable about sex and shares her information readily with her classmates.

Peter is a seventh-grader with a history of being "lazy," never completing his homework, acting impulsively and being easily distracted, losing his personal possessions, and having poor relationships with his peers. He has been assessed with numerous intelligence tests over the years and usually scores above average. His parents and teacher have given up hope; they can see no way to help him.

Rob's father lost his job six months ago and has not been able to find work. The family has had to move to a less expensive home. Their car has been repossessed, and Rob never has money for school supplies or activities. Rob tells his teacher of the bickering and fighting in his home. The teacher suspects physical abuse is occurring.

A Changing World

As we approach the 21st century, predictions about future events and conditions abound. What will the new decade bring? One prediction all forecasters seem to make is that the world will continue to change rapidly. Naisbitt and Aburdene (1990) indicate the following: (1) technological growth will continue; (2) the United States will move further from the Industrial Age into the Information Era; (3) "family" will be redefined to include many types of homes and relationships; (4) as more women enter the work force, more mothers of preschoolers and school-age children will be seeking good child care; (5) although the divorce rate has leveled off, over half of all children will live in a single-parent household at some time during their lives; (6) international events will continue to have a strong influence on the United States, and children will need to learn about other cultures in order to live and work with others effectively; (7) concern about substance abuse and addiction will continue to have high priority; and (8) environmental issues will bring about changes in living patterns.

Crabbs (1989, p. 160) believes it "is time to identify major social, political, educational, and economic influences that may have a direct impact on ... the counselor's role in the year 2000." He encourages counselors to identify "what is" in their counseling area and then to plan for the future and "what might be." Factors that Crabbs suggests be examined include the following:

1. violence on elementary and secondary school campuses;
2. experimentation with alcohol and drugs at young ages (approximately age 12);
3. increasing prejudice;
4. gang membership;
5. physical and sexual abuse;
6. a need for sex education due to increasing sexual activity;
7. increasing use of computer technology;
8. changing values and accompanying conflicts;
9. poor health practices in children (smoking, poor eating habits);
10. poverty that limits potential;
11. continuing instability in the family structure; and
12. new ways to treat childhood fears of the 21st century. [pp. 161–163]

Scher and Good (1990) point out that the influence of gender will be of great importance in the coming decade, but they fear that counselors are not as informed about the issue as they should be. Mintz and O'Neil (1990) contend that "while gender roles have a profound effect on individuals in our culture, there has been a dearth of research on the impact of counselor and client gender roles on the therapy process" (p. 381). However, Scher and Good contend that one's beliefs about gender can have a powerful influence in counseling and that clients must be understood within the "context of their conceptions about gender" (p. 389).

What we do know is that children have been exposed to gender-biased books, toys, teachers, and school curricula, as well as to a society that shapes gender roles and behaviors. Unfortunately, counselors, too, have supported gender stereotypes both in personal and career counseling through their use and interpretation of tests and methods of assisting young people to make choices, learn new ways of interacting, or develop their personal skills in other ways (Basow, 1986). Learned stereotypical attitudes and behaviors continue to influence the decisions and actions of individuals throughout their lives.

While researchers continue to debate what we do and do not know about the influence of sex and gender roles on a child's development and in the counseling environment, counselors are encouraged to examine their own attitudes toward masculine and feminine roles and expectations. This examination process includes discussion with colleagues about the issues, evaluation of one's own counseling styles, and continuing education through reading and attending seminars and workshops. Scher and Good (1990) argue that "counselors must be aware of the impact of gender on the way in which our society is defined, organized, and functions in order to do the best possible job for our clients. Ignoring the impact of conceptions of gender on our work is an invitation to disaster" (p. 388). Counselors who work with children as they develop physically, psychologically, socially, and emotionally have an increased responsibility to concern themselves with their influence on their clients during the formative years.

We like to think of our children as immune to the complexities and troubles of the world. It comforts us to believe that they are not sensitive to the stress produced by the rapid changes occurring in our adult world. The child's world is often viewed as one of carefree, irresponsible times, with no financial worries, societal pressures, or work-related troubles. Melton (1987) warns us that many adults who consider themselves child advocates do not understand a child's perception of the world. They do not believe a child's concerns matter much, and they believe that children are largely unaware of what is happening politically and economically. Melton presents research evidence to show that school-age children are effective decision-makers and problem-solvers and are "political beings by reason of their living in a political society" (p. 363).

Normal child development involves a series of cognitive, physical, emotional, and social changes. Almost all children, at some time during their development, will experience difficulty adjusting to the changes, and the accompanying stress or conflict can lead to learning or behavior problems. Normal child development brings tasks of achieving independence, learning to relate to peers, developing confidence in self, coping with an ever-changing body, forming basic values, and mastering new ways of thinking and new information. Wertlieb, Weigel, and Feldstein (1987) report that children face numerous factors in their lives that require them to adapt, including changes in home or school locations, death or divorce in the family, and major illnesses, as well as the usual "daily hassels." A high degree of stress has been found to be associated strongly with behavior symptoms. Add the stresses and conflicts of a rapidly changing society—a society even adults find difficult to understand—to normal developmental concerns, and the child's world does not look so appealing.

The American Home

According to developmental psychologists, children need warm, loving, and stable home environments in order to grow and develop in a healthy manner. Years ago, children lived in large and stable extended families. Fathers worked on the land, mothers in the home, and often an unmarried aunt or uncle lived with the family. Grandparents often lived with the children's family as well. Thus, many adults were around when a child needed to talk or needed to feel "special" to someone. Decisions about what to do for social activities, which career to choose, and whom to marry were relatively simple: the choices were restricted, and expectations were made clear.

In today's society, the home is not so simple. Grandparents may live 3000 miles away and be almost unknown to their grandchildren. Aunts and uncles seldom live nearby; in any case, they are busy pursuing individual interests and careers. Fathers work long hours to provide financial security for their families and then are expected to attend meetings or other community events at night. A majority of mothers of school-age children work to help support the family or for other reasons. Mothers still shoulder the primary responsibility for the care of the home, so they are often occupied at night with washing, ironing, or cleaning. And with the incidence of divorce in families remaining relatively high over the past few years, single parents are assuming the roles of both mother and father more frequently, doubling the burden on the parent, and leaving little free time for children. Thus, children may not be able to find someone to listen or to provide the care and guidance they need, even though adults are all around.

Societal Crises

Not only do many of our children live in insecure and unstable homes, but they are also continually confronted by an unstable, conflict-ridden society. Inflation and the high cost of life's necessities—food, shelter, clothing—are reported almost daily by the media. Unemployment rates are high, and new graduates often have difficulty finding jobs. Job opportunities change rapidly, and career planning is filled with uncertainties about the future demand for specific skills. Those adults with jobs are often dissatisfied and engage in slowdowns and strikes in conjunction with contract negotiations. The crime rate is on the upswing, and many neighborhoods are no longer safe for children or adults. The cost of vandalism to schools and other private and public property is astronomical. People are increasingly cynical and distrustful of local, state, and federal government. Once-respected public figures and government agencies have been found to be engaging in criminal or highly unethical practices. Some experts predict economic disaster because of the high national debt and unbalanced budget. Finally, we live in a world full of tensions generated by the buildup of war weapons, the seizure of hostages, and the threat of nuclear devastation.

Changing Values

Although change can be frightening or confusing, especially for a child, it can also be wondrous. A changing world can be exciting. It can bring new discoveries in medicine, new ideas for recreation, new and different jobs, new ways of living—all areas of life may be affected.

The children of today are forming values in a constantly and rapidly changing world. Our concept of what is "right" or "wrong" seems to change daily or vary with the person we are talking to. Who is right concerning standards of sexuality, cohabitation, alternative lifestyles, or abortion? Are the various "liberation movements" good or bad? How does a person behave in a world with changing sex roles? Will drugs seriously harm a person? Should society condone mercy killing? Is capital punishment justified? Adults with mature thinking processes and years of life experience have trouble making rational judgments on such ethical and moral issues.

Children in today's world are expected to grow, mature, and make critical decisions at a much younger age than before. Goodman (1990) laments the fact that because a 5-year-old cannot answer questions about what his or her parents do for a living, fill in the missing parts of an "incomplete man," name a certain number of animals in one minute, print his or her name, and number from 1 to 20, the child may be labeled "immature" and begin to believe that he or she is "dumb." Counselors are now seeing psychosomatic symptoms—stomachaches, headaches, fevers, and other physical symptoms—in "hurried" children.

The Frustrations of Childhood

Parents often give their children glowing reports of "when I was a child...," but we must question whether adults truly remember what it is like to be ordered to obey; to have rights and privileges extended only at the whim of an adult; to be treated as an object, or perhaps a prisoner; to try to understand a world that is inconsistent and continually changing; to feel the pressures to conform to the dictates of parents, school, and other authority figures without understanding; or to have feelings or emotions totally ignored.

How many adults would trade their present life for a world in which they were told what to eat and how to dress; in which they spent seven hours moving, working, and speaking at the orders or instructions of others; in which they were told where they could or could not go, when to be in, and with whom they could associate; in which someone constantly labeled them "good" or "bad"; in which daily events left them feeling insecure, anxious, and many times helpless and hopeless? Increasing incidences of school vandalism are one expression of the unhappiness and frustration children experience in school, and perhaps in life in general. Imagine yourself as a 4-foot-6-inch person looking up and out at a world you do not understand. Take away your present learning and life experiences from this small person, and then defend the idea that "happiness is a child's world" or that the United States is a child-centered society.

Obviously, some children in today's world enjoy secure childhoods that are preparing them well to meet the challenges of present-day society. The purpose of the pessimistic presentation of childhood is simply to discourage the idea that childhood is a carefree, irresponsible period and to encourage adults to seek to understand the reasons for the increase in learning and behavior problems, emotional problems, drinking and drug abuse, runaways, suicides, lack of commitment, and the multitude of other problems in today's population of children. Although every adult was once a child, a "generation gap" exists in understanding. As early as the days of Socrates and Aristotle, adults felt that the growing generation was "going to the dogs." However, past generations did not have to deal with a gap so compounded by the complexities of today's society.

THE PERSONAL WORLD OF THE CHILD

The various social and cultural conditions we have been discussing can have a profound effect on the child's personal and psychological world.

Maslow (1970) believes we all have certain basic needs that must be met in order for us to become "self-actualizing," or to reach our potential in all areas of development. If our lower level basic needs are not met, we will be unable to meet higher order needs. His ideas suggest some possible reasons why our children are experiencing an increased number of learning and behavior problems.

The first level of Maslow's hierarchy is comprised of physiological needs — the need for food, shelter, water, and warmth. We might be tempted to pass these needs by, believing that children of today are fed well and have adequate shelter and clothes. However, we must consider the number of children who participate in breakfast programs in schools or who do not get breakfast either at home or at school, and the poor diet of some children who may consume an adequate quantity of food. We are just beginning to learn about the relationship between diet and academic/behavioral problems. Evidence exists to support the idea that a poor diet may be related to such problems as hyperactivity and the inability to learn; recent research has suggested that an inadequate diet may contribute to mental illness in adolescents. Are we truly meeting the physiological needs of our children?

Maslow's second level is the need for safety. Again, we may be tempted to ignore this need at first glance. However, can we say that our children really feel safe, that they have little to fear? Some children feel afraid in their own homes; they fear for their very physical safety. Parents, frustrated that their own needs are not adequately met, may take their frustrations out on the child through physical or psychological abuse. Some adults who would not think of hurting a child physically will psychologically abuse children with demeaning and damaging words. Children may receive similar treatment in school, where teachers who are frustrated personally or professionally may use children as a safe target for their frustration. Not only are children afraid of adults; some are also afraid of their peers. Consider Tony, who is small for his age, rather shy, and has few friends. As Tony enters school one morning, several of the "bigger guys" tell him they will be waiting to "get him" this afternoon. Tony cannot be expected to learn 6 × 6 with this problem weighing on his mind!

Tony's fears for his safety may not be limited to home and school. For some children, the neighborhood can be a threatening place if the crime rate is high. In addition, the news media vividly portray the danger and effects of natural disasters such as hurricanes, tornados, and earthquakes. The threat of war, with the loss of loved ones, also seems ever-present.

Even if Tony feels safe and protected, his learning or behavior may be influenced by another need. The need to feel loved and to belong is the first higher order need, emerging after physiological and safety needs have been met. Humans are social beings and want to feel part of a group. We see this need being fulfilled in children's cliques, gangs, clubs, and other groups. The family also helps to satisfy the need for love and belonging. Wherever we are, most of us want to be loved and accepted, and we want to fit in with the group. Tony may not be getting positive attention from adults or peers, and he may think that no one likes him. Children sometimes attempt to hide their feelings of rejection or to compensate for the rejection with antisocial behavior; either defense can be destructive to learning and personal relationships.

Perhaps the need that our society has the most trouble fulfilling for children is the need for self-esteem — the fourth need in Maslow's hierarchy. Children are ordered, directed, commanded, criticized, devalued, ignored, and put down. You may have had the experience of being treated like a child. Your feelings probably included annoyance, inferiority, defensiveness, and anger. When adults are treated like children, they rebel, fight, or leave the scene. Such responses are not considered acceptable in children. All people — adults and children — need to be respected as worthwhile individuals, capable of feeling, thinking, and behaving responsibly. Children are developing their cognitive abilities and widening their range of experiences. They can be treated with the warmth and respect needed to encourage their learning within firm guidelines and expectations. Cruel and thoughtless remarks can be avoided; criticisms can be reduced; positive interactions can be accentuated to build self-respect and self-confidence.

The satisfaction of needs at the first four levels contributes to achievement of the fifth need in Maslow's hierarchy — self-actualization. Maslow states that a self-actualized person is moving toward the fulfillment of his or her inherent potential. Fulfilling this need implies that lower needs have been met; the child is not blocked by hunger, fear, lack of love or feelings of belonging, or low self-esteem. The child is not problem-free but has learned problem-solving skills and can move forward to becoming all that he or she can be.

Glasser (1986) believes that society is not meeting our children's needs. He contends that children are failing in school and in life, academically and behaviorally, because their needs are not being met. He lists five needs of all persons: (1) the need to survive and reproduce; (2) the need to belong and love; (3) the need to gain power; (4) the need to be free; and (5) the need to have fun. Glasser believes that children's problems relate to the inability to fulfill these needs. He emphasizes the teaching of reality, right and wrong, and responsibility.

Adlerian psychologists believe that children often attempt to meet their needs in a mistaken direction. They suggest that adults examine the "goals of misbehavior" and attempt to redirect the behavior to achieve more satisfying results.

Behavioral psychologists see academic and behavior problems as resulting from faulty learning. The child has learned inappropriate ways of behaving through reinforcement of those behaviors or from poor models. Helping the child succeed is a matter of unlearning or "extinguishing" inappropriate patterns and learning more appropriate behaviors.

Whatever the factors contributing to children's learning, behavioral, and social problems in today's society, parents, counselors, and other professionals must be prepared to assist and support children as they grow and develop in a complex and changing world. What to do about these children and their problems is an immediate concern.

WHAT COUNSELING CAN DO

Ask elementary classroom teachers to estimate the number of students in their rooms who are experiencing learning, emotional, or behavioral problems. Then ask these teachers to predict how many of the approximately 30 students in each class will have serious trouble with the law or other adjustment problems in the future. Multiply these figures by the number of classrooms throughout the United States, and the estimates will be overwhelming. We can change these statistics if we become more effective professionals.

Counseling with children is a growing area of interest for people in the helping professions. Developmental theorists have studied children's growth and development and the effect of childhood experiences on the adult. Child psychiatry has focused on seriously disturbed children. However, children with learning, social, or behavioral problems not serious enough to be classified as severely disturbed have been largely overlooked. Counseling can prevent "normal" problems from becoming more serious and resulting in delinquency, school failure, and emotional disturbance. It can create a healthy environment to help children cope with the stresses and conflicts of their growth and development. Counseling can also be a major remedial force for helping children in trouble through appraisal, individual or group counseling, parent or teacher consultation, or environmental changes.

The principles of counseling with children are the same as those used with adults; however, the counselor needs to be aware of the world as the child sees it. The counselor must adjust counseling procedures to suit the child's cognitive level, emotional and social development, and physical abilities. Each child is a unique individual with unique characteristics and needs.

Childhood should be a time for healthy growth, for establishing warm and rewarding relationships, for exploring a widening world, for developing confidence in self and others, and for learning and experiencing. It should contain some fun and carefree times. And it should also provide a foundation and guidance for the maturing person.

WHAT COUNSELORS DO: CAREERS IN COUNSELING

Counseling is performed by a variety of professionals trained in the helping professions. A person who works with children may be called a counselor, school counselor, school psychologist, social worker, marriage and family counselor, counseling psychologist, clinical psychologist, rehabilitation counselor, child-development counselor, or a combination of these titles. (See Table 1-1.) Duties may include performing individual counseling, group counseling, and/or consultation in a school, agency, clinic, hospital, criminal-justice facility, or other institutional setting to assist children with their personal, social/developmental, educational, or vocational concerns; collecting and analyzing data about an individual (personality, interests, aptitude, attitudes, intelligence, and so on) through interviews, tests, case histories, observational techniques, and other means; and using statistical data to carry out evaluative functions, research, or follow-up activities. A counselor can serve in an administrative role as the director of a school guidance unit or the head of an institutional counseling division or can be engaged primarily in teaching or research.

Some counseling positions require only a four-year baccalaureate degree with a major in psychology, social work, or a related area; however, most positions require a master's or doctoral degree. Accreditation standards and state laws governing the certification and licensure of counselors and psychologists are moving toward the requirement of a two-year master's degree, including a supervised practicum and internship. Doctoral programs, too, are raising their degree requirements to meet the demands for

TABLE 1-1   Careers in counseling

Career	Minimum degree requirement	Work setting
Human service worker	Baccalaureate	Human-service agencies
Juvenile justice counselor	Baccalaureate	Juvenile justice system
Child-development specialist	Master's	Community agencies
Clinical social worker	Master's	Private practice Community agencies Hospitals
Community agency counselor	Master's	Private practice Community agencies
Marriage and family therapist	Master's	Private practice Community agencies
Mental health counselor	Master's	Private practice Community agencies
Pastoral counselor	Master's	Churches Counseling centers Private practice
Rehabilitation counselor	Master's	Rehabilitation agencies Hospitals
School counselor	Master's	Elementary, middle, and secondary schools
Social worker	Master's	Community agencies Hospitals Schools
School psychologist	Educational specialist/ doctorate	Schools
Child psychologist	Doctorate	University Private practice Community agencies Hospitals
Clinical psychologist	Doctorate	University Private practice Community agencies Hospitals
Counseling psychologist	Doctorate	University Private practice Industry Community agencies Hospitals
Counselor educator	Doctorate	University Private practice Industry
Psychiatrist	Medical degree	Private practice Hospitals

highly qualified professionals and require additional supervised practica and internship experiences. Doctoral programs generally require five years study beyond the baccalaureate degree.

Many professionals use counseling skills in their jobs (for example, teachers use behavior modification procedures; ministers and nurses use active listening), but using these skills does not make one a professional counselor. Professional counselors have completed degree and credentialing requirements in their counseling specialty. Many states define and regulate the practice of professional counseling, psychology, and social work through certification (protection of title) and licensure (protection of practice).

The Council for Accreditation of Counseling and Related Educational Programs (CACREP), an accrediting body associated with the American Association for Counseling and Development (AACD), recommends a graduate training program that requires 48 semester hours of master's-level training, including competency in such areas as human growth and development, social and cultural foundations, helping relationships, group work, lifestyle and career development, appraisal, research and evaluation, and professional orientation. Their recommendations for doctoral training build on these competencies and include additional internship experiences.

The National Board for Certified Counselors (NBCC) administers the National Counselor Examination (NCE) as a component of the NBCC national professional counselor certification program, according to the guide to the NCE. This booklet also states that the NCE "has been selected by the majority of state-level counselor credentialing agencies to serve as a part of their respective licensure or registry processes" (1988, p. 3). The National Academy for Certification of Clinical Mental Health Counselors (NACCMHC), a branch of the AACD, also publishes a registry of certified mental health counselors. Special credentialing associations provide information about and recognition of counselors in many specialties. These professional associations can provide information about credentialing requirements to interested counselors.

REFERENCES

Basow, S. (1986). Gender stereotypes: Traditions and alternatives. In L. Mintz & J. O'Neil (1990), Gender roles, sex, and the process of psychotherapy: Many questions and few answers. *Journal of Counseling and Development, 68*, 381–386.

Bureau of the Census. (1990). *Statistical abstract of the United States: 1990* (110th ed.). Washington, DC: U.S. Department of Commerce.

Caldwell, B. (1989). Achieving rights for children: Role of the early childhood profession. *Childhood Education, 66*(1), 4–7.

Cohen, C., & Naimark, H. (1991). United Nations Convention on the Rights of the Child: Individual rights concepts and their significance for social scientists. *American Psychologist, 46*(1), 60–65.

Crabbs, M. (1989). Future perfect: Planning for the next century. *Elementary School Guidance and Counseling, 24*(2), 160–166.

Glasser, W. (1986). *Control theory in the classroom.* New York: Harper & Row.

Glosoff, H., & Koprowicz, C. (1990). *Children achieving potential: An introduction to elementary school counseling and state-level policies.* Washington, D.C.: National Conference of State Legislatures and Alexandria, VA: American Association for Counseling and Development.

Goodman, E. (1990, May). Out from the start. *Parenting,* pp. 104–110.

Hart, S. (1991). From property to person status: Historical perspective on children's rights. *American Psychologist, 46*(1), 53–59.

Maslow, A. (1970). *Motivation and personality* (2nd ed.). New York: Harper & Row.

Melton, G. (1987). Children, politics, and morality: The ethics of child advocacy. *Journal of Clinical Child Psychology, 16*(4), 357–367.

Mintz, L., & O'Neil, J. (1990). Gender roles, sex, and the process of psychotherapy: Many questions and few answers. *Journal of Counseling and Development, 68,* 381–386.

Naisbitt, J., & Aburdene, P. (1990). *Megatrends 2000: Ten new directions for the 1990's.* New York: Morrow.

National Board for Certified Counselors. (1988). *Your guide to the National Counselor Examination: How to prepare.* Alexandria, VA: Author.

Scher, M., & Good, G. (1990). Gender and counseling in the twenty-first century: What does the future hold? *Journal of Counseling and Development, 68,* 388–390.

Tuma, J. (1989). Mental health services for children: The state of the art. *American Psychologist, 44*(2), 188–199.

Wertlieb, D., Weigel, C., & Feldstein, M. (1987). Stress, social support, and behavior symptoms in middle childhood. *Journal of Clinical Child Psychology, 16*(3), 204–211.

CHAPTER 2

The Counseling Process

WHAT IS COUNSELING?

The American Psychological Association, Division of Counseling Psychology, Committee on Definition (1956), defined counseling as a process

> to help individuals toward overcoming obstacles to their personal growth, wherever these may be encountered, and toward achieving optimum development of their personal resources. [p. 283]

The National Conference of State Legislatures and the American Association for Counseling and Development (Glosoff & Koprowicz, 1990) defined counseling as

> a process in which a trained professional forms a trusting relationship with a person who needs assistance. This relationship focuses on personal meaning of experiences, feelings, behaviors, alternatives, consequences, and goals. Counseling provides a unique opportunity for individuals to explore and express their ideas and feelings in a nonevaluative, nonthreatening environment. [p. 8]

How Does Counseling Differ from Psychotherapy?

Distinctions between counseling and psychotherapy may be superficial in that both processes have similar objectives and techniques. Pallone (1977) and Patterson (1986) have outlined some of the differences between counseling and psychotherapy; Table 2-1 summarizes these differences. Differences between the processes of counseling and psychotherapy are often lost in the common ground they share. The key question about the domain of each process rests with counselors and therapists, who must restrict their practice to their areas of competence.

TABLE 2-1 Comparison of counseling and psychotherapy

Counseling is more for:	*Psychotherapy is more for:*
1. Clients	1. Patients
2. The less seriously disturbed	2. The more seriously disturbed
3. Personal, social, vocational, educational, and decision-making problems	3. Personality problems
4. Preventive and developmental concerns	4. Remedial concerns
5. Educational and nonremedial settings	5. Medical settings
6. Conscious concerns	6. Unconscious concerns
7. Teaching methods	7. Healing methods

What Is an Appropriate Working Definition of Counseling?

Counseling is a process that involves a relationship between two people who meet so one person can help the other to resolve a problem. One of these people, by virtue of his or her training, is the counselor; the person receiving the help is the client. The terms *counselor* and *client*, which are viewed by some as dehumanizing, can be replaced by words such as *helper* and *helpee, child, adolescent, adult,* or *person.* In fact, Carl Rogers referred to his client-centered counseling approach as *person-centered.* We believe the word *co-counselor* best describes the child's role in the counseling process — or the role of anyone who is seeking counseling — because we see counseling as a shared process. Counseling may also be a group process, in which the roles of helper and helpee can be shared and interchanged among the group members. The group counselor would then function as a facilitator as well as a counselor.

Coleman, Morris, and Glaros (1987) credit David Palmer of the Student Counseling Center at UCLA with the following definition of counseling:

> To be listened to
> & to be heard . . .
> to be supported
> while you gather your
> forces & get your bearings.
>
> A fresh look at alternatives
> & some new insights;
> learning some needed skills.
>
> To face your lion — your fears.
> To come to a decision —
> & the courage to act on it
> & to take the risks
> that living demands. [p. 282]

What Specific Types of Assistance Can Be Expected from the Counseling Session?

Counseling generally involves three areas: (1) thoughts and feelings about where you are in your life at present; (2) thoughts and feelings about where you would like to be in your life; and (3) if there is a discrepancy between (1) and (2), plans to reduce this discrepancy. The amount of emphasis given to each area varies according to the counseling approach being used. Nevertheless, most counseling approaches seem to share the ultimate goal of behavior change, although they may differ in the method used to attain that goal.

Perhaps the most important outcome for counseling occurs when clients learn how to be their own counselors. By teaching children the counseling process, we help them become more skilled in solving their problems, which in turn helps them become less dependent on others. In our view, counseling is a reeducative process designed to replace faulty learning with better strategies for getting what the child wants out of life. Regardless of the counseling approach employed, we believe it is necessary to listen for three pieces of information children bring to the counseling session: (1) their problem or concern, (2) their feelings about the problem, and (3) their expectations of what they want the counselor to do. Failure to complete this listening process will make further counseling a waste of valuable time and human resources.

Most problems brought to the counselor concerning children can be classified in one or more of five categories:

1. *Interpersonal conflict, or conflict with others.* The child has difficulty relating with parents, siblings, teachers, or peers and is seeking a better way to relate with them.
2. *Intrapersonal conflict, or conflict with self.* The child has a decision-making problem and needs some help clarifying alternatives and consequences involved in the conflict.
3. *Lack of information about self.* The child needs to learn more about his or her abilities, strengths, interests, or values.
4. *Lack of information about the environment.* The child needs information about what it takes to succeed in school or information concerning general career education.
5. *Lack of skill.* The child needs to learn a specific skill, such as effective study methods, assertive behavior, listening skills, or how to make friends.

In summary, counseling goals and objectives can range from becoming one's own counselor to positive behavior change, problem solving, decision-making, awareness, personal growth, remediation, and self-acceptance. A significant part of the counseling process for children in-

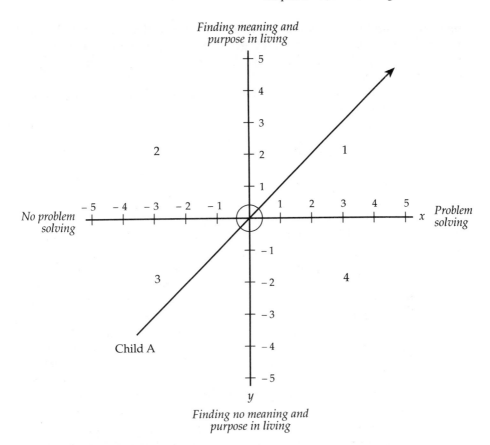

FIGURE 2-1   Counseling focus scale

volves training in life skills, such as communication, assertion, and effective study; however, counselors will choose the counseling focus that seems most appropriate to the child and the child's situation. The counselor's orientation will be determined by the proportionate counseling time given to people working in various areas. Figure 2-1 represents the possible areas of focus that counseling may take. Some counselors prefer to work in the general area of developing meaning and purpose in everyday living, whereas others prefer to work toward the solution of specific problems. Of course, many counselors try to accomplish both ends. Conceivably, Child A could start at point −5 on both the x- and the y-axis and move toward +5 on both axes.

In counseling with children in their middle childhood years (ages 5–12), for example, counselors may choose to work with problem areas in any or all of the quadrants represented in Figure 2-1. Some counselors prefer to work with the developmental and personal growth concerns found in quadrant 1. The children in quadrant 1 are solving their problems and seem to be finding considerable purpose in living. They are sometimes referred to as "stars" because they get along so well with their friends, teachers, and family. Quadrant 1 children seem to have a winner's script that spells success for them in achieving their goals. They usually do well in academic, athletic, social, and artistic endeavors. Working with these children is often a matter of staying out of their way. For quadrant 1 children, the primary focus of counseling would be to help them develop their full potential. The counselor's job would necessarily include some consultation and coordination to ensure that these children receive the appropriate teaching and parenting necessary for the development of their gifts and talents. This developmental model, emphasizing problem prevention over remediation, was pioneered by Herman J. Peters (Peters & Farwell, 1959). Peters encouraged counselors to focus on their clients' strengths as a way to facilitate their next steps up the developmental ladder. The developmental emphasis continues to be a popular theme in the counseling literature. Hoffman and McDaniels (1991) emphasize a developmental approach to career development for children. Parker and McDavis (1989) present a personal development model with 34 activities designed to facilitate development of black children's self-confidence, career development, social skills, work habits, problem-solving skills, and academic development. Myrick (1987, 1989) has written extensively on the developmental model for counseling children. He believes better counselor time-management skills to be the key to providing the best possible counseling to children in school settings. Myrick describes six counselor interventions for delivering developmental counseling services: individual and small-group counseling, large-group guidance, peer-facilitator training, consultation with teachers and parents, and guidance-activity coordination.

Quadrant 2 children find purpose in life and probably are finding meaning in the suffering they experience from not being able to solve a lot of their problems. The counselor's role with these children is remedial in the sense that counseling will be directed toward establishing problem-solving strategies. Frequently, these quadrant 2 children have good interpersonal relationships but experience problems with academic achievement and self-concept. They lack the success identity found in quadrant 1 children.

Quadrant 4 children are the people who do very well with their everyday problem solving but do not seem to find life exciting or challenging. Frequently, these children, being more introverted than extroverted, have little fun and few high points in their lives. A recent fourth-grade classroom discussion on the topic "My High Points from Last Week," led by one of the authors, revealed that 20 percent of the class had difficulty finding just one high point! Counseling plans for this group will be more developmental than remedial in that they will be directed toward building high points for each day of the child's life.

Quadrant 3 children represent the toughest counseling cases. They are not solving their problems, and they find little value in living their lives.

Children in this group suffer from depression, have a very low self-concept, and may be potential suicide victims. Frequently, the children in quadrant 3 have no one who really loves and cares about them, and consequently they have no one to love and care for in return. These are the children who have experienced a world of failure at home and at school. They are often in trouble with school and community authorities. Counseling with these children will be a highly remedial process, with a great amount of effort directed toward encouragement and the establishment of a positive, caring relationship between counselor and child. (This is not to say that the counseling relationship is not important to the children in the other three quadrants; it still remains the key ingredient in any counseling process.) Once a helpful relationship has been established, the counseling focus can be directed toward building success experiences in the child's life.

HOW MANY APPROACHES TO COUNSELING HAVE BEEN ESTABLISHED?

Harper (1959) described 36 systems of counseling and psychotherapy. Corsini and Wedding (1989) reported that, by 1984, 250 systems were documented in the literature. Two years later, Karasu (1986) wrote that the number of counseling systems exceeded 400. However, these myriad systems can generally be classified in four intervention categories: cognitive, behavior, affective, or some combination of categories referred to as "eclectic."

The type of help offered to children via counseling varies according to the model the counselor uses. Counseling theories often differ more in name and description than they do in actual practice. However, some counseling situations and some children are better suited to one approach than another. Counseling is basically a learning situation, and we each have our favorite style of learning.

WHICH APPROACHES TO COUNSELING ARE MOST EFFECTIVE?

In comparison studies of the different systems of counseling and psychotherapy, no one system has emerged as consistently more effective than others (Glass & Kliegl, 1983; Luborsky, Singer, & Luborsky, 1975; Shapiro & Shapiro, 1982; Smith & Glass, 1977; Smith, Glass, & Miller, 1980; Stiles, Shapiro, & Elliott, 1986; Teasdale, 1985). Rather, a range of counseling approaches, often based on different theories and emphasizing different methods, has been found effective for a wide variety of people with different problems.

Considerable support exists for training counselors in a variety of counseling approaches. Thompson and Campbell (in press), in a phenomenological study, surveyed 500 people on the nature of the self-help interventions people chose to alleviate mild depression. They found that these self-help interventions were spread fairly equally across affective, behavior, cognitive, and eclectic categories. However, there was a slight, but significant, preference for the affective category. These results were attributed to the fact that there were more females than males in the sample, and that females most often expressed preferences for affective interventions. Males, on the other hand, tended to favor cognitive interventions.

Further support for an eclectic approach to counseling comes from Lewis (1985) and Dimond, Havens, and Jones (1978), who point out that an individualized counseling plan is superior, but it is possible only when the counselor is able to draw upon a vast array of theory and technique and is not bound by any single approach. Lazarus (1981, 1984, 1990) makes essentially the same point in his argument that not only is behavior therapy not behaviorism, but neither behavior therapy nor behaviorism can account for all the events that occur in the counseling process. He recommends a multimodal, or comprehensive, eclectic framework for counseling that can be adapted to meet the needs of individual children. Lazarus developed his BASIC ID model to describe seven problem areas often treated in counseling:

B— Behavior:
　　　　Fighting
　　　　Disruption
　　　　Talking
　　　　Stealing
　　　　Procrastination
A— Affect:
　　　　Expression of anger
　　　　Anxiety
　　　　Phobias
　　　　Depression
S— Sensation/School:
　　　　Headaches
　　　　Backaches and stomachaches
　　　　School failure
　　　　Perceptual/motor problems
I— Imagery:
　　　　Nightmares
　　　　Low self-concept
　　　　Fear of rejection
　　　　Excessive daydreaming and fantasizing
C— Cognition:
　　　　Irrational thinking

      Difficulty in setting goals
      Decision-making problems
      Problem-solving difficulties
I— Interpersonal relationships:
      Withdrawing from others (shyness)
      Conflict with adults
      Conflict with peers
      Family problems
D—Drugs/Diet:
      Hyperactivity
      Weight-control problems
      Drug abuse
      Addictions to tobacco, alcohol, and other drugs

The Lazarus BASIC ID model covers most counseling problems that counselors working with children, adolescents, or adults are likely to encounter.

Keat (1990a, 1990b) and Gerler (1990) have written extensively on using multimodal approaches in schools and with children. Gerler (1990) edited and contributed to a special issue of *Elementary School Guidance and Counseling* (Gerler, Drew, & Mohr, 1990) on "Multimodal Approaches to Counseling in Schools," which reviewed multimodal research, applications, and changes. Gerler's special issue cites considerable research support for this eclectic counseling method.

Keat (1990a, 1990b) has specialized his multimodal writing on counseling children. He converted the BASIC ID model into the acronym HELPING. "H" refers to *health* issues (pain and sickness). "E" stands for *emotions* (anxiety, anger, feeling down). "L" is for *learning* problems (deficiencies, failing, and sensory shallowness). "P" stands for *personal relationships* (adult and peer relationships). "I" refers to *imagery* (low self-worth and poor coping skills). "N" is the *need* to know (despair, faulty thinking, lack of information). "G" stands for *guidance* of actions, behaviors, and consequences (behavior and motivation problems). After the problem areas are identified, interventions are designed to strengthen weak areas before they become more serious problems.

The counseling approaches presented in this book offer possibilities for helping counselors work with one or more of the seven areas presented in the BASIC ID model.

CLASSIFYING COUNSELING THEORIES

In the first two editions of this book, we attempted to classify the counseling theories presented on a cognitive/affective continuum. We explained away the behavior category by writing that considerable overlap exists

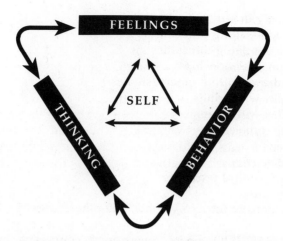

FIGURE 2-2   Classification of counseling approaches

among counseling theories; that put the behavior theories in the middle of our cognitive/affective ratings. A better way to classify counseling theories is to examine how the practitioners of each theory encounter their clients. Some counselors focus on the client's feelings, while others choose to intervene with the client's thoughts or behaviors. Change in any one of these three areas is likely to produce change in the other two. Therefore, rather than use a two-dimensional continuum, we propose a model showing the integrative relationship that exists among thoughts, feelings, and behaviors (see Figure 2-2).

By focusing on the point of intervention, we propose to classify the eight theories presented in this book as follows:

Affective (feeling)
    Person-Centered Counseling
    Gestalt Therapy
Behavior (behaving)
    Behavioral Counseling
    Reality Therapy
    Adlerian Counseling
Cognitive (thinking)
    Rational-Emotive Therapy
    Psychodynamic Counseling
    Transactional Analysis

It is not our intention to isolate feeling, thinking, and behaving from one another. Failure to integrate feelings, thoughts, and behaviors is one of the symptoms of schizophrenia, a diagnosis that describes a loss of contact with the environment, a split from reality, and a disintegration of personality. Rather, we will attempt to describe how effective intervention in one of the three areas helps the individual integrate the other two areas into a more fully functioning lifestyle.

Our purpose in classifying the various approaches to counseling is to provide the reader with a framework for examining the similarities and differences among the approaches discussed in the text. We believe the approaches presented provide a variety of techniques that can be adapted to the learning styles of the children being counseled. The cognitive, affective, and behavior classifications should help counselors match children with appropriate counseling methods.

Stages of Cognitive Development

A key point in counseling children is awareness of the child's level of cognitive development (see Table 2-2). The work of Piaget and Inhelder (1969) has established that children in the 5-to-12 age group may be functioning in as many as three stages of cognitive development. Though age is no guarantee of a child's stage of development, it is helpful to remember that we can expect 5- and 6-year-olds to be on the verge of moving from the preoperational to the concrete stage of cognitive development and that 11-year-old children will be moving into the formal stage.

In the early stages of concrete cognitive thought, children face four blocks to further development of their thought processes:

1. *Egocentrism block:* the inability to see another's point of view. For example, children believe that everyone thinks the same way and does the same things they do. The egocentrism block prevents children from questioning their own thoughts and behaviors even in the face of conflicting evidence. The development of a sense of empathy in the child is made difficult by the egocentrism block.

2. *Centration block:* the inability to focus on more than one aspect of a problem. For example, a child may perceive a long line of five coins as having more coins than a short line of six coins. Children are perception-bound and cannot see the forest for the trees. The centration block makes problem solving in counseling more difficult; thus, more detail and explanation by the counselor are necessary.

3. *Reversibility block:* the inability to work from front to back and then back to front in solving a problem. Children may have difficulty in working such mathematics problems as 17 − ___ = 8. The reversibility block is also characterized by being perception-bound. Children often lose track of quantity when the shape of a substance changes—believing, for example, that a clay ball flattened into a pancake contained more clay when it was in the form of a "taller" ball. Children generally do not understand the concept of irreversibility until after the age of 7; consequently, children's

TABLE 2-2   Piaget's four stages of cognitive development

Stage	Type of development	Age	Cognitive traits
Infancy	Sensori-motor	0–2	Children learn through their senses by touching, hitting, biting, tasting, smelling, observing, and listening. They begin to learn about the invariants in their environment (for instance, chairs are for sitting). Language begins to take form, habits develop, and children begin to communicate symbolically. Children make distinctions between self and other objects. They have the ability to think about things, and they engage in planned and purposeful behavior. At the midpoint of this stage, children achieve a sense of object permanence. Toward the end of this stage they begin to do some trial-and-error problem solving.
Childhood	Preoperational	2–7	Children are not able to conserve when solving problems. For example, children are not able to account for the quantity of a solid or liquid when it changes shape. This is the period of greatest language growth during childhood. Children are trial-and-error problem solvers in this stage and tend to focus on only one stimulus at a time. These children are able to classify objects more than one way (for instance, size, shape, color, and texture). They have trouble with reversible thinking and prefer to learn things in ascending order before descending order. They tend to be egocentric thinkers; play with other children can serve as a way of overcoming this egocentrism. Children are able to use mental images, imagination, and symbolic thought. They are capable of understanding simple rules; however, rules are regarded as sacred and unchangeable.

(continued)

reactions to loss or death may seem uncaring or inappropriate. Once again, any block to formal thinking necessitates a better "teaching" job by the counselor.

4. *Transformation block:* the inability to put events in the proper order or sequence. Children often have difficulty seeing the relationship between events or understanding cause and effect. Children may find it hard to predict the consequences of their behavior and to evaluate the effect of

TABLE 2-2 Piaget's four stages of cognitive development (*continued*)

Stage	Type of development	Age	Cognitive traits
Pre-adolescence	Concrete	7–11	Children in this stage have conservation skills and can do reversible thinking. Reasoning is based on perception, which causes these children difficulty with abstract reasoning, but they are able to appreciate the viewpoint of others. Concrete objects, pictures, diagrams, and examples are helpful learning aids. There is a reduction in egocentrism as children move toward more logical thought and away from intuitive thinking. Rules are regarded as changeable. Reality is distinguished from fantasy. Problem-solving strategies are strengthened through a larger capacity for concentration, attention, and memory. Children are capable of understanding that distance equals rate times time.
Adolescence through adulthood	Formal	11+	These people do not need to manipulate objects to solve problems. They are capable of abstract thought and scientific experimentation, which includes generation of hypotheses and alternatives, plus the ability to design and implement a series of problem-solving procedures. These people are capable of understanding ethical and moral principles and can apply this understanding to the establishment and revision of rules. They are also capable of self-reflective thought, high levels of empathic understanding, and a sense of what is best for society.

their behavior on themselves and others. In addition, children faced with the transformation block have difficulty seeing the gray areas in a given situation; they view events as black or white, right or wrong, regardless of the situation.

The counselor must know the level or stage of the child's cognitive development if successful learning is to result from the counseling experience. Most important is the degree to which a child is able to engage in abstract reasoning, a characteristic of the formal-thinking stage. Children in the concrete-thinking stage will need explicit examples, learning aids, and directions that are not required for formal-stage thinkers. The concrete thinker is able to walk through a series of directions but has difficulty drawing a map of the same route.

Counseling methods need to be matched with the child's cognitive ability if counseling is to be effective. For example, a child limited by the egocentrism block will have great difficulty empathizing with another person's situation. Piaget characterizes the preoperational child's behavior and thinking as egocentric; that is, the child cannot take the role of or see the viewpoint of another (see Wadsworth, 1989). Preoperational children believe that everyone thinks the same way and does the same things they do. As a result, preoperational children never question their own thoughts; as far as they are concerned, their thoughts are the only thoughts possible and consequently must be correct. When they are confronted with evidence that is contradictory to their thoughts, they conclude that the evidence must be wrong because their thoughts cannot be. Thus, from the children's point of view, their thinking is always logical and correct. This egocentrism of thought is not egocentric by intent; children remain unaware that they are egocentric and consequently see no problem in need of resolution.

Wadsworth (1989) adds that it is not until around age 6 or 7, when children's thoughts and those of their peers clearly conflict, that children begin to accommodate to others and egocentric thought begins to give way to social pressure. Peer-group social interaction, the repeated conflict of one's own thoughts with those of others, eventually jars the child to question and seek verification of his or her thoughts. The very source of conflict — social interaction — becomes the child's source of verification. To be sure, verification of one's thoughts comes about only through comparison with the thoughts of others. Thus, peer social interaction is the primary factor that acts to dissolve cognitive egocentrism. The work of Piaget strongly supports the use of group counseling to assist children with the egocentrism block.

Stages of Personal and Social Development

Erikson (1963, 1968) and Havighurst (1961) have written extensively about the stages of human development. Erikson described eight stages of human development that range from birth through adulthood beyond the age of 50. Havighurst wrote in a similar vein as he described expectations and developmental tasks over the life span. Effective counselors are well-informed about human development and know how to incorporate this knowledge into their counseling methods.

Using Erikson's (1963, 1968) and Havighurst's (1961) systems as a frame of reference, counselors can compare expectations, human needs, and developmental tasks of humans across the childhood years. Table 2-3 shows developmental tasks to be completed and necessary interventions for each of the eight stages of human development. The two basic tasks for people are to learn how to cope with the demands and expectations of others when these demands and expectations conflict with their own needs and how to meet these demands with the limited abilities they have in each developmental stage.

TABLE 2-3 Developmental tasks and interventions for the eight stages of human development

STAGE I: BIRTH TO AGE 1½
Basic Trust versus Basic Mistrust

TASK: Children need to develop trust in their environment and in their parents and caregivers. Through their trust, children learn that their world is a safe, secure, consistent, predictable, interesting, friendly place.

INTERVENTIONS: Children need parents and caregivers with all the traits mentioned in the Task column to help them achieve trust in their world and in others. Children need affectionate, consistent, predictable, and high-quality care to help them learn to bond with other people.

STAGE II: AGES 1½ TO 3
Autonomy versus Shame and Doubt

TASK: Children need to gain a sense of self-control as well as control over their environment.

INTERVENTIONS: Children need to experience success in doing things for themselves: expressing themselves, feeding, developing toilet behaviors, and performing various other motor tasks with hands and feet. Children often express their new feelings of autonomy by saying "no" to all requests and through frequent use of "me," "mine," and "I." They respond well to choices.

STAGE III: AGES 3 TO 6
Initiative versus Guilt

TASK: Children need to develop a sense of initiative, as opposed to feelings of guilt about never doing the right thing.

INTERVENTIONS: Children need to begin setting goals, taking leadership, and carrying out projects. Parents need to empower children and let them participate in family work activities and projects. When children's initiative carries them into unacceptable thoughts and behaviors, parents need to correct these behaviors in a loving, caring way as they teach their children what is and what is not acceptable. Discipline based on logical consequences should help these children develop a sense of purpose and goal-directedness.

STAGE IV: AGES 6 TO 11
Industry versus Inferiority

TASK: Children need to learn a variety of skills that will help them find a place in the adult world. The necessary skills range from academic and social to physical and practical.

INTERVENTIONS: Children need large doses of encouragement and praise to help them achieve the competence they need to eventually find a place in the adult world. Academic, physical, social, and work skills are all important in developing healthy self-esteem. Children need nurturing adults who will help them discover and develop their special talents and abilities.

(continued)

TABLE 2-3 Developmental tasks and interventions for the eight stages of
human development (*continued*)

STAGE V: AGES 12 TO 18
Identity versus Role Confusion

TASK: Teenagers need to develop a
self-image. They need to know
who they are and how their roles
will fit into their future.

INTERVENTIONS: Teenagers need to feel that
they are accepted by others as they work
toward self-acceptance and a sense of
identity. Identity can be found in joining
a group or cause. Another way to
achieve a sense of identity is to find
things they do well in work and play. It
is often good to permit adolescents time-
out periods for self-study and exploration before making commitments to further education or training, jobs, careers,
and marriage.

STAGES VI, VII, AND VIII:
Adult Stages

TASK: The primary task in the
young-adult stage is to achieve
intimacy through sharing in a
close friendship or love relationship. Middle adulthood tasks revolve around proper care of children and a productive work life.
Older adults are concerned with
ego integrity, which involves an
acceptance of past life, a search
for meaning in the present, and
continued growth and learning in
the future.

INTERVENTIONS: Counseling interventions for
adults are most effective when they match
the client's learning style. As reported in
Thompson and Campbell (in press), client preferences for interventions are nearly
equally divided between affective, behavior, cognitive, and eclectic methods.
Once again, we must remember that age
does not guarantee that any particular
stage of development has been reached.
Many adults use concrete rather than abstract reasoning in solving problems and
making decisions. Issues in counseling
will often center on relationships, careers, and the search for meaning and
purpose in life.

WHAT DO EFFECTIVE COUNSELORS DO?

The counseling philosophy expressed in this book contends that effective
counselors have many practices in common regardless of specific orientation. This section presents a summary of these commonalities.

Preparing for the Interview

Before the client first enters your counseling environment, look around.
The counseling environment should contribute to a client's feelings of
comfort and ease. A very cluttered, highly stimulating, overly "busy" room
can be especially distracting to children. Their attention is easily drawn to
interesting objects in the room and away from the counseling interaction.

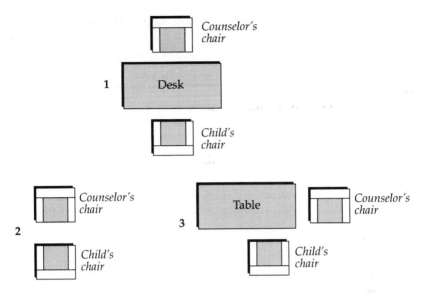

FIGURE 2-3   Seating arrangements for counseling children

Children who tend to be restless and highly distractible may be affected by brightly colored objects, mobiles, ticking clocks, outside noise, or even the darting fish in an aquarium. Inasmuch as counselors are part of the environment, you should check yourself for distracting jewelry such as necklaces or bracelets, highly colorful ties, or patterns in clothing that may affect children.

The furniture in the counseling room should be comfortable for both adults and children. We suggest that counselors not sit behind a desk or table during an interview because furniture can act as a barrier between child and counselor. Children also tend to see people sitting behind desks as authority figures—teachers, principals, and so on. We might add that, if you choose to use chairs in the counseling office, children prefer chairs that are low enough to allow them to keep their feet on the floor.

Counseling seems to work better if children can control the distance between themselves and the counselor. Adults are often too aggressive in trying to initiate conversations with children. Children prefer to talk with adults at the same eye level, so some care needs to be given to seating arrangements that allow for eye-to-eye contact and feet on the floor. Of the various seating arrangements (see Figure 2-3), two seem to be *least* effective: (1) having a desk between the counselor and child, and (2) having no barrier at all between counselor and child. The preferred seating arrangement (3) is to use the corner of a desk or table as an optional barrier for the child, allowing the child to retreat behind the desk or table corner or to move out around the corner when he or she feels comfortable doing so. A thick carpet, comfortable chairs, floor pillows, puppets, dollhouses, and other toys to facilitate communication are also recommended for the counseling room.

Effective counselors are skilled in creating a relaxed counseling environment and in building rapport with their clients. Making friends with the children you counsel may be the key to the entire counseling process. Play media have been effective in developing a relaxed atmosphere with younger children. A few counselors of children have employed large friendly dogs as icebreakers, with child and counselor sitting on a rug playing with the dog during the session (Levinson, 1962).

Check your appointment book to ensure promptness for scheduled sessions. Children (and adult clients) dislike being kept waiting for long periods of time. The counselor's tardiness may be interpreted as a lack of interest, or the delay can cause restlessness, fatigue, or irritability on the part of the child.

Just before the time for your counseling interview, check yourself as a counselor. Are you free from distracting worries and thoughts and ready to devote your attention to the child? Children are extremely sensitive to adult moods and can recognize insincerity or lack of concern quickly. Many counselors call their clients and reschedule appointments when they do not feel well rather than risk hurting the counseling relationship. If you have a cold, headache, or other minor ailment, you may want to admit to the child that you are not feeling up to par rather than have the child misinterpret your behavior as a lack of interest. Finally, alert those around you that you should not be disturbed, and you are ready to greet your child client.

What Are Some Things to Consider During the Initial Contact?

Seeing a new client can be unnerving for many counselors. Beginning counselors, facing a child client for the first time in a counseling situation, often have visions of ruining the child's life during the first session — saying something horribly wrong and doing irreparable psychological damage to the child — or they have a horror of the child sitting silently and staring into space. The child is no longer like any other child the counselor has ever known; this child is a *client!* Just remember that children who are clients are still children, with their own feelings, behaviors, problems, and expectations of counselors. They may come to counseling with fears of the unknown, just as the adult counselor may fear the new relationship. There are several methods counselors can use to allay these fears and to clarify what goes on in counseling for the child.

Children often have the idea that going for counseling means you are "sick," "mentally ill," or "weird" in some way. They may have heard the counselor referred to as a "shrink" or "head doctor." Many have erroneous ideas about counseling and the role of a counselor.

Some counselors prefer to ease the anxiety of the initial meeting by simply engaging in general conversation with the child for a few minutes.

After initial introductions, the counselor may start to talk with the child about home, school, friends, hobbies, or other interests. For nonverbal clients or extremely anxious children, the first session or two may include only techniques of play therapy. The counselor can begin to build a good relationship with the child while learning something about the child's world through these methods. Other counselors prefer to go directly to the problem: "Would you like to tell me why you have come to see me?" During the initial interview, a counselor may want to explain to the child the process of counseling and the counselor's expectations for himself or herself and for the child. The following is a sample dialogue:

Counselor: Do you know what counseling is?

Child: No. (If the child answers yes, the counselor might say "Tell me your ideas about what counseling is.")

Counselor: Well, at some time during our lives, most of us have things that worry or upset us—things we would like to talk to someone about. It could be something about school that concerns us, like another student in our class or our teacher; it could be a problem at home with our brothers or sisters, or perhaps we feel that our parents don't really understand how we feel; it could be that we are having trouble with friendships; it could be that we have some thoughts or feelings that it would be helpful to discuss with someone. A counselor listens and tries to help the other person work these things out. A counselor tries to think with that person about ways to solve these worries. Your job is to tell me whatever is bothering you. My job is to listen carefully and try to help you find ways to solve these problems.

The preceding statement is too long and wordy for children under the age of 7. Boat and Everson (1986) suggest that counselors use sentences with only three to five more words than the number of words in the child's average sentence.

For children who have been referred for counseling by others, the counselor may want to begin with a statement such as "Mrs. Jones told me that you were very unhappy since you moved here and that you might want to talk to me about it," or "Mr. Clifford told me that you would be coming by," and wait for the child to respond and tell what the trouble is.

In the first example, the counselor has informed the child that he or she is aware of the problem and is ready to discuss it. In the second example, the counselor is less directive and provides less structure, allowing the child to explain the problem, which may or may not be the one for which the child was referred. The counselor will want to consider the child's age; culture; and cognitive, social, and emotional development, as well as the type of presenting problem, before deciding which type of opening state-ment to use. The younger the child, chronologically and developmentally, and the more specific the problem, the greater the probability the child will respond more readily to a structured approach. Carlson (1990) prefers a direct approach when counseling "other-referred" children. For example, a counselor might say, "Let me tell you what your teacher shared with me that led to your being asked to see me." The counselor states the teacher's concern in a way that lets the child know that counseling is for helping and not for punishment. The counselor could say, for example, "Mr. Thompson is concerned about your behavior in class. He is afraid you will not learn all you need to know if you don't change what you are doing."

Carlson (1990) also believes that counseling needs to be defined for "other-referred" children in a language they can understand. For example, "Counseling is a time when you can talk to me about things that bother you. We can also talk about what we need to do to make things better." A counselor needs to assure children that what they talk about is confidential or "just between you and me unless I have to stop someone from getting hurt."

The preceding suggestions are only samples of what counselors might say. These examples can be modified to fit the situation, the age and maturity level of the child, and the counselor's personality.

The counselor may or may not think it necessary to structure the initial counseling session by defining the counselor's role and the child's expectations. Many children and counselors, however, feel more comfortable in a structured environment.

THE COUNSELING PROCESS

Step 1. Defining the problem through active listening.   The way the counselor listens to the child is an important factor in building rapport. An open, relaxed body posture is recommended as the best way to invite a child to talk. It is often helpful to suggest a time limit for your interview; the time will vary according to the attention span of the child. One way to start might be to say "Jimmy, we have 20 minutes today to talk about anything you'd like to discuss." In fact, several 20-minute periods might be used to build a friendship with Jimmy. We want to stress the importance of individualizing the counseling process to fit each child you counsel.

When the child wishes to discuss a concern or problem with you, it is necessary to listen for three significant points. Each child seeking help from a counselor has three things in mind: (1) a problem that has not been solved, (2) feelings about the problem, and (3) expectations of what the counselor should do about the problem. It is helpful if the counselor assumes the role of student and lets the child teach the counselor about these three topics. We believe that people learn best when they teach something to another person.

Counselors have the responsibility of letting the child know what they have learned as they help the child teach them. For example, the counselor should periodically respond with a statement such as "In other words, you are feeling _____ because _____ , and you want _____ ." This feedback to the child is referred to as *active listening;* it has the double effect of promoting better communication and of letting the child know you are paying attention. The active-listening process continues throughout the interview, but it is most important in helping to clarify the nature of the child's problem. When the child confirms your response as an accurate understanding of the problem, counseling can move to the next phase. (See Chapter 4 for a detailed explanation of the active-listening process.)

Step 2. Clarifying the child's expectations.   Counselors also need to let children know if they can meet their expectations for counseling. The counselor probably cannot have an unpopular teacher fired, for example. However, counselors can inform children what they are able to do and let the children determine if they want to accept or reject the service available. If the service is rejected, the counselor may want to explore other alternatives with the child about where or how the child can obtain the service.

Step 3. Exploring what has been done to solve the problem.   As we begin to look at what has been attempted to solve the problem, it is good to remember that open-ended questions generally elicit the best responses from the child. Closed questions that yield one-word answers such as yes, no, and maybe make the counselor's job much more difficult. As you will note in the text, many approaches to counseling avoid heavy questioning, while others rely strongly on a series of questions. We take the view that statements often work better than questions because statements have the effect of empowering the client by letting the client maintain the pace and direction of the interview. For example, rather than asking the child, "What have you done to solve the problem?" the counselor would say, "If you feel ready, we could begin by looking at what you have tried to do to solve the problem."

In exploring what the child has been doing to solve the problem, we find it is helpful to have children make a list of these behaviors if they can write; otherwise they can dictate their answers to the counselor. The list becomes important if we want the child to make a commitment to stop those behaviors that are not helping to solve the problem.

It is helpful to explore the possible rewards or payoffs the child derives from the ineffective or unhelpful behaviors. Change is facilitated when both the pluses and the minuses are examined. A "profit-and-loss statement" can be prepared to see if the behavior is actually worth the cost the child is paying. If the child decides it is not, the child may discard the behavior in favor of a more productive alternative.

Step 4. Exploring what new things could be done to solve the problem.   The next step could be a brainstorming session in which the counselor encourages the child to develop as many problem-solving alternatives as possible. Judgment is reserved until the list is finished; quantity of ideas is more important than quality in this first step. Thompson and Poppen (1992) recommend drawing a number of empty circles on a sheet of paper and seeing how many circles the child can fill with ideas. Many children may be blocked from thinking of possible new ideas. When this happens, we recommend that the counselor fill two circles with ideas as a way of encouraging the child to get started. The counselor thus allows the child to become a partner in the problem-solving process by choosing one of the counselor's two suggestions. Children seem to do best with a plan they have made or helped make. For example, if the plan involves learning a new skill such as assertion, effective study, or making friends, the counseling interview can be used for teaching and role-play rehearsal. After the brainstorming list is complete, children are asked to evaluate each alternative in light of its expected success in helping them get what they want.

Step 5. Obtaining a commitment to try one of the problem-solving ideas.   Building commitment to try a new plan may be one of the most difficult things to do in the counseling process. It is important that children achieve success with their first plan because they may be quite discouraged with previous failures to solve the problem. We suggest that the child not set impossible goals in this first attempt; the first plan should be achievable. Children will do better if they are asked to report the results of their plan to the counselor. When plans do not work, the counselor helps the child write new ones until the child achieves success. Plans can include a program of reinforcement when the child succeeds in meeting daily or weekly goals.

Step 6. Closing the counseling interview.   A good way to close the interview is to invite the child to summarize or review what was discussed in the session; for example, the summary might include what progress was made and what plans were developed. Summarizing by the child is also helpful when the interview becomes bogged down and the child cannot think of anything to say. Because the process seems to stimulate new thoughts, summarizing at the close of the interview should be limited to two to four minutes. We also recommend asking the child to summarize the last counseling interview at the start of each new interview. These counselor requests to summarize teach children to pay attention in the session and to review counseling plans between sessions; they have the effect of an oral quiz without the threat of a failing grade. The summary also helps counselors evaluate their own effectiveness. Finally, the counselor and the child make plans for the next counseling interview or for some type of maintenance plan if counseling is to be terminated.

QUESTIONS COUNSELORS ASK

What Does the Counselor Need to Know about Counseling Records?

Most counselors keep some record of interviews with their clients. Notes that summarize the content of sessions and observations the counselor makes can assist in recalling previous information. Before deciding which method of taking notes is appropriate, it is wise for counselors to become knowledgeable about their state's laws regarding privileged communication and the regulations contained in the Buckley Amendment (the federal Family Rights and Privacy Act of 1974). This amendment gives parents and young people of legal age the right to inspect records, letters, and recommendations about themselves. Personal notes do not fall under these regulations; however, for their own protection, counselors in institutional settings will want to become aware of the full requirements of the law.

It is also common practice to videotape or audiotape counseling sessions. This procedure not only provides a record of the interview but also aids counselors in gaining self-understanding and self-awareness. Counselors can listen to or watch their tapes with another counselor and continue to grow and learn by evaluating their own work. In addition, listening to and discussing some sessions with the client may aid in promoting growth.

Permission to record should be obtained from the child and the parents before the procedure is begun. If the material is to be used for instruction, or if anyone other than the counselor will hear the client, written permission should be obtained. Again, it would be advisable to read state laws pertaining to privileged communication and the Buckley Amendment before deciding on the use and storage of these records.

When introducing a recording system to children, it is usually best to show them the recorder, perhaps allow them to listen to themselves for a minute, and then place the equipment in an out-of-the-way place. Occasionally, children are unable to talk when they are being recorded; most, however, quickly forget the equipment. Should a child resist being recorded, the counselor may wish to pursue the reasons for this resistance. If circumstances indicate that recording is inhibiting the counseling process, the counselor may choose to remove the equipment. At the other extreme, some children become so excited and curious about the taping equipment that counseling becomes impossible. Again, the counselor may think it is best to remove the equipment, or a contract may be made with the child such as "After 30 minutes of the counseling work, Mickey may listen to the tape for 5 minutes." It is usually best to give as little attention to the recorder as possible after a brief initial explanation of its purpose and uses.

How Much Self-Disclosure Is
Appropriate for the Counselor?

Children are very often interested in their counselors as people. They may question counselors about their age, where they went to school, where they live, and whether they have children. Counselors are faced with the perplexing problem of how much personal information to share with the child. If counselors refuse to answer any personal questions, they run the risk of hurting the counseling relationship or being viewed by the child as a mysterious figure, bringing forth more questions. However, if counselors answer all personal questions, the interview time may be spent centered around the counselor rather than the client. With seriously disturbed or acting-out clients, revealing your address or where your children go to school could be bothersome or even dangerous. A general guideline might be to share some bits of personal information (favorite sport or TV show, number of children). When the questions become too personal or continue for an extended period, the counselor can reflect to the child, "You seem to be very interested in me personally," and explore the child's curiosity and pursuit of the subject. An understanding of the child's curiosity about the counselor could promote understanding of the child as a person. Questioning the counselor can be a defense for some children who wish to avoid discussing their own problems.

A second problem concerning self-disclosure relates to the counselor's feelings and emotions. Counselor-training programs are founded on the assumption that people are unique, capable of growth, and worthy of respect. These programs focus on listening and responding to clients with empathic understanding and respect. The programs also emphasize the idea that counselors should be genuine; however, genuineness is often interpreted as showing only genuine *positive* emotions and feelings. Counselor trainees are sometimes quite surprised when their supervisors encourage them to admit to the client their negative feelings, such as frustration or anger. Obviously, admitting emotions does not mean attacking and degrading the client; rather, it means admitting that the counselor is a person with feelings and is frustrated or angry over what is occurring ("I am really frustrated that we seem to be talking about everything but what occurred with your friend today").

The counselor's proper level of self-disclosure is a controversial issue in the profession. Some feel comfortable being completely open and honest about their feelings (high levels of self-disclosure); others think such openness can interfere with the counselor/client relationship and prefer low levels of self-disclosure. However, most counselors agree that self-disclosure is not "true confessions." Poppen and Thompson (1974) have summarized the arguments on both sides of the issue. The principal arguments in favor of high levels of self-disclosure are as follows:

1. If counselors are open and honest about their thoughts and feelings, this will encourage similar behavior by their clients.
2. Knowing that the counselor has had similar adjustment problems helps clients feel more at ease to discuss their own.
3. Children learn by imitation and can learn to solve their own problems through hearing about the experiences of others.
4. Counselors could be models for behavior.

On the other side of the issue, those opposing high levels of self-disclosure claim the following:

1. Clients are in the counselor's office for help with their problems, not to hear about the counselor's problems.
2. Counseling could become a time for sharing gripes or problems rather than a working session for personal growth.
3. Counselors can lose objectivity if they identify too strongly with the child's concerns.

Poppen and Thompson believe that

> self-disclosure is more beneficial when it takes a here-and-now focus — that is, when self-disclosure becomes an open and authentic expression of the counselor's or student's [child's] thoughts and feelings experienced at a particular time. Self-disclosure, when examined in the here-and-now context, means much more than dredging up the dark secrets of the past. [1974, p. 15]

What Types of Questions Should the Counselor Use?

Lay people often think they must ask children multitudes of questions when listening to their stories or problems in order to get the "whole story." Usually, these questions are of the "who," "what," "when," "where," and "what did you do next" variety. These questions may or may not be asked for the purpose of helping the child or for clarification; too often they arise out of general curiosity. Some questions may even be totally irrelevant and interrupt or ignore the child's thoughts and expressions. Questions can also be used to judge, blame, or criticize.

Child: The teacher called me a dummy in front of the whole class today!

Adult: (sarcastically) What did you say this time to make him call you that?

At that particular moment, the important fact is not what the child said, but the fact that the child was embarrassed, hurt, and possibly angered. By listening and understanding feelings and expressions rather than probing for details of who said what and when it was said, the adult will get the whole story eventually and will maintain a much friendlier relationship with the child. If counselors listen and respond with understanding, they will learn the child's important thoughts or problems. In other words, questions rephrased as statements work better.

Some counselors have a tendency to take over the counseling interview in their efforts to help the child. When counselors direct the interview, they run the serious risk of missing important feelings and thoughts. The counselor may guide the conversation in a totally meaningless direction.

Child: I hate my brother.
Counselor: Why do you hate your brother?
Child: Because he's mean.
Counselor: How is he mean?
Child: He hits me.
Counselor: What do you do to make him hit you? [accusation]
Child: Nothing.
Counselor: Come on, now. Tell me about when he hits you—and what your mother does when he hits you.

This example sounds more like an inquisition than a counseling session. The hitting and what the mother does may or may not be what is really troubling the child. What could be more important is the feeling that exists between the child and her brother. Is it really "hate" because he hits her, or could there be other problems in the relationship that the counselor will miss by focusing on hitting rather than listening to the child tell about her relationship with her brother? It is also possible that "hating brother" could have been a test problem to see if the counselor really would listen and be understanding. The true problem could be overlooked entirely by a counselor who guides the interview by questions; it may be revealed later if the child decides the counselor is a friend and can be trusted.

You may also have noticed in the preceding example that the child answered the counselor's questions but offered no further information. Children easily fall into the role of answering adults' questions and then waiting for the next question; thus, the pattern of a question-and-answer session is set. Rather than being the listener and helper that the counselor promised to be, suddenly the counselor is placed in the role of questioner. When the counselor runs out of questions, the interview may die if this pattern has been established.

Obviously, there are times in counseling when direct questions should be asked. The counselor may need factual information or clarification of what is being discussed. However, counselors will probably find that they get more information from children if they use open-ended questions. An open-ended question does not require a specific answer. It encourages the child to give the counselor more information about the topic but does not restrict replies or discourage further communication in the area.

Suppose a counselor was interested in learning about a child's social relationships. Rather than asking the direct, closed question "Do you have friends?" the counselor might elicit more information about the child's social relationships by saying "Tell me about what you like to do for fun—things that you enjoy doing in your free time." In this way, the counselor could learn not only about friends, but possibly also about the child's sports interests, hobbies, and other activities (or lack of activities). Another open-ended question that might help the counselor understand what is going on in the child's life is "Tell me about your family," out of which could come answers to such unasked questions as "Does your mother/father live in the home?" "How many people live in the household?" "What are your feelings about various members of the household?"

One further point should be made about questioning in counseling. Both Glasser (1969) and Benjamin (1987) caution adults about the use of "why" questions with youth. "Why" questions are associated with blame; "Why did you do that?" is often interpreted in the mind of a child as "Why did you do a *stupid thing* like that?" "Why" questions put people on the defensive; when asked why we acted a certain way, we feel forced to find some logical reason or excuse for our behavior. Glasser suggests that a better question might be a "what" question. Most of us are not really sure *why* we behaved a certain way, but we can tell *what* occurred. A "what" question does not deal with possible unconscious motives and desires but focuses on present behavior, allowing the client and counselor to look at what is happening now and what can be done.

Garbarino and Stott (1989) remind counselors that effective questions must be appropriate for the developmental level of their clients. They make the following suggestions for interviewing preschoolers.

- Use sentences that do not exceed by more than three or five words the number of words in a sentence the child uses.
- Use names rather than pronouns.
- Use the child's terms.
- Do not ask "Do you understand?" Ask the child to repeat your message.
- Do not repeat questions children do not understand, because they may think they have made errors and attempt to "correct" their answers. Rephrase the question instead.
- Avoid time-sequence questions.
- Preschoolers, being very literal, may give us answers that are easy to overinterpret.
- Do not respond to every answer with another question. A short summary or acknowledgement will encourage the child to expand on his or her previous statement.

In summary, counselors learn more by listening and summarizing than by questioning. The habit of questioning is difficult to break. When tempted to question, counselors might first ask themselves whether the questions they ask (1) will contribute therapeutically to their understanding of the child and the child's problems or (2) will inhibit the further flow of expression. In general, we find statements more useful than questions in the counseling process.

How Can Silences Be Used in Counseling?

Think a moment about the last time you were part of a group that suddenly fell silent. What happens at a party when the conversation begins to die? Most of us are very uncomfortable with silences. We have been socially conditioned to keep the conversation going; when conversation begins to ebb, we search through our thoughts for a new topic of interest to introduce to the group. Though silences can be very productive in a counseling interview, counselors often find them difficult to bear.

Benjamin (1987) suggests several productive uses of silences. He states that the child may need a few moments of silence to sort out thoughts and feelings, and "respect for this silence is more beneficial than many words from the interviewer" (p. 42). The child may have related some very emotional event or thought and may need a moment of silence to think about this revelation or regain composure. Benjamin further states that confusion can lead to a brief period of silence. The child or the counselor may have behaved or spoken in a confusing manner, and time may be required to sort things out.

On the other hand, silence can be a way of resisting counseling. The child may be reluctant to open up and talk with this stranger who promises acceptance or may simply be unwilling to admit and deal with the problem. Techniques such as play therapy, role-playing, or confrontation may be necessary to establish a better relationship and deal with the resistance.

Finally, Benjamin points out, silences can be used productively for problem solving. There are times when all of us need a few moments to collect our thoughts so we can work out problems that confront us or express our thoughts and feelings more clearly.

Silences can be productive, but how long should the counselor allow the silence to last? Obviously, an entire session of silence between child and counselor is not likely to be helpful. The child may begin spontaneously to speak again when ready. Children's nonverbal behavior may provide counselors with clues that they are ready to begin. The counselor may "test the water" by making a quiet statement reflecting the possible cause of the silence: "You seem a little confused about what you just told me." The child's response to this reflection should give an indication of whether he or she is ready to proceed.

Should Counselors Give Advice?

The role of a counselor has often been interpreted as that of an advice-giver, and some counseling theorists advocate giving advice to clients. Their rationale is that the counselor, who is trained in helping and is more knowing, should advise the less knowing client.

We prefer to view the role of the counselor as one of using skills and knowledge to assist another person in solving his or her own problems or conflicts. Counselors who believe in the uniqueness, worth, dignity, and responsibility of the individual and who believe that, given the right conditions, individuals can make correct choices for themselves will be reluctant to give advice on solving life's problems. Instead, they will use their counseling knowledge and skill to help clients make responsible choices of their own.

An illustration of the difference between giving advice and assisting in problem solving may help to clarify the point. Consider the example of a 12-year-old girl who tells her counselor she is ten weeks pregnant. You may be sorting through ideas to conclude what her best solution would be. Should this immature 12-year-old child have the baby and keep the child to bring up herself? Should she have the baby and place the child for adoption? Should she have an abortion? Should she marry the father? Perhaps her parents or his parents will adopt the child. Taking this example to the extreme, let's hypothesize that you advise the child and her parents that she should have an abortion because of her youth, immature body, and a multitude of other factors. Ten years later she sees you and confesses that she has experienced severe guilt and depression since the abortion because of her religious and moral beliefs. Abortion to her has been an unforgivable sin.

Using the same illustration, suppose you advise this 12-year-old and her parents that the best solution would be for the girl to have the baby and give the child up for adoption. Ten years later, she tells you she never sleeps at night without dreaming of her "lost" child and has spent the last three years diligently searching for the child.

Admittedly, this example is an extreme case; however, it is a very realistic counseling situation, especially as the rate of pregnancy among very young, unwed girls is rising rapidly. However extreme the example, the point is that each child client is an individual. Each has a different heredity, background, set of values, feelings, needs, and cultural mores. Because of these differences in lifestyle, temperament, and personality, only the individual with the problem can make the best choice for himself or herself—with the counselor's guidance and assistance.

A second example will emphasize the point further. Because most counselors believe in good communication between parents and children, they tend to encourage young people to talk with their parents about their concerns, feeling confident that parents will be supportive and understanding. Recall Tony in Chapter 1, who was threatened by neighborhood bullies who were going to beat him up on the way home from school. Tony confides his fear of fighting to the counselor, who advises him to talk this over with his parents—they will understand and will probably talk to the neighborhood boys' parents, and everything will work out fine. Tony is reluctant to talk to his parents, but the counselor persuades him they will understand and help. Tony returns later to relate that his father lectured him for being a "sissy" and instructed him to "go out and fight like a man." Tony is now more terrified than ever. He thinks that neither his parents nor the counselor understand his dilemma and that they cannot be counted on to support him. In this case, the counselor, not considering the client's home and culture, gave advice that intensified the problem. The counselor might have been more helpful by assisting Tony to think of ways of solving the problem—ways that Tony would choose.

Another possible disadvantage of counselors' giving advice is the problem of dependency. Counselors want their child clients to become responsible individuals, capable of solving their own problems. Children have a multitude of adults telling them how and when to act, but only a few assist them to learn responsible problem-solving behavior. In counseling, children learn the problem-solving process; they learn that they do not have to depend on adults to make decisions for them. The process can develop confident, mature, and independent individuals moving toward self-actualization.

Excessive advice-giving in counseling can foster dependency, overconformity, and low self-esteem. Counselors who encourage excessive dependency in clients might investigate their own motivations and needs. Most counselors find it extremely frustrating when clients depend upon them for decisions concerning their every move. A dependency relationship inevitably breeds hostility: the dependent person resents having to depend on the counselor; the counselor resents having to support the dependency of the client. This conflict is analogous to the typical adolescent struggle for independence. The attempt to resolve the dependence/independence crisis can result in poor parent/child communication and considerable conflict.

Since many people see the counselor's role as that of advice-giver, some clients may become frustrated and angry when counselors will not give advice. When asked what they think they could do to work out the conflict or problem, children typically are unable to think of possible solutions. It is a new experience for many children to be involved in solving their own problems. When pressed to give advice, a counselor could reflect the feeling that the child is not sure what to do and would like to have an answer, and then suggest again that they explore possibilities together. If the child is persistent and demands an answer, the counselor may wish to explore the reasons for this demand.

We need to point out, however, that counselors have a duty to protect their clients from any harm they might do to themselves as well as to prevent them from harming others. Therefore, counselors may need to give advice in emergency situations and to act on the advice they give.

Should Counselors Give Information?

Beginning counselors, believing that giving information is the same as giving advice, often give neither. Clients need good information to make good decisions, and it helps clients if counselors share what good information they have. For example, counselors should inform their clients of community and school resources where clients can receive assistance. The decision to seek assistance should be the client's. In other words, advice often takes the form of a suggestion to perform a certain behavior or to take some course of action. Information-giving, on the other hand, means providing data, facts, general knowledge, and to some extent, alternatives. Remember, lack of information about self and the environment are two primary problem causes. The counselor's role is to help clients find the information they need to solve their problems. Once again, we believe the more actively clients seek their own information, the better their learning experience will be.

How Does the Counselor Stay on Task during the Counseling Session?

Children soon discover that the counselor is a good listener who gives them undivided attention. Because many children are not listened to by adults, they often take advantage of the counseling situation to talk about everything except the reason for coming to counseling. With the least suggestion, the counselor may find the child rambling on about a TV show, last night's ballgame, a current movie, tricks his or her pet dog can do, or any number of other irrelevant topics. Children can ramble excessively when they wish to avoid a problem. Talkativeness then becomes a diversionary tactic either to avoid admitting what is troubling them or to avoid coping with the conflict. The conflict could be so traumatic or painful that the child does not want to face it.

Another possible reason for a counseling session becoming a gab session is that children do not understand their role in the counseling interview. If the purpose of counseling and expectations of the people involved are clearly defined in the initial interview, this will be less likely to occur.

Unfortunately, some counselors would rather chat with their child clients than "work" during the counseling interview. Counselors sometimes find it easier to engage in a superficial relationship and general conversation for the time they are with the child rather than to risk the involvement of caring and possibly uncovering and having to cope with intense feelings and emotions.

When counselors discover themselves being led into superficial or rambling conversations by their child clients, they may want to bring the conversation back to the problem at hand by reflecting to the child, "We seem to be getting away from the reason for our time together. I wonder if you could tell me more about . . . " If a child consistently wanders, it may be helpful to state that you notice the wandering and then to explore possible reasons for the avoidance. A tape recorder can be an excellent means of determining when, how, and why the distractions occur. A contract might be drawn up, such as "*(The counselor)* and I will work on *(the problem)* for 25 minutes. I can talk to *(the counselor)* about anything else for the last 5 minutes."

What Limits Should Be Set in Counseling?

In training, most counselors are taught to be empathic, respectful, genuine, accepting, and nonjudgmental—characteristics that writers such as Carl Rogers and Robert Carkhuff have defined as essential for a facilitative counseling relationship. Counselors may follow many other theories during the counseling process, but most believe that establishing a therapeutic relationship based on these ingredients is a necessary first step for effective counseling. The characteristics of empathy, respect, and genuineness have been operationally defined by Carkhuff (1969), and many training institutions teach counselors these behaviors according to his model. To define the counseling attitudes and behaviors involved in being accepting and nonjudgmental may not be quite so easy.

From the concepts of Rogers (1961), van Kaam (1965), and Frankl (1962), we may conclude that acceptance is born of genuine concern for people. Acceptance implies that counselors believe individuals have infinite worth and dignity, the right to make choices and decisions for their lives, and responsibility for their own lives. It is possible to accept an individual as a person of worth and potential without accepting that person's behavior. Children should be viewed as unique and responsible individuals, capable of making wise choices; however, adults cannot totally accept all child behaviors. Acceptance does not imply total permissiveness. Respect for the rights of all individuals involved must accompany acceptance, and counselors cannot allow children to infringe on their rights as people, or on the rights of other family members, friends, or acquaintances.

Being accepting and nonjudgmental can be difficult for some counselors, especially when moral and ethical issues are involved in the counseling. Counselors are human beings with their own attitudes, values, and beliefs. People sometimes make judgments very quickly, on the basis of little information, because of their values and beliefs. It is difficult to remain open-minded enough to really hear the client's entire story if a strong conflict exists between the client's values and those of the counselor.

Being nonjudgmental does not imply total permissiveness. Rather, it involves withholding those judgments we ordinarily make and allowing clients to tell their whole story without being threatened by the counselor's condemnation. Counselors attempt to refrain from blaming, accusing, criticizing, and moralizing, but they also attempt to teach responsible, reality-oriented behavior to their child clients. The counselor does not tell children they are "wrong"; the counselor's job is to help children explore the consequences, advantages, and disadvantages of their choices and, perhaps, discover better methods of resolving the conflict. For instance, rather than sermonizing to Tony that fighting is wrong, the counselor might be more helpful by thinking with him about what would happen if he challenged the bully to a fight and whether there were other ways to gain his father's acceptance and respect.

In summary, being accepting and nonjudgmental are essential characteristics of good counseling, but they must be combined with respect for the rights of others, the reality of the situation, and responsibility for one's own behavior.

What about the Issue of Confidentiality?

Most counselors are taught in their training programs that whatever is said in a counseling interview should remain confidential unless there is danger to the client, another person, or property. Many explain the principle of confidentiality to their clients during the first interview; others discuss confidentiality only if the child asks whether what is said will be told to parents or teachers. Should information indicating danger to a person or property be revealed during later interviews, counselors will want to remind children of the counselor's obligation to report such danger to the proper authorities. Counselors do not have privileged communication in their counselor/client relationships unless they are licensed by a state regulatory board. Counselors' records can be subpoenaed, and counselors can be called to testify in court proceedings should the information they possess be deemed necessary for a court decision. If counselors think that revealing the information required in their testimony could harm the child, they can request a private conference with the judge to share both the information and their reasons for wanting to keep the information confidential.

Some counselors who work with children do not think confidentiality is an important concern of children. Counselors with this orientation maintain that children and adults should be encouraged to communicate more openly with one another and that the counselor can facilitate this process in the counseling interview. They further contend that parents and other adults can provide insight and needed information about the child; the significant adult in the child's life can become a co-counselor. A signed contract with the parents to protect the confidentiality of the child's counseling sessions, though not legally binding, may help establish the interview content's confidentiality.

Careful evaluation of the child's presenting problem and the adults involved may help the counselor decide whether strict confidentiality should be maintained or if others should be included. To avoid misunderstanding and maintain the trust necessary for the counseling relationship, the decision to include others or share information should always be discussed with the child.

Is This Child Telling Me the Truth?

One counseling problem that can arise out of being an accepting person and a good listener is the question of whether the child is telling the counselor the truth or enhancing or exaggerating to get attention or sympathy. Children often tell their counselors of seeing people shoot one another, raging fires, and robberies. Unfortunately, many of these stories are true; however, children have vivid imaginations, and it is difficult to know how much to believe. Counselors do not want to be gullible, nor do they want to deny the truth.

If counselors doubt the truth of what they are hearing, soliciting more details of the incident (for example, by saying "Tell me more") may clarify whether the story is truth or fiction. When asked to give specifics, children may admit they were "only kidding" or "making it up." Counselors might also admit their genuine concerns: "I am really having trouble with this because I have never heard anything like it." An admission of this sort by a counselor expresses a genuine feeling and avoids labeling the child a liar or possibly denying a true story. It also provides the child with an opportunity to change the story while saving face. However, Garbarino and Stott (1989) point out that in cases of suspected child sexual abuse, the most effective approach is to be willing to believe the child. They recommend that we recognize that most child-initiated allegations are grounded in real experiences, even if these experiences in themselves do not constitute sexual abuse.

What Can Be Done When the Interview Process Becomes Blocked?

There will be counseling sessions when the child does not feel like talking. It is possible that things have been going well for the past few days and the child really has nothing to discuss. There may be a lull before new material is introduced. One way to avoid these unexpected empty periods is to be prepared for a session. Some counselors have general goals for their client (for instance, to increase assertiveness) and also define specific short-term goals for each session as counseling proceeds. Whether the counselor prefers to define objectives or not, notes of the previous session can be reviewed and a tentative plan made for the coming interview. Obviously, this plan is subject to change according to the content of the interview.

However, the best laid plans often go awry. When the child seems highly distracted, a short summary by the counselor or child of the previous conversation may stimulate further communication. If the child does not seem to want to talk, the techniques of play therapy (drawing, clay, games) may be beneficial. There may be times (illness, extreme excitability, or apathy) when it is best to end the session short of the designated time. The length of counseling sessions can vary from a few minutes to an hour depending on the client's age and presenting problem.

When sessions bog down, evaluate what is happening. Again, the tape recorder can be of assistance in assessing the lack of progress. Bogging down may be a sign that the child is ready for the counseling to conclude. It could be resistance on the part of the child client. It could come from the counselor's inadequate skills or lack of planning. Unproductive sessions will occur occasionally with all counselors, but frequent periods of nonproductivity should signal the counselor to investigate what is happening.

When Should Counseling Be Terminated?

How does a counselor decide when to end counseling? Does the counselor or the client decide? How does either party know when the client is ready to stand alone? If the counselor and client have clearly defined the problem brought to counseling and the goal to be accomplished, the termination time will be evident—when the goal is accomplished.

Termination may be difficult for children because they usually find the sessions to be a time when a caring adult gives them undivided attention. Deep friendships are often formed between counselor and child, and the child (and possibly the counselor) does not wish to end this pleasant relationship. In order to ease the break, client and counselor can discuss a possible termination date several weeks ahead of time. Plans can be made and rehearsed about how the child will react should problems occur again. The child can be left with a feeling that the counselor still cares and will be available should trouble arise again. Counselors may even consider building in a follow-up time when they ask their child clients to drop them a note or call to let them know how things are going. The counselor may want to schedule a brief follow-up visit. Any informal method of showing the child that a counselor's caring does not end with the last interview can signal the counselor's continued interest in the child's growth and development. Most successful counselors use a plan for maintaining the gains their child clients have achieved during counseling. Such maintenance plans require periodic follow-up contacts.

TABLE 2-4 Goal-attainment follow-up guide
Level at intake: √
Level at follow-up: ★

Scale attainment level	Scale 1: Working on task $W_1 = 20$	Scale 2: Disruptive behavior $W_2 = 30$	Scale 3: Punctuality $W_3 = 25$	Scale 4: Relationships $W_4 = 30$	Scale 5: Grade improvement $W_5 = 10$
a. Most unfavorable counseling outcome thought likely (−2)	Daydreams, leaves desk; ignores assignments √	Pushes, hits, leaves room, talks without permission	Fails to set clock and oversleeps √	Child gets into three fights per day √	Child continues to fail √
b. Less than expected success with counseling (−1)	Completes one assignment per day	Talks without permission	Shuts off alarm clock and goes back to sleep	Child gets into at least one fight per day	Child demonstrates "D" work
c. Expected level of counseling success (0)	Completes two assignments per day	Engages in appropriate behavior 75% of the time	Arises when alarm sounds	Child avoids all fights	Child demonstrates "C" work
d. More than expected success with counseling (+1)	Completes three assignments per day ★	Engages in appropriate behavior 85% of the time ★	Arises before alarm sounds; makes bed	Child develops one new friend ★	Child demonstrates "B" work ★
e. Best anticipated success with counseling (+2)	Completes four assignments per day	Engages in appropriate behavior 100% of the time	Arises in time to make bed and fix own breakfast ★	Child develops three new friends	Child demonstrates "A" work

★ Percentage figures based on spot-check observations during the school day.

How Can Counseling Be Evaluated?

One method of evaluation is goal-attainment scaling, which has the double advantage of facilitating the counseling process and evaluating counseling outcomes. Goal-attainment scaling (Kiresuk, 1973, 1976; Emmerson & Neely, 1988; and Smith 1976) is a process that allows counselor and client the opportunity to establish counseling goals cooperatively. The counselor's task is to help the child clarify these goals in measurable terms as a way of evaluating the distance between "what I have" and "what I would like to have." The tabulation and calculation of the data are the counselor's responsibility. Generally one to five goals are set, with five levels of attainment defined for each goal (see Table 2-4). In addition, each goal is given a weight to represent its importance to the client. Clients establish priorities for their goals, assigning weights to the most important and least important. For instance, goal number 1 may be three times more important than goal number 2. Intermediate goals are assigned weights representing their relative importance to the client. For example, if the most important goal is three times as important as the least important goal, it would receive a weight of 30 compared to a weight of 10 for the least important goal. Intermediate goals are then weighted on a scale of 10 to 30.

Levels of attainment for each goal range from a $+2$ for the best anticipated success to a -2 for the least favorable outcome. A 0 value is assigned for the middle level of expected outcome success. Values of $+1$ and -1 represent "more than" and "less than" expected levels of success, respectively.

The goals are defined in measurable and observable terms, with the level of entry checked on the goal-attainment follow-up guide. Following counseling, an asterisk is placed on the guide indicating where the client is after counseling. Follow-up data can also be recorded periodically on the chart.

Goal-attainment scores can be calculated for both the intake and follow-up levels. A follow-up goal-attainment score of 50 or better is considered successful. Kiresuk and Sherman (1968) adopted a conventional T-score scale with the mean set at 50 and a standard deviation set at 10 for their goal-attainment scale. The formulas on pages 53 to 55 are used to derive the goal-attainment scores for the guide in Table 2-4 (Kiresuk & Sherman, 1968).

Goal-Attainment Score
Calculation: Level at Intake

$\overline{X}$ = mean

s = standard deviation

p = probability

w = weight value

x = scale value

$\overline{X} = 50$

$s = 10$ (standard deviation)

$p = .3$

$1 - p = .7$

$w = 10$ to 30

$x = {}^-2$ to $^+2$

Goal-attainment score (T) = $50 + \dfrac{10\Sigma w_1 x_1}{\sqrt{(.7\Sigma w_1{}^2 + .3(\Sigma w_1)^2}}$

$50 + 10[(20 \times -2) + (30 \times -1) + (25 \times -2) + (30 \times -2) + (10 \times -2)]$

$50 + \dfrac{10 \times -200}{\sqrt{.7(20^2 + 30^2 + 25^2 + 30^2 + 10^2) + .3(20 + 30 + 25 + 30 + 10)^2}}$

$50 + \dfrac{10 \times -200}{\sqrt{.7(2925) + .3(13225)}}$

$50 + \dfrac{10 \times -200}{\sqrt{6015}}$

$50 + \dfrac{10 \times -200}{77.56}$

$50 + \dfrac{(-2000)}{77.56}$

$50 + (-25.78)$

$T = 24.22$

z score = $\dfrac{50 - 24.22}{10}$ = 2.58 standard deviations below the mean

Goal-Attainment Score
Calculation: Level at Follow-Up

$\overline{X}$ = mean $\overline{X}$ = 50
s = standard deviation s = 10 (standard deviation)
p = probability p = .3
w = weight value $1 - p$ = .7
x = scale value w = 10 to 30
                                        x = -2 to +2

Goal-attainment score (T) = $50 + \dfrac{10\Sigma w_1 x_1}{\sqrt{(.7\Sigma w_1{}^2 + .3(\Sigma w_1)^2}}$

$50 + 10[(20 \times 1) + (30 \times 1) + (25 \times 2) + (30 \times 1) + (10 \times 1)]$

$50 + \dfrac{10 \times 140}{\sqrt{.7(20^2 + 30^2 + 25^2 + 30^2 + 10^2) + .3(20 + 30 + 25 + 30 + 10)^2}}$

$50 + \dfrac{10 \times 140}{\sqrt{.7(2925) + .3(13225)}}$

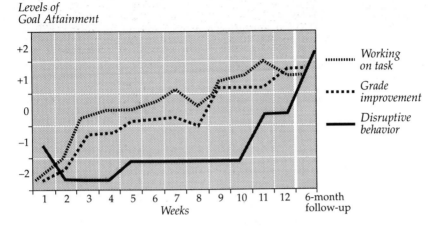

FIGURE 2-4 Weekly goal-attainment scale

$$50 + \frac{10 \times 140}{\sqrt{6015}}$$

$$50 + \frac{10 \times 140}{77.56}$$

$$50 + \frac{(1400)}{77.56}$$

$$50 + (18)$$

$$T = 68$$

z score $= \dfrac{68 - 50}{10} = \dfrac{18}{10} = 1.8$ standard deviations above the mean

Goal-attainment scaling (Dowd & Kelly, 1975) can be graphed to show weekly progress (see Figure 2-4). The graph can also be used to chart the results of periodic follow-up checks on the maintenance of counseling gains.

REFERENCES

American Psychological Association, Division of Counseling Psychology, Committee on Definition. (1956). Counseling psychology as a specialty. *American Psychologist, 11,* 282–285.

Benjamin, A. (1987). *The helping interview* (3rd ed.). Boston: Houghton Mifflin.

Boat, B., & Everson, M. (1986). *Using anatomical dolls: Guidelines for interviewing young children in sexual abuse investigations.* Unpublished manuscript, University of North Carolina, School of Medicine, Chapel Hill, NC.

Carkhuff, R. (1969). *Helping and human relations* (2 vols.). New York: Holt, Rinehart & Winston.

Carlson, K. (1990). Suggestions for counseling "other-referred" children. *Elementary School Guidance and Counseling, 24,* 222–229.

Coleman, J., Morris, C., & Glaros, A. (1987). *Contemporary psychology and effective behavior.* Glenview, IL: Scott, Foresman.

Corsini, R., & Wedding, D. (1989). *Current psychotherapies* (4th ed.). Itasca, IL: F. E. Peacock.

Dimond, R., Havens, R., & Jones, A. (1978). A conceptual framework for the practice of prescriptive electicism in psychotherapy. *American Psychologist, 33,* 239–248.

Dowd, E., & Kelly, F. (1975). The use of goal attainment scaling in single case study research. *Goal Attainment Review, 2,* 11–21.

Emmerson, G., & Neely, M. (1988). Two adaptable, valid and reliable data collection measures: Goal attainment scaling and the semantic differential. *The Counseling Psychologist, 16,* 261–271.

Erikson, E. (1963). *Childhood and society.* New York: Norton.

Erikson, E. (1968). *Identity, youth, and crisis.* New York: Norton.

Frankl, V. (1962). *Man's search for meaning: An introduction to logotherapy.* Boston: Beacon Press.

Garbarino, J., & Stott, F. (1989). *What children can tell us.* San Francisco: Jossey-Bass.

Gerler, E. (1990). Multimodal approaches to counseling in schools. *Elementary School Guidance and Counseling, 24,* 242.

Gerler, E., Drew, N., & Mohr, P. (1990). Succeeding in middle school: A multimodal approach. *Elementary School Guidance and Counseling, 24,* 263–271.

Glass, G., & Kliegl, R. (1983). An apology for research integration in the study of psychotherapy. *Journal of Consulting and Clinical Psychology, 51,* 28–41.

Glasser, W. (1969). *Schools without failure.* New York: Harper & Row.

Glosoff, H., & Koprowicz, C. (1990). *Children achieving potential: An introduction to elementary school counseling and state-level policies.* The National Conference of State Legislatures and the American Association for Counseling and Development.

Harper, R. (1959). *Psychoanalysis and psychotherapy: Thirty-six systems.* Englewood Cliffs, NJ: Prentice-Hall.

Havighurst, R. (1961). *Human development and education* (2nd ed.). New York: David McKay.

Hoffman, L., & McDaniels, C. (1991). Career development in the elementary school: A perspective for the 1990's. *Elementary School Guidance and Counseling, 25,* 163–171.

Karasu, T. (1986). The specificity versus nonspecificity dilemma: Toward identifying therapeutic change agents. *American Journal of Psychiatry, 143,* 688–695.

Keat, D. (1990a). Change in child multimodal counseling. *Elementary School Guidance and Counseling, 24,* 248–262.

Keat, D. (1990b). *Child multimodal therapy.* Norwood, NJ: Ablex.

Kiresuk, T. (1973). Goal attainment scaling at a county mental service. *Evaluation,* Special Monograph No. 1, 12–18.

Kiresuk, T. (1976). *Guide to goals: Goal setting for children* (Format Two). Minneapolis, MN: Program Evaluation Resource Center.

Kiresuk, T., & Sherman, R. (1968). Goal attainment scaling: A general method for evaluating comprehensive community mental health programs. *Community Mental Health, 4,* 443–453.

Lazarus, A. (1981). *The practice of multimodal therapy.* New York: McGraw-Hill.

Lazarus, A. (1984). Multimodal therapy. In R. Corsini (Ed.), *Current psychotherapies* (3rd ed.) (pp. 491–530). Itasca, IL: F. E. Peacock.

Lazarus, A. (1990). Multimodal applications and research: A brief overview and update. *Elementary School Guidance and Counseling, 24,* 243–247.

Levinson, B. (1962). The dog as co-therapist. *Mental Hygiene, 46,* 59–65.

Lewis, C. (1985). *Listening to children.* Northvale, NJ: Aronson.

Luborsky, L., Singer, B., & Luborsky, L. (1975). Comparative studies of psychotherapies: Is it true that "everyone has one and all must have prizes"? *Archives of General Psychiatry, 32,* 995–1008.

Myrick, R. (1987). *Developmental guidance and counseling: A practical approach.* Minneapolis, MN: Educational Media Corporation.

Myrick, R. (1989). Developmental guidance: Practical considerations. *Elementary School Guidance and Counseling, 24,* 14–20.

Pallone, N. (1977). Counseling psychology: Toward an empirical definition. *The Counseling Psychologist, 7,* 29–32.

Parker, W., & McDavis, R. (1989). A personal development model for black elementary school students. *Elementary School Guidance and Counseling, 23,* 244–253.

Patterson, C. (1986). *Theories of counseling and psychotherapy* (4th ed.). New York: Harper & Row.

Peters, H., & Farwell, G. (1959). *Guidance: A developmental approach.* Chicago: Rand McNally.

Piaget, J., & Inhelder, B. (1969). *The psychology of the child.* New York: Basic Books.

Poppen, W., & Thompson, C. (1974). *School counseling: Theories and concepts.* Lincoln, NE: Professional Educators.

Rogers, C. (1961). *On becoming a person.* Boston: Houghton Mifflin.

Shapiro, D., & Shapiro, D. (1982). Meta-analysis of comparative therapy outcome studies: A replication of refinement. *Psychological Bulletin, 92,* 581–604.

Smith, D. (1976). Goal attainment scaling as an adjunct to counseling. *Journal of Counseling Psychology, 23,* 22–27.

Smith, M., & Glass, G. (1977). Meta-analysis of psychotherapy outcome studies. *American Psychologist, 32,* 752–760.

Smith, M., Glass, G., & Miller, T. (1980). *The benefits of psychotherapy.* Baltimore, MD: Johns Hopkins University Press.

Stiles, W., Shapiro, D., & Elliott, R. (1986). Are all psychotherapies equivalent? *American Psychologist, 13,* 142–149.

Teasdale, J. (1985). Psychological treatments for depression: How do they work? *Behavior Research and Therapy, 23,* 157–165.

Thompson, C., & Campbell, S. (in press). Personal intervention preferences for alleviating mild depression. *Journal of Counseling and Development.*

Thompson, C., & Poppen, W. (1992). *Guidance activities for counselors and teachers.* Knoxville, TN: Kinko's Copies.

van Kaam, A. (1965). Counseling from the viewpoint of existential psychology. In R. Mosher, R. Carle, & C. Kehas (Eds.), *Guidance: An examination* (pp. 68–81). New York: Harcourt, Brace, & World.

Wadsworth, B. (1989). *Piaget's theory of cognitive and affective development.* New York: Longman.

PART TWO

COUNSELING THEORIES AND TECHNIQUES
Their Application to Children

CHAPTER 3

Reality Therapy

WILLIAM GLASSER

William Glasser graduated from Case Institute of Technology as a chemical engineer in 1944, at the age of 19. Later, he enrolled at Case Western Reserve University and, at 23, earned a master's degree in clinical psychology. At 28 he received a medical degree from the same institution. While serving his last year of residency at the UCLA School of Psychiatry and in a Veterans Administration hospital, Glasser discovered that traditional psychotherapy was not for him. Glasser voiced reservations about psychoanalysis to his last teacher, who reputedly responded "Join the club," although such an attitude was not common or popular among most of his colleagues. Denied a promised teaching position because of his rebellion against Freudian concepts, Glasser was quoted as saying that if he had had to rely on referrals from his alma mater, as most beginning psychiatrists do, he would have made about $8000 in the first 16 years of his practice.

In 1956, Glasser became head psychiatrist at the Ventura School for Girls, an institution operated by the State of California for the treatment of seriously delinquent adolescent girls. His first book, *Mental Health or Mental Illness?* (1961), laid the basic foundation for the techniques and concepts of reality therapy. For 12 years Glasser conducted a successful program at the Ventura School; the theory and concepts of reality therapy evolved out of this program. Glasser used the term *reality therapy* for the first time in April 1964 in a manuscript entitled "Reality Therapy: A Realistic Approach to the Young Offender." His widely read book *Reality Therapy* was published in 1965. In 1966, Glasser began consulting in California public schools for the purpose of applying reality therapy in education. These new ideas for applying reality therapy to teaching later became his third book, *Schools Without Failure* (1969).

In 1968, Glasser founded the Institute for Reality Therapy in Los Angeles. The institute offers training courses for selected professionals such as physicians, probation officers, police officers, nurses, lawyers, judges, teachers, and counselors. Both introductory and advanced courses and programs are offered on a regular and continuing basis. Teams of consultants provide a broad base for teaching the application of reality therapy in a variety of settings. Following the publication of *Schools Without Failure,* the Educator Training Center, a special division of the Institute for Reality Therapy, was established in Los Angeles in 1971. In 1970, the William Glasser La Verne College Center was established at the University of La Verne in southern California to provide teachers with an off-campus opportunity to gain graduate and in-service credits while working within their own schools to provide an exciting educational environment for children.

The Schools Without Failure Seminars, sponsored by the Educator Training Center, continue to draw large followings across the country. Glasser's books include *The Identity Society* (1972), *Positive Addiction* (1976), *Stations of the Mind* (1981), *Control Theory* (1984), *Control Theory in the Classroom* (1986), and *The Quality School: Managing Students Without Coercion* (1990). Glasser makes approximately 75 speaking appearances a year in addition to television interviews, writing, and videotaping.

William Glasser is married and has three children. He enjoys sports such as water skiing, sailing, and tennis. Glasser sees himself as a person who enjoys being a helper, one who takes an optimistic view of life and who is good at solving problems. He loves to daydream and has little use for intellectuals who make understandable ideas difficult to grasp. Glasser has an excellent sense of humor, which he uses skillfully in his teaching and counseling. It is not surprising that he enjoys Clarence Day's *Life with Father* and the humor of Charles Schulz in "Peanuts."

THE NATURE OF PEOPLE

Glasser believes that, despite varying manifestations of psychological problems, problems are the result of one factor: an inability to fulfill one's basic needs. Glasser (1965) believes that a correlation exists between people's lack of success in meeting their needs and the degree of their distress. He maintains that all psychological problems can be summed up by the fact that people deny the reality of the world around them.

Borrowing from Maslow's hierarchy of human needs, Glasser focuses his treatment plan on teaching people to meet the basic needs to love and be loved and to feel valued by oneself and others. Successful attainment of these two needs leads to a success identity. In fact, how well one is doing in these two important areas can be a quick index of one's mental health. Both needs are keys to healthy self-esteem; this theme runs through a book entitled *The Social Importance of Self-Esteem,* edited by Mecca, Smelser, and Vasconcellos (1989). Kronick and Hargis (1990) echo the same points in their prescriptions for preventing school failure and school dropouts. They focus on teaching children basic social skills to help them interact more effectively with their peers and with adults in the school setting. Building a network of friends and supportive people will put one well on the road to achieving a healthy sense of self-esteem, a journey that will be completed through success in the classroom. Kronick and Hargis also recommend treating children who have failure identities through training in time management and study skills as a way of ensuring academic success. "Schools without failure" has been a principal theme throughout Glasser's work.

Sharing Rogers's optimistic view of human nature, Glasser believes that people have the ability to learn to fulfill their needs and to become responsible individuals. He bases his system on what he calls the "three Rs:" responsibility, right and wrong, and reality. We believe two other Rs could be added: relatedness and respect. Mutual respect and relationship are the keys to a successful counseling partnership.

Glasser views adjusted people as those who are responsible, who can fulfill their needs without infringing on the needs or rights of others. A primary product of becoming a responsible person is an increased feeling of self-worth.

THEORY OF COUNSELING

Glasser was reacting against some of the principles of psychoanalytic theory when he developed reality therapy. Reality therapy differs from traditional psychoanalytic therapy in six ways.

First, reality therapy discards the concept of mental illness in favor of the concept of responsibility. Traditionally, it has been proposed that people behave irresponsibly because they are mentally ill. Glasser believes that people become mentally ill because they behave irresponsibly.

Second, reality therapy focuses on the moral issue of right and wrong— an issue often ignored in counseling because many believe that people already feel too guilty about various unresolved conflicts. In Freud's time, everyone talked about doing the right thing, so Freud thought it best to make psychotherapy a sanctuary free of moral judgments in order not to increase feelings of guilt in his patients. In reality therapy, moral issues are addressed head-on.

Third, the past is largely ignored in favor of dealing with the present and future. Most discussion in reality therapy is directed toward evaluating how present behavior is helping to meet one's needs. If present behavior is not working, future alternatives are examined, and commitments to change are made.

A fourth difference involves the idea of transference. In traditional psychoanalytic practice, transference is frequently used as a therapeutic mechanism for living through unresolved conflicts. In reality therapy, the counselor relates to the client on a person-to-person basis. The counselor does not encourage the client to relate to the counselor as someone other than a counselor; for example, the child does not relate to the counselor as a parent, teacher, or other authority figure.

Fifth, the unconscious is largely ignored in reality therapy, whereas it is generally the primary focus in psychoanalytic practice. According to Glasser, the unconscious is a fertile ground for excuses for misbehavior. He prefers to look at *what* is going on rather than at *why*.

Perhaps the most significant feature of reality therapy that distinguishes it from traditional practice is the aspect most dear to educators. It is our philosophy that the counseling we perform with children is primarily a teaching/learning situation. This is exactly what Glasser says about reality therapy: It is a teaching process, not a healing process. Counselors are in the business of teaching children a better way to meet their needs. From the reality therapy point of view, counseling is a matter of learning how to solve problems — teaching children, in effect, to become their own counselors.

COUNSELING METHOD

The practice of reality therapy follows eight steps. Step 1 concerns the most significant aspect of all counseling — building good relationships with the children we counsel. Glasser calls this first step becoming involved with the people we counsel, although *involvement* may not be the best word to describe this stage of counseling because it implies entangled or complex relationships. Counselors want to develop positive relationships that are honest, open, and unencumbered. In any approach to counseling children, the goal is to build the kind of trust and climate in which children feel free to express their innermost fears, anxieties, and concerns.

Step 2 is an examination of present behavior in a nonpunitive way. In Step 3, children are asked to evaluate what is going on in their lives and how they are helping themselves. In other words, is their behavior helping them get what they want from life? If not, then there will be a chance to ask "Do you want to change what is going on?"

This leads to the fourth step in reality therapy. The counselor and child now begin to look at the possible alternatives for getting what the child wants out of life. Step 4 follows a brainstorming format, in which the child is asked to look at better ways of meeting his or her needs. Step 5 involves selecting an alternative for reaching the child's goals. The child then makes a commitment to try the alternative. A key process in counseling children is helping them make commitments. When they are able to carry out present commitments, counselors can help them build on these successes to get more out of life. Therefore, children are first asked to make a relatively small commitment in which they can achieve success and have a basis on which to build.

In Step 6, counselor and client examine the results of the commitment. Often children will return for a second interview; say, "Well, I made a commitment to turn in one homework paper a day, and I did not meet my commitment"; and begin to list all the reasons they failed. Reality therapists do not dwell on rationalizing "whys." At this point, the counselor and child will discuss writing a new contract the child can handle; maybe one homework paper per day is too much for now, and a less demanding contract is needed. Counselors do not accept excuses if a child does not meet the commitments he or she made. Excuses are designed to avoid punishment, and when children learn they will not be punished for not meeting a commitment and for talking about what they do, there will be no need for excuses.

Step 7 entails the use of logical consequences—for instance, receiving a lower grade for failing to turn in a homework paper. Additional penalties that are not logical or natural consequences of failing to turn in the paper, such as paddling, are considered neither effective nor humane; however, logical and natural consequences are not to be permissively removed.

Step 8 requires that we do not become discouraged with our counseling failures and give up too soon. How long should we stick with children who seem bent on destroying our self-concepts as effective counselors? Glasser recommends that we work with such children three or four more times than they expect. We are not talking about a lifelong commitment when we say "Never give up." Rather, we should build on whatever relationship has been established in Step 1 and continue to build this relationship through the entire eight-step process. Glasser and his trainers modify the basic steps in reality therapy from time to time; however, we hold to the maxim, "If it ain't broke, don't fix it." The original version of reality therapy, with our own adaptations of the method, still works well for us.

The three key terms in reality therapy, which have been mentioned only briefly so far, are *reality, responsibility,* and *right and wrong*. In reality therapy, *reality* is generally defined as willingness to accept the logical, natural consequences of one's behavior. When we try to avoid these consequences, we deny reality and are prone to act irresponsibly. Glasser defines *responsibility* as the ability to meet one's needs without infringing on other people's rights to meet their needs. The third term is difficult to define, and Glasser's definition leaves us on somewhat shaky ground. Glasser defines *right and wrong* as something you know by how you feel; this is one of the few areas in which Glasser works with the concept of feelings. He would say that our feelings are good indicators of when we are behaving in responsible and correct ways. For example, if we feel good about what we are doing and most other people also feel good about it, then we are probably doing the right thing. One problem with defining right and wrong in terms of others' opinions is that many people have made significant contributions in the face of mass criticism.

At this point, we should examine some of the basic questions asked in the counseling process. The first step—and one that must continue throughout the counseling process—is to build a warm relationship that helps you become friends with the child. A number of things can help you do this, but genuine interest in the child is the key ingredient.

There is a series of five questions often asked in reality therapy that may be posed in different ways: (1) What are you doing? (2) Is what you are doing helping you get what you want? (3) If not, what might be some other things you could try? (4) Which idea would you like to try first? (5) When? The dialogue below is an example of how you can begin.

Counselor: Mary, can you tell me a little bit about your life right now here at school?

Mary: What do you mean?

Counselor: Well, Mary, it seems as though you get sent to the office a lot to talk to me about problems you're having with your teachers. Tell me what you're doing, and let's talk about it.

Mary: Well, I guess I talk out of turn in class too much sometimes. But my classes are so boring.

Counselor: OK, so you talk out a lot in class, and the teachers don't like what you're doing. Do you do anything else that seems to get you in trouble with Mr. Thompson and Mrs. Rudolph?

Mary: No, I don't think so.

Counselor: Are you happy with what happens to you when you do these things?

Mary: I do the same old things that keep getting me in trouble, but I feel good for the moment.

Counselor: I know you do feel better for a while. Are the good feelings worth the price you have to pay for them?

Mary: I guess not, because I'm sure tired of spending so much time in the office.

Counselor: Would you like to work on a better plan?

Mary: OK. Why not?

Counselor: Let's start by thinking of some things you could do to get along better in your classes and some ways to make them less boring, too.

Mary: Well, I could stop talking out of turn! I know the teachers would like that.

Counselor: Stopping unhelpful things is usually a good way to start. What about some things you could begin doing in class?

Mary: Doing more assignments would please the teachers, but I don't like all the work.

Counselor: Your two suggestions will probably help you with the teachers, but they won't do much to make the class more enjoyable for you. Can you think of something to help you like school more?

Mary: Some of the kids get free time or get to go to the library when they turn in their work. Could I do this, too?

Counselor: We can ask your teachers about that today. That might be a way to please both you and the teachers. Can you think of other ideas to try?

Mary: I guess that's about all for now.

Counselor: OK, Mary, how many of these ideas do you want to try?

Mary: I think I can do all of them if I can get free time, too.

Counselor: When do you want to start?

Mary: Today, if I can.

Counselor: We can try. Can you go over these with me one time before we leave?

Mary: I think so. No more talking out of turn, and do enough work to earn some free time.

Counselor: That sounds good to me. Do you want to shake hands and make this an agreement between you and me?

Mary: OK.

Counselor: Good. I'd like to talk with you a little each day to see how your plan is working. If it doesn't work, we'll have to make another plan. See you tomorrow?

Mary: OK, see you.

The above is a typical interview following the reality therapy philosophy and technique. Identifying and evaluating present behavior are followed by making a plan and building a commitment to follow through on it. Each step in the reality therapy process is supported by a relationship of trust, caring, and friendship between the counselor and the child.

As we mentioned in Chapter 2, we believe that the counseling process works better when the counselor uses statements rather than questions. Questioning tends to make the interview more counselor-centered because the questions move the interview from a dialogue toward a teacher/student question-and-answer session. We believe statements provide a better result with more acceptance of a plan that is the client's rather than the counselor's. For example,

Counselor: Wendy, I understand there has been a problem in your math class. If you feel up to it, we can spend some time talking about it.

As for each theory presented in Part Two, we have included an actual transcript from a case brought to a counselor as a way of demonstrating how the theory can be put into practice.

CASE STUDY

Identification of the Problem

Wendy Smith is a 12-year-old girl in the seventh grade at White Oak School. She was referred to the counselor because she was cheating on a mathematics test.

Individual and Background Information

Academic.   School records indicate that Wendy is a high achiever, with an overall "A" average on her elementary-school record. She also has an "A" average for the first two grading periods in the seventh grade. During the third grading period, which is almost over, Wendy has had some erratic test scores in mathematics. The test she was caught cheating on was an important test that could have brought up her low grades had she done well on it.

Family.   Wendy is the only child of older parents, both of whom are professionals. Teachers have indicated that the parents seem to expect Wendy to make the highest grades in her class.

Social.   According to teachers' reports on cumulative records, Wendy was well liked by most of the children in her classes in elementary school. She did not seem to have a close friend then, but this year she has developed a close friendship with a girl in her class. A sociogram done in her sixth-grade class last fall shows she is well accepted by her peers.

Counseling Method

The counselor used the reality therapy counseling method to help Wendy evaluate her behavior and identify some things she could do to meet more of her needs socially and emotionally without creating problems in other areas of her life.

The five basic steps followed by the counselor in this case are: (1) establishment of a relationship; (2) identification of present behavior—what is being done, or has been done; (3) evaluation of present behavior—is it helping the client get what he or she wants? (4) development of plans that will help; and (5) commitment from the client to try at least one of the plans.

Transcript

Counselor: Wendy, I understand that there has been a problem in your math class. Would you like to talk about it?

Wendy: I guess so.

Counselor: You're feeling somewhat embarrassed about the problem and uncomfortable about talking with me.

Wendy: Yes, I am, but I know I need to talk about it.

Counselor: Would you like to tell me what happened?

Wendy: Miss Waters caught me cheating on my math test. I have some bad grades in math this period. I knew I had to do well on this test, but I wasn't ready for it.

Counselor: How did you see cheating as helping you?

Wendy: I was feeling a lot of pressure because I wasn't prepared, and my parents expect me to do well.

Counselor: Can you tell me what you've been doing that kept you from being prepared for the test?

Wendy: I'm just getting to know Susan, and I've been spending a lot of time talking with her and not enough time studying.

Counselor: Susan's friendship is very important to you.

Wendy: Yes. I've never had a really close friend before.

Counselor: What might be some ways you could still be friends with Susan and also keep up with your studies?

Wendy: Well, I guess I could spend less time talking to her and more time studying.

Counselor: You believe that you can spend less time with Susan and still be close friends?

Wendy: Yes, I'm sure she'd understand.

Counselor: What are some other things you could do that might help?

Wendy: Maybe we could spend time together studying instead of talking so much.

Counselor: Would you like to try one of these plans for the next week and see how it works?

Wendy: OK. I'd like to try studying with Susan.

Counselor: All right. Let's meet next Tuesday at 1:00 and see how well your plan worked.

THE TEN-STEP REALITY THERAPY CONSULTATION MODEL

The ten-step reality therapy consultation model (Thompson & Poppen, 1992) has been an effective tool for counselors to use with teachers and parents who seek the counselor's assistance with their children's behavior and motivation problems. The ten steps are divided into three phases, each phase having a special objective. Phase I, consisting of three steps, is designed to assist the teacher or parent in building a better relationship with the child.

Step 1. List what you have already tried with the child that does not help. Stopping these ineffective interventions often stimulates a positive change in the child's behavior.

Step 2. If Step 1 is unsuccessful, make a list of change-of-pace interventions that are designed to disrupt the expected interactions between the adult and the child. For example, catch the child behaving appropriately; act surprised when the child repeats the same old irritating behavior; ask yourself what the child expects you to do and then do *not* do it; try a paradoxical counseling strategy, such as asking the child to increase the behavior you would like to eliminate.

Step 3. If Step 3 is necessary, make a list of things you could and would do to help the child have a better day tomorrow. For example, give the child at least three 20-second periods of your undivided, positive attention; ask the child to run an errand for you; give the child some choices in how to complete a task or an assignment; ask the child's opinion about something relevant to both of you; give the child an important classroom or household chore; negotiate a few rules (fewer than five) that you and the child think are fair to both of you.

Phase II, consisting of three steps, is devoted to counseling the child. In most cases we find that successful interventions will happen in the first phase. When this does not occur, we ask the adult to move to Step 4.

Step 4. Try one-line counseling approaches such as the following:
  a. Ask the child to stop the undesirable behavior. Use as few words as possible, relying instead on nonverbal gestures. Do not use threats.
  b. Try the "Could it be?" questions recommended by the practitioners of individual psychology (see Chapter 10).
  c. Acknowledge the child's cooperative efforts, but do not thank the child for behaving responsibly as if it were a favor to you.

Step 5. Use reality therapy questions that emphasize the rules on which agreement was reached in a previous negotiation.
  a. What did you do?
  b. What is our rule?
  c. What were you supposed to do?
  d. What will you do?

Step 6. Use the standard reality therapy questions that end with a written contract or a handshake.
  a. What did you do?
  b. How did it help you?
  c. What could you do that would help you?
  d. What will you do?

Have the child dictate or write and sign a contract, and have a follow-up meeting. If the contract is broken, have the child write or dictate a contract that he or she can meet. Punishment should be eliminated in favor of letting the child experience the logical consequences of appropriate and inappropriate behavior.

Phase III, consisting of four steps, is designed for children whose behavior makes it difficult for the teacher to teach and for the other children to learn. In the home setting, Phase III would be used when the child's behavior is infringing on the rights of other family members. It is hoped that we can solve our consultant problems in the six steps before Phase III. The primary intervention in Phase III is isolation.

Step 7. In-class time-out is recommended. A quiet corner, study carrel, or private work area may be used. Time-out should not be in a punishment area or a "dunce's corner." The child has two choices: to be with the group and behave or to be outside and sit. When the misbehavior occurs, send the child to the quiet area firmly with no discussion. The rest of the group does not have to be aware of the intervention. Have the child make a plan before returning to the group. The child's room may be used for time-out at home.

Step 8. Some children may require a time-out outside the classroom. The procedure is basically the same one described in Step 7. Some schools use a time-out room, and others use an in-school suspension room. Contracts or plans for making a successful return to the classroom group can follow the questions employed in the reality therapy method.

Step 9. Step 9 is designed for children who have difficulty making it through the entire school day without disrupting the class. Individual educational plans (IEPs) for these students may list four or five expectations or rules that the school has for all students. If the child fails to meet one of these rules, have the child's parents remove the child from school for the remainder of the day. Allow the child to return the next day and to remain as long as he or she follows the rules. Community agencies have been used when home isolation was not possible. Once again, no punishment in addition to the logical consequence of isolation needs to be administered. IEPs such as this require the input of teachers, parents, administrators, the child, and the counselor.

Step 10. Step 10 often involves taking the child on a field trip to juvenile court to observe the probable consequences of continuing present behavior patterns. Interviews with the judge, other court officials, counselors, teachers, and inmates increase the child's awareness of logical consequences existing outside the home and school settings. Failure to meet consultation goals with a child who has not reacted positively to the ten-step method may mean that the child should be referred to a community agency better equipped to solve the child's problem.

RESEARCH AND REACTIONS

The research and reactions summary for each counseling approach summarizes the literature regarding how the approach is used to work with children. However, because it is difficult to work with children without knowing how to work with their families, we have included some literature on families, adolescents, and adults. We have also included literature on general topics related to each theory because we believe such related material aids in generalization of the theory and approach to other case settings.

Perhaps the best validation of reality therapy is found in the success Glasser achieved at the Ventura School for Girls. Before Glasser's tenure at Ventura, the school's recidivism rate approached 90 percent; in a relatively short time this rate fell to 20 percent. What was the secret of changing the orientation of these young women into success identities? Glasser gave them the experience of personal responsibility and success by assigning them tasks they could handle and by making each girl responsible for her own behavior. Punishment was discarded in favor of logical consequences. Generous amounts of praise were given and sincere interest in each girl's welfare was displayed. Regardless of one's theoretical outlook, it would be difficult to argue with Glasser's formula for success. In fact, most counseling approaches will be effective if applied under Glasser's conditions, as described earlier in the chapter.

Control Theory

William Glasser continues to be a prolific contributor to the growing number of articles and books on reality therapy. In *Control Theory* (1984), he describes methods for taking control of one's life. The theory is based on the idea that people are responsible for their own choices, decisions, goals, and the general degree of happiness in their lives. We are not controlled by external events and people unless we choose to let this happen. If a person were to say "Mary Sue hurt me when she rejected me, and I am too depressed to want to continue my life," Glasser would point out that the person is "depressing" (using *depression* as a verb) as a last, desperate, but ineffective effort to regain control of a large part of his life that seems to be slipping away. Glasser would recommend reframing the mental image of life to include something more than a relationship with Mary Sue as one's raison d'être. This concept is similar to the methodology used in rational emotive therapy or rational behavioral therapy, which focus on reframing thoughts, self-talk, and visualization as ways of treating undesired emotional states such as depression. In fact, many points Glasser raises are similar to those in writings we find in Gestalt and existential theory regarding self-responsibility for living life. For example, rather than saying "I have a cold," one would say "I am doing a cold." Presumably, by taking control over having my cold, I can also take control over stopping it. Two themes run through *Control Theory:* (1) We control our mental images or pictures. We can put them in, exchange them, add to them, or throw them out. We can also choose which picture or goals we can and want to satisfy. (2) Whenever we choose to depress or develop a psychosomatic illness, we have the option of choosing something more satisfying. The chapter on control theory and rearing children, in which Glasser integrates his control theory points into the standard steps of reality therapy, is of particular relevance for counseling children. Perhaps the greatest help to parents, counselors, and teachers is the idea that we need to empower rather than overpower children if we are to win their cooperation when they grow too big to overpower.

The notion of empowering children is carried through to *Control Theory in the Classroom* (1986). In his best work for educators since *Schools Without Failure,* Glasser makes a strong case for the teacher functioning as a manager who motivates students by empowering them with the responsibility for learning. The principal motivation method is the establishment of two- to five-member learning teams designed to meet student needs for belonging, power, friendships, and achievement. The team idea has been presented elsewhere (Thompson & Poppen, 1972) and has been found successful. Glasser's principal contribution in *Control Theory in the Classroom* is the parallel he draws between successful managers in business and successful managers (teachers) in education. Glasser presents examples of the model with a sound explanation of why it works. He is highly critical of stimulus-response (S-R) learning; however, the team-learning approach, if well designed, seems an excellent example of creating the proper stimulus conditions to foster the desired learning response. Much of the research and writing on reality therapy is related to the school environment because counselors and teachers find the theory and practice of reality therapy to be most useful in working with student problems.

In 1990, Glasser continued his *Control Theory in the Classroom* ideas in a second book, *The Quality School: Managing Students Without Coercion.* The main difference in the two books is that the second book emphasizes the business metaphor derived from Edward Deming's work with Japanese factories. The factory/schools analogy suffers somewhat when one equates students with products (Toyotas, for example). However, the message of *The Quality School* is that managers and teachers have a lot in common in that the results you get depend on how you treat people (not Toyotas). The book presents two managerial models: the boss manager and the lead manager. Boss managers motivate by punishment rather than reinforcement, tell rather than show, overpower rather than empower, and rule rather than cooperate. Lead managers do the reverse. In short, Glasser makes a case for democratic teachers rather than autocratic ones. The model works equally well in homes, schools, businesses, and government because, regardless of setting, people generally give back, in full measure, what they receive.

In addition to Glasser's own writings on reality therapy (RT) in educational settings, many others have written and continue to write on the subject.

Educational Applications of Reality Therapy

One area of research focus is application of the ten-step RT process presented in this chapter to teaching discipline and to managing student behavior. The following people have reported success with varying versions of RT and the ten-step method: Gang (1976); Thompson and Cates (1976); Fuller and Fuller (1982); Engelhardt (1983); Chance (1985); Johnson (1985); Dempster and Raff (1989); Hart-Hester, Heuchert, and Whittier (1989); and Heuchert (1989).

Another successful application of reality therapy to educational settings has been the use of classroom meetings and cooperative learning teams described in Glasser's books on schools. Omizo and Cubberly (1983) found classroom meetings helpful in working with learning-disabled children. Sullo (1990) outlined steps for introducing control theory and reality therapy into cooperative learning groups. McDonald (1989) described how she has taught control theory in Grades 1 through 3.

Reality therapy has also been applied to higher education settings. Fried (1990), in one such application, described a method for teaching college students the concepts of reality and self-control in decision-making and problem solving. However, Levy and Faltico (1977), in an attempt to use RT principles and teachings to establish a community support group for college students, found their application of RT lacking.

Cross-Cultural Applications of Reality Therapy

Reality therapy has also been proven to work with a wide variety of clients and cultures. Ford (1983) wrote that reality therapy is a recommended counseling approach for minority adolescents because the RT process is directed toward developing reason and logic to meet one's needs of love and self-worth without depriving others of the means to meet their own needs. McCrone (1983) proposed a modification of RT to fit the needs of deaf clients. He found RT to be an effective method for rehabilitation counselors as they try to assist their deaf clients in making choices and plans that lead toward the clients' career development. In addition to being straightforward and to the point, RT is easier to communicate than are many other approaches. Mainored (1976), Greenberg and Bassin (1976), and Hurvitz (1976) have all written articles that support McCrone's ideas about the helpfulness of the RT process in decision-making, problem solving, and behavior planning.

Applications of Reality Therapy to Community Settings

The practice of reality therapy has also found widespread acceptance in various community settings. Cohen and Sorda (1984) found RT effective with adult offenders, while Yarish (1985), Ross (1984), and Thatcher (1983) successfully counseled juvenile offenders with RT. Chance, Bibens, Crowley, Pouretedal, Dolese, and Virtue (1990) found the RT-based *Lifeline* program useful in treating drug and alcohol addiction in prisons. Honeyman (1990) found RT helpful in working with addicts in a residential treatment program.

Poppen and Welch (1976) demonstrated RT's effectiveness as a group-counseling strategy for weight loss in adolescent women. Dolly and Page (1981), in a study of the effects of RT and behavior modification on the behavior of emotionally disturbed, institutionalized adolescents, succeeded in helping their clients achieve several significant, positive behavior changes.

Geronilla (1985), also working in a hospital setting, has recommended reality therapy as a viable method for working with adult and youth patient noncompliance. The practice of RT should create an atmosphere in which treatment goals are negotiated rather than dictated, and value judgments of personal behavior are left to the patient. Responsibility must be given to noncompliant patients in order to win their cooperation in writing productive plans and making commitments to follow their plans.

Applications of Reality Therapy to Marriage and Family Counseling

Reality therapy is often used in marriage and family counseling. Bassin (1976) developed a theory of marriage counseling called *IRT therapy*, which represents a combination of integrity, reality, and transparency theories. Bassin leans heavily on the ideas that a person must (1) love, be loved, and feel worthwhile; and (2) meet personal needs without depriving others of their needs. Emphasizing Glasser's methods, he states that the focus should be on current evaluation of behavior in terms of its contribution to a satisfactory marriage and on working out plans to correct any apparent deficiencies.

Connor (1988) presented another RT-based model for helping troubled marriages. The model is based, in part, on the idea that negative feelings toward a person can be changed through positive behavior experiences with that person.

Thatcher (1988) addressed the question of how reality therapy can be used with survivors of spouse abuse. Once again, the treatment focused on evaluating the helpfulness of present behaviors in moving the client toward desired outcomes and goals.

Reality Therapy as a Preventive and Developmental Approach

Suicide

The need for counselors to be skilled in recognizing the signs and symptoms of potential suicide cuts across all client populations and settings. Counselors also need to know how to work with their clients in developmental steps that lead to recovery. Wubbolding (1989) detailed four stages of decision-making that clients need to complete in order to get rid of the desire to kill themselves. These stages follow the RT treatment plan. In the first stage, the counselor asks several questions to determine the lethality of the decision. These questions are: (1) "Are you thinking about killing yourself?" (2) "Have you previously tried to kill yourself?" (3) "Do you have a specific plan and the means available to kill yourself?" and (4) "Will you make a commitment not to kill yourself (for a specific amount of time)?" When the imminent danger has passed, the second stage can be devoted to exploring the behaviors that lead to thoughts of suicide. Listening to certain kinds of music might be one example. Behavior choices leading to better feelings are discussed, and short-term, attainable goals are set. As clients meet short-term goals, they begin to feel better and move into a third stage of more positive behaviors and feelings. Third stage people may still entertain ideas about suicide. By monitoring their daily feelings and behaviors in a journal, clients become encouraged about their progress in setting and attaining larger goals. If all goes well, clients move into the fourth stage, characterized by a zest for living, no suicide ideation, and plans for attaining love, belonging, self-worth, freedom, and fun in their daily living. Further discussion of suicide is presented in Chapter 14.

Personal Development

Dennis (1990) developed a life-equity ledger sheet to help people analyze the cost and return on investment of their behavior. Using principles of RT and control theory, Dennis pointed out that when people grow to like themselves and others, take good care of their physical well-being, and begin to define their self-worth internally as opposed to defining it by some outside standard such as financial worth, they are well on the road to living a healthy, balanced life.

Summary

Several articles supportive of RT have appeared in the literature. Patterson (1976), Schofield (1976), Swensen (1976), and Easson (1976), writing about the counselor/client relationship, support the relationship-building phase of RT. Mainored (1976), Greenberg and Bassin (1976), and Hurvitz (1976) have written articles about the helpfulness of the RT process in decision-making, problem solving, and behavior planning.

Not all of the literature supports RT. Masserman (1975) writes that RT may offer only illusory comfort to clients. Kovel (1976) sees RT as a system for manipulating people into conformity to the established order. Moravec (1965) attacks Glasser for his emphasis on right and wrong, and Wahler (1965) criticizes Glasser's strict emphasis on behavior change. Barr (1974) writes that Glasser's originality is marginal and that Glasser's work echoes that of Alfred Adler, B. F. Skinner, Norman Vincent Peale, Mary Baker Eddy, Thomas Szasz, and Horatio Alger. We might also include Abraham Maslow in the above list. In many ways, it does seem as though Glasser has reinvented the wheel. But to his credit, as Barr points out, Glasser's ideas are his own in the sense that he personally discovered them, put them together on his own, and created a system that works well for counselors and clients in many different settings. Glasser would, of course, object to any comparison that links RT to Skinner's behaviorism. Johnson (1989), in an article comparing the theories of Glasser and Skinner, states that while these theories have their differences, a significant amount of similarity and overlap exists between them. She concludes that both theories are identifiable within RT, and the degree to which one sees a Skinnerian influence in RT depends on the degree to which one subscribes to the existence and relevance of the "inner person" and the freedom of choice.

In interviews with Glasser, Evans (1982) and Cockrum (1989) bring to light several points that practitioners of reality therapy often experience. First, reality therapy is simple and easy to understand, but difficult and demanding to implement. The key to reality therapy is helping people accept responsibility for what they are doing now. Second, a pessimistic counselor will not be a successful reality therapist. Considerable effort, persistence, and optimism are required for both the client and the counselor who wish to make the reality therapy process work. Third, the definition of behavior should be expanded to include feelings and thoughts as well as what we actually do. The focus remains on what we can change about these three behavior components.

As is true with all counseling approaches, reality therapy has its supporters and critics. As might be expected, Glasser continues to find his greatest following among counselors, educators, psychologists, and social workers. He has yet to win large numbers of his fellow psychiatrists to the practice and support of reality therapy.

REFERENCES

Barr, N. (1974, February). The responsible world of reality therapy. *Psychology Today,* pp. 64–67, 104.

Bassin, A. (1976). IRT therapy in marriage counseling. In A. Bassin, T. Bratter, & R. Rachin (Eds.), *The reality therapy reader* (pp. 181–204). New York: Harper & Row.

Chance, E., Bibens, R., Crowley, J., Pouretedal, M., Dolese, P., & Virtue, D. (1990). Lifeline: A drug/alcohol treatment program for negatively addictive inmates. *Journal of Reality Therapy, 9*(3), 33–38.

Chance, E. W. (1985). *An overview of major discipline programs in public schools since 1960.* Unpublished doctoral dissertation, University of Oklahoma, Norman, OK.

Cockrum, J. (1989). Interview with Dr. William Glasser. *Journal of Human Behavior, 26,* 13–16.

Cohen, B., & Sorda, I. (1984). Using reality therapy with adult offenders. *Journal of Offender Counseling, Services, and Rehabilitation, 8,* 25–29.

Connor, R. (1988). Applying reality therapy to troubled marriages through the concept of permanent love. *Journal of Reality Therapy, 8*(1), 13–17.

Dempster, M., & Raff, D. (1989). Managing students in primary schools: A successful Australian experience. *Journal of Reality Therapy, 8*(2), 19–23.

Dennis, B. (1990). Living a balanced life. *Journal of Reality Therapy, 9*(2), 118–132.

Dolly, J., & Page, D. (1981). The effects of a program of behavior modification and reality therapy on the behavior of emotionally disturbed institutionalized adolescents. *The Exceptional Child, 28,* 191–198.

Easson, W. (1976). After psychotherapy. In A. Bassin, T. Bratter, & R. Rachin (Eds.), *The reality therapy reader* (pp. 144–153). New York: Harper & Row.

Engelhardt, L. (1983, April). *School discipline programs that work.* Paper presented at the National School Boards Association Convention, San Francisco.

Evans, D. (1982). What are you doing? An interview with William Glasser. *The Personnel and Guidance Journal, 60,* 460–465.

Ford, R. (1983). *Counseling strategies for ethnic minority students.* Unpublished manuscript, University of Puget Sound, Office of Equity Education, Tacoma, WA.

Fried, J. (1990). Reality and self-control: Applying reality therapy to student personnel work in higher education. *Journal of Reality Therapy, 9*(2), 60–64.

Fuller, G., & Fuller, D. (1982). Reality therapy: Helping LD children make better choices. *Academic Therapy, 17,* 269–277.

Gang, M. (1976). Enhancing student-teacher relationships. *Elementary School Guidance and Counseling, 11,* 131–134.

Geronilla, L. (1985). Handling patient non-compliance using reality therapy. *Journal of Reality Therapy, 5*(1), 2–13.

Glasser, W. (1961). *Mental health or mental illness?* New York: Harper & Row.

Glasser, W. (1965). *Reality therapy.* New York: Harper & Row.

Glasser, W. (1969). *Schools without failure.* New York: Harper & Row.

Glasser, W. (1972). *The identity society.* New York: Harper & Row.

Glasser, W. (1976). *Positive addiction.* New York: Harper & Row.

Glasser, W. (1981). *Stations of the mind.* New York: Harper & Row.

Glasser, W. (1984). *Control theory.* New York: Harper & Row.

Glasser, W. (1986). *Control theory in the classroom.* New York: Harper & Row.

Glasser, W. (1990). *The quality school: Managing students without coercion.* New York: Harper & Row.

Greenberg, I., & Bassin, A. (1976). Reality therapy and psychodrama. In A. Bassin, T. Bratter, & R. Rachin (Eds.), *The reality therapy reader* (pp. 231–240). New York: Harper & Row.

Hart-Hester, S., Heuchert, C., and Whittier, K. (1989). The effects of teaching reality therapy techniques to elementary students to help change behaviors. *Journal of Reality Therapy, 8*(2), 13–18.

Heuchert, C. (1989). Enhancing self-directed behavior in the classroom. *Academic Therapy, 24,* 295–303.

Honeyman, A. (1990). Perceptual changes in addicts as a consequence of reality therapy based group treatment. *Journal of Reality Therapy, 9*(2), 53–59.

Hurvitz, N. (1976). Peer self-help groups. In A. Bassin, T. Bratter, & R. Rachin (Eds.), *The reality therapy reader* (pp. 154–171). New York: Harper & Row.

Johnson, E. (1985). Reality therapy in the elementary/junior high school. *Journal of Reality Therapy, 5*(1), 16–18.

Johnson, E. (1989). The theories of B. F. Skinner and William Glasser: Relevance to reality therapy. *Journal of Reality Therapy, 8*(2), 69–73.

Kovel, J. (1976). *A complete guide to therapy: From psychoanalysis to behavior modification.* New York: Pantheon.

Kronick, R., & Hargis, C. (1990). *Dropouts: Who drops out and why—and the recommended action.* Springfield, IL: Charles C Thomas.

Levy, E., & Faltico, G. (1977). Reading, writing, and responsibility. *Together, 2,* 101–110.

Mainored, W. (1976). A therapy. In A. Bassin, T. Bratter, & R. Rachin (Eds.), *The reality therapy reader* (pp. 205–214). New York: Harper & Row.

Masserman, J. (1975). *Current psychiatric therapies.* New York: Grune & Stratton.

McCrone, P. (1983). Reality therapy with deaf rehabilitation clients. *Journal of Rehabilitation of the Deaf, 17*(2), 13–15.

McDonald, A. (1989). Me and my shadow: Teaching "control theory" in elementary school. *Journal of Reality Therapy, 8,* 30–32.

Mecca, A., Smelser, N., & Vasconcellos, J. (Eds.). (1989). *The social importance of self-esteem.* Berkeley and Los Angeles: University of California Press.

Moravec, M. (1965, May 1). Letters to the science editor. *Saturday Review,* p. 64.

Omizo, M., & Cubberly, W. (1983). The effects of reality therapy classroom meetings on self-concept and locus of control among learning disabled children. *The Exceptional Child, 30,* 201–209.

Patterson, C. (1976). Counseling as a relationship. In A. Bassin, T. Bratter, & R. Rachin (Eds.), *The reality therapy reader* (pp. 110–118). New York: Harper & Row.

Poppen, W., & Welch, R. (1976). Work with adolescent girls. In A. Bassin, T. Bratter, & R. Rachin (Eds.), *The reality therapy reader* (pp. 337–344). New York: Harper & Row.

Ross, R. (1984, April). *Education of the young officer: A dynamic approach.* Paper presented at the annual convention of the Council for Exceptional Children, Washington, DC.

Schofield, W. (1976). The psychotherapist as friend. In A. Bassin, T. Bratter, & R. Rachin (Eds.), *The reality therapy reader* (pp. 119–132). New York: Harper & Row.

Sullo, R. (1990). Introducing control theory and reality therapy principles in cooperative learning groups. *Journal of Reality Therapy, 9*(2), 67–70.

Swensen, C. (1976). The successful therapist. In A. Bassin, T. Bratter, & R. Rachin (Eds.), *The reality therapy reader* (pp. 133–143). New York: Harper & Row.

Thatcher, J. (1983). *The effects of reality therapy upon self-concept and locus of control for juvenile delinquents.* Unpublished doctoral dissertation, Kent State University, Kent, OH.

Thatcher, J. (1988). Spouse violence: Survivors. *Journal of Reality Therapy, 7*(2), 2–7.

Thompson, C., & Cates, J. (1976). Teaching discipline to students in an individual teaching-counseling approach. *Focus on Guidance, 9,* 1–12.

Thompson, C., & Poppen, W. (1972). *For those who care: Ways of relating to youth.* Columbus, OH: Merrill.

Thompson, C., & Poppen, W. (1992). *Guidance activities for counselors and teachers.* Knoxville, TN: Kinko's Copy Center.

Wahler, H. (1965, May 1). Letters to the science editor. *Saturday Review,* p. 64.

Wubbolding, R. (1989). Professional issues: Four stages of decision making in suicidal recovery. *Journal of Reality Therapy, 8*(2), 57–61.

Yarish, P. (1985). *The impact of a treatment facility utilizing reality therapy on the locus of control and subsequent delinquent behavior of a group of juvenile offenders.* Unpublished doctoral dissertation, Florida State University, Tallahassee, FL.

CHAPTER 4

Person-Centered Counseling

CARL ROGERS

Carl Rogers (1902–1987) was born in Illinois, the fourth of six children. His early home life was marked by close family ties, a strict religious and moral atmosphere, and an appreciation of the value of hard work. During this period, Rogers thought his family was different from everyone else because they did not mix socially with other people. In fact, Rogers had only two dates during his high school years.

When Rogers was 12, his parents moved to a farm to remove the young family from the "temptations" of suburban life. From raising lambs, pigs, and calves, Rogers learned about matching experimental conditions with control conditions and about randomization procedures, and he acquired knowledge and respect for the methods of science. Rogers's thinking was influenced by a number of teachers, from high school through graduate school, who encouraged him to be unique and original in thought.

Rogers started college at the University of Wisconsin in the field of scientific agriculture. After two years, however, he switched to the ministerial field as a result of attending some emotionally charged religious conferences. In his junior year, he was chosen to go to China for six months for an international World Student Christian Federation conference. During this period, two things happened that greatly influenced his life. First, at the expense of great pain and stress within his family relationships, he freed himself from the religious thinking of his parents and became an independent thinker, though he did not abandon religion entirely. Second, he fell in love with a woman he had known most of his life. He married her, with reluctant parental consent, as soon as he finished college so they could attend graduate school together.

Rogers chose to go to graduate school at Union Theological Seminary, a very liberal school, to prepare for religious work. While at Union, he became interested in courses and lectures on psychological and psychiatric work taught by Goodwin Watson and Marian Kenworthy, and he began to take courses at Teachers College, Columbia University, across the street from Union. He found himself drawn to child guidance while working at Union under Leta Hollingsworth. He applied for a fellowship at the Institute for Child Guidance and was accepted; he was well on his way to a career in psychology.

At the end of his internship at the Institute for Child Guidance, Rogers accepted a job in Rochester, New York, at the Society for the Prevention of Cruelty to Children, even though he had not completed his doctorate. Rogers spent the next 12 years in Rochester. His son and daughter grew through infancy and childhood there. Rogers once said that his children taught him far more about the development and relationships of individuals than he ever learned professionally.

Rogers spent his first eight years in Rochester completely immersed in his work, conducting treatment interviews and trying to be effective with clients. Gradually, he began teaching in the sociology department at the University of Rochester. He was also involved in developing a guidance center and writing a book, *The Clinical Treatment of the Problem Child* (1939). Rogers's belief in people's ability to solve their own problems, given the proper climate, was influenced by Otto Rank, with whose work he became acquainted while at the child guidance center.

In 1940, Rogers accepted a full professorship at Ohio State University. There he began to realize that he had developed a distinctive viewpoint, so he wrote the then-controversial book *Counseling and Psychotherapy* (1942). In this book, Rogers proposed a counseling relationship based on the warmth and responsiveness of the therapist. Rogers believed that, with such a relationship, clients would feel free to express their feelings and thoughts. This was a radical change in the field of psychotherapy, which had been dominated by psychoanalysis and directive counseling. In fact, Rogers developed the first truly American system of psychotherapy. He and his students at Ohio State made detailed analyses of counseling sessions and began to publish cases that used what Rogers called "client-centered therapy." The theory developed as Rogers and his colleagues began to test the hypotheses they formed from their case studies.

In 1945, Rogers moved on to the University of Chicago, where he organized the counseling center and spent the next 12 years doing research. It was while he was associated with the University of Chicago that he wrote his famous *Client-Centered Therapy*, published in 1951. Rogers describes his years at Chicago as very satisfying, but when an opportunity at the University of Wisconsin became available, he accepted. He saw himself as essentially a frontiersman.

At the University of Wisconsin, he was able to work in both the departments of psychology and psychiatry. This especially pleased him because he had long wanted to work with psychotic individuals who had been hospitalized.

Rogers left the University of Wisconsin in 1966, moving to the Western Behavioral Science Institute in La Jolla, California. In 1968, he and several colleagues formed the Center for Studies of the Person, also in La Jolla. Through the 1970s and into the 1980s, Rogers spent most of his time working with and writing about the use of person-centered therapy with groups. As we explained in Chapter 2, Rogers came to prefer the term *person-centered* to *client-centered* in writing about his approach.

THE NATURE OF PEOPLE

Carl Rogers and his person-centered school of thought view people as rational, socialized, forward-moving, and realistic beings. Negative, anti-social emotions do exist, but they are only a result of frustrated basic impulses; this idea is related to Maslow's hierarchy of needs. For instance, extreme aggressive action toward other people would result from failure to meet needs of love and belonging. Once people are free of their defensive behavior, their reactions are positive and progressive.

People possess the capacity to experience — that is, to express rather than repress — their own maladjustment to life and to move toward a more adjusted state of mind. Rogers believed that in moving toward psychological adjustment, people are moving toward actualization. Because people possess the capacity to regulate and control their own behavior, the counseling relationship is merely a means of tapping personal resources and developing human potential. It is believed that people will learn from their external therapy experience how to internalize and provide their own form of psychotherapy.

In summary, a person-centered counselor believes that people:

- have worth and dignity in their own right and therefore deserve respect;
- have the capacity and right to self-direction (self-actualization) and, when given the opportunity, will make wise judgments;
- can select their own values;
- can learn to make constructive use of responsibility;
- have the capacity to deal with their own feelings, thoughts, and behavior; and
- have the potential for constructive change and personal development toward a full and satisfying life (actualization).

THEORY OF COUNSELING

Person-centered therapy was first called *nondirective therapy* because of the therapist's encouraging and listening role. Later, the term *client-centered* was adopted because of the complete responsibility given to clients for their own growth. Only recently has the name *person-centered* been used in hopes of further humanizing the counseling process.

Reflecting Rogers's view of human nature, if a warm and accepting climate can be created in the counseling interviews, people will trust the counselor enough to risk sharing their ideas about their lives and the problems they face. During this sharing with a nonjudgmental counselor, people will feel free to explore their feelings, thoughts, and behaviors as these relate to their personal growth, development, and adjustment. Such explorations should, in turn, lead to more effective decision-making and to productive behavior by the client. Rogers (1951) writes that the counselor operates from the point of view that people have the capacity to work effectively with all aspects of their lives that come into conscious awareness. Expansion of this conscious awareness occurs when the counseling climate meets Rogers's standards and when clients realize that the counselor accepts them as people competent to direct their own lives.

Person-centered counseling deals primarily with the organization and functioning of self. The counselor becomes an objective, unemotional "mirror" that reflects the person's inner world with warmth, acceptance, and trust. This mirroring allows people to judge their thoughts and feelings and to begin to explore their effects on behavior. Thus, people are enabled to reorganize their thoughts, feelings, and behaviors so they function in a more integrated fashion.

The Rogerian model for helping, as modified by Carkhuff (1973), involves three general stages through which the client proceeds. In the first phase, self-exploration, people are encouraged to examine exactly where they are in their lives. This includes a type of self-searching in which people question themselves concerning their status at the present moment. In the second phase, people begin to understand the relationship between where they are in life and where they would like to be. In other words, they move from a type of discovery in self-exploration to an understanding. The third phase involves action. In this context, action is goal-directed; people engage in some program or plan in order to reach the point where they want to be. The only exception to the logical order of these three stages might be in helping children, for whom movement through the process may be more meaningful if action is followed by understanding and then self-exploration. Children find it easier to move from the concrete to the abstract in problem solving, and in Rogers's system self-exploration is the most abstract area of the process.

One can think of person-centered counseling in two dimensions: responsive/facilitative, which includes attending, observing, and listening; and initiative, which includes initiating, personalizing, and responding. The counselor must remain in control of the counseling process, becoming an "expert" in creating the nonthreatening environment vital to the counseling process. Empathy, respect, warmth, concreteness, genuineness, and self-disclosure all facilitate change in client behavior. The process works best when the counselor lets the client direct the interview—a first step in teaching clients how to direct their lives. The client is viewed as an expert whose task is to teach the counselor about the client's life situation. Clients thereby learn more about themselves, as teaching generally helps the teacher to learn. This may be the main reason person-centered therapy helps many people.

The main goal of person-centered therapy is to assist people in becoming more autonomous, spontaneous, and confident (Rogers, 1969). As people move to an awareness of what is going on inside themselves, they can cease fearing and defending their inner feelings. They learn to accept their own values and trust their own judgment rather than live by the values of others. Expectations of person-centered therapy include the discussion of plans, behavioral steps to be taken, and the outcome of the steps; a change from immature behavior to mature behavior; a decrease in current defensive behaviors; an increased tolerance for frustration; and improved functioning in life tasks (Poppen & Thompson, 1974).

The ultimate goal of person-centered therapy is to produce fully functioning people who have learned to be free. According to Rogers, learning to be free is the essential goal of education "if the civilized culture is to survive and if individuals in the culture are to be worth saving" (1969, p. 12). People who have learned to be free can confront life and face problems; they trust themselves to choose their own way and accept their own feelings without forcing them on others. Such individuals prize themselves and others as having dignity, worth, and value.

COUNSELING METHOD

The counselor as a person, of critical importance to all counseling approaches, is perhaps most vital to person-centered counseling. The conditions the counselor models become the ultimate counseling goals for all clients. Counselors, to be optimally effective as person-centered counselors, must possess the following personality traits and values: openness, empathic understanding, independence, spontaneity, acceptance, mutual respect, and intimacy. After clients move through the immediate counseling goals of self-exploration and subgoals such as improving a math grade or making a new friend, they begin to work toward achieving the ultimate counseling goals: actualization, acceptance of self and others, genuineness, intimacy, openness to experience, independence, and spontaneity—the same traits modeled by effective counselors.

Perhaps the strongest techniques in the person-centered counselor's repertoire are actually attitudes toward people: *congruence* (genuineness), *unconditional positive regard* (respect), and *empathy*. Congruence implies that the counselor can maintain a sense of self-identity and can convey this identity to his or her clients. In other words, the counselor is not playing an artificial role. Unconditional positive regard implies that the counselor accepts clients as people who have the potential to become good, rational, and free. Because people have self-worth, dignity, and unique traits as individuals, they require individualized counseling approaches. Thus, people direct their own counseling sessions. For the process to succeed, clients must feel they can reveal the person they are to the counselor in an atmosphere of complete acceptance. Empathy is the attitude that holds the counseling process together. By attempting to understand, the counselor helps convince people that they are worth hearing and understanding.

In general, the person-centered counselor refrains from giving advice or solutions, moralizing, and making judgments. Diagnosis and interpretations are considered detrimental to the counseling process. To do any of these things would defeat the plan for teaching clients how to do them for themselves. It would also imply that the counselors know and understand their clients better than the clients do themselves—an assumption common to many approaches but totally out of line with Rogers's view. Instead, person-centered counselors use the methods of (1) active and passive listening, (2) reflection of thoughts and feelings, (3) clarification, (4) summarization, (5) confrontation of contradictions, and (6) general or open leads that help client self-exploration (Poppen & Thompson, 1974).

The major technique for person-centered counseling is active listening, which lets the client know that the counselor is hearing and understanding correctly all that the client is saying. As we saw in Chapter 2, active listening is especially important for counseling children. If the counselor fails to receive the correct message, the child attempts to reteach it to the counselor. Once counselor and child agree that the counselor has the story straight and that the counseling service will be helpful, counseling can continue.

Carkhuff (1973, 1981) has systematized Rogers's concept of active listening (reflection) into a highly understandable, usable model (see Table 4-1). Carkhuff believes that counselors typically respond on any one of five levels relating to the three phases of counseling: (I) where you are now in

TABLE 4-1 Five levels of communication

Levels	Phase I	Phase II	Phase III
	Thoughts and feelings about where you are now	*Thoughts and feelings about where you would like to be*	*Plans for getting from where you are to where you would like to be*
1			
2			X
3	X		
4	X	X	
5	X	X	X

NOTE: The Xs indicate which phase of counseling is treated by each of the five levels of communication.

your life; (II) where you would like to be; and (III) planning how to get from Phase I to Phase II. He classifies Levels 1 and 2 as harmful, Level 3 as break-even, and Levels 4 and 5 as helpful. It is often assumed that the worst thing that can happen in counseling is that clients will show no change. However, this is not true. If clients receive a preponderance of Level 1 and 2 responses, they could grow worse as the result of counseling.

Level 1 and 2 responses in Carkhuff's model also appear in Gordon's (1974) "dirty dozen" list of responses that tend to close or inhibit further communication:

1. Ordering; directing
2. Warning; threatening; stating consequences
3. Moralizing; shoulds, oughts
4. Advising; giving suggestions and solutions
5. Messages of logic; counterarguments
6. Judging; criticizing
7. Praising; buttering up
8. Name-calling; ridiculing
9. Psychoanalyzing
10. Reassuring; giving sympathy; consoling
11. Probing: "who, what, when, where, why?"
12. Humor; distracting; withdrawing

Level 1 responses tend to deny a person's feeling and thinking with statements such as the following:

- "Oh don't worry about that. Things will work out."
- "If you think you have a problem, listen to this."
- "You must have done something to make Mrs. Jones treat you that way."

As such, Level 1 responses do not help with any of the three counseling phases in Table 4-1.

Level 2 responses are messages that give advice and solutions to problems. These responses are relevant in Phase III, but they are not considered helpful because they do not allow the counselor and the client to fully explore the problem situation. Clients are deprived of the opportunity of working out their own solutions to their problems because the active-listening process is totally ignored. Level 2 responses keep clients dependent on the counselor's authority and prevent clients from learning to counsel themselves. Typical Level 2 responses include the following:

- "You need to study harder."
- "You should eat better."
- "You should be more assertive."
- "Why don't you make more friends?"
- "How would you like to have your brother treat you the way you treat him?"

Even though the advice may be excellent, the client—child or adult—may not have the skill to do what you suggest. Moreover, rebellious children may work especially hard to show that your advice is ineffective, receiving some satisfaction from knowing that an "expert" counselor is no more successful than they are in trying to solve day-to-day problems.

Level 3 responses are classified as break-even points in the counseling process—neither harmful nor helpful. However, these responses provide bridges to further conversation and exploration in the counseling process; they are the door-openers and invitations to discuss concerns in more depth.

Level 3 responses reflect what the client is thinking and feeling about the present status of the problem—for example: "You are feeling *discouraged* because *you haven't been able to make good grades in math.*" Such responses are checkpoints for counselors in determining if they are hearing and understanding the client's problem. Either the client acknowledges that the counselor has understood the message correctly, or the client makes another attempt to relate the concern to the counselor. At this point in counseling, clients are teaching the counselors about their problems and are thereby learning more about their problems themselves.

According to Carkhuff's model, an aid to counselors in making Level 3 responses is to ask themselves if the client is expressing pain or pleasure. The next task is to find the correct feeling word to describe the pain or pleasure. Below are listed seven feeling words. To help build your counseling vocabulary in order to be able to describe feelings as precisely as possible, add three synonyms of your own under each word. In reflecting the client's feeling and thoughts, be sure to avoid parroting the exact words of the client. It is often helpful to call time-out for a summary and say to your client, "Let's see if I understand what you have told me up to now."

Strong	Happy	Sad	Angry	Scared	Confused	Weak
_____	_____	___	_____	_____	_____	____
_____	_____	___	_____	_____	_____	____
_____	_____	___	_____	_____	_____	____

Level 4 responses reflect an understanding of Phases I and II in Carkhuff's model. For example: "You are feeling *discouraged* because *you haven't been able to make good grades in math,* and you want *to find a way to do better.*" It is best to rephrase the responses in your own words as you summarize the client's thoughts and feelings.

Level 5 responses are appropriate when the client agrees that the counselor understands the problem or concern. Now it is time to assist the client in developing a plan of action. We find that reality therapy provides a good framework for planning after person-centered counseling has been used to help the client relate the concern to the counselor. Together, reality therapy and person-centered counseling provide a most effective method to the counselor. An example of a Level 5 response would be the following:

Person-centered therapy: You feel _____ because _____, and you want _____.

Reality therapy: Let's look at what you have been doing to solve your problem.

PC and RT: You feel *discouraged* because you *haven't been able to make good grades in math,* and you want to *find a way to do better.* Let's look at what you have been trying to do *to make good grades in math.*

We do not want to imply that the entire counseling interview can be accomplished in one response. Several sessions of Level 3 and 4 responses may be necessary before the problem is defined well enough for solving.

Because the success of the person-centered approach to counseling depends so much on the relationship between counselor and client, counselors may find themselves unsuccessful in using the approach with young children. Not every adult is capable of establishing true empathy with children or even of liking children. Children, to a greater degree than adults, are sensitive to the real feelings and attitudes of others. They intuitively trust and open up to those who like and understand them. Phony expressions of understanding will not fool a child for very long. A good example of a person-centered counseling method used with play therapy is presented in Virginia Axline's *Dibs: In Search of Self* (1964).

In order to help children effectively, the counselor must provide a warm, caring environment in which children can explore their emotions and verbally act out the consequences of alternative means of expressing these emotions. Together, counselor and child, or the child alone if he or she possesses sufficient maturity, can evaluate the alternatives and select the one most likely to be appropriate and productive.

In using the person-centered approach with young children, the counselor may be required to assume a somewhat more active role than in working with adults. Still, it is assumed that even young children can distinguish between positive and negative behaviors and that they are able to choose the positive once the counselor has established an open dialogue in which feelings and emotions can be aired and conflicts resolved.

It is important to stress once again that the counselor should employ active listening when dealing with children and that the child should be given the opportunity to release feelings without feeling threatened by the counselor. Listening carefully and observing the child will increase the counselor's ability to understand what the child is trying to communicate. All clients convey both verbal and nonverbal messages, and the counselor needs to be alert to them. With children, whose verbal skills may be relatively limited, nonverbal messages may be the most important clue to what the child is really feeling and trying to communicate.

Our contention is that the person-centered approach is most successful when clients take the role of teaching their counselors about their problem situations. Most learning seems to occur when one teaches the subject to be learned. The counselor's job, as the "student" being taught, is to take periodic oral quizzes (counseling summary/reflection statements) to let the client (teacher) know how well the subject matter is being understood. The subject matter consists of the problem, feelings about the problem, and expectations the client has for its solution.

Children, not having the verbal skills of most adults, can benefit from the incorporation of bibliocounseling, storytelling, and play therapy (see Chapter 8, "Psychodynamic Counseling") as aids to teaching about their problem situations.

CASE STUDY*

Identification of the Problem

Ginger Wood, an 11-year-old girl in the sixth grade at Hill Middle School, was referred to the school counselor because her grades had recently fallen and she seemed depressed.

Individual and Background Information

Academic.   School records show that Ginger is an "A" student and was chosen to be in an advanced group in third grade. On her last report card, however, her grades dropped to a "C" average.

Family.   Ginger is the elder of two children, having a younger brother who is 9. Her mother is an elementary-school teacher, and her father is a systems analyst. Her parents have recently separated.

Social.   Ginger is approximately 30 pounds overweight. She has a friendly personality, and teacher reports do not show that she has a problem relating to her peers.

Counseling Method

The counselor chose to use Rogers's (1965) person-centered counseling method. The counselor believes that Ginger's problem originates from emotional blocks. Her goal is to establish a warm relationship with Ginger

---

*The case of Ginger was contributed by Anne Harvey.

and aid her in clarifying her thoughts and feelings so she may be better able to solve her problems.

In this method, the counselor uses five basic techniques:

1. Unconditional positive regard
2. Active listening
3. Reflection
4. Clarification
5. Summarization

Transcript

Counselor: Hi, Ginger. I'm Susan Morgan. Your teacher, Ms. Lowe, told me that you might come to talk to me.

Ginger: Yeah, I decided to.

Counselor: Do you know what a counselor's job is?

Ginger: Yeah, Ms. Lowe told me that you help people with their problems.

Counselor: That's right. I try to teach people how to solve their own problems. Do you have something on your mind that you'd like to talk about?

Ginger: Well, I haven't been doing so well in school lately.

Counselor: Yes, Ms. Lowe said you are normally an "A" student.

Ginger: I used to be, but not now. I made "C's" on my last report card. My mom was really upset with me; she yelled at me and then grounded me.

Counselor: It sounds as though she was angry with you because your grades went down.

Ginger: Well, not so much angry as unhappy. She looked like she was about to cry.

Counselor: So she was disappointed that you weren't doing as well in school as you usually do, and this made you feel bad too.

Ginger: I guess so. She probably blamed herself some, too, and that could have made her feel worse.

Counselor: You mean that she felt responsible for your grades going down.

Ginger: Well, maybe. Things aren't going so well at home. Mom and Dad aren't living together right now, and they may get a divorce. She hasn't had a lot of time for us lately. I guess she's really been worried.

Counselor: The problem at home has made it tougher for you to do well at school because you're worried about what's happening.

Ginger: Yeah, I think about it a lot. It's harder to study when I'm worrying about it.

Counselor: It would be for me too. This must be a very hard situation for you to go through.

Ginger: It sure is; everybody's mad. My little brother doesn't understand what's going on, and he cries a lot. Mom does, too.

Counselor: So the whole family is upset.

Ginger: Well, I guess so. My dad doesn't seem to be, but why should he be? It's all his fault. He's getting what he wants.

Counselor: I guess he's the one who wants the divorce. It doesn't seem fair to the rest of you.

Ginger: Yeah. He's got a girlfriend. My mom didn't even know anything about her till Daddy said he was leaving. I hate him! (Starts to cry) And that makes me feel even worse cause I know I shouldn't hate my father. I wish he were dead!

Counselor: (handing her a tissue) So you're all torn up between the way you feel and the way you think you should feel.

Ginger: Yeah. It's so hard to sort everything out. Do you think that makes me a bad person for me to hate my father?

Counselor: I think you are a good person who doesn't know what to do with all of her feelings right now. I'm wondering if you think you are a bad person.

Ginger: No, I guess not. I mean, I think most of my friends would feel about the same way I do if they were in my shoes.

Counselor: Sure, it's a tough thing to handle.

Ginger: And I guess they're not all bad people. Thanks, Ms. Morgan. I'm glad we talked about it. I feel a little better now.

Counselor: I'm glad, Ginger. It sounds like you're beginning to work out your problems. Would you like to make another appointment to talk with me?

Ginger: OK. Could I come back during free time next week?

Counselor: That will be fine. You can see me any day when you want to talk.

Ginger: Bye, Ms. Morgan, and thanks.

Counselor: You're welcome.

INTEGRATING SELF-CONCEPT DEVELOPMENT INTO LIFE SKILLS**

Radd (1987) developed a process to integrate self-concept development into life skills education, a theme consistent with the application of person-

---

**Tommie R. Radd, a professor in the College of Education, University of Nebraska at Omaha, contributed the Life Skills section.

centered theory to education. The process includes a series of activities that focus on teaching children about self-concept and ways of applying that information to daily living.

The activities each have three steps. The counselor may choose to teach these statements in the first person or in the format given. The counselor begins by saying:

1. "All people are special and valuable because they are unique." This statement is discussed to teach the concept of unconditional valuing of people simply because they are people. For children in kindergarten through fourth grades, the words "special and different" are effective. "No matter what you do, you are still special because you are a person." For children in Grades 5 through 8, variations of the words "unique and valuable" are effective. "If everyone were the same, it would be boring." "It is impossible for people to be better than other people because everyone is unique." In other words, "I'm the best me there is."

The counselor continues:

2. "Because people are special and unique, they have a responsibility to *help* and *not hurt* themselves. People *show* if they remember that they are important by the way they *choose* to act. If people choose to hurt themselves or others, they are forgetting that they are special. Likewise, if people choose to help themselves or others, they are remembering that they are special. What is special to you? How do you treat it? Do you *help* or *hurt* the things you think are special? Are your toys and computer games more important to you than people? Toys and games can be replaced, but people are different and not replaceable. If you are remembering that you are as special as your toys, will you help or hurt yourself?"

When people help others, they are helping themselves. People hurt themselves when they hurt other people by forgetting that all people are special and unique. Possible consequences of hurting others include feeling bad about oneself and losing positive relationships, which result in self-concept erosion. What people give is generally what they receive. The point we want to teach is that if we like ourselves, we will not hurt ourselves or others.

The counselor continues:

3. "People are responsible for 'watching' their actions to determine if they are remembering the *truth* that they are special. People are 'with' themselves at all times and are accountable for remembering to treat themselves as important people. When people blame others for their actions, they are forgetting their responsibility to value themselves. Who is with you all the time? Who will live with you forever? Who decides what happens to you? Who is the only one you can change?"

Integrating Self-Concept Activities
with the Child's Life

After the self-concept activities are introduced into all environments children experience, the concepts are related to the children's daily life experiences. The concepts are associated with various situations, interactions, and other skills such as decision-making, self-control, and group cooperation.

The continuing process of relating self-concept activities to a child's life is the *self-concept series weave*. Picture the self-concept activities being introduced to children. After this information is taught and processed, the children experience the integration of these concepts into their daily life experiences. This weaving process makes the concepts about self alive and relevant for children.

The self-concept series weave process is implemented consistently regardless of counseling approach or setting. The self-concept activities and weave can become the core of classroom group guidance, small-group counseling, individual counseling, and positive-behavior management. The self-concept activities are introduced and taught. Then, each subsequent session begins with a brief review of the self-concept activities and a weave of the self-concept activities into the process of the group or individual session. The procedure is continued throughout the various teaching or counseling experiences with the children.

An example of the self-concept series weave process follows. Although the example is part of the second individual counseling session with a third-grade student, the same process is used in classroom group guidance, small-group counseling, and within the classroom behavior plan.

In the first session, the self-concept activities were introduced and woven throughout the session. Bill was referred to counseling because of his problems with work completion.

Bill: I'm still in trouble with my teacher this week.

Counselor: You are not feeling very good about this.

Bill: I think my teacher doesn't like me. She thinks I'm dumb.

Counselor: Your feeling bad comes from what your teacher thinks about you. I'm wondering how this fits in with what we talked about last week.

Bill: You said that I am special, no matter what I do, because no one else is like me anywhere in the world.

Counselor: It seems this week you are feeling as though you're not special.

Bill: I don't know. My teacher doesn't think so.

Counselor: So you think you are not important or special because you think your teacher does not think you are special.

Bill: Yeah. I know you think I'm special, but it is hard for me to think so when my teacher doesn't like me.

Counselor: You may be showing that you forget you are special by the way you have been acting in your class. You and your teacher told me you have been deciding not to complete your work. I'm wondering if you have been hurting yourself with your choices.

Bill: I've been hurting myself because I'm not doing my work. But other people aren't doing their work, and they don't get picked on.

Counselor: It sounds as though you feel cheated because the teacher likes the other children better than you and does not treat you fairly. Let's see if we can figure this out with the ideas we learned last week.

Bill: OK.

Counselor: I wonder if you remember what we said about whom children hurt when they choose not to do their work.

Bill: I think they are hurting themselves.

Counselor: So, we could take a look at what happens to you when you don't do your work.

Bill: I guess it hurts me.

Counselor: If you want to, we can think of some ways to help you stop hurting yourself.

Bill: OK. Maybe. I can ask the teacher for help when I get lost on my work, or I can get a friend to help me. I can ask for help remembering the homework, too.

Counselor: These ideas might help you. We need to know which ones you want to try.

Bill: I guess I just need to do what it takes to turn in all my assignments.

Counselor: Next week we can see if you've been remembering to do all those things you need to do to help yourself. Maybe you could show me the work you get done each day.

Bill: OK.

Self-Concept Activities

The self-concept activities and weave demonstrated in the preceding example are not intended to be isolated activities. Three activities for use in group settings follow.

Activity 1: Self-Concept
(Used for teaching the first step of the self-concept series)

Topic: Self-concept

Competency: Children will be able to identify and express characteristics that make them special and unique.

Indicator: Children will name three characteristics that make them special and unique.

Purpose: To discuss that all people are special and important because they are different from all other people.

Procedure for Grades K–3: Discuss the meaning of being "special." Ask the children to raise their hands if they are special and important. Discuss the fact that no two people in the world are exactly alike. Because everyone is different, each person is special and valuable. Repeat until the children understand this concept. Play a game with the children, asking "What makes you special?" until they respond with the unconditional response, "because no one else in the world is like me" or "because we are all different." An example of this process follows.

> *Facilitator:*   What makes you special?
> *Group:*   We listen to the teacher.
> *Facilitator:*   If you do not listen to the teacher, are you still special?
> *Group:*   Yes.
> *Facilitator:*   What makes you special?

Continue the questioning until the group realizes that what we do does not determine our value. Review this concept frequently.

Procedure for Grades 4–8: Discuss the meaning of being unique and valuable. Compare the value of each person to a famous painting or valued object. Compare the value of each person to famous people such as the president, a rock star, or sports star.

Process each grade-level approach by using cooperative groups. Ask the group to apply the concept in their day-to-day living experiences. Incorporate the evaluation of feelings about being special and important.

Activity 2: Responsibility for Self
(Used for teaching the second step
of the self-concept series)

Topic: Self-concept

Competency: Children will tell three feelings they have when they act in a way that helps them.

Purpose: To discuss how behavior choices either *help* or *hurt* people.

Procedure: Ask the group how they show they are remembering that they are special and unique. Ask the group how they treat or take care of something valuable. Use the words "special and important" for Grades K–3; use the words "unique and valuable" for Grades 4–8. (Substitute the language for Grades 4–8 into the following steps.)

1. Form a circle or sit so everyone can see one another's faces during the discussion.
2. Ask each group member to share something special. How do you treat it?
3. Discuss that we are more special than our toys.
4. Discuss how we help ourselves and others by positive, helpful ways of acting.
5. Be sure to separate the behavior from the person. People are always special. Behavior is positive or negative and either helps or hurts.
6. If people help and not hurt themselves or others, it is their choice.

Process each activity by using cooperative groups. Discuss the sharing from the cooperative groups. Agree on one way of practicing the ideas at school or at home.

Activity 3: Responsibility for One's Behavior
(Used for teaching the third step of the self-concept series)

Topic: Self-concept

Competency: Children will be able to identify personal needs (for example, the need to belong, the need for self-worth, the need for love, and the need for attention) and means with which to meet those needs.

Indicator: Children will name three behaviors that meet their need to be accepted by various groups such as school, family, and peers.

Purpose: To discuss one's responsibility to "watch oneself" because everyone is important.

Procedures for Grades K–3. Ask the group who people need to watch to have positive, helpful behavior because they are so important. Ask the children to point to themselves. While everyone is pointing to themselves, ask questions about behaviors that are a part of everyone's day-to-day life at school or home. The following are sample questions: "Whose talking do you watch?" "Whose listening do you watch?" "Whose finishing work do you watch?" "Whose tattling do you watch?"

Discuss that everyone is special even if they are not liked by the group.

Procedure for Grades 4–8. Discuss with the group how people feel after they help or hurt themselves or others. Discuss ways we build or erode our feelings about self. Discuss the fact that behavior is a choice and that we are responsible for our helpful and harmful decisions. Discuss ways to avoid blaming others when one makes a harmful choice. What can happen when a person takes responsibility for behavior choices? How does this relate to remembering that all people are valuable?

Use cooperative groups to discuss ways of applying the ideas generated from the discussion to everyday life. Agree to implement one idea.

The process of integrating self-concept with life skill development is most effective if it becomes the focus and foundation of group guidance, group counseling, behavior management, and individual counseling (Radd, 1990). The consistent exposure of children to self-concept activities related to life experiences will clarify and personalize these difficult concepts so they can become part of the children's knowledge base.

RESEARCH AND REACTIONS
Counseling Process

Numerous counseling-process studies have been conducted on person-centered counseling involving adults that lend support to the method. One of the most productive contributions to validating the approach was the process scale originally developed in 1958 by Rogers and Rablen (1979), which provided seven progress stages descriptive of the counseling process. Studies using the process scale showed that significant behavior variations were discernible over the course of counseling. Walker, Rablen, and Rogers (1960) and Tomlinson and Hart (1962) showed that counseling cases prejudged as more successful were highly distinguishable when ratings were made on the process scale; this would indicate a positive correlation between counselor ratings and the process scale.

Rogers (1967b), by listening to numerous recordings of successful person-centered cases, also noted a consistent pattern of change in clients: the most successful clients moved from a rather rigid and impersonal type of functioning to a level of functioning marked by change and acceptance of personal feelings.

In addition to Rogers, many other researchers have investigated person-centered therapy. Cartwright (1957) provided an annotated bibliography of 122 studies with adults that investigated both the process and the outcome of person-centered therapy. Shlien and Zimring (1970) published a similar overview of person-centered research supporting Rogers's theory. A few representative studies are mentioned below.

Raskin (1952) and Rosenman (1955) produced evidence that clients shifted their emphasis from others as a source of evaluation to themselves during the course of person-centered therapy. Positive evaluation of self increased, and evaluation of others decreased. Corsini and Wedding (1989) noted similar support for person-centered counseling in their review of Rogers's work.

Bergman (1951) also provided support for the person-centered approach when he found that structuring and interpretation by the counselor were significantly followed by an abandonment of self-exploration by the client, and reflection by the counselor was significantly followed by continued client self-exploration.

Mercier and Johnson (1984) used neurolinguistic programming as a methodology to determine if therapists track or accommodate their language usage with that of their clients. The study involved training judges to a 75-percent agreement level in identifying both predicate and representational systems used by counselors and clients. The judges reviewed and analyzed the film series *Three Approaches to Psychotherapy* (Shostrom, 1965) and transcripts of the films. It was found that the three therapists (Rogers, Perls, and Ellis) differed in the frequency of their use of representational systems (RSs). Rogers used the kinesthetic RS most often, while Perls and Ellis used the auditory RS most often. Rogers's session with the client (Gloria) had the fewest differences in RS predicates. Perls's session with Gloria varied during the first two-thirds of the interview; however, Perls used the kinesthetic RS more frequently during the last third of the session. Ellis and Gloria used the most different RSs. The study speaks well for the person-centered approach as one that lends itself to the client's style rather than molding the client to fit the counselor's style.

Mahrer, Stalikas, Fairweather, and Scott (1989) found significant relationships between intensity of feeling and categories of "good moments" of client movement, progress, or change during the counseling process. In fact, the maintenance of relatively low-intensity levels of feeling were found sufficient for maintaining the "good moments."

Williams and Lair (1991) presented a rationale and technique for using person-centered counseling with children who have a disability. They stressed the importance of using Rogers's three conditions (counselor genuineness, unconditional acceptance and caring, and deep empathic understanding) to help build self-acceptance in those who have a disability.

In a similar vein, Foreman (1988) recommended Rogers's three conditions for work with parents of handicapped children. She argued that these parents should be viewed in light of their potential for growth rather than as "in need" and lacking in skills and resources.

Lindt (1988) presented an argument for using holding as a person-centered method to restore contact between parent and child. Holding is one way to communicate Rogers's three conditions. It provides safety and abreaction; it helps break down imbalance in the division of power between parent and child. The Lindt article included a case study about holding a boy, age 7, who exhibits autistic-like behavior.

Ellinwood (1989) made a similar case for ensuring that Rogers's process conditions were present for every member of the family if person-centered counseling was the treatment of choice. She was especially concerned that children might be omitted from the conditions. Ellinwood based her argument on the experiences she has had with children (ages 8 to 9) in family therapy.

Counseling Outcomes

Although published counseling-outcome studies on person-centered coun-seling are not as numerous as process studies, several have been reported. Some outcome studies have been conducted in school settings; one of them involved Rogers himself.

Rogers (1967a) applied person-centered principles in an educational institution that was seeking positive and productive change. Plans were devised for small groups, including parents, faculty, students, and admin-istrators, to meet on an intensive basis. The results showed:

- A loosening of the categories of student, faculty, and administrator en-hanced communication.
- There was more student participation in decision-making at all levels, and more student-centered teaching occurred.
- More experimentation and innovation took place.

Wiggins (1982) found that person-centered counseling was effective in helping second-graders improve their behavior and maintain these gains up to four months after treatment. Using the Carkhuff system for rating counselor responses, Wiggins found that the clients of the higher-functioning counselors made greater gains; however, gains were also re-corded for the clients of counselors not scoring as high on the Carkhuff scale.

Support for a nondirective counseling approach can also be found in a study conducted by Bayer (1986), in which two approaches to affective education were compared (a directed condition versus a facilitated condi-tion) on the two dimensions of self-concept gains and student ratings of interest and value attached to the program. This well-designed experiment was conducted in 12 sessions with seventh-graders over a three-week period. One hypothesis was confirmed: the facilitated experimental group showed a significantly greater gain in self-concept. However, no significant difference was found between the two groups on perception of interest and value of the sessions.

Omizo and Omizo (1988), applying Rogerian principles of self-concept and interpersonal relationship development, found group counseling suc-cessful in enhancing self-concept and interpersonal relationship develop-ment with learning-disabled children ages 9 to 11. Group sessions focused on activities designed to accomplish both ends.

Kazdin, Bass, Siegel, and Thomas (1989) compared cognitive-behavior therapy with relationship therapy in the treatment of children referred for antisocial behavior. Children receiving person-centered relationship therapy remained at pretreatment levels of functioning; however, the cognitive-behavioral problem-solving skills group reduced antisocial behavior and increased prosocial behavior.

Outcome studies on person-centered counseling cover a variety of topics, ranging from the effects of the counseling relationship, counselor or therapist personality, empathy and expectations for counseling outcomes, to the effects of various person-centered training methods on educational and training outcomes. The following outcome studies span five decades of research on Rogers's work.

Baehr (1954) studied 66 hospitalized veterans to see if the type of person-centered therapy they received made any difference. One group of veterans received individual therapy, one group received group therapy, and one group received both individual and group therapy. Although all three groups showed improvement, the combined group (both individual and group) showed the most change.

Gallagher (1953) presented evidence that for 42 clients of person-centered therapy, anxiety, as measured on four different anxiety scales, decreased significantly. He also found that significant improvement occurred as measured on four scales from the Minnesota Multiphasic Personality Inventory (MMPI).

Aaronson (1953) found that the counselor's understanding of himself or herself and the client is the key to person-centered counseling.

Brown (1954) used a different technique, the Q-sort, to rank client/counselor pairs on their perceptions of the actual therapeutic relationship and the ideal relationship. High agreement was found between client and counselor for the ideal relationship, but only moderate similarity was found in the actual relationship. The outcome of counseling was highly correlated with the abilities of the client and the counselor to perceive their relationship in similar terms.

Halkides (1958) studied the relationship between the counselor's characteristics of congruence, positive regard, and empathy and the success of counseling. Judges rated ten cases found to be successful and ten found to be unsuccessful. Halkides found that the presence of the three counselor characteristics was significantly associated with successful outcomes.

Studies have been conducted on the relationship of empathy to social and cognitive development. Shantz (1975) summarized a variety of these studies on children and concluded that children have empathy for situations and people who are most similar to them. In other words, they show empathy for other children more readily than they do for adults—a finding that comes as no surprise to parents. Shantz did find that reliable accuracy in judging emotions does not usually appear until middle childhood. The person-centered counselor must consider these findings when using an empathy-based counseling method with children.

Perhaps the most conclusive support for Rogers's method comes from a study that compared psychotics (schizophrenics), neurotics, and normals (Rogers, 1967b). Rogers compared these three groups to see how effective person-centered counseling would be with each. Although the findings were complex, they included the following:

1. Empathic understanding by counselors and the extent to which they were perceived as genuine by schizophrenics were associated with involvement and constructive personality changes in clients.
2. Both psychotics and normals had more realistic perceptions of the therapeutic relationship than the counselor did.
3. The same qualities in the counseling relationship were facilitative for the schizophrenic as for the neurotic.
4. It was possible to identify the qualities of client in-therapy behavior that indicated change was in progress.
5. The process of change involved a chain of events. The quality of the therapeutic relationship facilitated improved inner integration in the client, which in turn facilitated a reduction in pathological behavior, which facilitated an improvement in social adjustment.
6. Early assessment of the relationship qualities provided a good indicator of whether or not constructive change would result.

Rice (1983), in a study of 34 males in a maximum-security psychiatric hospital, attempted to compare the effectiveness of a social-skills group with that of a person-centered group in improving inmates' social skills on the ward. The social-skills group was found to be superior in social-skill development during role-play situations. However, the person-centered group showed a significant improvement when rated by the ward staff. The learning from the social-skills group did not transfer to the ward. Two types of reinforcement were used in the study, and neither was shown to be a significant factor in the outcome.

Levant (1983) conducted a literature review on types of person-centered skills-training programs available for the family and on the effectiveness of these programs. He found that each program could be classified into one of three divisions: (1) training for treating another family member, (2) training as treatment, and (3) training for problem prevention or personal enhancement. Research conducted on person-centered approaches to family training programs supports the following conclusions: (1) effective person-centered communication skills can be taught in a relatively short time; (2) play-therapy skills produce positive results when applied by a parent to a disturbed child; (3) person-centered communication skills can be used effectively to treat dysfunctional parent/child and marital relationships; (4) these gains hold up over short- and long-term follow-up periods; and (5) person-centered approaches hold their own with behavioral methods and are found to be more effective than Gestalt and discussion-group approaches.

Shaffer and Hasegawa (1984) found that the use of an empathy algorithm with a role-played client was instrumental in increasing the number of person-centered Level 3 responses made by counseling students in an experimental group. In another counselor-training study, Elizabeth (1983) found that a person-centered training group experienced lower levels of anxiety during the treatment period than did participants in a psychoanalytic training program. Self-actualization scores were also significantly higher for the person-centered group. Gains by the person-centered group were maintained on follow-up testing.

Robinson and Hyman (1984), in a meta-analysis of human relations teacher training programs, found that 20 to 30 hours of training in human relations theories seemed to be the most effective program. They also found that such training produced positive changes in teacher attitudes and corresponding changes in improved classroom learning climates.

One can draw several conclusions from the literature on person-centered counseling:

1. Consistent patterns of change are discernible over the course of therapy: successful people move from rigid functioning to more flexible functioning.
2. Person-centered therapy can be helpful in educational settings.
3. People increase their positive evaluation of self as a result of therapy.
4. Improved versus nonimproved people show more relief from symptoms and more insight into self.
5. Reflection of feelings leads to continued self-exploration.
6. Significant decrements in anxiety as well as increased signs of adjustment occur as a result of successful therapy.
7. The success of therapy rests partly with the ability of the person and the therapist to perceive their relationship in similar terms.
8. A case is less likely to be successful if the person is seen for a short amount of time.
9. Successful therapists have an ability to understand themselves as well as other people.
10. A combination of group and individual counseling is most effective.
11. It is unnecessary to develop different theories and procedures for schizophrenics. They were found to respond constructively to person-centered therapy.

MULTICULTURAL COUNSELING

Criticisms of person-centered counseling center around the idea that it is too abstract both for young children and for adults who have not attained the ability to do formal thinking. The perfect clients for person-centered counseling have often been described as having the "YAVIS" syndrome; that is, they are young, attractive, verbal, intelligent, and sensitive. Such people may not need much counseling. Who, then, we might ask, will counsel the tough, nonverbal children? Others criticize the person-centered approach as one that becomes "bogged down" in feelings and does not move quickly enough into planned behavioral change. Another critical point directed to Rogers's system concerns his distaste for diagnostic tools and tests; critics argue that valuable data may be lost to counselors who do not use diagnostic methods. Hand in hand with Rogers's refusal to use diagnostic tests went his equally strong aversion to prognostication and prescription. Critics of person-centered counseling hold that counselors are experts who can dispense valuable advice as well as predict future behavioral patterns and personality development in their clients.

In rebuttal, Rogers (1977) pointed out how person-centered counseling relates to a wide variety of individual and group concerns that span diverse populations, including the areas of family counseling, couple relationships, education, politics, government, and business administration.

Follensbee, Draguns, and Danish (1986) studied the differential effects of affective responses and closed questions on adult client responses in an analog counseling setting. Affective responses were found to be superior to closed questions in facilitating client verbalizations focusing on the present, the client, and the client's feelings. This finding held true for clients in all three cultural groups studied: African American, Puerto Rican, and Anglo American.

Usher (1989), in an attempt to evaluate the utility of person-centered counseling across cultures, examined person-centered counseling against ten possible problems with cultural bias arising from the method. The point is made that, while not a perfect method for all cultures, person-centered counseling has some advantages. There is less risk of being judged by the dominant culture's definition of normality, because the client defines the goals and evaluates the process in person-centered counseling. Rogers also allowed for circularity of thinking, which allows culturally different clients to express feelings and thoughts within an open, nonjudgmental setting. Possible cross-cultural disadvantages of person-centered counseling include an emphasis on individualism that fails to accommodate the healthy dependencies on family members fostered in other cultures. Focusing on the self, subjective experience, and the "here and now" may be truly foreign or offensive to other cultures. The level of abstraction required in person-centered counseling conducted in English may also be too different to be helpful.

Waxer (1989), in an effort to research the multicultural implications for person-centered counseling, compared Cantonese and Canadian college students' reactions to Rogers and Ellis on the film, *Three Approaches to Psychotherapy* (Shostram, 1965). The Canadians preferred Rogers, and the Cantonese chose Ellis. While both groups of students viewed Ellis as more directive, paternalistic, and authoritarian than Rogers, the Cantonese students did not rate him as harshly as the Canadians did. The Asian preference could be for counselors who are more autocratic, paternalistic, and directive. North Americans, on the other hand, may view counseling as an open, exploratory, and democratic process.

The true proof of person-centered counseling as a viable cross-cultural counseling method is in the pudding of real-life experience. In an interview with Carl Rogers shortly before his death in 1987, Hill-Hain (Hill-Hain & Rogers, 1988) explored some of the basic challenges involved in a large-scale, cross-cultural application of person-centered group work with white and black South Africans that Rogers had started in 1986. Rogers believed that the facilitator must not only accept a great deal of responsibility for learning about the culture of the participants, but he or she must also be ready for surprises. Rogers also stressed the goal of relinquishing any attempt to control the outcome of the group experience, direction, or mood. However, group members are not to physically or psychologically abuse other group members. Rogers reported that his method seemed to accomplish its goals. The interview ended with Rogers posing the question: "Can I really be open to any little clue that might open up doors of new understanding?" That is how Rogers worked with individuals and groups.

Stipsits and Hutterer (1989) detailed another account of person-centered approaches making a successful crossover to another culture. They found that after two decades of experience with person-centered approaches, Austrian professionals and their clients were moving toward this U.S. system of working with people. One survey revealed that 35 percent of the professionals in Austria who work in psychosocial areas have a person-centered orientation, and 40 percent of all clients in Austria had been in person-centered therapy. The person-centered numbers are most impressive when considered in light of the fact that they were compiled in the homeland of psychoanalysis, individual psychology, and logotherapy. Finally, Combs (1988), in writing about current issues in person-centered therapy, summarized Rogers's work in cross-cultural settings by pointing out how people from groups with supposedly irreconcilable differences and prejudices apparently learned to appreciate and communicate with one another in Rogers's encounter groups.

SUMMARY

In an article on developing a more human science of the person, Rogers (1985) recommended several new scientific models that promise new research alternatives. These models include phenomenological research, heuristics, and hermaneutics. Rogers believed these introspective models have some common elements: (1) Traditionalists are beginning to accept them. (2) The methods are appropriate for answering difficult questions about an inexact science. (3) The approaches require the scientist to indwell the perceptions, attitudes, feelings, experiences, and behaviors of the participants. (4) Participants are viewed as co-researchers, not subjects. Once again we see Rogers's humanizing philosophy reflected in all parts of his work, whether in counseling, teaching, or research.

Herman (1990) and Aspy (1988) have discussed Rogers's contribution to teachers and learners and how person-centered theory and practice can humanize education. Hutterer (1990) has presented the same type of summary regarding applying Rogers's philosophy to conducting research. Rogers was actively working on world peace projects at the time of his death in 1987. Soloman (1990) points out that Rogers devoted the last 15 years of his life to working on ways to bring emotional honesty and personal congruence into international dialogue. Rogers firmly believed that the methodology of person-centered theory could be successfully applied to the negotiation process needed to achieve peace among people and nations.

REFERENCES

Aaronson, M. (1953). A study of the relationship between certain counselor and client characteristics in client-centered therapy. In W. U. Snyder (Ed.), *Group report of a program of research in psychotherapy.* University Park, PA: Pennsylvania State University. [Summarized in *Journal of Counseling Psychology* (1957), 4, 95.]

Aspy, D. N. (1988). Carl Rogers' contributions to education. *Person-Centered Review, 3,* 10–18.

Axline, V. M. (1964). *Dibs: In search of self.* Boston: Houghton Mifflin.

Baehr, G. (1954). The comparative effectiveness of individual psychotherapy, group psychotherapy, and a combination of these methods. *Journal of Consulting Psychology, 18,* 179–183.

Bayer, D. L. (1986). The effects of two methods of affective education on self-concept in seventh-grade students. *The School Counselor, 34,* 123–134.

Bergman, D. V. (1951). Counseling methods and client responses. *Journal of Counseling Psychology, 15,* 216–224.

Brown, O. H. (1954). *An investigation of the therapeutic relationship in client-centered therapy.* Unpublished doctoral dissertation, University of Chicago. [Summarized in *Journal of Counseling Psychology* (1957), 4, 93.]

Carkhuff, R. (1973, March). *Human achievement, educational achievement, career achievement: Essential ingredients of elementary school guidance.* Paper presented at the National Elementary School Guidance Conference, Louisville, KY.

Carkhuff, R. (1981, April). *Creating and researching community based helping programs.* Paper presented at the American Personnel and Guidance Association Convention, St. Louis, MO.

Cartwright, D. (1957). Annotated bibliography of research and theory construction in client-centered therapy. *Journal of Counseling Psychology, 4,* 82–100.

Combs, A. W. (1988). Some current issues for person-centered therapy. *Person-Centered Review, 3,* 263–276.

Corsini, R., & Wedding, D. (1989). *Current psychotherapies* (4th ed.). Itasca, IL: F. E. Peacock.

Elizabeth, P. (1983). Comparison of a psychoanalytic and client-centered group treatment model on measures of anxiety and self actualization. *Journal of Counseling Psychology, 30,* 425–428.

Ellinwood, C. (1989). The young child in person-centered family therapy. *Person-Centered Review, 4,* 256–262.

Follensbee, R. W., Jr., Draguns, J. G., & Danish, S. J. (1986). Impact of two types of counselor intervention on Black American, Puerto Rican, and Anglo-American analogue clients. *Journal of Counseling Psychology, 33,* 446–453.

Foreman, J. (1988). Use of person-centered theory with parents of handicapped children. *Texas Association of Counseling and Development Journal, 16*(2), 115–118.

Gallagher, J. J. (1953). MMPI changes concomitant with client-centered therapy. *Journal of Consulting Psychology, 17,* 334–338.

Gordon, T. (1974). *Teacher effectiveness training.* New York: Wyden.

Halkides, G. (1958). *An experimental study of four conditions necessary for therapeutic change.* Unpublished doctoral dissertation, University of Chicago.

Herman, W. E. (1990). Helping students explore the motives, medium, and message of Carl R. Rogers. *Person-Centered Review, 5,* 30–38.

Hill-Hain, A., & Rogers, C. (1988). A dialogue with Carl Rogers: Cross-cultural challenges of facilitating person-centered groups in South Africa. *The Journal for Specialists in Group Work, 13,* 62–69.

Hutterer, R. (1990). Authentic science: Some implications of Carl Rogers' reflections on sciences. *Person-Centered Review, 5,* 57–76.

Kazdin, A. E., Bass, D., Siegel, T., & Thomas, C. (1989). Cognitive-behavioral therapy and relationship therapy in the treatment of children referred for antisocial behavior. *Journal of Consulting and Clinical Psychology, 57,* 522–535.

Levant, R. F. (1983). Client-centered skills training programs for the family: A review of the literature. *The Counseling Psychologist, 11,* 29–42.

Lindt, M. (1988). Holding and the person-centered approach: Experience and reflection. *Person-Centered Review, 3,* 229–240.

Mahrer, A. R., Stalikas, A., Fairweather, D. R., & Scott, J. M. (1989). Is there a relationship between client feeling level and categories of "good moments" in counseling sessions? *Canadian Journal of Counseling, 23*(3), 219–227.

Mercier, M., & Johnson, M. (1984). Representational system predicate use and convergence in counseling: Gloria revised. *Journal of Counseling Psychology, 31,* 161–169.

Omizo, M. M., & Omizo, S. A. (1988). Group counseling's effect on self-concept and social behavior among children with learning disabilities. *Journal of Humanistic Education and Development, 26,* 109–117.

Poppen, W., & Thompson, C. (1974). *School counseling: Theories and concepts.* Lincoln, NE: Professional Educators.

Radd, T. R. (1987). *The Grow with Guidance system section: Classroom behavior management.* Canton, OH: Grow with Guidance.

Radd, T. R. (1990). *The Grow with Guidance video: A powerful system for maximizing youth potential.* Canton, OH: Grow with Guidance.

Raskin, N. J. (1952). An objective study of the locus-of-evaluation factor in psychotherapy. In W. Wolff & J. A. Precker (Eds.), *Success in psychotherapy.* New York: Grune & Stratton. [Summarized in *Journal of Counseling Psychology* (1957), *4,* 85.]

Rice, M. E. (1983). Improving the social skills of males in a maximum security psychiatric setting. *Canadian Journal of Behavioral Science, 15,* 1–13.

Robinson, A. W., & Hyman, I. A. (1984, April). *A meta-analysis of human relations teacher training programs.* Paper presented at the Annual Convention of the National Association of School Psychologists, Philadelphia. (ERIC Document Reproduction Service No. ED 253 521)

Rogers, C. R. (1939). *The clinical treatment of the problem child.* Boston: Houghton Mifflin.

Rogers, C. R. (1942). *Counseling and psychotherapy.* Boston: Houghton Mifflin.

Rogers, C. R. (1951). *Client-centered therapy.* Boston: Houghton Mifflin.

Rogers, C. R. (1965). *Client-centered therapy: Its current practice, implications, and theory.* Boston: Houghton Mifflin.

Rogers, C. R. (1967a). A plan for self-directed change in an educational system. *Educational Leadership, 24,* 717–731.

Rogers, C. R. (1967b). *The therapeutic relationship and its impact: A study of psychotherapy with schizophrenics.* Madison, WI: University of Wisconsin Press.

Rogers, C. R. (1969). *Freedom to learn.* Columbus, OH: Merrill.

Rogers, C. R. (1977). *Carl Rogers on personal power: Inner strength and its revolutionary impact.* New York: Delacorte Press.

Rogers, C. R. (1985). Toward a more human science of the person. *Journal of Humanistic Psychology, 25,* 7–24.

Rogers, C. R., & Rablen, R. A. (1958). *A scale of process in psychotherapy.* Unpublished manuscript, University of Wisconsin, Madison, WI. Reprinted in R. Corsini (Ed.) *Current Psychotherapies,* Itasca, Ill.: F. E. Peacock, 1979.

Rosenman, S. (1955). Changes in the representation of self, others, and interrelationships in client-centered therapy. *Journal of Counseling Psychology, 2,* 271–277.

Shaffer, W. F., & Hasegawa, C. S. (1984). Use of an empathy algorithm with a role-played client. *Journal of Clinical Psychology, 40,* 57–64.

Shantz, C. U. (1975). Empathy in relation to social cognitive development. *The Counseling Psychologist, 5,* 18–21.

Shlien, J., & Zimring, F. (1970). Research directives and methods in client-centered therapy. In J. T. Hart & T. M. Tomlinson (Eds.), *New directions in client-centered therapy* (pp. 33–57). Boston: Houghton Mifflin.

Shostrom, E. (Producer). (1965). *Three approaches to psychotherapy* [Film]. Orange, CA: Psychological Films.

Soloman, L. N. (1990). Carl Rogers' efforts for world peace. *Person-Centered Review, 5,* 39–56.

Stipsits, R., & Hutterer, R. (1989). The person-centered approach in Austria. *Person-Centered Review, 4,* 475–487.

Tomlinson, T. M., & Hart, J. T. (1962). A validation study of the process scale. *Journal of Consulting Psychology, 26,* 74–78.

Usher, C. H. (1989). Recognizing cultural bias in counseling theory and practice: The case of Rogers. *Journal of Multicultural Counseling and Development, 17,* 62–71.

Walker, A., Rablen, R., & Rogers, C. (1960). Development of a scale to measure process changes in psychotherapy. *Journal of Clinical Psychology, 16,* 79–85.

Waxer, P. H. (1989). Cantonese versus Canadian evaluation of directive and non-directive therapy. *Canadian Journal of Counseling, 23*(3), 263–271.

Wiggins, J. D. (1982). Improving student behaviors with Carkhuff-model counseling. *The School Counselor, 30,* 57–60.

Williams, W., & Lair, G. (1991). Using a person-centered approach with children who have a disability. *Elementary School Guidance and Counseling, 25,* 194–203.

CHAPTER 5

Gestalt Therapy

FRITZ PERLS

Fritz Perls's estranged wife, Laura, once referred to him as half prophet and half bum; Perls considered this an accurate description. In his autobiography, *In and Out the Garbage Pail* (1971), Perls wrote that, at the age of 75, he liked his reputation of being both a dirty old man and a guru. Unfortunately, he continued, the first reputation was on the wane and the second ascending.

Born in a Jewish ghetto on the outskirts of Berlin on July 8, 1893, Friedrich Solomon Perls was the third child of Amelia Rund and Nathan Perls. He later anglicized his first name to Frederick but is remembered more commonly as Fritz.

Perls disliked his eldest sister, Else. He thought of her as a clinger and was uncomfortable in her presence. Else also had severe eye trouble, and Perls disliked the thought that he might have to take care of her someday. He did not mourn much when he heard of her death in a concentration camp. Shepard (1975) speculates that Perls resented the extra attention and favor his mother offered Else because of her partial blindness. He did seem to enjoy and was close to his second sister, Grete.

After a difficult first few weeks of life, Perls seems to have led a happy and healthy life for his first nine years. Around the age of 10, Perls became rebellious. His parents were having bitter fights, and his father was away from home quite often. Perls even began to doubt his paternity and suspected that his actual father was a much-respected uncle; this remained an open question for Fritz until his death. His marriage was not much happier than his childhood, although he and his wife, Laura, remained married and worked together in the development of Gestalt therapy. Perls came to realize that the roles of husband and father gave him little satisfaction.

After some hard times in Europe, Perls found success as a training analyst in Johannesburg, South Africa. While there, he founded the South African Institute for Psychoanalysis. He learned to fly and got his pilot's license. During this time, in 1936, he flew to Czechoslovakia to deliver a paper to the Psychoanalytic Congress. He intended to meet with his hero, Sigmund Freud, but he was given only a cool four-minute audience while standing in Freud's doorway. Perls experienced another disappointment when his paper received an icy reception from most of the other analysts attending the Congress. From this point on, for 30 years Perls challenged the assumptions and directions of Freud and the psychoanalysts. In his final years, many people began to listen. Perls thought he had four main "unfinished situations" in his life: not being able to sing well, never having made a parachute jump, never having tried skin diving, and never having had the opportunity to show Freud the mistakes he had made.

Perls spent 12 years in South Africa, during which time he formulated all the basic ideas underlying what he would later call Gestalt therapy. At the age of 53, he moved his family to New York, where the "formal birth" of Gestalt therapy took place. Several people were involved with this birth, and a great debate developed among them to determine what to call the new theory. Perls held out for *Gestalt*. The new therapy took its name from a German term. *Gestalt* cannot be translated exactly into English, but the meaning of the concept can be grasped.

[Gestalt is] a form, a configuration or a totality that has, as a unified whole, properties which cannot be derived by summation from the parts and their relationships. It may refer to physical structures, to physiological and psychological functions, or to symbolic units. [English & English, 1958, p. 225]

In late 1951, Perls's book *Gestalt Therapy* was first published. Perls is listed as author, although Ralph Hefferline wrote nearly all of the first half of the book and Paul Goodman the second. At first, the new therapy had almost no impact. Perls began traveling to cities such as Cleveland, Detroit, Toronto, and Miami to run groups for professionals and lay people interested in the new idea. As he traveled about the country, he discovered that he was received far better on the road than he was at home in New York. At the end of ten years in New York, Perls decided to leave that city, and his wife, for the warmth of Miami. Laura Perls's interpretation of why Fritz left was that he was not the leading psychotherapist, nor even the leading Gestaltist, in New York.

Miami was very important to Perls because there he met "the most significant woman in my life," Marty Fromm. In Florida he also found LSD and became involved in the drug subculture. From Florida he moved to California, eventually Big Sur, where he became widely known. At the Esalen Institute, he had to compete with people such as Virginia Satir, Bernard Gunther, and Will Schutz. Perls contended that the techniques Gunther and Schutz employed used other people's ideas and offered "instant joy." Perls, who opposed quick cures and respected only originality, established his own Gestalt Institute of Canada at Cowichan on Vancouver Island in British Columbia.

Nine months after the center in Canada was begun, Fritz Perls died. Two biopsies the doctors had taken during a long operation came back negative, but an autopsy disclosed that he had suffered from advanced cancer of the pancreas. Perls died as he had lived. On the last evening of his life, March 14, 1970, Perls was attempting to get out of bed against the wishes of his nurse. "Don't tell me what to do," he said to her, fell back, and died.

Perls viewed the state of Gestalt theory as being in progress at the time of his death. Perls thought that theory development, like human development, was a process of becoming. He was not one to close the book on his theory and treat it as gospel. Rather, Perls revised the theory to fit his observations of human behavior.

THE NATURE OF PEOPLE

According to Gestalt theory, the most important areas of concern are the thoughts and feelings people are experiencing at the moment. Normal, healthy behavior occurs when people act and react as total organisms. Many people tend to fragment their lives, distributing their concentration and attention among several variables and events at one time. The results of such fragmentation can be seen in an ineffective living style, with outcomes ranging from low productivity to serious accidents. The Gestalt view of human nature is positive in that people are viewed as capable of becoming self-regulating beings who can achieve a sense of unity and integration in their lives.

Perls (1969) saw the person as a total organism—not just as the brain. His saying that people would be better off losing their minds and coming to their senses meant that our bodies and feelings are better indicators of the truth than our words, which we use to hide the truth from ourselves. Body signs such as headaches, rashes, neck strain, and stomach pains may indicate that we need to change our behavior. Perls believed that awareness alone can be curative. With full awareness, a state of organismic self-regulation develops, and the total person takes control.

Mentally healthy people are viewed as people who can maintain their awareness without being distracted by the various environmental stimuli that constantly vie for our attention. Such people can fully and clearly experience their own needs and the environmental alternatives for meeting these needs. Healthy people still experience their share of inner conflicts and frustrations, but, having achieved increased levels of concentration and awareness, they can solve their problems without complicating them with fantasy elaborations. Conflicts with others are likewise resolved when it is possible and dismissed when it is not. People with high levels of awareness of their needs and their environment know which problems and conflicts are resolvable and which are not. In Perls's theory, the key to successful adjustment is the development of personal responsibility—responsibility for one's life and response to one's environment. Much of the Perls's doctrine is summarized in his famous Gestalt Prayer (Perls, 1969):

> I do my thing and you do your thing.
> I am not in this world to live up to your expectations,
> And you are not in this world to live up to mine.
> You are you and I am I
> And if by chance we find each other, it's beautiful.
> If not, it can't be helped. [p. 4]

The healthy person focuses sharply on one need (the figure) at a time while relegating other needs to the background. When the need is met—or the Gestalt is closed or completed—it is relegated to the background, and a new need comes into focus (becomes the figure). The smoothly functioning figure/ground relationship characterizes the healthy personality. The dominant need of the organism at any time becomes the foreground figure, and the other needs recede, at least temporarily, into the background. The foreground figure is the need that presses most sharply for satisfaction, whether the need is to preserve life or is related to less physically or psychologically vital areas. For individuals to be able to satisfy their needs and close the Gestalt in order to move on to other things, they must be able to determine what they need, and they must know how to manipulate themselves and their environment. Even purely physiological needs can be satisfied only through the interaction of the organism and the environment (Perls, 1976).

Perls defined neurotic people as those who try to attend to too many needs at one time and, as a result, fail to satisfy any one need fully. Neurotic people also use their potential to manipulate others to do for them what they have not done for themselves. Rather than running their own lives, they turn them over to those who will take care of their needs. In summary, people cause themselves additional problems by not handling their lives appropriately in the following six categories:

1. *Lacking contact with the environment.* People may become so rigid that they cut themselves off from others or from resources in the environment.
2. *Confluence.* People may incorporate too much of themselves into others or incorporate so much of the environment into themselves that they lose touch with where they are. Then the environment takes control.
3. *Unfinished business.* People may have unfulfilled needs, unexpressed feelings, or uncompleted situations that clamor for their attention. (This may manifest itself in dreams.)
4. *Fragmentation.* People may try to discover or deny a need such as aggression. The inability to find and obtain those things one needs may be the result of fragmenting one's life.

5. *Topdog/underdog.* People may experience a split in their personalities between what they think they "should" do (topdog) and what they "want" to do (underdog) (see Passons, 1975).
6. *Polarities (dichotomies).* People tend to flounder at times between existing, natural dichotomies in their lives, such as body/mind, self/external world, emotional/real, infantile/mature, biological/cultural, poetry/prose, spontaneous/deliberate, personal/social, love/aggression, and unconscious/conscious (Sahakian, 1969). Much of everyday living seems to be involved in resolving conflicts posed by these competing polarities. Assagioli (1965) has identified five types of polarities:
   a. Physical—masculinity/femininity and parasympathetic/sympathetic nervous system
   b. Emotional—pleasure/pain, excitement/depression, love/hate
   c. Mental—parent/child, eros (feeling)/logos (reason), topdog/underdog
   d. Spiritual—intellectual doubt/dogmatism
   e. Interindividual—man/woman, black/white, Christian/Jew

THEORY OF COUNSELING

Any adaptation of Perls's system to counseling children would incorporate the five layers of neuroses proposed by Perls (1971; see also Fagan & Shepard, 1970). Perls devised these five layers to depict how people fragment their lives and prevent themselves from succeeding and maturing. The five layers form a series of counseling stages, or benchmarks, for the counseling process; in fact, they could be considered as five steps to a better Gestalt way of life.

1. *The phony layer.* Many people find themselves trapped in trying to be what they are not. The phony layer is characterized by many conflicts that are never resolved.
2. *The phobic layer.* As people become aware of their phony games, they become aware of their fears that maintain the games. This is often a frightening experience.
3. *The impasse layer.* This is the layer people reach when they shed the environmental support of their games and find they do not know a better way to cope with their fears and dislikes. People often become stuck here and refuse to move on.
4. *The implosive layer.* People become aware of how they limit themselves, and they begin to experiment with new behaviors.
5. *The explosive layer.* If experiments with new behaviors are successful, people can reach the explosive layer, where they find much unused energy that had been tied up in maintaining a phony existence.

Perls believed that progress through the five layers of neuroses could best be achieved by observing how psychological defenses might be associated with muscular position, or what he called body armor. He believed the client's body language would be a better indicator of the truth than the client's words. He also believed that awareness of hidden material could be facilitated by acting out feelings. Perls asked people to project their thoughts and feelings upon empty chairs representing significant people in their lives. People were often asked to play several roles in attempting to identify who was experiencing conflict. Perls expanded on Rogers's idea of feedback as a therapeutic agent by including body posture, voice tone, eye movements, feelings, and gestures.

Gestalt therapy emphasizes direct experiences. It focuses on achieving awareness of the here and now and frustrating the client in any attempt to break out of this awareness. As an experiential approach, Gestalt therapy is not concerned with symptoms and analysis, but rather with total existence and integration. Integration and maturation, according to Perls, are never-ending processes directly related to a person's awareness of the here and now. A "Gestalt" is formed in a person as a new need arises. If a need is satisfied, the destruction of that particular Gestalt is achieved, and new Gestalts can be formed. This is a basic concept of Gestalt therapy. Incomplete Gestalts are referred to as "unfinished situations."

Perls (1969) wrote that the aim of his therapy was to help people help themselves to grow up—to mature, take charge of their lives, and become responsible for themselves. The central goal in Gestalt therapy is the deepening of awareness, which promotes a sense of living fully in the here and now. Other goals include teaching people to assume responsibility for themselves and facilitating their achievement of personal integration. These goals are consistent with those of most counseling systems.

The aim of integration is to help people become systematic, whole persons whose inner state and behavior match so that little energy is wasted within the system. Such integration allows people to give their full attention and energy to meeting their needs appropriately. The ultimate measure of success in Gestalt therapy is the extent to which clients grow in awareness, take responsibility for their actions, and are able to move from environmental to self-support.

COUNSELING METHOD

The function of the Gestalt counselor is to facilitate the client's awareness in the "now." Awareness is the capacity to focus, to attend, to be in touch with the "now." The Gestalt counselor is an aggressive therapist, one who frustrates any attempt on the part of the learner to break out of the awareness of here and now. Retreats into the past and jumps into the future are either stopped or related to the immediate present.

Miller (1989) pointed out that Perls often used sarcasm, humor, drama, and shock to rouse people from neurosis. For Perls, Gestalt therapy was a search for a workable solution in the present. The counselor's job would be to assist the client in experimenting with authentic new behaviors rather than to explain and maintain the unhelpful or harmful behaviors of the past. Dolliver (1991), attacking "inconsistencies" in Perls's philosophy and style in the often-reviewed film, *Three Approaches to Psychotherapy* (Shostrom, 1965), would conclude that none of the counselor's objectives in Miller's statement were met with Gloria. Miller and others, no doubt, will disagree, and the controversy over the film will continue well into the 21st century. It may be said with confidence that Fritz Perls, in person or on film, never left anyone feeling neutral; he made us all think and react.

Gestalt Techniques

In order to maintain the present-time orientation of the counseling interview, several language, game, and fantasy methods may be used. Helpful resources available to the counselor include books by Lederman (1969), Passons (1975), and Fagan and Shepard (1970). Some of the following techniques have been used successfully by the present authors and their students with children in the 5-to-12 age group.

"I" language. The use of the word *I* is encouraged when the client uses a generalized *you* when talking. For example: "*You* know how it is when *you* can't understand math and the teacher gets on *your* back." When *I* is substituted for *you,* the message becomes, "*I* know how it is when *I* can't understand math and the teacher gets on *my* back." Such substitutions of *I* for *you* are tried on like a pair of shoes to see how they fit. They help children to take responsibility for their feelings, thoughts, and behaviors.

Substituting *won't* for *can't.* Again, the "shoes" are tried on for comfort: "I won't pass math" rather than "I can't pass math." How much of the responsibility the child will own is the question to be answered.

Substituting *what* and *how* for *why.* "*How* do you feel about what you have just done?" "*What* are you doing with your foot as we talk about your behavior?"

No gossiping. If the child must talk about someone not present in the room, let the talk, all in the present tense, be directed to an empty chair. For example, the child might say, "I think you treat me unfairly, Ms. Clark. I wish you would be as nice to me as you are to the other kids." The child can then move to the other chair and answer for Ms. Clark. "Joan, I would find it easier to like you if you would be more helpful to me during the day."

The dialogue between Joan and Ms. Clark would continue until the child was finished with her complaint and the anticipated responses from her teacher. Person-to-person dialogues not only update the material into the present but also serve to increase the child's awareness of the problem. Side benefits include a better picture of the situation for the counselor and rehearsal time for the child, who may wish to discuss the problem later with the teacher. Some appreciation for the teacher's side of the conflict may also emerge from the dialogue.

Changing questions into statements. This method has the effect of helping children to be more authentic and direct in expressing their thoughts and feelings. For example, rather than "Don't you think I should stop hanging around those guys?" the child should say "I think I should stop hanging around those guys," or "I think you want me to stop hanging around those guys." Perls believed that most questions are phony in that they are really disguised statements.

Taking responsibility. Clients are asked to fill in sentence blanks as another way of examining personal responsibility for the way they manage their lives. For example, "Right now I'm feeling _____, and I take _____ percent responsibility for how I feel." The exercise is quite an eye-opener for those clients who tend to view outside sources as the total cause of their good and bad feelings.

Incomplete sentences. These exercises, like the exercise on taking responsibility, help clients to become aware of how they help and hurt themselves. For example, "I help myself when I _____," or "I block or hurt myself when I _____."

Bipolarities. Perls applies the term *differential thinking* to the concept of thinking in terms of opposites. Much everyday life appears to be spent resolving conflicts posed by competing polarities.

Topdog versus Underdog

One of the most common bipolarities consists of what Perls (1969) labeled "topdog" and "underdog." The topdog is righteous, authoritarian, and knows best. The topdog is a bully and works with "you should" and "you should not." The underdog manipulates by being defensive or apologetic, wheedling, and playing crybaby. The underdog works with "I want" and makes excuses such as "I try hard" and "I have good intentions." The underdog is cunning and usually gets the better of the topdog because the underdog position appeals to the pleasure-seeking side of our personality.

Two chairs can be used to help children resolve "I want" versus "I should" debates. One chair is labeled topdog (I should), and the other chair is labeled underdog (I want). Children are asked to present their best "I should" argument while sitting in the topdog chair and facing the empty underdog chair. Upon completing the first "I should" point, the child moves to the underdog chair to counter with an "I want" argument. The debate continues back and forth until the child completes all arguments from both points of view. Processing the activity often reveals in which chair (or on which side of the argument) the child feels that the greatest integration of shoulds and wants occurs, thus allowing the client to have the best of both sides.

The topdog/underdog technique can be used individually or in a group. If the technique is used in a group, the counselor can divide the clients into two subgroups, the topdogs and the underdogs. The topdog group members list reasons they *should* do a certain thing, while the underdog group members think of reasons they *want* to do something. After the lists have been compiled, the activity should lend itself to much discussion. Children respond very well to this activity.

The best outcomes from the topdog/underdog debate occur when the client can identify areas in which the "I shoulds" and "I wants" are the same. For example, "I love my job, I want to go to work, and I should go to work." These synergistic solutions help people integrate their lives.

The Empty Chair Technique

The Gestalt technique of the empty chair is often used to resolve a conflict between people or within a person. The child can sit in one chair and play his or her own part; then, sitting in the other chair, the child can play out a projection of what the other person is saying or doing in response. Similarly, a child may sit in one chair and discuss the pros of making a decision, then argue the cons of the decision while sitting in the opposite chair.

For example, Sharon was having trouble deciding whether to tell of her friend's involvement in a destruction of property. She thought her friend had behaved wrongly and should not let other children take the blame for the incident, yet she was reluctant to tattle on the friend and get her in trouble. The counselor suggested that Sharon sit in one chair and talk about what would happen if she did tell on her friend, then move to the other chair to describe what would happen if she did not. The technique helped Sharon to look at the consequences of both acts and make her decision.

Thompson and Poppen (1992) suggest a variation of the empty chair. A problem can be explored in an individual or group situation by introducing the empty chair as a hypothetical person with behaviors and characteristics similar to those of the child and his or her particular problem. It is sometimes easier for children to discuss a hypothetical child and how this child feels or could change than to discuss their own feelings and behaviors. While discussing an imagined person, the children learn about themselves.

My Greatest Weakness

In another exercise, clients are asked to name their greatest weakness and to write a short paragraph on how their weakness is really their greatest strength. For example, "My greatest weakness is procrastination, but I'll never give it up because by putting things off I create the motivation I need for completing unpleasant tasks."

Once clients realize that their greatest "weakness" may in fact be the greatest strength they have going for them, they begin to realize that they control the weakness rather than vice versa. Clients also realize that the counselor who uses this technique is not pushing them to fix their "weakness."

Resent, Demand, and Appreciate

Another exercise involves listing the three people the client is closest to and, for each of the three, having the client think of one thing that is resented, one thing that is demanded, and one thing that is appreciated about each person. For example:

Name	I resent	I demand	I appreciate
John	that you don't spend enough time with me	more time	your company and friendship
Mary			
Sue			

Such an exercise helps clients become more aware of the mixed feelings they have about others, how it is possible to resent and appreciate a person at the same time, and how opposing thoughts and feelings can be integrated.

The purpose of working with these bipolarities, or splits in the personality, is to bring each side into awareness so a reorganization can take place that does not exclude either side. Gestalt therapy is directed toward making life easier by integrating the splits in existence; each side is necessary and has its place in the well-integrated personality.

Fantasy Games

Fantasy games can be great fun for children of all ages and can let them become aware of their feelings right now. As a group activity, have the children choose an animal they would like to be. Allow them to move around as they feel this animal would. Then have the children sit down in pairs and discuss what they would feel if they were this particular animal. As a culmination to the activity, ask them to write a story about how they would feel if they were actually the animal. By the end of the exercise, children should have a real awareness of how they feel and be able to discuss their feelings with the counselor, teacher, or parent.

Fantasy games can be devised from almost any object or situation. The rosebush and wise-person fantasies are two favorites. In the first, the client pretends to be a rosebush. The client is then asked to consider the following points:

1. Type of bush—strong or weak?
2. Root system—deep or shallow?

3. Number of roses—too many or too few?
4. Number of thorns—too many or too few?
5. Environment—bad or good for growing?
6. Does your rosebush stand out?
7. Does it have enough room?
8. How does it get along with the other plants?
9. Does it have a good future?

The wise-person fantasy involves asking a fantasized wise man or woman one question, which the wise person ponders for a few minutes before he or she answers—speaking through the client, of course. Both question and answer should add some awareness and understanding to the client's life. For example, a client might ask "What should I do with my life?" and answer, as the wise person, "Develop all your talents and skills as much as you can."

Clients are asked to discuss their fantasies in depth with the counselor in individual sessions and with groups of two to four if a group is meeting. A good follow-up procedure is to have clients complete the statement "I learned that _____" after each exercise. The fantasy games are enhanced when clients lie down and participate in relaxation exercises before the experience and continue to lie down in a comfortable spot during the fantasy exercises.

Heikkinen (1989) wrote a helpful article on how to reorient clients from altered states of consciousness (ASC), used in Gestalt and other therapies, in a way that avoids such uncomfortable aftereffects as unusual cognitive or emotional functioning and atypical body reactions. Clients may experience an ASC during activities such as the rosebush or wise-person fantasies. It is recommended that these activities end by having the counselor count backward slowly from ten or in the direction opposite to that used to reach the ASC. Imagining walking up steps, swimming to the top of the lake, or returning from a journey are all useful methods of reorienting clients. Directing clients in a group setting to look slowly around the area and become reacquainted with their environment is also effective.

Dreamwork

Dreaming is a way of becoming aware of the world in the here and now. And because awareness is the dominant theme of Gestalt, dreaming and Gestalt seem to work well together. Dreaming is a guardian of one's existence because the content of dreams is always found to relate to one's survival, well-being, and growth; therefore, Gestalt therapists have been able to help clients overcome impasses in their lives through serious consideration of dreams. The Gestalt approach to dreams is helpful not only to people suffering from dilemmas in their lives but also to the average "healthy" person. Most people spend many of their waking hours out of touch with the here and now by worrying compulsively about the future or doting on memories of failure or past pleasures.

Spontaneity is an important feature of Gestalt therapy, and, according to Perls, dreams are the most spontaneous expression of the existence of the human being. The Gestalt approach is concerned with integration rather than analysis of dreams. Such integration is achieved by consciously reliving a dream, taking responsibility for being the objects and people in the dream, and becoming aware of the messages the dream holds. According to Perls, all parts of the dream are fragments of the dreamer's personality that must be pieced together to form a whole. These projected fragments must be reowned; thus, hidden potential that appears in the dream will also be reowned. As clients play the parts of all the objects and persons in the dream, they may become more aware of the message the dream holds. They may act out the dream until two conflicting roles emerge—for instance, the topdog and the underdog. This want and should conflict is essentially the conflict from which the dreamer suffers.

Gestaltists believe there are hidden existential messages in dreams that, once discovered, can fill the voids in people's personalities. In the Gestalt framework, dreamwork holds many possibilities for solving the problems of life or for developing a better self-awareness.

Variations of the dreamwork method can be used with children. A volunteer can describe a dream, and other students can role-play the objects and people in the dream by expressing their thoughts and feelings. The volunteer can direct the dream enactment. The therapist's task in the integration of dreams is to concentrate on what clients are avoiding in their present existence and to help them act out painful situations and reintegrate the alienated parts of their personality into their lives.

Gestalt Activities Adapted for Children

Polster and Polster (1973) discuss contact functions that highlight everyday communication. *Contact* usually implies touching in the physical sense. However, the seven processes of contact functioning—looking, listening, touching, talking, moving, smelling, and tasting—are not all directly physical; contact can also be made through space. For example, seeing is being touched by light waves; hearing is being touched along the basilar membrane by sound waves; and so on. Although physical contact is one of the most obvious ways of reaching people, the opportunities for reaching people through space are certainly more available and can be very effective. Application of the contact function can be useful in the elementary school classroom. Children can become more aware of their present actions and feelings by participating in activities that will bring about contact functioning. Listening activities are particularly appropriate for creating a classroom atmosphere conducive to learning.

Music.   Teachers or counselors can play a melody on the piano or phono-graph. They ask the children to listen carefully to it and then to write down how the music makes them feel, what they think of when they hear it, and whether they like it or not. When the children have finished writing their ideas, the counselor can ask different children to read their papers and discuss their reactions. This exercise should allow the children to get in touch with their present feelings and evaluate what they hear and think as well.

Musical instruments.   These can be very helpful in allowing emotions to come forth that might otherwise be repressed. The counselor may choose a shy child to sit in the center of a circle of the other children. The child can select one of several noisy instruments, such as cymbals or drums, for leading the group in lively, strong-sounding music. The other children may either also play instruments or clap hands and stamp their feet in time to the music. It is then hoped that the shy child will lose himself or herself in the activity and, by banging away, express some emotions he or she usually hides. Leading the group may also enhance the child's self-confidence. This activity can also be used to elicit the opposite effect on a hyperactive or overaggressive child. The child could lead the group with a quiet instrument (perhaps the triangle) and play it during a soft song or lullaby. The counselor can encourage the rest of the group to close their eyes, think of peaceful things, and sway slowly to the music. This would give the child the experience of feeling peaceful and soothed.

Tone of voice, body movement.   This activity involves the contact functions of listening and looking. The counselor asks the children to select partners for role-playing certain emotions or feelings. The activity can be initiated as a result of some altercation between two youngsters. The group can discuss what emotions the two children were feeling or even role-play the actual situation that took place. The counselor asks the children to notice not only the words spoken but also the tones of voice and the body movements that express the emotion. After working out the bad feelings between the two children involved, the counselor can ask the children to think of other emotions and practice role-playing with their partners. When they have had a few minutes to practice a short scene that will display an emotion, the counselor can select different partners to demonstrate for the class, each time making the class aware of the fact that emotion is expressed in many ways and that we need to learn to recognize how people show their feelings.

Awareness-enhancing activities.

1. *"Feelings Awareness."* Give children the following directions: "For five minutes or so, focus your attention on the way things feel on your

skin . . . the way you feel as your weight presses on the chair . . . the feel of
your feet in your shoes and against the floor . . . the places where clothing
is tight. . . . Can you feel any draft? Are some places warmer or colder than
others? Now reach out and touch different things." Have a variety of
objects and textured surfaces available for touching. The children can be
asked to verbalize descriptions ("I don't like this, it feels squishy," "This
feels rough," and so on).

2. *"Taste Time."* Have several bite-sized bits of different foods available — carrots, apples, turnips, meat, and so on, and give children the
following directions: "For five minutes or so, focus your attention on the
way several mouthfuls of food feel, change, and taste. Try not to talk to
yourself as you do this. Feel the texture of the food with your tongue, lips,
teeth, and mouth. Try the difference between bland, soft foods and crisp,
strong-tasting foods. Toward the end of the exercise, take one bite of food
and chew it, focusing your awareness on it all the time until it is liquefied.
Don't swallow it until it is absolutely liquefied."

3. *"Mirror, Mirror."* Bring a good-sized mirror to the group and have
the children look into it one at a time. Have each child look without any
comment at all for 30 seconds or so, then ask the child to tell you what he
or she sees. Ask for more and more description. Be gentle, but persistent.
When it becomes difficult for the child to come up with any more comments, shift to another child. Polaroid snapshots, videotaping, and even
movies can be used in the same way to build self-awareness.

4. *"Now."* Give children the following directions: "As you sit quietly,
make statements to yourself about exactly what you are aware of at this
very moment. Make every statement begin with 'Now I . . . .' Be aware of as
many things as you can. Try writing things down. Then just talk to yourself. Finally, try to be aware without talking to yourself."

Art activities. For disturbed children who cannot verbalize emotions,
many art media can be used. The child can smear fingerpaint with hands or
feet, create and destroy images with clay, and draw or paint pictures to
express confusing feelings. When appropriate, the child can be encouraged
to verbalize after the artwork is completed. ("Tell me about your picture.")
Chapter 8 further elaborates on using the expressive arts in counseling.

Self-confidence–building activities.

1. *Touching Games.* Children need to be touched, to touch others play-
fully and affectionately, and to realize the difference between "good"
touch and "bad" touch. Hugs, pats on the back, and handshakes of various types should be a part of the counselor's reinforcement and encouragement repertoire. In addition, several touch games can be used with
children's groups. "Group Sitdown" requires that children form a circle
and sit on the lap of the person on their left. No chairs are used, and

if done correctly, the circle maintains itself without anyone falling on the floor. In another touching game, the group forms two parallel lines with children sitting on the floor back to back. With arms interlocked with their back-to-back partner's, each person attempts to stand up. Good teamwork brings about good results in both activities. Shoulder massages are also popular and can be done in a group setting with children standing in a circle massaging the shoulders of the person in front of them. The "Trust Fall" is often done to introduce the topic of trusting others not to let you down. Partners take turns catching each other as they fall with their backs toward their partners. The various touch games promote teamwork, trust, and experience with the good touch of nonsexual caring for one another.

"Applause! Applause!" The group gathers and sits in a circle with space cleared in the center of the floor. One at a time, children go to the cleared space and say their names aloud. At this, the rest of the group loudly cheers, claps, shouts "bravo!" and so forth. Children acknowledge the applause in whatever way they choose.

"Confidence Courses." This gentle form of obstacle course, designed to build confidence, uses combinations of pit jumps, incline balances, boxes, barrels, ladder climbs, rope slides, and the like. (Children can also be involved in constructing such a course.) As children attain better motor coordination and balance, they form better self-images, a feeling of mastery, and an "I can do it" attitude about themselves. They begin to feel they can solve problems and can deal with their world competently.

CASE STUDIES

Many short-term counseling sessions can be conducted with children using the empty chair technique. For example, consider the following method for working with anger.

Child: I hate my dad. He's mean. I hate his guts.

Counselor: Let's pretend your dad is sitting in that empty chair. What do you want to say to him? You can walk over there and say whatever you want.

Child: Get off my back! Leave me alone! I cleaned my room just as good as I could.

Counselor: Now sit in the other chair. Pretend to be your dad.

Child: I've told you and told you that this room looks like a pigpen.

Counselor: Now be yourself again.

Child: I cleaned my room good, Dad! Then you came in and said it still isn't good enough. Nothing was left out in the room but my toys!

Counselor: Now be your dad.

Child: This is the last time I'm telling you, Son. The room better be finished when I get back. That means toys, too.

Counselor: Now be you.

Child: You don't care about me! You don't care about how I feel. You just worry about the house being messed up. You get mad when I get out my toys. Kids are supposed to have toys! It's MY ROOM! Quit buggin' me! (accompanied by much nonverbal expression of anger as well as the overt angry verbal content)

The child has expressed his strong thoughts that his room should be his "territory," that it should be OK to have his toys out. A global "hatred" for the father has been reduced to anger about a specific recurring problem (the differing standards for the room held by the parent and the child). After release of the built-up anger, some problem solving could be undertaken to perhaps achieve a compromise about the room situation.

Another sample counseling session involves the topdog/underdog debate, using an empty chair for each "dog." This technique is useful when the child has a decision-making problem. Most decision-making problems involve a debate between the inner voice of "I should do . . ." (topdog) versus "Yes, but I want to do . . ." (underdog). An empty chair is assigned to each point of view.

Identification of the Problem

Susan is experiencing a conflict over whether to live with her mother or father when their divorce is final.

Individual and Background Information

Susan Adams is a 10-year-old in the fourth grade. Her mother and father are getting a divorce, and she has to decide whether to live with her mother or her father. Susan is the second of three children. This is the second marriage for Susan's mother and the first marriage for Susan's father. Her elder brother is not her father's son. Both parents work in factory jobs, but their income seems to be limited by the fact that Susan's father drinks up most of his paycheck. Susan is an average student in school, quiet, and has never been a behavior problem. She gets along well with her peers at school. Susan's physical health is good, but she has a vision problem that requires a new pair of glasses. Susan's parents say they do not have the money to buy the new glasses.

Transcript

Counselor: Susan, we have the next 30 minutes for our talk. Where would you like to start?

Susan: Well, you know my problem about having to decide whether to live with Mom or Daddy after their divorce is final. I just don't know what I'm going to do.

Counselor: I know that when we talked about this the other day, you were feeling really upset about this situation of having to choose between your mom and dad. I can tell you still feel this way.

Susan: Yes, I do. I did all the things we talked about—like talking to both of them. That made it even harder to decide because they both want me. I still don't know what to do. I wish they would stop the divorce.

Counselor: Well, it's a good feeling to know that they both want you, but a bad feeling to know you have to choose. You would really like to have them stay together.

Susan: Yes, I really would, but that's impossible! I've tried every way I can to keep them together.

Counselor: Susan, would you try an exercise with me that might help clarify your thinking about this decision?

Susan: I'll try anything to help.

Counselor: (explains and demonstrates the topdog/underdog technique) So, when you are in the topdog chair, you say "I should . . ." and when you are in the underdog chair, you say "I want. . . ." OK?

Susan: OK (goes to the topdog chair first).

   Topdog: I should go with Daddy because he'll be all alone.

   Underdog: Yes, but I want to stay with Mom because I hate to give up my room, and I want to stay with my sister.

   Topdog: What is Daddy going to do without anyone to cook for him and clean house?

   Underdog: Why can't he hire a maid, and I can visit him a lot, too?

   Topdog: If I don't live with Daddy, he won't have anybody, because he doesn't want Jake, and Sally is too young to move away from Mom.

   Underdog: Well, Daddy goes out and drinks a lot with his friends, and sometimes he gets sick and is not nice to be around when he gets drunk.

   Topdog: I think I should take care of him when he gets sick.

   Underdog: I think it is better not to be near him when he drinks. I would like to visit him when he is not drinking.

   Topdog: How can I live with Mom and help Daddy, too?

   Underdog: I just know things will be better if I live with Mom in my room and see Daddy as often as I can.

Counselor: Do you think you've finished with this argument, Susan?

Susan: Yes, I've said all I can think of.

Counselor: I'm wondering what you learned from doing this exercise.

Susan: Well, I think things will be better if I stay where I am with
Mom. But I'll need to see a lot of Daddy—as much as I can.
I love them both so much (starts to cry).
Counselor: I know this has to be a sad and rough time for you.
It really hurts, doesn't it?
Susan: It sure does. I need to be brave about this and not let it
make me so sad.
Counselor: It's OK to feel sad about this. You can always come in
here to talk to me when you want to.
(Counselor terminates the interview and schedules another session
for the next day.)

RESEARCH AND REACTIONS

Fritz Perls took pride in the fact that Gestalt therapists were doers, not
researchers and writers. One of his pet four-letter descriptive terms was
reserved for the material turned out by researchers and writers on the topic
of psychotherapy. In spite of Perls, the literature on Gestalt therapy continues to grow; however, very little of the literature contains research.

Skolnick (1990), noting the lack of research on Gestalt therapy, warns
against enshrinement of current philosophy and theory. Instead, he believes Gestalt therapy and theory need to be revitalized through good
research. Miller (1989), on the other hand, is concerned that Gestalt therapy
may lose its identity because it is being absorbed into other systems as
others rediscover the obvious, just as Perls did. Others are concerned about
the misuse of popular Gestalt techniques with fragile clients who cannot
handle the emotional intensity these methods generate.

Fagan and Shepard (1970) offered words of caution concerning the
Gestalt approach to severely disturbed or psychotic clients. They recommended caution, sensitivity, and patience. They believed it preferable in
the initial stages of therapy to limit therapeutic activity to procedures that
strengthen clients' contact with reality, their confidence in their own being,
and their faith in the counselor's goodwill and competence, rather than
involving them in role-playing or reenactment of past experiences of pain
or conflict. This seems to be sensible advice. Fagan and Shepard endorsed
activities that increase sensory, perceptual, and motor capacities toward
self-support. Such activities could be useful adjuncts to many other therapies with children and could be employed in a wide variety of settings.

Greenberg (1989) echoes similar concerns about using traditional Gestalt
therapy with people having borderline personality disorder. He recommends interactive group therapy over talking to a dead parent in an empty
chair and "hot-seat" confrontations. Therefore, the question of who should
receive Gestalt therapy is as important as the skill, training, experience, and
judgment of the therapist. A counselor who uses this approach must be

neither afraid nor inept in allowing the client to follow through and finish the experience of grief, rage, fear, or joy. Without such skill, the counselor may leave the client aborted, unfinished, opened, and vulnerable (Fagan & Shepard, 1970).

Aylward (1988), in an attempt to give readers a better understanding of Gestalt therapy, presented an actual transcript of a session complete with commentary on breakthroughs made toward helping the client overcome a decision-making block. This article is especially helpful in understanding the counseling process from a Gestalt viewpoint.

Another issue hinges on the questions of when, with whom, and in what situations Gestalt therapy should be used. In general, Gestalt therapy is most effective with overly socialized, restrained, constricted individuals. With less organized, more severely disturbed clients, long-term counseling is required. Limiting activities at first to those that strengthen a client's contact with reality is preferable to role-playing situations further removed from the here and now. Individuals whose problems lie in lack of impulse control, acting out, delinquency, and the like require a different approach. For these people, Gestalt therapy can reinforce the activities that are causing the problems.

Gestalt Methods with Children

Greater optimism for using Gestalt methods, particularly with children, is found in the writings of Oaklander (1978) and Owmby (1983).

Oaklander (1978) describes several Gestalt techniques she has adapted for children. She recommends projection through art and storytelling as a way of increasing the child's self-awareness. Fantasy and imagery, such as the wise-person fantasy, are described as good ways to tap intuitive thought in children and adults. Oaklander also uses the empty chair method frequently, as a helpful way to handle unfinished business, frustration, and anger.

Owmby (1983), in another article on Gestalt therapy with children, describes adaptations of the topdog/underdog technique, as well as projection and retroflection. The topdog/underdog method is suggested for angry children who can talk to their angry self in another chair and find out why they are so upset. Projection is suggested for the child who is afraid of an ugly monster. The child can become the monster and allow that creature to explain its motives for scaring children. Retroflection is giving voice to that part of the body that is exhibiting muscular tension. The counselor may ask a child who tightens up his or her mouth to say what the mouth would like to say.

Allan and Crandall (1986) found that the use of relaxation and visual imagery, drawing, and postdrawing inquiry to identify coping and noncoping students was accurate about 80 percent of the time for counselors trained in projective techniques. The study was conducted with fourth-

and fifth-grade students. In fact, it was suggested that the strategy (the rosebush visualization) could be effective in identifying sexually abused children.

Alexander and Harman (1988) report a successful application of a Gestalt approach to group counseling with middle school classmates of a student who committed suicide. Using the empty chair, writing, and artwork, children were able to say "goodbye" and to discuss their own fears and anxieties about suicide.

Outcome Research

Outcome research in Gestalt therapy tends to fall into the categories of training and treatment. Beginning with training, Simkin (1976), working with experienced therapists, found that training in Gestalt therapy could be successfully condensed into a three-month period. Greenberg and Sarkissian (1984) had similar success in teaching Gestalt counseling methods such as the two-chair dialogue to counselors in training. Simkin (1979) found that residential patients rated Gestalt therapy workshops more helpful than individual and group therapy. The nine-to-one preference for the workshops is a favorable point for conducting counseling as an educational enterprise.

Frew (1988) surveyed Gestalt therapists to ascertain the nature, frequency, and usefulness of group work in Gestalt therapy. Group skills were ranked second in importance to individual therapy skills by nine percentage points. Many therapists reported using individual methods within the group setting.

Holiman and Engle (1989) conducted some observational studies on Gestalt training through group supervision, with trainees role-playing the roles of therapists, client, and observer. The trainees were taught to attend first to the content of the client's story, second to the process, and third to the integration of content and process. Holiman and Engle concluded that Gestalt training should occur in groups in which trainees play all three roles and receive feedback from the group.

Several outcome studies on treatment with Gestalt methods have also been conducted and documented.

Conoley, McConnell, Conoley, and Kimzey (1983), working with college students, found both the empty chair technique of Gestalt therapy and the ABC technique of rational-emotive therapy (see Chapter 6) to be effective in anger reduction. Reflective listening did not prove to be as effective as the other two interventions.

Clarke and Greenberg (1986), working with adult clients, compared the Gestalt two-chair intervention with a cognitive-behavioral intervention on effectiveness in treating decision-making conflicts. The results of the study provide support for the two-chair intervention, which proved superior to the cognitive-behavioral intervention as well as to the no-treatment control group. The cognitive-behavioral group outperformed the control group in resolving indecision.

Greenberg and Webster (1982) used the Gestalt two-chair dialogue in a study with adolescents and adults on the process and outcome of resolving decision-making conflicts. Such conflicts, arising from underlying splits between the client's standards and values and personal wants and needs, were resolved through the two-chair method. The study also revealed two basic groups of clients—resolvers and nonresolvers—based on a pattern of in-session progress indicators. Resolvers reported greater resolution, less discomfort, greater mood change, and greater goal attainment than nonresolvers.

Serok and Zemet (1983) succeeded in increasing the reality perception of adult schizophrenic patients using Gestalt therapy methods. In one exercise, patients were asked to recall (with eyes closed) who sat next to whom and what each person wore. It was hoped that, through the group exercise, participants would be better able to perceive concrete elements in their environment. Miming was also used to help the participants perceive events occurring in a series.

Serok and Bar (1984), working with graduate students, compared a Gestalt group with a T-group and a lecture group on post-treatment gains in self-concept. The Gestalt group outgained the other groups in decisiveness, general adaptation, and self-criticism and self-concept. No group differences were found for self-identification or self-acceptance.

Wathney (1982), in a discussion on using paradoxical counseling strategies in transactional analysis and Gestalt therapy, proposed that paradoxical strategies give clients control over their problem behavior. The theory that forced change can actually inhibit change is basic to most counseling theories. Proponents of Gestalt theory contend that clients must be allowed to change spontaneously. Paradoxical counseling strategies allow spontaneous change. For example, a client comes to counseling wishing to be rid of grief over the loss of a loved one. Instead of providing relief, the counselor encourages the person to experience the grief more fully. The human tendency to rebel may, in fact, provide the relief. Wathney presents another application example in the case of an adolescent male suffering from insomnia. He was told to stay up past his usual bedtime so he could work on an unpleasant task (math homework). He was to follow the unpleasant task with a relaxation exercise. Success in sleeping was immediate; no report was given of his math grade.

Halfond (1989) employed Gestalt counseling with adolescent and adult male stutterers. Participants experienced an increase in social interaction and expression of affect. While the decrease in stuttering was minimal, the participants expressed increased interest in working with a speech therapist.

Hill, Beutler, and Daldrup (1989) attempted to study the relationship of process to outcome in Gestalt therapy. Two therapists conducted 18 sessions with 6 white, adult females who suffered from rheumatoid arthritis. The authors found that all patients improved in positive feelings. However, the therapist rated higher by patients for session smoothness (process) had patients who experienced lower levels of dependency and global severity (outcome).

SUMMARY

Saner (1989) voiced concerns about possible cultural bias existing in U.S. Gestalt therapy. He suggested several ways to make Gestalt therapy valid across cultures. First, he would drop the ethnocentric emphasis on the individual in favor of stressing reciprocal interaction by all participants in a social setting. Second, he would prefer psychodrama in group therapy to the hot-seat method of individual therapy within the group setting. Third, Saner would like to see practitioners of Gestalt therapy incorporate contributions from other disciplines in their theory and practice.

Enns (1987) made a similar argument for integrating the self-responsibility and individualism of Gestalt therapy with the feminist values of interrelatedness and interdependence. She considered Gestalt therapy helpful in meeting three important goals of feminist therapy: (1) definition of the self and empowerment, (2) awareness and constructive use of anger, and (3) discovery of alternatives. Enns concluded that all three of these would benefit everyone.

Because Gestalt techniques facilitate discovery, facing, and the resolution of the client's major conflict, often in a dramatically short time, the inexperienced therapist/observer or client might assume that Gestalt therapy offers an "instant cure." Even for experienced counselors, the temptation is to push the client to a stance of self-support too fast, too soon. The use of Gestalt therapy with groups is common, but frequently it amounts to individual counseling in a group setting. Another hazard is the counselor's assuming excessive responsibility for the direction of the group by too much activity, thus fostering client passivity and defeating the goal of client self-support. Extensive experience with Gestalt therapy may actually make clients less fit for or less adjusted to contemporary society. At the same time, however, they may be motivated to work toward changing the world into a more compassionate and productive milieu in which human beings can develop, work, and enjoy their full humanness.

Perls seems to have done well in his attempt to establish the philosophy and practice of Gestalt therapy. The approach is well grounded in and consistent with the principles of human behavior. Perls, by removing the mystique created by professional jargon, made Gestalt therapy comprehensible to the general public. Many counselors, while choosing not to become true believers or disciples of Gestalt therapy, use many of the procedures reported in the Gestalt literature. Most notable among these techniques are the two-chair dialogue, visualization, fantasy, and projection.

REFERENCES

Alexander, J., & Harman, L. (1988). One counselor's intervention in the aftermath of middle school student's suicide: A case study. *Journal of Counseling and Development, 66,* 283–285.

Allan, J., & Crandall, J. (1986). The rosebush: A visualization strategy. *Elementary School Guidance and Counseling, 21,* 44–51.

Assagioli, R. (1965). *Psychosynthesis.* New York: Viking Press.

Aylward, J. (1988). A session with Cindy. *Gestalt Journal, 11*(1), 51–61.

Clarke, K., & Greenberg, L. (1986). Differential effects of the Gestalt two-chair intervention and problem solving in resolving decisional conflict. *Journal of Counseling Psychology, 33,* 11–14.

Conoley, C., McConnell, J., Conoley, J., & Kimzey, C. (1983). The effect of the ABCs of rational emotive therapy and the empty chair technique of Gestalt therapy on anger reduction. *Psychotherapy: Theory, Research and Practice, 20,* 112–116.

Dolliver, R. (1991). Perls with Gloria re-reviewed: Gestalt techniques and Perls's practices. *Journal of Counseling and Development, 69,* 299–304.

English, H., & English, A. (1958). *A comprehensive dictionary of psychological terms.* New York: Longmans, Green.

Enns, C. Z. (1987). Gestalt therapy and feminist therapy: A proposed integration. *Journal of Counseling and Development, 66,* 93–95.

Fagan, J., & Shepard, I. (1970). *Gestalt therapy now.* Palo Alto, CA: Science and Behavior Books.

Frew, J. (1988). The practice of Gestalt therapy in groups. *Gestalt Journal, 11*(1), 77–94.

Greenberg, E. (1989). Healing the borderline. *Gestalt Journal, 12,* 11–55.

Greenberg, L., & Sarkissian, M. (1984). Evaluation of counselor training in Gestalt methods. *Counselor Education and Supervision, 23,* 328–339.

Greenberg, L., & Webster, M. (1982). Resolving decisional conflict through Gestalt two chair dialogue: Relating process to outcome. *Journal of Counseling Psychology, 29,* 468–477.

Halfond, M. (1989). Gestalt therapy with stutterers. *Folia Phoniatrica, 41,* 173.

Heikkinen, C. (1989). Reorientation from altered states: Please, more carefully. *Journal of Counseling and Development, 67,* 520–521.

Hill, D., Beutler, L., & Daldrup, R. (1989). The relationship of process to outcome in brief experiential psychotherapy for chronic pain. *Journal of Clinical Psychology, 45,* 951–956.

Holiman, M., & Engle, D. (1989). Guidelines for training in advanced Gestalt therapy skills. *The Journal for Specialists in Group Work, 14,* 75–83.

Lederman, J. (1969). *Anger and the rocking chair: Gestalt awareness with children.* New York: McGraw-Hill.

Miller, M. (1989). Introduction to Gestalt therapy verbatim. *Gestalt Journal, 7*(1), 5–24.

Oaklander, V. (1978). *Windows to our children.* Moab, UT: Real People Press.

Owmby, R. L. (1983). Gestalt therapy with children. *Journal of Gestalt Therapy, 6,* 51–58.

Passons, W. (1975). *Gestalt approaches in counseling.* New York: Holt, Rinehart & Winston.

Perls, F. (1969). *Gestalt therapy verbatim.* Moab, UT: Real People Press.

Perls, F. (1971). *In and out the garbage pail.* New York: Bantam Books.

Perls, F. (1976). *The Gestalt approaches and eye witnesses to therapy.* New York: Bantam Books.

Perls, F., Hefferline, R., & Goodman, P. (1951). *Gestalt therapy.* New York: Julian Press.

Polster, E., & Polster, M. (1973). *Gestalt therapy integrated: Contours of theory and practice.* New York: Brunner/Mazel.

Sahakian, W. (Ed.). (1969). *Psychotherapy and counseling: Studies in technique.* Chicago: Rand McNally.

Saner, R. (1989). Culture bias of gestalt therapy: Made-in-U.S.A. *Gestalt Journal, 12,* 57–71.

Serok, S., & Bar, R. (1984). Looking at Gestalt group impact on environment. *Small Group Behavior, 15,* 270–277.

Serok, S., & Zemet, R. M. (1983). An experiment of Gestalt group therapy with hospitalized schizophrenics. *Psychotherapy: Theory, Research and Practice, 20,* 417–424.

Shepard, M. (1975). *Fritz.* New York: Saturday Review Press.

Shostrom, E. (Producer). (1965). *Three approaches to psychotherapy: Part 2. Fredrick Perls* [Film]. Orange, CA: Psychological Films.

Simkin, J. (1976). *Gestalt therapy mini-lectures.* Millbrae, CA: Celestial Arts.

Simkin, J. (1979). Gestalt therapy. In R. Corsini (Ed.), *Current psychotherapies.* Itasca, Ill.: F. E. Peacock.

Skolnick, T. (1990). Boundaries, boundaries, boundaries. *Gestalt Journal, 13,* 55–68.

Thompson, C., & Poppen, W. (1992). *Guidance activities for counselors and teachers.* Knoxville, TN: Kinko's Copies.

Wathney, S. (1982). Paradoxical interventions in transactional analysis and Gestalt therapy. *Transactional Analysis Journal, 12,* 185–189.

CHAPTER 6

Rational-Emotive Therapy and Cognitive-Behavior Therapy

ALBERT ELLIS

Albert Ellis is currently executive director of the Institute for Advanced Study in Rational Psychotherapy in New York, a community agency chartered by the regents of The State University of New York. He is widely known as the founder or developer of rational-emotive therapy.

For the past several years, Ellis has given individualized remedial instruction—or what he calls emotional education—to several thousand adults, adolescents, and children. In addition, he has conducted group therapy with more than 2500 adults and adolescents.

Ellis was born in Pittsburgh, Pennsylvania, in 1913 and grew up in New York City. In spite of a difficult childhood, he managed to earn a degree in business administration from the City University of New York in 1934. He earned his living during the Depression first by working with his brother in a business that located matching pants for still-usable suit coats. Later he worked as the personnel manager in a gift and novelty firm.

Ellis's ambition was to write, which he did in his spare time. He collected material for two books on sexual adjustment, which were eventually published: *The American Sexual Tragedy* (1954) and *The Case for Sexual Liberty* (1965). His friends began to regard him as an expert on the subject and often asked his advice. He discovered he enjoyed counseling people as much as writing and decided to return to school. In 1942, Ellis entered the clinical psychology program at Columbia University and in 1947 was awarded his doctorate.

Ellis's early professional work as a therapist in state institutions in New Jersey employed classical psychoanalytic methods, but within ten years Ellis had set psychoanalysis aside almost completely. His change in philosophy came about when he discovered that clients treated once a week or even every other week progressed as well as those he saw daily. Ellis found that a more active role, interjecting advice and direct interpretation, yielded faster results than did passive psychoanalytic procedures. His own theory of counseling, however, did not emerge until after he had received his doctorate from Columbia and later received training as a traditional psychoanalytic therapist. Consequently, some of the origins of rational-emotive therapy (RET) can be traced to Freud and some to disillusionment with Freudian psychoanalysis.

After discovering that rationalist philosophy fit his temperament and taste, Ellis began concentrating on changing people's behavior by confronting them with their irrational beliefs and persuading them to adopt more rational ones. He now considers himself a philosophical or educational therapist and sees RET as a system that is uniquely didactic, cognition-oriented, and explicative. He believes that RET places people at the center of the universe and gives them almost full responsibility for their fate.

More than 400 books and articles, in addition to his Institute for Rational Living, have proceeded from Ellis's conceptualization of rational-emotive therapy. From its early days to the present, RET has continued to undergo modifications. Writing in 1977, Ellis noted that RET, once a limited rational-persuasive therapy, had grown into a cognitive-behavior therapy that consciously used cognitive, emotive, and behavioral techniques to help clients (Ellis, 1977). It can be said that Ellis was good at turning his failures into successes. Though not successful as a clothing salesman or a novelist, Ellis did develop an effective approach to counseling and proceeded to write volumes about the technique, with a great deal of success. In 1957, he published his first book on RET, *How to Live with a "Neurotic"* (1957/1975), and in 1960, his first really successful book, *The Art and Science of Love* (1960/1969a).

Dryden (1989a), in an interview with Albert Ellis, explored four topic areas that provide insights into Ellis's personal and professional life. The interview covered Ellis's early years, women and marriage, his personal characteristics, and reflections on his professional career.

THE NATURE OF PEOPLE

Rational-emotive therapy is based on the philosophy of Epictetus (ca. A.D. 55–ca. 135): "What disturbs men's minds is not events, but their judgment of events." Generally speaking, very young children and animals have limited emotional repertoires and tend to express emotions in a quick, unsustained manner. When children grow old enough to use language effectively, they acquire the ability to sustain their emotions and possibly keep themselves emotionally upset. RET does not concentrate upon the past events in one's life, but rather on present events and how one reacts to them. RET theory stresses that, as human beings, we have choices. We control our ideas, attitudes, feelings, and actions, and we arrange our lives according to our own dictates. We have little control over what happens or what actually exists, but we do have both choices and control over how we

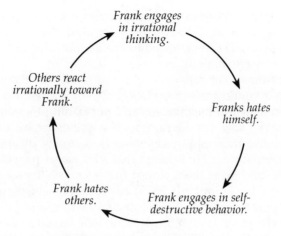

FIGURE 6-1   The circle of irrational thinking

view the world and how we react to difficulties, regardless of how we have
been taught to respond.

RET theory holds that people are neither good nor bad if they respond
to others with a rational belief system. If individuals react with irrational
beliefs, however, they will view themselves and others as evil, awful, and
horrible whenever they or others fall short of their expectations. Ellis (1987)
views humans as naturally irrational, self-defeating individuals who need
to be taught otherwise. They think crookedly about their desires and
preferences and escalate them self-defeatingly into musts, shoulds, oughts,
and demands. In assimilating these irrational beliefs, people become emotionally disturbed and feel anger, anxiety, depression, worthlessness, self-
pity, or other negative feelings that lead to destructive behavior. However,
Ellis has also stated that people can be "naturally" helpful and loving *as
long as they do not think irrationally.* In other words, Ellis has described a
circular process, as depicted in Figure 6-1. Irrational thinking leads to
self-hate, which leads to self-destructive behavior and eventually to hatred
of others, which in turn causes others to act irrationally toward the individual and thus to begin the cycle again.

Ellis believes that some of our irrational thoughts are biological in origin,
but the majority stem from our upbringing (parents, teachers, and clergy).
Ellis has described three areas in which people hold irrational beliefs: they
must be perfect, others must be perfect, or the world must be a perfect
place to live. The following examples describe in a nutshell what people
tell themselves when they interpret events with an irrational belief system.
A more rational replacement thought follows each irrational self-message.

1. Because it would be highly preferable if I were outstandingly competent, I absolutely should and must be; it is awful when I am not, and I
am therefore a worthless individual.

Alternative: It would be nice if I were outstanding in whatever I do, but if I am not, it is OK, and I will try my best anyway.

2. Because it is highly desirable that others treat me considerately and fairly, they absolutely should and must, and they are rotten people who deserve to be utterly damned when they do not.

Alternative: I would prefer people to treat me considerately. However, I realize this is not always the case, so I will not take it personally when they do not, *and* I will make it my business to be considerate.

3. Because it is preferable that I experience pleasure rather than pain, the world should absolutely arrange this, and life is horrible and I can't bear it when the world doesn't.

Alternative: I realize that in life there are both pleasurable moments and painful moments. Therefore, I will try to make the painful moments positive learning experiences so I can endure trials and even benefit from them.

THEORY OF COUNSELING

When interpreting daily events with one or more irrational philosophies, the individual is likely to feel angry or hostile toward others or to internalize these feelings with resulting anxiety, guilt, and/or depression. In essence, RET theory holds that people are primarily responsible for their feelings about themselves, others, the environment, and whether or not they want to be perpetually disturbed by them.

In their book *A New Guide to Rational Living,* Ellis and Harper (1975) write that, because humans naturally and easily think crookedly, express emotions inappropriately, and behave self-defeatingly, it seems best to use all possible educational modes dramatically, strongly, and persistently to teach them how to do otherwise. Ellis and Harper have compiled a list of irrational beliefs that cause people trouble:

1. It is a dire necessity for people to be loved or approved by almost everyone for virtually everything they do.
2. One should be thoroughly competent, adequate, and achieving in all possible respects.
3. Certain people are bad, wicked, or villainous, and they should be severely blamed and punished for their sins.
4. It is terrible, horrible, and catastrophic when things are not going the way one would like them to go.
5. Human unhappiness is externally caused, and people have little or no ability to control their sorrows or rid themselves of their negative feelings.
6. If something is or may be dangerous or fearsome, one should be terribly occupied with and upset about it.

7. It is easier to avoid facing many life difficulties and self-responsibilities than to undertake more rewarding forms of self-discipline.
8. The past is all-important, and because something once strongly affected one's life, it should do so indefinitely.
9. People and things should be different from the way they are, and it is catastrophic if perfect solutions to the grim realities of life are not immediately found.
10. Maximum human happiness can be achieved by inertia and inaction, or by passively and uncommittedly enjoying oneself.
11. My child is delinquent/emotionally disturbed/mentally retarded; therefore, I'm a failure as a parent.
12. My child is emotionally disturbed/mentally retarded; therefore, he or she is severely handicapped and will never amount to anything.
13. I cannot give my children everything they want; therefore, I am inadequate.

Goodman and Maultsby (1974, pp. 40–41) have drawn up a list of 26 consequences that may result from irrational thinking. We have cited 16 of them:

1. High degree of interpersonal difficulties
2. Persistence of emotionalism in reacting to daily problems
3. Desiring what one cannot have or is unlikely to get
4. Not wanting or appreciating what one has or could get
5. Tending to attribute all one's difficulties to others
6. Tending to see oneself as worthless
7. Pursuit of contradictory goals or behavior inconsistent with professed goals
8. Tolerating bad situations rather than taking steps to rectify or improve them
9. Remaining dependent on others past the point when it is necessary
10. Remaining angry or hurt past a reasonable period of time
11. Demanding perfection in one's own behavior or in that of others
12. Indulging in behavior that injures one's body or mind or impedes their functioning
13. Needless self-torment over past events or presumed failures
14. Chronic or intermittent states of depression or anxiety
15. Unreasonable fears
16. Excessive anger

Crawford and Ellis (1989) have provided further information on irrational beliefs and their consequences. They have compiled a dictionary of 36 self-defeating feelings accompanied by their corresponding rational and irrational beliefs. The rational beliefs appear first and are often followed by sequential irrational beliefs to form a chain of irrational beliefs. Crawford and Ellis have classified each irrational belief into one of five categories:

(1) *self-defeating* beliefs that interfere with basic goals and drives, (2) highly rigid and *dogmatic* beliefs that lead to unrealistic preferences and wishes, (3) *antisocial* beliefs that cause people to destroy their social groups, (4) *unrealistic* beliefs that falsely describe reality, and (5) *contradictory* beliefs that originate from false premises.

In an article entitled "What Rational-Emotive Therapy Is and Is Not," Ellis (1974) makes the following points about RET:

1. Anxiety is viewed not as "irrational" but as an inappropriate feeling that stems largely from irrational ideas. Feelings are not to be confused with ideas.
2. Clients have almost full or complete responsibility for their ideas and consequently for their feelings.
3. Clients, not early environment or conditioning or contemporary conditions, mainly choose to create their irrational ideas and consequent feelings. They can choose to change their ideas.
4. People are not to be blamed, damned, denigrated, or condemned for choosing irrational ideas, inappropriate feelings, or defeating behaviors.
5. The use of absolutes, such as *must, should,* and *ought,* is discouraged in clients' thinking. There are no absolutes (pun intended).
6. Therapists definitely do not determine whether clients' ideas or behaviors are rational or irrational.

The goal of rational-emotive therapy is to teach people to think and behave in a more personally satisfying way by making them realize they have a choice between self-defeating, negative behavior and efficient, enhancing, positive behavior. RET teaches people to take responsibility for their own logical thinking and the consequence or behavior that follows it.

COUNSELING METHOD

In the past, counselors have concentrated upon either the developmental events in one's life or the feelings one had about these events. Ellis did not believe these two main methods were totally erroneous, but he did not find either approach very effective. Neither approach explained why some people are rather well adjusted (that is, not too unhappy too much of the time regardless of the passage of events) and others are emotionally dysfunctional much of the time with the same passage of events.

Ellis theorized that individuals' responses or feelings toward the same events are predicated upon their belief systems. These individual belief systems are what people tell themselves about an event—in particular, an unfortunate incident. For example, 100 people may be rejected by their true loves. One of these people may respond: "I can't go on; I've lost my purpose in life. Because I've been rejected by such a wonderful person, I must really be a worthless slob. My only solution for getting rid of the unbearable pain I feel is to kill myself." Another may respond: "What a pain in the neck! I had dinner reservations and tickets for the show. Now I have to get another date for Saturday night. This surely sets me back. What an inconvenience!" Between these two extreme reactions are several other degrees of bad feelings growing from the various self-messages of the rejected 100. Such a wide variety of reactions to the same basic event suggests that one's view of the event and consequent self-message is the key to the counseling strategy. The same process happens to children who experience bad feelings from school failure, peer conflicts, and conflicts with adults.

The main goal of RET is to increase happiness and decrease pain. In order to achieve a prevailing happier state, RET has two main objectives. The first is to show the emotionally disturbed client how irrational beliefs or attitudes create dysfunctional consequences. Some of these consequences might include anger, depression, or anxiety. The second objective is to directively and intellectually teach clients how to dispute or crumble their irrational beliefs and replace them with rational beliefs. Once counselors lead the clients to dispute the irrational ideas, they guide them into adopting new expectations for themselves, others, and the environment. Ellis reasons that if the irrational, absolute philosophies and resultant feelings are replaced with more rational, productive thoughts, clients will no longer be trapped in a repetitive cycle of negative feelings. When children are no longer incapacitated by dysfunctional feelings, they are free to choose behaviors that eliminate the problem or at least lessen its disappointing impact.

Rational-emotive therapy is often referred to as the "A, B, C, D, and E" approach to counseling:

A is the activating event: "I failed my math test."
B is how you evaluate the event.
   B_1—irrational message: "I failed the test; therefore, I'm a total failure as a person."
   B_2—rational message: "I failed the test. This is unpleasant and inconvenient, but that is all it is. I need to study more efficiently for the next exam."
C represents the consequences or feelings resulting from your self-message at the B stage. The B_1 message will cause you to feel very depressed. The B_2 message won't make you feel great, but it will not be so overwhelming as to inhibit your performance on the next test.
D represents the disputing arguments you use to attack the irrational self-messages expressed in B_1. The counselor's function is to help you question these irrational self-messages once they have been identified.
E represents the answers you have developed to the questions regarding the rationality of your B_1 self-messages.

For example, counseling would proceed through the following steps:

A— something unpleasant happens to you.
B— you evaluate the event as something awful, something that should not be allowed to happen.
C— you become upset and nervous.
D— you question your B self-message:
  1. Why is it awful?
  2. Why shouldn't it be allowed to happen?
E— you answer:
  1. It's a disappointment.
  2. It's a setback, but not a disaster.
  3. I can handle it.
  4. I would like things to be better, but that doesn't mean I'm always supposed to get things done my way.

Ellis (1969b) provides another example of RET in action in an article entitled "Teaching Emotional Education in the Classroom." A student named Robert is so anxious about reciting in class, even though he knows the material, that he anticipates the event (A) and already feels the blocking and nervousness (C) just by anticipating the event (A). At point B_2 he tells himself: "It would be unfortunate if I did not recite well because the other children might think I did not know my lesson. They might even think I am a dummy, and I would not want that." At B_1, however, Robert usually adds another statement to his rational message: "It would be awful if I failed. No one would like me, and I would be a bum." The great anxiety felt at C caused by the B_1 message would sabotage Robert's efforts to recite in class the next time the teacher called on him.

Rational-emotive therapy is direct, didactic, confrontational, and verbally active counseling. Initially, the counselor seeks to detect the irrational beliefs that are creating the disturbance. Four factors are helpful in detecting irrational thinking:

1. Look for "awfulizing."
2. Look for something you think you cannot stand.
3. Look for absolute uses of *should, must, ought, always,* and *never.*
4. Look for damning of yourself and others.

Once the irrational beliefs are recognized, the counselor disputes and challenges them. Ultimately, the goal is for children to recognize irrational beliefs, think them through, and relinquish them. As a result of this process and therapy, children, it is hoped, will reach three insights. First, the present neurotic behavior has antecedent causes. Second, the reason original beliefs keep upsetting children is that they keep repeating these beliefs. Third, they can overcome emotional disturbances by consistently observing, questioning, and challenging their own belief systems.

People hold tenaciously to their beliefs, rational or not; consequently, the counselor vigorously attacks the irrational beliefs in an attempt to show the children how illogically they think. Using the Socratic method of questioning and disputing, the counselor takes a verbally active part in the early stages of counseling by identifying and explaining the child's problem. If counselors guess correctly, which often happens, they argue with and persuade the child to give up the old philosophical view and replace it with a new, essentially existentially oriented, philosophy.

Ellis (1962) suggests that, to the usual psychotherapeutic techniques of exploration, ventilation, excoriation, and interpretation, the rational therapist add techniques of confrontation, indoctrination, and reeducation. Counselors are didactic in that they explain how children's beliefs (which intervene between an event and the resultant feelings), rather than events themselves, are the cause of emotional disturbances. Because the counselor honestly believes that children do not understand the reason for their disturbance, the counselor enlightens and teaches. Counselors frequently assign homework for the child as an integral part of therapy. The homework may consist of reading, performing specific tasks, and taking risks.

There is little transference in RET. Contrary to classical psychoanalysis, the counselor serves as a model of rational thinking and behavior. The children are urged to resolve problems with significant people in their lives.

In addition, the counselor sometimes uses conventional methods such as dream analysis, reflection of feeling, and reassurance. All these methods are employed together, with the end result that the child's irrational thinking—which has resulted in irrational behavior—is destroyed and replaced with a saner belief system.

Rational-emotive counselors believe that the development of a person's belief system (which is defined as the meaning of facts) is analogous to the acquisition of speech. Just as language is learned by imitation and modeling, so is the belief system. Therefore, the belief system and attitudes children acquire are largely a reflection of the significant people in their lives. Furthermore, the belief systems incorporated into children's minds will determine whether they think rationally about facts. Continuing the analogy, it is suggested that, just as one continues to add vocabulary and modify one's speech, one can also change or replace one's belief system.

RET is modified when used with children because its style depends so much on verbal and abstract conceptualization skills. Working on the premise that people feel the way they think, the therapist attempts to change overt behavior by altering internal verbalization. A major disadvantage in using RET with children is that studies have shown that children do not generalize well from one situation to another; that is, the improved behavior is limited to the specific circumstances. Furthermore, Piaget's research would indicate that children in the preformal stages of cognitive development (see Chapter 2) might have difficulty relating to the rational-emotive counseling method.

Role reversal is one very effective technique used with children. In this technique, the child describes the activating event and the emotional consequences. Next, the counselor explains that it is the thoughts that are upsetting the child. Then they role-play the activating event, with the counselor playing the child. While acting out the event, the counselor demonstrates the appropriate behavior while uttering rational self-statements aloud. The roles are reversed again, with the child trying on new thoughts and being rewarded, preferably with social approval as reinforcement for rational statements and behaviors. It may be that the child will need to be rewarded for successive approximations.

An offspring of RET is rational-emotive education (REE). The objectives of REE are to teach how feelings develop, how to discriminate between valid and invalid assumptions, and how to think rationally in "antiawful" and "antiperfectionist" ways.

One study reported by Knaus (1974) illustrates quite effectively the results of reinforcing rational verbal expressions with disturbed children. The children became more rational not only in their verbal expressions and belief systems but also in their behaviors. The following are examples of beliefs that were reinforced by writing statements:

I don't like school, but I can stand it.
I did something bad, but I'm not a bad person.
I don't like being called insulting names, but being insulted is not awful.
Just because someone calls you a "dum-dum" does not mean you are one.

Some children in the experiment improved in their rational behaviors to the extent that they were recommended for dismissal from treatment.

Ellis believes that all children act neurotically simply because they are children. He states that childish behavior cannot be differentiated from neurosis until the age of 5. At this point, many children have integrated into their belief system the irrational belief that one should be thoroughly competent, adequate, and achieving in all possible respects if one is to be considered worthwhile. Ellis, Moseley, and Wolfe (1972) list several strategies for undermining this philosophy in children.

1. Teach children the joy of engaging in games that are worthwhile because they are fun. Deemphasize the importance of winning at all costs by teaching children that you do not have to win to have fun and to be a worthwhile person.

2. Teach children that significant achievements rarely come easily and that there is nothing wrong with working long and hard to achieve one's goals.

3. Teach children that they are not bad people when they do not meet their goals. It is important that children like themselves during periods of failure even when they may not be trying their best to achieve their goals. It is also important to teach children that there are important differences

between wants and needs. When we want something we cannot get, it does not mean that we are not getting what we absolutely need.

4. Teach children that, although it is good to strive for perfectionism in performance, perfectionism is not required for one to be a worthwhile person. It is not only OK to make mistakes, but making mistakes is a good way to learn why certain things happen and how to prevent them from happening again.

5. Teach children that popularity and achievement are not necessarily related, that it is very difficult to be liked by all people at all times, and that 100 percent popularity is not required to be a worthwhile person.

6. In summary, teach children not to take themselves and situations too seriously by turning minor setbacks into catastrophes. Positive reinforcement is recommended to balance constructive criticism when evaluating children's performances.

Cognitive-Behavioral Therapy

A common trend that is beginning to appear in the literature is the movement toward eclectic approaches to counseling. These eclectic approaches often involve the combination of two or more standard approaches into one treatment modality. We suggest that this has been happening in practice since the beginning of the counseling movement, and only now is the profession feeling sufficiently secure to admit that many practitioners have been eclectics all along. One such eclectic combination is represented by the unification of cognitive and behavioral approaches into cognitive-behavioral therapy (CBT). The practice of cognitive-behavioral therapy combines behavior-change methods with thought-restructuring methods to produce behavior and feeling change in clients. Such a marriage between two approaches results from deficiency in one or both of the methods in bringing about the desired counseling outcomes. The terms *cognitive restructuring, cognitive behavior modification,* and *stress inoculation* all represent current descriptions of Ellis's original work and some extensions of his work by Beck (1976), Maultsby (1984), and Meichenbaum (1977, 1985). These techniques combine various cognitive and behavioral approaches (Bernard, 1990). Stress-inoculation methods combined with role-playing provide an example of a cognitive-behavioral technique. In cases of test anxiety, the client might be asked to practice the following examples of self-talk: (1) "Tests are no fun, but all I want is to do the best I can." (2) "Though it would be nice to make an "A," it is not required for me to be a good and worthwhile person." (3) "All I need to do is prepare for the test and do the best I am able to do. If I fail, it will be inconvenient and no fun at all, but that is all it will be. For the moment, I just will not be getting what I want." Combining the self-talk with taking practice tests and visualization practice of the steps in the client's test-taking stimulus hierarchy (systematic desensitization) represents a typical cognitive-behavioral treatment plan.

Other stress-inoculation techniques include relaxation training, deep-breathing exercises, and reframing exercises that help children replace their anxiety with relaxation. Such reframing exercises help children perceive anxiety-provoking situations in a less threatening light. For example, rather than having the child focus on school as a place of potential failure and frightening teachers, the counselor teaches the child to focus on the friends and fun available at school.

Ritter (1985), in a review of cognitive therapies, summarizes the stress-inoculation training program designed by Meichenbaum (1977, 1985). The skills taught consist of four categories of coping self-statements designed to help people master difficult or highly stressful situations: (1) preparation for a stressor ("What is it you have to do? You can develop a plan to deal with it. Don't worry."); (2) confrontation and management of a stressor ("One step at a time; you can handle the situation. Relax, you are in control. Take a slow, deep breath."); (3) coping ("Don't try to eliminate fear totally; just keep it manageable. Keep the focus on the present; what is it you have to do?"); and (4) reinforcing self-statements ("It worked; you did it. It wasn't as bad as you expected. It's getting better each time.")

Winnett, Bornstein, Cogswell, and Paris (1987) developed a CBT model for treating childhood depressive disorders. The model consists of four levels of treatment: (1) behavioral procedures, such as contingent reinforcement, shaping, prompting, and modeling, to increase social interaction; (2) CBT interventions, which include pairing successful task completion with positive self-statements and reinforcement for those self-statements; (3) cognitive interventions, which are used with social-skills training, role-playing, and self-management; and (4) self-control procedures, such as self-evaluation and self-reinforcement.

Watkins (1983) has adapted Maultsby's (1976) rational self-analysis format to fit the developmental level of children (see Table 6-1). In Step 1, children write down what happened ("Jimmy called me a name because he doesn't like me."). In Step 2, children are asked to write, from the vantage point of a video camera, what they would see and hear ("Jimmy didn't like it when I didn't choose him for my team."). With the increased objectivity obtained in Step 2, children are then asked in Step 3 to write down their thoughts about what happened ("It's terrible when people talk mean to me," or "If people get angry at me, I'm a bad person."). In Step 4, children are asked to write how they felt (hurt, angry) and what they did ("I hit him."). In Step 5, children are asked to find out if they have been thinking "smart" thoughts by testing their thoughts with the five questions listed in Step 6 (for example, "Does my thought help me stay out of trouble with others?"). The yesses and noes are tabulated in the Step 5 box. If the noes win, the children go to Step 7 and list some of the feelings they want to feel (for example, a child may prefer to feel sad or disappointed instead of hurt, irritated, or angry). In Step 8, children are asked to write "smarter" thoughts that would help them feel better feelings ("I don't like it when

TABLE 6-1   Rational self-analysis for children

Step 1. Write down what happened.	**Step 2.** Be a video camera. If you were a video camera and recorded a videotape of what happened, what would you see and hear?	**Step 3.** Write down your thoughts about what happened. What did you think? A. B. C.

Step 4.
A. How did you feel?
 	
B. What did you do?
	Step 5. Decide if your thoughts are "smart." To do this, look at each thought you had and ask yourself the five questions in Step 6. Answer yes or no to each question and write your answers below.
	A. 1. B. 1. C. 1.
	   2. 2. 2.
	   3. 3. 3.
	   4. 4. 4.
	   5. 5. 5.
		Step 6. How do you know if you're thinking "smart" thoughts? Ask:
		1. Is my thought really real, say if I were a video camera, what would I see?
		2. Does the thought help me stay alive and in good physical shape?
		3. Does the thought help me get what I want?
		4. Does the thought help me stay out of trouble with others?
		5. Does the thought help me feel the way I want to?

Step 7. How do you want to feel?	**Step 8.** Write down thoughts you could have that would be "smarter" than those listed. A. B. C.	**Step 9.** What do you want to do?

SOURCE: Watkins, 1983; adapted from Maultsby, 1976.

others get upset with me, but things could be worse, and I don't have to let others control how I act."). Step 9 is reserved for a plan of action children can use the next time somebody does something to make them feel bad.

CASE STUDY

Jeff is a quiet, serious, 12-year-old seventh-grader at Smith County Middle School. He was referred to the counselor because he was very upset after receiving a failing grade on a language arts test. After the test, Jeff seemed to be firmly convinced he would fail the class.

Individual and Background Information

Academic.   School records indicate that Jeff is a high achiever. He had excellent grades ("B" and above) in all his classes for the first two grading periods of the year. Except for the "F" on the last test, he has also maintained an above-average grade in language arts this grading period.

Family.   Jeff is the youngest of three sons. His father is retired, and his mother works as a grocery-store cashier. Both of Jeff's older brothers, one of whom is a high school senior and the other a college sophomore, are excellent students. The family expects (or appears to expect) Jeff to excel also.

Social.   Jeff seems to get along well with his peers. He participates in group efforts and is especially good friends with one other student, John, also a good student with a quiet personality.

Counseling Method

The school counselor used rational-emotive therapy as a counseling method to help Jeff recognize and evaluate the erroneous messages he was giving himself (and which upset him) about his low grade in language arts. The counselor also taught Jeff to replace the erroneous messages with "sane" messages and to recognize "insane" messages when he encountered them again. The basic steps the counselor used included having Jeff examine each step along the way to becoming upset and look at the real message he was telling himself at each step.

Transcript*

Counselor: Jeff, why do you think you're going to fail language arts?

Jeff: Because I failed the last test.

Counselor: You mean if you fail one test, you're bound to fail the next one?

Jeff: Well, I failed that test, and I'm stupid!

Counselor: What are you telling yourself about your performance on that test?

Jeff: I remember thinking it was a really bad grade—not at all the kind I was used to getting. Then I thought how terrible it would be if I failed language arts and how my mom and dad and brothers would hate me and would think I was lazy and dumb!

*The case of Jeff was contributed by Sharon Simpson.

Counselor: It would be unpleasant and inconvenient if you failed language arts, but would this make you a hateful and dumb person?

Jeff: It makes me really worried about passing the next test that's coming up . . .

Counselor: I can understand how you would be worried about the next test, but does a bad grade make someone a bad or hated person?

Jeff: No, but it's not the kind of grade I usually get.

Counselor: OK, so a bad grade is unpleasant, and you don't like it, but it does not make you a bad person.

Jeff: *My* grade was an "F" and most of the other kids made "A's," so it made me look dumb.

Counselor: OK, it *was* a bad grade compared to the rest of the class, but does this mean you are the dumbest kid around?

Jeff: No, I make mostly "A's," a few "B's." One bad grade does not make me a dumb kid.

Counselor: So, compared to your usual grade and the class's grades, this *was* a bad grade, and that is all it is, right?

Jeff: Yeah.

Counselor: What else are you telling yourself about the low test grade?

Jeff: Well, like I said, I immediately thought how terrible it would be if I failed language arts, and . . .

Counselor: Stop there for just a minute, Jeff. Suppose you did fail language arts, even with your other high grades. It would be a bad experience, but would it be the end of the world?

Jeff: No, I guess I'd have to repeat the class, that's all.

Counselor: Right, it would be inconvenient and maybe embarrassing. It would not be pleasant, but you would go on living.

Jeff: Well, I guess that's right.

Counselor: Are you beginning to see what you told yourself about the consequences of *one* bad grade?

Jeff: Yeah, I guess I believed that one bad grade was awful—the end of the world—and that I shouldn't even try any more because I would fail the class anyway.

Counselor: Was that the correct information to give yourself about your grade?

Jeff: No!

Counselor: OK! Let's look at the rest of the message you gave yourself after you got that bad grade. Remember what was next?

Jeff: I think I thought my family would hate me and think I was dumb and lazy because I failed that test and would probably fail language arts.

Counselor: Do you think your family's love depends on your grades?

Jeff: No, Jimmy made an "F" on a chemistry test the first part of the school year, and nobody hated him.

Counselor: What did your parents do?

Jeff: Let's see. Oh, yeah, they got him a tutor—a friend of Dad's knew a student who was majoring in chemistry.

Counselor: What did your brother in college do when Jimmy failed the test?

Jeff: He offered to help Jim on weekends. He's a brain—a physics major!

Counselor: So when your brother failed a test, your family helped him out. They didn't say he was "dumb" or "lazy" or that they hated him for it!

Jeff: No, they didn't. And I guess they wouldn't say it to me, either; in fact, Dad and Jim ask every night if I need help with my homework. I can usually do it OK by myself.

Counselor: OK. Let's go back over some of these bad messages you've been giving yourself about your bad grade.

Jeff: I got a bad grade. I thought I would fail language arts no matter what I did. I decided my family would hate me and think I was dumb and lazy.

Counselor: Do you *still* believe those "crazy" messages you told yourself about failing and the way your family would react?

Jeff: No!

Counselor: Next time you mess up on something—maybe a ball game, maybe a test—what message will you give yourself?

Jeff: Well, I'm not exactly sure what I'll say, but I *won't* tell myself that it's a disaster and I'll never be able to do anything else. I'll probably say that I don't like what happened and that I'm not happy about it. That's all. Now I guess I'll go study and try to ace that next language arts test. Thanks a lot!

RESEARCH AND REACTIONS

Research relating to rational-emotive therapy began with Ellis's (1957) review of his own casework employing three different methods of psychotherapy. Ellis found that with orthodox psychoanalysis, 13 percent of his patients improved considerably, 37 percent showed distinct improvement, and 50 percent showed little or no improvement. With analytically oriented therapy, the figures were 18 percent, 45 percent, and 37 percent, respectively. Ellis found his system (then called *rational therapy*) to be the most successful, with figures of 44 percent, 46 percent, and 10 percent. In addition, Ellis found his system to be effective in one to five sessions as compared to the longer periods of therapy required for the other two approaches.

Belief Systems

In the development of RET, Ellis has postulated, among other things, a system of beliefs or philosophies common to our culture that are inherently irrational and conducive to maladjustment. Jones (1968) constructed an instrument to measure these beliefs. He was able to conclude on the basis of his data that his Irrational Beliefs Test was sufficiently reliable and valid as a measure of irrational beliefs for use in both research and specific clinical situations. Ellis's theoretical position with respect to irrational beliefs was substantially confirmed by the results of the study.

Master and Gershman (1983) verified the physiological reaction people get from making irrational statements in response to problems that have high relevance. Rational statements did not produce a higher level of emotional response than neutral statements produced.

Stoltenberg, Pace, and Maddux (1986) found that thinking-type students, as measured on the Myers-Briggs Type Indicator, tended to show a stronger preference than feeling types for the RET cognitive style of counseling. The finding is consistent with research on successful counseling resulting from counselor/client personality similarity.

Wolkersheim and Bugges (1982) found that college students, exposed to the treatment rationales of psychoanalysis and RET for severe nonreactive depression of a middle-aged woman and sample counseling tapes of each approach, chose RET as the method that seemed to hold the most promise for the client.

Thebarge (1989), differentiating RET from behavior modification, systematic desensitization, and traditional psychoanalysis, pointed out that RET treats underlying causes (irrational beliefs) of symptoms and not the symptoms themselves. Therefore, in successful RET, there will be none of the symptom substitution that may occur when treatment is focused on symptoms only. Behavior modification and systematic desensitization are two therapies that are directed toward symptom removal.

Dryden (1989b) discussed four types of chains people use to turn irrational beliefs into bad feelings and destructive behaviors. *Inference* chains occur when inferences are chained together and trigger emotions and irrational beliefs. The key to treatment is to find the most relevant inference. *Inference-evaluative belief* chains occur when a person holds an evaluative belief about each inference in the chain. The key to repairing this chain is to identify the earliest irrational belief that creates increasingly distorted beliefs. *Disturbance-about-disturbance* chains relate to how people become more upset by becoming upset about disturbances. In these cases, it is best to let the client choose the starting point in the chain. *Complex* chains are too difficult to handle by starting at the end of the chain. It is recommended that clients start at the beginning and replay the entire process in slow motion to see the ABC process.

DiGiuseppe (1990) detailed a method for using inference chaining as a technique for helping children reevaluate their automatic irrational beliefs. Children were asked to imagine or think about what would happen next if the automatic thought (for example, "I am stupid") were true and what it would mean to them. DiGiuseppe also recommended using deductive interpretation with children. In this method, the counselor and the child form and test hypotheses concerning the irrational belief. Both methods allow for self-discovery by the child.

Rational-Emotive Education

In recent years, many people have reported success with preventive programs that employ REE. Maultsby, Knipping, and Carpenter (1974) investigated the effectiveness of a rational-emotive educational program as a preventive mental health tool for high school and college students. The program was designed to teach students to use RET methods in analyzing their bad feelings and in developing strategies for solving their problems. The study was conducted with high school students already suffering from emotional upset. Following participation in the RET program, the experimental group improved significantly on several measures of personality assessment.

Rational-emotive education for children in the elementary school setting is of interest to those who believe it is important to teach children to think rationally about events before they are programmed to react irrationally. Several anecdotal studies have supported the view that the principles of RET can be effective in working with both disturbed and "normal" children (Ellis, 1969b, 1972; Ellis, Wolfe, & Moseley, 1966; Glicken, 1968; Hauck, 1967; Knaus, 1974). However, studies are needed to show that RET results in a generalized improvement in mental health. According to a survey of RET research by DiGiuseppe, Miller, and Trexler (1977), no evidence exists to support the idea that all children are able to acquire the principles of RET. As we have suggested earlier, many approaches to counseling will need to be adapted for those children functioning in the concrete cognitive stage.

Knaus and Boker (1975) and Albert (1972) investigated the effectiveness of RET education programs with elementary school children. Both studies showed lower scores for the experimental groups on the Anxiety Scale for Children, and the Knaus and Boker study showed an increase in self-esteem for the experimental group.

Omizo, Cubberly, and Omizo (1985) presented the results of a 12-week study designed to evaluate the impact of REE on self-concept and locus of control of children with learning disabilities. The REE objectives of the experimental group were: (1) learn the ABC format; (2) acquire basic problem-solving skills; (3) demonstrate that feelings are influenced by thoughts; (4) understand that feelings are not expressed in identical ways; (5) transfer learning to real life; (6) develop rational coping skills; (7) learn expression of feelings, not generalities; (8) be empathic to other group members; and (9) learn to dispute irrational thoughts. The experimental group differed significantly in a positive direction from the control group on three of five self-concept subscales and on the locus-of-control measure.

Roush (1984) proposed a version of rational-emotive therapy that could be adapted for use in institutional settings with younger children and other children having limited cognitive abilities. He noted three basic processes that are necessary for an effective RET intervention: (1) the ability to discriminate between rational and irrational beliefs; (2) possession of a working knowledge of core irrationalities; and (3) development of a usable system for identifying and disputing the components of irrational thinking. Roush developed four approaches geared to the readiness level of children and youth with lower levels of cognitive development.

Zoints (1983) has proposed a strategy for implementing REE in the classroom. Students are taught how their disturbing emotions develop from their thinking or belief systems. The students are also taught disputation in order to change the irrational beliefs that cause the disturbing emotions. Zoints recommends that the program be carried out in a problem-solving, group-discussion format, with the teacher taking an active/directive role. For example, the teacher would challenge the students with such questions as "How does failing a test make you a dumb jerk?"

Voelm, Cameron, Brown, and Gibson (1984) reported on the effects of REE on acting-out and socially withdrawn adolescents' self-concept, academic achievement, classroom behavior, and ability to comprehend and remember the concepts of REE over time. The REE group was compared with a transactional analysis group and a control group. The REE group (1) showed a dramatic increase in self-concept scores; (2) showed a significant increase in survey-of-rational-concepts scores; (3) scored significantly lower on an excessive-anxiety scale; and (4) were rated by their teachers as less aggressive, less resistant, and having control over anger and impulses.

Omizo, Lo, and Williams (1986) reported success in using REE with learning-disabled adolescents. The treatment group emerged with lower levels of anxiety and higher levels of aspiration, leadership, initiative, and internal locus of control.

Vernon (1990) designed a program for using REE with children and teachers. A workshop outline is presented for teaching teachers how to use REE in the classroom. Joyce (1990) and Bruner (1984) presented two different approaches for using REE with parent education and consultation.

Forman (1990) provided a literature review of RET and CBT strategies and training programs designed to help teachers become better managers of their own stress. Managing teacher stress might be the best way to manage student stress.

RET Outcome Research

Glass and Smith (1976) reviewed 375 outcome studies in psychotherapy, 35 of which were conducted with RET. In a ranking of ten types of therapy, RET placed second to systematic desensitization in outcome success, with behavior modification a close third. The other theories ranked were Gestalt, psychodynamic, transactional analysis, Adlerian, person-centered, implosion, and eclectic.

Carmody's (1977) study, "A Comparative Analysis of Rational-Emotive, Self-Instructional and Behavioral Assertion Training," employed 63 subassertive adult outpatients who participated in four 90-minute sessions of group assertion training. The three treatment groups did not differ significantly over the short term. At post-test, the RET group showed significantly more improvement on the self-report measure of unproductive cognitions than the other two training groups showed. The generalization of treatment gains was successfully demonstrated for all three training groups on role-played "generalization" assertive scenes; however, on a test of transfer of training at post-test, only the RET group evidenced significant generalization of treatment gains.

Ricketts and Galloway (1984) compared the effectiveness of three 1-hour approaches to reducing test anxiety among college students. Relaxation training, RET, and study skills were the three methods researched. Relaxation training was found to be the best test-anxiety reducer, followed by RET, study skills, and the placebo treatment, in that order. However, the sessions did not improve academic achievement.

Conoley, McConnell, Conoley, and Kimzey (1983) compared the ABCs of RET with the Gestalt empty chair method for effectiveness in achieving anger reduction. Systolic blood pressure and a feelings questionnaire were the dependent variables. A control group received active listening. Sixty-one undergraduate females were asked to discuss a high-anger-producing situation with a counselor. Both the RET and Gestalt participants outperformed the control group in anger reduction. There was, however, no significant difference between the RET and Gestalt groups.

Maxwell and Wilkerson (1982) found that weekly RET sessions over ten weeks were effective in reducing the anxiety of 24 female participants as measured by the Sixteen Personality Factor Questionnaire. Thurman (1983) studied the effects of RET on type-A behavior among college students. Following treatment, the experimental group significantly reduced self-reported levels of type-A speed and impatience, hard-driving, and competitive behavior; high self-expectation; anxious overconcern about the future; and perfectionism.

Sklare, Taylor, and Hyland (1985) recommend using an emotional control card (ECC) to facilitate the use of rational-emotive imagery outside the counseling session. Recognizing that rational-emotive imagery has been a helpful tool in RET, the authors believe it could be improved because clients may be likely to forget to apply newly learned imagery skills in real-life situations. The proposed ECC lists various situations and matches problem emotional responses with words to describe a more realistic or rational picture that leads to a less drastic emotional response. The ECC would provide the client with varied and numerous life situations in which to practice imagery. The authors present three successful case applications using the emotional control card.

Ellis (1989) presented a case-study report of how he successfully used RET for crisis intervention during a single interview with a suicidal client. The client, a 27-year-old female, was a successful resident in obstetrics and gynecology who was contemplating suicide after the loss of her last three lovers. Ellis described how he used RET, humor, contracting, and the homework assignment of singing some of Ellis's rational humor songs three times daily.

Dash, Hirt, and Schroeder (1989) reviewed and conducted a meta-analysis on 48 studies examining the effects of self-statement modification (SSM) in the treatment of child behavior disorders including attention-deficit hyperactivity disorder (ADHD), phobias, shyness, and behavior. While the evidence for the effectiveness of SSM is not conclusive, the data were most supportive of using SSM with adolescents and preadolescents and with children in the 5–7 age group. Children in the 8–10 age range did not fare as well.

CBT Outcome Research

Maultsby (1971) has significantly modified Ellis's basic system by focusing on homework assignments for clients. He refers to his system as *rational-behavior therapy*. In a study of 87 psychiatric outpatients receiving homework therapy for ten weeks, Maultsby found that 85 percent of the patients who were judged most improved rated the homework as effective in their treatment.

Bernard, Keefauver, and Kratochwill (1983) combined RET with a behavioral intervention to eliminate chronic hair pulling in a female client. The rational- or cognitive-behavioral treatment consisted of RET with self-instructional training. Partial success was experienced with RET used alone. Complete success was achieved with the addition of self-instructional training, including a self-monitoring program.

Gilchrist and Schinke (1983) found that young people given cognitive-behavioral treatment about sex and contraception possessed more sex-education knowledge and held more positive attitudes toward contraception than a control group receiving information on the topic. They also were observed to engage in more effective problem-solving and communication skills in videotaped role-plays.

Deutschle, Tosi, and Wise (1987) have successfully applied cognitive-experiential therapy (CET), or rational stage-directed hypnotherapy (RSDH), to the treatment of impulsivity in children. CET, or RSDH, is defined as a treatment modality that combines hypnosis, relaxation imagery, and cognitive restructuring. The technique is further enhanced through the use of metaphors designed to help children develop an objective, non-threatening identification with the elements of their experiential themes.

Bor, Dadds, Gordon, Morrison, Rebgetz, Sanders, and Shepard (1989) found CBT effective in treating recurrent nonspecific abdominal pain in children. Treatment included training in coping skills for self-managing pain, progressive muscle relaxation, self-monitoring of pain, and activities for redirecting children after a pain complaint. Mothers completed the eight sessions of training with their children.

Lochman and Lampron (1988) found CBT effective for aggressive boys in the 10–12 age range. A goal-setting component was added to the cognitive-behavioral interventions.

Warren, McLellarn, and Ponzoha (1988) found both RET and CBT effective in treating low self-esteem and related emotional problems. The authors conclude that RET needs to be combined with other methods, such as skills training, to obtain optimum effectiveness.

Summary

RET has received considerable recognition in the literature. A study by Berkowitz and Alioto (1973) demonstrated that activating events were not necessarily the causes of aggressive consequences. Rather, anger was found to originate in human cognitions. However, an article by Zajonc (1980) challenges this assumption by presenting evidence for emotion occurring without cognition.

A comprehensive review by Berkowitz (1970) of the literature on aggression points out the futility and danger of "acting out" aggressive impulses as a way of relieving these emotions. Aggression apparently begets more aggression; therefore, a more productive system for treating aggression is needed. Ellis believes RET is the answer.

Finally, in a reply to articles critical of rational-emotive therapy, Ellis (1981, 1984) wrote that RET or REP (rational-emotive psychology) remains within the field of science while at the same time resting on some evaluative assumptions. For example, the RET concept of unconditional humanistic self-acceptance is still valid even though it requires an operational definition. The REP philosophy does not conflict with all religions, only with those that are absolutist and that sabotage human health and happiness. Human nature has the potential to be both rational (scientific approach) and irrational (departure from science). The RET/REP concept of self-acceptance means that a person is more than a set of behaviors. That is, people are better off negating specific behaviors without labeling their entire self as good or bad.

REFERENCES

Albert, S. (1972). *A study to determine the effectiveness of affective education with fifth grade students.* Unpublished master's thesis, Queens College, Flushing, NY.

Beck, A. (1976). *Cognitive therapy and emotional disorders.* New York: International Universities Press.

Berkowitz, C. (1970). Experimental investigations of hostility catharsis. *Journal of Consulting and Clinical Psychology, 35,* 1–7.

Berkowitz, L., & Alioto, J. (1973). The meaning of an observed event as a determinant of its aggressive consequences. *Journal of Personality and Social Psychology, 28,* 206–217.

Bernard, M. (1990). Rational-emotive therapy with children and adolescents: Treatment strategies. *School Psychology Review, 19,* 294–303.

Bernard, M., Keefauver, L., & Kratochwill, T. (1983). The effects of rational emotive therapy and self instructional training on chronic hair pulling. *Cognitive Therapy and Research, 7,* 273–280.

Bor, W., Dadds, M., Gordon, A., Morrison, M., Rebgetz, M., Sanders, M., & Shepard, R. (1989). Cognitive behavioral treatment of recurrent nonspecific abdominal pain in children: An analysis of generalization, maintenance and side effects. *Journal of Consulting and Clinical Psychology, 57,* 294–300.

Bruner, G. (1984). Rational-emotive education for parent study groups. *Individual Psychology Journal of Adlerian Theory, Research and Practice, 40,* 228–231.

Carmody, T. (1977). A comparative analysis of rational-emotive, self-instructional and behavioral assertion training. *Dissertation Abstracts International, 38,* 1394B.

Conoley, C., McConnell, J., Conoley, J., & Kimzey, C. (1983). The effect of the ABCs of rational emotive therapy and the empty chair technique of Gestalt therapy on anger reduction. *Psychotherapy: Theory, Research and Practice, 20,* 112–116.

Crawford, T., & Ellis, A. (1989). A dictionary of rational-emotive feelings and behaviors. *Journal of Rational-Emotive and Cognitive-Behavioral Therapy, 7,* 3–28.

Dash, D., Hirt, M., & Schroeder, H. (1989). Self-statement modification in the treatment of child behavior disorder: A meta-analysis. *Psychological Bulletin, 106,* 97–106.

Deutschle, J., Jr., Tosi, D., & Wise, P. (1987). *The use of hypnosis and metaphor within a cognitive experiential framework: Theory, research, and case applications with impulse control disorders.* Paper presented at the American Society for Clinical Hypnosis, Las Vegas, NV.

DiGiuseppe, R. (1990). Rational-emotive assessment of school aged children. *School Psychology Review, 19,* 287–293.

DiGiuseppe, R., Miller, N., & Trexler, L. (1977). A review of rational-emotive psychotherapy outcome studies. *The Counseling Psychologist, 7,* 64–72.

Dryden, W. (1989a). Albert Ellis: An efficient and passionate life. *Journal of Counseling and Development, 67,* 539–546.

Dryden, W. (1989b). The use of chaining in rational-emotive therapy. *Journal of Rational-Emotive and Cognitive-Behavior Therapy, 7,* 59–66.

Ellis, A. (1954). *The American sexual tragedy.* New York: Twayne.

Ellis, A. (1957). Outcome of employing three techniques of psychotherapy. *Journal of Clinical Psychology, 13,* 334–350.

Ellis, A. (1962). *Reason and emotion in psychotherapy.* New York: Lyle Stuart.

Ellis, A. (1965). *The case for sexual liberty.* Tucson, AZ: Seymour Press.

Ellis, A. (1969a). *The art and science of love* (2nd ed.). New York: Lyle Stuart/Bantam.

Ellis, A. (1969b). Teaching emotional education in the classroom. *School Health Review, 1,* 10–13.

Ellis, A. (1972). Emotional education in the classroom. *Journal of Clinical Psychology, 1,* 19–22.

Ellis, A. (1974). What rational-emotive therapy is and is not. *Counselor Education and Supervision, 14,* 140–144.

Ellis, A. (1975). *How to live with a "neurotic"* (rev. ed.). New York: Crown.

Ellis, A. (1977). *How to live with—and without—anger.* New York: Reader's Digest Press.

Ellis, A. (1981). Science, religiosity and rational emotive psychology. *Psychotherapy: Theory, Research and Practice, 18,* 55–58.

Ellis, A. (1984). Rational emotive therapy and pastoral counseling: A reply to Richard Wessler. *Personnel and Guidance Journal, 62,* 266–267.

Ellis, A. (1987). The impossibility of achieving consistently good mental health. *American Psychologist, 42,* 364–375.

Ellis, A. (1989). Using rational-emotive therapy (RET) as crisis intervention: A single interview with a suicidal client. *Individual Psychology Journal of Adlerian Theory, Research and Practice, 45,* 75–81.

Ellis, A., & Harper, R. (1975). *A new guide to rational living.* Englewood Cliffs, NJ: Prentice-Hall.

Ellis, A., Moseley, S., & Wolfe, J. (1972). *How to raise an emotionally healthy, happy child.* North Hollywood, CA: Wilshire Books.

Ellis, A., Wolfe, J., & Moseley, S. (1966). *How to prevent your child from becoming a neurotic adult.* New York: Crown.

Forman, S. (1990). Rational-emotive therapy: Contributions to teacher stress management. *School Psychology Review, 19,* 315–321.

Gilchrist, L., & Schinke, S. (1983). Coping with contraception: Cognitive and behavioral methods with adolescents. *Cognitive Therapy and Research, 7,* 379–388.

Glass, G., & Smith, M. (1976, June). *Meta-analysis of psychotherapy outcome studies.* Paper presented at the annual meeting of the Society for Psychotherapy Research, Boston.

Glicken, M. (1968). Rational counseling: A new approach to children. *Journal of Elementary School Guidance and Counseling, 2,* 261–267.

Goodman, D., & Maultsby, M. (1974). *Emotional well-being through rational behavior training.* Springfield, IL: Charles C Thomas.

Hauck, P. (1967). *The rational management of children.* New York: Libra.

Jones, R. (1968). *A factored measure of Ellis' irrational belief systems with personality and maladjustment correlates.* Unpublished doctoral dissertation, Texas Technological University, Lubbock, TX.

Joyce, M. R. (1990). Rational-emotive parent consultation. *School Psychology Review, 19,* 304–314.

Knaus, W. (1974). *Rational emotive education: A manual for elementary school teachers.* New York: Institute for Rational Living.

Knaus, W., & Boker, S. (1975). The effect of rational-emotive education on anxiety and self-concept. *Rational Living, 10,* 7–10.

Lochman, J., & Lampron, L. (1988). Cognitive-behavioral interventions for aggressive boys: 7-month follow-up effects. *Journal of Child and Adolescent Psychotherapy, 5*(1), 15–23.

Master, S., & Gershman, L. (1983). Physiological responses to rational emotive self-verbalizations. *Journal of Behavior Therapy and Experimental Psychiatry, 14,* 289–296.

Maultsby, M. (1971). Systematic written homework in psychotherapy. *Psychotherapy, 8,* 195–198.

Maultsby, M. (1976). *Rational self-analysis format.* Lexington, KY: Center for Rational Behavior Therapy and Training, University of Kentucky.

Maultsby, M. (1984). *Rational behavior therapy.* Englewood Cliffs, NJ: Prentice-Hall.

Maultsby, M., Knipping, P., & Carpenter, L. (1974). Teaching self-help in the classroom with rational self-counseling. *Journal of School Health, 44,* 445–448.

Maxwell, J., & Wilkerson, J. (1982). Anxiety reduction through group instruction in rational therapy. *Journal of Psychology, 112,* 135–140.

Meichenbaum, D. (1977). *Cognitive behavior modification: An integrative approach.* New York: Plenum.

Meichenbaum, D. (1985). *Stress-inoculation training.* New York: Pergamon Press.

Omizo, M., Cubberly, W., & Omizo, S. (1985). The effects of rational emotive education groups on self-concept and locus of control among learning disabled children. *The Exceptional Child, 32,* 13–16.

Omizo, M., Lo, G., & Williams, R. (1986). Rational-emotive education, self-concept, and locus of control among learning-disabled students. *Journal of Humanistic Education and Development, 25,* 58–69.

Ricketts, M., & Galloway, R. (1984). The effects of three different one-hour single-session treatments for test anxiety. *Psychological Reports, 54,* 115–120.

Ritter, K. (1985). The cognitive therapies: An overview for counselors. *Journal of Counseling and Development, 64,* 42–46.

Roush, D. (1984). Rational emotive therapy and youth: Some new techniques for counselors. *Personnel and Guidance Journal, 62,* 414–417.

Sklare, G., Taylor, J., & Hyland, S. (1985). An emotional control card for rational-emotive imagery. *Journal of Counseling and Development, 64,* 145–146.

Stoltenberg, C., Pace, T., & Maddux, J. (1986). Cognitive style and counselor credibility: Effects on client endorsement of rational emotive therapy. *Cognitive Therapy and Research, 10,* 237–243.

Thebarge, R. (1989). Symptom substitution: A rational-emotive perspective. *Journal of Rational-Emotive and Cognitive-Behavior Therapy, 7,* 93–97.

Thurman, C. (1983). Effects of a rational treatment program in type A behavior among college students. *Journal of College Student Personnel, 24,* 417–423.

Vernon, A. (1990). The school psychologist's role in preventative education: Applications of rational-emotive education. *School Psychology Review, 19,* 322–330.

Voelm, C., Cameron, W., Brown, R., & Gibson, S. (1984, April). *The efficacy of rational emotive education for acting-out and socially withdrawn adolescents.* Paper presented at the annual meeting of the American Education Research Association, New Orleans, LA.

Warren, R., McLellarn, R., & Ponzoha, C. (1988). Rational-emotive therapy vs. general cognitive-behavior therapy in the treatment of low self-esteem and related emotional disturbances. *Cognitive Therapy and Research, 12,* 21–38.

Watkins, C. E. (1983). Rational self-analysis for children. *Elementary School Guidance and Counseling, 17,* 304–306.

Winnett, R., Bornstein, P., Cogswell, K., & Paris, A. (1987). Cognitive-behavioral therapy for childhood depression: A levels-of-treatment approach. *Journal of Child and Adolescent Psychotherapy, 4,* 283–286.

Wolkersheim, J., & Bugges, I. (1982). Effect of rationales for therapy on perceptions of clinical depression. *Psychological Reports, 50,* 314.

Zajonc, R. (1980). Feeling and thinking: Preferences need no inferences. *American Psychologist, 35,* 151–175.

Zoints, P. (1983). A strategy for understanding and correcting irrational beliefs in pupils: The rational emotive approach. *The Pointer, 27,* 13–17.

CHAPTER 7

Behavioral Counseling

DEVELOPERS OF BEHAVIORAL COUNSELING

Several names emerge as contributors to behavioral counseling, including Ivan Pavlov, John B. Watson, Edward L. Thorndike, Edward C. Tolman, Clark L. Hull, John Dollard, Neal E. Miller, H. J. Eysenck, L. Krasner, L. P. Ullman, Joseph Wolpe, Arnold Lazarus, and John Krumboltz. However, the name that is best known to the general public, as well as most controversial, is B. F. Skinner. Skinner, though he did not develop new principles of behaviorism, did the most to translate the theories and ideas of other behaviorists into an applied and useful technology. Skinner's methods are widely used today by psychotherapists, educators, counselors, and parents.

Burrhus Frederic Skinner (1904–1990) was born in Susquehanna, Pennsylvania. He majored in literature at Hamilton College in Clinton, New York. Skinner's goal was to become a writer. After a few years with little success, Skinner regarded himself a failure as a writer. Reflecting later on this time in his life, Skinner commented that the reason for his failure was that he had nothing to say. Giving up on writing, he entered Harvard University to study psychology. The behavior of humans and animals was of special interest to him. He received a master's degree in 1930 and a Ph.D. in experimental psychology in 1931. Following graduation, Skinner began his most productive career as a teacher and researcher at the University of Minnesota, followed by an appointment as chairman of the psychology department at Indiana University. He later returned to Harvard to accept a professorship, which he held until his death.

As he began to generate things to say in the field of behaviorism, Skinner's flair for writing returned. His numerous books include the following:

The Behavior of Organisms (1938)
Walden Two (1948)
Science and Human Behavior (1953)

Verbal Behavior (1957)
Schedules of Reinforcement (coauthored by C. Ferster, 1957)
The Technology of Teaching (1968)
Beyond Freedom and Dignity (1971)
About Behaviorism (1976)
Particulars of My Life (1976)
Reflections on Behaviorism and Society (1978)
The Shaping of a Behaviorist: Part II of an Autobiography (1979)
Skinner for the Classroom (1980, edited by R. Epstein)
A Matter of Consequences: Part III of an Autobiography (1983)
Upon Further Reflection (1987)

Skinner's contribution to knowledge is not strictly confined to the laboratory. He made considerable contributions to solving educational problems. He developed and advanced the concepts of programmed instruction, operant conditioning in classroom management, behavioral counseling, and the teaching machine (first developed by Sidney Pressey in 1923). Perhaps the most controversial of Skinner's works is *Beyond Freedom and Dignity*, in which he pictures a society where behavior is shaped and controlled by a planned system of rewards.

Skinner (1990a), in an article he completed the evening before his death, attacked those who would use introspection or brain analysis as methods for analyzing behavior. He asserted that behavior is the product of three types of variation and selection: natural selection, operant conditioning, and modeling. Skinner had little use for cognitive psychology because it has not contributed, as behavior analysis, to the design of better environments for solving existing problems and preventing future problems. Summing up his 62 years in the profession, Skinner (1990a) said that the point he tried to make is that it can be demonstrated that people choose behavior based on anticipated consequences. According to Skinner, this selection by consequences has negative implications for the world and its future unless some vital changes are made. He concluded by saying that "any evidence that I've been successful in that [fostering needed changes] is how I should like to be remembered" (Skinner, 1990a).

THE NATURE OF PEOPLE

A broad statement of the behaviorist view of the nature of people is probably best summarized by Skinner's (1971) belief that children are influenced and changed as biological entities by things that happen to them. He believed the idea that the child of our past is still contained within us was a form of animism that served no useful purpose in explaining present behavior. Behaviorists view human beings as neither good nor bad but merely as products of their environment. People are essentially born neutral (the blank slate, or tabula rasa, idea), with equal potential for good or evil and for rationality or irrationality.

Behaviorists view people as responders. They reject self-directing mentalistic concepts of human behavior. Behaviorists contend that people can make only those responses they have learned, and they make them when the stimulus conditions are appropriate.

Individuals, then, are viewed by behavioral counselors as products of their conditioning. The stimulus-response paradigm is the basic pattern of all human learning. People react in predictable ways to any given stimulus according to what they have learned through experience. Humans react to stimuli in much the same way animals do, except that human responses are more complex and are organized on a higher plane.

Skinner regarded the human being as an organism who learns patterns of behavior; these are catalogued within the individual's repertoire, to be repeated at a later date. To be more specific, the organism learns a specific response when a satisfying condition follows an action. The number of these responses mounts as time passes and satisfying conditions are repeated. The interest of the behaviorist is in the science of behavior as it relates to biology. Skinner believed that

> a person is a member of a species shaped by evolutionary contingencies of survival, displaying behavioral processes which bring him under the control of the environment in which he lives, and largely under the control of a social environment which he and millions of others like him have constructed and maintained during the evolution of a culture. The direction of the controlling relation is reversed: a person does not act upon the world, the world acts upon him. [1971, p. 211]

Since human behavior is learned, any or all behavior can be unlearned and new behaviors learned in its place. The behaviorist is concerned with observable events. These observable events, when they become unacceptable behaviors, can be unlearned. It is this unlearning or reeducation process with which the behavioral counselor is concerned. Behavioral-counseling procedures can be developed from social-learning theory.

THEORY OF COUNSELING

Behavioral counseling is a reeducation, or relearning, process. Adaptive or helpful behavior is reinforced, while maladaptive or unhelpful behavior is extinguished. The counselor's role is, through reinforcement principles, to help clients achieve the goals they have set for themselves.

Behavioral counseling includes several techniques based on principles of learning employed to manage maladaptive behavior. Today, behavioral counseling is used with covert processes (cognitions, emotions, obsessive ideation) as well as with traditional, overt behavior problems. Behavioral counseling involves two types of behavior: operant and respondent.

	Present	Remove
Positive stimuli candy praise free time	Positive reinforcement	Extinction
Negative stimuli spanking loss of free time criticism	Punishment	Negative reinforcement

FIGURE 7-1   Examples of operant conditioning

In operant conditioning, *operant behavior* refers to behavior that operates on and changes the environment in some manner. It is also referred to as "instrumental behavior" because it is instrumental in goal achievement. People who use operant conditioning wait until the desired behavior or an approximation of the desired behavior occurs and then reinforce it with a rewarding stimulus known as *positive reinforcement* (praise, money, candy, free time, and the like). *Negative reinforcement* (different from punishment) occurs when the operant behavior is reinforced by its capacity to stop an aversive stimulus. For example, rats will learn to press a bar to shut off an electric shock, and children will take their seats at school to shut off the aversive sound of their teacher's scolding. *Punishment,* like positive reinforcement, occurs after the behavior is emitted but tends to decrease its occurrence. *Extinction* is the process of eliminating a learned behavior by ignoring the behavior or by not reinforcing it through attention and other rewards. Figure 7-1 may help explain these four terms.

Behavior Analysis
Why People Behave as They Do

People behave in ways to achieve goals that meet the following hierarchy of needs (Maslow, 1970):

- self-fulfillment (the need to develop skills, interests, and talents)
- self-esteem (feeling worthwhile)
- social (belonging to a group, giving and receiving love)
- security (safety, shelter)
- physiological (food, sleep, oxygen, water)

People behave in ways that make sense to them and that maintain or enhance their self-image, regardless of whether their self-image is positive or negative.

TABLE 7-1 Determining causes of and solutions to performance problems

What category of problem?	Is it a problem of:	Is it due to:	Approach it by:
Performing a task *or* Dealing with people	Being unable*	Lack of knowledge about what, when, how	Providing training
		Obstacle in the environment	Removing the obstacle
	Being unwilling*	Lack of knowledge about why something needs to be done	Providing information/ feedback
		Simple refusal	Changing the balance of positive and negative consequences

NOTE: *Could he or she do it if his or her life depended on it?" No = unable; yes = unwilling.

Steps in Behavior Analysis

Principles of behavior

1. Behavior consists of three phases:
   - *antecedent,* the stimulus or cue that occurs before behavior that leads to its occurrence;
   - *behavior,* what the person says or does (or doesn't); and
   - *consequence,* what the person perceives happens to himself or herself (positive, neutral, and negative) as a result of his or her behavior.
2. Behavior problems are usually rooted in antecedents or consequences.
3. Behavior for which the consequences are known will usually be preferred to behavior for which the consequences are uncertain.

Four steps are followed when conducting a behavior analysis designed to determine causes of and solutions to performance problems: (a) identify the problem category, (b) identify the problem type, (c) determine the cause of the problem, and (d) select a problem solution (see Table 7-1). If the problem solution involves changing the balance of positive and negative consequences, the counselor needs to determine those things that reinforce the undesired behavior and those things that punish the desired behavior. Both reinforcement of the undesired behavior and punishment of the desired behavior must be decreased or eliminated while performance of the desired behavior is reinforced (see Figure 7-2).

As with most counseling, the ultimate goal of behavioral counseling is teaching children how to become their own counselors for changing their behavior to better meet their needs. Using a broad definition of behavior that includes both internal and external behavior, all behavior change can be attempted through behavioral counseling. Specific techniques are avail-

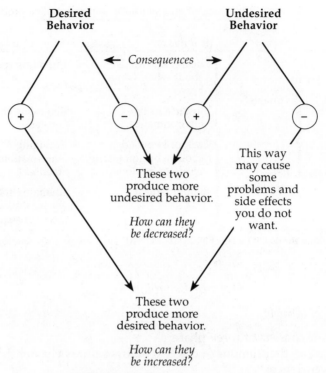

FIGURE 7-2 Balancing consequences

able for reducing and eliminating anxiety, phobias, and obsessive thoughts, as well as for reducing inappropriate, observable behaviors.

The goals of a behavioral counselor can be organized into three main categories (Krumboltz & Hosford, 1967):

1. Altering maladaptive behavior;
2. Teaching the decision-making process; and
3. Preventing problems.

A fourth goal, teaching new behaviors and skills, could also be added. The criteria for any set of goals in counseling children have been summarized by Krumboltz (1966):

1. The goals of counseling should be individualized for each child.
2. The counseling goals for each child should be compatible with, though not necessarily identical to, the values of the counselor.
3. The degree of goal attainment by each child should be observable and assessed.

After the problem has been identified and the desired behavior change agreed upon by counselor and child, the behavioral counselor is apt to employ a variety of counseling procedures to help the child acquire the behaviors necessary to solve the problem. The ultimate outcome of behavioral counseling is to teach children to become their own behavior-modification experts — in other words, to program their own reinforcement schedules (self-management). It would be even more desirable to encourage children to move from extrinsic to intrinsic reinforcement — to please themselves with their behavior rather than to constantly seek the approval of others. Training in self-management skills has proven to be a successful application of behavioral principles to counseling children.

Because behavioral counseling differs from traditional counseling principally in terms of specificity, the behavioral counselor prefers to state goals as overt changes in behavior rather than as hypothetical constructs. The basic counseling function involved in behavioral counseling is defined as discrimination — the differential responding to different situations (individuals, groups, institutions, and environmental settings). In behavioral counseling, the counselor's effectiveness is determined by continuing assessment of the effects of each counseling procedure upon outcomes rather than upon predetermined theoretical biases and/or counseling styles.

COUNSELING METHODS
Operant Techniques

Contingency contracting. Behavioral-counseling methods encompass a wide variety of techniques. One method, contingency contracting, can be broken down into six steps:

1. The counselor and the child identify the problem to be solved.
2. Data are collected to verify the baseline frequency rate for the occurrence of the undesired behavior.
3. The counselor and the child set mutually acceptable goals.
4. Specific counseling techniques and methods are selected for attaining the goals.
5. The counseling techniques are evaluated for observable and measurable change.
6. Step 4 is repeated if the selected counseling techniques are not effective. If the techniques prove effective, a maintenance plan is developed for maintaining the new behavior changes.

For example, Jerry completes no assignments in any of his school subjects. His grades are being lowered because of his unwillingness to complete these assignments. He is referred to the counselor.

Step 1. The counselor talks with Jerry about the problem. Jerry is not happy with his grades but still has trouble concentrating on completing his work. He would like to do better on these assignments and make better grades.

Step 2. A five-day period is set aside to determine the exact amount of work Jerry completes. The record verifies the teacher's report that Jerry does not complete any assignments, even though he starts about half of them.

Step 3. Jerry and the counselor agree that a good goal for a start would be to complete one assignment each day.

Step 4. For each assignment completed, Jerry will receive 10 points to be applied toward a total of 100 points, which can be exchanged for 30 minutes of free time during the school day.

Step 5. Evaluation of the contingency contract indicates that Jerry completed four assignments the first week, earning 40 points, and six assignments the second week, for a total of 100 points. He then received his 30 minutes of free time. The following week he earned 100 points and received a second 30 minutes of free time. He was also successful during week 3.

Step 6. The counselor and Jerry agree that it is not necessary to continue with the point system. Jerry's grades are improving and everyone seems happier—the teacher, Jerry, and his parents. As a maintenance procedure, Jerry agrees to check in with the counselor each Friday afternoon for reports on his completed assignments for the week, which he records on a pocket-sized scorecard. Of course, a good teaching procedure would be to continue to allow Jerry and his classmates to earn free time when they complete assigned work.

Self-management. An adaptation of the six-step method, the self-management plan is designed for children who are able to take more responsibility for their behavior. These plans also follow a step-by-step process: defining a problem in behavioral terms, collecting data on the problem, introducing a treatment program based on behavior principles, evaluating the effectiveness of the program, and appropriately changing the program if the plan is not working. The major difference between self-management and other procedures is that children assume major responsibility for carrying out their programs, including arranging their own contingencies or reinforcement when they have the skills to do so.

Steps in developing a self-management plan are as follows:

1. Choose an observable and measurable behavior you wish to change.
2. Record for at least one week (a) your target behavior, (b) the setting in which it occurs, (c) the antecedent events leading to the behavior, and (d) the consequences resulting from the behavior.
3. Set a goal you can achieve.
4. Change the setting and the antecedent events leading up to the target behavior.
5. Change the consequences that reinforce the target behavior.

6. Keep accurate records of your target behavior—your successes and failures.
7. Arrange a plan to maintain the goals you have reached.

Shaping. The basic operant technique of shaping is a general procedure designed to induce new behaviors by reinforcing behaviors that approximate the desired behavior. Each successive approximation of the behavior is reinforced until the desired behavior is obtained. To administer the technique, the counselor must know how to skillfully use (1) looking, (2) waiting, and (3) reinforcing. The counselor looks for the desired behavior, waits until it occurs, and reinforces it when it does occur. In essence, the counselor is catching the child in good behavior—a much more difficult task than catching the child in bad behavior.

Biofeedback. Biofeedback uses a machine to accomplish the three behaviors of looking, waiting, and reinforcing. Brain waves, muscle tension, body temperature, heart rate, and blood pressure can be monitored for small changes and fed back to the client by auditory and visual means. The more the child relaxes, the slower and lower the beeping sound on the monitor becomes. Biofeedback methods have been successful, for example, in teaching hyperactive children to relax. The equipment may provide feedback with electric trains and recorded music. Both stop when the child stops relaxing and restart when the child takes the first small step toward relaxing again.

Modeling. Modeling consists of exposing the child to one or more individuals, either in real life or in film or tape presentations, who exhibit behaviors to be adopted by the child. Counselors may be the models to demonstrate certain behaviors to the child, or peers of the child may be used.

Peers are an important part of a child's world, and their influence can be used quite effectively to help children change. Children usually imitate the behaviors of people they like. A model may be presented to the child through the use of TV, films, videotapes, or books. Other models include friends, classmates, adults, and the counselor.

For example, Charlene had mentioned a friend, Patty, a number of times during the counseling sessions. She indicated that she would like to be like Patty because Patty had a lot of friends, made good grades, and got along well with parents and teachers. The counselor asked Charlene to observe Patty's behaviors closely for one week and to write on an index card those she particularly liked and wanted to imitate. The next week Charlene brought back her list of six behaviors. The counselor and Charlene selected the most important one for Charlene (giving compliments) and began to work on that behavior. Role-playing and behavior rehearsal were included in the counseling to help Charlene learn the new behaviors. The observed behaviors were practiced and modified until they were appropriate for

Charlene. As the counseling progressed, Charlene continued to observe her model and to practice new behaviors until she became more like her idealized self.

Token economies.   Token economies are used on a group basis, as in a school classroom. The children earn tokens or points for certain target behaviors. These behaviors are classified as being either on task or socially appropriate. Tokens or points also may be lost for off-task and socially inappropriate behaviors. Children may periodically cash in tokens or points earned for such rewards as free time, game time, trinkets, sugarless candy, and the like.

Behavior-practice groups.   Behavior-practice groups have some advantages in counseling children. They provide a relatively safe setting in which the child can practice new behaviors before trying them out in real-life situations. These groups are also useful in supporting and reinforcing children as they attempt new behaviors and reach goals. Behavior-practice groups may focus on any of several behavior changes, including the following:

- weight loss
- study habits
- assertiveness training
- communication skills
- negative addictions such as drugs, alcohol, and smoking

In working with behavior-practice groups, the counselor needs to develop a lesson plan with behavioral objectives, instructional methods, reinforcement, and evaluation. A good lesson plan would maintain a balance among three teaching strategies: (1) tell me, (2) show me, and (3) let me try it. For example, a lesson plan in assertiveness training might have the following objective:

After ten weekly group meetings, each child in the group will have demonstrated in at least three real-life settings the ability to do the following:
1. make an effective complaint
2. give negative feedback
3. give positive feedback
4. make a reasonable request
5. say no to an unreasonable request

Role-Playing

Role-playing is a counseling technique not restricted to one theory and is used by many counseling professionals. Behavioral counselors often find that role-playing facilitates clients' progress in self-management programs; for example, it can help clients see their behaviors as others see them and obtain feedback about these behaviors. Role-playing can also provide practice for decision-making and exploring consequences.

Negative role-playing or rehearsal can be helpful in identifying what *not* to do. If children role-play negative behaviors and their consequences, it may help them evaluate objectively what is happening and the consequences of their behavior.

Role-playing to define a problem. Children often have trouble describing exactly what occurred in a particular situation, especially one involving interpersonal problems with parents, teachers, or peers. Moreover, they may be unable to see clearly how certain behaviors have evoked an unwanted response or consequence. For example, suppose Jerome tells the counselor that he and his mother are in constant conflict. She is unfair and never allows him to do *anything* he asks. Role-playing could provide some insight into what occurs when Jerome asks for permission.

Counselor: I'll be your mother, and you show me exactly how you ask your mother to allow you, for instance, to have a birthday party. Talk to me exactly as you would to your mother if you were to ask her for the party.

Jerome: Mom, you never let me do anything! You always say no to anything I want. I want a birthday party, and you'll be mean if you don't let me have one this year!

The counselor can now readily see that if a conflict already exists between mother and child, this demand will increase the conflict and is unlikely to get Jerome his birthday party.

Children having trouble with peers might be asked to describe what happened and then to role-play one or more persons in the incident. Verbal and nonverbal behaviors not adequately described in relating the incident often become more apparent when they are role-played.

Role reversal. When conflicts occur between children, adults frequently ask one child "How would you feel if he hit you like that (said that to you, bit you, and so on)?" The purpose of this admonition is to have the child empathize with the other. However, many cognitive theorists, especially Piaget, emphasize that young children up through the preoperational stage (11 years old) lack the cognitive development to be able to put themselves in another person's place. Because children understand better what they see, hear, or experience directly, role-playing other children's positions could promote a better understanding than a verbal admonition.

Counselor: Barbara, I understand from your sister that you hit her on the head quite often. Would you agree that this is what happens?

Barbara: Yeah, I can really make her move if I threaten to hit her good on the head!

Counselor: Would the two of you describe to me what happened
the last time you hit Judy? (The girls describe the incident.) Now
Barbara, I wonder if you would mind playing Judy and saying
and doing exactly what Judy did. I would like Judy to say and
do exactly what you did (remind the girls that hitting hard is not
allowed in the role playing because people are not for hitting).

The purpose of this role reversal is to help Barbara experience Judy's
feelings when Barbara hit her. It is hoped that Barbara will then want to
explore better methods of relating to Judy.

Role reversal can be effective when communication breaks down between parents and children, between teachers and children, between
peers, or between counselors and their clients. Each player can gain increased knowledge of the other's point of view.

Role-playing used as behavior rehearsal.   Most adults will rehearse a speech
before presenting it to an audience to refine the speech and ensure a
smooth presentation. Children, too, may feel more comfortable about trying a new behavior if they can practice it before actually facing the real
world.

Dave is a shy little boy who has no friends. In an effort to help Dave
make friends, the counselor may want to help him decide exactly how he
will approach another child and the things he will say to the child after the
opening "hello." To build confidence, the counselor could first role-play
another child and allow Dave to practice his new behaviors in a safe
atmosphere. When Dave feels secure in role-playing with the counselor,
another child can be involved in the role-play situation to help Dave gain
more realistic experiences in meeting other children.

Counseling Homework Assignments

Homework assignments may be given to children in counseling for a
variety of reasons. Homework can build continuity between sessions and
facilitate counseling by encouraging "work" on the child's problems between sessions. A homework assignment could be a commitment by the
child to keep a record of some particular feeling or behavior, to reduce or
stop a present behavior, or to try a new behavior. Homework assignments
provide the child with an opportunity to try out new or different behaviors
and discuss the consequences with the counselor. For example, after Dave
(in the preceding example) has rehearsed approaching a new person
within the counseling session, the counselor might ask him to approach
one new person during the coming week and try out this new behavior.
Dave could evaluate whether the new behavior was effective for him and
discuss the results with the counselor; if it was not effective, other methods
could be explored.

Assertiveness Training

There are children whose typical response to everyday interactions is withdrawal. Some of these children may have poor self-concepts and feelings of inferiority that inhibit them; others, having experienced negative consequences as a result of speaking out, are inhibited from doing so by their anxiety. Children who are withdrawn and passive need to be encouraged to recognize their rights as people as well as accept the rights of others.

Tim and Charles were close friends. However, Tim always took from Charles whatever he wanted or needed—toys, pencils, food, and so on. Charles responded passively, always allowing Tim to have his way. The counselor asked Charles to describe in detail the latest incident in which Tim had taken Charles's new bike, ridden it all afternoon, and brought it back scratched. The counselor encouraged Charles to formulate an assertive statement such as, "I want to ride my new bike. Would you go and get your bike to ride?" Charles and the counselor took several incidents from the past, and Charles was encouraged to state (1) his needs, and (2) what he would like to have happen in each situation. They then used behavior rehearsal to give Charles an opportunity to practice his assertiveness.

After several sessions, Charles made a commitment to try out his new response. He reported that he told Tim, "I want to use my Magic Markers now. Would you get your own?" and that it had worked. The counselor worked for several months on helping Charles learn how to become appropriately assertive. Each new situation was discussed and practiced in the counseling sessions before Charles actually tried it in daily living.

A word of caution is necessary to counselors teaching assertiveness to children. The adults in the child's life must be prepared for the child's new behavior. Parents who discipline children by authoritarian methods may not tolerate assertiveness on the part of their child. In order to avoid unpleasant consequences, the counselor will want to determine the effect of the child's behavioral change on the child's significant others or on the child's culture and environment before teaching the child this new skill.

Classical Techniques

Respondent behavior is associated with classical conditioning, in which learning occurs when a stimulus that already elicits a response (an unconditioned stimulus) is presented along with a neutral stimulus that elicits no response or a different response. With repeated pairings of the two stimuli, the neutral stimulus begins to elicit the same response as does the unconditioned stimulus. In the case of Pavlov's dogs, for example, the unconditioned stimulus of food was paired with the neutral stimulus of a bell. The response to the unconditioned stimulus was salivating. The neutral stimulus (the bell) became the conditioned stimulus, and the response to the conditioned stimulus became the conditioned response (salivating).

Systematic desensitization.   Systematic desensitization, developed by Wolpe (1958, 1969) from earlier work by Jacobsen (1938), is a procedure used to eliminate anxiety and fear. A response incompatible with anxiety, such as relaxation, is paired with first weak, then progressively stronger anxiety-provoking stimuli. The approach is based on the principles of counterconditioning. That is, if all skeletal muscles are deeply relaxed, it is impossible to experience anxiety at the same time.

A child may be experiencing anxiety related to specific stimulus situations such as taking tests, performing in front of a group, fear of high places, or fear of some animal. The first step is to develop a hierarchy of scenes related to the fear or phobia, with mildly aversive scenes at the bottom and progressively more aversive scenes at the top. The child is then taught the deep muscle-relaxation process and, while relaxed, is asked to visualize the various scenes in the hierarchy.

The relaxation exercises consist of successively tensing and relaxing 19 different muscle groups at six-second intervals until a high level of relaxation is achieved. The process is usually performed with the child in a recliner-type chair or stretched out on a soft rug. The child is asked to go as high as possible on the hierarchy without feeling anxiety. When the child feels anxiety, he or she signals the counselor by raising one finger, and the counselor reverts to a less anxiety provoking scene. Behavior practice facilitates the process. A child may successively practice giving a short speech in front of a mirror, with an audiotape recorder, with a videotape recorder, in front of a best friend, in front of a small group, and so on, until the child can give the speech in front of a class of 25 students. The child's stimulus hierarchy might look like this:

0. Lying in bed in your room just before going to sleep—describe your room
1. Thinking about speeches alone in your room one week before you give your speech
2. Discussing the upcoming speech a week before in class
3. Sitting in class while another student gives a speech one week before your speech
4. Writing your speech at home
5. Practicing your speech alone in room or in front of your friend
6. Getting dressed the morning of the speech
7. Eating breakfast and thinking about the speech before going to school
8. Walking to school on the day of your speech
9. Entering the classroom on the day of the speech
10. Waiting while another student gives a speech on the day of your presentation

11. Walking up before your classmates and looking at their faces
12. Presenting your speech before the class

The technique consists of asking the child to relax, imagine, relax, stop imagining, relax, and so on until, after repeated practice, the child learns to relax while visualizing each stage of the stimulus hierarchy.

Several relaxation exercises can be used with children. Following are two types of exercises frequently used.

1. Consciously "let go" of the various muscle groups, starting with your feet and moving to your legs, stomach, arms, neck, and head as you make yourself as comfortable as you can in the chair or lying down.
   a. Stop frowning; let forehead relax.
   b. Let hands, arms, and so on relax.
   c. Tighten six seconds, relax; tighten again six seconds, relax.
2. Form mental pictures.
   a. Picture yourself stretched out on a soft bed. Your legs are like concrete, sinking down in the mattress from their weight. Picture a friend coming into the room and trying to lift your concrete legs, but they are too heavy and your friend cannot do it. Repeat with arms, neck, and so on.
   b. Picture your body as a big puppet. Your hands are tied loosely to your wrists by strings. Your forearm is connected loosely by a string to your shoulder. Your feet and legs are also connected with a string. Your chin has dropped loosely against your chest. All strings are loose, your body is limp and just sprawled across the bed.
   c. Picture your body as consisting of a bunch of rubber balloons. Two air holes open in your feet and the air begins to escape from your legs. Your legs begin to collapse until they are flat rubber tubes. Next a hole is opened in your chest, and the air begins to escape until your entire body is lying flat on the bed. Continue with heads, arms, neck, and so on.
   d. Imagine the most relaxing, pleasant scene you can remember—a time when you felt really good and peaceful. If you remember fishing in a mountain stream, pay attention to the little things, such as quiet ripples on the water and leaves on the trees. What sounds were present? Did you hear the quiet rustling of the leaves? Is your relaxing place before an open fireplace with logs crackling, or is it the beach, with warm sun and breeze?

Continued practice will facilitate achievement of these images.

In summary, the technique of desensitization is based on a principle of learning referred to as *reciprocal inhibition*. That is, an organism cannot make two contradictory responses at the same time. If we assume that all responses are learned, they can be extinguished by relearning or reconditioning. Therefore, relaxation, being more rewarding than anxiety, can gradually replace anxiety as the response to the anxiety-evoking situation.

Wolpe (1989), attacking those who would practice cognitive therapy, made the point that if a habit has been acquired by learning, the logical approach is to treat it by a method based on learning principles. He wrote that the real difference between true behavior therapy and cognitive therapy is the cognitivists' failure to deny the possibility that some fears may be immediately triggered by a particular stimulus without the mediation of an idea of danger. Wolpe also criticized cognitive therapists for dispensing with the behavior analysis required for successful treatment of neurotic suffering.

Hypnosis.   A technique that incorporates deeper forms of relaxation, hypnosis has long been controversial; however, recent research indicates that it can be a useful tool for working with children. Children seem to be fascinated with the procedure and, therefore, are usually hypnotized more easily than are adults. Hypnotherapy has been used successfully with children experiencing anxiety, high blood pressure, asthma, and psychosomatic pain and to overcome such habits as nail biting, thumb sucking, tics, insomnia, and sleepwalking.

The danger of hypnotherapy, of course, comes when untrained persons attempt to use the procedure. Counselors may wish to investigate the possibility and availability of training in this area. Hypnotherapy appears to be a highly effective counseling tool for working with repressed conflicts, including memories of child sexual abuse.

Reactive or internal inhibition.   Reactive or internal inhibition, also referred to as *flooding,* is a process by which an anxiety-evoking stimulus is presented continuously, leading to fatigue and eventual unlearning of the undesirable response. When you were told to get back on your bike after a crash, you were being exposed to the flooding technique. Another application might involve taking a child with a fear of riding in cars on a four-hour trip. The initial response would be high anxiety or panic, which would, after a while, wear itself out.

Counterconditioning.   In counterconditioning, a stronger pleasant stimulus is paired with a weaker aversive stimulus as a procedure for overcoming the anxiety the aversive stimulus evokes. For example, a child may be given his or her favorite candy while sitting in the classroom. If the candy is sufficiently rewarding to the child, the anxiety evoked by the classroom should be diminished.

Aversive conditioning.   Aversive conditioning is the application of an aversive or noxious stimulus, such as a rubber-band snap on the wrist, when a maladaptive response or behavior occurs. For example, children could wear rubber bands around their wrists and snap them each time they found themselves daydreaming instead of listening to the teacher. When using the technique, it is recommended that opportunity be provided for helpful behavior to occur and be reinforced.

The following diagrams represent each of the four classical conditioning methods presented:

Key: ⊕ pleasant stimulus; ⊖ aversive stimulus

1. Desensitization

⊝⊝⊝ ⊖ ⊖ ⊖ ⊖ ⊖, where ⊖ is giving a speech.

The aversive stimulus is handled in small steps by visualization/ relaxation and by practice until increasingly larger steps can be handled.

2. Internal inhibition (flooding)

⊖ ⊖ ⊖ ⊖ ⊖ ⊖ ⊖ ⊖ ⊖ ⊖, where ⊖ is getting back on the bike after falling off.

The aversive stimulus is continually repeated until the fear response wears itself out.

3. Counterconditioning

⊕ and ⊖, where ⊕ is a candy bar and ⊖ is going to school.

The larger pleasant stimulus overcomes the anxiety or fear evoked by the smaller aversive stimulus.

4. Aversive conditioning

⊖ and ⊕, where ⊖ is a snap of a rubber band on the wrist and ⊕ is daydreaming during class.

The more painful stimulus overcomes the smaller reward gained from daydreaming in class.

CASE STUDY

Identification of the Problem

Sue is a 9-year-old in the fourth grade. She has exhibited some behavior problems in her classroom. She does not complete her classroom assignments, tells lies about her work and about things she does at home and at school, and is reported to be out of her seat constantly.

Individual and Background Information

Academic.   Sue has an above-average IQ. She is an excellent reader and has the ability to do any fourth-grade assignment.

Family.   Sue is an only child. Sue's parents are in their 30s. Sue comes from an upper-middle-class family; her father and mother manage their own business.

Social.   Sue seems to get along relatively well with the other children but has only one close friend, Marie. Sue has been caught telling lies by the other children, and they tell her they do not like her lies. She brings money and trinkets to share with Marie and even lets her wear her nice coats, sweaters, and jewelry. Sue has no other children to play with and is mostly around adults who let her have her own way.

Counseling Method

The counselor in this case used a behavioral-counseling technique to help Sue evaluate her behavior problems and to teach her to counsel herself. When using this method, a counselor has to determine carefully just how much right one has to influence the client's choices in modifying behavior. The criteria for determining when to use behavioral counseling are based on the frequency of the maladaptive behavior and the degree to which the behavior hinders the child's healthy development and that of the others in the class.

In this case, the counselor used the following steps:

1. Established a warm, talking relationship.
2. Wrote out the problems on paper.
3. Listed rewards and consequences of the plans.
4. Obtained a commitment from the client on the plan of action that would most likely help.
5. Used a behavior contract with positive reinforcement in the form of a social reward (praise) for desirable behavior and token reinforcement (points to exchange for fun-time activities). Positive reinforcers were withdrawn (by loss of points) when undesirable behavior occurred.
6. Drew up plans for a behavior contract. These plans were discussed with, agreed upon, and signed by the client, counselor, teacher, and parents because the child was exhibiting some of the undesirable behavior at home by not completing assigned tasks and telling her parents lies.

Transcript

Counselor: Sue, your teacher sent you to me because you seem to be having some problems in class. Would you like to tell me what kind of problems you seem to be having? I'll write them down in a list so we can see what could be done to help you here and at home.

Sue: I just can't seem to get my work done or turned in on time.

Counselor: How do you stop yourself from doing this?

Sue: I just can't seem to be able to sit still long enough to finish, and then time is always up before I finish.

Counselor: Who else is affected by your getting out of your seat?

Sue: I guess I'm keeping the others from working when I go to their seats, and it bothers my teacher because she stops what she is doing and tells me to sit down and get busy.

Counselor: What happens when you don't finish your work?

Sue: Well, nothing really happens, except I try to get out of being fussed at and being kept in during play period for not doing my work.

Counselor: What do you mean, Sue?

Sue: I make up stories about I can't find my paper or somebody took it when I really hadn't even started it, or I hide what I have started in my desk or notebook and take it home and do it and then turn it in the next day and say I found it.

Counselor: What do you tell your mom and dad about your work for the day when they ask you?

Sue: Well, I tell a story to them, too. I tell them I did all my work, and usually the same things I tell the teacher I tell them, too.

Counselor: How do you feel about telling untrue stories?

Sue: I don't really feel good about it, but I want Mom and Dad to be proud of me and I really do want to do my work, but I just can't seem to do it, so I just tell a story.

Counselor: OK, Sue, you say you want to change, so let's look at the list of things you want to change and see what you and I can work out together.

Sue: OK, I'd like that.

Counselor: Let me read your contract terms to you. If you think there is anything you can't live with, we'll change it until we get it the way we think will help you the most. This contract tells you what will happen when you are able to finish your work. Your teacher, your mom and dad, you, and I will all sign it to show you we are all willing to help you live up to the terms. Will you go over it with your mother and father and see if there is anything that needs to be changed?

Sue: I think it's OK just the way it is.

Counselor: OK, you and I will sign first, and I will send copies to your teacher and your parents to sign. We will try this for a week, and then you and I will meet at the same time next week to see how you are doing and if any changes need to be made.

Sue: OK.

Contract for Behavior and Learning

Positive Behaviors: *Points*

1. Bringing needed materials to class   5
2. Working on class or home assignment until finished   5
3. Staying in seat   5
4. Extra credit (reading SRA or laminated task sheets)   1, 2, 3, 4, 5

You may exchange points earned for positive behavior for time to do "fun" activities.

Fun Activities: *Points*

1. Writing on the small chalkboards   15
2. Playing Phonic Rummy   15
3. Playing with the tray puzzles   15
4. Getting to be the library aide for a day   15
5. Getting to use the cyclo-teacher   15
6. Playing Old Maid with classmates   10
7. Using the headphone and tape recorder to hear a story from   15
   tapes
8. Using clay, finger paints, and other art supplies   10

I, _____, agree to abide by the terms set forth in this contract. It is my understanding that my points earned will depend on my classroom work and behavior.

_____
Signature

We, your teacher, your parents, and your counselor, agree to abide by the conditions specified in the contract. It is our understanding that we will assist you in any way we can with your tasks and behavioral problems.

_____
Teacher

_____
Parents

_____
Counselor

Behavioral counseling helps individuals look at what they are doing and what happens when they do it. The contract helps children try different behaviors to see which ones will work for them. Parents are encouraged to adhere to the terms of the contract and to positively reinforce all desirable behaviors at home. If the child continues to receive positive reinforcement for socially desirable and classroom-adaptive behavior, a self-reinforcement system will be implemented gradually to help the child develop a sense of intrinsic reinforcement.

RESEARCH AND REACTIONS

Behavioral counselors have more supporting data available than counselors of any other school of counseling. As noted previously, behavioral counselors must collect accurate data if their procedures are to operate with maximum efficiency. Therefore, behavioral counselors have done a thorough job of validating their claims of success.

The purpose of behavioral counseling is to change the client's overt and covert responses (cognitions, emotions, physiological states). Bandura (1974) reacted to the oft-repeated dictum, "Change contingencies and you change behavior," by adding the reciprocal side: "Change behavior and you change the contingencies . . . since in everyday life this two-way control operates concurrently" (p. 866). Behavioral counselors work with behavior that is objective and measurable. Behavioral-counseling methods, not confined to one stimulus/response theory of learning, are derived from a variety of learning principles.

London (1972) declared that the distinguishing features of behavioral counseling include the functional analysis of behavior and the development of the necessary technology to bring about change. Thus, behavioral counseling is the application of specified procedures derived from experimental research to benefit an individual, a group, an institution, or an environmental setting.

Supporting research includes studies emphasizing a number of behavioral-counseling methods.

Contingency Management

Ayllon and Azrin (1965) demonstrated that tokens, when delivered contingent on specific behaviors, could have profound effects on the behavior of institutionalized psychotics. Many other applications have also been demonstrated (see Rimm & Masters, 1974).

The results of a study by Blechman, Kotanchik, and Taylor (1981) indicate that school-based contingency contracts written by families are helpful in inspiring inconsistent students to become more consistent in classroom performance, thus achieving the primary aims of home/school collaboration: better work and a more self-confident child.

Positive Reinforcement and Shaping

Harrop and McCann (1984) showed that shaping can improve the performance of third-year students in creative writing using the variables of fluency, elaboration, and flexibility. The skills were explained and shaped through the awarding of points and positive teacher comments.

Chirico (1985) describes three guidance programs in Providence, Rhode Island, that have been successful in building self-esteem and decreasing problem behavior and poor school attitudes. The programs included behavior management in addition to student-of-the-week and group guidance/puppetry programs.

Rosen and Rosen (1983), using stimulus control with a 7-year-old male, successfully extinguished his chronic stealing. The child's items were marked with green circles and checked at 15-minute intervals. Possession of marked items was reinforced, while possession of unmarked items (stolen goods) was punished. Points earned were usable at the classroom store.

Darveaux (1984) found that use of a good-behavior game plus merit points was effective in improving the behavior and motivation of two second-grade boys who were labeled as high risk for placement in a behaviorally impaired program. Using a two-team approach, with one boy on each team, the teacher recorded marks on the board when any team member violated a rule. Merit points were awarded for assignment completion and positive classroom participation. Merit points could be used to eliminate the "bad" marks on the board.

Positive Reinforcement

Holden, Lavigne, and Cameron (1990), assessing the impact on families from different socioeconomic levels of a parent/child training program that employed positive reinforcement (Wahler, Winkel, Peterson, & Morrison, 1965), found that program dropouts and difficulty in program completion occurred primarily in families having a greater number of problems, families from a lower socioeconomic level, and families from minority populations. One could conclude that parent training that focuses on "catching" children in cooperative behavior might need some adjustments to meet the needs of such families.

Punishment and Response Cost

Little and Kelley (1989), studying the effects of response cost procedures for reducing children's noncompliance with parental instructions, found removal of reinforcers to be effective.

Abramowitz and O'Leary (1990), in a study on delayed punishment, reported that immediate reprimands were superior to both delayed reprimands and a combination of immediate and delayed reprimands in reducing interactive off-task behavior by hyperactive children in Grades 1 and 2.

Stratton (1989), in an attempt to assess consumer satisfaction with three cost-effective parent-training programs for children with conduct problems, found that parents favored the "Time Out" program over both the "Ignore and Play" and the "Rewards and Commands" programs.

Whelan and Houts (1990), in a study on the effects of an hourly waking schedule on primary enuretic children with full-spectrum home training (FSHT), reported that the waking schedule did not shorten the time required to achieve success. FSHT requires the child to change bed linens, clean urine-alarm pads, remake the bed, and reset the alarm after each wetting. The child receives prearranged monetary rewards for success in postponing urination. Following 14 dry days, overlearning starts by having the child drink 16 ounces of water before bedtime. Success is defined as 14 dry nights.

Gumaer (1990), applying similar response cost procedures with positive reinforcement for the treatment of childhood encopresis, successfully treated the problem with a response cost contract. Briefly, punishment included washing dirty clothes, bathing immediately after soiling, doing extra chores, or losing privileges. Positive reinforcement included spending time in favorite activities with parents or receiving a toy or money.

Extinction

Williams (1959) demonstrated that several disruptive behaviors could be reduced with extinction. These behaviors included crying, tantrums, food throwing, and food spilling.

Richman, Douglas, Hunt, Lansdown, and Levere (1985) reported a 77 percent success rate in treating sleep disorders in children ages 1 to 5. The specific behavior techniques used included extinction, positive reinforcement, and consistent parental behaviors.

France and Hudson (1990) found similar success in using extinction to treat sleep disorders in children aged 20 months to 8 years. Basically, parents consistently ignored their children's crying during a four-week treatment period. Children with health problems that could cause sleep disturbances were excluded from the study.

Modeling

Lazarus (1966) compared the effectiveness of three treatments: behavior rehearsals, reflection/interpretation, and advice-giving. Behavior rehearsal included modeling by the therapist, practice by the client, and relaxation induction at the first sign of anxiety. He found that 92 percent of the behavior-rehearsal subjects showed improvement, compared with 44 percent and 32 percent improvement rates, respectively, for the other two groups.

Epstein and Borduin (1984) studied the effect of a children's feedback game with reinforcement on increasing the skill and frequency of giving and receiving positive and negative feedback to one another in a group therapy setting. Results of the study were positive and were maintained through practice and modeling of the group leader's behavior.

Barlow, Hay, and Hay (1981), employing covert modeling procedures in the treatment of a 10-year-old boy with gender-identity confusion, corrected target behavior in five areas. These behaviors were maintained throughout the six-month follow-up and were generalized to the home environment.

Self-Management and Behavior Skills Training

Goldiamond (1965) demonstrated the effectiveness of several self-control strategies for studying and marital difficulties, among other problems.

Genshaft (1982) used cognitive behavior therapy effectively to reduce math anxiety in seventh-grade girls. The three groups included in the study were a tutoring group, a tutoring group with training in self-instruction, and a control group. The group receiving self-instructional training was the only one that showed a significant improvement in computations and reported improved attitudes toward math.

Christie, Hiss, and Lozanoff (1984) found self-recording beneficial in changing the classroom behavior of hyperactive children. The teacher was able to decrease inattentiveness and other unacceptable forms of behavior by having children record their own behavior at varying time intervals convenient for the teacher.

Andrews and Feyer (1985) found behavioral therapy effective in treating stuttering behavior, as demonstrated in both posttreatment and 13-month follow-up evaluations. Clients maintained gains in fluency, rate, and positive personal feelings about their progress.

Kane and Kendall (1989), working with children having anxiety disorders, found a variety of behavioral and cognitive interventions effective in reducing anxiety. The children were given 16 to 20 one-hour treatments that included modeling, role-play, relaxation training, and coping strategies.

Mize and Ladd (1990), working with 4- and 5-year-old children who were experiencing mild peer rejection, were successful in training the children to perform useful social skills. Treatment included instruction, rehearsal, practice, and feedback. Hand puppets were used to model the target skills.

In a study on children's school-refusal behavior, Silverman and Kearney (1990) found that school refusal stemmed from four causes: fear, escape from social situations, attention-getting, and various types of positive reinforcement. The authors, in developing successful treatment programs for school refusal, made a case for basing treatment on the causes of the behavior (behavior analysis).

Kahn (1989), in researching a method for teaching self-management to children, reported that self-observation with an external feedback group outperformed a control group, an external feedback group, and a self-observation group. The dependent variable was staying on task during arithmetic classes.

Wurtele (1990), in a study designed to measure the effects on 4-year-old children of teaching safety skills to prevent sexual abuse, found no differences between the treatment and control groups on parent and teacher observation scales, children's attitudes toward their private parts, and a personal safety questionnaire. The positive finding from the study is that the program did not seem to have any negative effects on the children.

Wolfe, Gentile, and Wolfe (1989), studying the impact of sexual abuse on children, conducted behavior analyses on 72 children (ages 5 to 16) who had been referred for sexual abuse assessment. Sexually abused children were rated by their mothers as showing relatively high levels of internalizing and externalizing symptoms as well as high levels of posttraumatic stress disorder (PTSD) symptoms. However, the children did not report elevated levels of negative affect. Younger children showed more symptomology, were more distressed by sex-related situations, and were more likely to report stigmatization and anxiety.

Systematic Desensitization

Lang and Lazovik (1963) published the first controlled experiment that found greater reduction in the behavioral measure of snake avoidance for a desensitization group than for the no-treatment controls, who showed almost no change. Moreover, no evidence of symptom substitution appeared in a six-month follow-up.

Morris and Kratochwill (1985) reviewed the literature to find what behaviorally oriented fear-reduction methods were being used with children. They found systematic desensitization to be the most frequently used behavioral therapy. Variations of the method included contact desensitization, which combines elements of modeling and desensitization. Contact desensitization proved to be the most effective in the treatment of animal phobias. Morris and Kratochwill also encountered some use of self-controlled desensitization, which involves training children in developing coping skills. Contingency management, using positive reinforcement both alone and in combination with other operant procedures, was found effective, as was shaping, in decreasing fears and increasing approach behavior. Contingency-management procedures were most often used for social withdrawal, school phobia, and selective mutism. Modeling, in addition to being used for treating animal phobias, was also used for test anxiety and dental/surgical treatment. Self-control methods, under the labels of cognitive-behavior or rational-behavior therapy, involve the development of helpful thinking skills and were cited in both the behavioral and rational-emotive therapy literature as treatment methods for children's fears.

Fundudis (1986), in describing a case of anorexia nervosa in a preadolescent girl, found that a focused approach to treatment was likely to be more effective than a nonspecific or general-management approach. A combination of behavioral and cognitive-behavioral methods was used, including cognitive restructuring, environmental-stimulus control (for example, no exercising before completion of a group activity), and systematic desensitization for anxiety generated about the ingestion of food.

Aversive Control

Blakemore, Thorpe, Barker, Conway, and Lavin (1963) reduced transvestism by applying electric shock, which was administered while the client was putting on women's clothing.

Ashcraft, Jensen, Preator, and Peterson (1984) found that inappropriate touching in an autistic child can be reduced by overcorrection that is topographically related to and incompatible with appropriate behavior. The addition of question-asking to overcorrection pointed out the effectiveness of enhancing aversive techniques with alternate appropriate behavior.

Summary

We find the same eclectic theme running through the current literature on behavioral counseling that we find in all approaches to counseling. A balanced view of behavioral counseling can be found in Lazarus's article "Has Behavior Therapy Outlived Its Usefulness?" (1977). Lazarus suggests that behavioral-counseling methods by themselves are inadequate to treat the full range of human problems. He prefers a more eclectic approach such as his multimodal counseling, discussed elsewhere in this book. He does, however, see behavioral methods as valuable tools in the counselor's repertoire of methods.

Levine and Fasnacht's article "Token Rewards May Lead to Token Learning" (1974) makes the point that reinforcement methods may serve to extinguish desired behavior when the reward or token replaces any intrinsic reward a person might receive from engaging in the desired behavior. For example, if parents reward or reinforce a child's piano practicing, the message to the child may be that piano playing is not worth doing without pay and therefore is not worthwhile in itself.

Finally, Shapiro and Goldberg (1986) found that children prefer independent group contingencies over interdependent and dependent group contingencies. Independent group contingencies require the same response of all individuals in the group, but access to reinforcement is based only on each individual's response (for example, everyone scoring 90 percent gets a reward). Interdependent contingencies depend upon the collective performance of the group (for example, the entire group receives a reward if the group mean equals 90 percent or better). Dependent group contingencies are based on the performance of a selected member or selected members of the group (for example, if a paper drawn at random from a box containing all group members' test papers has a score of 90 percent or better, everyone receives a reward). Considerable evidence exists in the literature to support behavioral methods that use self-control, self-determination, and personal responsibility as motivators and reinforcers.

REFERENCES

Abramowitz, A., & O'Leary, S. (1990). Effectiveness of delayed punishment in an applied setting. *Behavior Therapy, 21,* 231–239.

Andrews, G., & Feyer, A. (1985). Does behavior therapy still work when the experimenters depart? An analysis of a behavioral treatment program for stuttering. *Behavior Modification, 9,* 443–457.

Ashcraft, P., Jensen, W., Preator, K., & Peterson, P. (1984). Overcorrection and alternate response training in the reduction of an autistic child's inappropriate touching. *School Psychology Review, 13,* 107–110.

Ayllon, T., & Azrin, N. (1965). The measurement and reinforcement of behavior of psychotics. *Journal of the Experimental Analysis of Behavior, 8,* 357–383.

Bandura, A. (1974). Behavior therapy and the models of man. *American Psychologist, 29,* 859–869.

Barlow, D., Hay, L., & Hay, W. (1981). Using covert modeling in a boy with gender identity confusion. *Journal of Consulting and Clinical Psychology, 49,* 388–394.

Blakemore, C., Thorpe, J., Barker, J., Conway, C., & Lavin, N. (1963). The application of paradic aversion conditioning in a case of transvestism. *Behavior Research and Therapy, 1,* 29–34.

Blechman, E., Kotanchik, N., & Taylor, C. (1981). Families and schools together: Early behavioral intervention with high risk children. *Behavior Therapy, 12,* 308–319.

Chirico, J. (1985). Three guidance programs in Providence, Rhode Island. *The School Counselor, 32,* 388–391.

Christie, D., Hiss, M., & Lozanoff, B. (1984). Modification of inattentive classroom behavior: Hyperactive children's use of self-recording with teacher guidance. *Behavior Modification, 8,* 391–406.

Darveaux, D. (1984). The good behavior game plus merit: Controlling disruptive behavior and improving student motivation. *School Psychology Review, 14,* 84–93.

Epstein, R. (Ed.). (1980). *Skinner for the classroom.* Champaign, IL: Research Press.

Epstein, Y., & Borduin, C. (1984). The children's feedback game: An approach for modifying disruptive group behavior. *American Journal of Psychotherapy, 1,* 63–71.

Ferster, C., & Skinner, B. F. (1957). *Schedules of reinforcement.* New York: Appleton-Century-Crofts.

France, K. G., & Hudson, S. (1990). Behavior management in infant sleep disturbance. *Journal of Applied Behavior Analysis, 23*(1), 91–98.

Fundudis, T. (1986). Anorexia nervosa in a pre-adolescent girl: A multimodal behavior therapy approach. *Journal of Child Psychology and Psychiatry, 27,* 261–273.

Genshaft, J. (1982). The use of cognitive behavior therapy for reducing math anxiety. *School Psychology Review, 11,* 32–34.

Goldiamond, I. (1965). Self-control procedures in personal behavior patterns. *Psychological Reports, 17,* 851–868.

Gumaer, J. (1990). Multimodel counseling of childhood encopresis: A case example. *The School Counselor, 38,* 58–64.

Harrop, A., & McCann, C. (1984). Modifying creative writing in the classroom. *British Journal of Educational Psychology, 54,* 62–72.

Holden, G., Lavigne, V., & Cameron, A. (1990). Probing the continuum of effectiveness in parent training: Characteristics of parents and pre-schoolers. *Journal of Clinical Child Psychology, 19,* 2–8.

Jacobsen, E. (1938). *Progressive relaxation.* Chicago: University of Chicago Press.

Kahn, W. (1989). Teaching self-management to children. *Elementary School Guidance and Counseling, 24,* 37–46.

Kane, M., & Kendall, P. (1989). Anxiety disorders in children: A multiple-base-line evaluation of a cognitive-behavioral treatment. *Behavior Therapy, 20,* 499–508.

Krumboltz, J. (1966). Behavioral goals for counseling. *Journal of Counseling Psychology, 13,* 153–159.

Krumboltz, J., & Hosford, R. (1967). Behavioral counseling in the elementary school. *Elementary School Guidance and Counseling, 1,* 27–40.

Lang, P., & Lazovik, A. (1963). Experimental desensitization of a phobia. *Journal of Abnormal and Social Psychology, 66,* 519–525.

Lazarus, A. (1966). Behavioral rehearsal vs. nondirective therapy vs. advice in effective behavior change. *Behavior Research and Therapy, 4,* 209–212.

Lazarus, A. (1977). Has behavior therapy outlived its usefulness? *American Psychologist, 32,* 550–554.

Levine, F., & Fasnacht, G. (1974). Token rewards may lead to token learning. *American Psychologist, 29,* 816–820.

Little, L., & Kelley, M. (1989). The efficacy of response cost procedures for reducing children's noncompliance to parental instructions. *Behavior Therapy, 20,* 525–534.

London, P. (1972). The end of ideology in behavior modification. *American Psychologist, 27,* 913–926.

Maslow, A. (1970). *Motivation and personality* (2nd ed.). New York: Harper & Row.

Mize, J., & Ladd, G. (1990). A cognitive-social learning approach to social skill training with low status pre-school children. *Developmental Psychology, 26,* 388–397.

Morris, R., & Kratochwill, T. (1985). Behavioral treatment of children's fears and phobias: A review. *School Psychology Review, 14,* 84–93.

Richman, N., Douglas, J., Hunt, H., Lansdown, R., & Levere, R. (1985). Behavioral methods in the treatment of sleep disorders: A pilot study. *Journal of Child Psychology and Psychiatry, 26,* 581–590.

Rimm, D., & Masters, J. (1974). *Behavior therapy: Techniques and empirical findings.* New York: Academic Press.

Rosen, H., & Rosen, L. (1983). Elementary stealing: Use of stimulus control with an elementary student. *Behavior Modification, 7,* 56–63.

Shapiro, E., & Goldberg, R. (1986). A comparison of group contingencies for increasing spelling performance among sixth grade students. *School Psychology Review, 15,* 546–557.

Silverman, W., & Kearney, C. (1990). A preliminary analysis of a functional model of assessment and treatment for school refusal behavior. *Behavior Modification, 14,* 340–363.

Skinner, B. F. (1938). *The behavior of organisms.* New York: Appleton-Century-Crofts.

Skinner, B. F. (1948). *Walden two.* New York: Macmillan.

Skinner, B. F. (1953). *Science and human behavior.* New York: Macmillan.

Skinner, B. F. (1957). *Verbal behavior.* Englewood Cliffs, NJ: Prentice-Hall.

Skinner, B. F. (1968). *The technology of teaching.* Englewood Cliffs, NJ: Prentice-Hall.

Skinner, B. F. (1971). *Beyond freedom and dignity.* New York: Knopf.

Skinner, B. F. (1976a). *About behaviorism.* New York: Random House.

Skinner, B. F. (1976b). *Particulars of my life.* New York: Beekman.

Skinner, B. F. (1978). *Reflections on behaviorism and society.* Englewood Cliffs, NJ: Prentice-Hall.

Skinner, B. F. (1979). *The shaping of a behaviorist: Part II of an autobiography.* New York: Knopf.

Skinner, B. F. (1983). *A matter of consequences: Part III of an autobiography.* New York: Knopf.

Skinner, B. F. (1987). *Upon further reflection.* Englewood Cliffs, NJ: Prentice-Hall.

Skinner, B. F. (1990a). Can psychology be a science of mind? *American Psychologist, 45,* 1206–1210.

Skinner, B. F. (1990b, August). *Cognitive science: The creationism of psychology.* Keynote address presented at the meeting of the American Psychological Association, Boston.

Stratton, C. (1989). Systematic comparison of consumer satisfaction of three cost-effective parent training programs for conduct problem children. *Behavior Therapy, 20,* 103–115.

Wahler, R., Winkel, G., Peterson, R., & Morrison, D. (1965). Mothers as behavior therapists for their own children. *Behavior Research and Therapy, 3,* 113–124.

Whelan, J., & Houts, A. (1990). Effects of a waking schedule on primary enuretic children treated with full spectrum home training. *Health Psychology, 9,* 164–176.

Williams, C. (1959). The elimination of tantrum behavior by extinction procedures. *Journal of Abnormal and Social Psychology, 59,* 269.

Wolfe, V., Gentile, C., & Wolfe, D. (1989). The impact of sexual abuse on children: A PTSD formulation. *Behavior Therapy, 20,* 215–228.

Wolpe, J. (1958). *Psychotherapy by reciprocal inhibition.* Stanford, CA: Stanford University Press.

Wolpe, J. (1969). *The practice of behavior therapy.* New York: Pergamon Press.

Wolpe, J. (1989). The derailment of behavior therapy: A tale of conceptual misdirection. *Journal of Behavior Therapy and Experimental Psychiatry, 20,* 3–15.

Wurtele, S. (1990). Teaching personal safety skills to four-year-old children: A behavioral approach. *Behavior Therapy, 21,* 25–32.

CHAPTER 8

Psychodynamic Counseling

SIGMUND FREUD

Sigmund Freud was born in Freiberg, Moravia, in 1856 and died in London in 1939. However, he is considered to have belonged to Vienna, where he lived and worked for nearly 80 years. Freud was the first-born of eight children by his father's second wife. There were two sons, 20-odd years older than Freud, by his father's first wife.

Freud graduated from the gymnasium at 17, and, in 1873, entered the medical school at the University of Vienna. He became deeply involved in neurological research and did not finish his M.D. degree for eight years. Never intending to practice medicine because he wanted to be a scientist, Freud devoted his next 15 years to investigations of the nervous system (Hall, 1954). However, the salary of a scientific researcher was inadequate to support a wife and six children. In addition, the anti-Semitism prevalent in Vienna during this period prevented Freud from achieving university advancement. Consequently, Freud was forced to take up the practice of medicine.

Freud decided to specialize in the treatment of nervous disorders. At the time, not much was known about this particular branch of medicine, and Freud spent considerable time learning the techniques associated with treatment of "aberrations of the mind." First, he spent a year in France learning about Jean Charcot's use of hypnosis in the treatment of hysteria (Stone, 1971). Freud (1925/1963) was dissatisfied with hypnosis because he thought its effects were only temporary and did not get at the center of the problem. Freud then studied with Joseph Breuer, learning the benefits of the catharsis or "talking-out-your-problems" form of therapy.

Noticing that his patients' physical symptoms seemed to have a mental base, Freud began to probe deeper and deeper into the minds of his patients. "His probing revealed dynamic forces at work which were responsible for creating the abnormal symptoms that he was called upon to treat. Gradually there began to take shape in Freud's mind the idea that most of these forces were unconscious" (Hall, 1954, p. 15). According to

Stone (1971), this finding was probably the turning point in Freud's career. To substantiate some of his ideas, Freud decided to undertake an intensive analysis of his own unconscious forces in order to check on the material he had gathered from his patients. "On the basis of the knowledge he gained from his patients and from himself he began to lay the foundations for a theory of personality" (Hall, 1954, p. 17).

After a period of being shunned by most doctors and scholars, as often happens to those with new and revolutionary ideas, Freud was accepted as a genius in the field of counseling. Many influential scientists, including Carl Jung, Alfred Adler, Ernest Jones, and Wilhelm Stekel, recognized Freud's theory as a major breakthrough in the field of psychology. However, though Freud's academic career with the University of Vienna began in 1883, it was not until 1920 that this institution saw fit to confer on him the rank of full professor. Freud's recognition by academic psychology came in 1909, when he was invited by G. Stanley Hall to give a series of lectures at Clark University in Worcester, Massachusetts.

Freud's writing career spanned 63 years, during which time he produced more than 600 publications. His collected works have been published in 24 volumes, under the title *The Standard Edition of the Complete Psychological Works of Sigmund Freud* (1953–1964). Among his more famous works are *The Interpretation of Dreams* (1900) and *The Psychopathology of Everyday Life* (1901).

Freud seemed never to think his work was finished. "As new evidence came to him from his patients and his colleagues, he expanded and revised his basic theories" (Hall, 1954, p. 17). As an example of his flexibility and capability, at 70 Freud completely altered a number of his fundamental views—he revamped motivation theory, reversed the theory of anxiety, and developed a new model of personality based on id, ego, and superego.

Freud developed his psychoanalytic model of people over five decades of observing and writing. The major principles were based on the clinical study of individual patients undergoing treatment for their problems. Free association became Freud's preferred procedure after he discarded hypnosis.

Psychoanalysis includes theories about the development and organization of the mind, the instinctual drives, the influences of the external environment, the importance of the family, and the attitudes of society. As useful as psychoanalysis is as a therapeutic tool, its impact and value reach far beyond its medical application. It is the only comprehensive theory of human psychology. Psychoanalysis has proven increasingly helpful to parents and teachers in the upbringing and education of children.

Although through the years psychoanalytic theory has been modified in some areas, its basic concepts still remain, and even today, it is recognized as very influential in counseling theory. Almost all counseling theories have extracted some of their basic premises from the psychoanalytic method. This alone shows the influence and durability of the theory.

THE NATURE OF PEOPLE

The concept of human nature in psychoanalytic theory found its basis in psychic determinism and unconscious mental processes. Psychic determinism implies that mental life is a continuous manifestation of cause-related relationships. Mental processes are considered the causative factors in the nature of human behavior. Mental activity and even physical activity may be kept below the conscious level. Freud (1933/1965b) noted that conflict, repression, and anxiety often go together, with the result that people often do not understand their feelings, thoughts, actions, or behaviors. Analysis on the basis of unconscious determinism is the base of psychoanalytic counseling. Counseling leading to catharsis will then lead to confronting the unconscious mind or to a way of learning to cope, understand, and grow in mental development.

Freud viewed people as basically evil and victims of instincts that must be balanced or reconciled with social forces to provide a structure in which human beings can function. To achieve balance, people need a deep understanding of the forces that motivate them to action. According to Freud, people operate as energy systems, distributing psychic energy to the id, ego, and superego. Human behavior is viewed as determined by this energy, by unconscious motives, and by instinctual and biological drives. Psychosexual events during the first five years of life are seen as critical to adult personality development.

Sugarman (1977), believing that Freud's concept of human nature is often misinterpreted, presents a contrasting view of Freudian theory in which a humanistic image of people is recognized in the following eight ideas:

1. People have a dual nature, biological and symbolic.
2. People are both individuals and related to others simultaneously.
3. People strive for goals and values.
4. One of the strongest human needs is to give meaning to life.
5. One's internal world, including the unconscious, is more important than overt behavior.
6. People are social creatures whose need for interpersonal relationships is supreme.
7. People are always evolving, always in process.
8. People have a certain amount of autonomy within the constraints of reality.

In summary, according to psychoanalytic theory, the basic concepts of human nature revolve around the notions of psychic determinism and unconscious mental processes. Psychic determinism simply implies that our mental function or mental life is a continuous logical manifestation of causative relationships. Nothing is random; nothing happens by chance. Though mental events may appear unrelated, they are actually closely interwoven and dependent upon preceding mental signals. Closely related to psychic determinism are unconscious mental processes, which exist as fundamental causative factors in the nature of human behavior. In essence, much of what goes on in our minds and hence our bodies is unknown, below the conscious level, so we often do not understand our feelings and/or actions. The existence of unconscious mental processes is the basis for much of what is involved in psychoanalytic counseling. Analysis leading to catharsis is employed to dredge up unconscious elements from within the recesses of the mind. By confronting these elements, the client can achieve growth and mental health.

THEORY OF COUNSELING

Freud's concepts of personality form the basis of a psychoanalytic counseling theory. The principal concepts in Freudian theory can be grouped under three topic headings: structural, dynamic, and developmental. The structural concepts are id, ego, and superego. The dynamic concepts are instinct, cathexis, anticathexis, and anxiety. The developmental concepts are defense mechanisms and psychosexual stages.

Structural Concepts

Freud believed human behavior resulted from the interaction of three important parts of the personality: id, ego, and superego.

Id. The id contains our basic instinctual drives, including thirst, hunger, sex, and aggression. These drives can be constructive or destructive. Constructive, pleasure-seeking (sexual) drives provide the basic energy of life (libido). In Freud's system, anything pleasurable was labeled sexual. Destructive, aggressive drives tend toward self-destruction and death. Life instincts are opposed by death instincts. The id, working on the pleasure principle, exists to provide immediate gratification of any instinctual need, regardless of the consequences. The id is not capable of thought but can form, for example, mental pictures of hamburgers for a hungry person. The formation of such images and wishes is referred to as *fantasy* and *wish fulfillment* (the *primary process*).

Ego. Often called the "executive" of the personality, the ego strives to strike a balance between the needs of the id and the superego in conjunction with the reality of the external world and transforms the mental images formed by the id (the hamburgers, for example) into acceptable behavior (purchasing a hamburger). These reality-oriented, rational processes of the ego are referred to as the *secondary process*. The ego, operating under the *reality principle,* is in tune with environmental constraints and adjusts behavior to meet these constraints.

Superego.   Composed of two parts — the ego ideal (the ideal rather than the real) and the conscience (developed from the child's concepts of parents' and/or other influential individuals' moral inclination) — the superego is, in essence, a person's moral standard. Often thought of as the judicial branch of the personality, the superego can act to restrict, prohibit, and judge conscious actions. Unconsciously, the superego can also act, and the unconscious process of the superego will often lead to detrimental forms of human behavior.

Ideally the ego, superego, and id systems work together as a cooperative unit, helping people fulfill their basic needs and desires and carry on satisfying relationships with others and efficient transactions with the environment. When the three systems are at odds, the individual is dissatisfied with his or her self and the environment, and efficiency is reduced. Extreme disunity may be labeled as maladjustment.

Dynamic Concepts

Instinct.   An instinct is an inborn psychological representation, referred to as a *wish,* which stems from a physiological condition referred to as a *need.* For example, hunger is a need that leads to a wish for food. The wish becomes a motive for behavior. Life instincts serve to maintain the survival of the species. Hunger, thirst, and sex needs are served by life instincts.

Libido. Libido is the energy that permits life instincts to work.

Cathexis.   Cathexis refers to directing one's energy toward an object that will satisfy a need.

Anticathexis.   Anticathexis refers to the force the ego exerts to block or restrain impulses of the id. The reality principle or superego directs this action of the ego against the pleasure principle emanating from the id.

Anxiety.   Anxiety refers to a conscious state in which a painful emotional experience is produced by external or internal excitation — a welling up of autonomic nervous energy. Closely akin to fear, but more encompassing, is the anxiety that originates from internal as well as external causes. Freud believed there were three types of anxiety: reality, neurotic, and moral. Reality anxiety results from real threats from the environment. Neurotic anxiety results from the fear that our instinctual impulses from the id will overpower our ego controls and get us into trouble. Moral anxiety results from the guilt we feel when we fail to live up to our standards.

Developmental Concepts
Defense Mechanisms

Defense mechanisms are the measures the ego takes to protect itself against heavy pressure and anxiety. Clark (1991) defined defense mechanisms as unconscious distortions of reality that reduce painful affect and conflict through automatic, habitual responses. Defense mechanisms are specific, unconscious, adjustive efforts used to resolve conflict and provide relief from anxiety. Counselors are generally able to detect when their clients are using defense mechanisms. Borrowing from Clark, we have provided examples of how an underachieving child might express a preference or lifestyle built around one, two, or a combination of defense mechanisms.

Identification. Identification refers to the development of role models that people identify with or imitate. They may choose to imitate either a few traits of the model or the total person. Identification often occurs with the same-sex parent and may be born out of love or power. For example, "I love dad so much I want to be just like him," or, "If I can't beat him, I'll join him until I get big too." The underachieving child might say, "I know a high school student who dropped out and is making a lot of money. He says school is a waste of time."

Displacement. Displacement means redirecting energy from a primary object to a substitute when an instinct is blocked. For example, anger toward a parent may be directed toward a sibling or another object because of the fear of reprisal from the parent. Freud believed that human behavior is motivated by basic instincts. He thought that the rechanneling of energy from the sexual instinct into productive activity, which he called *sublimation,* was the major reason for the advancement of civilization. Aggressive sports are sublimations of destructive impulses, and creative activities are sublimations of sexual impulses.

The underachieving child might say, "The stuff we study is so boring I'll never make good grades." The child may be redirecting hostile feelings from the teacher to the subject matter.

Repression and suppression. *Repression* forces a dangerous memory, conflict, idea, or perception out of the conscious into the unconscious and places a "lid" on it to prevent the repressed material from resurfacing. In discussing repression, we must consider the concepts of unconscious, preconscious, and conscious. *Conscious* refers to the part of mental activity that we are fully aware of at any given time. *Preconscious* refers to thoughts and feelings that are not immediately available but that can be brought back to consciousness with effort. The concept of the *unconscious* is the foundation of psychoanalytic theory and practice. This concept holds that, in a part of the mind that we are not aware of, drives, desires, attitudes, motivations, and fantasies exist. They are very important because they are responsible for many of our conscious feelings, thoughts, attitudes, and actions, and they influence our relationships with others. However, in repression, the person unconsciously bars a painful thought from memory. *Suppression* is a conscious effort to do the same thing. An underachieving child might say, "I don't remember missing any homework assignments this six weeks."

Projection.   Projection consists of attributing one's own characteristics to others or to things in the external world. For instance, a teacher may find it uncomfortable to admit he doesn't like the children in his class, so instead he says the children don't like him. Thus, he projects his dislike for his students onto the students.

An underachieving child may say, "My teacher doesn't like me; he thinks I'm stupid."

Reaction formation.   Reaction formation refers to the development of attitudes or character traits exactly opposite to ones that have been repressed. Anxiety-producing impulses are replaced in the conscious by their opposites. For example, "I love booze" is replaced by "Liquor should be declared illegal." An underachieving child may say, "I don't want to be a nerd; nerds suck up to the teacher just to make good grades."

Rationalization.   Rationalization is an attempt to prove that one's behavior is justified and rational and is thus worthy of approval by oneself and others. When asked why they behaved in a certain manner, children may feel forced to think up logical excuses or reasons. An underachieving child may say, "I could finish my homework if my little brother would stop bothering me."

Denial.   Denial is a refusal to face unpleasant aspects of reality or to perceive anxiety-provoking stimuli. Children may deny the possibility of falling while climbing high trees. An underachieving child may say, "Things are going fine; my grades will be much higher this time." Counselors need to remember that denial is common in young children but is maladaptive for adolescents.

Fantasy.   Fantasy is a way of seeking gratification of needs and frustrated desires through the imagination. A fantasy or imagined world may be a more pleasant place than a child's real world. An underachieving child may say, "Just wait, one of these days I'll become a doctor and show that teacher. She'll be sorry she made fun of my bad test score."

Withdrawal.   Withdrawal means reducing ego involvement by becoming passive or learning to avoid being hurt; examples of withdrawn children include the shy child or school-phobic child. A withdrawn, underachieving child will probably not say much as he or she tries to avoid "risky" situations.

Intellectualization.   Intellectualization is the act of separating the normal affect, or feeling, from an unpleasant or hurtful situation. For example, the grief of a child whose dog has been hit by a car might be softened by the child's saying, "Our dog is really better off dead; he was feeble and going blind." An underachieving child may say, "I learn best from doing things outside school," or "I don't learn from the boring things we do at school."

Regression.   Regression is a retreat to earlier developmental stages that are less demanding than those of the present level. An older child may revert to a babyish behavior when a baby arrives in the family. An underachieving child may say, "All we do is work; recess and lunch should be longer."

Compensation.   Compensation means covering up a weakness by emphasizing some desirable trait or reducing frustration in one area of life by overgratification in another area. For example, the class clown may compensate for poor academic performance by engaging in attention-getting behavior. An underachiever may be an attention-getting clown of the first order or may overachieve in another area to compensate for low grades (for example, sports, hobbies, or gang activities).

Undoing.   Undoing is engaging in some form of atonement for immoral or bad behavior or for the desire to participate in such behavior. For instance, after breaking a lamp, a child may try to glue it back together. An underachieving child may say, "I get in a lot of arguments with my teacher, but I always try to do something to make up for it."

Acting out.   Acting out means reducing the anxiety aroused by forbidden desires by expressing them. The behavior of a revenge-seeking child is one example. An underachieving child may engage in violence, vandalism, or theft as a way of expressing hurt feelings that he or she has been forbidden to express.

Psychosexual Stages

Freud (1940/1949) viewed personality development as a succession of stages, each characterized by a dominant mode of achieving libidinal pleasure and by specific developmental tasks. How well one adjusts at each stage is the critical factor in development. Freud believed that personality characteristics are fairly well established by the age of 6. Gratification during each stage is important if the individual is not to become fixated at that level of development. The key to successful adjustment in each stage is how well parents help their child adjust to the stage and make the transition to the next stage. The difficulty with Freud's system comes when counselors emphasize the extremes rather than the normal range of behaviors. The trick seems to lie in maintaining a balance between extremes. The five developmental stages are oral, anal, phallic, latency, and genital.

Oral stage (birth–1 year).   This stage encompasses two substages: oral erotic and oral sadistic. The oral-erotic substage is characterized by the sucking reflex, which is necessary for survival. The child's main task in the oral-sadistic substage is to adjust to the weaning process and learn to chew food. The mouth is characterized as an erogenous zone because one obtains pleasure from sucking, eating, and biting. Adult behaviors, such as smoking, eating, and drinking, and the personality traits of gullibility, dependency (oral-erotic), and sarcasm (oral-sadistic) originate in the oral period.

Anal stage (1–3 years).   During this time, the membrane of the anal region presumably provides the major source of pleasurable stimulation. Two substages are also evident in this stage: anal expulsive and anal retentive. The major hurdle in this stage is the regulation of a natural function (bowel control). Toilet training requires that the child learn how to deal with postponing immediate gratification. Again, the manner in which the parents facilitate or impede the process will form the basis for a number of adult personality traits. Stubbornness, stinginess, and orderliness (anal-retentive) and generosity and messiness (anal-expulsive) are among adult traits associated with the anal stage.

Phallic stage (3–6 years).   Self-manipulation of the genitals provides the major source of pleasurable sensation. The Oedipus complex occurs during this stage. The female version is sometimes referred to as the Electra complex. Sexual and aggressive feelings and fantasies are associated with the genitals. Boys have sexual desires for their mothers and aggressive feelings toward their fathers; girls develop hostility toward their mothers and become sexually attracted to their fathers. Attitudes toward people of the same sex and the opposite sex are beginning to take shape during this period. Freud has been attacked for his ideas about castration complexes. Criticisms range from labeling his castration ideas ridiculous to calling them projections of his own fears. In any case, Freud believed that boys are afraid that their fathers will castrate them for loving their mothers. Girls' castration complexes take the form of penis envy; compensation for lacking a penis comes with having a baby.

Latency stage (7–13 years).   Sexual motivations presumably recede in importance during the latency period as the child becomes preoccupied with developmental skills and activities. Children generally concentrate on developing their friendships with people of the same sex. Sexual and aggressive impulses are relatively quiet during this phase. (As for aggression, Freud obviously never taught a group of children in this age group.)

Genital stage (12–14 years).   After puberty, the deepest feeling of pleasure presumably comes from heterosexual relations. The major task of this period is the development of relationships with members of the opposite sex. This can be a risky task involving rejection and fear of rejection. Once again, the ease with which this task can be accomplished will have tremendous impact on future heterosexual relationships.

Oral, anal, and phallic stages are classified as narcissistic because children derive pleasure from their own erogenous zones. During the genital stage, the focus of activity shifts to developing genuine relationships with others. The goal is for the young person to move from a pleasure-seeking, pain-avoiding, narcissistic child to a reality-oriented, socialized adult.

COUNSELING METHODS

The primary goal of counseling within a psychoanalytic frame of reference is to make the unconscious conscious. The techniques used are directed toward discovering repressed conflicts and bringing them into the client's conscious awareness. Once repressed material has been brought to the conscious level, it can be dealt with in rational ways using any number of methods discussed in this book. Several methods are used to uncover the unconscious. Detailed case histories are taken, with special attention given to the handling of conflict areas. Hypnosis, though rejected by Freud, is still used to assist in plumbing the unconscious. Analyses of resistance, transference, and dreams are frequently used methods, as are catharsis, free association, and interpretation. All these methods have the long-term goal of strengthening the ego. The three principal counseling methods discussed in this chapter are catharsis, free association, and interpretation.

Catharsis

Freud, along with Breuer, first discovered the benefits of catharsis through hypnosis. Freud found that if, under hypnosis, hysterical patients were able to verbalize an early precipitating causal event, the hysterical symptoms would disappear. Freud soon discarded hypnosis because he was not able to induce in everyone the deep hypnotic sleep that enabled the patient to regress to an early enough period to disclose the repressed event. Freud discovered that for many people the mere command to remember the origin of some hysterical symptom worked quite well. Unfortunately, many of his patients could not remember the origin of their symptoms even upon command. Freud thus decided that all people were aware of the cause of their illness but that for some reason certain people blocked this knowledge. Freud believed that unless this repressed traumatic infantile experience could be dredged up from the unconscious to the conscious, verbalized, and relived emotionally, the patient would not recover. Because not everyone had the ability to find this unconscious material, the analyst had to use more indirect means to gain access to the unconscious mind. Freud developed free association and interpretation to bring everyone to the emotional state of catharsis that was necessary for cure.

Free Association

In traditional psychoanalysis, the client lies on a couch with the analyst at his or her head so the client is not looking at the analyst. The analyst then orders the client to say whatever comes to mind. It is hoped that through this means the unconscious thoughts and conflicts will be given freedom to reach the conscious mind. A great struggle takes place within the client to keep from telling the analyst his or her innermost thoughts. This resistance, as it is termed by psychoanalysts, is something the analyst must constantly struggle against.

During the time the client is trying to associate freely, the analyst must remain patient, nonjudgmental, and insistent that the client continue. The analyst must also look for continuity of thoughts and feelings. Although it may appear at first glance that the client is rambling idly, psychoanalysts believe there is a rational pattern to this rambling. In order to correctly interpret what the client is saying, the analyst must pay attention to the affect, or feeling, behind the client's verbalization, noting the client's gestures, tone of voice, and general body language during free association. The analyst, at this point, offers some interpretations of the client's statements in the hope that doing so will open another door for free association.

Interpretation

Free association, in turn, leads to another important technique—interpretation. Three major areas of interpretation are dreams, parapraxia, and humor.

Interpretation of dreams.   To Freud, dreams were a means of expressing a wish fulfillment. In order to correctly interpret the power of the id, the analyst must learn about and interpret the client's dreams. According to Freud, there are three major types of dreams: those with meaningful, rational content (almost invariably found in children), those with material very different from waking events, and those with illogical, senseless episodes. According to Freud, all dreams center around a person's life and are under the person's psychic control. Every dream reveals an unfulfilled wish. In children's dreams, the wish is usually very obvious. As the individual matures, the wish, as exposed in the dream, becomes more distorted and disguised. Freud said that the initial conscious wish is fought by the ego and thus is pushed back to the unconscious mind; it brings itself back into the conscious mind by means of a dream.

Freud's method of dream interpretation was to allow the client to freely associate. Certain objects in dreams were universal symbols for Freud. For example, a car in someone's dreams usually represented analysis, the number 3 represented male genitals, jewel cases were vaginas, peaches were female breasts, woods were pubic hair, and dancing and riding were symbols for sexual intercourse.

Freud (1901/1952) believed every dream to be a confession and a by-product of repressed, anxiety-producing thoughts. Freud thought that many dreams were representations of unfulfilled sexual desires and that many were also expressions of guilt and self-punishment from the super-ego. Nightmares, the most terrifying of all human experiences, result from the desire for self-punishment. Because we consciously and subconsciously are aware of those things that we fear most, we put these things into our nightmares to punish ourselves.

Parapraxia.   Parapraxia refers to what are popularly called "Freudian slips." They are consciously excused as harmless mistakes, but they are one of the id's ways to push unconscious material through to the conscious. The analyst must be very aware of any slips of the tongue while dealing with a client. The Freudians also believe there are no such things as "mistakes" or items that are "misplaced." According to psychoanalytic thinking, there is an unconscious motivation for everything we do. If we cannot remember a person's name, there is a reason for it. If we cut a finger while peeling potatoes, there is a reason for it. The analyst must take all these unconscious mistakes and arrange them into a conscious pattern.

Humor.   Jokes, puns, and satire are all acceptable means for unconscious urges to gain access to the conscious. The things we laugh about tell us something about our repressed thoughts. One of the fascinations of humor, according to psychoanalytic theory, is that it simultaneously disguises and reveals repressed thoughts. Repressed thoughts, released by humor, usually generate from the id or superego. Because sexual thoughts are usually repressed, many jokes are sexually oriented; because aggressive thoughts are usually repressed, they are expressed in humor by way of satire and witticisms.

Again, the counselor must watch for patterns. What does the client think is funny? How does the client's sense of humor fit into a pattern from the unconscious? According to Freud, the dream guards against pain; humor, on the other hand, serves to acquire pleasure.

PLAY THERAPY AND THE EXPRESSIVE ARTS

The greatest problems in applying psychoanalytic techniques to counseling children are children's relatively undeveloped verbal skills and inadequate cognitive development. Traditionally, raising unresolved and unconscious conflicts from the past to consciousness is achieved by free association and dream analysis and interpretation. Children are relatively receptive to dream analysis, as long as it is kept in the realm of metaphor. In that way it can remain in the child's realm of make-believe and thus be more under control and less threatening. Resolution of dreams involving conflict is a sign of therapeutic progress and emotional growth.

The problem of free association is more difficult. Children seem unable or unwilling to free-associate verbally. It is now widely believed that nondirective free play, particularly that involving symbolic make-believe (using dolls as particular real people, a stick as a gun, and the like) is closely analogous to free association. The assumption is that children will translate their imagination into symbolic play action rather than words. Some counselors use play therapy as a necessary prelude to verbal psychodynamic counseling and not necessarily as therapy in itself.

Play Therapy

Play techniques should be a primary method for counseling with children younger than 12 because of the children's limited cognitive development and ability to verbalize their thoughts and feelings and because play is a natural mode of expression and communication for children. Play techniques can be valuable to the counselor in many phases of the counseling process:

1. Play can be a means for establishing rapport. A child who is anxious, resistant, or suspicious of adults will usually relax and begin to talk more freely when the counselor uses play media.

2. Play can help counselors understand children and their relationships and interactions. For example, puppets will often reveal the types of interactions that occur between adults and children or between children and their peers.

3. Play can help children reveal feelings they are unable to verbalize. Children who are asked to draw a picture or build something with toys such as building blocks or clay may reveal their thoughts and feelings in their play. Children are often asked to draw pictures of themselves to determine how they perceive themselves or to draw their families to see how they perceive themselves in relation to other family members.

4. Play can be used to constructively act out feelings of anxiety or tension. The child can be allowed to release anger or hostility through play media such as hammer and nails, soft foam bats, war toys, or physical activities such as football, baseball, volleyball, or running.

5. Play can be an effective method for teaching socialization skills. Children participating in a counselor-guided play session can test limits,

gain insight about their behavior, explore alternatives, and learn about consequences in a protected environment.

Counselors may wish to consider carefully their objectives or goals for the use of play and to structure the counseling session accordingly, or they may wish to allow the child to determine the structure of play sessions. Because each child is unique, counselors will want to consider each situation to decide if the objective of the play could be achieved more readily through counselor-directed play or if child-directed play would be more productive.

Proponents of play therapy differ on the question of limits. Some counselors think no limits should be imposed on the child in a playroom–limits will hamper expression and understanding. Others propose that only limits to safeguard the welfare of the child and counselor and to protect property should be employed. Still other counselors would place limits on time, space, and certain behaviors. When limits are imposed, they should be clearly defined and discussed with the child before play begins. If counselors include play techniques in regular talking counseling sessions without moving to a playroom, there may be no need for a discussion of limits.

When selecting play media, counselors will want to consider the child's age and needs and the purposes for which play therapy will be used. Dolls, dollhouses, puppets, clay, punching toys, blocks, planes, soldiers, tanks, trucks, hammers, soft balls, sand, Magic Markers, or crayons may be helpful for working with younger children. Games such as chess, checkers, or backgammon, electronic games, published games (Life, Monopoly, Twister), paper-and-pencil games (tic-tac-toe), drawing supplies (paper and Magic Markers, blackboard and chalk), or games that require the child to construct or solve problems may be more helpful for working with older children. Physical activities may be incorporated into counseling sessions or given as homework assignments.

The play media selected should meet the following objectives:

- facilitate the relationship between counselor and child;
- encourage expression of feelings or thoughts;
- aid the counselor in gaining insight into the child's world;
- provide an opportunity for the child to test reality; and
- provide an acceptable means for expression of unacceptable thoughts or feelings.

The counselor may choose to become involved in the play or simply to observe the child during the play. The counselor's skills of listening, observing, and detecting and reflecting feelings and thoughts are as important during play sessions as they are during regular counseling.

Bibliocounseling

Bibliocounseling, or reading and discussing books about situations and children similar to themselves, can help children in several ways. Children unable to verbalize their thoughts and feelings may find them expressed in books. From selected stories, children can learn alternative solutions to problems and new ways of behaving. By reading about others similar to themselves, children may not feel so alone or different.

In an article citing the benefits of bibliocounseling for abused children, Watson (1980) suggests that children may become psychologically and emotionally involved with characters they have read about. Vicarious experiences through books can be similar to the child's own thoughts, feelings, attitudes, behavior, or environment. Directed reading can lead to expression of feelings or problem solving. Watson lists the goals of bibliotherapy as: (1) teaching constructive and positive thinking; (2) encouraging free expression concerning problems; (3) helping people analyze their attitudes and behaviors; (4) looking at alternative solutions; (5) encouraging the client to find an adjustment to the problem not in conflict with society; and (6) allowing clients to see the similarity of their problems to those of others.

When using bibliocounseling with children, counselors will want to discuss the stories with the child. Discussion focused around characters' behaviors, feelings, thoughts, relationships, cause and effect, and consequences will be more effective than just asking the child to relate the story. Counselors can guide children to see the relationships and application of the story to their own lives.

Bibliocounseling is another means of educating children about certain areas of concern such as sex, physical disabilities, divorce, and death. It is assumed that once children have enough information about a problem, their attitudes and behaviors will change. The ideas and facts presented in books should be discussed with the children to clear up questions that arise from the reading. Suggested books for bibliocounseling with exceptional children or children with special concerns are listed at the end of Chapters 14 and 15.

Storytelling

We have found storytelling to be an excellent counseling technique to help children deal with feelings or behaviors they are not ready to admit and to help children see unrecognized consequences of their behavior. An example follows:

> Marcia was a very bright child and had a very vivid imagination. Her parents and teachers complained that they never knew when she was telling the truth, and her peers were beginning to reject her because of her stories.

The counselor was also having trouble knowing when Marcia was telling the truth. Marcia would tell the counselor of things that had happened that could be true, yet the counselor had doubts about their occurrence. During one session, the counselor related a story to Marcia about a girl named Mary who was about Marcia's age and very similar to Marcia. The counselor went on to tell how Mary told exaggerated stories to everyone to try to make friends and impress them; however, no one who knew her believed anything she said. One day, Mary saw someone robbing the house down the street, but when she ran for help no one believed her. The counselor asked Marcia what she thought of Mary's situation and what she thought Mary could do to straighten it out. Before the discussion ended, Marcia stopped talking about Mary and substituted "I" in exploring alternatives and developing a new plan for making friends.

Davis (1986) presented two cases using this technique with children. It seems especially appropriate for working with children who have been sexually abused.

Incomplete Sentences

Psychodynamic counselors often use projective techniques such as the House/Tree/Person or Children's Apperception Test in an attempt to understand their clients' thoughts, behaviors, and feelings. For counselors not trained in test interpretation, asking children to complete stimulus statements about likes, dislikes, family, friends, goals, wishes, and things that make the child happy or sad is a technique to help counselors understand children and find problem areas. This procedure may be especially helpful in assisting counselors to become acquainted with children and to establish better rapport with those who are anxious, fearful, or reluctant to talk.

Examples

The thing I like to do most is _____.
The person in my family who helps me most is _____.
My friends are _____.
I feel happiest (or saddest) when _____.
My greatest wish is _____.
The greatest thing that ever happened to me was _____.
I wish my parents would _____.
When I grow up, I want _____.
Brothers are _____.
Sisters are _____.
Dad is _____.
Mom is _____.
School is _____.
My teacher is _____.

CASE STUDIES

Identification of Problem I[1]

Dennis, age 9, was considered a disturbed, slow, resistant boy who had to be pushed into doing everything he was supposed to be doing. He rarely participated in any family activities and had no friends in the neighborhood. His school records listed such problems as regression, playing with much younger children, thumb-sucking, daydreaming, soiling, bullying, and tardiness. An excerpt from the first counseling session begins with Dennis entering the playroom.

Transcript

Dennis: Well, what are we going to do today?

Counselor: Whatever you'd like. This is your time.

Dennis: Let's talk.

Counselor: All right.

Dennis: Let's go back in history. We're studying about it in school. I'm going to be studying about Italy next week. I can't think of anything to talk about. I can't think of one thing to say. Can you?

Counselor: I'd rather discuss something you suggest.

Dennis: I can't think of a thing.

Counselor: We can just sit here if you like.

Dennis: Good. Do you want to read?

Counselor: OK.

Dennis: You be the student, and I'll be the teacher. I'll read to you. Now you be ready to answer some questions. I don't like spelling. I like social studies, and I like history more than any other subject. I'd like being the teacher for a change. (Dennis asks counselor questions from a reading text.)

Counselor: You like to ask questions you think I'll miss.

Dennis: That's right. I'm going to give you a test next week. A whole bunch of arithmetic problems, and social studies, and other questions. Now, I'm going to read like my friend does. . . . Notice how he reads?

Counselor: He seems to read fast without pausing.

Dennis: Yes.

Counselor: You'd like to be able to read like that.

Dennis: Not much. Let's name the ships in the books. (Dennis names each type of boat.) I have so much fun making up those names. That's what we'll do next week. (Dennis begins reading again.) Stop me when I make a mistake or do something wrong.

Counselor: I'd rather you stop yourself.

---

[1] Michael Gooch contributed the case of Dennis.

Dennis: The teacher always stops me.

Counselor: I'm a listener, not a teacher.

Dennis: Be a teacher, all right? (Dennis begins reading again.) That reminds me I have three darts at home. The set cost me three dollars. Two have been broke. (The session is about to end. Counselor examines some darts and a board.) Oh boy, darts. Maybe we can play with them next week.

Counselor: You're making lots of plans for next time.

Dennis: Yeah.

Several counseling sessions followed this one. Dennis showed marked improvement at school and at home. Dennis's mother and teacher spoke more positively of him.

Comments

The counselor gave Dennis his complete, undivided attention, participating in his games, tasks, projects, and plans. Here was someone with whom Dennis could talk and share his interests and ideas at a time when no one else would understand and accept him. He needed someone who would let him lead the way and let him be important in making decisions and plans. Dennis played the role of the initiator, the director, the teacher. He needed to have someone else know how it felt to be the follower, the one who is told what to do, the one ordered into activity and made to meet expectations. He needed to gain respect and confidence in his ability to face tasks and problems and to see them through successfully. In short, he used the therapy experience to improve his relationships and his skills. He became a competent, self-dependent person by practicing behavior that gave him a sense of self-adequacy and self-fulfillment.

Identification of Problem II[2]

A family sought therapy for problems with Pete, their rebellious 12-year-old son. The boy and his younger sister were adopted five years earlier and had previously experienced a series of foster-care arrangements. The adopting couple had no children before the adoption.

A history-gathering first session with the adoptive parents revealed that Pete had been physically abused by his biological mother and by at least one subsequent foster mother. The parents described Pete as rebellious and disrespectful, especially toward his mother. During the second session, the counselor met separately with Pete to establish rapport and continue assessing the context of the presenting problem. Although the boy was 12 years old, his social and emotional development appeared to be more like that of a 6- or 7-year old. The counselor wanted to help Pete feel comfortable, as

[2] The case of Pete was contributed by Robert Lee Whitaker, a marriage and family therapist and doctoral student in counseling psychology at the University of Tennessee, and is reprinted by permission.

FIGURE 8-1 Pete's drawing

well as to elicit more information about his inner thoughts. With these objectives in mind and in view of Pete's apparent developmental stage, the counselor asked him to draw a picture of a person. Pete drew a hypermuscular, threatening-looking young adult (see Figure 8-1). After the picture was completed, the counselor asked Pete to make up a story about the picture. Pete then told the following story. Note how the story's themes describe metaphorically Pete's experiences and his frustrated efforts to cope with them.

Pete's Story

He was born in a hollow tree. His mom was a dog; his dad was a cat. He was green, and he was the strongest person who ever lived. People called him Starman. He could throw a car, and it wouldn't come down for a week.

Then one day he met a baby. The baby had a race with him in the Olympics and beat him. The baby asked if he thought he could beat him again. For two years, they competed, and the baby always won. So the guy trained for two more years to beat the baby, but by that time, the baby was so big his head went out of the earth. He could jump out of the earth. The guy knew he couldn't do anything about it, so he retired and went off to be a wimp and was never seen again. There were stories that he was beat up, killed, shot. And that was the last they saw of him.

A week later, the counselor asked Pete to tell the story of Starman's early life.

He lived in a jungle and helped his dad fight off the beasts that tried to attack his family. He's been alive 300 billion years. He was a god and a very powerful prince of the world then. His dad was the king. The prince made up the rules for the kingdom (which was communist). People could only work when the prince wanted them to work, and no family could have over $700. If so, they had to see him, and they couldn't leave the country.

The queen was named Laura. She was as skinny as a toothpick, and she was so powerful she could make it rain or snow or any kind of weather when she wanted. She could make people feel like they were dying and could make them grow old real fast. She could make them have nine lives or make them look ugly. She could change their bodies into beasts. She was very wicked.

The prince didn't like her because she was trying to overrule him and get all the power he had. So, the prince got all the other gods in all the world or universe and his dad and formed all their powers together and killed her. When she died, she turned into a planet called Saturn (her remains). The queen is dead now.

The prince grew up, and his dad died because of Zeus. Zeus gave him poison, and the prince was in charge from then on, except for Zeus (the god over all). The prince enforced all the laws the same way the lady did, and Zeus threatened to kill him. The lady had enforced the laws because Zeus threatened to kill her. The prince killed her because he didn't like the rules and what she was doing to the people, but he didn't know Zeus was making her do it by threatening to kill her.

The prince went on doing things the way Zeus wanted until he died. Now he is just a strong person.

Interpreting the Story

This story suggested to the counselor a need to explore issues of anger and powerlessness with Pete. "Starman," or "the prince," felt powerless against the exceptional power and influence of the queen and the baby. Queen "Laura" had absolute control over the environment and could make whatever kind of weather she wanted (usually bad), make people grow old quickly, make them experience a feeling of death, make them ugly, and even turn them into beasts. Leadership, no matter who was in power, was always threateningly authoritarian. The prince's battle for power or control is described as a violent act against the leader, made possible by combining the power of all oppressed victims.

The story appears to reflect the trauma of Pete's upbringing and the particularly negative feelings he has toward females with power over him. Further, the story seems to closely parallel his history of abuse and his development into an aggressive person involved in a power struggle with his adoptive mother. The information elicited from the story was useful in alerting the counselor to Pete's experience of the reported historical events. It is unlikely that Pete could have conveyed the impact of his history and its present relevance to his life in a form more insightful and descriptively meaningful than the story he told.

Intervention

On the basis of the initial assessment interview with Pete's parents and the issues identified within the story, the counselor decided upon the following initial interventions. First, he decided to continue combining direct-assessment procedures with picture-drawing and storytelling strategies to identify additional problematic areas for Pete. Second, the counselor began formulating a story to be used later about an abused person or animal who learned to adapt to a new environment by gradually learning to trust again. Third, he asked Pete's permission to share with Pete's parents the story and the counselor's impressions of it. He then used the story to show the parents the relationship between Pete's present behavior and the trauma of his early experiences. The parents appeared to expect Pete to behave like any normal 12-year-old and not manifest any significant behavioral deficits related to the care he received during the first seven years of his life. The counselor suggested that Pete was attempting to cope with these early experiences and that Pete's parents might be able to help him and themselves by reconsidering the long-range impact of such an experience, adjusting their expectations, mutually deciding upon and concentrating on just a few rules, giving Pete choices within limits they could accept, and selecting the roles each of them wanted to serve in Pete's life in light of what the story might suggest. Finally, the counselor suggested they try an experiment to begin their exploration of the new roles they wished to assume in Pete's life by letting the mother have a "vacation" from her job as the primary disciplinarian.

Rationale

The therapeutic intent of these interventions consisted of the following objectives: first, to reinforce consistency in the parents' rules and expectations; second, to empower Pete with choices his parents could accept; third, to empower Pete's mother by providing more involvement and support from his father in parenting; fourth, to foster an expectation of trust rather than distrust—"I know he'll do the right thing" instead of "I know he'll do the wrong thing"; fifth, to focus less on punishment and more on logical consequences for Pete's misbehavior; and finally, to do away with any "mystery" rules or consequences.

RESEARCH AND REACTIONS

Just as Sigmund Freud was the father of psychoanalysis, he was the grandfather of child psychoanalysis. His therapy with adults conducted at the Vienna Psychoanalytic Institute was continuous and lengthy, often requiring several years to complete. A school for children was established adjacent to the institute. Anna Freud, Sigmund Freud's daughter, began to take a great interest in these children and eventually devoted herself almost exclusively to the study of children. She stands today as the outstanding pioneer in the field. The institute also trained other prominent child analysts, most notable among them Peter Blos, Marianne Kris, and Erik Erikson, the last best known for his theory of sequenced tasks as the means to development of one's identity.

Supporting research and literature summaries in the area of child psychoanalysis include the following topics: the relationship, childhood depression, and expressive arts in counseling.

The Relationship

Maenchen (1970) saw the differences in technique between adult and child analytical psychotherapy lessening. She saw less reliance on play therapy, more emphasis on the therapist interpreting "the moment" with the child, and more use of verbal games to elicit free association. She also saw more emphasis being placed on the relationship between child and counselor. Pothier (1976) agreed with Maenchen by designating a special category for relationship therapy in her list of counseling methods.

Zelman, Samuels, and Abrams (1985), in an investigation of the effect of long-term psychoanalytic treatment on children diagnosed as having oppositional disorder of childhood (DSM-III) and developmental delays of expressive language, found that 10 of 11 children were able to improve their overall IQ scores from a mean of 84.9 to 112.8. All children had received the cornerstone therapeutic-nursery approach of having an analyst work one-on-one with the child in the classroom in conjunction with the teacher. Weekly therapy sessions, consisting of interpretative interactions, averaged 521 visits over 54 months. The mean age of the children was 44 months at the time of admission.

Bouman, Blix, and Coons (1985) presented a case study of a 14-year-old girl who developed multiple personalities after a family history of intercourse with her father. The authors point out that children who are physically and/or sexually abused may develop multiple personalities. Dissociation provides an effective way to cope with strong affects evoked by abuse. Reintegration of the dissociative mechanism protecting the ego was the treatment goal, and therapy was conducted over 13 months. Initial steps were directed toward building trust in the therapeutic relationship. Trust was built by providing help with routine teenage problems. Efforts were made to strengthen the child's tolerance of affect, and communication among personalities was encouraged while dissociation was discouraged. Hypnosis was used in the end to fuse all personalities.

Childhood Depression and Suicidal Behavior

Orbach (1986), in an article related to determinants of suicidal behavior in children, discussed the "insolvable problem" as a primary factor in children's feelings of being trapped and incapacitated. The characteristics of the "insolvable problem" may include one or more of the following: (1) a problem beyond the child's ability to resolve that is deeply rooted and long-standing in the life of the entire family; (2) limitation of solution alternatives, by the parents, down to only one possibility that is undesirable to the child; (3) a problem situation in which every resolution creates a new problem; and (4) a family problem that is disguised from the entire family, which brings pressure to bear on the child to blindly fight this invisible enemy.

Rosenthal, Rosenthal, Doherty, and Santora (1986) constructed a profile of nine depressed, hospitalized preschoolers. The children, ranging in age from 3½ to 5½, were admitted to a psychiatric hospital for suspected suicidal behaviors, self-injury, serious aggression toward others, and/or fire setting. Individual diagnostic-play assessments were made to clarify the psychodynamic ramifications of the ideation and intentionality of their behavior. DSM-III criteria and the Preschool Depression Scale were also used in the assessment. All the suicidal children demonstrated long-standing suicidal thoughts and repeated self-injurious behavior associated with angry feelings. Comparing inpatients with outpatients, inpatients tended to exhibit more attention-getting behaviors (such as setting fires and putting ropes around their necks), whereas outpatient suicidals tended to exhibit behaviors that might look like accidents (such as running into traffic and jumping from high places). Causes of the depression were linked to parents who tended to be depriving, punitive, rejecting, depressed, and drug abusers.

Nelson and Crawford (1990) point out that the stresses once identified with adolescence have now become prevalent in the lives of children. Increases in stress also increase anxiety, depression, and suicide ideation. The authors, surveying counselors in 123 elementary schools, found that counselors reported having made contact with 187 students who were considering suicide during the school year. Parental loss through separation or divorce was cited as the number-one cause of childhood suicide. Herring (1990) echoes Nelson and Crawford in an article on suicide among children in the middle school years. He points out that 200 suicides are committed annually in the United States by children younger than 14. Mentioning many of the stressors children face, Herring stated that depression stands apart from other psychological disorders in that suicide is often its tragic outcome.

Hart (1991) cites studies that show a 20 percent rate of depression among school-age children (5 to 12) and a 33 percent rate for other school-age populations. A 51 percent to 59 percent depression rate was cited for child-psychiatric settings. Hart offers several theoretical models explaining depression. Traditional psychoanalytic theory would not allow for childhood depression because children lack a judging, controlling superego. Lack of guilt and self-blame leads to no depression. From the contemporary psychodynamic view, the child's depressive difficulties relate to loss of self-esteem from feelings of helplessness or loss. Losses range from loss of contact with a primary caregiver to less traumatic losses, both actual and perceived. Children often respond to feelings of helplessness and loss by swallowing their anger. Depression is the result of anger turned inward.

A Literature Review of Play Therapy and the Expressive Arts

Jalongo (1990), writing on the child's right to the expressive arts, presents four well-referenced arguments for using this medium with children. According to Jalongo, the expressive arts do the following:

1. Foster learning from the inside out and provide authentic learning that changes behavior and encourages reflection.
2. Enhance the child's ability to interpret symbols. It is the symbolic ability of the child on which everything which is distinctly human will develop.
3. Promote growth in all areas of development.
4. Place the child in the roles of meaning-maker, constructor, discoverer, and embodiment of knowledge rather than that of a passive recipient of ready-made answers and advice.

Counseling through the expressive arts, such as play, bibliotherapy, drama, music, puppetry, and poetry, is used frequently to compensate for children's limited verbal abilities when describing problems, feelings, and expectations. Landreth (1987) suggests that play therapy is an essential tool for counselors working with children and that counselors will find the technique most rewarding. Johnson (1987) found that a computer helped one overly dependent young client to talk about painful feelings, gain self-confidence, and relieve his anxiety over losing parental support. Brand (1987) contends that writing "seems to proceed hand in hand with psychological growth, to reflect and enhance it, to deepen and extend it, and often to quicken the process" (p. 274). Irwin (1987) uses drama to understand the inner world of her clients—the "symbolization, conflict, characterization, and interaction" (p. 282). Even though the counselor may feel unmusical, Bowman (1987) believes music is a powerful tool for counseling children. James and Myer (1987) describe the use of puppets for counseling with children and offer some precautions for the novice. Allan and Berry (1987) suggest that sand play can be used by counselors who have basic skills in play therapy. Gladding (1987) recommends incorporating poetry and poetic forms into guidance activities to give children "an appreciation for creativity and a new perception of life events" (p. 310). Mazza (1986), too, strongly recommends the use of poetry and popular music to enhance counseling. These expressive forms of play therapy may provide counselors with additional tools that could add to their effectiveness in counseling and developing treatment plans for children.

The expressive arts in counseling and psychotherapy have been used over the past 70 years. Melanie Klein (1932) contributed to and enlarged upon the work done earlier at the Vienna Psychoanalytic Institute. She wrote of ways in which free play could be used with children in a manner similar to that in which traditional free association was used with adults. She also added to existing knowledge in the areas of working through displacements and transference verbally.

Virginia Axline (1947, 1964) did much to popularize the term *play therapy*. She developed the idea of helping the child develop the trust necessary for a therapeutic alliance by following the child's lead in free-play activities, not intruding into the process, and withholding interpretation. She felt that in this way the child would give symbolic messages that could later be expressed verbally and interpreted as the relationship developed. Ekstein (1966) expanded upon this concept somewhat. He, too, believed that verbal communication must often be bypassed for the sake of symbolic action, but he was not opposed to taking an active part in the child's play or acting-out fantasy. He believed that "playing" a make-believe situation with children encouraged them to act out and then talk about real-life situations that were bothering them. Less threat is present in make-believe than in direct talk with adults, the source of many of a child's anxieties.

Barrows (1984) presented a case study of an 8-year-old boy with severe learning disabilities who benefited from play therapy. He was seen four times a week for four years. The play therapy was self-directed by the child, and the activities were interpreted with insights into the child's inner conflicts. Issues were resolved sequentially as they arose, thereby facilitating conflict resolution. Conflict resolution helped release the child's ability to use his imagination and to learn.

Barlow, Strother, and Landreth (1985) presented a case of play-therapy treatment involving a 3-year-old who was pulling out her hair as a way of reacting to poor parenting practices. Treatment consisted of allowing the child to engage in self-directed play in a room filled with toys (dollhouse, family figures, furniture, animals, and so on). The child's capacity for self-direction was respected, and no attempt was made to direct or change the child. The parents were given three sessions on how to parent the child more effectively. Although no follow-up report was presented, Barrow et al. noted that the child's hair grew back in seven sessions. Self-directed play therapy provided a valuable assessment tool as well as a therapeutic experience for the child.

Kestenbaum (1985) examined mutual storytelling as a viable therapeutic method to use in counseling children. Three cases were presented that demonstrate how children with problems can remediate their troubles through storytelling. In two cases, the child dictated the stories and the teacher wrote them. In the third case, the child spoke into a tape recorder as though an original radio play were being produced. Transcripts from each case were typed and listened to during subsequent sessions. Story plots and characters were found to parallel events in the children's lives. Questions were asked about the characters, their backgrounds, and their motives, and the children's answers were recorded for use in future sessions.

Lawson (1987) presented a helpful method of using a story-within-a-story in working successfully with an overweight 8-year-old girl who was acting out in an attempt to handle rejection by her peers. The method involved telling a story about a similar girl who had no friends. No name was used in the story, but the counselor mentioned the client's name in nearly every sentence. For example, the counselor would say, "Ann, I once knew a little girl. . ." Next, the counselor began another story-within-a-story that had the same theme. For example, "Ann, this little girl had a dream about a little brown, black, and white puppy who had no friends because she was different than the other puppies who were all white, all black, or all brown." During the second story, a solution was worked out around the theme that being different and special is good. When the girl wakes from her dream about the puppy, she is excited about being special. She can't wait to take her new feelings to school, because, as in the puppy story, it didn't matter what the other children thought about her as long as she felt special.

Bertoia and Allan (1988), in an article on spontaneous drawings, described how the method was used successfully with a terminally ill 8-year-old girl. Based on the idea that the unconscious exists and that it can express itself through spontaneous or impromptu drawings, the authors described the counselor's role in helping children communicate through their drawings. The first step is to build rapport and create the safe, nonjudgmental climate discussed in Chapter 4. Children are given a choice of what to draw. If a child is short on ideas, the counselor might ask the child to draw a picture from one of his or her dreams. After the child has drawn the picture, the counselor thanks the child, acknowledges the effort, dates the picture, and asks for a title and a story. The drawings are kept in a file, and the stories are recorded on tape. The counselor's job is to help the child tell the story through active listening and summarizing remarks. The symbols in the picture relate to the child's thoughts, feelings, and expectations. The counselor can also help the child tell his or her story by pointing out the symbols and saying, "I noticed you have drawn a big bear; I wonder what the bear is thinking, feeling, and planning to do next." A follow-up statement might be, "I wonder why the bear would do that." The authors recommended some good sources for checking symbolic meanings of drawings (Cooper, 1978; Thompson & Allan, 1987).

Kottman (1990), in an article directed toward counseling middle school and junior high school students, pointed out the benefits of using therapeutic game play, stories or metaphors, and role-play/simulations to involve these children in the counseling process. All these activities, whether used one-on-one or in a group, provide diagnostic and therapeutic assistance. Even a game of checkers can provide information about a child's attitudes toward self, attitudes toward others, thoughts, feelings, and behavior patterns.

Kahn and Kahn (1990) recommend that counselors have children write their own books to help the children move through crisis periods in their lives. Through a process of expressive writing, children describe the origins, experiences, and adjustment strategies involved in coping with their own difficulties. The books can be illustrated in any art forms the children choose. The main point children learn from the experience is that feelings become less frightening when they are written down and understood.

Any of the expressive arts (mutual storytelling, doll play, drawing, painting, or puppet play) can help children work through unresolved psychic trauma or conflict without addressing their own problems directly. The key to the process may be selecting the medium most comfortable to the child and the counselor.

Tyson and Tyson (1986) present 11 case studies in which transference was viewed as the basis of the psychoanalytic process. Allowing the children to act out and discuss their feelings about past conflicts and frustration in a neutral environment helped them complete the old business of reacting in maladaptive ways to present-day conflicts. The transference process helped reduce maladaptive behavior in all 11 children treated.

Summary

Rutter (1975) points to four primary trends in analytic approaches to children: (1) a move to briefer treatment, which encourages clearer focus on problems, the setting of definite goals, and more definite strategies; (2) greater attention to conscious conflicts and current environmental stresses; (3) a shift away from treatment of the individual toward a focus on the family as a group; and (4) less preoccupation with the interpretation of intrapsychic mechanisms and a greater reliance on the counselor/child relationship itself as the main treatment agent. This last trend seems to have a consensus of support of professionals in the field.

To Rutter's list of four trends we would add a fifth: using the expressive arts in counseling children. As we become reacquainted with Freud's work, we find that much of what is being done in counseling today has its roots in his many contributions to counseling theory and practice.

REFERENCES

Allan, J., & Berry, P. (1987). Sandplay. *Elementary School Guidance and Counseling, 21*, 300–306.

Axline, V. (1947). *Play therapy.* Boston: Houghton Mifflin.

Axline, V. (1964). *Dibs: In search of self.* Boston: Houghton Mifflin.

Barlow, K., Strother, J., & Landreth, G. (1985). Child-centered play therapy: Nancy from baldness to curls. *The School Counselor, 32*, 347–363.

Barrows, K. (1984). A child's difficulty in using his gifts and imagination. *Journal of Child Psychotherapy, 10,* 15–26.

Bertoia, J., & Allan, J. (1988). Counseling seriously ill children: Use of spontaneous drawings. *Elementary School Guidance and Counseling, 22,* 206–221.

Bouman, E. S., Blix, S., & Coons, P. M. (1985). Multiple personality in adolescence: Relationship to incestual experiences. *American Academy of Child Psychiatry, 24,* 109–114.

Bowman, R. (1987). Approaches for counseling children through music. *Elementary School Guidance and Counseling, 21,* 284–291.

Brand, A. (1987). Writing as counseling. *Elementary School Guidance and Counseling, 21,* 266–275.

Clark, A. (1991). The identification and modification of defense mechanism in counseling. *Journal of Counseling and Development, 69,* 231–236.

Cooper, J. C. (1978). *An illustrated encyclopedia of traditional symbols.* London: Thames and Hudson.

Davis, J. (1986). Storytelling: Using the child as consultant. *Elementary School Guidance and Counseling, 21,* 89–92.

Ekstein, R. (1966). *Children of time and space, of action and impulse: Clinical studies on psychoanalytic treatment of severely disturbed children.* New York: Appleton-Century-Crofts.

Freud, S. (1949). *An outline of psychoanalysis* (J. Strachey, Trans.). New York: Norton. (Original work published 1940)

Freud, S. (1952). *On dreams* (J. Strachey, Trans.). New York: Norton. (Original work published 1901)

Freud, S. (1963). *An autobiographical study* (J. Strachey, Trans.). New York: Norton. (Original work published 1925)

Freud, S. (1965a). *The interpretation of dreams* (J. Strachey, Trans.). New York: Norton. (Original work published 1900)

Freud, S. (1965b). *New introductory lectures in psychoanalysis* (J. Strachey, Ed. and Trans.). New York: Norton. (Original work published 1933)

Freud, S. (1971). *The psychopathology of everyday life* (A. Tyson, Trans.). New York: Norton. (Original work published 1901)

Freud, S. (1976). *The complete psychological works.* Standard edition, 24 volumes (J. Strachey, Trans.). New York: Norton.

Gladding, S. (1987). Poetic expression: A counseling art in elementary schools. *Elementary School Guidance and Counseling, 21,* 307–311.

Hall, C. (1954). *A primer of Freudian psychology.* New York: Mentor.

Hart, S. (1991). Childhood depression: Implications and options for school counselors. *Elementary School Guidance and Counseling, 25,* 277–289.

Herring, R. (1990). Suicide in the middle school: Who said kids will not? *Elementary School Guidance and Counseling, 25,* 129–137.

Irwin, E. (1987). Drama: The play's the thing. *Elementary School Guidance and Counseling, 21,* 276–283.

Jalongo, M. (1990). The child's right to the expressive arts: Nurturing the imagination as well as the intellect. *Childhood Education, 66,* 195–201.

James, R., & Myer, R. (1987). Puppets: The elementary school counselor's right or left arm. *Elementary School Guidance and Counseling, 21,* 292–299.

Johnson, R. (1987). Using computer art in counseling children. *Elementary School Guidance and Counseling, 21,* 262–265.

Kahn, B., & Kahn, W. (1990). I am the author books (ITABS). *Elementary School Guidance and Counseling, 25,* 153–157.

Kestenbaum, C. J. (1985). The creative process in child psychotherapy. *American Journal of Psychotherapy, 39,* 479–489.

Klein, M. (1932). *The psychoanalysis of children.* London: Hogarth Press.

Kottman, T. (1990). Counseling middle school students: Techniques that work. *Elementary School Guidance and Counseling, 25,* 138–145.

Landreth, G. (1987). Play therapy: Facilitative use of child's play in elementary school counseling. *Elementary School Guidance and Counseling, 21,* 253–261.

Lawson, D. (1987). Using therapeutic stories in the counseling process. *Elementary School Guidance and Counseling, 22,* 134–142.

Maenchen, A. (1970). On the technique of child analysis in relation to stages of development. *The Psychoanalytic Study of the Child, 25,* 175–208.

Mazza, N. (1986). Poetry and popular music in social work education: The liberal arts perspective. *The Arts in Psychotherapy, 13*, 293–299.

Nelson, R., & Crawford, B. (1990). Suicide among elementary school-aged children. *Elementary School Guidance and Counseling, 25*, 123–128.

Orbach, I. (1986). The "insolvable problem" as a determinant in the dynamics of suicidal behavior in children. *American Journal of Psychotherapy, 40*, 511–520.

Pothier, P. (1976). *Mental health counseling with children.* Boston: Little, Brown.

Rosenthal, P., Rosenthal, S., Doherty, M., & Santora, D. (1986). Suicidal thoughts and behaviors in depressed hospitalized preschoolers. *American Journal of Psychotherapy, 40*, 201–211.

Rutter, M. (1975). *Helping troubled children.* New York: Plenum.

Stone, I. (1971). *Passions of the mind.* New York: Doubleday.

Sugarman, A. (1977). Psychoanalysis as a humanistic psychology. *Psychotherapy: Theory, Research, and Practice, 14*, 204–211.

Thompson, F., & Allan, J. (1987). Common symbols of children in art counseling. *Guidance and Counseling, 2*(5), 24–32.

Tyson, R., & Tyson, P. (1986). The concept of transference in child psychoanalysis. *Journal of the American Academy of Child Psychiatry, 25*, 30–39.

Watson, J. (1980). Bibliotherapy for abused children. *The School Counselor, 27*, 204–208.

Zelman, A. B., Samuels, S., & Abrams, D. (1985). I.Q. changes in young children following long-term psychotherapy. *American Journal of Psychotherapy, 39*, 215–227.

CHAPTER 9

Transactional Analysis

ERIC BERNE

Eric Lennard Bernstein was born May 10, 1910, at his family home in Montreal, Canada. His family consisted of his father, who was a general practitioner; his mother, who was a professional writer and editor; and a sister five years younger than he. Eric respected his father a great deal, and up to the time of his father's death, he was permitted to make rounds with him, house to house. He was 10 years old when his father died from tuberculosis, at which time his mother assumed responsibility for supporting the two children.

After receiving his medical degree from McGill University at the age of 25, Berne moved to the United States and began a psychiatric residency at Yale University. He became a citizen around 1938 and shortly thereafter changed his name to Eric Berne. Following a tour of service with the armed forces from 1943 to 1946, he began working to earn the title of psychoanalyst. His first book, *Mind in Action,* was published in 1946. In 1947, Berne began analysis with Erik Erikson.

Berne encountered several frustrations during his adulthood. Each of his three marriages ended in divorce. However, he did have seven children from his first two marriages; he found the role of parent rewarding and loved his children very much. It is said that he was overly permissive and more of a nurturing parent than an authoritarian, critical parent. One of the major rejections of his life occurred when, in 1956, his application for membership in the Psychoanalytic Institute was denied. It was recommended that he continue through four more years of personal analysis, then reapply later for the coveted title. This action greatly discouraged Berne but at the same time motivated him, and he immediately began work on a new approach to psychotherapy.

Although Berne first published information on the three ego states in "The Nature of Intuition" (1949), the core of transactional analysis (TA) was formed in 1954. At that time, Berne was involved in the psychoanalysis of a successful middle-aged lawyer he was treating by classic Freudian principles. During a session, the patient suddenly said, "I'm not a lawyer, I'm just a little boy," sparking the idea that each of us contains a child ego state accompanied by a parent and an adult ego state. After listening to his patients relating "games" for some 30 years, Berne decided to gather certain of these breezily named games into a catalog. Three years after its publication, *Games People Play* (1964) had been on the nonfiction best-seller list for 111 weeks—longer than any other book that decade. Some reviewers called the book psychiatric gimmickry, emphatically denying that it would ever be regarded as a contribution to psychological or psychiatric theory. Other reviewers found the book a real contribution to psychology, suggesting that Berne had offered a thesaurus of social transactions with explanations and titles. In 1967, Berne attributed the book's success to the recognition factor—some of us recognize ourselves in it, and some recognize other people.

Poker was Berne's favorite game because people play it to win. He had little patience with losers and was noted as saying that you might as well play to win if you are going to play. He saw losers as spending a lot of time explaining why they lost. Berne saw his mission as turning frogs back into princesses and princes—just as they were born. He viewed parents, other adults, and the environment as being responsible for turning children into frogs. He was not satisfied in just making frogs from frogs. In the final years of his life, Berne shifted his emphasis from games to life scripts.

Berne published 8 books and 64 articles in psychiatric and other periodicals and was editor of *Transactional Analysis Bulletin*. In an article in the *New York Times* magazine in 1966, Berne renounced the therapeutic value of shock treatment, hypnosis, and medication in favor of his easy-to-understand approach to psychotherapy. Today TA is an international organization with more than 10,000 members. Eric Berne died in 1970.

THE NATURE OF PEOPLE
AND THEORY OF COUNSELING

The nature of people and the theory of counseling are covered together in this chapter because the TA theory of counseling is basically a statement describing the human personality.

Berne had a positive view of the nature of people. He believed children were born princes and princesses, but shortly thereafter their parents and the environment turned them into frogs. He believed people had the potential to regain their royal status, providing they learned and applied the lessons of transactional analysis to their personal lives. Berne believed that the early childhood years were critical to personal development. During these early years, before children enter school, they form their basic life script, and they develop a sense of being either "OK" or "not OK." They also arrive at conclusions about other people's "OK-ness." In Berne's view, life is very simple to live. However, people upset themselves to the point that they invent religions, pastimes, and games. These same people complain about how complicated life is, while persisting in making life even harder. Life is a series of decisions to be made and problems to be solved. Berne believed that people have the rationality and freedom to make decisions and solve their problems.

The TA theory of human nature and human relationships derives from data collected through four types of analysis:

1. Structural analysis, in which an individual's personality is analyzed;
2. Transactional analysis, which is concerned with what people do and say to each other;
3. Script analysis, which deals with the specific life dramas people compulsively enjoy; and
4. Game analysis, in which ulterior transactions leading to a payoff are analyzed.

Structural Analysis

In explaining the TA view of human nature and the difficulties people encounter in their lives, we begin with the structural analysis of personality. Each individual's personality is divided into three separate and distinct ego states. These ego states, which are the sources of behavior, are called Parent, Adult, and Child, or P, A, and C for short. The ego states represent real persons who now exist or once existed and had their own identities. Therefore, the conflicts among them often cause inconsistencies as well as flexibility in people.

The Parent, Adult, and Child ego states Berne proposed are not concepts like the id, ego, and superego of Freud, but rather phenomena based on actual realities. They each represent skeletal/muscular and verbal patterns of behavior and feeling based on emotions and experiences perceived by people in their early years. The three ego states are defined in the following paragraphs.

Parent. This aspect of personality contains instructions, attitudes, and behaviors handed down mostly by parents and significant authority figures. It resembles a recording of all the admonitions, orders, punishments, encouragement, and so on experienced in the first years of life. Parents can take two different attitudes, depending on the situation: (1) Nurturing Parent, which manifests itself in nurturing or helping behavior; and (2) Critical Parent, which provides criticism, control, and punishment. The Parent feels and behaves as the one who raised you did—both critical and nurturing. The Parent admonishes "you should" or "you should not," "you can't win," "boys will be boys," or "a woman's place is in the home."

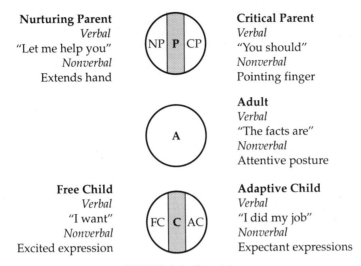

Nurturing Parent		Critical Parent
Verbal		*Verbal*
"Let me help you"		"You should"
Nonverbal		*Nonverbal*
Extends hand		Pointing finger

Adult
Verbal
"The facts are"
Nonverbal
Attentive posture

Free Child		Adaptive Child
Verbal		*Verbal*
"I want"		"I did my job"
Nonverbal		*Nonverbal*
Excited expression		Expectant expressions

FIGURE 9-1   Ego states

The Parent, wanting to be in control and to be right, acts with superiority and authority. But the Parent is also responsible for giving love, nurturance, and respect to the Child in you.

Adult.   This ego state operates logically and nonemotionally, providing objective information using reality testing and a computerlike approach to life. Your Adult uses facts as a computer does to make decisions without emotion. The Adult says "This is how this works" with mature, objective, logical, and rational thinking based on reality. The Adult ego state is not related to age. A child is also capable of dealing with reality by gathering facts and computing objectively.

Child.   Here we find all the childlike impulses common to everyone. The Child is an important part of personality because it contributes such things as joy, creativity, spontaneity, intuition, pleasure, and enjoyment. The Child has two parts: (1) Adaptive Child, which emerges as a result of demands from significant authority figures and is marked by passivity; and (2) Natural, or Free Child, which represents the impulsive, untrained, self-loving, pleasure-seeking part of the Child.

The Child part of us is an accumulation of impulses that come naturally to a young person and of recorded internal events or responses to what is seen and heard. There is an element of immaturity but also a source of deep feeling, affection, adaptation, expression, and fun. Figure 9-1 presents the ego states and their divisions in graphic form.

The well-adjusted person allows the situation to determine which ego state is in control, striking an even balance among the three. A common problem is seen in the person who allows one ego state to assume predom-

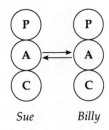

Sue   *Billy*

FIGURE 9-2   Complementary transaction

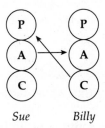

Sue   *Billy*

FIGURE 9-3   Crossed transaction

inant control. For example, the Constant Parent is seen as dictatorial or prejudiced; the Constant Adult is an analytical bore; the Constant Child is immature or overreactive. No age is implied by any of these states, as even the young child has Adult and Parent states, and senior citizens can evince a Child response.

Transactional Analysis

The second type of analysis—the study of the transaction—is the heart of TA. Any time a person acknowledges the presence of another person, either verbally or physically, a transaction has taken place. A transaction is often defined as a unit of human communication or as a stimulus/response connection between two people's ego states.

Transactions are grouped into three categories:

1. Complementary transactions, which Berne describes as "the natural order of healthy human relationships," occur when a response comes from the ego state to which it was addressed (see Figure 9-2).

Sue: Billy, have you seen my bike?
Billy: Yes, it is in the backyard.

2. Crossed transactions break communications. They occur when a response comes from one of the other two ego states (Figure 9-3).

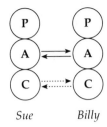

FIGURE 9-4   Covert transaction

Sue: Billy, would you help me find my bike?
Billy: Can't you see I'm watching my favorite program???

3. Covert, or ulterior, transactions involve more than one ego state of each person and are basically dishonest. On the surface, the transaction looks and sounds like number 1 or 2 above, but the actual message sent is not spoken (Figure 9-4). For example, the ulterior message being sent in number 1 could be on a social or overt level:

Sue: Billy, why don't you help me find my bike so we can go riding?
Billy: OK, it's a good day for a ride!

Or the ulterior message could be on a psychological, covert, or ulterior level:

Sue: I wish you would be my boyfriend.
Billy: I hope you like me better than the other boys.

Script Analysis

The nature of people can be further described by script analysis. A psychological script is a person's ongoing program for a life drama; it dictates where people are going with their lives and the paths that will lead there. The individual—consciously or unconsciously—acts compulsively according to that program. As mentioned before, people are born basically OK; their difficulties come from bad scripts they learned during their childhood.

Berne (1961) developed the theory of scripts as part of TA theory from its inception. A life script is that life plan your Child selected in your early years, based mostly on messages you received from the Child in your parents. For example, at the request of her mother, a little girl takes it upon herself to save her alcoholic father. The same script may emerge once again later in life as she tries to save an alcoholic husband in an attempt to regain some of the payoffs from the original experience. Although the Parent and Adult of your mother and father may have told you sensible things such as

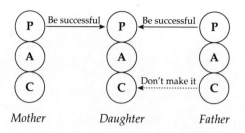

FIGURE 9-5   Life script: injunctions

"be successful," the unspoken injunction from the Child in your parents may communicate the message "You can't make it" (see Figure 9-5). Injunctions are prohibitions and negative commands usually delivered from the parent of the opposite sex. Injunctions are seldom discussed or verbalized aloud. Values we hold as guidelines for living may have come from injunctions. These injunctions determine how we think and feel about sex, work, money, marriage, family, play, and people.

The best way to learn about scripts is to examine how we spend our time and how we relate (transactions) with others. Scripts have main themes, such as martyring, procrastinating, succeeding, failing, blaming, distracting, placating, and computing. Reviewing your life will help you discover your theme. Basically there are three types of scripts: winner, loser, and nonwinner. A small percentage of our population seem to be natural winners; everything they touch turns to gold. Conversely, a slightly larger percentage of our population seem to be natural losers; everything seems to turn out badly for them. The vast majority of the population, perhaps 80–85 percent, follow the nonwinners' script. Nonwinners are identified by a phrase they often use: "but at least . . ." ("I went to school and made poor grades, *but at least* I did not flunk out").

TA borrows heavily from fairy tales for its terminology and analogies. For example, the Cinderella script is not an especially healthy plan because your prince or prize will not come if you sit around waiting. You have to make things happen. Even martyring yourself, as Cinderella did for her stepmother and stepsisters, won't help. The Santa Claus script is based on a similar myth. Again, you may have to be your own Santa. Since life scripts are formed in early childhood, considerable care needs to be given to the selection of children's stories. We have included a comprehensive list of books in this text that we believe to be helpful to children and their families (see Chapters 14 and 15).

In summary, Berne believed that scripts have five components: (1) directions from parents, (2) a corresponding personality development, (3) a confirming childhood decision about oneself and life, (4) a penchant for either success or failure, and (5) a pattern for behavior.

Game Analysis

Unfortunately, most of us in following our scripts learn how to use ulterior transactions. In other words, we play games. A game is an ongoing series of complementary ulterior transactions progressing to a well-defined, predictable outcome. Like every ulterior transaction, all games are basically dishonest, and they're by no means fun. One of the first games a child learns is "Mine is better than yours." The relatively benign outcome of "Mine is better" could range, in later years, to considerably more serious games. *Games People Play* offers a vastly entertaining, chilling overview of what might happen to a not-OK child.

Life Positions

On the basis of the transactions and scripts, children develop life positions that summarize their concepts of self-worth and the worth of others. The four life positions (described by Harris, 1969) are as follows:

1. *I'm not OK–You're OK.* This is the universal position of childhood. It represents the introjective position of those who feel powerless. Adults in this position often experience withdrawal and depression. The extreme of this position would be represented by a -5 on the x-axis and $+5$ on the y-axis in quadrant II of Figure 9-6.

2. *I'm not OK–You're not OK.* This is the arrival point of the child who cannot depend on parents for positive stroking (discussed later in this chapter). Already not OK, the child perceives Mom and Dad as not OK, too. Adults in this category are losers who go through a series of helpless, disappointing experiences and may even become suicidal or homicidal. The extreme of this position would be represented by a -5 on both the x- and y-axes in quadrant III of Figure 9-6.

3. *I'm OK–You're not OK.* The individual feels victimized in this position. The brutalized, battered child will end up here. It is the position of the criminal, the psychopath. Whatever happens, it's someone else's fault. The extreme of this position would be represented by a $+5$ on the x-axis and a -5 on the y-axis in quadrant IV of Figure 9-6.

4. *I'm OK–You're OK.* This is the position of mentally healthy people. They possess realistic expectations, have good human relationships, and are capable of solving problems constructively. It is a "winner's" position. A winner is defined as an authentic being. The extreme of this position would be represented by a $+5$ on both the x- and y-axes in quadrant I of Figure 9-6.

Among the many games Berne identified, some are to be especially avoided in the counseling interview.

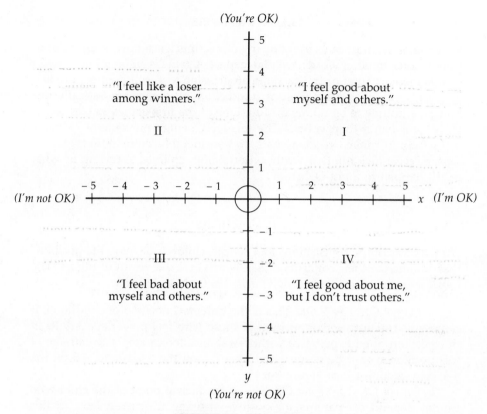

FIGURE 9-6 Life positions

1. *Why don't you; yes, but . . .*

The counselor's Adult is tricked into working for the client's Child or Parent when you as the counselor give advice.

Counselor: Why don't you ask your teacher to give you some extra help with math?

Client: Yes, but what if she says she doesn't have time?

The payoff comes to the client in spreading bad feelings, as in the misery-loves-company game. "I am not OK, and you aren't either because you can't help me solve my problem."

2. *I'm only trying to help you.*

This is a game that counselors sometimes play with their clients. The message to the client is: "You are not OK, and I know what is good for you." The payoff is for the counselor, who holds the faulty belief that "If I straighten my client out, then maybe I can get my own life in order." A truly helpful counselor offers help when it is requested, but believes that help can be accepted or rejected. When help fails or is rejected, the helpful counselor does not respond derogatorily, "Well, I was only trying to help you."

3. Courtroom

The courtroom game puts the counselor in the position of judge and jury if two clients can manipulate the counselor into placing blame. The payoff is bad feelings for all—persecutor, victim, and rescuer—because the rescuer (counselor) usually ends up being victimized by the other two players.

4. Kick me and NIGYYSOB

Counselors may find that some clients enjoy playing the game of "kick me" with the counselor, just as they do with their bosses, colleagues, and spouses. They seem to enjoy being victimized. These clients work at getting themselves rejected. They even work at getting themselves terminated from counseling before any gains have been made. Kick-me players manipulate others into playing NIGYYSOB (now I've got you, you son-of-a-bitch) when they react to the bids for the negative attention the kick-me players make.

NIGYYSOB can be played by itself when a person tries to trap others in a double bind—damned if you do and damned if you don't.

Mother: Johnny, do you love me?
Johnny: Yes, I do.
Mother: How many times have I told you not to talk with your mouth full?!

5. Gossiping

Gossiping refers to talking about people who are not present. In a counseling interview, the counselor may wish to have clients role-play dialogue between themselves and a missing person, as was suggested in Chapter 5. For example, a child complaining about a teacher could role-play a conversation between the two of them, with the child playing the role of the teacher and then responding as he or she would in the classroom. The technique uses an empty chair to represent the missing person. Role-playing and role-reversal methods have a way of limiting gossip while creating greater awareness of the problem situations as well as the proper assignment of responsibility for the problem.

6. Wooden leg

The wooden-leg game is a display of the inadequacy pattern described in the following chapter on individual psychology. Clients playing wooden-leg games work to increase their disabilities as a way of avoiding responsibility for taking care of themselves. These clients are experts at making people give up on them. Children are adept at convincing parents that they cannot handle certain chores and school subjects.

Paradoxical strategies, effective at times with these clients, focus on harnessing their rebellion into productive activity. The counselor might say, for example, "Frank, you've got me convinced that you really can't make it." The rebellious client, Frank, will often rise to the occasion to show that you, the counselor, are the total idiot he has always believed you to be and begin to succeed where you predicted he could not.

For clients who are really defeated and not rebellious, we stick to our advice of offering large doses of unconditional encouragement. Counselors of welfare and rehabilitation clients often find themselves in the wooden-leg game. The payoff goes to the client, who justifies not getting better, or even getting worse, as a way of increasing welfare payments.

7. *If it weren't for you . . .*

Related to the wooden leg, this game is another way of avoiding the assumption of responsibility for one's life and its unsolved problems. The client says, for example, "If it weren't for you and your good cooking, I could lose ten pounds." The counselor may want to examine with the client the payoffs of being overweight and even develop a rationale of how being fat may be the preferred and "best" lifestyle for the client.

The Pursuit of Strokes

Human beings need recognition; in order to obtain it, they exchange what Berne calls *strokes*. When people acknowledge the presence of another, they give a stroke. The stroke can be either positive or negative. It is usually obvious which is which, except in the case of ulterior transactions. Young children receive positive or negative physical strokes when they are cuddled or spanked, whereas adults obtain primarily symbolic strokes in conversations or transactions with others. Positive strokes, such as compliments, handshakes, open affection, or uninterrupted listening, are the most desirable, but negative strokes, such as hatred or disagreement, are better than no recognition at all. A middle ground is maintenance strokes, which keep transactions going by giving recognition to the speaker but give neither positive nor negative feedback. All these strokes can be either conditional or unconditional — given as a result of some specific action or given just for being yourself. Unconditional regard — "I like you" — has more positive stroke value than conditional acceptance — "I like you when you are nice to me."

The pattern of giving and receiving strokes an individual uses most is determined by the person's life position, as explained in the section on life positions. How people view themselves and others controls their ability to give and receive conditional and unconditional positive and negative strokes.

People engage in transactions to exchange strokes. According to Berne (1964), there is an inherent psychological hunger for stimulation through human interactions and stroking, and any act implying recognition of another's presence is a means of satisfying these hungers. Failure to fulfill these needs may cause a failure to thrive in infants (James & Jongeward,

1971) and feelings of abandonment and not-OK-ness in both children and adults. Satisfied hunger yields feelings of OK-ness and release of creative energy (Phillips & Cordell, 1975). Thus, it is important to become aware of our psychological hungers and to satisfy them adequately.

Negative strokes such as lack of attention, shin kicking, and hatred send "You're not OK" messages. Diminishing, humiliating, and ridiculing strokes all treat people as though they were insignificant.

Positive strokes are usually complementary transactions. They may be verbal expressions of affection and appreciation, or they may give compliments or positive feedback; they may be physical, like a touch, or they may be silent gestures or looks. Listening is one of the finest strokes one person can give another (James & Jongeward, 1971). All yield reinforcement to the I'm OK–You're OK position. Maintenance strokes, though lacking in meaningful content, at least serve to give recognition and keep communication open.

Structuring Time

People have six options for structuring their time in pursuit of strokes:

1. Withdrawing, in which no transaction takes place. It involves few risks, and no stroking occurs.
2. Rituals, which involve prescribed social transactions such as "Hello" and "How are you?" These are fairly impersonal transactions.
3. Pastimes, which provide mutually acceptable stroking. Pastimes are a means of self-expression but often involve only superficial transactions or conversations. Examples are baseball, automobiles, shopping, or other safe topics of conversation.
4. Activities, in which time is structured around some task or career. Activities are a way to deal with external reality.
5. Games, in which the need is met in a crooked way. Intense stroking is often received, but it may be unpleasant. Games are considered destructive transactions.
6. Intimacy, which provides unconditional stroking. It is free of games and exploitation.

Obviously, some of these ways of structuring time are good and some are bad, depending on the time and energy given to each. One of the goals of TA therapy is to help people learn productive ways of structuring their time.

Withdrawing may be the Adult's decision to relax or be alone, the Parent's way of coping with conflict, or the Child's adaptation to protect itself from pain or conflict. It is fairly harmless unless it happens all the time or when someone such as your boss is talking to you. Withdrawing into fantasy may allow one to experience good stroking when the present setting does not appear to hold any.

Harris (1969) observes that a ritual is a socially programmed use of time in which everybody agrees to do the same thing. Brief encounters, worship rituals, greeting rituals, cocktail-party rituals, and bedroom rituals may allow maintenance strokes without commitment or involvement. The outcome is predictable and pleasant when you know you are doing the "in-step" thing, but most people need more intense stroking.

James and Jongeward (1971) believe that pastimes are, as they imply, ways to pass time. They are superficial exchanges without involvement that people use in order to size one another up. Conversations concerning relative gas mileage, the weather, or potty training may yield minimal stroking at the maintenance level while allowing one to decide whether to risk a more intimate relationship.

Doing work or activities, according to Phillips and Cordell (1975), is time spent dealing with realities of the world. It is getting something done that one may want to do, need to do, or have to do. Activities allow for positive strokes befitting a winner.

Berne (1964) defines games as an ongoing series of complementary ulterior transactions progressing to a well-defined, predictable outcome. When your message to another person is ulterior, for some hidden purpose, you are playing a game. The Adult part of you is unaware that the Child or Parent has a secret reason for playing or wanting to play. Harris (1969) believes all games derive from the Child's "mine is better than yours" attempt to ease the not-OK feeling — to feel superior while the other feels put down. A game can be recognized by the payoff. When you think you've won, but part of you knows you took unfair advantage — that's a game. Games are differentiated from rituals and pastimes in two ways: (1) their ulterior quality and (2) the payoff. Games are a way, too, of using time for people who cannot bear the stroking starvation of withdrawal and yet whose not-OK position makes the ultimate form of relatedness — intimacy — impossible (Berne, 1964; Harris, 1969).

James and Jongeward (1971) define intimacy as a deep human encounter stemming from genuine caring. Steiner (1974) views intimacy as the way of structuring time when there is no withdrawal, no rituals, no games, no pastimes, and no work. Conditions favorable for intimacy include a commitment to the I'm OK–You're OK position and a satisfying of psychological hungers through positive strokes.

Rackets

Some people find themselves involved in what is known in TA theory as a "stamp-collecting enterprise," in which they save up archaic, bad feelings until they have enough to "cash in" for some psychological prize. The bad-feelings racket, or stamp collecting, works in much the same way that supermarket stamp collecting works. People save brown stamps for all the bad things others have caused them to suffer and gold stamps for all the favors others owe them. Gray stamps refer to lowered self-esteem, red stamps symbolize anger, blue stamps mean depression, and white stamps connote purity (James & Jongeward, 1971). When the bad-feelings stamp books are filled, they may be cashed in for such things as a free divorce, custody of children, nervous breakdown, blowup, drunken binge, depression, tantrum, runaway, or love affair. Good-feelings stamps are used to justify playtime, relaxation, and breaks from work. According to McCormick and Campos (1969), stamp collecting is a racket we learn from our parents. The collector uses the stamps as excuses for behavior and feelings, and the suppliers may not even be aware they are giving them out. I'm OK–You're OK people do not need stamps because they need no excuses.

COUNSELING METHOD

Transactional analysis is the ideal system for those who view the counseling process as teaching. As is evident from the previous section, TA abounds with terms, diagrams, and models. Clients are taught the TA vocabulary so they can become proficient in identifying ego states, transactions, and scripts. The counselor's role includes teaching and providing a nurturing, supportive environment in which clients feel free to lift or eliminate restricting injunctions, attempt new behaviors, rewrite scripts, and move toward the I'm OK–You're OK life position. Contracting between counselor and client is a large part of the TA process.

TA involves teaching the principles of transactional analysis to participants and then letting them use these principles to analyze and improve their own behavior. TA concepts have been taught to people of all age and ability levels, from the very young to the very old and from mentally retarded children to gifted children. The following TA points are most useful in counseling children:

1. Definition and explanation of ego states
2. Analysis of transactions between ego states
3. Positive and negative stroking (or "warm fuzzies" and "cold pricklies")
4. I'm OK, You're OK
5. Games and rackets
6. Scripts

Put simply, the primary goal in transactional analysis is to help the person achieve the I'm OK–You're OK life position. One can use a variety of methods and techniques to accomplish this aim. Because children can easily learn and understand the terms and concepts of TA, the approach has become popular in helping school-age children.

The I'm OK–You're OK life position is one the child chooses to take. The other three positions more or less evolve of themselves; the child feels no sense of free choice in the matter. According to Harris (1969), the first three positions are based on feelings; the fourth position—I'm OK–You're OK—is based on thought, faith, and initiation of action. The first three have to do with "why"; the fourth has to do with "why not." We do not drift into a new position; it is a decision we must make. Using the graph in Figure 9-6, we can plot a person's progress in moving from one quadrant to another, providing each step on the number axis is defined in operational terms. The x-axis refers to gains and losses in self-esteem; the y-axis indicates the same for our relationships with others.

Ideally, the role of a transactional analyst is that of a teacher. Once children have been taught how to speak the language of TA, the counselor can help them analyze their own transactions and see how their behavior affects others and vice versa. Children learn to identify the source of the reasoning that goes into their decisions; that is, they learn how to use their Adult in dealing with the demands of their Parent and Child.

Probably the most important concept to remember when dealing with children is that we all grow up feeling not OK. Children function on the basis of the OK-ness they see in their parents. If Mommy frequently responds to the child with *her* not-OK Child, the stage is set for the establishment of the I'm not OK–You're not OK position. In the case of the severely abused child, the extreme I'm OK–You're not OK position is a real possibility. One of the best ways for youngsters to develop strong Adult ego states is to observe their parents use their Adults in handling inappropriate responses from the demanding Parent or Child.

TA principles can be effectively taught to children using a variety of tools such as posters, pictures, humorous role-playing, and so on. Alvyn Freed and Margaret Freed have given examples in their books *TA for Kids* (1974a) and *TA for Tots* (1974b). The kids learn how to be "prinzes" instead of "frozzes." They also learn how to give and get warm fuzzies (positive strokes) and how to avoid giving and getting cold pricklies (negative strokes). Of course, in getting strokes, one must not play games.

As mentioned before, the goal of TA counseling with children is to help them learn to control their responses with their Adult, thereby achieving the I'm OK—You're OK life position. It must be remembered, however, that strengthening a child's Adult will cause his or her role in the family to shift. It is hoped that the child will no longer be as active in playing the destructive games that dominate many families. Other family members' roles will of necessity shift also. For this reason, the child's parents must be included in the counseling process in order to achieve lasting results.

Children can learn all about warm fuzzies and cold pricklies, but because of the tremendous influence of their parents, it is next to impossible, without effective intervention, for them to reverse the "loser" life script their parents may have given them. Everything parents do and say to children tells them they are OK or not OK, depending on what life position the parents themselves occupy. People attract not what they want but what they are. People also rear not the children they want but the children who reproduce what they, the parents, are.

Positive stroking and respect are two things we all need in building a winner's script. The child needs positive strokes, both conditional ("We'll have some ice cream after you put away your toys") and unconditional ("I love you no matter what"). Children come to see themselves as OK because their parents treat them that way.

As a positive stroke, it's hard to beat respect. The conclusion a child reaches is this: if my OK parents think I'm OK, then I really must be OK. If you want the Adult in your youngsters to grow, you must respect your children.

Another useful TA principle for both teachers and parents is to teach "do" and not "don't." It baffles children when parents and adults attempt to teach appropriate behavior by catching children doing inappropriate behavior. Since Mommy is OK, a child thinks "It must be all my fault, and I must be not OK."

A slightly different aspect of the same idea is that in counseling and teaching children that they must "do more" or "do better," it is also important to let the child know *what*. The Parent in all of us admonishes "do better." It is our Adult who supplies the "do *what* better."

As children and their families become better acquainted with the whys of their relationships, they learn to avoid undesirable ways of structuring time. Again, the goal of TA is to help the individual learn to lead a full, game-free life. And everyone has that choice. The usefulness of the P-A-C model comes in creating awareness of how the Parent, Adult, and Child function in decision-making.

As mentioned earlier, several techniques for teaching TA to children have been developed. The concepts of positive and negative stroking have been taught with smiling and frowning faces as well as with fuzzy yarn balls and sharp, prickly plastic objects to connote warm fuzzies and cold pricklies. The warm fuzzy/cold prickly fairy tale (Steiner, 1975) was written for the Child in all of us. A summary of the fairy tale follows:

> There once existed a town where people shared their warm fuzzies without fear of running out of their supply of fuzzies. One day a wicked witch appeared and planted the idea that people should hoard their fuzzies in case there happened to be a shortage of fuzzies. When the townspeople did this, their backbones began to shrivel up. The witch cured the shriveling backbones by giving everybody a bag of cold pricklies to share. The sharing of cold pricklies continued until a good witch arrived and put the townspeople back on the right track, sharing their warm fuzzies.

Counselors and teachers can follow the story by bringing a bowl of sugar-free candy to class and telling the children that the only way they can have a piece of candy is if someone gives them a piece. The counselor or teacher serves as a model in the exercise, making sure each child receives a piece of candy.

Posters can be made with representations of the various ideas of TA (stroking, ego states, I'm OK–You're OK, lists of games with appropriate illustrations, lists of scripting phrases, and so on). The use of puppets, dolls, and make-believe stories can be successful with younger children who cannot yet read.

A three-step process is effective in teaching TA to any child. First, explain the principle, using a story, a poster, puppets, or other age-appropriate methods. Second, ask the children to "read" back what they understand of the TA principle (correcting them as you go along). Third, ask the children to give examples of the principle from their own experience ("What positive strokes have you received today?") or to identify examples of the principle you gave them ("What ego state does 'You must always go to bed early' come from?").

Teach children who are having conflicts with others new stroking patterns. They first need to analyze the other person's behavior. What response does parent, teacher, friend give to the child's positive or negative strokes? What strokes does the other person like? Teach children new ways of stroking from among these categories:

1. Self-stroking—doing nice things for yourself
2. Physical strokes—hugs, kisses, pats, backrubs, handshakes, "high fives" (be sure to distinguish between good and bad touching)
3. Silent strokes—winks, nods, waves, smiles
4. Verbal strokes—"I like you," "Good job," "Thanks"
5. Rewards or privileges—letting younger siblings go with you, playing with them, doing something for parents

Young children (5–7 years) may not be able to symbolize stroking and ego states as well as older ones, and less technical language may be necessary. Young children can understand "warm fuzzy" if a stroke feels good, and "cold prickly" if they feel bad after someone says or does something to them. They may need permission to ask for a warm fuzzy instead of manipulating for a cold prickly when they feel bad. Likewise, small children can understand "my bossy part," "my thinking part," "my angry part," or "my happy part" rather than the ego states, which they sometimes confuse with actual people.

Ego-grams are bar graphs showing children "how much" of each ego state they use (see Figure 9-7). An ego-gram can indicate where changes might be made. If a child thinks that he or she wants to make a change, the child can work on strengthening low ego states by practicing appropriate behaviors. See if the child thinks the ego-gram differs in various situations—at home, at school, playing with friends.

Once children understand ego states, they can learn to distinguish complementary, crossed, and ulterior transactions. If they bring in a situation that illustrates one of these, have them diagram it. In the case of crossed or ulterior transactions, encourage children to use their Adult to figure out ways to obtain a more successful result.

Some other methods for teaching the various TA techniques are described in the following list.

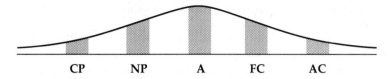

CP	NP	A	FC	AC

Key:

P The Parent refers to a person's values, beliefs, and morals.

    CP The Critical Parent finds fault, directs, orders, sets limits, makes rules, and enforces one's value system. Too much CP results in dictatorial or bossy behavior.

    NP The Nurturing Parent is empathic and promotes growth. The NP is warm and kind, but too much NP becomes smothering, and children will not be able to learn how to take care of themselves.

A The Adult acts like a computer. It takes in, stores, retrieves, and processes information. The A is a storehouse of facts and helps you think when you solve problems, but too much Adult is boring.

C The Child can be fun, expressive, and spontaneous, and sometimes it can be compliant and a follower of rules.

    FC The Free Child is the fun and spontaneous part of the child. When you cheer at a ballgame, you are in the Free Child part of your personality. However, too much FC might mean that you have lost control of yourself.

    AC The Adapting Child is the conforming, easy-to-get-along-with part of your personality. Too much AC results in guilt feelings, depression, other bad feelings, and robotlike behavior.

FIGURE 9-7 Ego-gram

1. Talk about the feelings and behaviors that go with each ego state. Have children identify their own ego states and the ego states of others. This can easily be done by relating the ego states to what children tell you about their experiences.

   Child: My brother always tells me what to do. He's not my father.
   Counselor: You feel rebellious when your brother acts like a bossy
     parent.

As children become aware of their ego states and can discriminate them, their Adult can gain control of which ego state is expressed and give them permission to replace destructive ideas with constructive ones.

2. The OK Corral diagram below is useful in helping children identify how they feel and think about themselves and other people. Children are

able to discuss what OK-ness and not-OK-ness mean to them in terms of specific behaviors.

3. Games intrigue children. Once they have the concept, they can readily pick up on games in themselves and others and describe them. Any time children describe a pattern of games or recognize that "this always happens to me," the counselor can introduce the concept of games as a way of getting negative strokes to replace the positive strokes children think they cannot get. You can use such interventions as "You seem to mess up a lot. How do you manage that?" "What does this mean about you?" "How did it feel after it happened?" "What do you really want? How could you get it better?" "What 'bad' (scary) thing does this game prevent?"

Children can also identify the three game roles of persecutor, rescuer, and victim and learn to stay out of them. The persecutor role can be demonstrated by having the child try to "put someone down" by pressing straight down on his or her shoulders. It is very difficult to put people down by doing this unless they lean over or bend their knees. One can demonstrate the rescuer role by trying to pick up a limp person (of about the same size). It is very difficult to hold up a person who does not want to stand. The victim role is demonstrated in relation to the other two by the partner's "giving in" and lying down and staying limp.

4. Racket feelings can be discussed in terms of stamp collecting. Children can usually identify the bad feelings they save up and the prize they get. Hypothetical situations such as the following create bad feelings: "Did you ever have a rotten day? Your mom yells at you at breakfast, your teacher catches you talking, the other guys play keep-away with your hat, and you drop your books in the mud when your dog jumps on you because he's so glad to see you home. All day long you have felt mistreated and hurt, and that is the last straw. So you pick a fight with your little sister." Talk about how it feels to cash stamps in and how it feels to get dumped on. As small people, children are often the target of stamp cashing. Being aware of this can help children stop collecting stamps (child abuse is the worst form of stamp cashing). Two main ways of not collecting stamps are learning to talk about bad feelings with someone you can trust and asking for and receiving the positive strokes you need.

5. For counselors working with script issues, useful questions for figuring out a child's script include many of the same questions used in the Adlerian lifestyle interview (see Chapter 10):

What are the "hurt" points in your family? (G)
Who is in your family? (BP)
What are the people in your family like? (BP)
Has anyone else ever lived with you? (BP)

What were they like? (BP)
Who is boss in your family? (PI, P)
What is your mother's (or father's) favorite saying? (PI, CI)
Describe yourself in three words. (BP, D)
What words would other people in your family use to describe you? (PI, CI, BP)
What bad feeling do you have a lot? (R)
What good feeling do you have a lot? (BP)
Who is your mother's favorite? (PI, CI)
Who is your father's favorite? (PI, CI)

The preceding questions are coded to fit parts of the life script.

BP—Basic life position regarding how I feel about myself and others
PI—Parental injunction (message from parent's Child): "Don't do as I do"
CI—Counterinjunction (message from parent's Parent): "Do at least try"
G—Games (getting strokes at others' expense)
R—Racket (bad feelings)
D—Decision (how I have chosen to live my life)
P—Program (how to obey injunctions)

6. Most people have kept a diary or journal at some time during their lives in which they have recorded their innermost feelings, thoughts, and other events. Children respond well to a homework assignment of keeping a diary. The diary provides the counselor and child with a record of feelings, thoughts, and life script to be explored. Keeping a journal or diary may also provide the child with a feeling of closeness to the counselor between sessions.

7. What *not* to do: If you are not in a position to protect a child from negative consequences, do not interfere with script behavior that still serves a purpose in the family. Do not ask children to give up their games or rackets before they learn more appropriate ways to get strokes. Do not decide for children what they "should" do. Do not encourage children to play TA counselor with people who have power over them and may not appreciate it.

All the preceding exercises can be used in group and family counseling as well as in individual counseling. Role-playing and acting out games are very effective group techniques. Families in TA counseling come to recognize where their transactions become crossed, how and when scripting occurs, and how stroking behavior can change family feelings.

CASE STUDIES[1]

Transcript I

Jim, age 5, is being seen by the school counselor because Jim has been fighting with other children in his kindergarten class. Jim has only recently started this.

Counselor: Jim, remember when I came to your class and read the story about the warm fuzzies and the cold pricklies? (Jim nods.) Well, everybody, kids and grown-ups, needs to get some of these to live. Sometimes people do things to get cold pricklies like slaps or frowns, or being yelled at. Would you like to find out how to give yourself and other people nice warm fuzzies like smiles and hugs, and get them back from others?

Jim: Yes. Everybody doesn't like me now.

Counselor: What do you do to get hugs and smiles from your mommy?

Jim: I don't do anything, she just gives them to me. Or sometimes I hug her first or say "I love you."

Counselor: Sometimes mommies are busy. What do you do to get her attention then?

Jim: Well, I get a hug from Grandma. But if I can't get one, I make my little sister yell. Then somebody comes to see what's happening.

Counselor: If you can't get a warm fuzzy, you get them to give you a cold prickly?

Jim: Yeah.

Counselor: What do kids in your class have to do to get a hug?

Jim: They hug you if you fall down. But I don't fall down, so nobody hugs me.

Counselor: If you can't get a hug or other warm fuzzy when you want one, what do you do to get attention?

Jim: I make one of the other kids yell.

Counselor: Sometimes getting yelled at is better than nothing, huh?

Jim: Yeah.

Counselor: Do you think any of your teachers would give you a warm fuzzy?

Jim: Miss Sally has a nice face.

Counselor: So when you feel bad inside and need a warm fuzzy, you could get one from Miss Sally?

Jim: Yeah, like when I miss my mommy. I could tell Miss Sally that and ask her to hug me.

---

[1] The case study transcripts and several teaching ideas in the "Counseling Method" section were contributed by Mary Wells Holbrook (Transcript II) and Jean Wycoff (Transcript I).

Counselor: That sounds like a good plan, Jim. And if you feel bad, or sad, or lonely, or angry, and need to talk about it, you can come here and talk to me about it.

Jim: OK.

Counselor: (gives Jim a hug) I give warm fuzzies, too.

Counselor feedback to Jim's teacher should include talking about giving Jim some strokes when he is being good and not making a bid for negative feedback.

Transcript II

The child in this interview is a 10-year-old boy.

Counselor: Christopher, you've read Dr. and Ms. Freed's book about stroking. Can you explain to me what they mean by strokes?

Christopher: Stroking is when somebody does some type of action, physical or verbal, that makes you feel either good or not so good.

Counselor: I think that's a very good definition. Can you give me some examples of a positive stroke?

Christopher: Patting somebody, or hugging them, or saying something nice.

Counselor: Like what?

Christopher: You really did well today.

Counselor: Can you think of a positive stroke you've given someone today?

Christopher: Not really.

Counselor: How about when I came in, and you looked up and smiled?

Christopher: I guess. I smiled at most everybody in the class today.

Counselor: You have to remember that they don't have to be verbal; just a smile is a positive stroke. Can you think of any negative strokes you've given anyone today?

Christopher: No.

Counselor: That's good. Of course, the same holds true for negative strokes—if, without realizing it, you looked at someone and gave them a hard frown or something, that could be a negative stroke that you didn't realize you gave.

Christopher: I don't see why I would have given any, even by accident. There wasn't any reason to give any.

Counselor: Well, good. Can you think of any positive strokes anyone gave you today?

Christopher: When I got 100 on our test today, Mrs. Kincaid said that that was very good.

Counselor: I'm glad. Any negative strokes?

Christopher: No.

Counselor: Well, I told you your hands and face were dirty and I didn't like you coming downtown like that, right? You think you've got the idea about how positive and negative strokes work?

Christopher: Yes.

Counselor: How would you use stroking?

Christopher: Well, whenever I thought somebody did a good job on something, I could tell them.

Counselor: You know, there's such a thing as giving strokes that are not asked for, strokes that you just offer freely. Can you give an example of one of those, maybe?

Christopher: Just saying something nice when they don't even really need it . . . well, they do need it. Just saying it, but just saying it even if they haven't done anything.

Counselor: Be more specific.

Christopher: Well, if you meet somebody, you can say "I like your shoes," or "Your hair looks nice," or something like that.

Counselor: Yes, those would be nice to hear. Can you tell me how you might use nonverbal positive strokes?

Christopher: By patting somebody, or smiling at them, or giving them a hug.

Counselor: How do you think you would feel if you started giving more positive strokes and getting more positive strokes?

Christopher: All covered over with strokes.

RESEARCH AND REACTIONS[2]

Literature and research summaries on transactional analysis are directed toward several topics central to TA theory and practice.

Consultation Strategy

Kenny and Lyons (1980) researched the usefulness of TA as a model for school consultation. A 14-year-old girl in a class for students with learning disabilities and her teacher were the subjects in this study. Following consultation with the teacher on how to use and practice using the Nurturing Parent and Free Child ego states with the student, the student's oppositional behavior declined. The increased use of the two ego states in interactions with the student remained through a five-day follow-up pe-

---

[2] Connie O'Connell and Linda VanBeke summarized the 1970s research studies.

riod. TA interventions have the immediate goal of rebalancing the ego states.

Kenny (1981), in a follow-up effort, studied the effect problem students have on teacher ego states. Two teachers, each with an identified problem student, were the subjects in this study. Three teacher ego-state behaviors were targeted and monitored on the days the students were present and absent. The three ego states were Nurturing Parent (approval, praise, rewards), Critical Parent (disapproval, punishment), and Free Child (laughter, surprise, pleasant excitement). Both teachers exhibited more Nurturing Parent behaviors and Free Child behaviors with their classes when the problem student was absent. The teachers' Critical Parent behaviors toward the class increased when the problem student was present.

Discipline

Erskine and Maisenbacher (1975) found that a one-semester TA course for "worst-problem" high school students resulted in an increase in overall grade average, fewer discipline referrals, and a marked decrease in truancy for each student.

Bloomfield and Goodman (1976) studied the effects of a "feelings" course designed to improve communication skills in emotionally disturbed preadolescent children. Informal chartings by teachers showed a decreased incidence of maladaptive behaviors following the course. The greatest decrease was in verbally aggressive behaviors.

Amundson and Sawatsky (1976) studied elementary school teachers (Grades 3 to 6) who agreed to present basic transactional analysis with children's material in their classrooms. Several teachers indicated that the program had a significant effect on their lives, especially with regard to their relationship with their students. The program was very effective with poorly behaved children in the classes.

Jesness (1975) studied 983 adolescent delinquents assigned to two institutions. The program of one institution was based on TA; that of the other was based on the principles of behavior modification. Improvement on psychological measures favored participants in the TA program; behavior ratings slightly favored the behavioral program. Periodic follow-up observations provided evidence that both groups were doing significantly better than the comparison groups of the same age assigned to other institutions.

Adams (1974) evaluated a TA program administered to adult male prison inmates in 1971. Ninety-five percent of the participants felt they had gained control of the destructive aspects of their behavior and had attained a more positive feeling toward themselves and others. During the six months of therapy, the punishment-incident rate for each person in the group dropped by about 50 percent.

Parent Education

Bredehoft (1986) studied the effect of TA parent education on family members' self-esteem, adaptability, cohesion, and conflict. The classes were conducted in ten 2-hour sessions. Fathers who attended the class perceived their families as more adaptable and were more satisfied with family cohesion. Significant changes occurred in both average family empathy and mother's empathy with father. No significant changes were recorded in the area of self-concept.

The Glen family (1982) described an interesting family-counseling technique incorporating TA techniques to improve their family-system functioning. Basically, they agreed to spend one half-day period practicing role reversal, in which the two children could select parent roles while the parents took the children's roles. The roles came complete with duties. The parent role included setting limits for the children, cooking, and putting the children to bed. Role reversal offers a good way to exchange positive and negative feedback, as well as to build empathy for the other family members. Communication and interaction was facilitated by role reversal.

Bredehoft (1990) researched the effectiveness of a TA parent-training program on the self-esteem and communication skills of abusive parents. The program was successful in building self-esteem; however, there was no evidence that communication skills were improved.

Strokes

Horwitz (1982), using a sample of 52 female and 27 male adult subjects who had applied for counseling services, studied the relationship between positive stroking and self-perceived symptoms of distress. Distress was defined as a self-reported lapse of memory, lower back pains, headaches, low self-esteem, bad temper, or loss of desire for physical encounters. It was hypothesized that people who frequently get positive strokes by asking for them will show fewer symptoms of distress than those who view themselves as recipients of infrequent positive strokes. Self-reported symptoms of distress were found to decrease as receipt of positive strokes increased.

Allen and Allen (1989), writing on stroking and its relationship to biological well-being, pointed out that, while a lack of strokes may not cause your spinal cord to shrivel up, it could relate to other biological conditions as well as to depression and failure to thrive. The authors argued that if TA is to continue to "thrive," it is important to use it as a framework in developmental and longitudinal research on real children and to begin integrating TA with current developments in biological research.

Self-Esteem

Golub and Guerriero (1981), in a study of the effects of TA training on the self-concept of learning-disabled boys from Grades 2 to 4, found that 18 sessions of 30 minutes each were sufficient to help the boys achieve a significant positive change in their Coopersmith Self-Esteem Inventory scores. Role-playing and practice sessions gave the learning-disabled students the opportunity to successfully demonstrate application of their TA understanding.

Ego States

Goldberg and Summerfield (1982) tested the assumption that a person's personality depends on the amount of time that person spends in a given ego state. Two hypotheses were tested: (1) observers' judgments on neuroticism and extroversion would depend on the ego state of the videotaped stimulus person; and (2) a significant difference would appear between managers and students on the judgments stated in the first hypothesis. The Child ego state was rated significantly more extroverted than the Parent ego state. The Parent ego state was rated more neurotic and less extroverted. No significant differences between managers' and students' ratings were found in the videotaped ratings. Gilmore (1981), in an attempt to go beyond the clinical observation of ego states, measured physiological responses to the three ego states. Subjects were to respond orally to a questionnaire composed of questions designed to evoke Child, Adult, or Parent ego states. Each category required answers to 15 questions. Ego state 1 compared Child/Adult, ego state 2 compared Child/Parent, and ego state 3 compared Adult/Parent. Monitors recorded skin temperature, respiration, and heart rate. Significant changes occurred in half the comparisons made. A significant change was detected in skin-surface temperature and respiration rate with ego states 2 and 3. There was also a significant difference between heart rate and skin conductance for ego state 1.

White (1983) proposed a three-chair version of the Gestalt topdog/underdog debate. The client would be asked to speak from chairs representing Parent, Child, and Adult. Presumably the same "I should" versus "I want" debate would still take place until the Adult ego state takes over, evaluates the data, and makes a decision.

Kleinewiese (1980) conducted a study comparing two methods for teaching TA to children. One method employed visual models of the ego states, and the other was the traditional lecture approach. The visual-model group required an average explanation time of 3.75 minutes on each of the ego states. The other group required 10.75 minutes to accomplish the same task. Visual aids are always superior for teaching and counseling children who have not attained formal thinking skills.

Bala (1986) described a TA treatment method for autistic children and offered a four-step plan: (1) attachment—developed on a physical level, followed by an emotional level, by nurturing the child; (2) Child ego state—work on body image and a sense of "me" and "not me" by increasing contact with the outside world; (3) Adult ego state—special-education classes in perception, language, communication, and motor ability; and (4) Parent ego state—after language skill develops, the child can integrate good and bad objects. For example, TA with play therapy can be used to integrate the child's perception of mother as sometimes good and sometimes dangerous. The counseling session can be used to work on new responses to the mother's behavior.

Manning and Manning (1988), in an attempt to study the quantity and content of the private self-talk of preservice teachers, found that 65 percent of the self-talk characterized the Adult ego state, 55 percent indicated an external locus of control, and negative self-talk exceeded positive self-talk. The increased levels of stress involved in teaching would be better handled by positive self-talk, an internal locus of control, and adult problem-solving logic.

Hazell (1989), in describing five driver responses as mediators of stress, crossed over into RET territory. The five drivers, or self-messages, are Be Pleasing, Be Perfect, Be Strong, Hurry Up, and Try Harder. As is the case with most irrational thoughts, these driver responses usually get their user exactly what they try to avoid. Extremes of each driver parallel a variety of personality disorders. Be Pleasing, associated with seeking love while avoiding rejection, relates to histrionic, avoidant, and dependent disorders. Be Perfect, associated with gaining respect while avoiding looking bad, is linked with obsessive-compulsive and narcissistic disorders. Be Strong, associated with hiding feeling, is related to schizoid disorders. Hurry Up, associated with gaining control, is compared to impulse-control disorders. Try Harder, associated with avoiding being controlled, is linked to passive-aggressive, antisocial, and paranoid personality disorders.

Craig and Olson (1988), in researching changes in ego states following treatment for drug abuse, found that ego states, as measured by the Adjective Checklist, changed from the Adaptive Child to the Adult. Before treatment, the participants were characterized by higher needs for succorance, abasement, heterosexuality, exhibitionism, deference, nurturance, and change. Following treatment, the participants' scores were higher for achievement, dominance, endurance, and orderliness.

Relationships

Thweatt (1974) found that 78 percent of the students in a psychology course integrated with TA reported an increase in self-awareness, and more than 50 percent reported improvement in personal or family relations (specific changes).

Windell and Woollams (1974) studied people who had been involved in TA training and therapy since 1971. Results of a questionnaire that dealt with perceived changes in relationships with spouse and other individuals showed that the participants perceived that their relationships with other people, especially their spouses, had changed markedly. Eighty-four percent believed that their marriages had improved.

Spencer (1977) studied employees who had received an introductory TA course. Overall morale, interpersonal relationships, and productivity improved.

Gormly and Gormly (1984), in a study on reactions to emotions, found that the most likely reaction to anger, anxiety, or happiness is to seek out others. For depression, the most likely reaction is avoiding people. Their results have implications for counselors using transactional analysis.

Nykodym, Rund, and Liverpool (1986) investigated whether or not TA training would be an effective pre–quality-circle strategy to improve communication skills. An experimental group received six half-day sessions of TA training. Two hypotheses were affirmed: (1) TA training will improve perception of co-worker communication, and (2) interaction of group members will improve after TA training. A control group showed no change on either dimension.

Games

Douglas (1986) reviewed the current literature on adolescent suicide in an attempt to find support for the theory that it is a third-degree game in the TA system. (The third-degree game is a magnification of inflexible, tenacious, and intense game patterns that constitute mental disturbance. The victims in the game include family and friends who must suffer when the teenager commits suicide.) Some conclusions reached in the review were: (1) adolescent suicide attempts, whether successful or not, are attempts to gain strokes from others; (2) suicide attempts are often preceded by rebelling, withdrawing, or running away; (3) parent/child relationships are not good and are often characterized by too much parental control or no control at all; (4) parent/child relationships often lack closeness; and (5) the third-degree game requirements are met.

Zalcman (1990), in an update of Berne's concepts of game and racket analysis, reemphasized that games undermine the stability of relationships. Strokes are the motivation for games, and the need for strokes often turns an honest transaction into a game. Rackets are described as ego-state switches within the intrapsychic structure of an individual. Game analysis deals with transactions between two people. A racket could be the procrastination racket of "I'll do it tomorrow," where the child masquerades as the adult. An example of a game would be "why don't you; yes but . . ." where a person says "help me," the helper gives advice, and the helpee says "Yes, but that won't work."

Choy (1990), in an article on how to move from Karpman's Drama Triangle (DT) to the Winner's Triangle (WT), made the point that the persecutor, rescuer, and victim points of the drama triangle correlate to the respective assertive, caring, and vulnerable roles in the winner's triangle. "Vulnerable" is distinguished from "victim" in that the vulnerable person, maintaining contact with the adult's logical problem-solving capability, works out a solution to the problem. Assertive people see negotiation as a viable part of problem solving and have no interest in punishing or cheating others. Persecutors, on the other hand, will satisfy personal needs by discounting the victim's importance and feelings. People in both the rescuer and the caring roles act out of genuine concern; however, the rescuer's motivation is the need to feel superior or reassured that, "I'm OK." Counselors can avoid the rescuer role if they maintain adult-to-adult communication in counseling interviews. Active listening, coupled with no advice giving, should also help the counselor avoid the rescuer role.

Reparenting

Wilson, White, and Heiber (1985) compared the TA technique of "reparenting" with traditional psychotherapy in treating adolescent and young adult schizophrenics. The hospital patients in both groups received five 2-hour sessions per week. The reparenting patients were held and fed by bottles and allowed to regress to earlier developmental stages when proper nurturance was not available to them. Pretreatment and posttreatment data were collected on the Minnesota Multiphasic Personality Inventory (MMPI) and DSM-III evaluations. The reparenting group made significant positive changes in mental condition and level of adaptive functioning. The reparenting group was rated slightly higher than the traditional-treatment group in both areas.

Smith (1989) conducted a study of clinicians who use regressive work in their therapy. Regressive work is based on the TA concept of reparenting, where new parent messages replace old, counterproductive messages as a new, healthy life script begins to take shape. Results of the survey indicated that regressive work is most effective with adults 18–40 and is seldom used with children under 12. Regression therapy was rated to be 30 percent effective with adolescents. Women seemed to benefit from it more than men, 74.6 percent to 54.1 percent.

Moroney (1989) described five reparenting strategies for providing clients with new parent messages to replace the inadequate or dysfunctional ones they received in childhood. Total regression reparenting is a 24-hour, comprehensive approach in which the client lives with the therapist throughout treatment. Through regression to early childhood periods of conflict, the client is provided with a nurturing and protective environment until he or she reaches psychological adulthood. The Child's needs are met, and a complete change in the client's unhealthy Parent ego state results. Reparenting with time-limited regression can take place in a series of two-hour group sessions. Spot reparenting is a focused approach targeted toward less severely disturbed patients and toward traumatic incidents rather than developmental periods. Self-reparenting does not attempt to replace the entire Parent ego state. Instead, the counselor affirms the positive aspects of the client's Parent ego and gives the Child ego comfort and support. Reparenting using parents of origin involves the client in playing the reparenting role. Here, the dysfunction of the defective Parent ego resulted from defective communication rather than from bad parenting.

Clarkson and Fish (1988) discussed "rechilding" as creating a new past in the present as a support for the future. The individual regresses to a younger age in which development deficits occurred. There, deficit periods are recreated in ways that allow clients to react with positive, healthy responses. Briefly, when stressed, a person may move from the Adult to either the Child or Parent ego state. If neither can support the stressed Adult, script regression may occur. Reparenting and rechilding allow the Adult to find greater stability under stress.

Script Analysis

Stapleton and Murkison (1990), in a study with implications for career development, found evidence of early scripting in college business majors. Over 50 percent of the business students studied entertained their first entrepreneurial fantasies and thoughts during their middle teens. Comparing students to actual entrepreneurs, they found that only 35 percent of the entrepreneurs had experienced similar fantasies and thoughts before age 19. Fewer business failures occurred for those people whose entrepreneurial fantasies appeared after age 21.

Price (1990), writing on borderline disorders, emphasized the role the family plays in these cases. Borderline disorders are defined as an inability to integrate the good and bad aspects of self and others. Things are either all good or all bad; there are no gray areas or in-betweens. This all-or-nothing approach to living, which can shift immediately from one extreme to the other, results in an inability to acquire a coherent sense of self and others. Price lists four causal family factors of borderline disorders: (1) rewarding Child behavior and punishing independent, assertive Adult behavior; (2) stressing the importance of the family myth—for example, in cases of child sexual abuse, the abuse is justified or denied; (3) sending double-bind messages, where the child is forced to deny or distort the truth—for example, the reality of abuse and its cover-up; and (4) activating the child's "protect my parent" defense mechanism, in which the child protects and preserves the idealized image of the abusive parent.

With a "perfect" parent, any problem must be the fault of the "bad" child victim.

Olia (1989), in an article on treating adult survivors of sexual abuse, focused on memory retrieval. She pointed out that approximately 27 percent of women and 16 percent of men have been victims of sexual abuse and that many victims have handled the trauma by denial or dissociation. *Denial* is defined as blocking the event from consciousness. *Dissociation* allows victims to desensitize their bodies or remove themselves altogether from the event. Memory work for survivors is similar to that done for amnesiacs where loss of knowledge, rather than of memory, is the problem. Asking clients to "guess" or "tell a story" often helps them regain the lost knowledge. Two other methods are also used: (1) recall, requiring a client to consider a stimulus possibility before determining its familiarity; and (2) recognition, determining whether a stimulus seems familiar to the client. Olia provided some guidelines for recognizing adult survivors of sexual abuse. Although the indicators are not sure signs of childhood sexual abuse, most survivors suffer depression, phobias, anxiety disorders, sexual dysfunction, and difficulty maintaining close, intimate relationships.

Osnes and Rendack (1989), in a related article on abuse survivors, stated that we live our lives in four script areas: body, mind, emotion, and spirit. Childhood abuse affects each area's function and development. Bodies may be neglected by excessive eating or physical illness. Minds may be affected by faulty reasoning. Emotional lives may be disjointed, and spiritual involvement may run from hyperreligiosity to complete atheism. The recommended treatment is ego-state education, where the Parent and Adult ego states are aligned with the counselor as advocates of the not-OK Child ego state. Trust-building and maintenance, while important in all counseling, is especially critical to success in counseling abuse survivors.

Summary

The practitioners of transactional analysis continue to enjoy wide popularity for improving relationship and communication skills between individuals and within groups of various types. However, Douglass (1990), in a survey of TA literature available to college students, found that Gestalt therapy is represented more often than TA. Students had a 37 percent chance of studying TA and a 66 percent chance of studying Gestalt. Douglass was also concerned that TA was not well defined, nor were its techniques properly integrated with theory. In fact, many authors had difficulty agreeing on where to place TA in relation to philosophical orientation. Douglass recommended that standards and guidelines on TA information be developed in an effort to ensure TA's survival and proper professional presentation.

REFERENCES

Adams, L. (1974). Uses of TA with adult male prison inmates. *Transactional Analysis Journal, 3,* 18–20.

Allen, J., & Allen, B. (1989). Stroking: Biological underpinnings and direct observations. *Transactional Analysis Journal, 19,* 26–31.

Amundson, N., & Sawatsky, D. (1976). An educational program and TA. *Transactional Analysis Journal, 6,* 217–220.

Bala, J. (1986). "Mama stop doing MMMMMMM": TA in the treatment of autistic children. *Transactional Analysis Journal, 16,* 234–239.

Berne, E. (1949). The nature of intuition. *Psychiatric Quarterly, 23,* 203–226.

Berne, E. (1961). *Transactional analysis in psychotherapy.* New York: Grove Press.

Berne, E. (1964). *Games people play.* New York: Grove Press.

Bloomfield, B., & Goodman, G. (1976). A TA approach to children's feelings. *Transactional Analysis Journal, 6,* 323–325.

Bredehoft, D. (1986). An evaluation of self-esteem: A family affair. *Transactional Analysis Journal, 16,* 175–181.

Bredehoft, D. J (1990). Self-esteem: A family affair. *Transactional Analysis Journal, 20,* 111–116.

Choy, A. (1990). The winner's triangle. *Transactional Analysis Journal, 20,* 40–45.

Clarkson, P., & Fish, S. (1988). Rechilding: Creating a new past in the present as a support for the future. *Transactional Analysis Journal, 18,* 51–59.

Craig, R., & Olson, R. (1988). Changes in functional ego states following treatment for drug abuse. *Transactional Analysis Journal, 18,* 43–48.

Douglas, L. (1986). Is adolescent suicide a third degree game and who is the real victim? *Transactional Analysis Journal, 16,* 165–169.

Douglass, H. (1990). Transactional analysis in American college psychology textbooks. *Transactional Analysis Journal, 20,* 92–109.

Erskine, R., & Maisenbacher, J. (1975). The effects of a TA class on socially maladjusted high school students. *Transactional Analysis Journal, 5,* 252–254.

Freed, A., & Freed, M. (1974a). *TA for kids.* Sacramento, CA: Freed.

Freed, A., & Freed, M. (1974b). *TA for tots.* Sacramento, CA: Freed.

Gilmore, J. R (1981). Psychological evidence of ego states. *Transactional Analysis Journal, 11,* 207–212.

Glen, R., Glen, O., Glen, L., & Glen, A. (1982). Upside-down day: A family role reversal experience. *Transactional Analysis Journal, 12,* 277–279.

Goldberg, H., & Summerfield, A. (1982). The perception of Parent and Child ego states. *Transactional Analysis Journal, 12,* 223–226.

Golub, S., & Guerriero, L. (1981). The effects of a transactional analysis program on self-esteem in learning disabled boys. *Transactional Analysis Journal, 11,* 244–246.

Gormly, A., & Gormly, J. (1984). A psychological study of emotions. *Transactional Analysis Journal, 14,* 74–79.

Harris, T. (1969). *I'm OK—you're OK.* New York: Harper & Row.

Hazell, J. (1989). Drivers as mediators of stress response. *Transactional Analysis Journal, 19,* 212–222.

Horwitz, A. (1982). The relationship between positive stroking and self-perceived symptoms of distress. *Transactional Analysis Journal, 12,* 218–221.

James, M., & Jongeward, D. (1971). *Born to win.* Reading, MA: Addison-Wesley.

Jesness, C. (1975). Comparative effectiveness of behavior modification and transactional programs for delinquents. *Journal of Consulting and Clinical Psychology, 43,* 759–779.

Kenny, W. (1981). Problem-student effects on teacher ego state behavior. *Transactional Analysis Journal, 11,* 252–253.

Kenny, W., & Lyons, B. (1980). A TA model of school consultation: An empirical analysis. *Transactional Analysis Journal, 10,* 264–269.

Kleinewiese, E. (1980). TA with children: Visual representation model of the ego states. *Transactional Analysis Journal, 10,* 259–263.

Manning, B., & Manning, P. (1988). Analysis of private self-talk of preservice teachers. *Educational Research Quarterly, 12,* 46–50.

McCormick, P., & Campos, L. (1969). *Introduce yourself to transactional analysis.* Stockton, CA: San Joaquin Transactional Analysis Study Group.

Moroney, M. (1989). Reparenting strategies in transactional analysis therapy: A comparison of five methods. *Transactional Analysis Journal, 19,* 35–41.

Nykodym, N., Rund, W., & Liverpool, P. (1986). Quality circles: Will transactional analysis improve their effectiveness? *Transactional Analysis Journal, 16,* 182–187.

Olia, A. (1989). Memory retrieval in the treatment of adult survivors of sexual abuse. *Transactional Analysis Journal, 19,* 93–99.

Osnes, R., & Rendack, S. (1989). Therapy with long-term abuse survivors. *Transactional Analysis Journal, 19,* 86–91.

Phillips, P., & Cordell, F. (1975). *Am I OK?* Niles, IL: Argus Communications.

Price, R. (1990). Borderline disorders of the self: Toward a reconceptualization. *Transactional Analysis Journal, 20,* 128–133.

Smith, S. (1989). A study of clinicians who use regressive work. *Transactional Analysis Journal, 19,* 75–79.

Spencer, G. (1977). Effectiveness of an introductory course in TA. *Transactional Analysis Journal, 7,* 346–349.

Stapleton, R., & Murkison, G. (1990). Scripts and entrepreneurship. *Transactional Analysis Journal, 20,* 193–197.

Steiner, C. (1974). *Scripts people live.* New York: Grove Press.

Steiner, C. (1975). *Readings in radical psychiatry.* New York: Grove Press.

Thweatt, W. (1974). Integrating transactional analysis with a university psychology course. *Transactional Analysis Journal, 3,* 23–25.

White, A. (1983). Three-chair parenting. *Transactional Analysis Journal, 13,* 110–111.

Wilson, T., White, T., & Heiber, R. (1985). Reparenting schizophrenic youth in a hospital setting. *Transactional Analysis Journal, 15,* 211–215.

Windell, J., & Woollams, S. (1974). The effects of training on marriage. *Transactional Analysis Journal, 4,* 209–213.

Zalcman, M. (1990). Game analysis and racket analysis: Overview, critique, and future development. *Transactional Analysis Journal, 20,* 4–19.

CHAPTER 10

Individual Psychology

ALFRED ADLER

Alfred Adler, the founder of individual psychology, was born in Vienna, Austria, on February 7, 1870, the second eldest of six children. When Adler was 10 years old, he was found to be doing very poorly in mathematics. His teachers suggested to Adler's father that Alfred be removed from school and assigned as an apprentice to a cobbler. As is often true with paradoxical counseling strategies, Alfred became angry, studied harder, and placed first in his class. As a child, Adler suffered from rickets, pneumonia, and several accidents. The resulting frequent contact with doctors and illness influenced Adler to study medicine.

Adler spent his entire youth in Vienna and received his medical degree from its university in 1895. In addition to medicine, Adler was also knowledgeable in psychology and philosophy as well as the Bible and Shakespeare. Two years after his graduation, Adler married Raisa Timofeyeuna Epstein, an intellectual and friend of Freud's, who had come from Russia to study at the University of Vienna (Alexander, Eisenstein, & Grotjahn, 1966).

In the fall of 1902, Adler joined Sigmund Freud's discussion group, which was to become the first psychoanalytic society. Adler was not a proponent of Freud's psychosexual theory, and his writings about "feelings of inferiority" in 1910 and 1911 initiated a break with Freud. In 1910, in an attempt to reconcile the gap between himself and the Adlerians, Freud named Adler president of the Viennese Analytic Society and appointed him co-editor of a journal published by Freud. Nevertheless, Adler continued to disagree with Freud's psychosexual theory; Adler was the first psychoanalyst to emphasize human nature as being fundamentally social. Upon Freud's demand that his entire staff accept his theory without any conditions, Adler resigned, along with seven others, and founded the Society for Free Psychoanalysis. In 1912, Adler changed the name to the Society for Individual Psychology (Orgler, 1965).

After World War I broke out, Adler served for two years as a military doctor and later was appointed the head of a large hospital for the wounded and shell-shocked. In 1926, Adler accepted a visiting professorship at Columbia University in New York, and in 1935 he moved his family to the United States. His children, one son and one daughter, became psychiatrists and worked with the principles of individual psychology. On May 28, 1937, while giving a series of lectures in Scotland, Adler suddenly collapsed on the street and died of heart failure.

Adler achieved a great deal in his lifetime. In 1912, he founded the *Journal for Individual Psychology*, which was first published in North America in 1935. In 1919, he organized the first child-guidance clinics in Vienna. The staff of these clinics included physicians, psychologists, and social workers. Adler introduced the term *inferiority feelings*, and he developed a flexible, supportive psychotherapy to direct those emotionally disabled by inferiority feelings toward maturity, common sense, and social usefulness.

Adler originated the network of child-guidance clinics called *Erziehungsberatungsstellen*, which means literally "places to come for questions about education" — parent-education centers. He originated the idea of group discussions with families. Many people believe Adler to have been 50 years ahead of his time; present-day emphasis on group counseling and parent education supports this claim.

Perhaps the most helpful adaptations and development of Adler's work were contributed by Rudolf Dreikurs, a leading proponent of individual psychology until his death in 1972. Dreikurs was professor emeritus of psychiatry at the Chicago Medical School, director of the Alfred Adler Institute in Tel Aviv, and visiting professor at many universities in North America and abroad.

Dreikurs was a pioneer in music therapy and group psychotherapy, which he introduced into private psychiatric practice in 1929. A former student and collaborator of Alfred Adler, Dreikurs developed specific technical procedures, based on Adlerian principles, in many fields of human relations. His literary works include nine books and numerous papers (Mosak, 1973). Dreikurs's most significant contribution to the field of counseling children was his ability to translate theory into practice. Dreikurs developed many of Adler's complex ideas into a relatively simple applied method for understanding and working with the behavior of children in both family and school settings.

THE NATURE OF PEOPLE

If Freud had done nothing more than stimulate thinking and reactions in other theorists, he would have made a significant contribution to the field of counseling and psychotherapy. Like many others, Adler reacted against Freud's ideas and developed a new theory. Freud attempted to interpret all behaviors and problems as extensions of sex, pleasure, and the death instinct. Adler, on the other hand, believed that all people develop some sense of inferiority because they are born completely helpless and remain that way for a rather long childhood. Such feelings of inferiority may be exaggerated by body or organ defects (real or imaginary), by having older and more powerful siblings, or by parent neglect or rejection. One way to cope with feelings of inferiority is through compensation or through gaining power to handle the sense of weakness. The effects of organ inferiority are reduced through development of skills, behaviors, traits, and strengths that tend to replace or compensate for these thoughts of weakness and powerlessness.

Adler viewed human behavior as falling on a continuum between his concepts of masculinity, representing strength and power, and femininity, symbolizing weakness and inferiority. What he called *masculine protest*, a striving for power, was common to both sexes, especially women. Adler replaced Freud's concept of sexual pleasure as the prime motivator of behavior with the search for power.

According to Adler, personality development progresses along a road paved with evidence of either personal superiority or inferiority. As infants — small, helpless, inexperienced — we are especially subject to others' whims and vulnerable to inferiority feelings. As we grow older, both family and society emphasize the advantages of size, beauty, and strength. Therefore, there develops within us a continual conflict between our wishes and dreams for superiority, our attempts to achieve it, and the social realities that may make us feel inferior. This striving for power (masculine protest) occupies a place in his theory similar to that of the Oedipus situation in Freudian theory. A person develops into a normal adult or a neurotic or psychotic personality as the result of this struggle between the masculine protest and social reality.

The Need for Success

Adler was struck by the importance of the hunger for success in human life — the ways by which people seek power and prestige and strive for goals associated with social approval. He was very concerned with the problems of competition, blocked ambition, feelings of resentment and hostility, and impulses to struggle and resist or to surrender and give in. Adler shifted his clinical attention from a primary focus on clients' psychosexual history to an examination of their success/failure pattern, or style of life. Adler's term *style of life* emphasizes the direction in which the individual is moving. Style-of-life analysis involves an assessment of children in terms of their habitual responses to frustration, to the assumption of responsibility, and to situations that require the exercise of initiative.

Goals of Behavior

Adler's individual psychology emphasizes the purposive nature of human strivings. All behavior, including emotions, is purposive, or goal directed. According to Adlerian theory, the cause of behavior is not the issue; the important thing is to determine what children want to accomplish, either in the real world or in their own minds. Behaviors will not be continued over time unless they "work" for the children. By looking at the consequences of their behavior, adults can determine their goals. Adler's conception was that people are guided by a striving for ideal masculinity. Adler described what he termed the *neurotic search for glory:* neurotics are characterized by an unrealistic goal of masculinity and mastery that they strive to overcome or attain. He also anticipated later psychoanalytic groups in his emphasis upon the social as well as the constitutional determinants of one's style of life. In fact, the term *individual psychology* is based on Adler's emphasis on the uniqueness of the individual and the creation of a personal lifestyle as opposed to Freud's emphasis on instincts common to all people. The individual's style of life is built from an interaction between heredity and environment; these lifestyle building blocks are used to fit oneself into life as one perceives it.

Lifestyle

Behavior is holistic, according to Adler. Usually by the age of 4 or 5, children have drawn general conclusions about life and the "best" way to meet the problems life offers. These conclusions are based on their biased perceptions of the events and interactions that go on around them and form the basis for their lifestyle. The style of life, unique for each individual, is the pattern of behavior that will predominate throughout that person's life. Only rarely will a person's lifestyle change without outside intervention. It is important that children understand their lifestyle—that is, the basic beliefs they have developed at an early age to help organize, understand, predict, and control their world.

The amount of social interest one possesses is, according to Adler, a good barometer of mental health. Social interest is a feeling for and cooperation with people—a sense of belonging and participating with others for the common good. Everyone has a need to belong to a group. Although social interest is inborn, it does not appear spontaneously but must be encouraged and trained, beginning with the relationship between the newborn infant and the mother. Children who feel they are part of a group will do useful things that contribute to the well-being of that group, while those who feel left out, and therefore inferior, will do useless things in order to prove their own worth by gaining attention. From this concept comes the idea that misbehaving children are discouraged children—children who think that they can be known only in useless ways.

Because children behave within the social context, their behavior cannot be studied in isolation. The study of human interaction is basic to individual psychology.

Many of life's problems center around conflicts with others. Solutions for these problems involve cooperating with people in the interest of making society a better place in which to live. A strong point in Adler's theory is his understanding of the implications of the social structure of life. Because every individual is dependent upon other people for birth and growth, for food and shelter and protection, for love and companionship, a great web of interdependence exists among people. Thus the individual, Adler points out, owes a constant debt to society. Each of us is responsible to our group, and those who do not learn to cooperate are destroyed. Adler believed that we cannot violate the love and logic that bind us together without dire consequences for the health of our personality. Pronounced egocentricity (the opposite of social interest) leads to neurosis, and the individual becomes healthy again only when this egocentricity is renounced in favor of a greater interest in the well-being of the total group. Critics of Adlerian theory who hold a less positive view of human nature point out that even though people know they should cooperate, they ordinarily do not do so until forced. Cross-cultural research evidence exists to support this view.

Environment

Three environmental factors affect the development of a child's personality: family atmosphere, family constellation, and the prevalent methods of training. Through the family atmosphere, children learn about values and customs and try to fit themselves into the standards their parents set. Children also learn about relationships by watching how their family interacts and about sex roles by seeing the patterns adopted by their parents. The family constellation is important in that children formulate unique personalities based on how they interpret their positions in the family relative to other siblings. The following example illustrates one possible pattern. The first-born child, when dethroned by a new baby, tries very hard to maintain the position of supremacy and seeks recognition by whatever means possible. The second child feels inadequate because there is always someone ahead and seeks a place by becoming what the older child is not. This child may feel squeezed out when a third child comes and may adopt the position that life is unfair. The youngest child may take advantage of being the youngest and become outstanding in some respect, be it good or bad. Youngest children may even seek a place by becoming openly rebellious or helpless.

In summary, Adler believed that the principal human motive, a striving for perfection, could become a striving for superiority and thus an overcompensation for a feeling of inferiority. Children are seen as self-determining persons able to create a style of life in the context of their family constellation. By trial and error and observation, children form their own conclusions about life and their place in it.

THEORY OF COUNSELING

Adler (1964, first published in 1938) held the point of view that four ties create reality and meaning in people's lives:

1. People are on earth to help ensure the continuance of the human species.
2. Our survival depends on our need to cooperate with our fellow human beings.
3. Human beings each live in two sexes—the masculine, powerful side of our nature and the feminine, weak side of our nature.
4. Human problems can be grouped into three categories: social, occupational, and sexual.

Adler viewed the counselor's job as helping the child substitute realistic goals for unrealistic life goals and instilling social interest and concern for others.

As with most approaches to counseling, the goal of establishing a positive sense of self-esteem is primary. To achieve this feeling of self-esteem, children need to feel good about finding a place in life and about their progress in overcoming the unpleasant sense of inferiority associated with the dependence, smallness, and vulnerability introduced in early childhood. In the Adlerian view, the ideal or well-adjusted child would exhibit the following qualities:

1. Respects the rights of others
2. Is tolerant of others
3. Is interested in others
4. Cooperates with others
5. Encourages others
6. Is courteous
7. Has a strong, positive self-concept
8. Has a feeling of belonging
9. Has socially acceptable goals
10. Exerts genuine effort
11. Is willing to share with others
12. Is concerned with how much "we" can get rather than how much "I" can get

In response to the specific pattern of inferiority feelings experienced by a child in a specific home situation, one unitary way of coping with the problem is discovered; one fundamental attitude is developed; and one mode of compensation is achieved. Thus, a style of life is formed early in one's childhood—a style that is unitary, dependable, and predictable.

Adler recognized two fundamental styles of life: a direct and an indirect approach to the good things. We may choose to conquer through strength and power or to conquer through weakness. We usually try power first; if power is blocked, we choose another road to our goal. The second road is paved with gentleness and bids for sympathy. If both roads fail to take us to our goals, secondary feelings of inferiority arise. These secondary inferiority feelings, which Adler considered more serious than the primary, universal inferiority feelings, may be seen as ego problems, which can be the most burning problems of all. The focus of counseling, therefore, is directed toward harnessing this drive to compensate for weakness so positive, constructive behavior will result. Freud held that the backbone of civilization was sublimation. Adler thought that talent and capabilities arise from the stimulus of inadequacy.

Adlerians believe that because children are pulled by their goals, adults need to know these goals. Knowledge of children's goals is a major key to understanding their behavior. We need to observe behaviors because movement tends to be more reliable than words. Adlerians work with priorities. For example, the need to belong has four possible priorities:

1. *To be comfortable.* The main objective of seeking comfort is to avoid stress. Such behavior may be irritating to others, and the price you pay for comfort may be reduced productivity.
2. *To please others.* The main objective of pleasing others is to avoid rejection. Although other people may find it quite easy to accept a "me last" person, the price for this behavior is stunted growth.
3. *To control.* The main objective of trying to control others, yourself, and your environment is to avoid unexpected humiliation. Controlling others tends to make them feel challenged, with the resulting price of increased social distance between you and other people. Too much self-control results in a very structured life with little spontaneity.
4. *To be superior.* The main objective of trying to be superior is to avoid meaninglessness in your life. Such an attitude of superiority tends to make others feel inadequate. The price for superiority may be an overloaded lifestyle. The child may become overly responsible and perfectionist, with all the resulting worry and anxiety when things are not perfect.

The Family Constellation

One goal of counseling is to construct a picture of the child's lifestyle and how that style was developed. Such a lifestyle analysis necessitates an examination of the family dynamics and the child's place in the family constellation. Ordinal position in the family constellation is a key to the lifestyle pattern developed by the child and may have a significant effect on how that child perceives reality. Although certain characteristics are associated with each child's position in the family, we know that many exceptions exist; not all first-borns are alike. However, we know that children, in an effort to find their special place in the family, tend to select different roles, behaviors, and interests. In general, some stereotypic behaviors based on birth order have been cataloged by Adlerians over the past 80 years. Some of these generalizations are summarized in the following paragraphs.

The only child.   The only child enjoys some intellectual advantages by not having to share mother and father with any siblings. Language development is usually accelerated because the child learns adult language patterns. However, the reverse is sometimes true in an extremely child-centered home where everyone talks baby talk. Frequently, only children may experience difficulties outside the home when peers and teachers do not pamper them in the manner to which they have become accustomed. Only children may be skillful in getting along with adults but experience difficulty in making friends with children their own age. They enjoy being the center of attention. It is helpful in understanding these children to observe how they gain the approval and attention to maintain their center-stage position. Have they developed skills, do they elicit sympathy by being helpless, or do they act shy? Only children are more likely to have problems with the egocentrism block. They are usually interested only in themselves and may resort to tantrums and uncooperative behavior if their requests are not granted. Finally, only children may become overly dependent on adults because they are not taught to do things on their own. An exception to the rule are those only children who learn to play ball and other games by themselves when they have not had an opportunity to be around friends.

First-born and second-born children.   Often considered the special child, or "Christ child," by the family, especially if they are male, first-borns enjoy their number-one ranking but often fear dethronement by the birth of a second child. First-borns work hard at pleasing their parents. They are likely to be conforming achievers, defenders of the faith, introverted, and well behaved. Twenty-three of the first 25 astronauts were first-born males. NASA was interested in recruiting high-achieving followers for the space program; there was no need for "creative astronauts" who might decide to take the scenic route home. First-borns often find themselves functioning as substitute parents in larger families.

Second-born children may be those extroverted, creative, free-thinking spirits that NASA was trying to avoid. More often than not, second-borns look at what is "left over" in the way of roles and behavior patterns that the first-born child has shunned; it may be easier to pick another role than to compete with the older sibling who has such a large head start. Second-borns may get lower grades in school even though they may be brighter than Number One. Parents are often easier on second-born children, showing less concern with rules. In fact, second-borns may be the family rebels—with or without a cause! In any case, a second-born will usually be the opposite of the first child. It is easy for second-borns to become discouraged when trying to compete with successful, older, and bigger first-borns. The more successful first-borns are, the more likely second-borns are to feel unsure of themselves and their abilities. They may even feel squeezed out, neglected, unloved, and abused when the third child arrives.

The youngest child.   Often referred to as Prince or Princess Charming, the youngest child could find a permanent lifestyle of being the baby in the family. Youngest children often get a lot of service from all the other family members. They may become dependent or spoiled and experience a lag in development. It is easy for youngest children to develop real feelings of inferiority because they are smaller, less able to take care of themselves, and often not taken seriously. The really successful charmers may learn how to boss subtly or to manipulate the entire family. They will decide either to challenge their elder siblings or to evade any direct struggles for superiority.

When a five-year difference exists between two children in a family, the situation changes. With a gap of five years or longer, the next-born child often assumes the characteristics of a first-born; apparently, the five years remove the competitive barriers found between children who are closer in age.

Extreme behavior patterns are often observed in children who find themselves the only boy or girl among siblings of the opposite sex. They may tend to develop toward extremes in either masculinity or femininity. Sex roles children assume often depend on roles perceived as most favored in our culture.

Large families appear to offer some advantages in child-rearing by making it tough for parents to overparent each child. Children in large families frequently learn how to solve their own problems, take care of themselves, and handle their conflicts because their parents cannot always give personal service and attention to each and every problem. Large families are probably good training grounds for learning how to be independent.

Many factors enter into the perceptions children have of their particular roles in their family:

1. The parents may have a favorite child.
2. The family may be required to move.
3. Parents become more experienced and easygoing as they grow older.
4. Some homes are single-parent homes because of death or divorce.
5. The children may have a stepparent living in the home.

6. The family climate changes with each addition to the family.
7. Chronic illnesses or handicaps may be a problem in the family.
8. A grandparent may live in the home.

The Family Atmosphere

Dreikurs, in his book *Children: The Challenge* (1964), examined the importance of the family atmosphere in the development of the child. Whereas the family constellation is a description of how family members interact with one another, the family atmosphere is the style of coping with life that the family has modeled for the child.

The following 12 family atmospheres indicate how a negative family atmosphere can affect children adversely.

1. *Authoritarian.* The authoritarian home requires unquestioned obedience from the children. Children have little or no voice in family decisions. Although these children are often well behaved and well mannered, they also tend to be more anxious and outer-directed. What was once a shy child may turn into a rebel with a cause in later life.

2. *Suppressive.* In tune with the authoritarian home is the suppressive family atmosphere, in which children are not permitted to express their thoughts and feelings. Expression of opinion is limited to what the parents want to hear. Frequently children from such a family have a difficult time expressing feeling when it is allowed in situations outside the home, such as counseling. Close relationships are not encouraged in this type of family atmosphere.

3. *Rejective.* Children feel unloved and unaccepted in this family atmosphere. Some parents do not know how to show love and frequently have difficulty separating the deed from the doer. Children and parents need to know and understand that love can be unconditional and not tied to unacceptable behavior: "I love you, but I am still angered by your irresponsibility." It is easy for a child to become extremely discouraged in the rejective family.

4. *Disparaging.* Children criticized by everyone else in the family often turn out to be the "bad egg" everyone predicted they would be. Too much criticism generally leads to cynicism and an inability to form good interpersonal relationships.

5. *High standards.* Children living in the high-standards atmosphere may think such things as "I am not loved unless I make all 'A's.' " Fear of failure leads to the considerable distress perfectionist people experience. The tension and stress these children experience often prevent them from performing as well as they are able.

6. *Inharmonious.* In homes with considerable quarreling and fighting, children learn that it is important to try to control other people and keep others from controlling them. Power becomes a prime goal for these chil-

dren. Discipline may be inconsistent in these homes, depending on the mood of the parents.

7. *Inconsistent.* Inconsistent methods of discipline and home routines are often sources of confusion and disharmony in the home. Lack of self-control, low motivation, self-centeredness, instability, and poor interpersonal relationships are often attributed to inconsistency in parenting practices.

8. *Materialistic.* In this type of home, children learn that feelings of self-worth depend on possessions and on how much you own in relation to your peers. Interpersonal relationships take a backseat to accumulating wealth in the materialistic family.

9. *Overprotective.* Children are often prevented from growing up in these homes because parents do too much for them. They protect the children from the consequences of their behavior and, in doing so, deny the reality of the situation. This overindulgence by parents leads to feelings of helplessness and dependency in the child. Dependent children fall into the class of outer-directed people who rely on others for approval.

10. *Pitying.* Like overprotectiveness, pitying also prevents children from developing and using the resources they have for solving their problems. Such may be the case with handicapped children, especially, who may be encouraged to feel sorry for themselves and to expect favors from others to make up for their misfortunes.

11. *Hopeless.* Discouraged and "unsuccessful" parents often pass these attitudes on to their children, who make hopelessness a part of their lifestyle. A pessimistic home atmosphere may be due to economic factors, especially if the breadwinners lack financial resources.

12. *Martyr.* Martyrdom is another pessimistic viewpoint possessed by people suffering from low self-esteem, hopelessness, and discouragement. Once again, children may learn that life is unfair and that people should treat them better. As with other types of negative family atmosphere, martyrdom is a breeding ground for dependency.

When looking at the various types of family atmosphere, it is important to remember that atmosphere is not the total cause of behavior. Behavior is most influenced by the child's biased perceptions of the family climate.

Goals of Misbehavior

As children grow and interact with their environment, they gradually develop methods for achieving their basic goal of belonging. Several factors, including the child's place in the family, the quality of parents' interaction with the child, and the child's creative reaction to the family atmosphere, are critical in the development of coherent patterns of behaviors and attitudes.

Dreikurs (1964) has made an especially insightful and useful analysis of the immediate goals by which children attempt to achieve their basic goal of belonging. Children who do not have a pattern of misbehavior have an immediate goal of cooperation and constructive collaboration. These children find their place and feel good about themselves through constructive cooperation. They generally approach life with the goal of being a collaborator, and their usual behavior is socially and personally effective. On the other hand, children who have a pattern of misbehavior are usually pursuing one of four mistaken goals: attention, power, revenge, and inadequacy or withdrawal. An understanding of the goal for which a misbehaving child is striving helps put the behavior in perspective and provides a basis for corrective action.

Attention.   All children seek attention, especially those of preschool age. However, excessive attention getting should diminish in the primary school years. Excessive attention-getting behavior that continues beyond the primary grades becomes a problem to teachers, parents, and peers. The child's goal is to keep you busy, and your natural reaction is to feel annoyed and provide the service and attention the child seeks. Attention getting appears in four forms:

1. *Active constructive.* This child may be the model child, but the goal is to elevate self, not to cooperate. This is the successful student whose industrious and reliable performance is for attention only.
2. *Passive constructive.* This is the charming child who is not as vigorous as the active-constructive child about attention getting. This child is a conscientious performer and a prime candidate for teacher's pet.
3. *Active destructive.* This is the nuisance child — the prime candidate for the child most likely to ruin your day. This is the class clown, showoff, and mischief-maker.
4. *Passive destructive.* This is the lazy child who gets your attention through demands for service and help. This child often lacks the ability and motivation to complete work.

Power.   These children have an exaggerated need to exercise power and superiority. They take every situation, debate, or issue as a personal challenge from which it is necessary to emerge the winner; otherwise, these children think they have failed. The child's goal is to be the boss. Your reaction ranges from anger to feeling threatened or defeated. The child acts in a stubborn, argumentative way and may even throw tantrums. This child will likely lead the league in disobedience. Power-struggling has two forms:

1. *Active destructive.* This child is the rebel who has the potential of leading a group rebellion.
2. *Passive destructive.* This child is stubborn, forgetful, and could also be the lazy one in the group.

Revenge. These children feel hurt and mistreated by life. Their goal is to get even by hurting others. They achieve social recognition, although they usually make themselves unpopular with most other children. The child's goal, then, is to even up the score, and the adult's reaction is usually to feel hurt. Revenge has two forms:

1. *Active destructive.* This child is violent and resorts to stealing, vandalism, and physical abuse to extract revenge. This child is a candidate to become a leader of a juvenile-delinquent gang.
2. *Passive destructive.* This child is also violent, but in a passive way. This is the quiet, sullen, defiant child. Both of these revenge types believe their only hope lies in getting even.

Inadequacy or withdrawal. These children often feel inferior and think they are incapable of handling life's problems. Their deficiencies may be either real or imagined. By giving up, they hope to hide their inferiority and to prevent others from making demands on them. The child's goal is to be left alone, and the adult's reaction is to give up because of a feeling of help-lessness. Inadequacy has only one form:

Passive destructive. These children are usually described as hopeless. They often put on an act of being stupid just to discourage the teacher from asking them to recite and do work. They may have an unwritten contract with their teachers that says, in effect, "I'll leave you alone if you leave me alone."

Manly (1986) has adapted the four goal questions into an informal inventory she likes to use with students who have been referred to her for behavior or attitude problems. Manly tells her students that the inventory will help her know them better and know what they think. The inventory may be taken as a pencil-and-paper client list or as an interview between counselor and client. Students are asked to indicate which of the following sentences are true for them.

Goals inventory.

Attention

_____ I want people to notice me.
_____ I want people to do more for me.
_____ I want to be special.
_____ I want some attention.

Power

_____ I want to be in charge.
_____ I want people to do what I want to do.
_____ I want people to stop telling me what to do.
_____ I want power.

Revenge

_____ I think I have been treated unfairly.

_____ I want to get even.

_____ I want people to see what it is like to feel hurt.

_____ I want people to feel sorry for what they have done.

Display of Inadequacy

_____ I want people to stop asking me to do things.

_____ I want people to feel sorry for me.

_____ I want to be left alone. I can't do it anyway.

_____ I know I'll mess up, so there's no point in trying.

The questions may be intermixed or administered in the above groupings. The four goal labels are not meant to be included on the inventory.

COUNSELING METHOD

The counseling methods Adler pioneered were based on his experiences and philosophy about the nature of people. Many of Adler's original ideas have been used and modified by later Adlerians, including Rudolf Dreikurs, Heinz Ansbacher, Harold Mosak, and Don Dinkmeyer.

In Adlerian counseling, no distinction is made between conscious and unconscious material. The counselor uses dreams, for example, to discover the lifestyle of a client—that is, the type of defense used to establish superiority. The counselor tries to analyze the inferiority feelings that stem from real or fancied personal deficiencies, particularly so-called organ deficiencies (such as defective vision) or organic inferiority (weak heart), some form of which everyone is assumed to possess. Next, the counselor proceeds to examine the client's academic, extracurricular, and social adjustments. It is helpful to see how the client has maintained or achieved superiority in each of these major areas of life and to examine the inferiority feelings that may plague the client. A primary goal of Adlerian counseling is to point out to the client the overcompensation and defensive patterns the client is using to solve problems and to find more successful ways of solving problems related to school, play, and other social concerns.

A summary of the main points in the Adlerian counseling method with children is presented in the following paragraphs.

Main Aspects

Counselor/client relationship.   As with many counseling methods, the establishment of the counselor/client relationship is the key step in the process. The counselor's job is to reeducate children who have developed mistaken ideas about some concepts of their lives. The counseling relationship is based on the assumption that the counselor and child are equal partners in the process and that the child is a responsible person who is capable of learning better ways to meet personal needs. The positive view of human nature is indicated through the counselor's faith, hope, and caring attitude toward the child.

Life as holistic.   Adlerians believe that lives are holistic. Dinkmeyer, Pew, and Dinkmeyer (1979) refer to the concept of *teleoanalytic holistic theory,* which regards any troubled or troublesome behavior as a reflection of one indivisible, unified, whole organism moving toward self-created goals. The foremost task of Adlerian counselors is to prove this unity in people, in their thinking, feeling, and behavior—in fact, in every expression of their personality (Ansbacher & Ansbacher, 1956). Adlerians believe that children are the artists of their own personalities and are constantly moving purposefully toward self-consistent goals. One technique that can be used with children is the lifestyle-interview analysis, which consists of present and past (early) recollections of the children themselves and their families, how they fit in, and how they perceive siblings and parents in relation to themselves. Questions often used include the following:

1. What type of concern or problem would you like to discuss, and how did this problem develop?
2. On a five-point scale, how are things going for you:

	Great	Medium	Poor
	1 2	3 4	5

   in school?_____
   with your friends?_____
   with your hobbies?_____
   with your parents?_____
   with your brothers and sisters?_____
   with your fun times?_____
3. Can you tell me about your mother and father? (Separate the answers for mother and father or for any other parent figures living at home.)
   What do they do?
   What do they want you to do?
   How do you get along with them?
   How are you like your parents?
   How are you different from your parents?
4. Are there things in your family that you would like to be better? What? How?
5. Can you tell me about your brothers and sisters? (Make a list of children in the family, from eldest to youngest, with their ages.) Of all your brothers and sisters, who is:
   a. most like you? How?
   b. most different from you?[1] How?

[1] The sibling most different from your client usually has the greatest influence on your client's lifestyle.

6. What kind of child are you?
7. What kind of child did you used to be?
8. What scares you most?
9. What used to scare you most?
10. Have any of your brothers or sisters been sick or hurt?
11. What does each of the children in your family do best?
12. Who is the:

smartest?	best in spelling?[2]
best athlete?	best in penmanship?[2]
mother's favorite?	most stubborn?
father's favorite?	best looking?
hardest worker?	friendliest?
best behaved?	strongest?
funniest?	healthiest?
most spoiled?	best musician?
best in mathematics?[2]	best with tools?

The counselor uses these and other questions initially to explore the pictures children have painted of their lives. Later they are used to help children understand their present lifestyles.

Early Recollections (ERs)

Early recollections are also used to understand the child's earliest impressions of life and how the child felt about them. Children are asked to remember as far back as they can. It is good to obtain recollections of specific incidents, as detailed as possible, including the child's reaction at the time. "If we took a snapshot when that happened, what would we see? How did you feel?" It is helpful to elicit three to six of those early recollections as a way of finding a pattern in the lifestyle. These recollections tend to reflect a prototype that is apparent in the lifestyle analysis. Although the occurrences related by children may not be factually accurate, they are true insofar as they reflect the children's memories and feelings. This gives the counselor a clearer idea of the child's basic view of life and how some attitudes may have mistakenly crystallized. Examples of themes that may appear in these recollections and the child's accompanying mistaken beliefs include the following:

1. Early dangers—be aware of the many hostile aspects of life.
2. Happy times with adults around—life is great as long as many people praise and serve me.
3. Misdeeds recalled—be very careful that they do not happen again.

---

[2] These three school subjects relate to the child's personality development. Good mathematics students are good personal problem-solvers. Good spellers and good writers (good in penmanship) are generally well-behaved children who follow rules and cooperate with the social order.

Myer and James (1991) present a useful set of guidelines on how to use ERs as an assessment technique to help counselors discern children's behavior patterns. If the child is nonverbal, ERs may be obtained by drawings and other types of play media. Counselors can make ERs a memory game or a "make up a story about when you were small" game. It may be helpful for the counselor to model what he or she wants the child to do. At least three ERs are needed to find a child's pattern of behaviors. The process should not be rushed. The counselor's job is the same as we have recommended throughout the book: to help the child teach the counselor about his or her situation by being a good summarizer of content and feelings. Open-ended statements are good if the counselor is not leading the child into one of the counselor's own ERs. Myer and James recommend that the counselor pay attention to context (for example, if the child is alone, that may indicate isolation), content (for example, recurring topics such as food, water, animals, and wearing boots have special significance for the child), persons (for example, family members left in and out of the story), movement (for example, passivity and compliance may indicate discouragement), and feelings (for example, hot and cold feeling words tell much about the child's outlook on life). The counselor must be careful to avoid overinterpreting or underinterpreting ERs in planning interventions for children.

Understanding.   Counselors must use a great deal of understanding with children. No matter what they are doing, they are probably doing the best they can at the moment. Ways of relieving some anxiousness and conflict include helping them interpret what is happening and giving the problem, child, or action a "handle." Use encouragement. Change negative situations to positive ones by telling fables where appropriate. "The Miller and the Donkey" is one story that helps children understand they will never be able to please everyone, even by absurdly attempting the impossible. "The Frogs in the Milk" is another useful tale. It tells about two frogs who jumped into a barrel of milk and simply paddled until they made butter; they were then able to jump out easily.

Confrontation.   In some cases, confrontation is necessary when children are unable to change the mistaken ideas behind their behavior (Myer & James, 1986). Children can be confronted with educated guesses about the goals they are trying to achieve at others' expense. Be aware also of the child who is using depreciation. This often occurs when the counselor is viewed as an obstacle. Typically, the child is unwilling to move in a direction indicated by the counselor and attempts avoidance or wastes time. Counselors are advised to stay out of these power struggles.

Stages.   Actual changes in children's perspectives occur in stages. First, children are limited to afterthoughts of insight: they can clearly see what they are doing to cause mistaken ideas or unhappiness to persist, but only after they have misbehaved. In the second stage, children become able to catch themselves in the act of misbehaving. Added awareness enables them to sensitize themselves to inappropriate behavior. In the next stage, children have developed a heightened sense of awareness that enables them to anticipate the situation and plan a more appropriate behavior or response.

Practical Methods

In helping children, parents, counselors, and teachers have used methods Dreikurs and Dinkmeyer developed from Adler's original ideas. These methods were designed for practical application and use. The four goals of misbehaviors were designed to aid parents' and teachers' understanding that *how they feel* about what the child is doing will most clearly explain what the child's mistaken goal is.

Dreikurs's analysis and description of the four mistaken goals, the ways of identifying them, and the methods of correction have resulted in an impressive array of guidance and counseling approaches to help discouraged children and their often-discouraged families. The steps he outlines for determining a child's mistaken goals are both penetrating and simple. They involve answering the following questions in relation to a child's misbehavior: What is the adult's corrective response? What is the child's reaction to correction? When the child's goal is understood, it is possible, through counseling with the child and parents, to help the child develop a constructive goal and appropriate behavior.

In describing and analyzing specific immediate goals, Dreikurs and his colleagues have focused primarily on preadolescents. Dreikurs notes that, in early childhood, the children's status depends on the impression they make on adults. Later, they may develop different goals to gain social significance in their peer group and, later still, in adult society. These original goals can still be observed in people of every age. However, they are not all-inclusive; teenagers and adults have other goals of misbehavior based on irrational self-messages (see Chapter 6). Dreikurs reminds us that status and prestige can frequently be achieved more easily through useless and destructive means than through accomplishment.

Dreikurs advocates modifying the motivation rather than the behavior itself. When the motivation is changed, more constructive behavior follows automatically.

To use the "four-goal technique," one must take the following steps:

1. Observe the child's behavior in detail.
2. Be psychologically sensitive to your own reaction.
3. Confront the child with the goal of the behavior.
4. Note the recognition reflex.
5. Apply appropriate corrective procedures.

It is important to remember that misbehaving children are discouraged children trying to find their place; they are acting on the faulty logic that their misbehavior will give them the social acceptance that they desire. Goal 1, attention getting, is a manifestation of minor discouragement; Goal 4, display of inadequacy, is a manifestation of deep discouragement. Sometimes a child will switch from one kind of misbehavior to another. This is often a signal that the discouragement is growing worse.

In identifying young children's goals, it is most helpful to observe your own immediate response to their behavior. Your immediate response is in line with their expectations. The following four examples of behaviors show how you may feel, what the child may be thinking, what alternate behaviors exist, and what questions may come to mind about the child's behavior.

Attention
You are annoyed; you begin coaxing, reminding.
Charlie thinks he belongs only when he is noticed.
You can (1) attend to the child when he is behaving appropriately; or
          (2) ignore misbehavior (scolding reinforces attention-getting behavior).
You can ask: Could it be that you want me to notice you?
Power
You are angry, provoked, and threatened.
Linda thinks she belongs only when she is in control or boss.
You can withdraw or "take your sail out of her wind" by leaving the room.
You can ask: (1) Could it be that you want to be the boss?
             (2) Could it be that you want me to do what you want?
Revenge
You are deeply hurt and want to get even.
Sally thinks her only hope is to get even.
You can (1) use group and individual encouragement; and
          (2) try to convince her she is liked.
You can ask: Could it be that you want to hurt me?
Inadequacy
You are feeling helpless and don't know what to do.
Tom thinks he is unable to do anything and that he belongs only when people expect nothing of him.
You can show genuine faith in the child and use encouragement.
You can ask: Could it be that you feel stupid and don't want people to know?

A counseling interview that uses the four "Could it be?" questions might go as follows:

Counselor: Alice, do you know why you did [the misbehavior]?
Alice: No. (This may be an honest response.)
Counselor: Would you like to work with me so that we can find

out? I have some ideas that might help us explain what you are trying to get when you do _____. Will you help me figure this out?

Alice: OK.

Counselor: (using one question at a time, in a nonjudgmental, unemotional tone of voice):

1. Could it be that you want Mr. Jones to notice you more and give you some special attention?
2. Could it be that you would like to be boss and have things your own way in Mr. Jones's class?
3. Could it be that you have been hurt and you want to get even by hurting Mr. Jones and others in the class?
4. Could it be that you want Mr. Jones to leave you alone and to stop asking you all those questions in math?

All four of these questions are always asked, sequentially, regardless of the child's answers or reflex because the child may be operating on more than one goal at a time. The counselor observes the body language and listens carefully for the response in order to catch the "recognition reflex." An accurate disclosure of the child's present intentions produces a recognition reflex, such as a "guilty" facial expression, which is a reliable indication of his or her goal even though the child may say nothing or even say "no." Sometimes the confrontation itself helps the child change. Another indication of the child's goal is the child's response to correction. If children are seeking attention and get it from the teacher, they will stop the misbehavior temporarily, then they will probably repeat it or do something similar. If children seek power, they will refuse to stop the disturbance, or even increase it. If they seek revenge, their response to the teacher's efforts to get them to stop will be to switch to some more violent action. A child with Goal 4 will not cooperate but will remain entirely passive and inactive.

Once the counselor suspects the goal of the child's misbehavior, it is most important to confront the child. The purpose of this confrontation is to disclose and confirm the mistaken goal of the child. The emphasis is on "for what purpose," not "why."

Corrective Procedures

The next step after identifying the goal of misbehavior is for the adult to choose and use appropriate corrective procedures. These may range from encouragement to logical consequences.

Encouragement.   Dreikurs (1964) wrote that encouragement implies faith in and respect for children as they are. One should not discourage children by having extremely high standards and being overly ambitious for them. Children misbehave only when they are discouraged and believe they cannot succeed by useful means. In fact, one way to evaluate counseling would be to measure how far the child has moved from feeling discouraged toward feeling encouraged. Children need encouragement as plants need water and sunshine. Telling children they can be better implies they are not good enough as they are.

Problems with Dreikurs's ideas on encouragement arise when parents ask how they are supposed to *not* expect their children to do better when they are performing below their ability levels. The answer seems to be in loving children unconditionally in spite of their behavior and performance. You do not have to love their misbehavior or pretend that you do.

Encouragement is advocated in place of praise and reinforcement. Adlerians see praise as a message that tells children that, under conditions determined by you, they are OK. Praise focuses on the product. Encouragement, however, tells children you accept them where they are; it focuses on the process. Encouragement occurs *before* the child completes, or even starts, a task.

- "I am proud of you."
- "That's a rough one, but I think you have what it takes to work it out."
- "I know you can do it; let me help you get started."

Praise (reinforcement) occurs *after* the child performs a behavior or completes a task.

- "You certainly did a good job."
- "That was great work you did in math."
- "I like the way you handled that."
- "You played a good game."

Adlerian counselors believe that reward and punishment have detrimental effects on the development of the child, particularly in the democratic atmosphere that prevails today. Only in an autocratic society are reward and punishment systems an effective and necessary means of obtaining conformity; they presuppose a certain person is endowed with superior authority. Children may see rewards as one of their rights and soon demand a reward for everything they do if they are trained under this system. Punishment of children may be interpreted as their right to punish others. In fact, children often are hurt more by their retaliation than they are hurt by the punishment. They are experts in knowing how to hurt their parents, whether by getting into trouble or making low grades. Therefore, reward and punishment methods that focus on extrinsic reinforcement are rejected by Adlerians, who favor encouragement, intrinsic reinforcement, and logical consequences.

Natural and logical consequences.   Natural and logical consequences are Adlerian techniques favored over reward and punishment because they allow children to experience the actual consequences of their behavior.

Natural consequences are a direct result of children's behavior. If children are careless and touch the hot stove, they get burned. They will be more careful of stoves in the future.

Natural consequences of irresponsible behavior are those unfavorable outcomes that occur naturally without any prearranged plan or program. For example, if Sue leaves her baseball glove outside and it is ruined in a rainstorm, she has experienced a natural consequence. If I am late in making my airline reservation, I may find I cannot take the flight I want. Natural consequences to irresponsible behavior happen on their own, or naturally, without being planned and administered by others.

Logical consequences, established through rules and family policy, are fair, direct, consistent, and logical results of a child's behavior. For example, if Frank comes home late for dinner, he will find that his plate has been removed because it has been assumed that if he were hungry, he would have been home on time to eat or would have called. Frank will be allowed to fix any food he can as long as he cleans up after himself.

As another example of a logical consequence, if Mary breaks someone's window, she will be asked to repair the damage or pay to have the damage repaired. If the cash or skill required to repair the damage is not available to Mary, she could work off her debt by performing other jobs. In school, if John interferes with someone's right to learn, he will be moved to a place where he cannot continue to do so (some form of isolation). In other words, the consequence will fit the misbehavior; that is, it will be a logical consequence. Punishment, as defined by Adlerians, is any illogical consequence for irresponsible behavior. For example, if Frank is late for dinner, he gets paddled and sent to bed. The punishment or consequence does not match the crime, but it teaches children that bigger people get to overpower smaller people. Children reared under a punishment-by-power system become very impressed with power and will use it whenever they can to get what they want.

Both natural and logical consequences allow children to experience the results of their behavior instead of arbitrary punishment exercised through the parent's personal authority. These two techniques help direct children's motivation toward proper behavior through personal experience with the social order in which they live. We are not recommending, however, that adults not protect children in dangerous situations—we do not want to teach children about the dangers of street traffic through personal experience!

Natural and logical consequences focus on the Adlerian belief that people are responsible and capable of leading full, happy lives. Consequences allow the child to understand an inner message that is more likely to be remembered than punishment that can harm the relationship with a child.

Using natural and logical consequences gives children the message that you believe they are capable of making their own decisions. It allows them an opportunity for growth through weighing alternatives and arriving at a decision. When overly severe limits are set, the child is deprived of making decisions that foster self-respect and responsibility. One should allow children to do for themselves that which they are capable of doing.

Family counseling.   Adlerian methods are well suited for counseling the entire family. The following interview guide is suggested:
1. Interview the parents on the following topics (while their children are observed in a playroom situation):
   a. Describe your children (use a blackboard)—their respective ordinal positions, schoolwork, hobbies, athletics, and so on.
   b. How does each child find his or her place in the family?
   c. What problems revolve around getting up? mealtime? TV? home-work? chores? bedtime?
   d. Is there something in your family that needs to be better?
   e. Would you like to make a change?
   Before the counselor gives suggestions, it is preferable that the parents admit they are bankrupt in child-rearing ideas; that is, nothing has worked in improving the particular family concern.
2. Interview the children on the following topics (parents leave the conference room):
   a. Do you know why you are here today?
   b. Is there anything that bothers you in the family that you would like to change?
   c. How can we make things better at home?
   d. Who is the good child?
   e. Who is father's favorite?
   f. Who is mother's favorite?
   g. Who is best in sports?
   h. What does each of you do best?
   i. Which are your best school subjects?[3]
   j. Which are your worst school subjects?[3]
   Use "Could it be?" questions when appropriate. Ask who is in charge of discipline.
3. Interview the entire family. Summarize plans for the coming week, clarifying roles, behaviors, and expectations. Recommendations for each family generally include the following:
   a. Provide individual parent time for each child, each day.
   b. Have one family conference per week.
   c. Do one family activity per week.
   d. Each family member does chores.

[3] Once again, you may want to discuss with the family the three school subjects that relate to personality development (see p. 262). These assumptions about mathematics, spelling, and writing hold true for students who have the ability to do better and are not true for children handicapped by a particular learning or perceptual disability.

RESEARCH AND REACTIONS

Considerable research has been done on Adler's individual psychology. Possibly it would be more accurate to say that considerable research has been done on Dreikurs' modification of Adler's work. Dreikurs deserves much of the credit for putting Adlerian theory into practice. Research topics covered in the present summary include consultation, parent education, family counseling, early recollections, social interest, goals of misbehavior, birth order, and encouragement.

Consultation

Bundy and Poppen (1986) reviewed research on the effectiveness of elementary school counselors as consultants. In 10 of 13 studies done with teachers, the counselor's consultation proved helpful. In eight successful studies with parents, four counselors used Adlerian psychology, three used parent effectiveness training, and one used a multimodal approach.

Gamble and Watkins (1983) presented an excellent case for combining the best of individual psychology and reality therapy in designing intervention plans for children. Using a case-study approach, they integrated motives, goals, and logical consequences with client self-evaluation, classroom meetings, and written contracts to design a successful intervention for a 12-year-old boy experiencing peer-relationship problems and problems with school attendance and stealing.

Pepper and Roberson (1983) integrated individual psychology and behavioral approaches in working with eight males (ages 12 to 14) in special-education classes. The students were described as being disruptive and engaging in power struggles with others. Encouragement, group discussions, and logical consequences were used with shaping (positive reinforcement and extinction) to bring about positive behavior change.

Parent Education

Weaver (1980) and Pelley (1980), in separate studies, have shown the effectiveness of the Adlerian method in training parents to parent more effectively. Both studies employed the STEP kit designed by Dinkmeyer and McKay (1976) for use with parent groups. Weaver found the method more effective with mothers from middle socioeconomic levels and somewhat less effective with mothers from lower socioeconomic levels. Pelley found the method effective in stimulating more group interaction in parent groups using the materials compared with groups not using the materials. Both studies supported the transferability of group learning to the home setting.

Krebs (1986), comparing research on behavioral, Adlerian, and communications approaches to parent training found the Adlerian approach fostered more democratic parenting practices. Systematic Training for Effective Parenting (STEP), based on the Adlerian model, was effective with both parents and children. Children became more responsible and considerate and better problem-solvers. Behavioral programs, based on rewards and punishment, were seen as more difficult to implement and too heavily focused on behavior as opposed to courses of behavior. The communications approach, similar to parent effectiveness training (PET), was found effective in moving parents away from a power model to a cooperation model of parenting. However, as Dembo, Switzer, and Lauritzen (1985) discovered, parent-training programs are not well researched.

Family Counseling

Croake and Hinckle (1983), in an attempt to evaluate the outcome of Adlerian family counseling, followed the family-study-group model. They administered the MMPI, Child-Rearing Practice Scale, and Attitudes Toward the Freedom of Children Scale as pretest and posttest measures of the family-counseling experience. They found significant positive changes on each of the scales, with married parents scoring the highest.

Berry (1983) used an Adlerian family-counseling case-study approach with two families having difficulty adjusting to rearing a handicapped child. Emphasis was placed on each child's strength and increased family involvement through the encouragement process.

Watkins (1984) presented a model for Adlerian family counseling as a viable alternative for treating crimes committed within the family (such as child abuse). Watkins describes a child-abuse case in which two major Adlerian principles were successfully applied: (1) offering nothing for the client to resist and (2) building on family and personal strengths rather than focusing on weaknesses. Specific counseling steps included (1) breaking down the resistance between client and counselor, (2) discovering family strengths, and (3) planning and implementing activities that focus on family strengths.

Kern and Carlson (1981) suggested four Adlerian constructs for counselors to understand and implement in their work with families: (1) All problems are social problems; interpersonal relationships are more important than intrapersonal factors. (2) All behavior is purposeful; misbehavior has a way of maintaining the family at its present level. (3) Knowledge of the family constellation is necessary, as is how children perceive their position in the constellation. (4) Each family member strives to move from an inferior position to one of competence.

Nicoll (1984) provided a rationale for school counseling programs to provide family-counseling services. He based his argument on the following points: (1) Referred families rarely follow through with counseling. (2) Counseling in the school setting may be less threatening. (3) Family counseling is more effective and economical than individual or group counseling. (4) The school counselor is able to add perceptions and input from the child's school behavior.

Casper and Zachary (1984) pointed out that cases of anorexia nervosa, bulimia, and obesity may be the result of a family's inability to solve problems or conflicts effectively. Eating disorders may be communicating symbolically a sense of inadequacy that stems from the child's failure to learn skills that enable the child to live effectively with others. Casper and Zachary provided checklists of effective family and co-parenting goals to help family members recognize their role behavior and the family reactions to these roles.

Main and Oliver (1988) researched complementary, symmetrical, and parallel personality priorities as indicators of marital adjustment. Symmetric relationships occur when spouses' first priorities match each other. Complementary relationships are defined as "opposites attract." Parallel relationships are a mixture of symmetric and complementary. The Langenfeld Inventory of Personality Priorities and the Dyadic Adjustment Scale were used in this research. Couples having parallel relationships had significantly higher marital adjustment scores than did couples in complementary relationships.

Dinkmeyer (1988) outlined a unique type of family therapy, based on Adlerian psychology, that he entitled "marathon family counseling." The process, completed in one 8-hour day, focuses on family constellation, mutual respect, encouragement, and taking responsibility for one's behavior. Dinkmeyer described four stages:

Stage I: Orientation and organization
   a. Determine if this type of counseling is suitable for the family.
   b. Obtain family background information.
   c. Arrange for family members to participate.
Stage II: Exploration
   a. Give overview and summary of Stage I.
   b. Obtain an overview of the family's life circumstances.
   c. Explore problems in more depth.
Stage III: Action
   a. Encourage family members to commit to doing something to improve the family situation.
   b. Confront family members who are reluctant to change.
   c. Encourage family members to take responsibility for their own behavior.
Stage IV: Termination
   a. Have family members talk about their commitments to change and how they will accomplish their goals.
   b. Thank family members for participating in the session.
   c. Talk individually with family members who want more counseling.

Pew (1989) outlined another method for conducting brief marriage therapy, Adlerian style, that may extend over several sessions.

1. The counselor and couple discuss reasons why the couple is seeking counseling.
2. The counselor and couple discuss the couple's goals for counseling.
3. The counselor shares expectations.
4. The counselor draws a family constellation for each person and uses this and ERs to construct a lifestyle form for each client.
5. The couple works on the basic marriage skills of conflict resolution, communication, and doing fun things together.
6. The couple uses the paradoxical strategies of practicing at home those things that annoy each partner.
7. The couple keeps daily journal entries of feelings, thoughts, and behaviors.

Early Recollections

Lord (1982), in a study of the validity of early recollections for clinical use, asked ten children (ages 6½ to 8) to write one early recollection each. Ten graduate students were asked to do the same. The recollections were rated according to 13 variables: success/failure, active/passive, we/I, confident/inferior, praise/blame, participant/observer, obedient/defiant, benevolent/hostile, reward/punishment, secure/jeopardize, pampered/mistreated, cheerful/depressed, and pleasure/pain. Any of these categories voted as not appearing in the recollection were rated as neutral (absence ratings). Two hypotheses were tested: (1) Children do not have sufficient thematic apperceptions to use in lifestyle analysis. (2) Children's thematic apperceptions vary so much in clinical interpretation that the content cannot be communicated as well as that of adults. Both hypotheses were proven false, indicating that grounds exist for using early recollections in analyzing children's lifestyle and behavior goals.

Further support for using early recollections appears in a study conducted by Kopp and Der (1982). They compared the early recollections of two groups of adolescents who had been referred for counseling. The two groups, classified as active and passive, were asked to rate six early recollections on the Role/Activity Scale in Early Recollections, which indicates the degree to which a person is active in memory and if the person is an initiator or a responder. The scores on the Role/Activity Scale were significantly higher for the active group, indicating support for early recollections analysis as a viable method for examining present lifestyle.

Grunberg (1989), investigating early recollections and criminal behavior in mentally ill homeless men, found that very few of their ERs were positive. Most ERs (occurring before age 8) involved conflict, loneliness, defiance of authority, or victimization. Of those participants who reported negative ERs, 92 percent had been convicted of a crime. It is possible that the ERs might be more reflective of a person's present rather than past condition. However, that is not a problem when counselors try to obtain a picture of how their clients view life.

Coram and Hafner (1988) found that hypnosis produced ERs that contained more themes about mothers, misdeeds, hostility, motor activities, and mastery. It also produced qualitatively different recollections with more detail. Coram and Hafner found that hypnosis did not affect productivity.

Jorgensen and Newlon (1988), analyzing the lifestyle themes of ten unwed, pregnant adolescents who chose to keep their babies, found that all felt a lack of self-esteem and a need for positive attention. Pregnancies were hypothesized to be deliberate attempts to gain closeness and excitement. Birth order, found not to be a determinant in who would deliberately become pregnant, was a factor in how pregnancy was handled. The ERs of first-borns and only children focused on life's "shoulds" and responsibilities. ERs of later-born children emphasized being the center of attention and blaming others for their behavior.

Hyer, Woods, and Boudewyns (1989), studying the ERs of Vietnam veterans with posttraumatic stress disorder (PTSD), found that their ERs contained more negative themes and less social interest when compared to the average range of responses. Each participant recounted two ERs that occurred before age 8. Participants were asked to give their ERs a title that expressed their feelings about the event. The first ER was scored for goals; attitudes; themes; action/passivity; and the positive, negative, or neutral outcome of the ER.

Social Interest

Hjelle's (1975) research supported the hypothesis that high social interest, internal locus of control, and high self-actualization are positively related. Reimanis's (1974) research found that young criminals showed higher levels of anomie and more childhood-experience memories suggesting interference with development of social interest than other youths showed.

Barkley, Wilborn, and Towers (1984), in an attempt to foster social interest in a peer-counseling training program, selected 20 adolescent student volunteers for a study group that met 45 minutes per day, 5 days per week, over an 18-week period. The students received training in communication skills, and the sessions stressed the importance of caring for and helping others. Following nine weeks' training, the students worked in a helping relationship with two other people drawn from an elementary school, junior high school, or nursing-home population. A social-interest index was administered at the beginning, middle, and end of the program to both experimental and control groups. Although females outperformed males in the experimental group, all members of the experimental group were observed to have improved their social-interest skills and behaviors.

Leak and Gardner (1990), in attempting to study relationships between sexual and love attitudes and social interest, reported that high social interest was related to a companion love style, nonpermissive sexual attitudes, and characteristics of mature love. Eros was not found to be a characteristic of people high in social interest.

Fish and Mozdzierz (1988) found that the Sulliman Scale of Social Interest (SSSI) correlated directly with measures of adjustment and inversely with measures of maladjustment. However, the SSSI did not appear to be more accurate than the Social Interest Index and the Social Interest Scale.

Meunier and Royce (1988), using the Social Interest Scale, demonstrated that social interest continues to increase with age at the same rate for elderly persons as for younger persons. Inasmuch as mental health and personal adjustment directly relate to social interest, we can conclude that older adults experience high levels of personal adjustment.

Leak and Williams (1989b) found social interest to be positively correlated to positive perceptions of one's family. Social interest was also linked to multicultural orientation and a sense of religion or morality. Leak and Williams (1989a) also found a positive correlation between social interest and the psychological-hardiness areas of commitment and control. They found a negative correlation between social interest and feelings of alienation.

Considering that Adler believed that social interest was exhibited through such qualities as friendliness, cooperation, and empathy, these findings are not surprising. Social-interest development, being associated with so many good things, seems a worthwhile pursuit for clients of all ages.

Goals of Misbehavior

Mattice (1976) found that teachers and children considered the four goals of misbehavior a reasonable explanation of human behavior. She also found that children did better at formulating interpersonal goal statements about misbehavior than did teachers. School psychologists were found to have difficulty categorizing the misbehavior goals. We might ask if it could be that our education interferes with our common sense.

Nystul (1986) recommended that counselors look beyond the goals of children's misbehavior to the special reasons for misbehavior. He makes three assumptions about people: (1) Human nature is positive. (2) The child's most basic psychological need is positive relationships with significant others. (3) The child has four life choices: to be a "good somebody," a "good nobody," a "bad somebody," or to have severe mental health problems (a "bad nobody"?).

Adlerians have long stated that asking children why they misbehave is not helpful. Porter and Hoedt (1985), in a study of fourth- and fifth-grade students from inner-city schools, found that 70 percent of the children replied "I don't know" when asked why they misbehaved. Focusing on the goal of misbehaviors (for example, asking "Could it be that you want to be the boss?") was more effective when combined with action plans that increased children's understanding of the goals.

Brannon and Jacques (1989) studied the goals of misbehavior for 150 male, adolescent, juvenile offenders committed to a state facility. The percentage for each goal was as follows: attention, 28 percent; power, 32 percent; revenge, 24 percent; and inadequacy, 14 percent. (Two percentage points were missing from the totals.) Treatment teams, trained in identifying the goals of misbehavior, conducted the study.

Kottman and Stiles (1990) described how mutual storytelling can be incorporated into Adlerian counseling. They provided a useful framework for developing stories about how children use various misbehaviors to achieve the four goals. The stories also include ways to achieve goals with acceptable, responsible behavior.

Kottman and Warlick (1989) wrote a helpful article on how to adapt play therapy to the Adlerian model. Their play therapy model consists of four phases:

Phase I: Building a democratic relationship with the child:
  a. Tracking behavior ("I see you are building a house.")
  b. Restatement of content
  c. Reflection of feeling
Phase II: Exploring the child's lifestyle through the parents, child, observation, and drawings:
  a. Family atmosphere
  b. Family constellation
  c. Early recollections
Phase III: Allowing the child to gain insight about relationships and behavior:
  a. Four goals of misbehavior ("Could it be . . .")
  b. Lifestyle ("Let's look at how others feel when you blow up.")
  c. Parallels of behavior inside and outside the playroom
Phase IV: Reorienting the child toward better ways to achieve goals:
  a. Alternative behaviors
  b. Encouragement
  c. Consultation with parents

Birth Order

Horn and Turner (1975), in a study of unwed mothers, found a higher incidence of first-born women reporting premarital sexual intercourse—a finding that was interpreted to mean that first-born women are more likely than later-born women to model the wife/mother role. Nystul (1974) found no significant effect of birth order on self-concept as measured by the Tennessee Self-Concept Scale used on Oregon State University students. Fakouri (1974) found that a relationship between birth order and achievement existed but that a relationship between birth order and dogmatism was not significant.

Recent research on birth order has not been as supportive of fixed birth order as it once was. In fact, exceptions seem to be the rule. Phillips, Bedeian, Mossholder, and Touliatos (1988) found no relationship between first-born and later-born accountants on managerial potential, work orientation, achievement by independence, and sociability. First-borns did, however, score slightly higher on the California Personality Inventory (CPI) in dominance, good impressions, and achievement by conformity.

Stein, DeMiranda, and Stein (1988) researched the relationship between substance abuse, criminality, and birth order by correlating first-born, intermediate-born, and last-born substance abusers on the three dimensions. Being a first-born male was significantly correlated with substance abuse and criminality. No other relationships were identified among the three birth-order groups.

Encouragement

Pety, Kelly, and Kafafy (1984), in an attempt to discover children's preference for praise or encouragement, administered the Praise/Encouragement Preference Scale to 277 students in Grades 4, 6, 8, and 10. Praise was defined as emphasizing the worth of the child (for example, "Good boy" or "Good job"). Encouragement was defined as emphasizing nonjudgmental observations of achievement, improvement, or appreciation (for example, "You must be very proud of yourself"). Children in the fourth through eighth grades preferred receiving praise, but as children matured they began to prefer encouragement to a greater degree. Males preferred praise over encouragement to a higher degree than females.

Rathvon (1990), studying the effects of encouragement on off-task behavior and academic performance of children, found that encouragement decreased off-task behavior for all five first-grade children in the study but failed to increase academic performance in six out of ten measures. Two types of encouragement were used with approximately equal success: proximal, defined as encouraging remarks given within approximately 1 meter of the student when the student was engaging in off-task behavior; and, distal, defined as the same treatment delivered from approximately 7 meters from the off-task child. Examples of encouragement included "You can do it," "Keep trying," "If you get stuck on one question, try the next," and "Keep it up."

Summary

Critics of the Adlerian system agree that although it explains much of our behavior, the theory tends to oversimplify some of the complex human behaviors brought to the counseling interview. Not everyone can be sorted into a birth-order category or a particular goal of misbehavior. Many Adlerian assumptions are nothing more than broad generalizations. Are we not all motivated by power and the drive to compensate for our inferiority as we seek to find a place in this world? Furthermore, a contradiction exists in the Adlerian system. On one hand, the basis of learning potential is the striving to compensate for feelings of inferiority; on the other hand, the pessimist or the one who poses the greatest learning problem is characterized by deep feelings of inferiority. Adlerian counseling, like psychoanalytic counseling, puts the child on the spot: the child is wrong, and the counselor is right.

Despite these criticisms, the Adlerian counseling system offers a wealth of techniques for counseling children and families. Many other counseling theorists have borrowed, both knowingly and unknowingly, from Adler's work. Many of his commonsense ideas on effective counseling have been with us since the early 1900s.

REFERENCES

Adler, A. (1964). *Social interest: A challenge to mankind.* New York: Capricorn Books.

Alexander, F., Eisenstein, S., & Grotjahn, M. (1966). *Psychoanalytic pioneers.* New York: Basic Books.

Ansbacher, H., & Ansbacher, R. (1956). *The individual psychology of Alfred Adler: A systematic presentation in selections from his writings.* New York: Basic Books.

Barkley, H., Wilborn, B., & Towers, M. (1984). Social interest in a peer training program. *Individual Psychology: The Journal of Adlerian Theory, Research, and Practice, 40,* 295–299.

Berry, J. (1983). Adlerian family counseling: A strengths approach. *Individual Psychology: The Journal of Adlerian Theory, Research, and Practice, 39,* 419–424.

Brannon, J., & Jacques, R. (1989). The mistaken goals of adolescence in residential group treatment of juvenile offenders. *Individual Psychology: The Journal of Adlerian Theory, Research, and Practice, 45,* 376–380.

Bundy, M., & Poppen, W. (1986). School counselors' effectiveness as consultants: A research review. *Elementary School Guidance and Counseling, 20,* 215–222.

Casper, D., & Zachary, D. (1984). The eating disorder as a maladaptive conflict resolution. *Individual Psychology: The Journal of Adlerian Theory, Research, and Practice, 40,* 445–452.

Coram, G., & Hafner, J. (1988). Early recollections and hypnosis. *Individual Psychology: The Journal of Adlerian Theory, Research, and Practice, 44,* 472–479.

Croake, J., & Hinckle, D. (1983). Adlerian family counseling education. *Individual Psychology: The Journal of Adlerian Theory, Research, and Practice, 39,* 247–258.

Dembo, M., Switzer, M., & Lauritzen, P. (1985). An evaluation of group parent education: Behavioral, PET, and Adlerian programs. *Review of Educational Research, 55,* 155–200.

Dinkmeyer, D. (1988). Marathon family counseling. *Individual Psychology: The Journal of Adlerian Theory, Research, and Practice, 44,* 210–215.

Dinkmeyer, D., & McKay, G. (1976). *Systematic training for effective parenting.* Circle Pines, MN: American Guidance Service.

Dinkmeyer, D., Pew, W., & Dinkmeyer, D., Jr. (1979). *Adlerian counseling and psychotherapy.* Monterey, CA: Brooks/Cole.

Dreikurs, R. (1964). *Children: The challenge.* New York: Hawthorn Books.

Fakouri, M. (1974). Relationships of birth order, dogmatism, and achievement motivation. *Journal of Individual Psychology, 30,* 216–220.

Fish, R., & Mozdzierz, G. (1988). Validation of the Sulliman Scale of Social Interest with psychotherapy outpatients. *Individual Psychology: The Journal of Adlerian Theory, Research, and Practice, 44,* 307–315.

Gamble, C., & Watkins, C., Jr. (1983). Combining the child discipline approaches of Alfred Adler and William Glasser: A case study. *Individual Psychology: The Journal of Adlerian Theory, Research, and Practice, 39,* 156–164.

Grunberg, J. (1989). Early recollections and criminal behavior in mentally-ill homeless men. *Individual Psychology: The Journal of Adlerian Theory, Research, and Practice, 45,* 289–299.

Hjelle, L. A. (1975). Relationship of social interest to internal-external control and self-actualization in young women. *Journal of Individual Psychology, 31,* 171–182.

Horn, J. M., & Turner, R. G. (1975). Birth order effects among unwed mothers. *Journal of Individual Psychology, 31,* 71–78.

Hyer, L., Woods, M., & Boudewyns, P. (1989). Early recollections of Vietnam veterans with PTSD. *Individual Psychology: The Journal of Adlerian Theory, Research, and Practice, 45,* 300–312.

Jorgensen, J., & Newlon, B. (1988). Life-style themes of unwed, pregnant adolescents who chose to keep their babies. *Individual Psychology: The Journal of Adlerian Theory, Research, and Practice, 44,* 466–471.

Kern, R., & Carlson, J. (1981). Adlerian family counseling. *Elementary School Guidance and Counseling, 15,* 301–306.

Kopp, R., & Der, D. (1982). Level of activity in adolescents' early recollections: A validity study. *Individual Psychology: The Journal of Adlerian Theory, Research, and Practice, 38,* 213–222.

Kottman, T., & Stiles, K. (1990). The mutual storytelling technique: An Adlerian application in child therapy. *Individual Psychology: The Journal of Adlerian Theory, Research, and Pratice, 46,* 148–156.

Kottman, T., & Warlick, J. (1989). Adlerian play therapy: Practical considerations. *Individual Psychology: The Journal of Adlerian Theory, Research, and Practice, 45,* 433–446.

Krebs, L. (1986). Current research on theoretically based parenting programs. *Individual Psychology: The Journal of Adlerian Theory, Research, and Practice, 42,* 375–387.

Leak, G., & Gardner, L. (1990). Sexual attitudes, love attitudes, and social interest. *Individual Psychology: The Journal of Adlerian Theory, Research, and Practice, 46,* 55–60.

Leak, G., & Williams, D. (1989a). Relationship between social interest, alienation, and psychological hardiness. *Individual Psychology: The Journal of Adlerian Theory, Research, and Practice, 45,* 369–374.

Leak, G., & Williams, D. (1989b). Relationship between social interest and perceived family environment. *Individual Psychology: The Journal of Adlerian Theory, Research, and Practice, 45,* 362–367.

Lord, D. B. (1982). On the clinical use of children's early rehabilitations. *Individual Psychology: The Journal of Adlerian Theory, Research, and Practice, 38,* 198–206.

Main, R., & Oliver, R. (1988). Complementary, symmetrical, and parallel personality priorities as indicators of marital adjustment. *Individual Psychology: The Journal of Adlerian Theory, Research, and Practice, 44,* 324–331.

Manly, L. (1986). Goals of misbehavior inventory. *Elementary School Guidance and Counseling, 21,* 160–161.

Mattice, E. (1976). *Dreikurs' goals of misbehavior theory: Child and teacher generation of a neo-Adlerian construct.* Unpublished doctoral dissertation, University of Tennessee, Knoxville.

Meunier, G., & Royce, S. (1988). Age and social interest. *Individual Psychology: The Journal of Adlerian Theory, Research, and Practice, 44,* 49–52.

Mosak, H. (1973). *Alfred Adler: His influence on psychology today.* Park Ridge, NJ: Noyes Press.

Myer, R., & James, R. (1986, February). *Confrontation: A strategy for counseling.* Paper presented at the Tennessee Association for Counseling and Development State Conference, Gatlinburg, TN.

Myer, R., & James, R. (1991). Using early recollections as an assessment technique with children. *Elementary School Guidance and Counseling, 25,* 228–232.

Nicoll, W. (1984). School counselors as family counselors: A rationale and training model. *The School Counselor, 31,* 279–284.

Nystul, M. S. (1974). The effects of birth order and sex on self concept. *Journal of Individual Psychology, 30,* 211–215.

Nystul, M. S. (1986). The hidden reason behind children's misbehavior. *Elementary School Guidance and Counseling, 20,* 188–193.

Orgler, H. (1965). *Alfred Adler: The man and his work.* New York: Capricorn Books.

Pelley, A. (1980, March). *Family involvement in guidance programs.* Paper presented at the American Personnel and Guidance Association Convention, Atlanta, GA.

Pepper, F., & Roberson, M. (1983). The integration of Adlerian behavioral approaches in the classroom management of emotionally handicapped children. *Individual Psychology: The Journal of Adlerian Theory, Research, and Practice, 39,* 165–172.

Pety, J., Kelly, F., & Kafafy, A. (1984). The praise-encouragement preference scale for children. *Individual Psychology: The Journal of Adlerian Theory, Research, and Practice, 40,* 92–101.

Pew, M. (1989). Brief marriage therapy. *Individual Psychology: The Journal of Adlerian Theory, Research, and Practice, 45,* 191–200.

Phillips, A., Bedeian, A., Mossholder, K., & Touliatos, J. (1988). Birth order and selected work-related personality variables. *Individual Psychology: The Journal of Adlerian Theory, Research, and Practice, 44,* 492–501.

Porter, B., & Hoedt, K. (1985). Differential effects of an Adlerian counseling approach with pre-adolescent children. *Individual Psychology: The Journal of Adlerian Theory, Research, and Practice, 41,* 372–385.

Rathvon, N. (1990). The effects of encouragement on off-task behavior and academic productivity. *Elementary School Guidance and Counseling, 24,* 189–199.

Reimanis, G. (1974). Anomie, crime, childhood memories, and development of social interest. *Journal of Individual Psychology, 30,* 53–58.

Stein, S., DeMiranda, S., & Stein, A. (1988). Birth order, substance abuse, and criminality. *Individual Psychology: The Journal of Adlerian Theory, Research, and Practice, 44,* 500–506.

Watkins, E. C. (1984). Court ordered treatment in a case of child abuse. *Individual Psychology: The Journal of Adlerian Theory, Research, and Practice, 40,* 209–212.

Weaver, C. (1980, March). *The STEP program: A comparison of its effectiveness with middle and lower socio-economic status mothers.* Paper presented at the American Personnel and Guidance Association Convention, Atlanta, GA.

CHAPTER 11

Family Therapy:
An Overview

The term *family therapy* covers a wide body of knowledge. Definitions of family therapy range from one-person family therapy to multiple-family therapy. Between the two extremes we have nuclear and extended families, not to mention eight other family organizational structures: blended, common-law, single-parent, communal, serial, polygamous, cohabitational, and homosexual (see Goldenberg & Goldenberg, 1985).

Lacking agreement on who participates in family therapy as clients, we are not surprised to find that opinions on the proper number of family therapists participating per session range from one up to a "full team." The question of what family therapists do to help their clients stimulates a variety of answers ranging the full length of the eclectic-counseling continuum. Although "schools" of family practice have developed, there appears to be wide divergence within each school or theory. Fish and Piercy (1987) surveyed 14 structural and 14 strategic family therapists for the purpose of identifying similarities and differences in the theory and practice of these two systems.

Structural therapy is based on the assumption that families are evolving, hierarchial organizations with rules and behavior patterns for interacting across and within subsystems. Families get themselves into trouble when their members either become overly enmeshed in each other's business or totally disengaged from each other. The key to a functional family seems to be finding a healthy balance between these two extremes. One way to find the needed balance is to define and clarify the boundaries that exist among the subsystems within the total family system. For example, a family has a spousal subsystem, a sibling subsystem, and a parent/child subsystem. Each system contains its own subject matter that should remain within that subsystem. Spouses will discuss matters that do not belong in the other two subsystems. The same is true for siblings, who will have their own content, and for parent/child interactions. Families who understand and respect the differences between healthy and unhealthy boundaries and rules do well.

Those who do not understand and respect these differences find themselves in a dysfunctional state of being disengaged from or enmeshed in the family business. Therapy is directed toward changing the family organizational structure as a way of resolving the presenting problem or changing family-member behavior patterns. For example, Dad might be asked to give up his role of being in charge of the children's homework assignments. The structural therapist actively directs the session and participates as a family member. Salvador Minuchin is a proponent of structural family therapy.

Strategic family therapy is based on the assumption that family-member behavior, which is ongoing and repetitive, can only be understood in context. Symptoms are developed and maintained by the family's ineffective problem-solving ability. The counselor's role is to design a strategy for solving the presenting problem. Milton Erickson, Jay Haley, Cloe Madanes, and the Milan associates are affiliated with strategic family therapy.

Virginia Satir's method could fit very well into a systems approach or into a communications approach for counseling families. She focused much of her work on developing better family communication. To accomplish her task, she made family members aware of how others in the family react to their communication styles. Satir saw improvement in communication skills as leading to better family conflict resolution and problem-solving.

Although we have focused on differences among the schools and proponents of the various family therapies, similarities do exist. First, all agree that families operate somewhat like an engine with interdependent parts. When one part malfunctions, the total engine is adversely affected; that is, one malfunction may cause other parts to malfunction as well. Therefore, if lasting behavior change is to occur, the entire family may need to change. Second (to mix our metaphors), the family may be like a canoe floating downstream. Although the canoe is balanced, it may be maintaining its balance only because one member of the family is leaning way out over the right side and two other members are tilted slightly to the left. In other words, the canoe *is* balanced, but uncomfortably so. The goal of family therapy is to relieve the pain by finding a more comfortable balance without upsetting the canoe. Families often say, "Stabilize us, but do not change anything." Third, to bring about successful change, the canoe may need to be upset; the counselor's job is to ensure that the emergency process is a safe one. Fourth, all family therapy approaches borrow heavily from the material discussed in the previous chapters as well as from sources outside the present text. Once again, as with the other theories, we see the eclectic theme continued in the current literature on family therapy. In this chapter, we present an overview of Satir's theory and method for counseling families, with briefer coverage of contributions by Minuchin, Erickson, Haley, and Madanes.

VIRGINIA SATIR

When Virginia Satir (1916–1988) was 5 years old, she decided to become a detective for children to help figure out parents. She was not sure what she would be looking for, but even at this age she knew that more strange things were going on in families than met the eye. Over half a century later, after working with thousands of families, Satir reported that she still found a lot of puzzles in families.

Satir viewed family life as being like an iceberg. Most people are aware of only one tenth of what is happening in the family–the tenth that they can see and hear. Like the fate of the ship that depends on the captain's awareness of the total iceberg, the family must depend on the total awareness of the family structure if it is to survive. Satir referred to the hidden 90 percent as the family's needs, motives, and communication patterns. In four books, Satir shared some of the answers she found to the puzzles over the years: *Conjoint Family Therapy* (1967), *Peoplemaking* (1972), *Helping Families to Change* (Satir, Stachowiak, & Taschman, 1975), and *Step by Step* (Satir & Baldwin, 1983). Some of the early concepts in *Conjoint Family Therapy* have been embellished, according to Satir, as a result of her work with the Gestalt concepts presented by Fritz Perls and the body-awareness work of Bernard Gunther.

Virginia Satir's qualifications as a certified detective on parents were well founded. She received formal academic training in psychological social work at the University of Chicago. She worked as a teacher, consultant, and practitioner in psychiatric clinics, mental hospitals, family-service centers, growth centers, and private practice. In 1959, she joined with two psychiatrists to form the initial staff of the Mental Research Institute in Palo Alto, California. She also served as the first director of training at the Esalen Institute in Big Sur, California. Satir lectured in most parts of the world. She was a visiting professor to at least ten universities and a consultant to the Veterans Administration and to several other agencies and schools. As is true with many theorists presented in this book, she was most effective in demonstrating her methods rather than in lecturing about them.

THE NATURE OF PEOPLE

Satir had a positive view of human nature. After studying thousands of families in depth, she was convinced that, at any time, whatever people are doing represents the best they are aware of and the best they can do. She believed that people are rational and have the freedom and ability to make decisions in their lives. Although Satir viewed people as being basically free, she considered the extent of their knowledge as the biggest limitation on personal freedom. People can learn what they do not know and can change their ways of interacting with others. People can also make themselves healthier by freeing themselves from the past. Like Maslow, Satir believed that people are geared to surviving, growing, and developing close relationships with others. Although some behavior may be labeled psychotic, sick, or bad, Satir saw it as an attempt to reach out for help.

Self-esteem plays a prominent role in Satir's system. She believed that self-esteem and effective communication beget one another. Conversely, low self-esteem and dysfunctional communication are also correlated. Satir saw self-esteem, which she defined as the degree to which people accept both their good and their bad points, as the basic human drive. Self-esteem is a changing variable that fluctuates up and down within a healthy range, depending on the amount of stress one is experiencing. It is related to one's participation in the family interaction. When individual family members are experiencing stress, their ability to communicate openly, to give and receive feedback, and to solve problems will depend on the collective self-esteem of the family. Family members may try to block communication in order to protect their own self-esteem in times of stress or in crisis situations. Family members having low self-esteem are likely to create disturbances to make the others feel as bad as they do. For example, parents guilty of child abuse often have a low sense of self-esteem and may unconsciously internalize the following rationale: "One way to punish myself for my wasteful ways is to punish that same behavior in one of my children."

Behavior, according to Satir, is directly related to one's family position and one's view of that position. If we feel good or bad about ourselves, then we are probably communicating that feeling to others. Satir viewed people as mature and functional when they behave in acceptable and helpful ways and when they take responsibility for their actions. Failure to communicate effectively and to behave responsibly were seen by Satir — as by Adler and Glasser — as symptoms of a low self-concept. Therefore, self-esteem needs to receive a strong focus if a person's mental and physical assets are to be developed to their fullest. An examination of one's place in life relates closely to self-esteem.

Satir made the point that a high degree of self-esteem is necessary for a person to qualify as a good marriage partner. People with a healthy self-concept view their partners as enhancing their self-esteem by the two personalities' complementing each other. However, if people have low self-esteem, they look to their partners as extensions of themselves. A marital relationship will be dysfunctional if one partner looks to the other as one who will supply what is missing in the self. In this dysfunctional couple relationship, the marriage or partnership is seen as a place for getting and not giving. For example, marriage may be entered into as a type of therapy for strengthening one's inadequate personality. However, the general outcome of a "taking" relationship is disappointment and an even lower sense of self-esteem.

By the same token, the birth of a child to parents having low self-esteem may be another way of compensating for feelings of inferiority. The child may be used as a mechanism for demonstrating the parents' worth to the community and their self-worth as parents, and also as an extension of themselves. Unconsciously they seem to be thinking, "If I did not fulfill many of my life's aspirations, perhaps I can relive them through my child." In such situations, children are never viewed as individuals with separate worth, value, and identities. Children of parents deficient in self-esteem have a heavy, difficult burden to bear. They are expected to live out their parents' fantasies. Success and failure are viewed from the vantage point of the parent. Children who show individuality and different points of view may be accused of not loving their parents. They receive such messages as "After all I have done for you, how could you do this to me?" or "If you loved me, you would practice the piano more."

Satir (1967) held the view that children are the third angle of the family triangle. As such, they may find themselves in an intolerable position similar to the persecutor/victim/rescuer triangle described in transactional analysis (see Chapter 9). When the parents are in conflict, any direction in which the child turns will be considered as being for or against one of the parents. Given this state of affairs, Satir wrote, if children seem to side with one parent, they run the risk of seeming not to love the other parent. Because children need both parents, making such a choice inevitably hurts them. Both parents have interlocking roles to play in the process of educating children emotionally, and failure of one angle of the family triangle, or one parent, results in disturbance of the entire system and frequently results in disturbed children.

A further complication in the triangle is the fact that the child has already established an identity with the same-sex parent, and the hurt of taking sides is further compounded by the stunted or stifled psychosexual development that may occur. Children need the opposite-sex parent to admire, respect, and love; the same-sex parent needs to be a good role model. When the parents are divided, arguing, and fighting, children cannot achieve these identity and interpersonal goals. If there is no parental coalition, or cooperation between father and mother to fulfill their respective roles as man and woman and husband and wife, the child may need counseling to fulfill unsatisfied wishes. Satir conceptualized this child as the *identified client*, even though the entire family will be counseled.

Satir did not believe in the concept of triangular relationships; that is, she believed there is no such thing as a relationship "among" three people. There are only shifting two-person relationships, with the third member in the role of observer. The building blocks of Satir's system are two-person, interacting relationships. The key to success or failure in this system is the relationship between husband and wife. If the system is dysfunctional and they are not acting in parental coalition, then both mates may look to the child to satisfy their unmet needs in the marital relationship.

According to Satir, children who are triangled into a marital situation in the role of "ersatz mate" — an ally who is wooed seductively by the parent of the opposite sex — are not happy. The child has loyalties to and needs for both parents. Although a child may appear closer to one parent, such an alliance is illusory. Children cannot unambivalently side with either parent.

Satir wrote that one develops a sense of self-esteem in the early childhood years. Beside the obvious physical needs, children need a warm, ongoing, predictable mastery over their world and a validation of themselves as distinct and worthwhile people. Finally, they require a sense of what it is to be male or female and an acceptance of this role. If parents consistently show that they consider their children masterful, sexual people, and if they also demonstrate a gratifying, functional male/female relationship, their children acquire self-esteem and become increasingly independent. In every way, self-esteem, independence, and individuality go together.

Satir viewed mature people as those who are fully in charge of their feelings and who make choices based on accurate perceptions of themselves and others. Once choices have been made, the mature person takes full responsibility for them. In summary, Satir regarded mature people as (1) being in touch with their feelings, (2) communicating clearly and effectively, and (3) accepting differences in others as a chance to learn.

THEORY OF COUNSELING

Satir believed there are four components in a family situation that are subject to change and correction: the members' feelings of self-worth, the family's communication abilities, the system, and the rules of the family. The rules are the way things are accomplished in the family. They are the most difficult component to uncover during therapy sessions because they usually are not verbalized or consciously known to all members of the family. Satir's goal was to have all members of a family understand the rules that govern their emotional interchanges. These rules include: (1) freedom to comment, (2) freedom to express what one is seeing or hearing, (3) freedom to agree or disapprove, and (4) freedom to ask questions when one does not understand. The family unit becomes dysfunctional when the unwritten rules are not understood. Satir told families that were having problems with one of the members that there are no bad family members who cause pain, only bad rules. She believed that what goes on at a given moment is the natural consequence of the experience of one's own life; consequently, there is hope that anything can change. However, Satir believed that change is not a "have to" but is one possibility of several. She believed in risk-taking, controlling the counseling process, and leaving the outcome to the family.

In family systems theory, the main idea is that the family functions as a unit, with certain rules, expectations, and emotions. Members of the family unit are interdependent; therefore, when stress is applied to one part of the system or to one family member, it will be felt throughout the system by all the other members in varying degrees. The family system has both the potential to share and deal with the stress in a healthy, open, and productive way and the potential to close the communication process by focusing blame for the stress on one family member (the identified client).

To bring about changes in a family's functioning, analyzing the interaction processes between the family members and the family system is as important as analyzing the communications content. Questions of who is "right" and who is "wrong" border on value judgments and have no place in the process of family growth and further development. The focus is on discovering how individuals can adjust to the various events occurring within the family in such a way as to achieve satisfaction for its members and to avoid withdrawing from facing problems openly.

Satir emphasized the necessity of developing trust before any meaningful change process can begin. When there is a willingness to take a risk, trust can be assumed. The second step is the development of awareness, or knowing what one is doing. With awareness comes understanding and the application of this new understanding to effective decision-making. At this point, the new decision-making behavior can be put to use. The underlying theme is the development of self-worth and the freedom to comment.

Satir believed that whether a family grows or not is primarily the responsibility of counselors and their input. They must be able to put clients in touch with themselves at a feeling level. The counselor assumes the role of teacher to reeducate the family to new ways of thinking, feeling, and communicating. The challenge is to bring about in clients a curiosity and a willingness to change and explore.

Communication is the most important factor in Satir's system. She viewed communication as the main determinant of the kinds of relationships people have with one another and of how people adjust to their environment. Communication is the tie that binds the family together. When a family is operating smoothly, communication among family members is open, authentic, assertive, and received. Conversely, when a family system is in trouble, communication is blocked or distorted in a futile attempt to ward off anxiety and tension.

Fear of rejection is a common source of anxiety, and because people fear rejection, they resort to one response pattern or to a combination of patterns in communicating with others. These universal response roles are the placater, the blamer, the computer, the distractor, and the leveler. The last response, leveling, is the one that helps people develop healthy personalities; all the others are used to hide real feelings for fear of rejection. In such situations, people feel and react to the threat of rejection, but because they do not want to reveal "weakness," they attempt to conceal it. Satir (1971) agreed with Gestalt theory on nonverbal behavior:

the body expresses where you are in terms of your whole integration. Each response pattern is accompanied by a unique body posture and nonverbal behaviors. A brief description of each pattern follows.

Placater.   These people placate so others do not get angry. Their motto is "peace at any price." They talk in ingratiating ways to try to please, or they apologize. They never disagree and even take on the air of a "yes-person." They have a low sense of self-esteem. They are unable to negotiate solutions of mutual benefit because the process is too threatening. In other words, placaters negate self in the interest of serving others and staying within the context of the situation. Nonverbal messages of the placater include "Whatever you want is okay with me; I am just here to make you happy."

Blamer.   These people are the faultfinders, directors, and bosses. They also do not feel good about themselves. They may feel lonely and unsuccessful and attempt to compensate for these feelings by trying to coerce others into obeying them so they can feel that they amount to something. Blaming is also a good way to create distance and prevent others from getting too close. The blamers are good guilt inducers: "After all I have done for you, how could you do this to me?" Blamers negate others while focusing on the context of the situation and on themselves. Nonverbal messages from the blamer include "You never do anything right. What is the matter with you?"

Computer.   These people are calm, correct, show no feelings, and speak like a recording. They pretend there is no conflict when there is. Computers are the "super-reasonable" people. Their bodies reflect their rigid personalities. They negate self and others in order to concentrate on context. They cover up their vulnerability by using big words to establish a sense of self-worth. Nonverbal messages from the computer include "I am cool, calm, and collected." They may also take the position of "see it my way" at the expense of others and the context of the situation.

Distractor.   These people make statements that are completely irrelevant to what is going on. They change the subject and never respond to the point. Their strong point is evading the issue. They may even resort to withdrawing from the situation to avoid a crisis. Distractors negate all three elements of reality: self, others, and the context of the situation. Nonverbal messages from distractors include "Maybe if I do this long enough, the problem will really go away."

Leveler.   These people communicate their honest thoughts and feelings in a straightforward manner that addresses self, others, and the context of the situation. Their verbal messages and nonverbal body posture are consistent. Leveling occurs when all aspects of communication are congruent: body, vocal tone, context, and facial expression. Levelers do not cover up, nor do they put other people down in the name of being open and honest. They are not phonies. Their communication proceeds in a natural, healthy flow. Their relationships are free and honest, so there are few threats to self-esteem. The leveling response is the truthful message for a particular person at a given time. It is single and straight. There is an openness and a feeling of trust in interactions with a person who is leveling. This response allows people to live as complete persons who are really in touch with their behavior, thinking, and feelings. Satir (1972) stated that being a leveler allows a person to have integrity, commitment, honesty, intimacy, competency, creativity, and the ability to solve real problems in a real way. The other four forms of communicating result in doubtful integrity, commitment by bargain, dishonesty, loneliness, incompetence, strangulation by tradition (inability to change traditional patterns), and destructive ways of dealing with fantasy problems.

Our society does not encourage people to use leveling responses. Although people would like to be honest, they are afraid to and play games instead. Satir outlined a variety of experiences to help family members become aware that they can choose to change their responses and understand how they can do so. Levelers can choose to use one of the other four response patterns if they are willing to accept the consequences; but for them such responses would not be the automatic response of people locked into a particular pattern. Levelers can choose to placate, blame, compute, or distract; the difference is that they know what they are doing and are prepared to accept the result of their behavior.

The message of the leveler is consistent. If a leveler says "I like you," the voice is warm and the eye contact and body speak the same message. If the leveler is angry, the voice is harsh, the face is tight, and the words are clear: "I am mad as hell at you!"

Satir pointed out that every person she has seen with a behavior or coping problem was a member of a family in which all significant communication was double-level—that is, phony or hidden (Satir et al., 1975). If people can learn to recognize harmful communication patterns and learn to level with their family members, then the family has a chance to make its members' lives better and to solve problems more efficiently. As mentioned previously, Satir's system is based on two-person, interacting relationships. However, there are three parts to every couple: you, me, and us. In order for the relationship to continue and for love to grow, each part has to be recognized without being dominated by the other two. Although love is the feeling that begins a marriage, the process is what makes it work. The process is the "how," and it is this "how" that Satir taught her clients.

Satir divided all families into two types: nurturing or troubled. There are varying degrees of each type. Her main objective was for her clients to recognize which type they are and either to change from troubled to nurturing or to become more nurturing. The nurturing family helps develop feelings of self-worth in its members, whereas the troubled family diminishes these feelings. In every family, factors to be considered include feelings of self-worth, communication, rules, and links to society.

According to Satir (1972), nurturing families are marked by aliveness, honesty, genuineness, and love. These families have the following characteristics:

1. People are listened to and are interested in listening to others.
2. People are not afraid to take risks because the family understands that mistakes are bound to happen when risking.
3. People's bodies are graceful, and their facial expressions are relaxed.
4. People look at one another and not through one another or at the floor.
5. The children are friendly and open, and the rest of the family treats them as people.
6. People seem comfortable about touching one another and showing their affection.
7. People show love by talking and listening with concern and by being straight and real with one another.
8. Members feel free to tell one another how they feel.
9. Anything can be discussed — fears, anger, hurt, criticism, joys, achievements, and so on.
10. Members plan, but if something does not work out, they can adjust.
11. Human life and feelings are more important than anything else.
12. Parents see themselves as leaders and not as bosses. They acknowledge to their children their poor as well as their good judgment, their hurt, anger, or disappointment as well as their joy. Their behavior matches their teaching.
13. When nurturing, parents need to correct their children. They rely on listening, touching, understanding, and careful timing, being aware of children's feelings and their natural wish to learn.
14. Nurturing parents understand that children can only learn when they are valued, so they do not respond in a way to make the child feel devalued.

COUNSELING METHOD

The counseling method of conjoint family therapy involves the entire family and is based on communication, interaction, and general information. The approach Satir taught to families is both physical and emotional. Those counselors who prefer to work less with emotions and more with behavior will find the Adlerian method more comfortable.

Satir's goals for family counseling were to establish the proper environment and to assist family members in clarifying what they want or hope for themselves and for their family. She wanted them to explore how it is now for the family and who plays which roles. She sought to build everyone's self-esteem. Satir also worked to help families operationalize their definitions of words like *respect* and *love*. For example, she would ask a family member, "What would be happening that would let us know you were getting the respect and love you desire?" Or, "What must be done for you to make you feel respected and loved?" Satir also used reframing as a way of turning negatives into positives. This allowed clients to view difficult situations in a better light and see possibilities for cooperation, conflict resolution, and change.

Satir led the family in role-playing both family situations and each other's actions and reactions to the happenings in a typical day in the family's life. She used some Gestalt techniques of "sculpting" a family argument or interaction, believing that the body is often a more honest reflection than the verbal message (see the following example). Satir used videotape replay to teach the concepts of communication discussed in the previous section. In her role-play dramas, she used various props, such as rope ladders and stepladders, to demonstrate and analyze the types of family interactions that exist. These dramas were staged to help family members learn how to level with each other in expressing their emotions by using honest, direct language. Satir examined the family history by drawing family trees to look at how past and immediate family styles are passed on from parent to child. She used ropes to demonstrate the complicated process of communication between parents and children.

Even with a multitude of techniques, Satir proposed no formula for therapy because therapy involves human feelings and the ability to respond on a human level. Satir viewed the family as a "people-making factory" in which people are made by a process that is crude at best and destructive at worst.

An Example of Satir's Method

The following family-therapy scene is typical of Satir's work:

A 40-year-old woman sits in a fetal position on the floor, hiding behind a sofa. Her husband, sitting in a chair, points an accusing finger at her across the room. One daughter, with arms outstretched, tries to make peace. Two children sit with their backs to the group, and a fourth child rubs his mother's back. Satir breaks the silent role-play, rests her hand on the father's shoulder, and asks how he feels right now. She has asked the family to act out silently how each person in the family feels during a family argument. This sculpting method is excellent in creating awareness of personal feelings as well as awareness of the feelings of other family members.

The Importance of Including Children

Including children is imperative for the success of family counseling in Satir's system. Satir advocated inclusion of all the children, not just the child who has a problem, because all are a part of the family homeostasis—a process by which the family balances forces within itself to achieve unity and working order. Satir operated from the assumption that when dysfunction exists within the family, all members feel it in some way. Therefore, the counselor works with all members of the family to help them redefine their relationships. Family members have their own perceptions of what is going on in the family, and input from each member is vital in building a functional family. The counselor works with the family's interpersonal relationships, discovering how the members interact so they can strengthen their bonding.

Before bringing the children in, Satir suggested meeting with the marital pair. She made the couple aware of themselves as individuals as well as mates and parents. She also suggested preparing the parents in the initial interview for bringing the children into the counseling sessions. After the parents agreed that the role of the children in family counseling was important, the children were included.

When working with children, the counselor must consider many things. The counselor needs to be fully aware of the children's capabilities and potentialities. The counselor can plan the length of counseling sessions in accordance with the ages of the children. Children have short attention spans, and the counseling process must hold their interest. Counselors confronted with these obstacles can work within them, making the counseling process beneficial, productive, and enjoyable for all.

The counselor should begin by recognizing all the children, repeating their names, ages, and birth order to let the children know they are being heard. The counselor will also want to set rules for the sessions—for example, no one may destroy property within the room, no one may speak for the others, all must speak so they can be heard, everyone must make it possible for others to be heard, and so on. When the ground rules have been established, in-depth discussion can begin.

The counselor should set the mood by asking questions in a warm, specific, matter-of-fact way. The counselor should create a setting in which people can take the risk of looking clearly and objectively at themselves and their actions. Satir suggested that the counselor ask many questions; however, they should be questions that the children are able to answer. During this time, the counselor must be sure the children understand what is happening and what the family is striving to gain. The children need to feel comfortable and to be aware of themselves as individuals, different from one another. They need to be made aware of the importance of communicating with one another—for example, to feel free to agree or disagree with other family members, to say what they think, and to bring disagreements out in the open. The children need to know that they will be treated as people with perceptions and feelings.

The counselor should demonstrate the idea of individuality by speaking to each child separately, differentiating each child, and restating and summarizing what each child says. Counselors need to convey their sincerity in honoring all questions from each child, demonstrating that questions are not troublemaking and illegitimate, that all should ask questions about what they do not know or are unsure about. Counselors should convey their expectations of the children to increase the likelihood of the children's rising to meet them. Children listen, are interested, and are able to contribute to the discussions.

It is important for the counselor to ask the children their ideas about why they are in counseling. The counselor should repeat what each child says to make sure the child's meaning is understood. The counselor may proceed by asking the children where they got their ideas about why they are there, who told them, and what was said. From this exchange, the counselor can gain some insight into the methods of communication within the family. The counselor encourages the children to talk about themselves and their feelings in relation to each family member. The counselor also helps the children express frustration and anger and has the children ask their family members for answers to any questions they may have. The counselor may use confronting questions to provoke thought in the child. As the counseling sessions advance, questions concerning family rules and roles will arise. After establishing good rapport and a comfortable atmosphere, the counselor may begin to bring out underlying feelings and confront family members concerning the elements causing the family's dysfunctioning. The basis for further probing and confronting must be established between counselor and parent; counselor and child; parent and child; and counselor, parent, and child in the initial interviews. From the initial interviews, the counselor must gain the child's confidence in order to move forward.

The counselor wants to see where each child fits into the family unit. In the beginning, to build self-esteem within the children, the counselor will focus on the children, not ignoring the parents but having the parents respond intermittently. Counselors help children understand their parents as parents and people and themselves as children and people.

Three Keys to Satir's System

Satir's approach to family counseling focused on three key ingredients:

1. Increasing the self-esteem of each family member by facilitating ways in which the family as a whole can better understand its systems and learn to implement changes toward open systems and nurturing attitudes and behaviors;

2. Assisting the family in discovering ways to improve and open communication patterns by helping family members better understand and
analyze their encounters with each other and learn the leveling
response; and
3. Using experiential learning techniques in the counseling setting to help
the family understand present interactions, thus encouraging personal
responsibility for one's own actions and feelings.

Satir viewed the counselor as a facilitator, a change agent, who assists in
the process of moving toward a more open family system, and thereby, a
nurturing family. The counselor is not the "expert." The process should
help family members become the experts on the family's problems and
growth.

Satir's Technique

A family therapist will use a variety of techniques to assist the family in
self-discovery. Satir's method is designed to help family members discover
what patterns do not work and how to better understand and express their
feelings in an open, level manner. Rather than have them rehash past
hurts, Satir would have the family analyze its "systems" in a present
interaction in the counseling setting. The counselor might accomplish this
analysis in many ways. The following are several examples:

1. The counselor asks the family to describe a situation that causes the
difficulties that have brought them to counseling or asks them to describe a typical situation from their recent experience that usually results
in the problem. Family members enact the situation.
2. The counselor might have the family sit in a circle in chairs to simulate
a family decision, such as deciding together where to go on their next
vacation.
3. The family participates in a family sculpture, as in the example presented earlier. The counselor asks someone to describe a typical family
argument, then has that person "sculpt" the argument by placing each
family member in appropriate positions—complete with gestures, facial
expressions, touching, and so on. The counselor might follow this by
asking each of the other members how he or she would change it and
letting each make the changes. It is essential to follow this process with
discussion aimed at leveling and participation by each family member.
4. Each family member takes some long ropes, one for each of the other in
the family, and ties all of them around his or her waist. Next, the
counselor instructs them to tie one rope to each of the other family
members. Discussion of the resulting tension and mass of ropes can help
the family better understand the complexity of its relationships and
crossed transactions.

5. Role-playing and reverse role-playing are useful for stimulating family discussion.
6. Videotaped family sessions and discussions help family members achieve a better understanding of the reactions and responses of all members.
7. Use of games includes (a) the simulated-family game, (b) the systems game, and (c) communication games.

Satir's games, which are used for counselor training as well as family therapy, are based upon her definition of a *growth model*. The growth model is based on the assumption that an individual's behavior changes as a process that is represented by transactions with other people. People will function fully when they are removed from the maladaptive system or when the system is changed to promote growth. This model differs greatly from the *sin model*, which proposes that the individual's thinking, values, and attitudes are wrong and therefore must be changed; and the *medical model*, which purports that the cause of the problem is an illness located in the patient.

Satir developed various games to deal with the family's behavior when family members operate within these three models. It is again imperative to state that all family members are present during the family counseling process.

The simulated-family game. In this game, various family members simulate each other's behavior; for example, the son plays the mother. The family members may also be asked to pretend that they are a different family. Following this enactment, the counselor and family members discuss how they differ from or identify with the roles.

Systems games. These games are based upon either open or closed family systems; learning and insight can be obtained from both family types. Satir believed that emotional and behavioral disturbances directly result from a member's being caught in a closed family system. The closed system does not allow any individual the right to honest self-expression. Differences are viewed as dangerous, and the overriding "rule" is to have the same values, feelings, and opinions. In the open-system family, honest expression and differences are received as natural occurrences, and open negotiation occurs to resolve such differences by "compromise," "agreeing to disagree," "taking turns," and so on.

One game entails having family members take roles revolving around the five interactional patterns of behavior discussed earlier: (1) the placater, (2) the blamer, (3) the distractor, (4) the computer, or (5) the leveler. On the basis of these interactional patterns, various games have been constructed.

1. *Rescue game.* Behaviors 1, 2, 3, and 4 are played. Who plays each role is variable, but each member must remain in this role throughout the session.
2. *Coalition game.* Behaviors 1 and 2 are played. Two people always disagree and gang up on the third person.
3. *Lethal game.* Behavior 1 is used. Everyone agrees.
4. *Growth vitality game.* Each person includes himself or herself and others by honest expression and by permitting others to express themselves (leveling).

These techniques can be broadened beyond the initial family triad by incorporating all family members into a prescribed family situation and assigning various roles to each member. These sessions are extremely vital for younger children who have been ruled by the adage "Children should be seen but not heard." The games aid families in understanding the nature of their own family system. They also allow family members to experience new interactional patterns through identification of where they are and insight into possible alternatives. By using the growth vitality game and the leveling role, families can experience the movement from a pathological system of interaction to a growth-producing one.

Communication games.   These games are aimed at establishing communication skills. Satir believed that it is almost impossible to deliver an insincere or phony message if the communicator has skin contact and/or steady eye contact with the listener. One communication game involves having two members sit back to back while they talk. Next they are turned around and instructed to stare into each other's eyes without talking or touching. Satir (1967) reported that this type of interaction leads to many insights concerning the assumptions that each makes about the other's thoughts and feelings. Next, the participants continue to stare and then touch each other without talking. This process continues in steps until each partner is talking, touching, and "eyeballing" the other. Assuming these positions, they are asked to disagree with each other. Satir found that this was nearly impossible. People either enjoy the effort or are forced to pull back physically and divert their eyes to get angry.

The counselor's role is one of the most important parts of these games. Throughout and after each session, the counselor intervenes and discusses each member's responses, feelings, and gut reactions in relation to his or herself and to other family members.

The Counselor's Role

In Satir's approach to family counseling, the counselor is a facilitator who gives total commitment and attention to the process and interactions. The counselor does not take charge and must be careful not to manipulate the participants' reactions and verbalizations. By careful and sensitive attention to the interactions, transactions, and response (or lack of response) of each family member, the counselor can intervene at certain points to ask whether the messages are clear and correct and how a particular person is feeling, giving each person a chance to interact or make corrections. For example, the counselor might interrupt the dialogue when one person makes a statement about how another feels or thinks by asking the second person if the statement is accurate and how he or she feels at that moment.

In short, the counselor will intervene to assist leveling and taking responsibility for one's own actions and feelings. The counselor will also intervene to give quieter family members permission to talk and be heard. By focusing on understanding and analyzing a present interaction in the counseling setting, family members should be better able to understand past hurts and problems. They should also be better able to understand past hurts and problems by understanding what patterns produced the trouble. With experience in openness and leveling, communication between family members can change, and growth can occur. The family is then better able to continue the discussions, come to new insights, and implement appropriate changes.

CASE STUDIES

The ability of people to assume other roles in the family-group situation supports the idea that people can change their response roles and that families can change their ways of interacting and solving problems. Family members need to learn how to share both positive and negative feedback in ways that do not hurt or belittle one another. The following is a family role-play transcript in which the leveling response is omitted:

Don (father/husband, blaming): Why isn't our dinner ready?

Sandy (mother/wife, blaming): What are you yelling about? You've got as much time as I have.

Bill (son, blaming): Aw, shut up. You two are always yelling. I don't want any dinner, anyway.

Don (blaming): You keep your trap shut. I'm the one who makes the rules around here because I'm the one who makes the money.

Sandy (blaming): Says who? Besides, young man, keep your nose out of this.

Or:

Don (placating): Maybe you'd like to go out to dinner for a change?

Sandy (computer): According to the last issue of *Woman's Day*, they say eating out is cheaper than cooking the same things at home.

Don (placating): Whatever you would like to do, dear.

Bill (placating): You always have good ideas, Mother.

Sandy (computer): That's right. I have a list of the restaurants offering specials this week.

Perhaps one good leveling response by any of the family members could have helped these short exchanges. Perhaps Sandy could have said that she needed a rest from a long, hard day and would like to have dinner out. Don could have made a statement rather than asking a phony question. Perhaps a leveling remark by Don might have informed Sandy that he was wondering what she wanted to do about dinner tonight. Bill could have made a small change in his remark to "I really worry when we argue and fight in this family, and I would like this to stop." The counselor's job would be to rehearse these leveling responses until the problem is solved in the role-playing setting. Then plans are made to try the leveling response in real life.

Let's examine a second family session with the counselor present. The Frazier family is seated clockwise around the counselor in the following order: Jody, the wife/mother, 43 years old; Frank, the 11-year-old son; Larry, the husband/father, 44 years old; Joyce, the 14-year-old daughter; and Kathy, the 16-year-old daughter.

Kathy: Mom, just say yes or no. Am I going to be allowed to go out on weekdays or not?

Jody: Why don't you do what you want? You always do anyway.

Counselor (to Kathy): How does this make you feel?

Kathy: Angry. I'd like to be able to do what the rest of the kids are doing, but I know Mom and Dad don't approve.

Counselor: That sounds funny because I heard your mom say it was up to you. (To Jody) Is that what you said? Maybe it was the expression on your face and the way you spoke your message to Kathy that made her think you didn't really mean "Do what you want to do."

Kathy: Yes, her stern face said "no."

Counselor: What did she do with her face to tip you off?

Kathy: Well, she squinted her eyes and wrinkled up her nose.

Counselor: It's hard to read your mom's mind, but I am guessing that she thinks nobody listens to her very much. We can check this with her later. But I'm wondering if you have ever felt this way.

Kathy: Sometimes.

Counselor (to Jody): Do you ever have this feeling?

Jody: I think maybe we've hit on something new.

Counselor: Do you think no one listens to you?

Jody: I have a rough day just keeping house for this family. Larry comes home from work too tired to talk, and all I ever talk to the children about are their fights and arguments. I have to handle all the family problems.

Larry: Well, my job is all I can handle.

Jody: See, no one listens to my side of the story.

Counselor (to Larry): Were you aware of what Jody was saying when she said that? What did it feel like, Larry?

Larry: It irritates me that everybody thinks it's my fault that things don't go better in our family.

Counselor: Hold it one minute. Frank is doing something over here.

Larry (to Frank): Settle down over there and shape up.

Counselor: Let's take some time out and find out what's going on with Frank. I haven't been paying much attention to Frank and Joyce. (To Frank) How did you feel about what was going on over here?

Frank: Well, I, uh . . .

Joyce (blaming Frank): You weren't even paying attention.

Kathy: Frank, if you move over here with me, we can get along better.

Jody (to Larry): Can't you do anything to make him mind me? It's all your fault he acts like he does.

Counselor (to Kathy and Larry): An interesting thing happened before Frank started acting up. I was wondering, Kathy, how you felt when your father said to your mother, "That it's all my fault that things don't go better in our family."

In this short segment, the counselor attempts to look at present communication patterns and the feelings these patterns conceal. After achieving awareness of the communication blocks, the family can begin to practice leveling as an alternative way of communicating.

CONTRIBUTIONS OF SALVADOR MINUCHIN
Background

Salvador Minuchin brings a rich, wide variety of background experiences to the role of family therapist, theorist, and educator. He was born in 1921 to Russian Jewish parents in a small Argentinian town. According to Simon (1984), Minuchin benefited from two cultures: the transported European community of Russian Jews and the alien Argentine culture from which he learned the rituals of Latin pride. Minuchin developed an active role in social-interest activities early in life. As a university student, he joined a Zionist student organization and was arrested for taking part in a student protest against Juan Perón in 1943. After spending three months in jail, Minuchin was expelled from the university. Forced to continue work on his medical degree in Uruguay for a time, he was able to return later to complete his degree in Argentina. Next came a residency in child psychiatry and an 18-month tour of duty as a doctor with the Israelis in their 1948 War of Independence. Minuchin came to the United States with the intention of working with Bruno Bettelheim in Chicago's Orthogenic School; however, he met Nathan Ackerman in New York and eventually decided to work in Ackerman's child-development center. Minuchin sandwiched in three years of work with African and Asian immigrant children in Israel before receiving more analytic training and becoming director of family research at the Wiltwyck School for Boys in New York.

It appears that Minuchin's best training did not come from books and classes. As so many therapists have soon noticed, traditional psychoanalytic methods do not often work with populations similar to the delinquent boys found at Wiltwyck. The recidivism rate seemed to be close to 100 percent, with the young men repeating their delinquent behaviors upon their release. Noticing that some families produced several delinquent children, Minuchin concluded that families must be making a significant contribution to the problem. Therefore, Minuchin began to develop an approach for working with inner-city families who did not have sufficient verbal skills for traditional psychotherapy, focusing on the nonverbal communication techniques that have become standard practice in individual, group, and family therapy.

Much of what Minuchin learned about families he learned by observation through a one-way glass and in collaboration with his colleagues at the school. In an approach similar to the Adlerian method for working with families, Minuchin and his colleagues developed a three-step approach, with two counselors meeting with the entire family followed by one counselor meeting with the parents and the other with the children. The process culminated in a final stage in which everyone gathered to share information and plans for change. Further observation and study led to the development of a language for describing family structure as well as a system of interventions designed to change unhelpful, and even harmful, patterns of family organization. Just as Glasser wrote his first successful book based on his experience at the Ventura School for Girls, Minuchin wrote *Families of the Slums* (1967) based on his experiences at Wiltwyck.

Minuchin's next project was transforming the Philadelphia Child Guidance Clinic into a model family therapy center. In describing this stage of his career, it is possible to compare Minuchin's various roles at the clinic with roles in the theater. He is often described as having a flair for the dramatic. As an administrator/supervisor, he was highly critical of seminar case presentations that did not meet his standards—much like a play director dissatisfied with the author's efforts. As a practicing family therapist, he was often viewed as writer, director, stage manager, and actor all rolled into one. He would set the family scene, assign roles, start and stop the action, and take a leading or supporting role himself. It is not surprising to learn that he has a fondness for the theater and that he has written plays. Perhaps the ability to diagnose and remediate a bad script or scene is the same ability required to fix a bad family script.

Working with Jay Haley, Minuchin developed the clinic's family orientation and the Institute for Family Counseling, which was designed to train paraprofessionals. Perhaps his most notable accomplishment during this period was the treatment he developed for psychosomatic families, particularly those of anorexics. He wrote *Families and Family Therapy* (1974) during his ten years as director of the clinic. Stepping down as director, Minuchin served as head of the training center until 1981. His next book, *Psychosomatic Families,* was published in 1978. In recent years, Minuchin has continued family research with "normal" families, written several plays, and written a book for the lay public about families entitled *Family Kaleidoscope* (1984).

Theory and Practice

Minuchin has been praised for rescuing family therapy from intellectuality and mystery. His pragmatic approach has contributed both to the understanding of how families function and to productive interventions for correcting malfunctions in the family system. As Papp (1986) points out, Minuchin was willing to work with children and families written off by the psychiatric community as unsuitable for treatment. His achievements are rooted in his philosophy of putting clients first and in his total commitment to their cases.

It would appear that once Minuchin diagnoses a flaw in the family system, he will go to any length to bring about a needed change. His techniques range from gentle persuasion to outright provocation and confrontation. He views psychosomatic illness as a symptom brought on and maintained by the family. He has had successes in treating eating disorders, asthma, and uncontrolled diabetes. As mentioned previously, the structural family therapy approach Minuchin developed is directed toward changing the family structure or organization as a way of modifying the behavior of the family members. The counselor makes interventions by becoming an active "family" member.

Marcus (1977), quoting Minuchin, described the difference between traditional psychotherapy and structural family therapy as being the same as the difference between a technician using a magnifying glass to focus on a small part of the total field and one with a zoom lens who can focus on the entire family or zoom in for a close-up of any one family member as part of the larger system. Leaving the family belief system in place, the structural therapist works with this belief system to effect behavior changes between people. Rule changes may be the immediate goal as three questions are explored: (1) How do family members relate to one another? (2) Who is allied with whom against whom? and (3) What is the nature of the parental dyad? The idea is to change the immediate context of the family situation in such a way that the family members' positions are changed. The cognitive-dissonance principle operates much the same way.

For example, Minuchin (1978) describes the case of an asthmatic 12-year-old girl whose asthma was psychosomatically triggered. She had a history of heavy medication, missed school days, and several trips to the emergency room. During the first family interview, the counselor directed the family's attention to the eldest sister's weight problem. The family's concern then shifted to the newly identified patient. The result was a diminishing of the asthmatic's symptoms, requiring less medication and no lost school time.

Minuchin refers to the preceding case as the foundation of family therapy. The family structure had changed: it moved from two parents protectively concerned with one child's asthma to two parents concerned with one child's asthma and one child's obesity. The asthmatic child's position in the family had changed, and that changed her experience.

As with all counseling approaches, the counselor's first step is to establish a trusting relationship with the family. Minuchin recommends three ways: (1) tracking—demonstrating interest in the family by asking a series of questions about the topics they bring up; (2) mimicry—adapting your communication style to fit the family's; and (3) support, which includes 1 and 2 plus acceptance of the problem as presented by the client.

Minuchin's style is to get the family to talk briefly until he identifies a central theme of concern and the leading and supporting roles in the theme. At this point, he operates like a play director or group-dynamics consultant in determining what roles are being played, what is interrupting the flow, what is silencing communication, and what diverting maneuvers are blocking the family-group interaction.

Next, boundaries or family rules are examined. These rules define (1) who participates in what, and how; (2) areas of responsibility; (3) decision-making; and (4) privacy (Lewis, 1986). When rules have been broken, the family works on them with the help of "stage directions." A family member may be asked to observe the family interaction but not interfere. Minuchin paces the family by adopting their mood and tempo and gradually changes it as the interview proceeds. He asks questions in the enactive mode: not "Why doesn't your mother talk to you?" but "See if you can get your mother to talk to you" (Ferber, Mendelsohn, & Napier, 1970).

The counselor might assign tasks related to the manipulation of space. For example, a child might be asked to move his chair so he can't see his mother's signals. A husband might be asked to sit next to his wife and hold her hand when she is anxious. Assigned tasks can be used to dramatize family transactions and to suggest change.

Minuchin (1974) shares a case about an anorexic girl and her family to illustrate how he conducts family therapy. Once again, like a play director, the stage is set. The family of six and Minuchin sit down at the table to have lunch.

Minuchin begins to develop the crisis in the family by announcing that Sally must eat or she will soon die. He assigns her father the task of helping her eat. The father tries bribery with ice cream and a soft drink, to no avail, and is "rewarded" by a minor tantrum from Sally.

Next, her mother is given the assignment to help Sally eat. Mother's pleas, guilt inducements, and lectures go unheeded except for more tantrum behavior in the corner of the room (including slapping Mother).

Minuchin begins a new stage in the process when he stands up and orders Sally to sit at the table. At this point, the family is exhausted and searching for a way to solve the problem. The reality-therapy philosophy that no one stops any behavior until thorough disgust sets in may come into play at this stage.

The therapist offers a way out of the trap. He offers a negotiation model that will allow Sally to negotiate with a pediatric resident, who will present several choices from all the required food groups from which Sally can select her daily meals. Any attempt by the parents to intervene in the process is blocked by the therapist, resulting in a separation between Sally and her parents and the creation of a therapeutic dyad between Sally and the therapist. The one rule of the game remains: Sally must eat. The strategy of offering alternatives empowers Sally with a control over her life that she has attempted to achieve through not eating. In one month, she returns to her normal weight.

CONTRIBUTIONS OF MILTON ERICKSON, JAY HALEY, AND CLOE MADANES

The contributions of each of the family therapists mentioned in this section could fill many books. Our purpose is merely to highlight some of their strategies and review some of the literature evaluating these methods.

Jay Haley, the director of the Family Therapy Institute of Washington, D.C., was a longtime colleague and student of Milton Erickson. He describes Erickson as his mentor and major source of ideas about therapy. Since Erickson's death in 1980, Haley is perhaps his best interpreter. Haley also worked closely with Salvador Minuchin at the Philadelphia Child Guidance Clinic. For the past several years, Haley's work has been closely associated with that of his wife, Cloe Madanes. They founded the Family Therapy Institute and now conduct lectures and workshops on strategic family therapy. Thus, we can observe some common roots among those who have contributed to structural family therapy (Minuchin), strategic/ structural approaches (Haley and Madanes), systemic therapy (Selvini-

Palazzoli of the Milan and Ackerman Institute groups), and brief family therapy (Watzlawick and the Palo Alto group).

To the strategic family therapists, *strategic* refers to the development of a specific strategy, planned in advance by the therapist, to resolve the presenting problem as quickly and efficiently as possible. Erickson promoted the idea that insight, awareness, and emotional release are not necessary for change. Rather, people need to solve their immediate problems and eliminate bothersome symptoms in order to move ahead with their lives. Followers of Erickson's approach would probably not have personal growth and development of the client as a therapeutic goal. Problem solving through minimal intervention is the key goal for the strategic group.

According to Feldman (1985), Erickson's approach incorporates three other principles in addition to discounting the importance of achieving insight: (1) the therapist uses the client's reality rather than attempting to fit the client to the views of the world, or even to those of the therapist; (2) both the therapist and client play active roles in the action-oriented process; and (3) minimal change must occur in one or more areas of the client's life in order for change to result in the family system. It would seem that eclecticism is alive and well in family therapy practice as the therapist works to construct strategies to implement the needed changes.

Erickson and Zeig (1985) presented one of Erickson's cases concerning a mother and her 61-pound anorexic daughter, Barbie, who was limiting her daily diet to one oyster cracker and a glass of ginger ale. Initial treatment began with routine questions for Barbie, which her mother answered. Erickson allowed the mother's behavior to continue for two days as a way of building rapport and establishing a pattern before initiating an intervention. The next stage began with Erickson's scolding the mother in front of Barbie for answering all of Barbie's questions. Barbie developed a new perspective on her mother. The next step was to punish Barbie for keeping her mother awake at night with her whimpering. The punishment was forcing Barbie to eat scrambled eggs — acceptable to her because she viewed eating as punishment. In the next stage, Erickson used storytelling as a way of changing Barbie's maladaptive behavior patterns by replacing them indirectly with good associations of food in various social settings. He altered her role as victim by placing her in other roles in the stories such as rescuer or persecutor. Barbie's treatment was successful and remained so during a lengthy follow-up period.

Haley (1976) described a family case involving a young boy's fear of dogs. A problem of family dynamics was that the boy was close to his mother but disengaged from his father. Haley's first step was to get father and son to interact by having them talk about the dangers of dogs in the neighborhood. When the mother tried to interrupt, Haley neutralized her by explaining that this was Dad's area of expertise. The second step was to get a dog into the home to help in three areas: (1) to continue the father/

son interaction, (2) to achieve systematic desensitization of the dog phobia, and (3) to stimulate change in the family dynamics. Haley accomplished step 2 by asking the boy to pick out a dog who was afraid and to work with his father on teaching the dog not to be afraid.

The preceding case illustrates a common malfunction in a child-centered family structure. Generally one or more overinvolved dyads exist, one of which usually includes the "problem" child. Haley (1973) described three ways to handle the overinvolved dyad: (1) act on the relationship between the child and his mother (neutralize mother); (2) modify the relationship between father and child (interact about the dog); and (3) change the relationship between spouses (bring the dog into the home for the son to care for and teach with the father's help).

Stone and Peeks (1986) provided another application of the same three steps, using a method Haley (1984b) refers to as "ordeal therapy." The case concerned a 17-year-old male who was engaging in seriously disruptive behavior in one class at school. After individual counseling had failed to resolve the problem, the counselor embarked on the three-step plan incorporating an ordeal consequence to change the young man's behavior and, indirectly, to improve the parental relationship (described as argumentative). The ordeal was presented to the family as follows:

> When Frank misbehaves at school, he will be sent to me with a note of explanation. I will call you, Dad, at your office to pick up Frank, take him home, and supervise his digging of a 3- by 3- by 3-foot hole in your flower bed. Upon completion of the digging, Frank is to place one of his record albums or tapes in it, fill the hole, tramp it down, clean the shovel, and return the shovel to the garage. You will then return Frank to me, and I will return him to his class. At the end of the day, you, Dad, are to have a talk with your wife about Frank's behavior for that day.

The treatment plan solved both problems: the son's behavior improved both at school and at home.

RESEARCH AND REACTIONS[1]
Introduction

Writing in 1976, Keebler was critical of the lack of research supporting family therapy during the three decades of its existence. Keebler also complained of the difficulty in defining family therapy because the definition varied with the practitioner. More than a decade later, we find a growing body of research studies that support the various forms of family therapy. However, we continue to find a wide variance in its definition and practice.

Treatment times for family therapy range from weekly visits for one

---

[1] Edward C. Bloser edited and contributed to the writing of this section.

year to monthly visits for four years to brief, one- to ten-session programs. Therapists and counselors from all three extremes claim they are effective. From this we can conclude that human beings are too complex for any one counseling approach to be effective for all.

Green and Kolevzon (1982) surveyed 1000 members of the American Association for Marriage and Family Therapy and the American Family Therapist Association on the belief and action systems of therapists identifying with the communication, structural/strategic, or systems approach to family therapy. Respondents, categorized according to theoretical orientation, were placed in four groups: (1) eclectic (38.1 percent), (2) communication (28.1 percent), (3) structural/strategic (18.2 percent), and (4) systems (15.6 percent). Theoretical preferences were found to show considerably more divergence than actual therapist style. Wilcoxon (1989), in a study on family therapists' application of family-of-origin concepts, found that 82 percent of his survey respondents made moderate to considerable use of family-of-origin theory and its concepts.

Rosenthal and Glass (1990) conducted a longitudinal study to assess the impact of day treatment and family therapy as alternatives to placement of 93 children aged 12–17. The alternative treatments were effective in reducing the incidence of placement outside the home. The most significant factor related to family therapy was a great reduction in the amount of money spent per child. There was also a reduction in the amount of delinquency following the alternative treatments. However, school performance changed very little, and parents reported less satisfaction with the in-home treatments than the control group did with out-of-home services. Szykula and Fleischman (1985) conducted a similar study with children aged 3–12. They found family interventions more effective than placement in about 50 percent of the cases and also cited tremendous cost benefits in family interventions as opposed to placement.

Training

Haley (1984a) has proposed that marriage counselors and family therapists should be brought together under common standards of organization, theory, and training. Rather than the two groups' competing, Haley believes they should correct discrepancies in training and skills through standardized training and competency requirements in systems analysis and psychodynamics.

Isaacs, Embry, and Baer (1982) implemented a training program in which therapists were paired with a parent and a preschool-age child. They were trained in the clinic to use and teach several behavioral skills to the parents. An analysis of the experimental results showed that after the training program (1) therapists increased their rates of instructing, praising, and informing the parents; (2) all the parents increased attention to compliance, decreased attention to noncompliance, and increased rates of praise to their children; and (3) all the children increased their compliance and decreased their noncompliance.

Eclectic Approaches

Satir cited several contributors to the development of her system–including Harry Stack Sullivan's interpersonal theory of the 1920s (an individual's behavior is influenced by his or her interaction with another) and the growth of group therapy, whose major contributors were J. L. Moreno and S. R. Slavson, also during the 1920s. Gregory Bateson and Murray Bowen began to look at families to discover why individuals became "schizophrenic." They believed that a person possibly represented the family situation. Bateson, of the Mental Research Institute, contributed the idea of double leveling. Much of Satir's theory has roots not only in classic theories of clinical psychology and psychiatry, but also in her past research at the Mental Research Institute and the National Institute of Mental Health. Satir appeared to be synthesizing older and newer theories while adding highly developed original techniques. Her eclectic approach is unique in the field of family counseling. In her four books, Satir wrote about her successes with more than 12,000 families. She also reported research data that showed that blood pressure, galvanic skin response, and EEG were significantly affected when people changed their stance and body posture and held them for at least 10 seconds during role-play demonstrations with double-level communication. For example, assuming the blamer posture caused a physiological as well as an emotional response after 10 seconds. In other words, people engaging in harmful role behavior over a period of time could make themselves sick.

Ross, Baker, and Guerney (1985) researched the efficacy of relationship-enhancement therapy as compared to the therapist's traditional approach to counseling couples. The study, conducted over ten weeks, found that the relationship-enhancement therapy group scored significantly higher than the preferred-treatment group on communication, general relationships, and marital adjustment.

Greenburg and Johnson (1986) made a strong case for working with feelings in family counseling. They believe that simply talking about past emotional experiences does not create change or intimacy in a relationship. Instead, focusing on and heightening primary emotions in the "here and now" are necessary for any changes to occur. Primary emotions are defined as those about which most people are unaware. Primary emotions are also those that individuals are least likely to discuss. This is unfortunate because it is these emotions that are biologically adaptive and valuable sources of information for decision-making and problem solving. The counselor's role, then, is to block or bypass secondary and instrumental emotions in favor of exploring and expressing these primary emotions to facilitate positive change in family interaction patterns.

Koch and Ingram (1985) conducted research supporting a trend toward eclectic approaches to family therapy, or at least combinations of two or more approaches. The two components of behavioral marital therapy (behavior exchange and communication/problem-solving training), when offered in isolation from each other, were found initially effective during posttest evaluation, as was a combination of the two approaches. However, the combination-approach client group continued to improve on follow-up evaluation while the other two client groups declined. It was noted that although the behavior-exchange group had the best posttreatment gains, they also showed the greatest decline at follow-up. The communication/problem-solving group, having significant but smaller gains at posttest, showed only minimal decline at follow-up.

Chasin, Roth, and Bograd (1989), in an article on action methods in systemic therapy, described a counseling method that would be quite at home in Gestalt counseling; perhaps their Gestalt orientation to therapy with couples underscores the eclectic nature of the profession. The authors discuss an approach to therapy that involves deemphasizing the problems. The main focus is on looking for clients' strengths and using various action strategies to open up new perspectives and discussions. Chasin, Roth, and Bograd provide a five-step outline:

1. Therapists and clients contract to promote safe, voluntary participation. The clients have the right to disclose at the level they choose and can refuse to answer any question or participate in any given activity.
2. Each participant is invited to list his or her individual strengths and the strengths of the relationship.
3. Participants enact three dramatizations. First, the couple enacts what would happen if the goals for the relationship were reached. Second, each client enacts a painful past experience. Third, each client enacts the painful past experience "as it should have been." The partner's roles in this enactment are preventive, protective, and/or resolving.
4. Each participant states what he or she perceives to be the problem in the relationship.
5. The therapist recommends the next step (homework, follow-up appointment, and so on) based on what happened during the session.

Duncan, Parks, and Rusk (1990), writing on eclectic strategic practice, emphasized a theme that runs throughout this book — counselors adapting to their clients rather than vice versa. The eclectic strategies offer a fuller menu for setting a context for change and empowering clients to independently discover and select better alternatives to meet their needs.

Duncan and Solovey (1989), in an attempt to integrate strategic brief therapy with insight-oriented therapy, restated that therapists are more similar than dissimilar and that they should not close themselves off from potentially helpful methods in other systems. The authors believe that considerable overlap exists between reframing and therapist-ascribed meaning (interpretation) designed to achieve insight. Reframing refers to charging the framework ("view work") of a situation to make it more workable and manageable.

Coche (1990), writing on resistance in existential-strategic marital therapy, defined resistance as all those behaviors in the therapeutic system that interact to prevent the system from achieving the family's goals for therapy. Strategists intervene by encouraging resistance, thereby making the resistance "cooperative." Four stages for handling resistance were presented: (1) the halo effect and cynical disbelief (clients bring considerable cynicism and doubt to counseling); (2) joining the couple and reframing the problem; (3) pulling for despair (where despair is used as a change agent—a person could have the assignment of deliberately experiencing despair for two days); and (4) turning the corner when the decision is made not to live unhappily ever after.

Conjoint Family Therapy

Taylor (1984) developed a seven-stage, structural, conjoint family-therapy approach for use in spouse-abuse cases. The treatment schedule is directed toward relearning about anger and appropriate expression of anger, positive self-talk, awareness of anger and stress levels, structural raising of self-image and marriage image, and learning of autonomy, assertiveness, and decision-making skills. Five major topic areas are targeted: (1) stress and anger management, (2) positive expression of anger through assertion, (3) problem solving, (4) positive interaction and relationship climate, and (5) values, expectations, and jealousy.

Gentry and Eaddy (1980) proposed a similar method that uses a family systems approach for spouse-abusive families. They recommend a therapeutic/educational program that focuses on safety, long-term planning, child guidance, children's fears, relationship skills, and conflict management.

Pevsner (1982) divided into two groups 15 families with children aged 5–13. One group received individual treatment, and the other group received both individual and group family treatment. Those with the additional treatment did better on posttest instruments that measured knowledge of behavioral principles, but every family showed a decrease in frequency of targeted behaviors. A nine-month follow-up revealed that the gains made regarding targeted behaviors were maintained by every one of the participating families.

Szapocznik, Kurtines, Foote, Perez-Vidal, and Hervis (1986) presented evidence to suggest that one-person family therapy can be done successfully with the problem-source individual in the family. Drug-abusing adolescents were the problem-source people in the 35 families under study.

With half of the families receiving conjoint family therapy and the other half one-person family therapy, the researchers found both treatments equally effective in reducing family discord.

Gurman and Kniskern (1986), in a review of literature on the comparative effectiveness of individual versus conjoint family therapy, found more support for conjoint family therapy. Specifically, they concluded that (1) there is very little acceptable evidence of the inefficacy of individual marital therapy; (2) there is no evidence, acceptable or otherwise, of the efficacy of individual marital therapy; and (3) there is a large body of acceptable evidence of the efficacy of conjoint marital therapy.

Brach and O'Leary (1986) compared the treatment effectiveness of conjoint behavioral marital therapy with individual cognitive therapy for couples experiencing discord and depression (by the wife). Comparing a conjoint treatment focusing on social learning with a cognitive treatment focusing on self-talk, the researchers found the behavioral approach significantly superior to the cognitive approach and the control-group waiting list in reducing marital discord and depression.

Structural Family Therapy

Kurtines (1989) researched the differential effects of structural family therapy and psychodynamic child therapy on problematic Hispanic American boys aged 6 to 12. The two systems were also compared with a recreational group that served as a control group for the study. In structural family therapy, the families were seen conjointly, with emphasis on modifying maladaptive patterns of interaction. In individual psychodynamic child therapy, the child was seen in a playroom, while the mother was seen briefly as an aid in this process. Emphasis was placed on feelings, limit setting, transference interpretations, and insight as a mechanism to change. Both treatment groups outperformed the recreational group and were basically equal in lowering behavioral and emotional problems in the boys. While both approaches used the corrective-experience approach, the structural-family approach helped parents change their own behaviors and become the source of the corrective experience.

Fish (1989) compared structural, strategic, and feminist-informed therapies to determine whether family therapists consider feminist and gender issues in their therapy. The structuralists attempt to restructure a family's present organization in order to achieve their goals of broadening the family's resources to cope. Strategists, on the other hand, focus on solving the presenting problem. Feminist-informed therapists want to broaden sex roles for men and women. Survey results from the three groups revealed that men have been discouraged from participating in family life and that women should give up being the sole emotional support in the home. Structuralists would solve the problem using unbalancing, creating a crisis, boundary-making, restructuring, and escalating stress. Strategists would use reframing, positive connotation, and indirect techniques. The feminist-informed approach would emphasize co-responsibility in the family.

Enns (1988), in an examination of how to integrate family systems and feminist concepts, wrote that the strategic techniques of reframing and restraining can be compatible with a feminist perspective. Reframing vulnerability, neediness, and helplessness as sensitivity to others and the power of empathy may help clients realize that they do have strengths on which to build a better life.

Strategic Family Therapy

Bergman (1983) explored the use of paradoxical interventions or invariant prescriptions with families displaying dysfunctional symptoms of fusion in their family systems. Bergman presented two family case studies involving symptoms of systemic fusion. The specific symptoms differed for the two families: suicidal depression in one family and refusal to attend school in the other. Intense criticism between parents and children was characteristic of both families. Failing to overcome resistance to change with structural techniques, the author prescribed parental criticism in an attempt to shift the fusion in each family to a more functional reorganization of family dynamics. The presenting symptoms of dysfunctional fusion in both families were eliminated and remained absent through a one-year follow-up period. The prescribed parental criticism was effective in blocking the ongoing parental criticism, leading to the development of more functional patterns of family interactions. The therapist succeeded in harnessing family resistance to work for change rather than against it.

McColgan, Puch, and Pruitt (1985) reported successful treatment of a 9-year-old boy (diagnosed with primary encopresis) and his family. Treatment consisted of an initial family-assessment interview, six family sessions, and five individual 10-minute prefamily sessions with the boy. Structural changes were made by the therapist forming an alliance with the disengaged stepfather, which unbalanced the system by increasing the stepfather's authority. This served to block the boy's attempt to detour marital conflict with his encopresis. The strategic intervention was conducted in the 10-minute sessions with the boy, which focused on allowing him to take complete and private responsibility for his toilet habits and any cleanup that might occur after an "accident." The family agreed to not interfere with his encopresis. Three- and 18-month follow-up reports revealed only occasional episodes of encopresis.

Mirkin (1983) presented a successful family-treatment approach for anorexia nervosa. In the case study review, anorexia nervosa was viewed as an illness that stemmed from an overprotective family, leading to suppression of autonomy in the adolescent and surfacing in the form of an illness rather than outward rebellion. Two interventions were used to treat the anorexic adolescent, Cathy: (1) Cathy's refusal to eat was termed "disobedient behavior" and was dealt with as unacceptable by the parents, and (2) parental intervention in her eating habits was prevented. Cathy's defiance of the parental rules surfaced in her eating habits. She controlled the family by manipulating her eating behavior. Therapy with the entire family focused on discussing, negotiating, and resolving difficult family issues. The children were given more autonomy and responsibility for their decisions, and the parents spent more time with each other. Any weight gain Cathy showed was reinforced by allowing her more autonomy. Weight loss was punished by loss of new privileges. In other words, Cathy's eating behavior now controlled only her own autonomy and the number of privileges available to her.

DeShazer and Molnar (1984) have described a useful team approach for prescribing four common interventions in their practice of brief family therapy. The therapy hour is divided as follows: (1) a 40-minute interview with the family, (2) a 10-minute consultation time with the team, and (3) a 10-minute delivery of the intervention message and closing of the session. The first intervention, designed for families who focus on the perceived stability of their problem pattern, requires family members to observe one another between sessions so that "you can tell us next time what happens in your family that you want to continue to have happen." The second intervention is for families who are bankrupt of ideas about how to solve the problem. The therapist requests that they "do something different." The third intervention is for clients who believe their problem is out of their control. The therapist asks them to "pay attention to what you do when you overcome the temptation or urge to _____." The fourth intervention works well for clients who are convinced they are doing the only logical thing. The therapist's response is, "A lot of people in your situation would have _____." All four interventions are designed to help clients experience changing.

Morgenson (1989) presented an excellent example of how strategic methods can be used with children. Morgenson met with parents of a 7-year-old girl who was described as whiny, argumentative, and stubborn. The parents viewed this behavior as bad behavior, but the daughter did not. Without the child's recognition that the behavior was bad, the door was open for the counselor to use the age-metaphor technique. The girl was brought into the office with the parents, and the counselor asked her age.

After the child told him she was 7, the counselor looked incredulously at the mother and father. He then shook his head and said to the parents, "This can't be, for this girl is 7 and this is the behavior of a 5-year-old." With a puzzled look, the counselor asked the girl how old she was on her last birthday and would be on her next birthday. The counselor noted that the behavior she was exhibiting during the session was that of a 7-year-old, and he asked the parents to keep a log of the child's behavior for one week. This direct challenge of age appeals to children's needs to look their age or older.

Peeks (1989) supported the use of behavior metaphors in solving children's problems and presented several examples. One, entitled straightforward reorganizations, corrects a problem by altering the usual course of action the family takes. A young girl, unable to walk, suffered from a swollen leg that was diagnosed as psychosomatic. The therapist advised the mother to disengage herself from taking care of her widowed father to give structure back to her marriage. The therapist viewed the girl's swollen leg as a metaphor of her mother's situation. The reorganization of the family resulted in a rapid cure of the swollen leg.

Breit, Im, and Wilner (1988), in defending strategic therapy, provided more good examples of its application. One case concerned a 10-year-old girl who was driving her parents to high levels of stress by constant talk about dirt and feces. The parents were told to set aside 30 minutes to listen to their daughter talk about this. If approached outside the time frame, they told their daughter to hold the dirt and feces talk until the scheduled time. The problem disappeared in a few days because the child was caught between disobeying her parents by not talking about feces or obeying her parents and talking about it with their blessing. She chose to "disobey" and not talk about feces at any time.

Dysfunctional Families

The impact of the family-systems approach on counseling has grown steadily as a result of successful research with families that have produced children with emotional disorders. By focusing on the family as the source of pathology, this approach has also moved in the direction of the marital therapists, for it has been found rather consistently in family therapy that problem children come from homes in which husband/wife relationships are disturbed. According to Keebler (1976), most family therapists agree that family therapy is not effective with every individual or family. Families that are too rigid or have broken completely with reality will probably not benefit from family therapy. Like most counseling, it works best with those people capable of taking action. In a review of psychosocial interventions for antisocial children and their families, Duman (1989) reports that only a small number of programs provide evidence that positive changes in antisocial behavior were brought about by family therapy.

Zuk and Zuk (1989) described how the conflict cycle can be used as an organizing principle in helping counselors who work with families make assessments and plan interventions. The conflict cycle has four steps: (1) the dispute; (2) blaming; (3) shame, guilt, or denial; and (4) reparation, reconciliation, or retaliation. The authors illustrated how the conflict cycle operated in four conflicts experienced by a 15-year-old white male in crisis: (1) adolescent versus parent, (2) adolescent versus community, (3) parent versus parent, and (4) good self versus bad self.

Robertson and Simons (1989), writing on adolescent depression, noted that perceived parental rejection is positively correlated with adolescent low self-esteem, and in turn, low self-esteem is positively correlated with adolescent depression. The authors, emphasizing the importance of a confidant in preventing depression, pointed out that peers cannot fill this role because of their ambivalent and unsure feelings. Thus, adolescents depend on their parents for needed support. If it is absent due to parental rejection, the resulting low self-esteem may become depression. The preventive cure is plenty of parental nurturing during childhood and adolescence.

Forehand (1990), writing on families with a conduct-problem child, questioned whether parenting skills provide the needed answer. While it is true that parents with poor parenting skills usually have children who develop a deviant behavior, good parenting skills don't always solve the problem. Forehand recommends a thorough assessment of five areas before recommending parent education: (1) child's behavior, (2) parents' behavior coercing the child's behavior, (3) parents' parenting skills, (4) family atmosphere (that is, depression and conflict), and (5) research related to the problem.

Long and Forehand (1990) reported research studying the relationship between parental divorce, parent conflict, and the adjustment of individual family members. They found that not all divorces affect children the same way because of mediating factors: the child's age, the time elapsed since the divorce, and the child's gender. Behavior problems increase during the first two years after divorce, and there tends to be more anger and a stronger need for emotional stability. Boys seem to have a more difficult time adjusting. Some researchers believe the decrease in income may be more significant in causing maladjustment than the divorce. In fact, conflict over finances, visitation, child rearing, and relationships with other partners appears to be more related to the frequency of child behavior problems than does the divorce itself.

Functional Families

Gottman (1990), studying the characteristics of close personal relationships, found three patterns. First, more negative affect exists among dissatisfied couples than among satisfied couples. Second, a higher level of reciprocity of negative affect exists in dissatisfied couples. Third, the interactions of satisfied couples are less structured than are those of dissatisfied couples.

Ponzetti and Long (1989), reviewing the literature on healthy family functioning, found strong spousal relationships to be the most prominent indicator of healthy families. Other universal healthy traits include mutual interests, effective communication, problem-solving capability, adaptability to change, the ability to have fun together, mutual respect, and shared responsibilities.

Wuerffel, DeFrain, and Stinnet (1990), in a study on how strong families use humor, found that stronger families use wit, fun, and jokes to the benefit of their family. Put-down humor was seldom used by stronger families. Strong families reported negative effects when humor was used to put down other family members.

SUMMARY

We conclude our research and literature review with still another approach to family therapy. Bahatti, Janakiramariah, and Channabasvanna (1982) have proposed employing multiple-family group therapy as a way of capturing the support and help a family can get from an extended family living experience. Mutual support, belongingness, and common goals are some of the advantages listed for the group approach. The authors believe that group members act as allies of the therapist. These allies provide an objective framework in which to view difficult and conflicting intrafamily themes. Finally, the entire group serves as a resource for problem solving in generating, evaluating, and selecting alternative plans of action.

It is evident from our review that family therapy ranges from one person to multiple families and from brief interventions to multiple sessions and stages covering a variety of personal growth topics. It is also evident that research support exists for all types of family therapy and that it will be some time before a unification of family therapists occurs—unless they unite under the common banner of eclecticism.

REFERENCES

Bahatti, R. S., Janakiramariah, N., & Channabasvanna, S. (1982). Group interaction as a method of family therapy. *International Journal of Group Psychotherapy, 32*, 103–113.

Bergman, J. S. (1983). Prescribing family criticism as a paradoxical intervention. *Family Process, 22*, 517–521.

Brach, S. R., & O'Leary, K. D. (1986). The treatment of depression occurring in the context of marital discord. *Behavior Therapy, 17*, 43–49.

Breit, M., Im, W., & Wilner, R. S. (1988). In defense of strategic therapy. *Contemporary Family Therapy: An International Journal, 10*, 169–181.

Chasin, R., Roth, S., & Bograd, M. (1989). Action methods in systemic therapy: Dramatizing ideal futures and reformed pasts with couples. *Family Process, 28*, 121–136.

Coche, J. M. (1990). Resistance in existential-strategic marital therapy: A four-stage conceptual framework. *Journal of Family Psychology, 3*, 236–250.

DeShazer, S., & Molnar, A. (1984). Four useful interventions in brief family therapy. *Journal of Marital and Family Therapy, 10*, 297–304.

Duman, J. (1989). Treating antisocial behavior in children: Child and family approaches. *Clinical Psychology Review, 9*, 197–222.

Duncan, B. L., Parks, M. B., & Rusk, G. S. (1990). Eclectic strategic practice: A process constructive perspective. *Journal of Marital and Family Therapy, 16*, 165–178.

Duncan, B. L., & Solovey, A. D. (1989). Strategic-brief therapy: An insight-oriented approach? *Journal of Marital and Family Therapy, 15*, 1–9.

Enns, C. (1988). Dilemmas of power and equality in marital and family counseling: Proposals for a feminist perspective. *Journal of Counseling and Development, 67*, 242–248.

Erickson, M., & Zeig, J. (1985). The case of Barbie: An Ericksonian approach to the treatment of anorexia nervosa. *Transactional Analysis Journal, 15*, 85–92.

Feldman, J. (1985). The work of Milton H. Erickson: A multi-system model of eclectic therapy. *Psychotherapy, 22,* 154–161.

Ferber, A., Mendelsohn, M., & Napier, A. (1970). *The book of family therapy.* New York: Aronson.

Fish, L. S. (1989). Comparing structural, strategic, and feminist-informed family therapies: Two delphi students. *The American Journal of Family Therapy, 17,* 303–314.

Fish, L., & Piercy, F. (1987). The theory and practice of structural and strategic family therapies: A delphi study. *Journal of Marital and Family Therapy, 13,* 113–125.

Forehand, R. (1990). Families with a conduct problem child. In G. Brody & I. Sigel (Eds.), *Methods of family research: Biographies of research projects: Vol. II. Clinical populations* (pp. 1–30). Hillsdale, NJ: Lawrence Erlbaum Associates, Publishers.

Gentry, C. E., & Eaddy, V. B. (1980). Treatment of children in spouse abusive families. *Victimology: An International Journal, 5,* 240–250.

Goldenberg, I., & Goldenberg, H. (1985). *Family therapy: An overview.* Monterey, CA: Brooks/Cole.

Gottman, J. M. (1990). Finding the laws of close personal relationships. *Methods of Family Research, 1,* 249–263.

Green, R. G., & Kolevzon, M. S. (1982). Three approaches to family therapy: A study of convergency and divergence. *Journal of Marital and Family Therapy, 8,* 39–50.

Greenburg, L., & Johnson, S. (1986). Affect in marital therapy. *Journal of Marital and Family Therapy, 12,* 1–10.

Gurman, A., & Kniskern, D. (1986). Commentary: Individual marital therapy—Have reports of your death been somewhat exaggerated? *Family Process, 25,* 51–62.

Haley, J. (1973). *Uncommon therapy.* New York: Norton.

Haley, J. (1976). *Problem-solving therapy.* New York: Harper & Row.

Haley, J. (1984a). Marriage and family therapy. *American Journal of Family Therapy, 12,* 3–14.

Haley, J. (1984b). *Ordeal therapy: Unusual ways to change behavior.* San Francisco: Jossey-Bass.

Isaacs, C., Embry, L., & Baer, D. (1982). Training family therapists: An experimental analysis. *Journal of Applied Behavior Analysis, 15,* 505–520.

Keebler, N. (1976). Family therapy: A profusion of methods and meanings. *APA Monitor, 7,* 4–5, 17.

Koch, A., & Ingram, T. (1985). The treatment of borderline personality disorder within a distressed relationship. *Journal of Marital and Family Therapy, 11,* 373–380.

Kurtines, W. (1989). Structural family versus psychodynamic child therapy for problematic Hispanic boys. *Journal of Consulting and Clinical Psychology, 57,* 571–578.

Lewis, W. (1986). Strategic interventions with children of single parent families. *The School Counselor, 33,* 375–378.

Long, N. & Forehand, R. (1990). Parental divorce research. In G. Brody & I. Sigel (Eds.), *Methods of family research: Biographies of research projects: Vol. II. Clinical populations* (pp. 135–137). Hillsdale, NJ: Lawrence Erlbaum Associates, Publisher.

Marcus, M. (1977, July). The artificial boundary between self and family. *Psychology Today,* pp. 66–72.

McColgan, E. B., Puch, R. L., & Pruitt, D. B. (1985). Encopresis: A structural/strategic approach to family treatment. *American Journal of Family Therapy, 13,* 46–53.

Minuchin, S. (1967). *Families of the slums.* New York: Basic Books.

Minuchin, S. (1974). *Families and family therapy.* Cambridge, MA: Harvard University Press/London: Tavistock Publications.

Minuchin, S. (1978). *Psychosomatic families.* Cambridge, MA: Harvard University Press.

Minuchin, S. (1984). *Family kaleidoscope.* Cambridge, MA: Harvard University Press.

Mirkin, M. D. (1983). The Peter Pan syndrome: Inpatient treatment of adolescent anorexia nervosa. *International Journal of Family Therapy, 5,* 179–189.

Morgenson, G. (1989). Act your age: A strategic approach to helping children change. *Journal of Strategic and Systemic Therapies, 8,* 52–55.

Papp, P. (1986). Letter to Salvador Minuchin. In *Evolving models for family change* (p. 207). New York: Guilford Press.

Peeks, B. (1989). Strategies for solving children's problems understood as behavior metaphors. *Journal of Strategic and Systemic Therapies, 8,* 22–25.

Pevsner, R. (1982). Group parent training versus individual family therapy: An outcome study. *Journal of Behavior Therapy and Experimental Psychiatry, 13,* 119–122.

Ponzetti, J. J., & Long, E. (1989). Healthy family functioning: A review and critique. *Family Therapy, 14,* 43–49.

Robertson, J., & Simons, R. (1989). Family factors, self-esteem, and adolescent depression. *Journal of Marriage and the Family, 51,* 128–138.

Rosenthal, J., & Glass, G. (1990). Comparative impacts of alternatives to adolescent placement. *Journal of Social Services Research, 13,* 19–37.

Ross, E. R., Baker, S. B., & Guerney, B. G. (1985). Effectiveness of relationship enhancement therapy versus therapist's preferred therapy. *American Journal of Family Therapy, 13,* 11–20.

Satir, V. (1967). *Conjoint family therapy: A guide to theory and technique* (rev. ed.). Palo Alto, CA: Science and Behavior Books.

Satir, V. (1971, January). Conjoint family therapy. In G. Gazda (Ed.), *Proceedings of a symposium on family counseling and therapy* (pp 1–14). Athens, GA: University of Georgia.

Satir, V. (1972). *Peoplemaking.* Palo Alto, CA: Science and Behavior Books.

Satir, V., & Baldwin, M. (1983). *Step by step.* Palo Alto, CA: Science and Behavior Books.

Satir, V., Stachowiak, J., & Taschman, H. (1975). *Helping families to change.* New York: Tiffany.

Simon, R. (1984, November/December). Stranger in a strange land. *The Family Networker,* pp. 21–31, 66–68.

Stone, G., & Peeks, B. (1986). The use of strategic family therapy in the school setting: A case study. *Journal of Counseling and Development, 65,* 200–203.

Szapocznik, J., Kurtines, W., Foote, F., Perez-Vidal, A., & Hervis, O. (1986). Conjoint versus one-person family therapy: Further evidence for the effectiveness of conducting family therapy through one person with drug-abusing adolescents. *Journal of Consulting and Clinical Psychology, 54,* 395–397.

Szykula, S., & Fleischman, M. (1985). Reducing out-of-home placements of abused children: Two controlled field studies. *Child Abuse and Neglect, 9,* 277–283.

Taylor, J. W. (1984). Structured conjoint therapy for spouse abuse cases. *Social Casework, 65,* 11–18.

Wilcoxon, S. A. (1989). Application of family-of-origin concepts by marital and family therapists: A qualitative study. *Family Therapy, 16,* 207–213.

Wuerffel, J., DeFrain, J., & Stinnet, N. (1990). How strong families use humor. *Family Perspective, 24,* 129–141.

Zuk, C. V., & Zuk, G. H. (1989). The conflict cycle in the case of an adolescent in crisis. *Contemporary Family Therapy, 11,* 259–266.

PART THREE

COUNSELING WITH CHILDREN: SPECIAL TOPICS

CHAPTER 12

Consulting Techniques

INTRODUCTION

Dougherty (1990) states that "mental health consultation is based on the idea that society's mental health can be promoted through the efforts of consultants who work with deliverers of human services (such as counselors) or with administrators of human services programs (such as the director of a factory's employee assistance program" (p. 220). According to Dougherty, consultation in the mental health field began in the late 1940s with the passage of legislation that established the National Institute of Mental Health (NIMH). Because the need for mental health services exceeded the availability of such services, consultation became a method of providing preventive treatment in an attempt to meet mental health needs.

Kurpius and Robinson (1978) agree that the practice of consultation is relatively new, appearing shortly after World War II. In 1979, Kahnweiler reviewed the literature in four major journals published by the American Personnel and Guidance Association (now the American Association for Counseling and Development) to examine the history of consultation. The first articles on the counselor as a consultant appeared in these journals in 1957 and focused on consultation as an alternative to direct-service counseling. Models for consultation did not appear until several years later, and many of the early models were vague and abstract (Kahnweiler, 1979).

In spite of the need to share information with a wide variety of professionals attempting to meet the needs of adults and children, interest in consultative models and processes appeared to be limited for many years. In fact, according to Myrick (1987), some critics believe that consultation takes valuable time away from more important functions, such as counseling; that consultation is less difficult than counseling; and that children's needs could be ignored while counselors worked with adults. Despite the fact that consultation is a method whereby counselors may be able to help adults (parents, teachers, or others) work more effectively to meet the needs of a greater number of children, helping professionals have not widely accepted and used consultation. In many instances, consultation has been deemed unworthy of the counselor's time and interest. Blocher (1987) now believes that consultation is a rapidly growing method for providing human services. However, a cursory review of counseling books, journal articles, and other resource material indicates the paucity of research and writing in this area.

CONSULTATION DEFINED

In 1984, Dustin and Blocher wrote that *consultation* is often used to "describe almost any kind of activity that the user wishes to dignify and endow with benign and respectable characteristics" (p. 752). They found it difficult to review the research on consultation because of the "ambiguity that surrounds the term" (p. 752). Bundy and Poppen (1986) also found it difficult to review the research on elementary school consultation; they could not find agreement on the definition of the term *consultation*. Dougherty (1990) contends that the most consistently recognized definition of mental health consultation is one developed by Gerald Caplan, a psychiatrist who has studied and written extensively in the field, and published in his 1970 book, *The Theory and Practice of Mental Health Consultation*. Caplan defines consultation as follows:

> a process of interaction between two professional persons—the consultant, who is a specialist, and the consultee, who invokes the consultant's help in regard to a current work problem with which he is having some difficulty and which he has decided is within the other's area of specialized competence. The work problem involves the management or treatment of one or more clients of the consultee, or the planning or implementation of a program to cater to such clients. [Caplan, 1970, p. 19, cited in Dougherty, 1990]

The counselor working with children would, of course, reword Caplan's definition to address any problems of children rather than limiting consultative services to "work problems."

In 1968, Dinkmeyer attempted to clarify and define consultation by focusing on the processes or behaviors involved. Dinkmeyer suggested that "consultation involves sharing information, ideas, coordinating, comparing observations, providing a sounding board, and developing tentative hypotheses for action" (Myrick, 1987). Like Dinkmeyer, Myrick emphasized the planning and collaboration functions of consultation. He suggested that the consultant and consultee discuss the problem and develop a plan of action. Then the consultee takes appropriate steps to implement the agreed-on actions.

The AACD *Ethical Standards* in Appendix C defines consultation as "a voluntary relationship between a professional helper and help-needing individual, group or social unit in which the consultant is providing help to the client(s) in defining and solving a work-related problem or potential problem with a client or client system" (1988, Section E). The AACD code further states that the "consultant must have a high degree of self-awareness of his/her own values, knowledge, skills, limitations, and needs" and that "the focus of the relationship [is] on the issues to be resolved and not on the person's presenting problems" (Section E, 1).

SCHOOL CONSULTATION MODEL

According to Glosoff and Koprowicz (1990), consultation by counselors working primarily with children typically involves the following:

- Conducting professional development workshops and discussions with teachers and other school personnel on subjects such as substance or child abuse;
- Assisting teachers in working with individual students or groups of students;
- Providing relevant materials and resources to teachers, especially relating to classroom guidance curriculum;
- Helping to identify and develop programs for students with special needs;
- Participating in school committees that address substance abuse, human growth and development, school climate, and other guidance-related areas;
- Designing and conducting parent-education classes;
- Interpreting student information, such as results of standardized tests for students and team members; and
- Consulting regularly with other specialists (for example, social workers, psychologists, and representatives from community agencies).

By the end of the 1960s, models for behavioral consultation, Adlerian consultation, teacher-consultation groups, in-service training, and classroom observation had appeared in the literature (Kahnweiler, 1979).

Myrick (1987) presents three models of consultation: crisis, remedial, and developmental. According to Myrick, crisis consultation addresses urgent, critical issues. Remedial consultation focuses on intervening to avert a crisis. Developmental consultation is preventive in that it is designed to set up conditions that facilitate children's effective growth and development. (Parenting classes are an example of developmental consultation.) Myrick (1987) also defines four approaches to consultation. The diagnostic-prescriptive approach is probably used more often by school psychologists than by other helping professions. Information about the client/consultee is presented and analyzed, alternatives are considered, and a recommendation (prescription) is made. A school psychologist who suspects that a child has an attention-deficit disorder might present the results of interviews with a child's parents and teacher, observations of classroom behavior, and the results of a battery of tests for a team of experts to consider. The consultants would discuss various options for helping the child and make a recommendation for helping the child find better ways of learning and behaving.

Myrick (1987) points out that often adults lack knowledge or skills to work effectively with children. He suggests the *staff development and training* consultative approach to teach school personnel new skills and to review and refine those already present. A consultant might provide information on techniques for discipline problems, understanding developmental stages of children, teaching children with learning disabilities, classroom management, or a variety of other topics. Although Myrick calls this approach "staff development," the method of consultation could be effective for other adults working with children. Parenting classes that address developmental issues, methods for disciplining children, and ways to cope with children's special needs could be helpful to many adults, both professional and nonprofessional, who interact with children.

X According to Myrick (1987), the *case-management* approach considers one particular case and is similar to the case group, or C-group, which Poppen and Thompson (1975) describe as follows:

1. A brief description of the case is presented.
2. A discussion of the present situation follows.
   a. What is happening?
   b. What behavior is helpful or hurtful?
3. How does the child view himself or herself and the situation?
   a. View of self
   b. Goals
   c. Self-evaluation of behaviors
4. How are others involved? What are their reactions?
5. What are alternative or new behaviors?
6. What helpful resources are available?
7. Design a specific plan of action.

This is a sharing group; there is no expert advice, no diagnostic labeling, no blame placed. Participants share feelings and experiences and help each other find new ways of coping with the presenting problem.

Myrick (1987) points out that sometimes children's problems are not necessarily their own problems but are a function of the environment in which they live—home, classroom, or social system. In these cases, he suggests that consultants help children increase their awareness of events in the environment or values of a system, assess how the children respond, and evaluate their strength and weakness for effecting change. He calls this consultative technique the *process approach*. A counselor may want to examine the child's environment with the teacher or parents to determine if it is contributing to his or her hyperactivity, stealing, aggression, poor self-image, or other problems.

Myrick believes that, although counseling and consultation involve many of the same processes, different factors should be considered before one enters a consultation relationship.

1. *Who is the client?* Deciding this question will affect the focus of discussions, interventions selected, and possibly issues of confidentiality.
2. *Which consultation approach should be used?* Would the diagnostic-prescriptive approach, staff (or parent) training, case group, process, or a combination of approaches be most effective?
3. *When and where does consultation happen?* Is individual or group consultation preferred or necessary because of certain conditions?
4. *Who initiates the consultation?* Teachers, parents, and other adult consultees involved with the child may not be willing to discuss the case openly and without defensiveness.
5. *What are some pitfalls?* Myrick lists a number of behaviors to avoid—eliciting excessive guilt and defensiveness, giving advice freely, displaying too much self-disclosure, and other behaviors that good counselors (and good consultants) avoid (Myrick, 1987).

MENTAL HEALTH CONSULTATION

Caplan's (cited in Dougherty, 1990) mental-health consultation model and Bergan's (cited in Dougherty, 1990) behavioral-consultation model have enjoyed wide support for a number of years (Meyers, 1981; Dustin & Blocher, 1984; Dougherty, 1990; Dougherty, Dougherty, & Purcell, 1991). Dougherty (1990) presents a detailed description of Caplan's model and its application to individual and administrative situations. Blocher (1987) cautions that mental health consultation should not be seen as supervisory —that is, as having a more highly trained professional take over the case. Rather, the purpose is to help the consultee analyze and understand his or her interactions with the client, treatment approach and responses, and to provide support to the consultee.

Mental health consultation, according to Caplan (cited in Dougherty, 1990), focuses on primary prevention and involves helping professionals and nonprofessionals. Caplan believed that people seek consultation for four reasons: lack of understanding, lack of skills, lack of confidence, and lack of objectivity. Meyers (1981) suggested that consultants provide knowledge regarding child development, interpersonal dynamics, and abnormal psychology to help the adult understand the child. To enhance skills, he encourages consultants to develop the ability to observe and analyze the environment and interactions and, based on these observations, assist the adult to develop intervention skills.

For counselors interested in a more structured behavioral model, Brown,

Pryzwansky, and Schulte (1991) have developed general interview guidelines for noncrisis and crisis consulting situations. The consultant in a noncrisis situation (developmental interview) focuses on the following:

1. Establishing clear general objectives;
2. Reaching agreement with the consultee in the relationship between general objectives and more specific ones;
3. Generating with the consultee clearly defined, prioritized performance objectives;
4. Deciding how accomplishment of performance objectives will be assessed and recorded; and
5. Deciding on follow-up meetings.

In a crisis or problem-centered interview, the outline focuses on the following:

1. Identifying and describing problematic behavior(s) by collecting data from several sources concerning the nature of the problem;
2. Determining the conditions under which these behaviors occur, their antecedents, and their consequences. The consultant and consultee either analyze the setting or interpersonal factors that contribute to the problem, or they analyze the client's skill deficits;
3. Deciding on assessment procedures. The consultant and consultee design a plan to deal with the problem by identifying objectives, selecting behavioral interventions, considering barriers to be overcome, and evaluating progress; and
4. Scheduling future meetings. [pp. 75–76]

Combining the work of several writers in the field of consultation (Meyers, 1981; Keller, 1981; Blocher, 1987), we believe that consultation and counseling can be compared, as in Table 12-1. To enhance adult confidence, Meyers proposed that consultants listen carefully and support the adults' effective ideas. To promote objectivity, the consultant might act as a role model by objectively and calmly gathering good and bad data about the case or use an indirect technique to recognize the adult's involvement in the case, such as relating a similar interpersonal problem with the child or a story that indirectly points out the negative interaction. A direct discussion of the problem, using supportive empathy and confrontation, may also be effective (Meyers, 1981).

Behavioral consultation, as described by Bergan (1977), is indirect in its process and involves a series of clearly defined steps: problem identification, problem analysis, plan implementation, and problem evaluation. According to Keller (1981), problem identification and analysis are usually accomplished by assessing or measuring behaviors in multiple settings through interview techniques, behavior checklists, rating scales, or recording of periodic observations. A variety of behavioral techniques are used in the plan-implementation stage, including feedback and reinforcement, self-monitoring, modeling, role-playing, and parent training. Evaluation is an

TABLE 12-1 A comparison of counseling and consultation roles

Counseling	Consultation
Directly involved with client.	Not directly involved with the identified client.
Professionally and ethically responsible for outcome.	Not professionally and ethically responsible for outcome.
Relationship is therapeutic.	Relationship is professional, not therapeutic.
Establish rapport by listening and communicating understanding and respect.	Establish rapport by listening and communicating understanding and respect.
Identify consequences: "How does this help (or hurt) you in reaching your goal of _____?"	Identify consequences: "What happens when Jenny does this?"
Evaluate past solutions: "What have you tried to solve this?"	Evaluate past solutions: "What have you (or Jenny) tried to solve this?"
Develop alternatives by encouraging the client to brainstorm. The counselor may provide information: "What could you be doing?"	Develop alternatives by brainstorming with the client. Provide information and advice: "Can you think of other things that might help?"
Contract—make a plan: "Which alternative will you choose, and when will you do this?"	Contract—make a plan. "Which alternative will you choose, and when will you do this?"
Follow up to evaluate results of the plan.	Follow up to evaluate results of the plan.

ongoing process in behavioral consultation, and when the goals established in the initial stage are accomplished, the consultation is terminated (Keller, 1981). Behavioral-analysis and self-management models are presented in Chapter 7. In addition, a ten-step reality-therapy model is described in Chapter 3.

Blocher (1987) contends that the most frequently used model is triadic consultation, which involves a "mediator" with whom the consultant works. This mediator provides service to the ultimate client; the consultant may never see the client. Although we believe the skills of the counselor and consultant to be similar (see Table 12-1), Blocher differentiates the process by pointing out that:

1. The consultant is not fully responsible professionally and ethically for the client's outcome; therefore, the consultant must be careful to maintain his or her distinct role and not infringe on the mediator/client relationship.
2. The consultant/consultee relationship is not therapeutic, but professional.

CONSULTATION INTERVENTIONS

Consulting can help counselors reach more children by teaching adults (parents, teachers, and other significant persons in the children's lives) to behave in more helpful ways. Providing indirect services to children through consultation can be an important part of the counselor's role; unfortunately, few counselors are using their skills in this area. Following are techniques counselors may wish to try in their consultative efforts with the adults in the child's world. Not every technique will work with every child. Each child's uniqueness and specific needs must be considered before selecting any counseling or consulting procedure.

Role Shift

Simply changing one's own behavior may elicit a behavior change in another person. Adults who change their response to children's behaviors may cease to reinforce them or may present children with an unexpected response, which causes them to change.

Thompson and Poppen (1992) suggest that adults be asked to list *everything* they have tried with the child that has been ineffective. The adults are then asked to commit themselves to never again trying any one of these ineffective techniques with this child. The list should be kept as a reminder of "what not to do" with the child.

When the child has behaved inappropriately, adults can stop and ask themselves, "What response does this child expect?" Does the child expect the adult to be shocked, outraged, or angry? For instance, Glen reacted to his mother's scoldings by drawing grotesque pictures of her and placing them around the house. He took great delight in watching her reactions when she found the pictures. The mother decided that Glen enjoyed her outrage when he got back at her with the grotesque pictures. The next time she found a picture, she calmly commented to him, "I must have really made you angry when I scolded you for you to draw me like this." The mother left the picture up and went on with her work. Glen quietly removed his pictures later in the day. This technique seems to work best when the child expects to get attention, to shock (as with curse words or dirty language), to frustrate, to anger, or to seek revenge.

Descriptive Discussions of Children

Many times adults have become so frustrated with a child's problems that the child is perceived as "all bad." Counselors can gain some understanding of adults' perceptions and expectations of children by asking them to describe the children and their behaviors in some detail (Thompson & Poppen, 1972). If the entire description focuses on negative traits or behaviors, the counselor might ask the adult if there is *anything* good about the child. The adult can then be asked to make a list of any strengths the child may have. It is hoped that focusing attention on the child's positive side will help the adult decrease attention to the negative and increase awareness of the positive.

Listing of Behaviors

A technique similar to the descriptive discussion to change an adult's perceptions of children is listing of behaviors. For instance, Mr. Jones told the counselor that Sherry was a crybaby; she cried at *everything* that did not go her way. The counselor asked Mr. Jones to keep an exact count of the times that Sherry cried during the next week. The next week Mr. Jones admitted that, according to his count, Sherry had cried only three times that week—once when she fell, once when she was told to go to bed, and once when she was refused a request. Mr. Jones began to change his perception of Sherry as a crybaby.

Listing the number of times a behavior occurs can also provide a baseline count to determine if an intervention has helped reduce an inappropriate behavior or increase an appropriate one.

Logical Consequences

Proponents of Adler's individual psychology advocate allowing children to experience the natural or logical consequences of their behavior, rather than punishment, as the preferred form of discipline (see Chapter 10). They suggest that adults who punish children become authority figures and lose the friendship of the child. They also point out that natural or logical consequences are reality-oriented and teach the child the rules of society, whereas punishment may teach unwanted lessons such as "power is authority."

Obviously, adults cannot allow children to experience the consequences of all their behavior; children cannot learn that busy streets are dangerous by being allowed to play in streets. However, a thoughtful adult can find ways to arrange for children to see the consequences of inappropriate behavior. When Peter colors on the walls instead of on paper, for instance, Peter is handed the sponge and cleanser to remove the coloring. The natural consequence of being late is to miss an event or a meal. The logical consequence of damaging someone's property is to earn enough money to replace it. The logical consequence of behaving inappropriately in a group is usually rejection by the group or isolation. Discipline with logical consequences teaches children the order and rules of society very quickly.

Isolation Techniques

There may be times when children's behaviors become so unacceptable that they must be removed from the group (the classroom, family, or peer group). For many years, parents have sent children to their rooms when they acted out. Our society isolates adults who behave inappropriately by ostracism and, in extreme cases, by imprisonment. Isolation techniques are a form of logical consequences.

Four steps of isolation have been outlined by Thompson and Poppen (1987). For children with minor problems of maintaining attention, a second seat may be arranged away from the group, in a quiet place but not out of sight. When children are not directing attention toward the task of the group, they may be quietly reminded that their present seat, seat 1, is for working on science, participating in a group discussion, and the like, and that they will have to move to seat 2. Children are given the choice of returning to the group when they are ready to participate in the group activity. The success of this technique is based on the premise that children like to be part of a group and will change their behavior in order to remain within the group.

The second step of isolation is the quiet corner. Some children are highly distractible and highly distracting to their peers. They must be completely screened from the group in order to accomplish their work. A quiet corner can be made with screens, study carrels, bookshelves (books facing outward), or large, decorated furniture cartons. The quiet corner should contain a desk, chair, books, puzzles, or other quiet materials. There should be no windows or doors in a quiet corner. When a child misbehaves, the adult can signal the child quietly that the behavior is not appropriate and ask the child to go to the quiet corner. Children should have the choice of returning to the group when they are ready to participate more acceptably. A short time limit of 10 to 15 minutes may have to be imposed before allowing children this choice.

For more severe problems, counselors may wish to suggest a time-out room. This procedure can be used when children need to be completely away from the group. Thompson and Poppen (1992) suggest that time-out be used not as a punishment but as a "cooling-off" time. Children can be instructed to make a plan while they are in the time-out room for avoiding the trouble in the future.

When children's problem behaviors are so severe that the first three isolation procedures have not worked, they may be asked quietly to leave the premises (school, church, club, recreational center) and come back tomorrow to try again. The children should be aware of what behaviors are acceptable and unacceptable and of the conditions for remaining in the group. Because this procedure often requires the assistance of parents, school personnel, or other community workers, a written agreement among all parties is advisable. Many schools use "in-house suspension" to provide a place where children who cannot remain in the group can go for supervised study. Other community resources providing youth services may cooperate in arranging for supervision.

There are times when adults may need a time-out. Dreikurs, Grunwald, and Pepper (1971) have suggested that parents who find themselves as referees in children's conflicts with others take a time-out in the bathroom. It is their contention that children try to involve adults in their conflicts to get attention and that unless there is danger of physical harm or property destruction, children will learn to settle their differences (and learn the consequences) more effectively without relying on adults.

Isolation techniques are designed to teach children the logical consequences of their behavior. Acceptable and unacceptable behaviors should be clearly defined for children. Adults are encouraged not to nag, lecture, or scold when using the procedures. Isolation techniques should be viewed not as a punishment but as a positive method of discipline.

Parent Training

Gordon (1970) described a model for consulting with parents about their children's behavior in his book, *Parent Effectiveness Training* (PET). PET, based on empathic listening and responding, outlines the steps for effective problem solving.

Gordon advised parents when to listen with empathy and when to assert their rights as a parent using "I" statements. He suggested that when children need acceptance, parents should use the techniques of active listening, or they may demonstrate acceptance through nonintervention or passive listening. He discussed the "roadblocks" to communication, such as ordering, directing, commanding, warning, threatening, giving solutions, lecturing, criticizing, ridiculing, and analyzing, and shows why these typical methods of communicating with children are ineffective. When children's behaviors interfere with the rights of others, Gordon suggested that parents or other adults should use "I" statements to allow children to know how they really feel. His writings give examples of how to use these messages to improve communication without tearing down the child's self-esteem, talking too much, resorting to negative messages, or engaging in a power struggle.

Gordon described three ways of resolving parent/child conflict: I win–you lose, you win–I lose (both ineffective), and the effective win–win situation in which both parent and child resolve the conflict and feel good about the gains. He gave case examples of why each method was ineffective or effective and demonstrated the use of good problem-solving techniques.

Gordon has presented evidence to demonstrate the efficacy of his method for consulting with parents, and the popularity of PET programs across the country suggests it has value for helping parents deal with children's problems. Because the steps for communication and problem solving are outlined in an easily accessible book, it is an efficient method for helping parents.

Dinkmeyer and McKay (1976) developed a similar program. *Systematic Training for Effective Parenting* (STEP) is based on Adlerian theory as popularized by Rudolf Dreikurs. It emphasizes principles of logical consequences over punishment and of using cooperation rather than power as a child-rearing method. The STEP program also teaches parents to recognize the goals of misbehavior. Weekly family meetings, daily individual time with the parent, and a weekly fun activity are all a part of this program.

EVALUATION OF CONSULTING

Parsons and Myers (1984) have constructed a Consultee Satisfaction Form that asks consultees to rate, on a four-point scale, the efficacy of consultation with regard to goal definition, data gathering, and the appropriateness of the intervention plan; the consultant's expertise with regard to content and presentation; the consultant's administrative skills in using time, providing feedback, and assigning work; and the consultant's interpersonal style (good listener, pleasant, encouraging, and so on). Information from checksheets or other evaluative forms helps consultants develop and maintain an effective consulting relationship.

All writers point out the need for further research to evaluate the results of consultation techniques. Dustin and Blocher (1984) conclude that "at the present time there is simply not a sufficient body of credible empirical research upon which to assess the overall effectiveness or ineffectiveness of consultation" (p. 777). They believe, however, that more recent studies have been encouraging in that they have used more sophisticated research designs. Meyers (1981) and Keller (1981) also call for more carefully controlled studies to determine the efficacy of consultative models and techniques. Bundy and Poppen (1986) have found that 18 of the 21 studies of elementary school consultation they reviewed reported positive effects. Of the 18 showing positive results, the two most commonly used methods were the Adlerian model and behavioral consultation. Dougherty (1990) believes that mental health consultation has "a broad and positive impact," but agrees that "it is not without criticism" (p. 251).

SUMMARY

Although problems exist with theoretical foundations and evaluative research on consultation, we believe the technique should not be overlooked as a possible means for helping children in need. Helping techniques presented to significant people in children's lives through small groups, psychological education, outreach programs, and preventive education may reach children to whom direct services would not be available by the counselor working alone. For our purposes, consultation will refer to the one-to-one interaction between the counselor and a significant adult in the child's life or to a counselor-led group of significant adults, with the purpose of finding ways to assist children toward functioning more effectively or becoming more self-actualizing.

REFERENCES

American Association for Counseling and Development. (1988). *Ethical standards* (rev. ed.). Alexandria, VA: Author.

Bergan, J. (1977). *Behavioral consultation.* Columbus, OH: Merrill.

Blocher, D. (1987). *The professional counselor.* New York: Macmillan.

Brown, D., Pryzwansky, W., & Schulte, A. (1991). *Psychological consultation: Introduction to theory and practice.* Boston: Allyn & Bacon.

Bundy, M., & Poppen, W. (1986). School counselors' effectiveness as consultants: A research review. *Elementary School Guidance and Counseling, 20,* 215–222.

Dinkmeyer, D., & McKay, G. (1976). *Systematic training for effective parenting.* Circle Pines, MN: American Guidance Service.

Dougherty, A. (1990). *Consultation: Practice and perspectives.* Pacific Grove, CA: Brooks/Cole.

Dougherty, A., Dougherty, L., & Purcell, D. (1991). The sources and management of resistance to consultation. *The School Counselor, 38,* 178–185.

Dreikurs, R., Grunwald, B., & Pepper, F. (1971). *Maintaining sanity in the classroom.* New York: Harper & Row.

Dustin, D., & Blocher, D. (1984). Theories and models of consultation. In S. Brown & R. Lent (Eds.), *Handbook of counseling psychology* (p. 752). New York: Wiley.

Glosoff, H., & Koprowicz, C. (1990). *Children achieving potential: An introduction to elementary school counseling and state-level policies.* Washington, DC: National Conference of State Legislatures and American Association for Counseling and Development.

Gordon, T. (1970). *Parent effectiveness training.* New York: Wyden.

Kahnweiler, W. M. (1979). The school counselor as consultant: A historical review. *Personnel and Guidance Journal, 57,* 374–379.

Keller, H. (1981). Behavioral consultation. In J. C. Conoley (Ed.), *Consultation in schools: Theory, research, procedures* (pp. 59–89). New York: Academic Press.

Kurpius, D., & Robinson, S. (1978). An overview of consultation. *Personnel and Guidance Journal, 56,* 321–323.

Meyers, J. (1981). Mental health consultation. In J. C. Conoley (Ed.), *Consultation in schools: Theory, research, procedures* (pp. 35–58). New York: Academic Press.

Myrick, R. (1987). *Developmental guidance and counseling: A practical approach.* Minneapolis, MN: Educational Media.

Parsons, R., & Myers, J. (1984). *Developing consultation skills.* San Francisco: Jossey-Bass.

Poppen, W., & Thompson, C. (1975). *School counseling: Theories and concepts.* Lincoln, NE: Professional Educators.

Thompson, C., & Poppen, W. (1972). *For those who care: Ways for relating to youth.* Columbus, OH: Merrill.

Thompson, C., & Poppen, W. (1987). *Guidance activities for counselors and teachers.* Knoxville, TN: Authors.

CHAPTER 13

Group Counseling with Children

INTRODUCTION

Many counselors suggest that groups are a more natural setting for working with people than individual counseling. Children and adults function as members of groups in their daily activities—in the family, the classroom, the work setting, or the peer group. Our beliefs and perceptions of self are formed from the feedback of significant people in groups—family, friends, and peers. Psychologists such as Alfred Adler emphasize that people are "social beings" and that their development is influenced significantly by the groups around them. Therefore, according to these writers, group counseling is more reality-oriented than individual counseling. Different types of groups appear to be increasing in popularity as loneliness and separation from family and friends increase in our society. At one time, group counseling was considered an effective method of counseling because the counselor could help a number of children more economically. However, a more important reason is that children can unlearn inappropriate behaviors and learn new ways of relating more easily through interaction and feedback in a safe practice situation with their peers.

This chapter is not intended to be a comprehensive guide for training counselors in conducting groups. Complete books have been written about group counseling, and most counselors have coursework and supervised practica to help them develop skills. This chapter presents an overview of the area, with suggestions for those who already possess the basic knowledge and skills required for conducting groups or intend to pursue further training.

GROUP COUNSELING DEFINED

Johnson and Johnson (1987) reviewed the literature for a definition of a group. They found that various definitions incorporated several components:

334

a group may be defined as two or more individuals who (a) interact with each other, (b) are interdependent, (c) define themselves or are defined by others as belonging to the group, (d) share norms concerning matters of common interest and participate in a system of interlocking roles, (e) influence each other, (f) find the group rewarding, and (g) pursue common goals. [p. 7]

They believe that "any effective group has three core activities: (1) accomplishing its goals, (2) maintaining itself internally, and (3) developing and changing in ways that improve its effectiveness" (p. 8).

Dyer and Vriend (1980) have operationally defined group counseling with children as a model that includes the following elements:

1. Children identify thoughts or behaviors that are self-defeating and set goals for themselves with the help of the counselor/facilitator and other group members.
2. The counselor and the group assist children in setting specific and attainable goals.
3. Children try new behaviors in the safe atmosphere of the group and make commitments to try the new behaviors in the real world.
4. Children report the results of homework assignments during the next session and decide either to continue the new ways of thinking and behaving or to reject them for further exploration of alternatives.

The model of group counseling defined by Dyer and Vriend is similar to the process of individual counseling presented in this book.

In his description of group counseling as a helping process, Ohlsen (1977) pointed out that in groups children learn to help other people and to accept their help and learn to talk openly about themselves and give up facades. Groups encourage members to take risks and to accept responsibility for their growth and the growth of others. Ohlsen's definition of group counseling closely follows the Dyer and Vriend model. Ohlsen, too, viewed group counseling as providing a safe atmosphere for children to discuss their concerns, to define goals, and to try new behaviors.

TYPES OF GROUP COUNSELING

The number of group counseling methods is almost equivalent to the number of counseling theories. Most approaches or orientations to counseling can be adapted to a group counseling setting.

Theoretically Oriented Group Counseling

Adlerian counselors used group work in their child-guidance center in the early 1900s for group discussions involving parents (see Chapter 10). Because Adlerians believe that people are essentially social and need to belong to a community or group, it would be reasonable for them to see group counseling as a natural environment for helping children see the reality of the situation and meet their needs through social interactions in the group.

The principles of *behavioral counseling* are also used in groups when the clients' goals are similar or when it is believed that the members can help one another by providing feedback, support, or reinforcement to alter maladaptive behaviors, learn new behaviors, or prevent problems. Relaxation training, assertion training, modeling techniques, and self-management programs to control overeating or other negative behaviors are examples of behavioral techniques that can be used effectively in group settings.

Because *rational-emotive therapy* (RET) attempts to teach people to think rationally about events and assume responsibility for their feelings, the techniques of this theory can be applied very effectively in groups. Members are encouraged to recognize and confront their irrational thoughts and feelings, take risks, try new behaviors, and use the feedback of others to learn new social skills. Members are taught to apply the principles of RET to one another.

The principles of *reality therapy* adapt effectively to group work because the group is a microcosm of the "real" world. The members provide feedback about the reality of the behavior and plans for change. They reinforce one another in their commitments and check on the completion of homework assignments. A quick review of the literature on the effectiveness of reality therapy shows that it has been a popular method for helping groups of children and adolescents in schools, those confined to correctional institutions, substance abusers, and those with handicaps.

Transactional analysis (TA) is an ideal counseling method for use in groups; in fact, treatment in groups is the choice of most counselors adhering to the principles of TA. This method focuses on analysis of life scripts, games, and interactions among people, and the ideal setting for this teaching and learning is within a group that simulates life's interactions.

Gestalt therapy focuses on the here and now and on maintaining personal awareness. Some Gestalt counselors ask for volunteers and focus on one client at a time within the group; for example, the "hot seat" technique requires the counselor to work with one person in the presence of the other group members. Structured interaction between other group members may be encouraged at certain times.

Other counseling methods have their place in group work but do not adapt as readily as those already mentioned. The relationship skills set forth by *person-centered* counselors are appropriate in an individual or group setting. The therapeutic relationship is an essential ingredient for all clients to feel free enough to explore their world and make changes;

however, the techniques of person-centered counseling are probably more effective in changing behavior when focused on an individual during the entire counseling session.

Group Counseling Models

Many labels are used for the types of group work carried out in various settings. Group processes can also be described according to the type of group conducted. Some theorists differentiate between group therapy and group counseling.

Group therapy deals with unconscious motivations and seeks to effect personality changes. Group therapy is usually of longer duration and includes people who are more severely disturbed. *Group counseling* is conducted in schools, institutions, or mental health agencies and deals primarily with personal, interpersonal, educational, career, or social issues. The members of counseling groups are "normal" people who are experiencing some stress in their daily lives; no attempt is made to deal with severe psychological or personality disorders.

Personal-growth groups are often formed for healthy people who wish to function better in life. Their goals may include helping people communicate better, learn assertion skills, improve relationship skills, develop leadership skills, learn to think positively, or develop other personal attitudes or abilities to adjust more effectively. Some groups are structured so the only goal is to assist members to learn one skill (such as assertiveness or relaxation) or to cope with one type of problem (alcoholism in the family, parental divorce, sexual abuse, or eating disorders).

Self-help groups usually are not led by professionals but are structured by persons who have experienced the common problem. The members share experiences and provide understanding and support for one another. Groups such as Alcoholics Anonymous, Alateen, and Weight Watchers serve an important function in our society.

Group guidance focuses on prevention of problems and is more developmental compared to other groups, which are more remedial. Group guidance is conducted with large groups and is primarily didactic. The intent is to provide children with information they will need to make informed decisions and adjust to the requirements of their developmental stage. Topics covered may include study skills, living peacefully with brothers and sisters, communicating with parents, saying "no" to drugs, physical and emotional changes of an age stage, or interpreting test scores on an aptitude or interest test. Group guidance is discussed in greater detail later in this chapter.

The counseling skills and techniques discussed in Chapter 2 also apply to the group counseling setting. However, the group counselor has the additional tasks of directing communication traffic, facilitating the group process, blocking harmful group behaviors, connecting ideas, obtaining a consensus, moderating discussions, summarizing, and supporting the children who need encouragement and reinforcement.

GROUP COUNSELING
Forming a Group

Because of reports of people being verbally attacked and hurt in groups using extreme methods, parents or children may have reservations about participating in a group. It is helpful for counselors to explain fully the purpose of the group and the experiences planned in order to allay fears and clarify possible misconceptions. By providing this information to children before starting the group, the counselor can inform the children of their roles and what is expected of them and explain the role and expectations of the counselor as well. Explaining the process will provide the structure needed to facilitate interaction once the group is begun. Following is an example of an informative statement:

> We are forming a group made up of young people about your age in order to talk about things that bother or upset us. Many of us have similar concerns, and it is often helpful to share these worries and help each other try to find ways of solving them. Each member will be expected to talk about what bothers him or her and try to figure out what can be done about the situation. In addition, members will be expected to listen carefully to each other and try to understand the other members' worries and help them solve their problems. The counselor, too, tries to understand what all the members are saying or feeling, to help them explain and clarify their thoughts and feelings, and to find solutions to their concerns.
>
> Most group members learn they can trust the others in the group and feel free to discuss things that worry them. Members are free to talk about anything or anyone that bothers or upsets them. However, the group will not be a gripe session, a gossip session, or a chatting session. We will be working together to find solutions to what is upsetting you. There may be very personal information or feelings that you would prefer not to discuss in the group. You should not feel pressured to disclose these feelings or thoughts to the group. Whatever is said in the group cannot be discussed with anyone except the counselor. If there is anyone you would rather not have in a group with you, discuss this with the counselor.

Intake Interview

Many group leaders prefer to hold an individual conference or intake interview with prospective members before forming the group. Other group leaders think that anyone should be eligible to join a group and that the intake interview is unnecessary. An intake interview allows the leader an opportunity to talk privately with prospective members, to learn a little about them and their concerns, and to define some possible goals. It also gives the leader an opportunity to determine if the child will benefit from a group experience or if individual counseling would be more helpful.

Group Membership

Some counselors, such as those following the Adlerian method, hold that anyone who wishes to participate in a group should be allowed to do so, with attention being given only to similar, age-related levels of interest and intellectual abilities of members. Other counselors attempt to select members of a group to provide for either heterogeneity or homogeneity. Homogeneity may be desired for common-problems groups, such as children whose parents are divorced. However, a homogeneous group of underachievers or drug users probably would be counterproductive because no peer model and peer reinforcement for improved behaviors would be present. For children with problems of acting out or withdrawal, a heterogeneous group would be more helpful to provide for active discussion and role models. As to whether to include boys and girls in the same group, most counselors prefer to include a balance of both sexes unless the problem to be discussed is such that the presence of the opposite sex would hinder discussion—sex-education topics, for example. The counselor should seriously consider the possible consequences before including in groups children who are highly dissimilar in interests or maturity levels and children who are extremely dominating, manipulative, gifted, or mentally retarded. Children with extreme behaviors may be better candidates for individual counseling, especially during the initial stages of counseling.

The number of children selected to participate in the group will depend on age, maturity, and attention span. Children of 5 and 6 years have a very short attention span and are unable to give much attention to the concerns of others. Counselors may want to limit group size at this age to three or four and to work with the children for only short periods of time at frequent intervals—for example, 20 minutes two or three times a week. As age and maturity levels increase, counselors will be able to work with more children for longer periods of time—for example, six children, ages 10 and 11, for 30 minutes twice a week. The maximum number of children in a group that functions effectively seems to be eight. However, the classroom-meeting concept developed by Glasser (1969) has proven effective with an entire class of 30 students for periods of 20 to 30 minutes.

The Group Setting

A room away from noise and traffic is best. In addition, children should not fear being overheard if they are expected to talk openly about their concerns. Groups should be conducted with all members sitting in a circle. We always ask our groups to arrange the circle in such a way that everyone can see everyone else's face. Some counselors prefer to have the children sit around a circular table; others think tables may serve as a barrier to interaction. Many counselors prefer to have groups of children sit in a circle on a carpeted floor. A carpeted floor provides easy access for counselors to move the group into play therapy.

The First Session

Part of the first counseling session will be devoted to establishing ground rules and agreeing on some guidelines for the group. The frequency of the meetings, the length of each meeting, the setting, and the duration of the group should be determined, either by consensus of the group or by the leader. Members will also want to discuss confidentiality and what might be done if confidentiality is broken by a member; what to do about members who do not attend regularly; and whether or not to allow new members to join should a member drop out.

Confidentiality is an important concept to be discussed with children. They often do not understand the necessity for "keeping what is discussed in our group" and not talking to others about what happens. The leader may want to provide specific instances of other children asking about their group and have participants role-play their responses.

The group leader will want to remind members that they are expected to listen carefully to each other, to try to understand each other's feelings and thoughts, and to help one another explore possible solutions to problems. The children can be encouraged to wait until members seem to have explored and discussed their concerns thoroughly before changing the subject. The group leader can provide the role model for listening and reflecting feelings and content and can reinforce these behaviors in group members.

By establishing ground rules and structuring the group during the initial session, the group leader defines expected behaviors. When inappropriate behaviors occur, the leader can ask the group, "What was the ground rule?" or can present the problem to the group for their discussion and resolution. Groups are formed to help the members. The leader is the facilitator but should not take over as disciplinarian and authoritarian.

Group members may be reluctant to begin by bringing up concerns or worries for discussion, especially if the participants are not acquainted with one another. The leader could reflect their feeling of reluctance and, if appropriate, try an "icebreaker" counseling technique. For example, the leader might ask members of the group to introduce themselves and describe themselves using three adjectives. Or members might be asked to introduce themselves and complete a statement such as "If I had three wishes, I would wish _____." Another icebreaker is to complete the statement "I am a _____, but I would like to be a _____," using animals, vegetables, automobiles, flowers, or other nonhuman categories. (Example: "I am a dandelion, but I'd like to be a long-stemmed rose.")

These activities can be done in the entire group or in dyads; either method will ease the tension of the first session and promote interaction.

Building cohesiveness and trust is an important concern for counselors. Children have had little experience listening to one another and trying to help one another solve problems. Unless these behaviors are taught, the group experience will be little more than a time to play and chatter. Bergin (1989) suggests a series of cooperative activities to build group cohesiveness. These include using only the sense of touch in communication, learning-to-listen activities, group planning, and cooperative physical activities.

Guidelines for the Remaining Sessions

Before the second group session, counselors will want to review thoroughly the content of the first meeting (names, behaviors, concerns, other personal information) and develop a plan for guiding the second meeting. At this point, the counselor should have tentative goals in mind for each member based on the initial interview and should be aware of who in the group will facilitate the group process—a good listener, encourager, problem-solver—and who will distract—dominating, too talkative, silly, confrontive, and so on. The counselor may want to develop plans for dealing with distracting behaviors should they occur. The second session opens with a brief summary of what occurred in the initial meeting. If homework was assigned, the results should be shared. The group is then ready to address one of the member's concerns, either one that was identified earlier or a situation that occurred between meetings that is of concern to a member. If no one volunteers to discuss a problem or concern, those concerns identified in the pregroup interviews can be suggested by the counselor: "Pam, when we talked in our interview before the first meeting of the group, you shared with me that you were worried because your younger brother is so sick all the time. Would you like to tell the group about your brother's illness?"

Just as in individual counseling, a group leader will want to establish a therapeutic counseling atmosphere by demonstrating the facilitative skills of empathic understanding, genuineness, and respect for group members. Counselors can demonstrate their caring by being nonjudgmental and accepting and by providing encouragement, support, and guidance. Counselors will want to be adept at identifying, labeling, clarifying, and reflecting group members' feelings and thoughts. This process becomes difficult as the group size increases. The counselor/facilitator must be concerned about and aware of the reactions of each child in the group. As the leader models facilitative behaviors, group members will begin to participate in the helping process and become more effective helpers for one another.

The group counseling process will follow closely the format for individual counseling:

1. Establishing a therapeutic relationship
2. Defining the problems of the member or members
3. Exploring what has been tried and whether it has hurt or helped the situation
4. Deciding what could be done — looking at the alternatives
5. Making a plan — goal setting
6. Trying new behaviors by implementing the plan
7. Homework
8. Reporting and evaluating the results

Also as in individual counseling, the counselor/facilitator is responsible for helping children identify and define their problems and the accompanying feelings and thoughts. The process of defining what is happening in the child's life and looking at alternatives for solving the conflict is enhanced in the group setting because of the other group members. Ideally, the child will have a number of counselors to listen, understand, and help search for solutions, while enjoying the acceptance, encouragement, support, and feedback of a number of helpers. The counselor must be skilled in facilitating these interactions and suggesting appropriate interventions. The counselor must also possess information about group dynamics and counseling skills to intervene and facilitate progress through the various steps of the counseling process.

As with individual counseling, it can be helpful to the counselor and to group members to audiotape or videotape the session. Such tapes provide a record of what occurred in the session, enable the counselor to review the dynamics of the group, and help counselors evaluate their leadership skills.

The process and techniques used in individual counseling (role-playing, role rehearsal, play therapy, homework assignments, contracting, and so on) are just as appropriate for use in group counseling. In fact, individual counseling is often conducted in groups, as the following example shows.

Karen, Susan, Peggy, Mark, Ken, and Mike are 11-year-olds participating in a counseling group. This is their fourth session with the counselor.

Counselor: Last time we met, Susan told us about the misunderstanding she was having with her neighbor, Mrs. Jackson. As I remember, Susan, you were going to offer to use your allowance to replace the storm window you broke playing baseball or offer to babysit free of charge for her until the bill was paid. Can you bring us up to date on what's happened?

Susan: Well, she decided she would rather have me babysit for her to pay for the window. I babysat one hour last week. We are keeping a list of the times I sit and how much will go toward the cost of the window.

Counselor: It sounds as though you and Mrs. Jackson have worked things out to the satisfaction of both of you.

Susan: Yeah, she really liked the idea of my babysitting to pay for the window.

Counselor: Good. Is there anyone else who has something they would like to discuss today?

All six children: Mr. Havens!

Counselor: You all sound pretty angry at Mr. Havens. Could one of you tell me what's happened?

Ken: We were all going on a trip to the ice-skating rink next week. Yesterday, somebody broke some equipment that belonged to Mr. Havens. No one would tell who did it, so he is punishing us all by not letting us go ice-skating.

Counselor: You think Mr. Havens is being unfair to punish everyone because of something one person did. You'd like to find out who broke the equipment.

Karen: That's right. We didn't break his equipment, so why should we have to miss the trip?

Counselor: Have you thought of anything you could do to work this out?

Mike: Yeah, break the rest of his old equipment!

Counselor: How would that help you get to go skating?

Mark: It wouldn't. It would just make him madder.

Peggy (timidly): We could tell him who did it.

Other five children: You know who did it? Who?

Peggy (very upset): If I tell, I'll be called a tattler, and no one will like me. Besides, I don't want to get anyone in trouble.

Counselor: Peggy, it sounds as though you are really feeling torn apart by this. You just don't know what to do. If you don't tell, the whole group will miss the skating outing. If you do tell, you'll get someone in trouble, and your friends might think you're a tattler and not want you around.

Peggy: Yeah, I don't know what to do!

Counselor: What do you think you could do?

Peggy: Well, I could tell who did it.

Counselor: What would happen if you told? (Silence.) Let's help Peggy think of all the things that could happen if she told who broke Mr. Havens's equipment.

The group thinks of all the possible positive and negative results of Peggy's telling who broke the equipment: the group might still get to go skating; the person might beat up Peggy or try to get back at her in some other way; she might not be believed; the person could deny it and say Peggy broke the equipment; and so on.

Counselor: We've listed all the things that could happen if Peggy told. What will happen if Peggy does *not* reveal who broke the equipment?

Karen: We won't get to go skating, and the person will get away with it!

Other possibilities—such as Mr. Havens's distrust of the whole group, or the person thinking he or she "can get away with anything"—are brought out and discussed.

Counselor: Can anyone think of any alternatives to solve this other than Peggy telling or not telling Mr. Havens?

Ken: She could write him an anonymous letter telling him who did it.

Counselor: What would happen if she did?

Mike: He probably wouldn't believe an anonymous letter.

Counselor: What do the rest of you think about that?

They all agree by nodding their heads that Mike is probably right.

Counselor: Is there anything else you could do to straighten this out?

Susan: Peggy could tell you [the counselor], and you could tell Mr. Havens.

Counselor: How would my telling Mr. Havens help you all solve your problem?

Mark: Mr. Havens would believe you, and we'd get to go skating!

Counselor: I would have to tell Mr. Havens how I knew and give him some details to assure him that I was right. I really think this is the group's problem. What can you do to work it out?

Karen: Seems like it's up to Peggy, then.

Counselor: You all think it's up to Peggy to decide whether or not to tell.

The group agrees it is Peggy's decision.

Counselor: Peggy, we have looked at the consequences of your telling on the other person and not telling, and we've tried to think of other alternatives. Have you made any decision about what to do?

Peggy: No, I still don't know.

Counselor: So far, it seems that we have come up with two possible alternatives—to tell on the person or not to tell. I wonder if there are any other alternatives you can think of that might help Peggy. (Silence.) Well, our time is about up for today, but this is really important. Let's meet together tomorrow and try to help Peggy come to some decision at that time. Peggy, I wonder if you would go over the list of alternatives and think about them before tomorrow. (Peggy agrees.) How would the rest of you feel about trying to put yourselves in Peggy's place and think of what you would do if you knew who broke Mr. Havens's equip-

ment? Also, you might think about how you would feel if you
were the person who broke the equipment. What would you
want Peggy to do?

The group agrees and adjourns.

The counselor has checked on the results of the last homework assignment for the group, listened, and reflected the group members' angry
feelings that Mr. Havens is unfair. The counselor has then helped them
clarify and define the problem and look at possible alternatives and the
consequences of these alternatives. No decision has been reached, but the
group has agreed to a homework assignment of thinking further about the
problem. Possibly the next session will bring new ideas and a resolution.

GROUP COUNSELING STAGES

Tuckman and Jensen (1977) reviewed studies of group development and
concluded that groups typically progressed through five stages: forming,
storming, norming, performing, and adjourning. During the forming period, members try to learn the group's structure and rules and find their
place. Tensions begin to rise during the storming phase, and resistance to
accomplishing goals and tasks may arise. During the third stage, norming,
group cohesiveness should grow and members should begin to work together more easily. In the fourth stage, performing, the group begins to
function effectively and move toward accomplishing tasks and solving
problems. In the final stage, adjourning, issues related to termination,
breaking the emotional bond within the group, and going on with life are
addressed.

Using the information developed from studies such as those of Tuckman
and Jensen, Johnson and Johnson (1987) described seven stages of group
development:

1. Defining and structuring procedures and becoming oriented (defining
   what is expected of group members and what will happen);
2. Conforming to procedures and getting acquainted (goals and procedures are leaders' rather than owned by group members);
3. Recognizing mutuality and building trust (taking responsibility for one's
   own learning as well as that of others; feeling freedom to discuss ideas
   and feelings);
4. Rebelling and differentiating (establishing their autonomy; challenging
   the authority of the leader);
5. Committing to and taking ownership for the goals, procedures, and
   other members (ownership of the group is members' rather than
   leaders'; developing commitment to one another); and
6. Functioning maturely and productively (all members participate in leadership and decision-making).

7. Terminating (deal with separation and move toward new experiences) [pp. 363–364]

These stages may not be so apparent in children's groups, depending on the members' ages. In addition, Tuckman and Jensen reviewed groups with more nondirective leaders, while group leaders who work with children will need to be more structured and directive. Nevertheless, the present writers believe children's groups will go through processes similar to those described by Tuckman and Jensen.

Johnson and Johnson (1987) believe that all groups need to set aside time to process what is occurring: (1) how well members are achieving their goals; and (2) how well the group is maintaining effective working relationships among members. They believe this processing will improve the group's effectiveness by reminding members of their tasks and goals and providing feedback to members about their participation and interactional skills.

GROUP GUIDANCE

Gazda (1973) has emphasized the preventive orientation of groups, suggesting that information-giving and human-development education be pursued through group processes. Through group guidance procedures, counselors can help children become more involved in school and with classmates, understand themselves and their feelings, learn to share ideas and feelings, and develop decision-making and problem-solving skills. The development of such skills will promote self-confidence in the children and build competencies for more effective functioning in daily living.

Group guidance units can present information about study skills, making friends, drugs, or any other area in which children need help to grow and develop in a healthy manner. Guidance activities designed to help children with self-concept development, peer relationships, improved adult/youth relationships, academic achievement, and career development can be found in *Guidance Activities for Counselors and Teachers* by Thompson and Poppen (1992).

Poppen and Thompson (1975) also describe group activities that enhance self-concept by focusing on children's strengths. One such activity is to have members of the group share something about themselves, such as three adjectives that describe them and why, or their favorite activity and why they enjoy it, and then have group members write all the good points observed about each member on a 4-by-6-inch card. Another is to have each group member draw something he or she does well and wear the drawing for the rest of the day. Children seldom have their good points recognized, and these exercises create good feelings and serve as a stimulus for group guidance activities.

One interesting new idea for facilitating group guidance is described by Bowman (1986). He points out that counselors have long known that attention-getting techniques such as puppets, art, music, books, dramatics, humor, and yoga are effective in working with children. He suggests adding magic to this list of attention-getting devices. He reviews the literature on programs that have used magic to help increase self-concept, eye/hand coordination, patience, attending behavior, and interpersonal skills; stimulate creative thinking and increase children's curiosity; and introduce and reinforce lessons on safety. He suggests using magic to "break the ice," to reward or reinforce behavior, to focus attention during guidance lessons, and to help withdrawn or alienated children.

Classroom Meetings

Glasser (1969, 1986, 1990) contends that children's needs for love and self-worth are not being met in our society and suggests the need for classroom meetings and discussions in the schools to help meet these needs. Glasser has suggested three types of classroom meetings: the open-ended meeting, the problem-solving meeting, and the educational-diagnostic meeting. He advocates that counselors or teachers use all three types of meetings to help children feel loved and worthwhile. The meetings can be adapted to the age and developmental level of the children involved.

Open-ended meetings can be held to discuss anything relevant to the children's lives in order to stimulate understanding and thinking. Topics may include "What is a friend?" "What would you do if all schools closed tomorrow and you never had to go again?" or "What would you do if you inherited a million dollars today?" Open-ended meetings can also be used to discuss situations involving moral decisions and values — "What would you do if you saw your best friend cheating on a test?" — or social issues such as prejudice. The leader's job is to remain nonjudgmental, directing the discussion in a way that stimulates thinking and helps the children set goals, look at consequences, and make plans. The leader uses frequent "what," "where," "when," "who," and "how" questions and encourages members to think of what they would do in the situation under discussion. All the children are encouraged to express their opinions. The leader's opinions, judgments, and criticisms are *not* interjected.

A behavior problem-solving meeting can be used to encourage the group to help one of its members solve a behavior problem or a group problem. The leader/counselor can present the problem and ask the group to think of ways to handle the conflict. Children often can decide on better methods for handling conflicts than adults can. Again, it is the leader's responsibility to facilitate understanding and clarification of the problem, stimulate the children to think of alternative solutions and their consequences, and encourage commitment to a plan of action. Glasser cautions teachers and counselors not to use the behavior problem-solving meeting too frequently because the attention a child receives from being the focus of the discussion may reinforce the unwanted behavior.

Educational-diagnostic meetings provide a method for teachers to quickly evaluate a unit of learning to determine the degree to which the children have understood what has been taught and the relevance of the material for their lives. Glasser criticizes schools for emphasizing memorization of facts rather than understanding and relevance. Educational-diagnostic meetings enable the teacher to assess how well the concepts of a unit are understood before and after the unit is taught. For example, before beginning a unit of study on photosynthesis, the teacher might ask how many of the children can define photosynthesis and give examples of how it works. Following the unit, a second meeting could be held to see what the children now understand about photosynthesis.

Group Meetings: Seven Levels

Poppen (see Thompson & Poppen, 1992) has suggested that children's groups work well with structured activities, provided the activities are presented in a developmental fashion that allows the children to move from easy to more difficult tasks. He proposes seven levels of group meetings:

1. *Involvement meetings.* These meetings are designed to help children participate freely in the group and build a sense of belonging to the group. For example, children can make name tags that describe some of their favorite things and share these name tags with the group.

2. *Rules meetings.* These meetings are used to discuss what ground rules the group needs. The meaning of rules and why they are necessary or not necessary may also be discussed.

3. *Thinking meetings.* These group sessions are directed toward helping children develop their cognitive skills. "What if" topics are often used. For example, children may be asked to discuss the question "What if you had one pill that would allow you to live for 200 years? Would you take the pill? Why or why not? What information would you need before making your decision?" Educational-diagnostic meetings would be included on this level.

4. *Values-clarification meetings.* These meetings are designed to help children examine and understand their present systems of values, not to destroy them or build new value systems. Children may be asked to write newspaper ads for themselves, describing the kind of people they are, or to vote on how well they like school and then discuss why they voted as they did.

5. *Hypothetical problem-solving meetings.* These meetings are designed to give children some group experience in solving practice problems. The primary aim in teaching group problem solving is to help children learn

how to generate alternative solutions to problems. Too often children tend to cling to one problem-solving idea even if it is not working. A sample activity at this level is to ask three children to simultaneously play the role of a child in their age group who is having problems with his or her parents. Six other students could play the child's father and mother as the family members try to work out their difficulties. The rest of the children in the group would evaluate the interaction and make suggestions on how to play the roles better.

6. *Actual problem solving.* When children are ready for this level of group interaction, the counselor lets them work with actual problems. Perhaps one child has a real family- or school-related problem for the group's consideration.

7. *Group council.* The highest level for children to attain in this seven-stage sequence is the group-council procedure recommended by Adlerian psychologists. The group is essentially governed on a democratic basis by a rotating three-member council that represents the entire group. This type of group uses all the skills developed in the preceding six levels of group interaction. All group problems, from discipline to next week's picnic, are brought before the council for discussion. However, the counselor retains veto power over solutions that might endanger the children or others.

Evaluation of Group Meetings

Bruckner and Thompson (1987) provide a model for evaluating weekly group counseling sessions with children in the elementary school. This model could be adapted for use with group counseling programs in any setting. They developed an instrument containing the following six incomplete statements and two forced-choice items:

1. I think coming to the group room is _____.
2. Some things I have enjoyed talking about in the group room are _____.
3. Some things I would like to talk about that we have not talked about are

   _____.
4. I think the counselor is _____.
5. The counselor could be better if _____.
6. Some things I have learned from coming to the group room are _____.
7. If I had a choice, I (would) (would not) come to the group room with my class.
8. Have you ever talked with your parents about things that were discussed in the group? (yes) (no)

Some of these items may be used as a needs survey for future group sessions. Two independent persons rate student responses on a five-point scale, ranging from a rating of 5 for statements showing an outright positive, accepting attitude toward the item, to a rating of 1 for statements showing an outright rejecting, negative attitude toward the item. A rating of 3 is awarded to neutral, ambivalent, or evasive responses. Limited positive and limited negative responses receive ratings of 4 and 2, respectively. Raters should reach 85 percent levels of agreement and generally experience little difficulty in obtaining agreement on the remaining 15 percent.

Group Crisis Intervention

Two classmates are killed in a fiery car wreck.
A 12-year-old puts a gun to his head and commits suicide.
The mother of a 9-year-old dies of cancer.
The father of a 7-year-old is murdered.
War breaks out, and the television shows bombings on 24-hour newscasts.
Economic recession hits, and many parents lose their jobs.
Reports of an earthquake forecast send feelings of fear and panic throughout the population.
A hurricane devastates an entire section of the state.

In recent years, professionals have been asked to provide crisis counseling to children in schools, churches, and clubs and through other activities. Incidents such as those just described stimulate feelings of fear, helplessness, loss, sadness, and shock. Children worry about the loss of their parents (their security), their friends ("Could it happen to me? Why did it happen?"), and their security ("Where will I go if I lose my home?"). In some cases, their parents may be coping with their own loss or grief, and be unable to help the children. In other cases, the situation may be related to the school, church, or an organizational group, and children may feel that their parents do not really understand the situation. Some parents may not realize their children are worried; some children are not able to verbalize their pain. Those who work with children recognize that young people cannot learn or perform their daily activities with these fears and concerns. They become irritable and restless, moody or agitated. They have difficulty concentrating and sleeping. They may experience physical symptoms such as nausea or diarrhea. Someone has to help them cope, and this is usually effected through group discussion and group counseling.

Gilliland and James (1988) propose six steps for crisis counseling that are similar to the reality counseling model described in previous chapters of this book. In addition, they urge that counselors take steps to ensure the physical, emotional, and physical safety of the client, and, as the child develops a plan, to assist him or her in identifying additional support systems, coping mechanisms, and actions to take.

Gilliland and James (1988) emphasize the need for the crisis counselor to assess the severity of the crisis subjectively (as the child views it) and objectively (as the counselor views it). They also caution that consideration should be given to the child's emotional state and his or her ability to cope with the problem. There may be a possibility of suicide in a crisis situation, and factors in the child's family and emotional history, as well as the seriousness of the thought and plan, will help counselors determine the possibilities of such an action. (See "Suicidal Behaviors" in Chapter 14.) Crisis counseling is short-term, and counselors should carefully consider the need for referrals for some children or other arrangements to ensure that each client successfully copes with the crisis in the days and weeks to follow.

Graham (1990) presented a plan for helping children after a trauma, such as a hurricane or plane crash, which affects the families of numerous children. Incorporating ideas presented by Graham with those of Gilliland and James (1988), we suggest the following outline for group crisis counseling:

I. Introductory phase
   A. Ask members to introduce themselves and tell why they are in the group.
   B. Help members clarify their goals regarding what they would like to accomplish in the meeting.
   C. Discuss confidentiality—what group members talk about stays in the group. Get a commitment from all members to maintain confidentiality.
   D. Discuss basic rules:
      1. Take a bathroom break first because no one can leave the room after the group begins.
      2. Encourage group members to stay the entire time. The group will generally run for two hours; the time will depend on the ages of the children.
      3. Elect or appoint a co-leader or a peer leader to keep the gate (that is, not let people in or out).
      4. Remind the group that no group member holds rank over any other group member and that everyone's participation is valued equally.
II. Fact phase
   A. Focus on discussing what happened.
   B. Encourage everyone to participate.
III. Feeling phase
   A. Ask "What happened then?"
   B. Ask "What are you experiencing now?"
IV. Clients' symptoms
   A. Ask "How is this affecting you?" (Is the member having trouble sleeping or studying, or is the member worrying too much?)
   B. Ask "How is this affecting your grades, your studies, your health, and so on?"
V. Teaching phase
   A. Explore the common responses to this incident.
   B. Brainstorm about how people have been responding to the incident.
   C. Discuss how each response is helpful or not helpful to people.

VI. Summary phase
  A. Raise questions and provide answers.
  B. Summarize what has been learned and shared.
  C. Develop action plans for individuals and/or the group if needed.
  D. Provide support for group members to ensure their physical, emotional, and psychological safety. An action plan should be made to protect any group member needing protection.
  E. Conduct a follow-up meeting in three to five days to see how well the group members are coping.
  F. Arrange individual counseling sessions for group members who need further assistance.

In conclusion, group counseling can be a highly effective method for changing children's lives or, better still, for helping prevent excess stress and conflict in their lives. It is rewarding for children to find their place in a group and to help one another. It is rewarding for the group counselor to watch the children grow and develop into caring, functioning group members.

REFERENCES

Bergin, J. (1989). Building group cohesiveness through cooperation activities. *Elementary School Guidance and Counseling, 24,* 90–94.

Bowman, R. (1986). The magic counselor: Using magic tricks as tools to teach children guidance lessons. *Elementary School Guidance and Counseling, 21,* 128–136.

Bruckner, S., & Thompson, C. (1987). Guidance program evaluation: An example. *Elementary School Guidance and Counseling, 21,* 193–196.

Dyer, W., & Vriend, J. (1980). *Group counseling for personal mastery.* New York: Sovereign Books.

Gazda, G. (1973). Group procedures with children: A developmental approach. In M. M. Ohlsen (Ed.), *Counseling children in groups: A forum* (pp. 118–130). New York: Holt, Rinehart & Winston.

Gilliland, B., & James, R. (1988). *Crisis intervention strategies.* Pacific Grove, CA: Brooks/Cole.

Glasser, W. (1969). *Schools without failure.* New York: Harper & Row.

Glasser, W. (1986). *Control theory in the classroom.* New York: Harper & Row.

Glasser, W. (1990). *The quality school: Managing students without coercion.* New York: Harper & Row.

Graham, C. (1990, November). *A normal response to an abnormal situation: The crisis debriefing.* Paper presented at the meeting of the Southern Association for Counselor Education and Supervision, Norfolk, VA.

Johnson, D., & Johnson, F. (1987). *Joining together: Group theory and group skills* (3rd ed.). Englewood Cliffs, NJ: Prentice-Hall.

Ohlsen, M. (1977). *Group counseling* (2nd ed.). New York: Holt, Rinehart & Winston.

Poppen, W., & Thompson, C. (1975). *School counseling: Theories and concepts.* Lincoln, NE: Professional Educators.

Thompson, C., & Poppen, W. (1992). *Guidance activities for counselors and teachers.* Knoxville, TN: Kinko's Copies.

Tuckman, B., & Jensen, M. (1977). Stages in small group development. *Group and Organizational Studies, 2,* 419–427.

CHAPTER 14

Counseling Children
with Special Concerns

Chapter 1 described some of the difficulties inherent in our complex present-day society—difficulties with which children must cope during their major years of growth and development. Counselors obviously cannot supply all the answers to these problems; however, several concerns seem pressing and are seen frequently by counselors. The purpose of this chapter is to suggest methods for working with children with these special needs and problems. The suggestions should be incorporated into a caring, accepting counseling atmosphere and modified to meet the unique needs of the child and the presenting concern. The reader may wish to refer to Appendixes A and B for special procedures for handling problem behaviors that may accompany these societal problems. The following problems will be considered: child abuse, divorce, stepfamilies, single-parent homes, death and dying, cultural barriers, alcoholism, latchkey children, homeless children, suicidal behaviors, satanic cults, and AIDS.

CHILD ABUSE

Congress has defined *child abuse* as the "physical or mental injury, sexual abuse, negligent treatment or maltreatment of a child under the age of 18 by a person who is responsible for the child's welfare under circumstances which indicate the child's health or welfare is harmed or threatened" (U.S. Department of Health, Education, and Welfare, 1975, p. 1). Kavanagh (1982) points out that most definitions of emotional abuse and neglect focus on parental fault and/or the condition of the child, with some states emphasizing parental behavior (failure to provide proper care) and other states focusing on the child's condition (the child's having been denied proper care or parental love). Kavanagh expresses some concern about the diagnoses being made because of these definitions.

According to Hart, Germain, and Brassard (cited in Neese, 1989), actions associated with psychological abuse may include mental cruelty (verbal abuse, unrealistic expectations, discrimination), aspects of sexual abuse and exploitation, living in unstable or dangerous environments, drug and substance abuse condoned by adults, negative models, cultural bias or prejudice, neglect or stimulus deprivation, and institutional abuse.

The American School Counselors Association (ASCA) published a position statement on child abuse in 1988, defining the act as "the infliction by other than accidental means of physical harm upon the body of a child, continual psychological damage or denial of emotional needs" (p. 262). Examples of child abuse given in the statement include extensive or patterned bruises, burns, lacerations, welts, or abrasions; injuries inconsistent with explanation; sexual abuse, molestation, or exploitation; emotional disturbances caused by friction or discord in the home or mentally ill parents; and cruel treatment. ASCA defined child neglect as "the failure to provide necessary food, care, clothing, shelter, supervision, or medical attention for a child" (p. 262) and described this behavior as lack of supervision or medical attention; irregular and illegal school absences; overworking or exploiting child; lack of nurturance; or abandonment (ASCA, 1988).

Because of the variety of laws defining child abuse and because of the large number of unreported child abuse cases, Hart, Germain, and Brassard (cited in Neese, 1989) believe that relatively few cases of psychological maltreatment are reported. Citing 1979–1980 statistics from the National Center on Child Abuse and Neglect, they report a conservative estimate of 200,000 cases of emotional abuse and neglect for the one-year period. Conte (cited in England & Thompson, 1988) reports that in 1984 there were 100,000 reports of child sexual abuse; however, Conte believes this may be a gross underestimate of actual cases. In 1985, Elliot reported that in the U.S. child sexual offenders average 73 assaults before they are reported (cited in Tennant, 1988). The largest number of victims are girls. Schaefer, Briesmeister, and Fitton (1984) point out that child abuse occurs at all levels of social, economic, and educational status and that in 80 to 90 percent of the cases the offender is a male relative or friend of the family. The offender may use bribes, threats, guilt, or coercion to ensure secrecy. In order to protect the family and this relative or friend, the abuse may be ignored or "hushed up" in a variety of ways. Whatever the cover-up means, the incidents are never reported or recorded, and the child and family never confront the issue or receive treatment.

Several hypotheses have been advanced to explain the causes of child abuse. Hart, Germain, and Brassard (cited in Neese, 1989) reviewed some of the research describing the characteristics of abusers. They found that abusers tend to be a heterogeneous group; however, their characteristics include a low frustration tolerance, nonempathic relationships, unmet dependency needs, power/authoritarianism problems, low self-esteem, depressed emotions, learned helplessness, and self-isolating tendencies. Abusers tend to respond to others' distress in an aversive, unsympathetic manner. From their research on the characteristics of abusers, Roehl and

Burns (1985) suggest that the "abuser usually exhibits poor impulse control, immature behavior, jealousy or favoritism toward the child, rigid and authoritarian belief systems, and few social skills" (p. 20). Abusers may attempt to dominate the family, feel uncomfortable in relationships with adult females or anyone outside the family, possess average or above-average intelligence, and probably abuse alcohol or other drugs. Mothers in incestuous families are usually very dependent, are frequently absent from home for long periods of time, show little involvement with the family, may be disenchanted with their role as wife and mother, and may be seriously ill or disabled (Roehl & Burns, 1985).

Families in which child abuse occurs often are experiencing multiple problems (marital, financial, occupational, parent/child), but the adults lack the resources and coping skills necessary for efficient resolution of these problems. Community and cultural factors—for example, economic stress; social isolation; acceptance of domestic violence and corporal punishment; socialization of men to view women as sex objects and inferior persons; and disrespect for minorities, their lifestyles and culture—may also contribute to the incidence of child abuse (Germain et al., cited in Neese, 1989). Research indicates that the following characteristics are often associated with higher incidences of abuse: poverty, blue-collar employment, unemployment, two-children families, parents who were victims of abuse, families going through stressful change (moving, work, health, marital), and families that are more punitive and less empathic (Germain et al., cited in Neese, 1989). Kavanaugh, Youngblade, Reid, and Fagot (1988) found that abused children talked less than nonabused children did, and abusive parents reacted less often to the communication of their children than nonabusive parents reacted. Abusive parents also spent less time in positive interactions with their children than did nonabusive parents. When these factors are present and abuse is suspected, the child should be considered to be at greater risk.

Psychological Maltreatment

Hart, Germain, and Brassard (cited in Neese, 1989) reviewed the literature to determine the destructive effects of psychological maltreatment on the lives of children. Their lists include many of the above symptoms, as well as conditions or characteristics such as a poor appetite, lying and stealing, low self-esteem, emotional instability, incompetence or underachievement, depression, prostitution, suicide, and homicide. They believe strong evidence exists to indicate that psychological maltreatment results in serious emotional and/or behavioral disorders. Neese (1989) is also concerned about psychological maltreatment, believing that this type of abuse increases the risk of developing serious behavioral and/or emotional disorders because it affects the victim's view of self and others as well as his or her expectations for the future. For this reason, Neese advocates that "counselors and other professionals involved in the total development of children must study the aspects of prevention and intervention as they relate to psychological maltreatment" (p. 194).

Garbarino, Guttmann, and Seeley (1986) believe psychological maltreatment of children is a significant problem in our society. They have attempted to define the issue more clearly and to link the definition to prevention and treatment. The writers suggest that psychological maltreatment "is a concerted attack by an adult on a child's development of self and social competence, a *pattern* of psychically destructive behavior" (p. 8). According to Garbarino et al., psychological maltreatment manifests itself in five forms: rejecting, isolating, terrorizing, ignoring, and/or corrupting the child. They present numerous methods for assessing the child's situation in addition to prevention and intervention techniques for individual and families and ways to mobilize community resources. Counseling techniques such as marital counseling, family therapy, parent/child interventions, methods for working with socially isolated families, and educating the public are suggested and described to assist the professional working with psychological maltreatment.

Neese (1989) found evidence in the literature suggesting that the educational system may be perpetrators of child psychological maltreatment. Teachers may be abusive through disparaging remarks, threats, and punishments; the curriculum may be structured to overemphasize theoretical or academic goals while neglecting social development; and school bullies are a significant factor in the psychological victimization of children (Neese, 1989). Hart, Germain, and Brassard (cited in Neese, 1989) recommend that school systems address the issue through preservice and inservice programs and through clear policy statements. Neese calls attention to the AACD Ethical Standards to guide counselors in the resolution of ethical conflicts with their employing institutions and in their relationships with their child clients but points out that these standards do not specifically address psychological maltreatment. Counselors must keep informed about issues and legislation through continuing education efforts (Neese, 1989).

Child Sexual Abuse

Kohn (1987) suggests that "as many as 40 million people, about one in six Americans, may have been sexually victimized as children" and "as many as a quarter of these people may be suffering from a variety of psychological problems, ranging from guilt and poor self-esteem to sexual difficulties" (pp. 55–56). Holtgraves (1986) reports that one in four girls and one in ten boys are sexually abused before they reach age 18. Adams and Fay (1981) believe that children are acquainted with their attackers in 85 percent of the sexual assaults, and that attacks made by an acquaintance place children at a greater risk than those committed by strangers. Children who are in frequent contact with their abusers have additional problems in maintaining and balancing the relationship, as well as coping with the trauma of the abuse.

England and Thompson (1988) describe a number of myths associated with childhood sexual abuse:

1. *Myth number 1: Incest rarely occurs, but when it does, it is found mainly in lower socioeconomic, poorly educated families.* The writers report that their review of literature indicates that sexual abuse is *not* restricted to a social class, educational level, or ethnic group.

2. *Myth number 2: Child molesters are attracted sexually to their victims.* England and Thompson state that sexual abuse is believed to be an act of power rather than of sex. Male clients treated by one of these writers were found to have poor interpersonal relationships, to experience problems at work, and to feel worthless about themselves. In other words, they seemed to feel they had little control in their lives; engaging in sexual behavior with children was their way of showing power and control.

3. *Myth number 3: Most child molesters are strangers (unknown) to their victims.* Unfortunately, most offenders are related to their victims; in fact, according to a 1985 Committee for Children report, the majority of offenders are persons that the child loves and trusts (such as a parent), who use the child's innocence, dependence, and fear to gain control (England & Thompson, 1988).

4. *Myth number 4: Child sexual abuse is a modern phenomenon, probably resulting from the sexual revolution.* Finkelhor (1979) found it has been quite common throughout history for children to be sexually abused by adults. Child pornography had been readily available for years before the sexual revolution and continues to flourish, as does childhood prostitution.

5. *Myth number 5: The sexual abuse of a child is usually a single violent incident.* The abuse is *not* usually a single incident resulting from the overuse of drugs or alcohol or loss of control for other reasons. Studies have revealed that the abuse moves through several phases unless the child reports the incidents. England and Thompson (1988) contend that most children do not "tell," and the abuse continues until the child leaves home.

6. *Myth number 6: Children frequently make up stories about engaging in sexual activities with adults.* There is general agreement among researchers in the field that children tend to tell the truth in reporting sexual abuse. In fact, Finkelhor (1979) believes that most sexually abused children grow into adulthood without ever revealing their "secrets" because of guilt, threats, and the perceived consequences of such revelations. Unfortunately, there have been a few cases of adult-reported child sexual abuse that proved false (England & Thompson, 1988).

Tennant (1988) lists physical signs of possible sexual abuse such as vaginal discharge, discomfort in the genital area, difficulty walking or sitting, and venereal disease or pregnancy in a child under 13. Behavior changes may include sleep disturbances (fear, nightmares, bedwetting); eating problems; changes in school behavior, performance, or attendance; unusual sexual behavior for the child's age; sudden dependency; or fear of losing a particular person (Tennant, 1988). From her review of the literature, she offers the following suggestions to teachers, parents, and counselors:

1. Listen to the child carefully.
2. Be sure you understand the meaning of words used by the child and he or she understands your meanings.
3. Discuss examples of "good" and "bad" touching.
4. Talk about the child's rights with regard to his or her body or touching someone else's body, and explain that "bad" touches can come from those close to us.
5. Teach the child to say "no" to inappropriate touching.
6. Discuss the importance of telling someone about any incidents that confuse the child or make him or her uncomfortable. Reassure the child that telling is appropriate and that he or she will not be blamed. [Tennant, 1988, p. 51]

Sexually abused children are probably more difficult clients to work with than physically or emotionally abused children. They, too, have learned not to trust people; they have been deeply hurt by those they love. The counselor may have a difficult time developing a relationship of trust in order to help the child.

Hollander (1989) believes that "an aware child is a safe child" (p. 184). She presents a preventive educational program that uses bibliocounseling. The program should be developed jointly by school personnel and parents. The books selected should be part of a structured curriculum and should be used as a follow-up to a presentation by local protective or enforcement agencies. The materials should be readily available to the children, and they should be aware of professionals in the school able to answer questions that result from their reading (see the list of suggested readings at the end of this chapter). Puppets or role-playing may be used to reenact situations in books if children need help talking.

Vernon and Hay (1988) were also interested in developing a preventive approach to child sexual abuse. After reviewing the literature on sexual abuse and receiving permission from parents and the school system, they implemented activities to address accepting oneself, developing vocabularies to discuss feelings about abuse, responding to inappropriate and appropriate touching, making decisions about self-protection, using assertiveness in saying "no," and finding help. They felt the response from parents and children was positive and contend that children become less vulnerable physically and psychologically when they know the issues and the methods for coping with them.

Counseling Strategies for Working with Abused Children

Society's first priority has traditionally been to punish the offender. Until recently, there was a tendency to forget the victim once medical attention had been given for the physical problem and the child had been removed from the abuser's custody. Recently, more assistance has been given to the victims of abuse because of educational information in churches and schools, reporting and information provided by the news media, and the increased willingness of victims to tell their story in the hope that it will help another victim. Courtois (1980) believes that increased attention is being focused on the victims of incest (and probably all forms of abuse) "due to pressure from a number of sources: (1) victims who are refusing to remain silent and who, alone or with other family members, are seeking assistance in increasing numbers; (2) the Women's Movement and the attention it has brought to all forms of violence against women; and (3) the Child Welfare Movement" (p. 323). Also, as can be seen from a review of recent literature, empirical research on factors associated with abuse is increasing.

Much of the recent research suggests that some long-term psychological and behavioral problems may result from unresolved issues surrounding child abuse. Browne and Finkelhor (cited in Germain et al., 1985) suggest that emotional symptoms may include anger, denial, repression, fear, self-blame, self-doubts, helplessness, low self-esteem, guilt, dejection, and apathy; inappropriate behavioral symptoms may include acting out, withdrawal, somatic symptoms, nightmares, and phobias; and the child's belief system may be affected in such a manner as to make the world unpredictable and hostile. Some children may be referred to counselors because they are aggressive and have behavioral problems; they model the abusive behavior of their parents. Others may be referred because they are extremely withdrawn, isolated, or have academic or social problems.

Abused children are not easy clients. They have learned not to trust themselves, other people, or their environment. The world and the people in it are inconsistent and hurt them. It is safer to withdraw from this painful world and not chance relationships. Building friendship and trust may be a difficult step.

The child will need to ventilate his or her feelings, ask questions, and replay abusive incidents in order to resolve issues. Children have been taught that caregivers and other adults in their lives act in their best interest. It is difficult for them to understand that people who are supposed to love and care for them can also harm them. Their dependency on parents and other adults for care and security intensifies the conflict. Many children believe they deserve the punishment they receive. Elkind (1980) points out that young children in Piaget's concrete operations stage (ages

7–11) will say their parents are good parents even though they are abusive. Their view of reality is that their parents are kind and loving; they cannot verbalize their feelings because of their limited view of the world. This cognitive assumption often interferes with counseling children of abusive parents.

Specific suggestions for counseling with abused children follow.

1. In counseling all abuse victims, counselors must be prepared to become totally involved with the child client and be prepared for the child's repeated testing of their caring.

2. Counseling techniques for overcoming the feelings of worthlessness and guilt and methods for building self-esteem must be found. Holtgraves (1986) suggests using visual imagery to help children develop positive attitudes toward life. This imagery might include situations in which they successfully encounter and resolve uncomfortable or dangerous circumstances. Emphasis should be placed on developing strengths and positive attributes. Holtgraves reminds readers that pride in physical appearance is important for a good self-concept and recommends that children be encouraged to stand tall, make good eye contact, use a strong voice, and project an image of strength.

3. England and Thompson (1988) suggest that a playroom, rather than an office, is a better location for interviewing children suspected of experiencing abuse. The play media will assist children in their efforts to communicate their feelings, and the natural environment will help the child client feel safe and in control. Gunsberg (1989) also believes that play can be used effectively to help abused or neglected children. He reports that the play behavior of these children is likely to be primitive and disorganized (making them a behavior problem), and they often see themselves as powerless to affect the behavior of others. He describes a contingency play format to teach impulse control and maintain enjoyable interactions with adults.

4. Sexually abused children will require extra consideration, understanding, and support from the counselor. Often the children are initially unable to discuss the problem with the counselor because of intense feelings of guilt, believing that somehow they provoked the attack or could have done something to prevent it. They may feel worthless and ashamed of having been used or abused in such a manner. They may be more affected by the questions and reactions that follow than by the act itself, and they often feel intense guilt at having gotten a parent or other adult "in trouble," "in jail," or barred from the home because they "told."

5. Ask for clarification of words or nonverbal expressions you do not understand, but avoid influencing the child's statements by asking leading or closed questions (England & Thompson, 1988).

6. Specific techniques such as bibliocounseling, role-playing, play therapy, or group counseling may be considered, depending on the child's

maturity. Counselors will need to be cautious about placing sexually abused children in groups, especially if the trauma is very recent. The child may not be ready to share intense feelings with others.

7. Children may need information about what is appropriate and inappropriate touching or treatment and to be assured that certain parts of their bodies are private. They may need to be told that the adult's sexual or punishing behavior was inappropriate. Because of children's limited cognitive development and understanding, and to allay the anxiety surrounding the topic, most programs designed to teach children about child abuse use a variety of activities such as role-play, puppets, coloring books, film-strips, movies, and so on. The vocabulary used is not explicit, but instead refers to *touching* and *private areas*. The programs are not designed for sex education but are developed to give children information and strategies for coping with abusive situations. Finkelhor (1984) suggests that prevention programs are useful for children who have been abused as well as children who have not, because they give both groups information and confidence to handle situations. Those programs described earlier (Hollander, 1989; Holtgraves, 1986) may help counselors with ideas for developing preventive education presentations in their own areas.

8. Assertiveness training that focuses on how to say "no" or handle potentially abusive situations may be necessary. The child will need to be helped to determine the warning signs of abuse and to plan ways for coping with the situations (for example, calling a special person when father or mother begins to drink). Role-playing these strategies will prepare children to handle such situations more effectively.

9. Children need to be encouraged to tell someone right away when an abusive situation occurs. Adults who abuse children sexually often warn the children to keep "their secret." Children will need help discerning when they should "tell a secret" and when information should be kept confidential. They will also need assistance in deciding whom they should tell and what to do if the adult does not believe their story the first time.

10. Issues of trust must be dealt with at some point in counseling abused children. Developmental theorists have emphasized the importance of children developing trust in people and their interactions in order to live effectively. Yet children receive a multitude of daily messages, designed to protect them, that imply that the world and the people in it are dangerous. Eisenberg and O'Dell (1988) recommend group discussions and activities to help children decide whom to trust and when to be cautious. They also suggest parent-education programs with this theme because parental fears are extremely influential in children's lives.

Childhood abuse is a part of an overall pattern of abusive behavior, and the family network, as well as the personality of the abuser, must be considered. In addition, family reactions to the child who has been abused will enhance or interfere with counseling treatment and progress. Counselors may want to consider family therapy at an appropriate time in their treatment plans.

England and Thompson (1988) write that counseling interviews with the child who has experienced sexual abuse can be destructive if the counselor exhibits shock and disapproval of the child, the parents, or the content of the story the child tells. They caution that the counselor should tell the child what will be done with the information and what will happen next.

Counselors working with abused children must be prepared to provide understanding and support for all persons involved. It is a natural reaction to feel anger at anyone who hurts a child; however, these feelings must be recognized and resolved if the counselor is to work effectively with the child and the family, particularly the abuser. Counselors who are overly sympathetic with abused children lose objectivity and the ability to help the child; counselors who are extremely angry at and judgmental of the family of an abused child (for allowing this to happen), or who have strong feelings of anger toward the abuser, can never establish the relationship necessary to help these individuals. Before beginning counseling with victims of abuse, counselors may need to examine their own feelings and views about the case.

Child Abuse Hysteria?

Although most professionals report that a high percentage of child abuse reports are valid, because of a personal experience, Spiegel (1988) has written convincingly that our society is now involved in child abuse hysteria, which has resulted in significant related problems including "good faith but overzealous reporting, professionals looking for abuse in otherwise innocuous behaviors, and parents using accusations of sexual abuse in divorce and custody proceedings" (p. 276). Spiegel warns that the hysteria has resulted from sensationalized media reports, televised awareness programs, newspaper articles, television movies, children's programs on touching, puppet shows, lectures, and a variety of other media. He reports that a shared paranoia develops when overzealous attitudes toward abuse become prevalent and children's perceptions are directed by a biased adult eager to save the child. Spiegel summarizes the body of "backlash literature" that has resulted from what he describes as overzealous attention to the issue of child abuse and warns counselors they can no longer simply report cases and withdraw. Spiegel believes that counselors working with children have to be aware of this hysteria and see that investigations are completed thoroughly and objectively. Sandberg, Crabbs, and Crabbs (1988), in their article on the legal issues involved in child abuse, also believe counselors have a responsibility to remain alert in cases where there are chronic problems, but warn against a "zealous crusade." They report being aware of an increasing number of false allegations of child abuse in divorce/custody cases but caution about making general assumptions about false reporting.

CHILDREN OF DIVORCE

The incidence of divorce has been increasing rapidly in the United States during the past several decades, although there are indications of a leveling-off at the present time. Strangeland, Pellegreno, and Lundholm (1989) report that close to one third of children under 18 will be affected by the divorce of their parents. Because divorce and marital separation are emotionally comparable to losing a parent through death (Wallerstein, 1983), and because divorce, separation, and remarriage bring about rapid and multiple changes in the family (Goldman & King, 1985), it is a traumatic and painful process for all involved.

Adults frequently seek help to cope with the hurt associated with divorce through individual and group counseling or through organized helping groups such as Parents Without Partners. In past years, little direct help was given to the children of divorce; in fact, in most instances, the children were told as little as possible about family affairs and were instructed to keep the breakup secret for as long as possible. Recently, because of the noticeable effects of family separation on children, more attention has been directed to the needs of children going through this traumatic event.

The lives and relationships of children in a divorcing family are profoundly affected — socially, economically, psychologically, and even legally. Children must adjust to the separation from one parent and formation of a new and different relationship with the other. A change in the family's economic status, possibly a change in the home and school environment, different parenting styles, custody battles, and sometimes a totally different lifestyle bring about a variety of feelings that may be positive or negative. Often, mothers who have been totally involved in the care of children and home have to go to work; many are unskilled and have to accept low-paying jobs. Children may be torn by conflicting loyalties, or they may learn to manipulate the parents in an effort to get their own way. Children of divorced parents may be asked to assume the role of the absent parent and to fulfill physical or emotional responsibilities beyond their maturity level. For some families, the separation and divorce bring relief from tension and strife; for other families, the breakup brings more stress, pressure, and overwhelming burdens (Kupisch, Rudolph, & Weed, 1984).

Several leading researchers have pioneered the research efforts on children of divorce. Wallerstein and Kelly (1980) followed 60 divorcing families, with 131 children, for ten years. More recently, Wallerstein and Blakeslee (1989) conducted follow-up interviews with at least one member of 52 of these families to determine their current reactions to the divorce. Hetherington, Cox, and Cox (1978) studied 46 preschool children and their families for two years. Kurdek and Berg (1983) and Kurdek, Blisk, and Siesky (1981) are now working with 74 families. Guidubaldi (1984) and Guidubaldi, Perry, Cleminshaw, and McLoughlin (1983) are attempting to follow a national sample of elementary school children going through divorce. According to Goldman and King (1985), these are the major researchers in the area, and their studies have yielded most of the data concerning the effects of divorce on children.

Wallerstein and Kelly (1980) note that the "central hazard of divorce" is that it may adversely affect the child's development. Numerous studies have suggested that the child's developmental level is related to the reaction that follows the separation. Wallerstein and Kelly (1980) and Wallerstein and Blakeslee (1989) suggest that infants respond mainly to the emotional reactions of their caretaker; for example, mothers or fathers under stress convey their feelings to the infant through handling and verbal communication with the infant. Very young children seem to have many of their needs met regardless of the stress of the caretaker. Very young children are dependent and demand attention to their needs. Preschoolers (ages 3–5) have only a vague understanding of the family situation because of their limited cognitive development; thus, they often feel frightened and insecure, experience nightmares, and regress to more infantile behaviors. School-age children, who have more advanced cognitive and emotional development, see the situation somewhat more accurately. However, children aged 6–8 often believe the divorce was their fault ("If I had not been bad, Dad would not have left"), and children at this age often hold unrealistic hopes for a family reconciliation. They may feel loss, rejection, guilt, and loyalty conflicts. The ages of 9–12 are a time when children are developing rapidly and rely on their parents for stability. They may become very angry at the parent they blame for the divorce or may take on a supportive role as they worry about their troubled parents. Because of their anxiety, they may develop somatic symptoms, engage in troublesome behaviors, or experience a decline in academic achievement. The parents' divorce during children's adolescent years brings a different set of developmental problems. Young people at this age are striving for independence and exploring their own sexuality. They need structure, limits, and guidance in dealing with their sexuality. They also may worry about their own relationships and the possibility of repeating their parents' mistakes.

The results of research relating risk to age have been contradictory. Hetherington et al. (1978) believe that children of younger ages suffer more detrimental effects of a divorce. In her ten-year follow-up, Wallerstein (1984) found that children who were very young at the time of the divorce seemed to have suffered less—they remembered less about that time in their lives. It could be that a multitude of factors other than developmental level will influence the effect of divorce on the child, including the amount of tension and conflict in the home, the length of time the child has lived with the conflict, the parents' reactions to the conflict, and the parents' personal adjustment to divorce and the resumption of parenting roles.

Most researchers have reported that children going through a divorce experience academic problems, especially boys (Guidubaldi, 1984; Werner & Smith, 1982). School is usually the second most stable environment for the child, and when the home environment is disrupted, it is natural for a child to turn to the school and teachers for support and comfort. Guidubaldi et al. (1983) found that an orderly, structured, and predictable school environment was related to the resumption of student achievement. Some evidence exists that children who were achieving well before the family disruption and who had no previous serious personality or behavioral disorder resume their good adjustment within one to two years after the divorce. It is possible that children just entering school at the time of the divorce may be at greater risk academically, because these are the years when the foundations for learning are formed. However, academic achievement is probably related more closely to other factors, such as socioeconomic status, than to the incidence of divorce.

Wallerstein (1983) and Wallerstein and Blakeslee (1989) describe "psychological tasks" children of divorce must successfully resolve. A knowledge and understanding of these tasks will help counselors choose effective methods for working with children experiencing family breakup. Following is a summary of these tasks, with counseling suggestions for each.

Acknowledging the reality of the marital rupture.   As has been pointed out, young children often experience terrifying fantasies, feel abandoned, and tend to deny the reality of the family situation. Because of their own stress, parents often fail to reassure the children and help them understand the situation and their future. Older children, too, may experience some fantasies of disaster, reduced ability to think and cope, and even psychosomatic symptoms indicating their anxiety. Supportive counseling techniques, including listening, reflection, clarification, and problem solving; and perhaps stress-reduction techniques, such as relaxation or guided imagery, are suggested for children working through this task. Oehmen (1985) believes the child should be confronted with the situation quickly and forcefully and provided an opportunity to discuss, process, and resolve his or her feelings about the divorce to avoid being overwhelmed by negative feelings.

Wallerstein and Blakeslee (1989) believe the most critical factor in helping children through divorce is parental support. They suggest that both parents should talk with all the children in a group about the decision to divorce several days before one parent leaves the home. Children should be provided with a clear explanation about why their parents are divorcing, although they need not be told the details of an infidelity or other sexual problem. The parents should convey that, unfortunately, they have made a mistake in their marriage, but they will remain committed to the family. The writers state that helping the child understand the divorce and its consequences is the first psychological task for children of divorcing families.

Disengaging from parental conflict and distress and resuming customary pursuits. The resolution of this task calls for the children to distance themselves from the crisis in their household and resume their normal learning tasks, outside activities, and friendships. Parents must work to help children keep their lives in order and not let the divorce overshadow all their activities. As has been reported by other researchers, Wallerstein (1983) saw a significant decline in academic achievement in more than half of her sample of children during the ages of 7 to 11 following a marital separation. Group counseling and individual techniques directed toward improving academic achievement (for example, contingency contracting) may assist children at this level. Consultation sessions with teachers to plan for a structured class environment may bring stability to the child's life and encourage achievement.

Resolution of loss. Divorce not only brings the loss of a parent, it often brings other losses, such as the loss of familiar surroundings and possibly of a more comfortable lifestyle. Wallerstein (1983) believes the task of resolving these losses may be the most difficult. "At its core this task demands that the child overcome his or her profound sense of rejection, of humiliation, of unlovability, and of powerlessness which the one parent's departure so often engenders" (p. 237). Wallerstein and Blakeslee (1989) suggest that a consistent pattern of visitation by the absent parent, with emphasis on building a new and positive relationship, can help children through this stage. Unfortunately, many children do not have this relationship with the absent parent and remain disappointed for years, feeling rejected by the absent parent and thus unlovable and unworthy. Roleplaying, puppetry, writing, drawing, feeling charades, and other techniques can be used to encourage children to express their feelings. Individual and group sessions focusing on building self-esteem may be helpful—for example, strengths testing, peer teaching, finding the child a "buddy," and the techniques of cognitive restructuring.

Resolving anger and self-blame. Because divorce is a voluntary decision by one or both parents, children tend to blame the parents for being selfish and unresponsive to their needs, or they may blame themselves for the breakup of the family. Intense anger at one or both parents is characteristic of children of divorce, especially older children. The researchers found that the child's ability to forgive himself or herself for perceived blame for the divorce or failure to achieve a reconciliation was a significant step toward forgiving the parents and reconciling the relationship. Some excellent books are available for children that will help them understand the divorce process and the reality that they are not to blame for the divorce. Most of these books emphasize that sometimes adults just cannot live together or resolve their differences. Counselors may want to recommend specific books for the developmental level of their clients and discuss the books with the children. The child's intense anger often results in acting-out behavior. A consistent, structured environment at home and at school will provide some of the security the child needs during this period of turmoil and change. Group counseling that focuses on role-playing, play therapy, drawing, and writing can help children express their anger and feelings of guilt. Group problem-solving discussions will help children find constructive ways of handling their feelings.

Accepting the permanence of the divorce.   Wallerstein (1983) points out that the fantasy of the family being reunited persists tenaciously for children of divorce, even though the parents may have married other partners. Whereas there is a finality about losing a parent through death, the fact that both partners are alive contributes to the continuing fantasy of restoring the intact family. Counseling using the techniques of reality therapy may help the child accept the permanence of divorce. Group counseling with other children going through divorce or who have experienced a family divorcing may also help. Drawings showing the family before the divorce and at the present time, good and bad family changes since the divorce, and filmstrips and books about divorce and other family lifestyles (the stepfamily or single-parent family) often stimulate excellent discussions.

Achieving realistic hope regarding relationships.   During the adolescent years, the child of divorce must resolve issues surrounding relationships — learning to take a chance in relationships knowing that they might be fulfilling or that they might fail. This requires that the child feel he or she is lovable and worthy. It has been noted already that children often feel rejected, unlovable, and unworthy because they feel guilty over the divorce or because they believe that one or both parents rejected them and cared little about their feelings and welfare. Wallerstein and Blakeslee (1989) note that some adolescents engage in acting-out behavior (promiscuity, alcohol or drug abuse, and the like) that indicates low self-esteem. An important task for adolescents is realizing they can love and be loved. They must learn to be open in relationships while knowing that divorce or a loss is possible. Wallerstein and Blakeslee believe that effective resolution of this last psychological task of "taking a chance on love" leads to freedom from the psychological trauma of divorce, and provides "second chances" for children of these families. Wallerstein and Blakeslee conclude that the effects of divorce are much more pervasive and longer lasting than originally thought. In earlier research, Wallerstein and Kelly (1980) had reported that boys showed more signs of trauma from the divorce during their developmental years than girls did. Wallerstein and Blakeslee (1989) found a "sleeper effect" — the girls' problems became more apparent as they entered young adulthood. Twenty years after Wallerstein began her initial research, she found parents' continuing anger still a factor in their children's lives. Many of the sample of children, now adults, were underachievers or drank heavily; a few had been involved in serious crimes. One third of the girls had relationship problems.

Guidubaldi (1989) reported the results of his study on children of divorce to the National Committee for Children's Rights. He found that elementary-grade children, especially boys, experience poor academic and social adjustment after divorce. He concludes that poor financial conditions and the lack of a male role model contribute to these problems. Guidubaldi suggests that special measures, including joint custody, frequent visitation rights, and the father's involvement in school activities, may help children of divorce better adjust to the breakup.

Counselors working with the parents of children involved in a divorce can be of assistance by providing consultative advice. Some of the following suggestions for parents may help:

1. Talk with the child about the divorce at his or her cognitive level (counselors may want to rehearse this with the parents). Explain what has happened at the child's level of understanding, and try to relate the experience to one that the child may have had. Emphasize that the child is not at fault. Keep the lines of communication open so the child's misconceptions or fears will be recognized immediately. Avoid blaming or criticizing the other parent and relating all the unpleasant details.

2. Plan for ways to make the child's life as stable and consistent as possible, even though changes may be necessary. Household routines, school schedules, and consistent discipline will help children understand that their world is not completely wrecked. Involve teachers, counselors, ministers, grandparents, and other support systems.

3. Avoid using the children as a go-between to carry messages ("The child-support check is late!") or to find out about the other parent's life ("What does her/his apartment look like?"). Children love both parents and are torn by conflicting loyalties already.

4. Arrange for regular visits from the absent parent to assure the children that they are loved by both parents. Children will sometimes be disappointed by absent parents who fail to call or come for a visit. Custodial parents will need to provide a lot of love and reassurance at these times.

5. Talk with the children about the future. Involve them in the planning without overwhelming them with the problems. They need to know what to expect.

6. Children experiencing a divorce in their family are still children at a particular developmental level. Avoid asking them to assume responsibilities beyond their capabilities—being "the man of the family," babysitting younger children, or taking on excessive household chores.

Parents and counselors need to remember that the child's adjustment after a divorce will take time and will require continuing efforts of understanding and reassurance. Parent-group meetings can help parents understand the problems their children are experiencing, learn new methods for communicating with their children, try new methods of discipline, and resolve some of the parents' own frustration.

Omizo and Omizo (1987) found that group counseling benefited parents by encouraging a more positive child-rearing attitude toward the children, which, in turn, resulted in the children feeling more positive about themselves.

As in counseling with any problem in which values, beliefs, and attitudes may affect the counselor's objectivity, counselors may want to assess their feelings about divorce and their potential reactions to both the parents and the child. Children who are the victims of divorce have been hurt by adults they trusted and will be quick to detect uneasiness, anxiety, or insincerity in the counselor's behavior.

CHILDREN IN STEPFAMILIES

For years, the intact nuclear family has been considered the ideal or "norm." With the present rate of divorce and the number of adults remarrying each year, this idealized view of the family must be adjusted. Kantrowitz and Wingert (1990) reported that, according to census data released in 1985, 6.8 million children lived in stepfamilies. According to these writers, demographers are predicting that one third of the children born in the 1980s will live with a stepparent.

A stepfamily has been defined as a family in which at least one adult has had a child prior to the couple's marriage (Kupisch, 1984). The joining of two families into one presents children with another set of unique problems with which to cope at a time when the effects of the biological parents' divorce may still be troublesome. Bryan, Ganong, Coleman, and Bryan (1985) conclude that, with the number of stepfamilies increasing, it is reasonable to expect mental health professionals to become more involved with stepfamilies and the problems of the adults and children in these families. Kantrowitz and Wingert (1990) state that until the 1970s, researchers focused their attention on nuclear, intact families. Stepfamilies or single-parent families were virtually ignored, but researchers have shown that these families are very different in structure, interactional modes, and functioning from nuclear, intact families.

Because the stepfamily is not considered a "normal" family, expectations and relationships are more ambiguous and complex. Not only are cultural and social guidelines unclear, but when children are members of two households, moving in and out, the home guidelines and schedules may also be ambiguous and complex. Adults and children experience changes in roles, alliances, parenting arrangements, household responsibilities, rules, expectations, and demands. For children who are attempting to regain stability after the first family breakup, this lack of structure may bring additional stresses and strains.

Kupisch (1984) contends that the stepfamily is not recognized as an equal to the ideal first-marriage family. She points out that some religious groups sanction only the first-marriage family and do not support alternative families fully. Legally, stepparents do not have protected parental rights; for example, they are not authorized to grant permission for medical aid to their stepchildren. Socially, stepparents are often treated as "extra baggage" by uncomfortable hosts at school functions, family gatherings, or parties with friends. The children in stepfamilies are often labeled "maladjusted" or "delinquent" because they have experienced divorce and the reorganization of a family. School activities are built around the intact, first-marriage family, especially activities related to Mother's Day, Father's Day, or other occasions that call for honoring parents. The lack of acceptance toward stepfamilies, and especially toward the children in these families, adds to the stress of coping and establishing a new and stable home life for all members.

Gardner (1984) describes certain disturbances that children in stepfamilies may experience. He believes hostility and anger are extremely common reactions found in these children. The hostility may be felt toward the natural parent and displaced onto the stepparent because the stepparent is a less dangerous target. Having been "abandoned" by one parent, and perhaps feeling unrealistic guilt for the divorce, the child can displace anger and hostility onto the stepparent without worrying about the "loss" of this person.

While ordinary sibling rivalry is "fierce," according to Gardner, rivalry between stepsiblings will be "even more virulent." He points out that under ordinary circumstances, older children have an opportunity to get used to the idea of a new brother or sister. When remarriage occurs, the stepsiblings "descend in a horde all at once."

Love in the stepfamily does not occur immediately; it takes time and work. Gardner suggests that counselors work with children to help them understand the concepts of compromise and the degrees of love—that loving one person does not take away love for another, nor does it mean that we always agree with the person we love.

Gardner includes in his writings suggestions for stepmothers and stepfathers; however, he emphasizes strongly the importance of joint counseling in the stepfamily situation. The child is a part of a family network, and the problems that concern the child are enmeshed in family interactions. Prosen and Farmer (1982), too, stress the importance of including the stepparents in the counseling process. These authors mention a number of outreach groups for stepparents designed to increase knowledge and acceptance of family differences, to build positive attitudes toward the new family, to develop competency in handling new situations, and to provide support for the new family.

Fuller (1988) has summarized writers' and researchers' findings regarding stepfamilies. She reports there is general agreement that younger children adjust more readily to the stepfamily situation; that adolescents seem to have the most difficult time, especially if the stepparent is not the same sex as the adolescent; that children adjust better to a stepfamily after the death of a natural parent than after a divorce; and that cooperation and support among spouses and former spouses will contribute to the children's adjustment. Fuller cautions that stepfamilies' strengths are often overlooked because of the focus on problems. She suggests that being a child in a stepfamily can (1) promote flexibility because children often must adjust to new situations, (2) provide multiple role models, (3) teach conflict-resolution skills, (4) extend the number of people who care about the child, (5) improve the child's standard of living, (6) increase the child's happiness with his or her parents, and (7) provide additional siblings for enjoyment and learning.

Kupisch (1984) contends that counselors can facilitate a satisfactory level of functioning in a stepfamily by helping the stepfamily accomplish six critical tasks.

1. *Finding realistic, appropriate role models for stepparents.* The stepparent role is different from the parent role and must be negotiated in the new family. Both adults and children need to clarify and understand the stepparent's role.

2. *Redefining financial and social obligations.* Although a marriage may end, financial responsibility for the children does not end, nor do the social relationships that were established prior to the remarriage. Resentment over support payments or continued relationships with former friends or relatives (such as grandparents) often present problems for the new family. Children in the middle of these conflicts may be "used" by adults for personal gain.

3. *Arranging custody and visitation patterns.* Finding ways to allow the children to maintain "contact with both parents requires logistical planning, flexibility and continuous open communication across households," according to Kupisch (p. 41). Custody battles and arguments over visitation rights are not uncommon in stepfamilies, and the child is often the pawn.

4. *Establishing consistent leadership and discipline.* Maintaining consistency in discipline patterns with an increased number of authority figures and two households requires open communication and planning. Some

research indicates that discipline controversies and divided loyalties are the most stressful conflicts for children in stepfamilies.

5. *Dispelling myths and tempering idealism.* Counselors can help new stepparents understand that the love of stepchildren is not instant but requires time and patience.

6. *Forming emotional bonds within the new family.* It requires time and work to develop emotional bonds for all members of a new family. "The couple bond is particularly crucial for continuance of the stepfamily, and it is important for the children's sense of family security," according to Kupisch (p. 41).

In a more recent article, Kupisch (1987) added a seventh task—that of dealing with sexuality in the home. The newly married adults may demonstrate more sexual behavior, which young children may model as a way to gain affection and attention.

Kupisch believes groups can be a "dynamic vehicle" for helping families as they reorganize. She presents guidelines for stepparents and stepchildren and suggests that these guidelines be used as topics for group discussions. Stepchildren are encouraged to recognize the following:

1. They should express their feelings and thoughts honestly.
2. They should ask parents about expectancies and routines.
3. Marriage and divorce are adult decisions, and they are not responsible.
4. They do not have to divide their loyalties and choose between parent and stepparents (love can be shared).
5. They can be members of two households.
6. Love for stepkin may take time. [p. 43]

Kupisch also encourages counselors to pursue in their interviews issues surrounding the family constellation: the frequency and amount of significant change in the child's life; living, visitation, and custody arrangements; reactions to family disruption and remarriage; typical behavioral reactions to stress; significant emotional attachments; relationship with the absent parent and extended family; acceptance of new family members; discipline arrangements between and within both households; and other stressful life events. She suggests the kinetic family drawing as a helpful technique for understanding family dynamics.

Manning and Wooten (1987) asked a small group of 23 stepparents attending a chapter meeting of the Stepfamily Association of Louisiana what they thought schools should know about stepfamilies. Three themes emerged from this survey. Stepfamilies wanted improved communications between the school and family and hoped this would lead to greater understanding and information about the family. The stepfamilies also asked for greater understanding from teachers concerning the amount of stress in the family. It was suggested that community resources be identified so teachers could use them for referral sources. School groups for children in stepfamilies were highly praised for their helpfulness. The participants' third request was that schools be especially sensitive to including stepparents and noncustodial parents in school life (Manning & Wooten, 1987).

Diamond (1985), too, has written about the necessity for "sensitizing" teachers and other school personnel to the needs of children in stepfamilies. She suggests that to avoid confusion and embarrassment, teachers must have information about students' living arrangements. A class list with parents' names should provide the teacher with information about the child's home. Schools, and especially teachers, should make every effort to get parents' names correct to avoid awkwardness. Special occasions and holidays can cause problems for children in stepfamilies; teachers should ask them how they wish to handle these occasions. Teachers should make every effort to respect the family's privacy and avoid embarrassing questions. Teachers are cautioned to become more aware that many students in their classes live in nontraditional homes and to reorient their thinking so as not to make erroneous assumptions about the child's home life or to feel uncomfortable about interacting with families other than two-parent families (Diamond, 1985).

Carter (1988), in her presentation to the American Association for Marriage and Family Therapy, stated that many problems in stepfamilies stem from traditional assumptions about the woman's role in a family; for example, competition between the stepparent and stepchildren for the spouse's attention, the woman's role of being responsible for the emotional well-being of the family, and the perception that men should take financial care of the family. She recommends a "new paradigm to allow for complex relationships and roles in remarried systems," including: (1) open lines of communication and permeable boundaries between households; (2) support for the parenting responsibilities of new spouses; and (3) a revision of traditional roles for men and women that allows for shared day-to-day responsibilities.

Kupisch (1984) urges counselors in both school and community mental health settings to assess their personal attitudes about all types of families and to use supportive counseling methods such as support groups, educational workshops, family therapy, and bibliotherapy to help the adults and children in these families.

Periodically, we too have emphasized that counselors need to examine their attitudes and beliefs about certain clients in order to maintain the highest levels of effectiveness. Visher and Visher (1979) believe that negative stereotypes of stepparents are common, and even those trained in the helping professions may not be immune to these biases. Bryan et al. (1985) attempted to investigate counselors' attitudes toward stepparents and stepchildren. The results of their study indicated that experienced counselors did not view stepfamilies and nuclear families differently; however, counselors with limited experience viewed stepparents and stepfamilies more negatively than they did members of an intact family. The researchers suggest several explanations for this difference: inexperienced counselors may have a more unrealistically positive view of nuclear-family life; experienced counselors may not accept stereotypes as readily as inexperienced counselors do; experienced counselors may be more hesitant to make judgments about cases with only the minimal amount of data given in the experimental study; and finally, experienced counselors may have had more frequent contact with stepfamilies in a clinical setting, thus reducing the impact of the stereotype. Bryan et al. (1985) recognize the limitations of their study but express concern that "if inexperienced counselors view stepfamilies significantly more negatively based on the minimal cues provided in this study, it is likely they will view their stepfamily clients somewhat negatively at the first and subsequent meetings" (p. 282). Whether the counselor is inexperienced, experienced but has had little contact with stepfamilies, or experienced with a substantial amount of contact with stepfamilies, unrecognized biases can slip into counseling practices. It would behoove all of us in the helping professions to evaluate our counseling periodically.

CHILDREN IN SINGLE-PARENT HOMES

Blum, Boyle, and Offord (1988) present discouraging news about children in single-parent families. They surveyed 1,800 families with children 6–12 years of age; 304 of these children lived in single-parent homes. Children with conduct disorders, emotional problems, attention-deficit disorder with hyperactivity, and poor school performance were 1.7 times more likely to live in a single-parent home. A low income level was also a strong factor in these homes. The researchers cautioned that their study did not indicate whether the children's disorders followed or preceded the child's living in a single-parent home. However, Shreeve, Goetter, Bunn, Norby, Stueckle, Midgley, and de Michele (1986) found that children of average intelligence earned lower grade point averages and class standings than those in two-parent households.

In 1988, Glick projected that 26 percent of minor children would be living in a single-parent household by 1990. Barney and Koford (1987) suggest that schools examine how they are meeting the needs of these families. In their article, they ask a series of questions designed to stimulate thinking about interactions and activities that could make members of single-parent families feel uncomfortable. These questions include concerns about to whom communications are addressed, timing of parent conferences, child care, teaching activities to support children in single-parent homes, and referral resources.

Counseling strategies to help children in single-parent homes are similar to many described for children of divorce. The counselor must deal with the child's feelings of loss, whether the loss resulted from divorce, separation, or death. Emotions must be recognized and discussed. These children need stability, security, and consistency in their lives. Therefore, counselors may want to recommend to the child's parent and other family members that they join a support group to help the family reorganize effectively after the loss. Counselors in schools can provide group activities for children of single-parent homes to help these children discuss their fears, concerns, and feelings about having only one parent in the home. Crosbie-Burnett and Pulvino (1990) describe a classroom guidance program for children in nontraditional families that focuses on eight aspects of nontraditional families and includes topics such as having less money, feelings of anger or sadness, questions friends ask, time alone, and other concerns.

As stated previously in this section, a considerable amount of research exists to substantiate that children from single-parent homes have a higher rate of conduct disorders and other adjustment problems than do children from intact homes. However, there are well-adjusted children who live in single-parent homes. Counselors must be careful not to allow generalizations or personal bias to interfere with their objectivity in working with these children.

COUNSELING WITH CHILDREN ABOUT DEATH AND DYING

Death has been a taboo subject for discussion in our society. When asked about death or dying, most adults try to find ways of avoiding the subject or excuse themselves by expressing their inadequacy to discuss such a subject with young people. Discussions about death seem to be accompanied by a great deal of discomfort, anxiety, vagueness, and avoidance behavior on the part of the adult. Because of these reactions to the topic, children may become confused about the facts and emotions that accompany death and show their own grief inappropriately (Frears & Schneider, 1981). In fact, Cunningham and Hare (1989) suggested that teachers and other adults may unwittingly interfere with the grieving process by refusing to answer questions, using diverting techniques, or making negative nonverbal responses to the child's attempts to talk about death and dying.

Only recently have we begun to realize that talking about death may help us accept it as a part of life and cope with the feelings that accompany death. Every child will be affected by the death of pets or grandparents, or perhaps by an even closer loss of parents, friends, or siblings. Counselors need to be prepared to help children accept the reality of death as a part of life. In order to work effectively with children on the issue of death, counselors must first examine their own attitudes toward death. A counselor in conflict will not be able to provide the support and understanding the child needs.

Children have trouble understanding death for many reasons. As Piaget points out, children are limited in understanding by the stage of their cognitive development. Young children are unable to understand the finality and irreversibility of death; they feel they are immortal. They may be concerned about their own basic needs ("Who will care for me?"), or they may wonder about the needs of the deceased (Bertoia & Allan, 1988). As children grow, they begin to question death and its causes. It may be recognized as inevitable and final, but it is still difficult for the child to comprehend the process. Children often believe that only old people die. Matter and Matter (1982) have written an informative article, based on Piaget's work, that describes children's understanding of death at different cognitive levels of development. They point out that the preoperational child holds an egocentric view of death and uses fantasy and magical thinking to explain the occurrence. The concrete-operational child may be more specific in understanding death. According to the writers, these children will note specific ways of inflicting death by act or weapon and show some interest in the details of death. Bertoia and Allan (1988) recommend that explanations be clear and specific and at a level understandable to a child in the concrete-operations stage. They suggest that explanations should be made only after listening carefully to the child for his or her thoughts. The child in the formal-thought stage "is capable of conceptualizing death in an abstract manner, and using logic in reasoning about its causes" (p. 113). It is at this stage that the child understands that everyone dies and that death is not reversible.

Many factors in the child's environment may encourage faulty concepts concerning death. The mass media often portray death violently. Adults in the child's life may react negatively to death. Often they attempt to "protect" the child from death by refusing to discuss the subject and by hiding their own feelings. It may be difficult for children to understand adult reactions. They may think they caused or contributed to the death in some way or decide that death is a punishment for something "bad" they have done. Unfounded fears and anxieties can arise out of these misunderstandings. Euphemistic explanations often cause misconceptions in children. If told that the person is "only asleep" or that "God has called her," children can learn to fear sleep or fear that God will call them away from their world.

For the most part, children have difficulty learning effective ways of handling death. Adults may not provide the answers needed or demonstrate appropriate behaviors. Unresolved grief can result in personal, interpersonal, or social problems in the future.

Segal (1984) describes children's responses to loss and death in an excellent article on expressing grief through symbolic communication. He states that, following the trauma, children may respond with denial, assume responsibility for the loss and feel guilty, internalize or act out their anger over the loss, withdraw, repress their feelings, become obsessed with fear about future losses, seek spiritual comfort ("Mom is in heaven"), feel confused about the facts, become dependent, or develop a closer relationship with a friend or sibling to gain emotional support. Segal points out that feelings are communicated nonverbally and suggests that counselors especially need to be aware of some primary modes of nonverbal communication that may indicate problems:

1. *Kinesics*—communication through body movement. The grieving or depressed child may be lethargic, rigid, or listless or may exhibit restricted movement.
2. *Oculesics*—communication through eye movements. The confused or anxious child may show involuntary eye movements, eye twitching, a blank gaze, or inability to maintain eye contact.
3. *Vocalics*—communication by tone, pitch, and rate of articulation. A grieving child may block words, stutter, or talk in low, soft tones or in a flat, colorless manner.
4. *Haptics*—communication through touch. Grieving children may withdraw from touching or kissing, distancing themselves from close human relationships.
5. *Chronemics*—communication through use of time. Segal points out that resistive children may come late for counseling or other appointments to distance themselves from human contact; alternatively, an anxious, insecure child may be upset at the possibility of being late for any appointment, fearing punishment or rejection.

Segal believes that counselors can understand their clients more fully by attending to nonverbal communication but cautions that cultural lifestyles and family styles may also prompt these behaviors. Counselors must use care in interpreting nonverbal communication.

Segal (1984) recommends a number of games and communication exercises to help children express feelings related to losses. He suggests passing out small blank cards and pencils to children in a group and asking them to write down a question about death or dying. Assurances should be given that the writer's name will not be revealed. The group leader reads the questions, and the children discuss their thoughts about the questions. Segal provides some sample questions. The group leader may prefer to write the questions on cards ahead of time and ask each child to draw a card, read the question, and answer it with his or her views. Art techniques, including crayon drawings, clay, or hand puppets, may help children portray their conflicts. Children can be asked to sculpt or carve a figure representing someone for whom they have a great deal of love; usually the figure will be the person they have lost. These drawings, carvings, or hand puppets can express the pain of the loss more easily than the child can verbalize it. Segal describes a technique for illustrating feelings with paper and music. The children draw "peaceful" views of death on one side of the paper while listening to soft music; they then draw "harsh" views of death on the other side of the sheet while listening to dissonant music. Phototherapy—having the child respond to different photographs of men, women, or children—may also be used to stimulate discussion concerning losses of loved ones. The use of all nonverbal means of communication should be followed with a discussion of their meaning and of coping strategies for the various problems revealed.

From her work with terminally ill patients, Kübler-Ross (1969) has defined the stages that most patients and their families go through in facing death. The first reaction is denial—"This is not happening to me." Second, the patient and family will experience anger over the situation—"Why did this have to happen to me and not to somebody else?" Third comes a stage of bargaining. People may try to make a bargain with God to be a better person if God will let them or their loved one live. When the inevitability of death must be faced and the pressures become a harsh reality, depression commonly occurs. When these feelings can be worked through successfully, one can achieve a quiet acceptance of death.

Swander (1987) suggests there are only three stages of grief:

1. *Shock*—This stage is evident by the child's mechanical behavior and such emotional reactions as disbelief, denial, numbness, and concern for self.
2. *Suffering*—The child shows despair, depression, sadness, hurt, anger, and anxiety and may experience loss of concentration or memory, feelings of worthlessness, suicidal thoughts, fatigue, and a variety of psychosomatic symptoms.
3. *Recovery*—The child begins to look ahead and become involved with life once again but may regress into a previous stage during holidays, anniversaries, or other special reminders of the dead loved one.

Swander stated that the grieving child may move back and forth through the stages, and the duration of any stage depends on the individual and his or her relationship to the deceased.

Bertoia and Allan (1988) suggest that counselors consider four areas when they work with children coping with death or dying issues. Counselors can encourage communication with open-ended statements that reflect care, understanding, and a willingness to listen. Counselors, teachers, and others should model accepting behavior by not treating the child in a different way and by providing support. Normal routines should be continued to provide structure and security, but they should be flexible enough to provide time for emotions and changes in behavior. Bertoia and Allan remind counselors that each child experiences different reactions to death.

In summary, counseling strategies for helping children who have experienced a loss through death include the following:

1. Listen carefully to children's thoughts, feelings, and concerns, and respond clearly and objectively with statements at their level of understanding. Clarify children's questions or statements that may have a double meaning or suggest a hidden concern.
2. Allow children to express their grief, talk freely, and ask questions. Play therapy, the use of puppets, role-playing, creative artwork, bibliocounseling, a visit to a nursing home, videos on dealing with loss, family-drawing, relaxation and imagery, letter writing to say good-bye, the open-chair technique, and individual or group discussions may be helpful counseling techniques for working with these children. Counselors can also recommend books, pamphlets, or other resources to adults who provide support for these children. Children experiencing a loss through death may feel abandoned or insecure. They will need extra amounts of time, energy, and reassurance.
3. Children sometimes have trouble understanding concepts such as "heaven" and "eternity." They may be confused about why "God takes away loved ones." Counselors may want to consult with the family's clergy leader for assistance in dealing with this sensitive topic.
4. Counselors are often asked if children should attend the funeral of someone who has died. The answer depends on the child's age, the kinship of the deceased, and the child's reaction to the death. Children need to learn that death is part of the natural order of life. They need the opportunity to say good-bye to a close loved one. But the child's reaction to death and his or her concern about attending the funeral should also be considered.

There is a paucity of literature describing effective methods for counseling with children and their reactions to death and dying, especially empirical studies. Perhaps researchers avoid the subject as do parents and other adults. The severity of pain associated with the death and dying of a loved one would indicate a need for study of both the short-term and long-term effects of the trauma.

COUNSELING WITH CHILDREN FROM DIFFERENT CULTURES

The child who enters the counselor's office may be African American, white, Native American, Asian American, Hispanic American, or from a number of other cultures or subcultures. The counselor is most often white and middle class. How can these two uniquely different individuals eliminate cultural barriers and form the facilitative relationship necessary for effective counseling?

For counseling to be effective, most researchers would agree, the essential ingredients of understanding and respect must be present. Counselors attempt to understand the child's world as the child perceives it, and they have faith in the child's ability to grow and fulfill his or her potential, given the proper support and guidance. In theory, counselors respect each person's uniqueness and potential. In practice, however, barriers may consciously or unconsciously interfere with this facilitative counseling relationship. Ivey (1987) cautions counselors not to forget that they are working with a unique person in the counseling interview and suggests that counselors must also be aware of cultural and group differences. He believes that without this awareness of cultural variations, the counselor may risk offending clients, because the meaning of certain behaviors such as eye contact and other attending behaviors differs among cultures. Ivey concludes that a counselor cannot really understand the individual unless he or she has some degree of cultural awareness.

Lloyd (1987) is concerned that multicultural movements that emphasize differences among groups may encourage counselors to hold on to preconceived beliefs and prevent them from treating the individual as a unique person. He points out that differences among people within a cultural group may be greater than differences among groups. Lloyd agrees, however, that some information about different cultures is helpful in "minimizing social blunders concerning mores, religious ceremonies, and social graces" (p. 165). Hood and Arceneaux (1987) remind readers that no one person is a sole representative of the cultural group to which he or she belongs. Lee and Richardson (1991) also caution against the danger in assuming that all people of one group are the same and that one counseling approach is appropriate for all.

Lee and Richardson (1991) define multicultural counseling as "a helping process that places the emphases for counseling theory and practice equally on the cultural impressions of both the counselor and the client" (p. 3). They believe counselors must consider differences in language, social class, and culture in order to be effective, and they describe the culturally skilled counselor as one who "uses strategies and techniques that are consistent with the life experiences and cultural values of clients" (p. 5), as well as one who is knowledgeable of the issues of cultural diversity. According to Lee and Richardson, general themes counselors should consider when working with any client of a different culture include the level of ethnic identity and acculturation, family influences, sex-role socialization, religions and spiritual influences, and the immigration experience.

Sue (1977) states that cultural, class, and language factors discriminate against the culturally different and suggests that a "culturally competent counselor" is one who is knowledgeable of cultural and class factors and is able to use differential counseling approaches that are consistent with the client's lifestyle. Sue also advocates that counselors examine what they do in counseling (that is, the process) and the goals they hold for their clients to determine their appropriateness for the client and his or her culture.

Sue (1978, p. 451) lists the characteristics of a culturally effective counselor as follows:

1. Understanding his or her own values and philosophy concerning the nature of people and their behavior, realizing that others may differ;
2. Recognizing that "no theory of counseling is politically or morally neutral";
3. Understanding that sociological and political forces external to the person have shaped culturally different persons;
4. Being able to view the world as the client does, avoiding being "culturally encapsulated"; and
5. Being truly eclectic, drawing on techniques and methods of counseling appropriate to the culture and lifestyle of the client.

Sue and Sue (1977) suggest that three cultural barriers may hinder cross-cultural counseling: language barriers, class-bound values, and culture-bound values.

1. *Language barriers.* Much traditional counseling has emphasized the establishment of rapport through verbal and nonverbal communication. Children from other cultures or subcultures may be disadvantaged in their ability to communicate their thoughts or feelings accurately. Counselors often are not familiar with the informal language or slang of other cultures. The meaning of body language, such as eye contact or personal space, varies from culture to culture. These factors may make communication between counselor and child extremely difficult and lead to misconceptions and misunderstanding.

2. *Class-bound values.* Class-bound values may hinder counseling because of conflicting attitudes and different expectations from counseling. Some of the areas of concern investigated by Wrenn (1976) may be aspects of this barrier (attitudes toward women, sexuality, work, and education).

3. *Culture-bound values.* Cultures hold different attitudes, values, beliefs, mores, and customs. Counselors may consciously or unconsciously communicate that these differences are inferior or a handicap to be overcome.

Smith (1982) believes that counseling interventions should not be selected on the basis of the client's race, but rather on the basis of other factors, such as the client's degree of acculturation, sex, socioeconomic status, and value system. In working with children, developmental and cognitive levels must be considered also.

Ponterotto and Benesch (1988) criticize multicultural counseling as being fragmented and providing conceptually inadequate models for training counselors. They suggest a framework based on the work of Torrey:

1. Identify the problem—problems will vary in different cultures.
2. Portray the personal qualities necessary for effective counseling—

some counselors believe Rogers's core relationship conditions are universal.

3. Meet client expectations—listening, directing, giving advice, and so on, will also vary with the culture.
4. Seek ways to improve counselor credibility—perceptions of credible characteristics will vary with culture.
5. Use appropriate counseling interventions—the effectiveness of active or passive interventions will vary with culture.

Ponterotto and Benesch believe this model will provide effective guidelines for counseling white or culturally diverse clients. They emphasize that although these principles may apply to all races and cultures, "culture-specific knowledge is needed to accurately conceptualize and understand the client's 'place' in each stage" (p. 239).

Gibbs and Huang (1989) caution that ethnicity issues influence the development of minority children by shaping their belief systems about mental illness or health, the manner in which they manifest and cope with symptoms, the method they use to seek help, and the way they respond to treatment. The writers suggest that although minority children are vulnerable because of factors such as poverty and prejudice, they may also have available to them "protective factors" such as extended families, social or religious networks, or traditional sources of help within their own culture.

African American Children

Sue and Sue (1990) have pointed out that many people of color are reluctant to seek counseling because it has been seen as a sociopolitical force. African American families are often required to go for counseling as a consequence of encounters with the law or their interactions with other community agencies that are providing services. Counseling may be perceived as a punishment rather than as a helpful process. According to Allen and Majidi-Ahi (1989), the traditional clinical or medical model, which focuses on a person's weaknesses or deficits, is not appropriate for working with African American children because many of them adjust well despite poverty, prejudice, and other barriers to their development. Allen and Majidi-Ahi prefer a social-ecological approach with an emphasis on understanding how economic status, education, health care, housing, racism, and other ecological factors affect the child. Other issues that counselors who work with African American children must be aware of include the following:

• Differences in perception of time—clients may consistently be late for appointments.
• Differences in communication styles—African Americans often communicate while involved in an activity and do not maintain eye contact.

- Early termination—African Americans tend to drop out of treatment at much higher rates than do white clients, probably due to problems of miscommunication and misunderstanding.

Richardson (1991) contends that counseling professionals must recognize nontraditional means for providing services to their clients and suggests that African American churches can be effective tools for enhancing self-esteem, self-respect, and community. Richardson provides guidelines for counselors as they attempt to develop relationships with the African American churches for the benefit of clients.

Native American Children

According to Lazarus (1982), the U.S. Office of Education estimates a total of approximately 326,000 Native American school-age children in the United States. Although these children compose a small proportion of the total population, their problems have been and continue to be significant. He suggests that counselors working with Native American children need to be aware of their particular values in order to prepare them for the difficulties of growing up in the present-day world. Each Native American tribe is different, but Lazarus (1982, p. 84) lists from the literature conclusions to use as general guidelines for understanding values:

1. Children are respected to the same degree as adults.
2. Cooperation and harmony are valued.
3. Generosity and sharing are important, and individuals are judged on their contributions.
4. Competition is encouraged so long as it hurts no one.
5. The Native American lives in the present, with little concern for planning for tomorrow.
6. The school culture for children is strange; some behaviors are considered ill-mannered (loud talking and reprimands).
7. Older people are respected for their wisdom and knowledge.
8. Ancient legends and cultural traditions are important.
9. Peace and politeness are essential; confrontation is rude.

Lazarus suggests that counselors will have little success with "talking therapy" and that play and art may be more effective. Tribal-made materials can be incorporated into the play techniques. Rather than confrontation, Lazarus advocates communication and social control through gossip and chitchat to promote change. Counselors are cautioned to be silent and allow time for children to speak, because Native American children feel no need to fill time with idle words. Disapproval and reluctance to talk are also indicated by silence. Teachers and counselors are encouraged to avoid individual correction or praise but to recognize group efforts. The behavioral techniques of ignoring undesirable behavior and reinforcing good behavior (of the group) are effective. Because the aged are highly respected, counselors may want to consider involving them in classrooms, in the counseling process, or in working with institutionalized children.

LaFromboise and Low (1989) caution that Native American children may believe that going to a counselor is a sign of weakness or an avoidance of cultural values such as social responsibility, honesty, independence, kindness, and self-control. Native American cultural values may differ from traditional white values. Some tribes do not value competitiveness and individualism. LaFromboise and Low point out that because of tribal differences, it is difficult to make generalizations about counseling with Native Americans. Some research indicates, however, that Native American youths prefer someone who understands their culture and can help them with their lives. The writers report that social-cognitive procedures may be effective because they tend to be less culture bound.

Herring (1991) reminds readers that the history of Native Americans has been characterized by military defeat, ethnic demoralization, and forced displacement—forces that negatively influence Native American youth. The Native American family is often faced with overwhelming poverty and unemployment, family dissolution due in part to federal government policies, and educational failure. Herring cautions that young clients will be evaluating the counselor from the first moment—his or her manner of greeting, appearance, communication style, and knowledge of the Native American culture. He also suggests that community and tribal leaders can be a valuable source of help in counseling Native American youth, as can bias-free media resources that show realistic, accurate portrayals of Native American culture.

Asian American Children

Asian Americans may have roots in China, Japan, Korea, Vietnam, or Cambodia. Although they come from different countries, Lee and Richardson (1991) believe all Asian American groups are influenced by old religious traditions that are passed down through the generations, including issues related to moderation of behavior, self-discipline, patience, humility, honor, and respect.

Stereotypes of Asian American culture would have us believe that all adults are hardworking and successful and all Asian children are high achieving (Sue & Sue, 1990); however, some Asian American families live in poverty and feel the stresses of discrimination (Huang & Ying, 1989). To visit a counselor for help with their problems may be viewed as shameful and embarrassing and may produce a sense of failure; therefore, the number of clients in treatment is low, and research on effective therapeutic interventions is limited.

Counselor credibility can be an issue with Chinese American children because it is often based not only on therapeutic skills, but also on cultural roles related to age and gender. Counselors will want to communicate thoroughly with Chinese American families about what is going on in counseling in order to enlist their support (Huang & Ying, 1989). Sue and Sue (1990) advises counselors that "issues such as independence, the necessity of eliciting emotional reactions, and the equality of family members must be seen from a cultural perspective and not as a given" (p. 89).

Much of the Japanese culture evolved from the philosophies of Confucianism and Buddhism. These teachings continue to influence the lives of Japanese Americans and are factors that must be recognized in counseling (Tomine, 1991):

- The family is more important than the individual.
- The family roles and rules for behavior are formalized, and adherence to these roles and rules is expected in order to avoid shame and loss of face.
- The father is the leader and authority; the mother is the nurturing parent.
- Communication is usually indirect and confrontation is avoided.
- Problems are kept within the family, and all problems are solved within the family unit.

In addition to possible enculturation concerns and problems of coping with prejudices, Japanese American children may be dealing with lingering anger over World War II internment issues in the family. They may also feel the impact of other political and economic decisions that affect American-Japanese relationships (Nagata, 1989).

Tomine (1991) cautions counselors to attend carefully to the personal, cultural, and defensive factors that influence the coping mechanisms of Japanese Americans. The counselor needs a wide range of skills to be able to adapt to the client's needs. Expression of feelings must be dealt with carefully by encouraging the children to express only a little more than they are comfortable with. Because of the strong family orientation, family members may serve as a nontraditional means of providing counseling, but the family may also hinder the process, preferring to solve problems within the nuclear structure.

Lee and Cynn (1991) contend that Korean Americans have cultural values similar to those of Chinese Americans and Japanese Americans. The primary adjustment problems of children from this group may be due to the rate of acculturation. Young persons adopt American values and behaviors more quickly than do parents who have only recently immigrated. Lee and Cynn call on counselors to recognize this problem and the expectations placed on children by both the old and new cultures. If adjustment problems can be described as a normal part of the acculturation process, the family can "save face" and continue counseling with a more positive attitude. Counseling strategies must be consistent in degree of acculturation and stage of ethnic-identity development.

Mexican American Children

According to Baron (1991), labels have psychological meaning for groups. He uses the terms *Chicano* and *Mexican American* interchangeably in his writings. Arredondo (1991) suggests that both scientific and political concerns exist about generic categories such as *Hispanic* or *Latino* and points out that *Hispanic* is a governmental designation. Because this section focuses on those people having ethnic origins in Mexico, the term *Mexican American* is used here.

According to Ramirez (1989), the Mexican population in the United States numbers about 12 million. Their reported income levels are significantly below those of non-Hispanic groups. These families usually have more children and less formal education than do other groups. A large number of Mexican Americans live in large cities, primarily in California, Texas, New Mexico, Arizona, Colorado, and Illinois.

Because Mexican Americans are reluctant to seek mental health treatment, there is little information about the most prevalent types of problems and most effective treatment modes. However, cultural issues about which counselors need to know include the following (Ramirez, 1989):

- Mexican Americans prefer close physical contact more than many other minority groups do.
- Mexican Americans tend to self-disclose very slowly and may need encouragement through storytelling, anecdotes, humor, and proverbs.
- The client will need evidence of the counselor's personal warmth and acceptance of the client's ideas and behaviors, especially in the initial phase of counseling. Ramirez recommends that counselors praise strengths and family dignity and avoid interpretations and confrontations during this stage. The treatment plan should be carefully explained and should possibly involve the family as a support system. Counselors need to be aware that some aspects of the treatment plan may be accepted in order to be polite and that the child and family may not agree with objectives or procedures.

Biracial Children

According to Sebring (1985), "the stresses on an interracial marriage can be severe, and the parents' abilities to cope with these pressures can and usually do affect the lives of their children. In addition, each parent brings a racial 'set' into the marriage, and there are implications here for further discord" (p. 4). Her conclusions are relevant for counselors working with interracial children. She believes that early formation of a healthy self-esteem will provide a good foundation for coping with the issues to be faced later in life. She cautions that masculine and feminine stereotypes may become confused with racial stereotypes (such as "African American is nurturing") and suggests that role models from both races are essential. According to Sebring, the child's lack of identification with both races can lead to guilt about rejecting one parent and his or her heritage; in fact, she states that "ambivalence over ethnic identity seems to be the most significant problem faced by interracial children" (p. 7). Suggestions for counseling children of interracial marriages include seeing the family in its culture, capitalizing on family strengths, becoming aware of the ethnic factors operating in the marriage, clarifying ambiguities, finding techniques for managing anger, and facilitating the parenting experience.

Hill and Peitzer (1982) worked with biracial families in groups. The stated purpose of these groups was to help parents raise their children with strong, positive African American identities and self-concepts. They encouraged the biracial parents of African American children to examine their own self-esteem and self-concept, to identify their own racism and that of others, and to recognize how racism influenced their lives.

Gibbs (1989) believes that in addition to having unique characteristics and the potential for problems because of their dual ancestry, biracial children may have problems of identity related to their ambiguous ethnicity. They may encounter problems with family approval, acceptance in the community, discrimination, and isolation. Gibbs enumerates their conflicts:

1. Racial/ethnic identity—"Who am I?"
2. Social marginality—"Where do I fit?"
3. Sexuality—"What is my sexual role?" (with regard to orientation, gender identity, and sexual activity).
4. Autonomy—parents may have attempted to protect or isolate children from reality.
5. Educational and occupational aspirations—"Where am I going?" and whether children's expectations are realistic in the light of prejudices and discrimination.

Gibbs encourages counselors to assist children in exploring their ancestry and recognizing the impact of their heritage on their present and future functioning.

Summary

This section has discussed the characteristics and needs of some of the many cultures that professionals may encounter when they work with children. As we have seen, research on the counseling needs of culturally different clients is limited. Counselor-education training programs have only begun to prepare more culturally aware professionals. Materials and resources are limited, although books, media, and special programs are beginning to appear. Myer, James, and Street (1987) published a series of lesson plans to ease the adaptation of internationally adopted children to the classroom culture. Lee and Richardson (1991) mention resources in their discussion of many cultures. The literature describes successful peer counseling programs. The number of minority group members living in the United States will continue to grow in the 21st century. Counselors must be prepared to bridge cultural gaps and adopt techniques and procedures to meet the needs of many different children and families.

CHILDREN IN ALCOHOLIC FAMILIES

One group of children in our society who receive little attention is children living in alcoholic families. Brake (1988) points out that significant attention has been paid to the fetal alcohol syndrome, adolescent alcoholics, adult children of alcoholics, and co-dependence; however, she states, "there continues to be a dearth of material on one of alcoholism's tragic victims, children of alcoholic parents" (p. 106). The children of alcoholics are often left out of an alcoholic parent's treatment, and if children are treated by agencies for other problems, alcoholism in the family is often not recognized (Lawson, Peterson, & Lawson, 1983). Buwick, Martin, and Martin (1988) report that 6.5 million children under 10 live in homes with alcoholic parents. From her research review, Brake (1988) estimates that one in five children lives in an alcoholic family; thus, the lives of approximately 8 million children revolve around alcohol. Wilson and Blocher (1990) caution that sons of alcoholics are five times more likely to become alcoholics as compared to sons of nonalcoholics, and daughters of alcoholic mothers are three times more likely to become alcoholic than girls living in a nonalcoholic environment.

The children of alcoholic parents frequently do not have their physical or psychological needs met in the family. Money needed for food and shelter may be spent on alcohol; but even if there is money, the parents may not be attentive to the child's physical needs because of preoccupation with alcohol. The child's need for love, belonging, and security cannot be met by parents who have lost control over their lives and frequently dislike themselves for their behavior. Children who live in homes where rules are consistently broken and family members cannot be relied upon to provide love and nurturance cannot be expected to grow and develop into fully functioning, well-adjusted individuals.

Clinicians have identified several general characteristics to assist counselors and other helping professionals in recognizing children of alcoholic families. Weddle and Wishon (1986) divide symptoms into three categories: general, physical, and emotional. They point out that these characteristics may occur singularly or in combination and that children with other problems may exhibit similar symptoms; however, their presence should alert counselors to the possibility of an alcohol-related problem. Because of parental inconsistency in the home, the child may adopt certain roles such as "hero," "scapegoat," "lost child," or "mascot." Additionally, children in alcoholic families may become isolated, fearful, approval-seeking, overly responsible, overly nurturant, passive, and extremely self-critical; they may hide their feelings, fear abandonment, and show physical or nutritional neglect. All writers reviewed pointed to the extremely harmful effects of inconsistent parental attitudes, behaviors, and discipline techniques and to the lack of attention and nurturance for the children.

Newlon and Furrow (1986) add that lack of attention, trouble with concentration, growing up too soon, "walking on pins and needles," "keeping it all inside," embarrassment, shame, and guilt are conditions of children living in alcoholic families. They quote Cork's (1969) study of 113 children, which indicated that familial and peer relationships suffered; school achievement decreased; the children were anxious, easily upset, and lacked self-confidence; and many experienced physical problems resulting from the stress.

Buwick, Martin, and Martin (1988) describe the children in alcoholic families as angry and hostile toward their parents; as usually having low-ered self-esteem, an external locus of control, and learning disabilities; and as believing they do not receive adequate affection. Buwick et al. state that as these children grow older, they may exhibit antisocial behaviors, alcohol abuse, delinquency, or suicidal tendencies. It is believed that these symptoms result from the conflict and stress present in the home of alcoholics. Brake (1988) summarizes research that indicates these children are affected less by the conflict and stress in the home than by how they perceive what is happening. They may feel guilty, believing they have done something to contribute to the alcoholism. However, Wilson and Blocher (1990) describe children in alcoholic homes as being under considerable stress due to family quarreling, abuse or neglect, inconsistent discipline, inadequate or unpredictable environments, disruption of family holidays or rituals, early assumption of adult roles, a denial of reality that makes understanding the real world difficult, isolation, shame, and embarrassment.

Wegscheider (1981) has described extensively the roles and responses of children in alcoholic families. Her comprehensive work has relevance for understanding and counseling with children. The roles adopted by children in alcoholic families direct behavior and family interactions and form foundations that will influence adult functioning. According to Wegscheider, the role assumed is often related to ordinal position. For example, the eldest child may assume the role of "hero," becoming overly responsible, overly compliant and helpful, and a parent surrogate; such a child may suffer from pervasive feelings of guilt and inadequacy. The "scapegoat" behaves irresponsibly, drawing attention away from the alcoholic conflict. This child is the opposite of the "hero" and gets attention through acting-out behavior. The "lost child" or "loner" does not ask for attention or nurturance and appears independent and self-reliant; however, this child is confused and fearful, and feels lonely and inadequate. "Lost children" make no demands on anyone and therefore receive very little love, attention, and support. The "mascot" draws attention away from the alcoholic conflict by providing comic relief. This child gets attention by entertaining everyone, a role that inhibits the development of mature behaviors.

Black (1981) has developed a similar model of descriptive roles assumed by children in alcoholic families. Her model includes the "responsible" role (similar to the "hero"), the "adjuster" (Wegscheider's "lost child"), and the "placater" (comparable to both the "mascot" and the "scapegoat"). Both writers point out that these roles may shift over time and that no one role may fit exactly the child's pattern of behavior.

Bepko (1985) believes this evolution and shifting of roles is detrimental to the child's development because it prevents the child from developing a distinct identity, thus "perpetuating the legacy of addiction" (p. 202). Goals for treatment Bepko suggests include (1) educating the child about drinking and life in an alcoholic family; (2) providing a safe environment for the expression of feelings about the alcoholic situation; (3) determining the neglect or deprivation occurring in the family, including the possibility of abuse; (4) intervening to ameliorate any symptomatic problem behaviors in the child; (5) assessing family interactional patterns, parenting styles, and the role or roles the child assumes; and (6) assisting parents in developing appropriate parenting skills and providing proper nurturance.

Bepko cautions that when and if the parent stops drinking, the problems for the child do not cease. Roles previously assumed now become inappropriate and ineffective. She suggests that treatment goals during this period should be (1) to provide an atmosphere in which children can express their feelings about the change in the family; (2) to help the child adjust to the change and find a new, more appropriate place in the family; and (3) to provide instruction and support to the parents to help them find new ways of responding to the children and repairing the damage that may have been caused during the period of alcohol abuse. She cautions that children's typical reactions will include anger, jealousy, competitiveness, and a sense of betrayal or abandonment. The children are divested of their "power" and must learn new roles, often more subordinate ones. The initial period of sobriety can be as filled with turmoil as the alcoholic phase — until new and more appropriate roles and patterns of family interaction are established.

The effects of parental alcoholism do not end when the parent assumes sobriety or the child becomes an adult. Wegscheider's (1981) research suggests that twice as many children of alcoholics marry before they reach 16 years of age; juvenile delinquency is higher in alcoholic families; there is twice as much mental illness in children with alcoholic families; and the suicide rate is higher than that of disadvantaged children. According to Newlon and Furrow (1986), their review of the literature suggests that "children who come from alcoholic environments suffer from a high incidence of behavioral, emotional, and psychological problems, not to mention the high risk of becoming 'problem drinkers' themselves or choosing an alcoholic spouse" (p. 287). They believe the logical place to provide early assistance and intervention for children from alcoholic homes is the school. They describe identification procedures and step-by-step guidance lessons to help these children understand alcoholism as a family disease and the necessity for all members to seek help.

Brake (1988) believes that children of alcoholics need a counselor to help them understand they can love their parents without liking their behavior and that these children need help in feeling worthwhile as individuals. She suggests group counseling preceded by an individual session. Films and books may be needed to encourage talking because these children have learned to avoid conflict by not talking. Time and patience will be required to build trust. Buwick, Martin, and Martin (1988) add to the preceding strategies the counseling techniques of modeling consistency to provide limits and add stability to the children's lives, responding to both positive and negative behaviors, and arranging conditions to involve children in success experiences. Wilson and Blocher (1990) suggest that counselors conduct developmental support groups incorporating bibliotherapy, role-play of problem situations, RET techniques for assessing behavior and coping more effectively, Gestalt activities to express feelings, assertiveness to express needs and rights, and relaxation techniques to reduce stress. O'Rourke (1990) provides an outline for a children's support group that includes attention to the preceding needs and provides information about alcoholism for young participants. We would add that these children need activities to improve their self-esteem, assertiveness training to teach them to say "no" to drugs and alcohol, and help with developing problem-solving and decision-making skills. Excellent drug education programs are now available to counselors working with these children.

Lawson, Peterson, and Lawson (1983) emphasize that in looking at the problem, "it is impossible to avoid the idea of prevention. Treating the behavioral or emotional problems of children who have lived with an alcoholic parent is surely a major step in preventing these high-risk children from becoming alcoholics themselves" (p. 185). They recommend that prevention procedures include either treatment centers that will provide group support for the children or educational programming and support groups in the schools. They point out that parents have modeled drinking to get drunk or avoid reality—not responsible behaviors to teach children; therefore, parents will need help in becoming more aware of the models they present to their children. Parents can be encouraged to educate their children about alcoholism and to develop effective communication skills in order to become more aware of their children's concerns about drinking. Parents need to develop new parenting strategies, assist their children to improve self-esteem, and teach them to make good choices. Lawson et al.'s (1983) "prevention fraction" includes coping skills competence, self-esteem, and support networks.

In 1985, an Associated Press article cited a study by *Family Circle* and the Parent's Resource Institute for Drug Education indicating that drug and alcohol abuse is spreading into grammar schools. According to this study, more than 500,000 children 10 to 13 years old admitted getting drunk once a week. Information published by Cumberland Heights Alcohol and Drug Treatment Center (n.d.) reports that over 50 percent of seventh graders have tried alcohol and that 13 is the average age at which young people begin to drink. These children learned at least some of their behavior from parent models who were or are alcoholics. The problem must be addressed, and counselors are in an excellent position to help.

LATCHKEY CHILDREN

There has been increasing concern for the past few years about the number of children left at home unsupervised while parents work. These children are called *latchkey children* because they carry a key to lock the house as they leave after their parents in the mornings or to unlock the house when they return before their parents in the afternoon. Some experts believe that 15 to 20 percent of early–elementary schoolchildren carry their own latch-key, and approximately 45 percent of late elementary schoolchildren are unsupervised for some period in the day (Peterson & Magrab, 1989). Experts conclude that the developmental implications of children's self-care are uncertain because of the lack of research in this area.

The children's activities during these times of being on their own can be problematic because of the risk of injury, emotional reactions to being alone, and poor selection of activities (Peterson, 1989). Peterson concludes from her review of the literature that children are more likely to be injured when an adult is not present in the home; that although research is not clear on children's emotional reactions to staying alone, many experience negative feelings (anxiety, worry, fear); and that children spend their unsupervised hours watching too much television, not getting enough physical exercise, snacking inappropriately, and postponing homework and chores until later in the evening. She suggests as alternatives programs for preparing children for self-care, "neighborhood mothers," activities in or near the school, and expanded child care in schools or businesses. In addition, Peterson provides a checklist for checking the home for security from strangers, from fire, from poisoning, and for safe use of equipment.

Unfortunately, most children do not know how to care for themselves adequately, and direct instruction is necessary for them to learn to handle situations effectively. Bundy and Boser (1987) have developed a group guidance unit to address self-care issues, focusing on how parents and children could develop a self-care plan, personal safety at home, handling emergency and nonemergency situations, and "being in charge." This unit resulted in positive effects for both parents and children.

Society has generally felt that being a latchkey child will negatively affect the child's development. Peterson and Magrab (1989) point out that some indict "working mothers" for leaving their children, but they suggest that communities must recognize the changing values and lifestyles of the present and find ways to support working families. Research by Lovko and Ullman (1989) comparing latchkey children to non-latchkey children indicates there are no differences in levels of anxiety, social ability, or behavior problems. Any variance in the two groups' adjustment levels was accounted for by the demographic and background variables of sex, income, and interaction with other children. The researchers are quick to point out the limitations in their study and suggest that adjustment depends on many variables still not clearly defined.

Counseling with latchkey children may include listening for fears and anxieties about being left alone and helping the child cope with these feelings. The child may have concerns about what to say when the phone or doorbell rings, who will care for the child if he or she gets hurt or sick, or what to do about boredom or loneliness. O'Brien (1989) reports that many families make a large chart for the child, listing activities that should be carried out during unsupervised periods to overcome boredom or loneliness. Group discussions with role-play will provide an opportunity for children to voice their concerns and to practice appropriate techniques for answering the door or phone, reacting to emergency and nonemergency situations, and coping with other problems that may arise.

HOMELESS CHILDREN

Concerns about the increasing number of homeless families are increasing for many communities. Eddowes and Hranitz (1989) report that Children's Defense Fund statistics indicate that there are approximately three million homeless people in America, with more than a third of this number including families with children. Dail (1990) describes these families, based on her review of the literature. Although most homeless people in the past have been male, a growing number today are single-parent families headed by women. She states that approximately 50 percent of the women heading homeless families are between 17 and 25 years of age; the majority have never been married or are separated or divorced. Most have some high school education, and a few attended college for a period. These mothers have few social or family support systems and tend to distrust people. About 50 percent of homeless children are under 5 years old. They are typically undernourished, and many experience delayed development with symptoms of acting-out behavior and physical problems (Dail, 1990). They may have difficulty with language, attention to the task, physical-coordination problems, and symptoms of anxiety. Over one half of the children over 5 years need mental health treatment. School performance is low because of poor attendance and confused lives. These children may be abused physically or psychologically because of their parents' stress (Dail, 1990).

Eddowes and Hranitz (1989) suggest denial of education is the most critical problem of homeless children. They contend that these children are prohibited from entering school because of requirements such as residency, proof of age, immunization, and school records. Eddowes and Hranitz point out that if the children do enter school, they are often ridiculed by their peers and not accepted by their teachers; in addition, they receive little support from their parents.

The U.S. Congress passed a law in 1987 requiring that homeless children be admitted to schools. Eddowes and Hranitz (1989) suggest that communities could also provide greater access to day care, counseling, and nutritional and educational support for homeless children.

Counseling tasks include facilitating the child's entrance into school, helping the child and his or her family find some kind of stability in their lives, assisting the child to overcome excessive fears and distrust of people, and being alert to the possibility of abuse. Counselors will need a variety of referral resources to help the child meet physical needs such as shelter, food, and medical care. Assessing the child's educational level and helping him or her develop social skills will require time, energy, and patience.

The counselor will want to avoid being influenced by such generalizations about the homeless as that they are mentally ill, are unmotivated, could find a job if they wanted to, or abuse alcohol or drugs. Education is the best method for overcoming the problems of the homeless, but it will require a broad spectrum of services within the school and community. The counselor may be called on to coordinate these services and act as an advocate for the child.

SUICIDAL BEHAVIORS

There is a popular misconception that children's lives are so carefree they do not have suicidal thoughts and do not commit suicidal acts. Professionals working with children know this is not true. Herring (1990) states that nearly 200 children younger than 14 years commit suicide each year. Nelson and Crawford (1990) report that suicide is the second most likely cause of death in 15- to 19-year-olds. In a survey Nelson and Crawford conducted, counselors in one state indicated they had made contact with 187 elementary-grade students considering suicide, and 26 of these students had actually attempted the act. Most researchers question the statistics relative to the incidence of child suicide, pointing out that they are probably underestimates because of a reluctance in our society to admit that our children commit suicide.

Herring (1990) suggests that child suicide attempts are "silent" many times. Parents and physicians may conceal the suicide to avoid embarrassing the family. Many "accidents" are actually child suicides (Stefanowski-Harding, 1990). Children sometimes run in front of vehicles or jump off high places when they want to commit suicide (Herring, 1990). Stefanowski-Harding (1990) also reports that an increasing number of children under 12 are treated for "accidental overdoses." She points out that children rarely leave suicide notes because they cannot write or are not in the habit of writing their communications.

The question of why a child would attempt suicide is complex. Some researchers believe that suicidal children are highly sensitive, have a low tolerance for frustration, and have feelings of depression, guilt, hostility, and anger that they are unable to express (Stefanowski-Harding, 1990). Nelson and Crawford (1990) asked counselors to indicate the factors they thought contributed to suicidal attempts and completions in the group they saw. Family problems such as divorce, separation, and parental alcoholism were rated as highly probable contributors. Peer pressure and pressure to achieve academically were ranked second and third. Drug abuse, physical handicap, and economic stress were ranked very low. Stefanowski-Harding (1990), too, found several researchers who indicated that family problems related to death, divorce, separation, physical assault, rejection, or a suicidal parent were probable factors related to child suicide. Herring (1990) reports that children who have a family history of suicide are nine times more likely to take their own life than those who do not have this history. Boys are more likely to complete the suicidal act than girls because boys use more violent means in their attempts. Stefanowski-Harding (1990) cautions that children with learning disabilities or other learning difficulties that cause constant frustration are more likely to attempt suicide and that gifted children may attempt suicide because their advanced intellectual ability can make it difficult for them to relate to children their own age.

Thoughts of, or attempts to commit, suicide often accompany a poor self-concept and feelings of hopelessness, worthlessness, depression, or guilt. A depressed or suicidal child may be extremely quiet and withdrawn or highly active and agitated. Depression may be masked by overactivity, gaiety, or acting-out behavior. Feelings of depression leading to self-destructive attempts or acts frequently follow the death of loved ones, significant personal or material losses, events that profoundly affect self-esteem, or other traumatic life crises. Clues may include chronic sleeplessness, loss of appetite, withdrawal, or any extreme behavioral change.

The incidence of child suicide has increased dramatically during the past few years. No comment or sign indicating depression and thoughts of self-destruction should go unnoticed.

1. If you feel a child could be seriously contemplating suicide, suggest to the parents that they consult a doctor or psychiatrist.

2. Never hesitate to consult with or refer suicidal children to someone thoroughly trained in suicide prevention — suicide-prevention centers, clinics, or psychiatrists.

3. Use techniques to enhance the self-concept of children who exhibit suicidal tendencies.

4. Children with self-destructive or self-mutilating tendencies, such as head banging, holding of breath, and hair pulling, have responded to behavior modification techniques in which acceptable behaviors are rewarded and destructive tendencies punished by penalties such as withdrawing privileges or ignoring the behaviors. Children with severe tendencies usually require full-time supervision and psychotherapeutic intervention in a residential situation (Blanco, 1972).

5. Never ignore threats, hints, and continued comments about destroying oneself, "leaving this world," "you're going to miss me," or "life's not worth living." These comments may be attention-getting, but if children must use these techniques to get attention, they need help. Follow up the "threat" immediately with active listening in an attempt to discover the feelings or events that brought on the self-destructive feelings (see Chapter 4).

6. At a time of crisis, listen to the child carefully, in a nonjudgmental manner. Have the child tell you *everything* that has happened during the previous few hours or days. You may gain some understanding or knowledge of factors contributing to the depression.

7. Suicidal children need permission to call, and the phone number of, a person (the counselor or another close and understanding friend) they feel they can talk with in times of distress.

8. The parents of a suicidal child should be made aware of the child's feelings and thoughts and helped to understand the situation without panic or guilt. Counsel with the parents about how to listen to and talk with the child. Consult with them concerning danger signals, and make a plan for handling crises should they arise.

9. If you suspect a child has suicidal tendencies, confront the child with your thoughts and feelings. You will not be placing the thought in the child's mind, but you may provide an opening and opportunity for the child to discuss the troublesome thoughts and feelings.

10. Talk with suicidal children about what has happened in their lives recently. Losses of loved ones, pets, and other significant objects in the children's lives; feelings of personal failure; feelings of extreme shame or grief; or other traumatic events contribute to suicidal thoughts. Allow children to express their feelings without being judgmental, glossing over, or denying their right to these feelings.

11. If suicidal children admit to self-destructive thoughts, ask about their plan. A well thought out plan is a significant danger signal.

12. Ask suicidal children to tell you about their fantasies or dreams.

Ask them to draw a picture or write out their thoughts. These techniques often give the adult some insight into the child's thoughts and feelings.

13. Often children do not understand death as final and irreversible; therefore, any child who is seriously disturbed or depressed needs careful attention. The months following the threat are also crucial, and careful attention should be continued until the conflict is completely resolved.

14. A sudden "recovery" after severe depression may be a warning signal. It often means a decision has been made to end one's life.

Many writers in this area suggest psychological education and peer-group counseling as preventive measures. In addition to forming peer-counseling groups, Herring (1990) suggests that counselors advocate that psychological education become a part of the middle school curriculum, that parents be involved in training sessions to help them understand the issue of suicide, and that counselors serve in a consultant role, providing information and knowledge about what to do and where to refer clients.

Siehl (1990) believes that all schools should have a "disaster plan" to use in the event of a suicide, just as they have a plan for hurricanes, tornados, earthquakes, and other traumatic events. Siehl advocates that schools do the following:

1. Develop a team of resource people to handle the emotional crisis;
2. Present inservice training programs to the entire staff on the causes, warning signs, and sources of help for suicidal persons;
3. Establish a network to inform all faculty of the facts of the tragedy;
4. Designate special crisis centers for children needing additional help;
5. Develop a checklist of activities to be included in the classroom announcement;
6. Plan for cautions about the dangers in the days following a suicide;
7. Carry out home visits;
8. Schedule special events or memorial services to help everyone draw closer;
9. Develop guidelines for media coverage; and
10. Develop procedures to continue alertness for several months.

Because helping professionals are aware that children may "imitate" other children who commit suicide, such a plan, along with psychological education and group counseling, is appropriate for counselors to consider.

CHILDREN IN SATANIC CULTS

Although the typical young person involved in cults or satanic rituals is usually an adolescent, Rudin (1990) states that the satanically involved can be as young as 11 years of age. In addition, some children are born into satanic cults that have been practicing rituals for generations. The typical youth involved in devil worship is one who is troubled and alienated from his or her significant groups. The young person who might be attracted to the drug culture is also a prime candidate for the occult.

Rudin (1990) describes the typical cult member as being very intelligent, idealistic, and high achieving. The young person involved in satanic worship is also intelligent and curious but is usually an underachiever with low self-esteem. These people have feelings of powerlessness, have few friends, and are often isolated from their families. They are drawn to negative groups because of their need for friendships and power. Rudin cautions school personnel to watch for black clothing; jewelry with satanic symbols; drawings or symbols of demons, death, and mutilation; satanic literature; and other paraphernalia. Wheeler, Wood, and Hatch (1988) describe such common symbols as the abbreviation DW for "devil worship," the number 666, upside-down crosses, dripping blood, candles, daggers, and a goat. Young people in satanic cults may like heavy-metal music because of its emphasis on death and destruction.

Rudin (1990) warns that child abuse is prevalent in cults because children are not valued. These children may or may not attend school. However, Rudin strongly recommends that school personnel learn to recognize the signs of satanic involvement and schedule educational programs for staff and students. The International Cult Education Program (P.O. Box 1232, Gracie Station, New York, NY 10028) will provide speakers, literature, resource lists, and other materials to assist with educational programs.

Wheeler, Wood, and Hatch (1988) suggest that counselors help the young person to understand the motivation for his or her involvement and to verbalize his or her feelings of anger, pain, frustration, or alienation. They recommend that counselors help their clients find new and better ways to feel power in their lives and to develop better personal relationships. Family counseling is helpful, because most children feel alienated from parents and other family members. Children deeply involved in satanic rituals or the occult may need to be removed from all contact with their present environment. They will require intense, continuing efforts to improve their self-esteem, to help them to find positive relationships within their families and peer groups, and to establish some control over their lives.

It is not unusual for young people to have a casual interest in reading about the occult; however, parents, teachers, counselors, and friends should become concerned when the young person retreats from more positive group relationships and shows changes in behavior that indicate alienation and withdrawal.

Counselors working with children involved in the occult should be aware of these children's feelings of alienation, powerlessness, and low self-esteem. Such children will need to be listened to intently in order to understand all the underlying reasons for their involvement.

COUNSELING CHILDREN ABOUT AIDS

Because of the widespread media coverage of concerns related to Acquired Immune Deficiency Syndrome (AIDS), Holcomb (1990) sought to ascertain how elementary schoolchildren feel about AIDS and what information they have about the issues. He surveyed 224 fourth-grade children, asking them questions to assess their basic knowledge and attitudes about AIDS. Holcomb's results indicate that these children knew AIDS was transmitted by direct sexual contact, by direct blood-to-blood contact, and by sharing needles with an infected person. Most knew that one does not contract AIDS by hugging or shaking hands with an infected person. They were less sure about whether people contract AIDS from toilet seats, food prepared by an AIDS-infected person, and swimming pools. Kissing was very risky, according to these children, as was drinking from the glass of an AIDS-infected person. Some expressed concern over mosquito bites and donating blood. Over 50 percent of the children interviewed feared or worried about AIDS, and 72 percent said they would be worried about a child with AIDS in their classroom. Holcomb recommends that counselors make sure AIDS education is included in their curriculum, that they find out the areas of misinformation and provide correct information, and that educational groups be held for parents to help them learn to talk with their children. He also encourages counselors to hold classroom groups to discuss fears and worries about AIDS and to form small groups for children with excessive fears and worries.

A Kappan special report on AIDS (Reed, 1988) estimates that, by 1991, 10,000 to 20,000 children under 13 years may be infected with the disease. In spite of the statement by the Centers for Disease Control (CDC) that casual contact between schoolchildren poses no risk, fear of AIDS-infected children prevails among many parents. The American Academy of Pediatrics issued a statement similar to that of the CDC, recommending that children with AIDS be allowed to attend school except in cases where the child bites, cannot control bodily functions, or has open lesions (Reed, 1988). The Deputy Director of the National Association of State Boards of Education (NASBE), Brenda Welburn (1989), states that it is now known "that HIV is not transmitted through saliva or urine" and that the "possibility that the AIDS virus would be transmitted through simple exposure to blood is extremely low."

In spite of assurances that AIDS is not communicated through casual contact, the fear of AIDS has caused children with the virus to be ostracized from school and playmates. Bruhn (1989) states that public fears are unjustified in most cases because the HIV virus is fragile. These fears result from ignorance about the disease and are present in people of all educational levels (Bruhn, 1989). Protecting children is an emotional issue that troubles parents, teachers, and other school personnel. Parents often believe their children can contact AIDS by sharing toys or school supplies or by touching a child with AIDS (Walker & Hulecki, 1989) and therefore have protested strongly when a child identified as having AIDS is in the school system. Schools interested in developing clear policies and procedures regarding attendance, confidentiality, mandatory testing, and guidelines for dealing with AIDS cases in the school may wish to contact NASBE to obtain their publication developed in cooperation with the Centers for Disease Control, *Someone at School Has AIDS: A Guide to Developing Policies for Students and Staff Members Who Are Infected with HIV*, published in 1989.

Most writers advocate AIDS education for teachers, parents, and other children as the best way to help children with AIDS. However, AIDS education requires discussion of topics such as homosexuality, drugs, and condoms. Parents often do not want these topics discussed with their children, fearing that such discussion might encourage sexual acting-out (Kirp & Epstein, 1989). Communities that do provide educational programs usually accept children with AIDS more readily and with less fear. Bennett (1987) recommended that children should be helped to develop clear standards of right and wrong, as well as tough ways of resisting pressure to engage in dangerous activities. He also advised adults to set a good example and to teach children about AIDS. Shaffer, Godwin, and Richmond (1987) suggest that when talking to children about AIDS, adults should provide credible information appropriate to the age level of the children without overwhelming them with information. Books, videos, pamphlets, and other materials may be used to clarify misunderstandings and stimulate discussions.

Counselors also must be ready to deal with the feelings of children with AIDS about themselves and their disease, as well as with the range of emotions that accompany the realization that one has a fatal disease. Daily activities for the child can be problematic because he or she may be isolated from friends and not physically able to participate in games and sports. Children with AIDS will need supportive counseling as well as counseling to deal with specific concerns.

As with other issues that affect children, counselors will want to examine their own feeling about children with AIDS. Counselors who have not resolved their own fears about contracting AIDS or who hold values that interfere with acceptance of the child should resolve these personal issues before working with children who have AIDS.

SUGGESTED READINGS FOR
CONCERNS OF CHILDREN*

Abandonment

Byars, Betsy. *The house of wings.* Illustrated by Daniel Schwartz. New York: Viking Press, 1972 (142 pages).

A wounded crane and the care an old man gives it teach Sammy to love the grandfather he couldn't understand before. Ages 10–12.

Clymer, Eleanor. *Luke was there.* New York: Holt, Rinehart & Winston, 1973 (74 pages). Julius and his brother Danny are sent to a children's home when their mother has to be hospitalized. Already abandoned by his father, uncle, and stepfather, Julius is further upset when Luke, a counselor at the home, has to leave. Ages 8–12.

Furlong, Monica. *Wise child.* New York: Knopf, 1987 (228 pages). Nine-year-old Wise Child goes to live with the witch woman Juniper after her parents abandon her. Ages 11 and up.

Hahn, Mary Downing. *Tallahassee Higgins.* New York: Clarion Books, 1987 (180 pages). Tallahassee Higgins has to come to grips with a new lifestyle after her mother, Liz, leaves her with an aunt and uncle in Maryland so Liz can pursue a career in Hollywood. Ages 11 and up.

Howard, Ellen. *Edith herself.* New York: Atheneum, 1987 (131 pages). After her mother's death, Edith goes to live with her elder sister and dour brother-in-law. Their stern Christian household makes it difficult for her to adjust, and her epileptic seizures seem to be recurring. Ages 10–12.

Adoption/Foster Homes

Cohen, Miriam. *Robert and Dawn Marie 4ever.* New York: Harper & Row, 1986. Fourteen-year-old Robert is a "throwaway"—unwanted by his mother and out on the street again after her latest rejection. His wandering brings him to Margaret Mary, a motherly, chatty woman. Ages 11–14.

Greenberg, Judith E. *Adopted.* New York: Watts, 1987 (32 pages). Sarah asks questions about her own adoption as an infant when her parents adopt a baby boy. Sarah's parents and extended family explain that everyone is special not because of the way he or she joins a family, but because of each person's uniqueness and loving behavior. Ages 6–9.

Howard, Ellen. *Her own song.* New York: Atheneum, 1988 (160 pages). Teased by her classmates for being adopted, Mellie is friendless and lonely. Because her adoptive mother is dead, Mellie is raised by her fa-

*Sincere appreciation and gratitude are given to Elinor Brown and Flo Plemmons, Linden Elementary School, Oak Ridge, TN; to Pamela Viator Strange and Beth Eades, Farragut Intermediate School, Knoxville, TN; to Katrina Cannon, Flenniken Elementary School, Knoxville, TN; to Harriet W. Thompson, Knoxville, TN; and to Margaret Sumner and Jan Walker, Austin Peay State University, Clarksville, TN; for their diligent efforts in compiling this list of suggested readings for children. Sincere appreciation and gratitude is also extended to Alicia Barber, librarian at Barksdale Elementary School, Clarksville, TN, for updating the suggested readings for this edition.

Annotations are derived from the following sources:

1. Booklist—including *Reference Books Bulletin.* New York: American Library Association, 1985, 1986, and 1987.

2. *The Elementary School Library Collection: A Guide to Books and Other Media.* Williamsport, PA: Brodart, 1984.

3. Dreyer, Sharon Spredemann. *The Bookfinder: When Kids Need Books.* Circle Pines, MN: American Guidance Service, 1985.

4. Yaakov, J. (1987). *Children's Catalog: 1987 Supplement to the Fifteenth Edition.* New York: H. W. Wilson.

5. Goldberg, J. (1988). *Children's Catalog: 1988 Supplement to the Fifteenth Edition.* New York: H. W. Wilson.

6. Goldberg, J. (1989). *Children's Catalog: 1989 Supplement to the Fifteenth Edition.* New York: H. W. Wilson.

ther, Bill, a stern and undemonstrative man, and by her aunt. She develops a friendship with the Chinese laundryman whom everyone despises. It is through the laundryman that Mellie is able to gain a new sense of self-worth and discover the truth behind her dreams. Ages 10 and up.

Hughes, Dean. *Family pose.* New York: Atheneum, 1989 (184 pages). David runs away from his uncaring foster family and ends up sleeping in the warm hallway of the Hotel Jefferson. He is found by Paul, the bellboy, who is a reformed alcoholic. Paul risks losing his job by letting David stay in an unused room. Eventually David reveals his name and why he is a runaway on the Seattle streets. Paul and his coworkers are good to David, and they consult Paul's friend at Social Services about David's future. Ages 11 and up.

Johnston, Norma. *To Jess, with love and memories.* New York: Bantam/Starfire, 1986 (120 pages). Sixteen-year-old Jess learns that she is adopted and that her beloved late Aunt Faith was her natural mother. Ages 12–15.

Krementz, Jill. *How it feels to be adopted.* New York: Knopf, 1982 (107 pages). Interviews with adopted children and adoptive families about their experiences and feelings concerning adoption. Ages 8–12.

Mills, Claudia. *Boardwalk with hotel.* New York: Macmillan/Collier, 1985 (131 pages). Eleven-year-old Jessica Jarrel has always known she was adopted, but her babysitter gives her an interesting insight into why her parents wanted her: "They were trying to have kids and they thought they couldn't," so they adopted her. Ages 10–12.

Myers, Walter Dean. *Me, Mop and the Moondance Kid.* New York: Delacorte Press, 1988 (154 pages). Eleven-year-old T. J. and his younger brother Billy, a.k.a. the Moondance Kid, have been living with their adoptive parents for about six months and are settling in well. They are worried that their friend Mop may be transferred to an orphanage some distance away. Mop decides to join T. J.'s Little League team in order to get close to the coach and his wife, whom Mop suspects are interested in adopting her. Ages 10–12.

Child Abuse

Anderson, Deborah, and Finne, Martha. *Jason's story.* Minneapolis, MN: Dillon Press, 1986 (45 pages). A young boy is taken from his neglectful mother as a baby and placed in foster care. The mother claims her child again when he is 2 but then becomes abusive; Jason is sent to another foster family until his mother is really able to care for him. Ages 7–10.

Anderson, Deborah, and Finne, Martha. *Michael's story.* Minneapolis, MN: Dillon Press, 1986 (45 pages). Michael is an emotionally abused child. His parents continually berate him, and as a result he believes himself to be stupid as well as unloved. A supportive school counselor suggests that Michael and his parents undergo family counseling. Ages 7–10.

Byars, Betsy. *The pinballs.* New York: Harper & Row, 1977 (136 pages). Three children of diverse backgrounds are placed with the Masons, who have taken care of many other foster children, and begin to help one another accept things as they are. Ages 11 and up.

Hall, Lynn. *The boy in the off-white hat.* New York: Scribner's, 1984 (87 pages). Nine-year-old Shane becomes involved in a tragic relationship with a businessman who is new in town. Only through the sensitivity of his friend and the ultimate support of his mother is he able to confess the relationship and get the help he needs to cope with it. Ages 11–14.

Kehoe, Patricia. *Something happened and I'm scared to tell.* Seattle: Parenting Press, 1987 (26 pages). This book is designed to encourage child victims to speak out and to give them the concepts that will help their recovery. It is written for the very young child who is a suspected victim of sexual or physical abuse. Ages 3–7.

Newman, Susan. *Never say yes to a stranger: What every child should know to stay safe.* Photographs by George Tiboni. New York: Putnam/Perigee, 1985 (128 pages). A book aimed at teaching the dangers of strangers and what children should do when they find themselves in trouble. Ages 4–10.

Quiri, Patricia. *Stranger danger.* New York: Messner, 1985 (40 pages). Strangers come in all shapes and sizes. A stranger is someone you have never seen before; a stranger is someone whose name you do not know. This book presents many tips to keep children safe from strangers who mean to harm them. Ages 6–12.

Roberts, Willo Davis. *Don't hurt Laurie!* New York: Atheneum, 1977 (176 pages). Laurie's mother, Annabelle, blames the girl's continual burns, bruises, broken bones, and knife cuts on clumsiness until Laurie dares to tell her stepbrother and grandmother of the real and growing problem of Annabelle's unstable and violent temper. Ages 10–13.

Russell, Pamela, and Stone, Beth. *Do you have a secret?* Illustrated by Mary McKee. Minneapolis, MN: CompCare Publications, 1986 (24 pages). The simple text effectively presents the concepts of secrets and trust in a manner that encourages an abused child to seek help. Ages 10–14.

Stanek, Muriel. *Don't hurt me, Mama.* Niles, IL: Albert Whitman, 1983 (32 pages). A young girl narrates the story of how her mother begins neglecting and beating her until school officials intervene with a connection to the community health center. Ages 5–8.

Wachter, Oralee. *Close to home.* Illustrated by Jane Aaron. New York: Scholastic, 1986 (46 pages). Wachter addresses the child-safety issue, this time in a quartet of stories that portray abduction situations. In a nonthreatening vignette, a girl and her babysitter take a ride in the sitter's friend's car — without Mother's knowledge or permission. Ages 8–11.

Weik, Mary. *The jazz man.* New York: Aladdin, 1977 (48 pages). The wonderful music from a room across the court in his Harlem tenement alleviates the loneliness of a lame 9-year-old boy until his parents' absence threatens to become abandonment. Ages 8–12.

Woolverton, Linda. *Running before the wind.* Boston: Houghton Mifflin, 1987 (152 pages). Thirteen-year-old Kelly finds running to be her only outlet for her confused feelings of love and hate for her abusive father, particularly after his sudden death brings both relief and guilt. Ages 12 and up.

Children's Worries

Dunn, Phoebe, and Dunn, Tris. *Feelings.* Words by Judy Dunn. Mankato, MN: Creative Educational

Society, 1971 (40 pages). Text interprets and photographs illustrate various emotions. Ages 7–12.

Leiner, Katherine. *Both my parents work.* Photographs by Steve Sax. New York: Watts, 1986 (45 pages). Nine children who have families in which both parents work outside the home talk about what their parents do and, as a result, how their own days are structured. Ages 7–10.

Levine, Abby, and Levine, Sarah. *Sometimes I wish I were Mindy.* Pictures by Blanche Sims. Niles, IL: Albert Whitman, 1986 (32 pages). Some people are rich and some aren't, and that's the truth of the matter—a truth that won't go away no matter how you look at it. A wise, humorous look at a common situation. Ages 4–6.

Little, Jean. *Different dragons.* New York: Viking/Kestrel, 1987 (123 pages). Ben faces many challenges on his first stay away from home without his family. He visits his Aunt Rose, whom his brother said was mean. He has to sleep alone. The bossy girl next door, a thunderstorm, and a big dog are other challenges Ben must deal with. Ages 9–11.

Morrison, Carl V., and Nafus, Dorothy. *Can I help how I feel?* Drawings by James and Ruth McCrea. New York: Atheneum, 1976 (124 pages). The authors use case histories to illustrate the distressful emotions of young people. Ages 7–12.

Oram, Hiawyn. *Jenna and the troublemaker.* Illustrated by Tony Ross. New York: Holt, Rinehart & Winston, 1986 (27 pages). For children who wonder where their troubles come from, Oram introduces the Troublemaker. A variant on an old Yiddish folktale, this message-laced story is lightened by Ross's zany cartoon-style artwork that brings out all the story's wry humor. Ages 5–7.

Rosenberg, Maxine B. *Living in two worlds.* Illustrated with photographs by George Ancona. New York: Lothrop, 1986 (46 pages). Ancona's searching camera zooms in on children of biracial heritage as Rosenberg's thoughtful text introduces five subjects and uses their experiences to explain notions of race and describe common attitudes toward racial mixing. Ages 8–12.

Schwartz, Joel L. *Shrink.* New York: Dell/Yearling, 1986 (119 pages). When Mike's parents take him to a psychiatrist because of poor grades, he finds that needing someone to talk to is not the disgrace he thought it would be. Humorous and warm. Ages 11–14.

Shaw, Diana. *Make the most of a good thing: You!* Boston: Atlantic Monthly Press, 1986 (209 pages). Shaw addresses preteen girls on the basics of taking good care of themselves as they pass into their teenage years. The tone is warm and positive, and the information and advice are sensible. Sections cover physical changes experienced by girls. Ages 11–14.

Smith, Robert Kimmel. *Mostly Michael.* New York: Delacorte Press, 1987 (184 pages). Michael's diary reflects the ups and downs of his 11th year as he copes with braces, the school play, a little sister not yet potty trained, and a big spelling bee. Ages 10–12.

Stolz, Mary. *Storm in the night.* New York: Harper & Row, 1988 (unpaged). Thomas, his grandfather, and Ringo the cat go out on the porch after a power failure during a thunderstorm. Grandfather tells Thomas a story of his own childhood fear of storms and how concern for his equally frightened pet helped him overcome it. Ages 6–9.

Viorst, Judith. *The good-bye book.* New York: Atheneum, 1988 (unpaged). Full-color pictures show parents going about the business of getting ready for an evening out as their small boy throws a tantrum in the foreground. Ages 6–8.

Weller, Frances Ward. *Boat song.* New York: Macmillan, 1987 (169 pages). Eleven-year-old Jonno already feels alienated from his family because he is quieter than his brothers and sisters and overawed by his father's "renaissance" brilliance. A summer vacation in Maine emphasizes the father-son conflict, but a Scottish bagpiper named Bob Loud reaches out to Jonno with his music, stories, and individualistic perspective. Ages 10–12.

White, Ruth. *Sweet Creek Holler.* New York: Farrar, Straus & Giroux, 1988 (215 pages). Ginny Short, her elder sister June, and their mother come under the hostile scrutiny of new neighbors when the family moves out of their coal-mining town to a house farther down the valley. Ginny must adjust to a new life, school, and friends. Ages 11 and up.

Children with AIDS

Colman, Warren. *Understanding and preventing AIDS.* Chicago: Children's Press, 1987 (123 pages). Surveys the history and symptoms of the deadly disease and discusses how it spreads, how it may be prevented, and how it may eventually be cured. Ages 11 and up.

Hausherr, Rosmarie. *Children and the AIDS virus: A book for children, parents, and teachers.* New York: Clarion Books, 1989 (48 pages). The author

examines the lives of two children who have AIDS. She seeks to explain what a virus is, how the AIDS virus affects the body, and how it is contracted. Ages 6–9.

Silverstein, Alvin. *Learning about AIDS.* Hillside, NJ: Enslow Publishers, 1989 (64 pages). This book provides an introduction to the causes and treatment of AIDS. Ages 10–12.

Death

Barker, Peggy. *What happened when Grandma died.* Illustrated by Patricia Mattozzi. St. Louis, MO: Concordia, 1984 (28 pages). A tenderly pictured yet forthright story about the death of a beloved relative. A message to parents is appended. Ages 5–8.

Bauer, Marion Dane. *On my honor.* New York: Clarion Books, 1986 (112 pages). In this powerful, soul-stirring novel, Joel comes to understand the power of choice after his daredevil friend drowns in a forbidden, raging river. Ages 10–13.

Boyd, Candy Dawson. *Breadsticks and blessing places.* New York: Macmillan, 1985 (210 pages). A young African American girl, Toni Douglas, faces the challenges of adolescence with no more than the usual trepidation until her best friend, Susan, is killed by a drunken driver. Ages 11–14.

Cleaver, Vera. *Belle Pruitt.* Philadelphia: Lippincott, 1988 (169 pages). Eleven-year-old Belle is left to cope with the devastating effects on her family when her adored baby brother suddenly dies of pneumonia. Ages 10–12.

Clifton, Lucille. *Everett Anderson's good-bye.* Illustrated by Ann Grifalconi. New York: Holt, Rinehart & Winston, 1983 (32 pages). A little boy whose father has died experiences the five stages of grief. Ages 4 and up.

Coerr, Eleanor. *The Josefina story quilt.* Pictures by Bruce Degen. New York: Harper & Row, 1986 (64 pages). Soon after the family arrives in California by wagon train, Faith's pet hen, Josefina, dies. The family creates a special patchwork quilt that recalls the events of Josefina's trip. Ages 4–8.

Cohen, Janice. *I had a friend named Peter: Talking to children about the death of a friend.* New York: Morrow, 1987 (unpaged). Peter is run over while chasing a ball into the street, and Betsy's parents have the sad task of telling their daughter and helping her cope with the tragedy. The feelings and questions that arise when a child's playmate dies are presented in the gently told story. Ages 6–10.

Cohen, Miriam. *Jim's dog Muffins.* Illustrated by Lillian Hoban. New York: Greenwillow Books, 1984 (32 pages). Jim's friends exhibit a wide variety of reactions after his dog is killed by a garbage truck, but Jim is helped in accepting the death. Ages 5–8.

Fayerweather Street School Staff. *The kid's book about death and dying: By and for kids.* (Edited by Eric E. Rofes.) Boston: Little, Brown, 1985 (119 pages). Based on a yearlong discussion group on death and dying with children ages 11–14. This book should do much to foster learning about and acceptance of death. Ages 10–14.

Gould, Deborah Lee. *Grandpa's slide show.* New York: Lothrop, Lee & Shepard Books, 1987 (unpaged). Sam and Douglas always watch a slide show when they visit their grandpa. After grandpa dies, they watch the show to remember him. Ages 6–9.

Krementz, Jill. *How it feels when a parent dies.* New York: Knopf, 1981 (110 pages). Twenty children speak openly and honestly about their experiences and emotions when one of their parents died, in a book designed to help other children deal with their own emotional upheaval. Ages 8–12.

Le Tord, Bijou. *My Grandma Leonie.* New York: Bradbury Press, 1987 (unpaged). The special relationship between a child and a live-in grandmother is presented in this story. The child reminisces about the grandmother, who has died, and the times they shared. Ages 6–9.

Richter, Elizabeth. *Losing someone you love: When a brother or sister dies.* New York: Putnam, 1986 (80 pages). Richter presents young people of various races, from ages 10 to 24, who talk about the death of a brother or sister. They describe how their sibling died (disease, accident, suicide, murder), their relationship before the death, and how they are dealing with their grief. Ages 10–14.

Rogers, Fred. *When a pet dies.* New York: Putnam, 1988 (unpaged). This book explores the feelings of sadness, loneliness, and frustration a youngster may feel when a pet dies. Ages 5–7.

Talbert, Marc. *Dead birds singing.* Boston: Little, Brown, 1985 (168 pages). Matt's mother is driving him home from a swim meet when a drunken driver runs head-on into their car, killing his mother instantly and fatally injuring his sister. Talbert follows Matt's stages of grief as the seventh grader is adopted into his best friend's family. Ages 12–15.

Thomas, Jane Resh. *Saying good-bye to Grandma.* New York: Clarion Books, 1988 (48 pages). Seven-year-old Suzie takes a trip to her grandparents' house to attend her grandmother's funeral. Her feelings about her grandmother and her relationship with her grieving grandfather are presented in this story. Ages 3–9.

Divorce/Separation/Blended Families

Bates, Betty. *Thatcher Payne-in-the-neck.* Illustrated by Linda Strauss Edwards. New York: Holiday, 1985 (130 pages). Kib and Thatcher, longtime friends at their summer lake cottages, hatch a plan to get her father and his mother to marry. Things go exactly as they plan—much to their surprise—but after the ceremony takes place and they all move in together, Kib has second thoughts. Ages 9–12.

Bawden, Nina. *The outside child.* New York: Lothrop, Lee & Shepard Books, 1989 (232 pages). Thirteen-year-old Jane Tucker suddenly and accidentally learns that her widowed father, a ship's engineer, is remarried and has two other children. She defies her adoptive aunts in order to locate her half-sister and half-brother. What she doesn't expect to find is a dark secret that seems to spark violent hostility from her stepmother. Ages 12 and up.

Betancourt, Jeanne. *Puppy love.* New York: Avon/Camelot 1986 (89 pages). Aviva Granger, who was being shuttled between her divorced parents in *Turtle Time,* is still bothered by her divided life. She spends one week with her mother and her new stepfather and one week with her father. Ages 10–12.

Boyd, Lizi. *The not-so-wicked stepmother.* New York: Viking/Kestrel, 1987 (unpaged). Hessie is going to spend the summer with her father and stepmother. She plans to act horrible and mean because she knows that stepmothers are supposed to be horrible and mean. To her surprise, her stepmother is kind and loving, which brings much confusion and conflicting feelings. Ages 6–9.

Brown, Laurene Krasny, and Brown, Marc. *Dinosaurs divorce: A guide for changing families.* Boston: Atlantic Monthly Press; dist. by Little, Brown, 1986 (32 pages). The text is excellent, briefly getting to the heart of the feelings and problems common to children during and after divorce; making point after point succinctly; and offering sound, practical advice in a friendly tone. Ages 3–8.

Carrick, Carol. *What a wimp!* Drawings by Donald Carrick. New York: Clarion Books, 1983 (89 pages). Barney, his brother, and their mother move to a new town after his parents divorce. Barney must adjust to a new school and a classroom bully, Lenny. Ages 8–11.

Christiansen, C. B. *My mother's house, my father's house.* New York: Atheneum, 1989 (unpaged). A child of divorce tells what it is like when she spends four days at her mother's house and three days at her father's house. Both houses are home, but neither parent will visit the other. Ages 6–9.

Conrad, Pam. *Holding me here.* New York: Harper & Row, 1986 (185 pages). This drama has no heroes, only victims—whose rightful interests clash painfully. "Parents shouldn't leave their kids. Never! They should never leave their children," sobs Robin, revealing her own pain at her parents' separation. A sad, powerful story of loves gone awry. Ages 12–15.

Danziger, Paula. *It's an aardvark-eat-turtle world.* New York: Delacorte Press, 1985 (132 pages). Rosie Wilson's mother is moving in with the father of Phoebe, Rosie's best friend. Rosie, the child of a white mother and a black father, experiences the joys of a first love and is exposed to a racist who does not like seeing her with a white boy. Ages 11–14.

Drescher, Joan. *My mother's getting married.* New York: Dial Press; dist. by Dutton, 1986 (32 pages). In picture-book format, Drescher describes a common problem in today's society—a child who resents a parent's remarriage. Ages 6–10.

Fox, Paula. *The moonlight man.* New York: Bradbury Press, 1986 (179 pages). Catherine spends an unusual summer with her father, a writer and, she discovers, an alcoholic. He is divorced from her mother, and Catherine finds her feelings for him conflicting and confusing. Ages 13 and up.

Katz, Welwyn Wilton. *False face.* New York: Macmillan/Margaret K. McElderry Books, 1988 (196 pages). Laney's parents' bitter divorce has left her confused and vulnerable. She discovers a small Indian ritual mask and takes it home. It creates tension between her mother, a successful antiques dealer, and her father, a professor determined to preserve Indian relics. The mask and its larger companion mask harbor an evil power that seems to be corrupting her mother. Resentments between Laney's parents due to soured love, divorce, and her own envy are presented convincingly. Ages 12 and up.

Krementz, Jill. *How it feels when parents divorce.* New York: Knopf, 1984 (115 pages). Nineteen boys and girls, 8 to 16 years of age, share the experiences and feelings they had while adjusting to divorced families. They represent several ethnic and economic groups and a wide variety of

experiences, ranging from a background of violence in the home to resolutions of friendly joint custody. Ages 9–14.

Osborne, Mary Pope. *Last one home.* New York: Dial Press, 1986 (147 pages). Bailey Evans's father is remarrying, and she's determined not to become part of his new family. She heartily resists, refusing to warm up to Janet, her father's fiancee, and doing her best to stall the move to Janet's house. Ages 11–14.

Park, Barbara. *My mother got married (and other disasters).* New York: Knopf, 1989 (139 pages). Adjusting to a new stepfather, stepsister and stepbrother, 12-year-old Charles is presented with many difficult experiences. It isn't until a near-tragedy tempers his feelings that Charles is willing to give up his anger. Ages 10–12.

Pevsner, Stella. *Sister of the quints.* New York: Clarion Books, 1987 (177 pages). Natalie Wentworth is living with her father and his new wife, Jean, and quintuplets. She is convinced that her life has been ruined by her father's newest children. Natalie's mother has recently moved to Colorado, and Natalie must make a painful choice when she decides to live with her mother. Ages 12 and up.

Drug and Alcohol Abuse

Christopher, Matt. *Tackle without a team.* Boston: Little, Brown, 1989 (145 pages). Scott was unjustly dismissed from the football team for drug possession. He learns that he can clear himself with his parents only by finding out who planted the marijuana in his duffel bag. Ages 11 and up.

Dolan, Edward F. *Drugs in sports.* New York: Watts, 1986 (128 pages).

School counselors as well as students will be interested in this straightforward overview of a much-publicized topic. Ages 12–14.

Fishman, Ross. *Alcohol and alcoholism.* New York: Chelsea House, 1986. For junior high libraries needing solid material on this devastating problem. Ages 12–15.

Hawkes, Nigel. *The heroin trail.* Illustrated by Ron Hayward Associates. New York: Gloucester Press; dist. by Watts, 1986 (32 pages). This discussion of heroin pulls no punches. Young readers will be plunged into the world of heroin addiction with this book's first two-page pictorial spread: a needle going into a junkie's arm. A useful overview for junior high students. Ages 11–14.

Hurwitz, Sue, and Shniderman, Nancy. *Drugs and your friends.* New York: Rosen, 1991 (64 pages). Both drugs and friends involve making choices, and making good choices is up to each individual child. This book helps children make sound judgments on some vital choices that will affect the rest of their lives. Ages 10 and up.

Hyde, Margaret Oldroyd. *Alcohol: Uses and abuses.* Hillside, NJ: Enslow Publishers, 1988 (96 pages). The author describes medical and social problems that alcohol causes alcoholics and the community. Hypothetical cases and simulated situations equip readers with information on how to get help for the alcoholic or for themselves as children of alcoholics and how to act in social situations. This book emphasizes that sometimes there are no right answers and that not all stories have a happy ending. Ages 12 and up.

McFarland, Rhonda. *Drugs and your brothers and sisters.* New York: Rosen, 1991 (64 pages). When addiction takes over, the trust that exists in a family breaks down, and every member of the family is affected. A sibling's influence can be either extremely harmful or helpful. The author tells children how to benefit from the latter. Ages 10 and up.

McFarland, Rhonda. *Drugs and your parents.* New York: Rosen, 1991 (64 pages). Millions of kids are children of alcoholics or addicts. McFarland gives kids practical advice on how to cope and survive. Ages 10 and up.

Newman, Susan. *You can say no to a drink or a drug.* Photographs by George Tiboni. New York: Putnam/Perigee, 1986 (128 pages). Through ten vignettes, the author shows kids ways of saying no to drugs and alcohol even in the face of strong peer pressure. Ages 10–14.

Nielsen, Nancy. *Teen alcoholism.* San Diego, CA: Lucent Books, 1989 (96 pages). Teen use and abuse of alcohol is a widespread problem that destroys many young people's lives each year. This book explores the issue of alcohol abuse and presents solutions for the future. Ages 10–13.

Rosenberg, Maxine B. *Not my family: Sharing the truth about alcoholism.* New York: Bradbury Press, 1988 (97 pages). The author of this book interviewed eight youngsters referred to her through treatment centers and six adult children of alcoholics about their family experiences. The bibliography is addressed to adults as well as to children, and the book contains a list of seven national organizations that one can contact for help. Ages 10 and up.

Woods, Geraldine, and Woods, Harold. *Cocaine.* New York: Watts, 1985 (68 pages). Beginning with two case histories, this book examines the effects of cocaine, describes how people become addicted, and gives an overall history of the drug. Ages 10–14.

Family

Aliki. *Jack and Jake.* New York: Greenwillow Books, 1986 (32 pages). When Jack and Jake are born, no one can tell the twins apart. The unnamed narrator, the boys' older sister, chronicles the way parents, grandmother, friends, and relatives mix up the twins. Even as the boys grow older, the confusion remains; it is up to their sister to set everyone straight. Ages 4–6.

Blume, Judy. *Letters to Judy: What your kids wish they could tell you.* New York: Putnam, 1986 (288 pages). Although this book is directed at parents, Blume's correspondence will be of most interest to her young fans, and they may be the ones to bring the book to the attention of the adults in their lives. Ages 11–14.

Cameron, Eleanor. *The private worlds of Julia Redfern.* New York: Dutton, 1988 (218 pages). Julia is on the verge of 15. She is secure in her accomplishments as a writer and is exploring her talents as an actress. She comes to terms with her father's death, her stepfather, the frailties of her beloved Uncle Hugh, her first love, and the death of her friend Rhiannon. Julia finds that her perceptions and relationships grow more complex as she grows older. Ages 12 and up.

Carey, Mary. *A place for Allie.* New York: Putnam, 1985 (250 pages). Life in Nova Scotia is comfortable and secure until Allie Hughes's father is killed in a boating accident. Her mother, who counted on Allie's father more than anyone knew, is un-able to carry on after his death and makes some hasty decisions that are repented at leisure. Ages 11–14.

Cleary, Beverly. *Ramona forever.* Illustrated by Alan Tiegreen. New York: Morrow, 1984 (192 pages). Ramona is an impulsive, enthusiastic third grader with a zest for life, yet she finds growing up can be difficult. Several personal experiences are important in helping her realize just how special she really is. Ages 8–12.

Danziger, Paula. *Everyone else's parents said yes.* New York: Delacorte Press, 1989 (115 pages). Matthew is always playing practical jokes on his sister and all the girls in his class at school, so by the time the party for his 11th birthday takes place, they have all declared war on him. Ages 10–12.

Flournoy, Valerie. *The patchwork quilt.* Pictures by Jerry Pinkney. New York: Dial Press; dist. by Dutton, 1985. A comforting sense of strong family bonds is at the heart of this story about a young African American girl named Tonya and her grandmother, who decides to make Tonya a quilt. Ages 6–8.

Fox, Paula. *The village by the sea.* New York: Orchard Books, 1988 (147 pages). Emma experiences the devastating effects of envy and the power of love and forgiveness when she is sent to stay with her fractious aunt and eccentric uncle. Ages 11 and up.

Gauch, Patricia Lee. *Christina Katerina and the time she quit the family.* New York: Putnam, 1987 (unpaged). Christina Katerina has been unjustly accused of just about everything. She decides to change her name to Agnes and quit the family. Ages 6–9.

Gifaldi, David. *One thing for sure.* New York: Clarion Books, 1986 (172 pages). Dylan deeply resents his father for breaking the law and ending up in jail and secretly harbors a fear that he might follow in his father's footsteps. Ages 10–13.

Goble, Paul. *Buffalo woman.* Illustrated by the author. New York: Bradbury Press; dist. by Macmillan, 1984 (32 pages). Turning away from his own family, a young brave joins his wife's people, the Buffalo Nation, in this stunning, stylized depiction of a Native American legend. Ages 6–9.

Hahn, Mary Downing. *The jellyfish season.* New York: Clarion Books; dist. by Ticknor & Fields, 1985 (168 pages). Kathleen is leaving Baltimore. Her father, who has lost his steel-mill job, has found temporary employment in the city, but it will be cheaper for Kathleen, her three younger sisters, and her mother to live with relatives in a beach town on Chesapeake Bay. Ages 10–13.

Heide, Florence Parry. *Treehorn's wish.* Illustrated by Edward Gorey. New York: Holiday House, 1984 (64 pages). Treehorn is having a birthday. He is sure he will receive many presents this year because last year he received so few. Ages 8–13.

Heitler, Susan M. *David decides about thumbsucking: A motivating story for children, an informative guide for parents.* Photographs by Paula Singer. Denver, CO: Reading Matters, 1985 (26 pages). David, who looks about 6 or 7, realizes he is too old to continue his habit. When his father tells him it is time to stop, David is angry, but he asks his sister and brother how they quit. Ages 4–8.

Hines, Anna Grossnickle. *Daddy makes the best spaghetti.* Illustrated by Clarion Books. New York: Ticknor & Fields, 1986 (30 pages). Corey and his father enjoy a close relationship that is aptly demonstrated in pic-

ture and story. Youngsters may wish their own fathers were as funny as this one is. Ages 3–5.

Honeycutt, Natalie. *The best-laid plans of Jonah Twist.* New York: Bradbury Press, 1988 (115 pages). Jonah is in third grade. His best-laid plan is to convince his mother to let him keep a kitten. The kitten stays, but it is accused of devouring Woz, a hamster belonging to Jonah's older brother. Jonah and Granville plan to be partners for an animal habitat study, and they are assigned to work with the bossiest girl in class. When Jonah goes to visit an elderly neighbor, the neighbor is missing. Many themes are comfortably woven into the plot. Ages 10–12.

Hurwitz, Johanna. *Rip-roaring Russell.* Illustrated by Lillian Hoban. New York: Morrow Junior Books, 1983 (80 pages). Hurwitz is a practiced hand at rendering convincing vignettes of childhood and family life. Ages 8–10.

Hurwitz, Johanna. *Hurricane Elaine.* Illustrated by Diane de Groat. New York: Morrow Junior Books, 1986 (107 pages). Fifteen-year-old Elaine Sossi's life revolves around family, school, and friends. She is dubbed Hurricane Elaine by her father because of her impulsiveness—a characteristic that underlies most of Elaine's predicaments. Ages 9–12.

Janeczko, Paul B. *Bridges to cross.* New York: Macmillan, 1986 (162 pages). James Marchuk's first year at Our Lady Queen of Angels High School is a year of growing up the hard way. Rules at home and at school suddenly seem unbearably oppressive, and James is champing at the bit for a measure of independence. At home, his mother is the problem; she is unbending in her expectations and narrow in her views. Ages 11–14.

Kent, Jack. *Joey runs away.* Englewood Cliffs, NJ: Prentice-Hall, 1985 (30 pages). Nagged by his mother to clean his room, Joey jumps in, but he takes one look at the mess and decides it would be easier to run away from home. Ages 2–6.

Kinsey-Warnock, Natalie. *The Canada geese quilt.* New York: Dutton, 1989 (60 pages). Ten-year-old Ariel is worried that the coming of a new baby and her grandmother's serious illness will change the warm, familiar life on her family's Vermont farm. Ariel combines her artistic talent and her grandmother's knowledge to make a special quilt. Ages 9–12.

LeShan, Eda. *When grownups drive you crazy.* New York: Macmillan, 1988 (121 pages). Explores the misunderstandings and conflicts that occur between adults and children and offers advice to youngsters on understanding and dealing with the things adults do that distress them. Ages 10 and up.

Levinson, Riki. *I go with my family to Grandma's.* Illustrated by Diane Goode. New York: Dutton, 1986 (32 pages). Grandma's house embodies the ideal of a loving, secure home — a vivid celebration of long-ago family life in the city. Ages 4–6.

Lowry, Lois. *Anastasia on her own.* Boston: Houghton Mifflin, 1985 (131 pages). Anastasia copes with domestic crisis and seventh-grade romance. Pacing and character are excellent, and the humor varies from laugh-out-loud farce to wry insights into a loving family. Ages 10–13.

Lowry, Lois. *All about Sam.* Boston: Houghton Mifflin, 1988 (135 pages). Sam is Anastasia Krupnik's younger brother. This book tells of Sam's adventures from his first day as a newborn through his mischievous times as a toddler. Ages 10–12.

Martin, Ann M. *Me and Katie.* Illustrated by Blanche Sims. New York: Holiday, 1985 (152 pages). Ten-year-old Wendy is in competition with her sister, Katie, who is a year and a half younger, and it's Katie who comes out on top every time. Ages 8–12.

Martin, Jacqueline Briggs. *Bizzy Bones and Moosemouse.* Illustrated by Stella Ormai. New York: Lothrop, 1986 (38 pages). This charming story soothes the pangs of being away from home for the first time. Ages 4–8.

Miklowitz, Gloria D. *Love story, take three.* New York: Delacorte Press; dist. by Doubleday, 1986 (136 pages). Sixteen-year-old Valerie has been encouraged in her acting career by her ambitious mother and her influential agent, but Val herself is not sure what she wants. The story teaches self-assertion. Ages 11–14.

Mitchell, Joyce Slayton. *My mommy makes money.* Illustrated by True Kelley. Boston: Little, Brown, 1984 (30 pages). Despite the strident title (with its implications about mothers who don't make money), this book may have some bibliotherapeutic use for the children of mothers who work outside the home. Ages 4–7.

Murphy, Jill. *Five minutes' peace.* New York: Putnam, 1986 (32 pages). This is a very funny book — at least for parents who long for a moment's peace from their offsprings' raucous presence. There's a good chance that older children may see their parents in a new light, too. Ages 8–11.

Naylor, Phyllis Reynolds. *The keeper.* New York: Atheneum, 1986 (228 pages). A compelling psychological drama that portrays an adolescent boy named Nick as he struggles to deal with his father's schizophrenia and its terrible effect on their family. Ages 11–13.

Naylor, Phyllis Reynolds. *Maudie in the middle.* New York: Atheneum, 1988 (161 pages). Maudie is 8, and she is the middle child of seven children in her family. She feels she is either too young or too old for everything. And because she is a lively child and often in trouble, she despairs of ever being appreciated or being special in any way. Ages 9–12.

Rosenberg, Maxine B. *Being twins.* Photographs by George Ancona. New York: Lothrop, 1985 (48 pages). Rosenberg focuses on twins' mutual support and companionship. She also presents the problems of competition for parents' and friends' attention and the difficulty of achieving separate individual identities. Ages 5–7.

Sawicki, Norma Jean. *Something for mom.* Lothrop, Lee & Shepard Books, 1987 (unpaged). Mother loses patience with little Matilda when she doesn't come to breakfast when called. Then mother discovers that Matilda has been wrapping her birthday present. The story is told in dialogue, and details are skillfully provided by the illustrator. The fact that this is a single-parent family is a definite bonus, as is the warm and realistic tone. Ages 6–9.

Shyer, Marlene Fanta. *Here I am, an only child.* Pictures by Donald Carrick. New York: Scribner's, 1985 (32 pages). A young boy's sprightly monologue considers the pros and cons of being an only child. Ages 4–6.

Sirof, Harriet. *The real world.* New York: Watts, 1985 (194 pages). Cady Stanton's mother is a staunch feminist, and Cady pretty much subscribes to her views that marriage enslaves women, that people are more important than things, and that

"doing what's right is more important than getting ahead." Ages 11–14.

Smith, Robert Kimmel. *Bobby baseball.* New York: Delacorte Press, 1989 (165 pages). Bobby is 10 years old, and passionate about baseball. He is convinced he is a great player; his only problem is proving his skill to his father. Ages 9–12.

Spotts, Audra. *Standing ovation.* New York: Berkley/Ace/Tempo, 1983 (167 pages). Fifteen-year-old Darlene Stewart is feeling lost as a middle child in a family of six, so she decides to break away from the pack by pursuing her interest in the trumpet. Ages 11–15.

Stiles, Martha Bennett. *Sarah the dragon lady.* New York: Macmillan, 1986 (91 pages). When Sarah's illustrator mother decides she must go to Kentucky to paint horses for her new book, Sarah has to leave her fashion-designer father in New York for life in the boonies. The question mark in her parents' marriage bothers Sarah, as does much of small-town life. Ages 9–12.

Sussman, Susan. *Casey the nomad.* Illustrated by Joelle Shefts. Niles, IL: Albert Whitman, 1985 (110 pages). Nine-year-old Casey is eagerly awaiting the return of his father, a computer specialist who has been on a code-breaking assignment for the army. Information offered about secret codes and the lifestyle of nomads are extra tidbits children will enjoy. Ages 8–11.

Terris, Susan. *Octopus pie.* New York: Farrar, 1983 (166 pages). A lighthearted story about sibling rivalry. Ages 10–13.

Titherington, Jeanne. *A place for Ben.* New York: Greenwillow Books, 1987 (unpaged). Ben desperately needs private space because baby Ezra's crib has just been moved into his room. Ben establishes a niche in the garage, furnishes it with his favorite toys and cereal, and then becomes lonely. Everyone in the family is preoccupied, but there's one person who wants to come and play—Ezra! Ages 6–9.

Tyler, Linda Wagner. *When daddy comes home.* Pictures by Susan Davis. New York: Viking/Kestrel, 1986 (33 pages). A story for every child whose father does not work regular hours. Ages 3–5.

Walter, Mildred Pitts. *Justin and the best biscuits in the world.* New York: Lothrop, 1986 (128 pages). This warm story is especially welcome for its positive portrayal of African American family life. Justin learns that "it doesn't matter who does the work, man or woman, when it needs to be done." Ages 4–6.

Friendship/Sense of Belonging

Blume, Judy. *Just as long as we're together.* New York: Orchard Books, 1987 (296 pages). Stephanie, in her first year of junior high, is distressed by her parents' trial separation. Rachel is Stephanie's special friend, but both girls like a newcomer (Alison, a Vietnamese adoptee) enough to make it a triumvirate. Ages 11 and up.

Carle, Eric. *The mixed-up chameleon.* New York: Harper/Crowell, 1984 (32 pages). A funny story about a chameleon that tries changing into other animals but finds that it is best just to be itself. Ages 4–7.

Carris, Joan. *Rusty Timmons' first million.* Illustrated by Kim Mulkey. Philadelphia: Lippincott; dist. by Harper & Row, 1985 (179 pages). When Rusty is replaced in his friend Dan's life by newcomer Tiffany Smeltzer, Rusty decides to take action. After Rusty gets a summer job and becomes partners with Ruthann Miller, he discovers a surprising camaraderie with a girl. Ages 11–13.

Conford, Ellen. *Why me?* Boston: Little, Brown, 1985 (124 pages). G. G. Graffman has a crush on him? That's all Hobie needs. He has absolutely no interest in this bright but, as far as he can see, slightly nerdy girl who wants to be a marine biologist. The interactions of these besotted characters form a comic romance of sorts, and Hobie winds up realizing that there is more to love than lusting after good looks. Ages 11–14.

Dantzer-Rosenthal, Marya. *Some things are different, some things are the same.* Pictures by Miriam Nerlove. Niles, IL: Albert Whitman, 1986 (30 pages). Young children are quick to notice differences between their homes and the homes of their friends. This simple story takes advantage of the fact and turns it into an engaging lesson in self-understanding. Ages 4–6.

Diggs, Lucy. *Everyday friends.* New York: Atheneum, 1986 (255 pages). A novel about a developing friendship between two 13-year-old girls who both love horses and riding. Occasionally each girl's problem strains the fabric of their friendship, but accepting people as they are, faults included, is what friendship means. Ages 11–14.

Edwards, Pat. *Little John and Plutie.* Boston: Houghton Mifflin, 1988 (172 pages). John is delighted to have the resourceful, courageous Plutie as his first real friend. However, he begins to realize a close relationship between blacks and whites is discouraged in their rural Southern environment. Ages 10 and up.

Gaeddert, Lou Ann. *Your former friend, Matthew.* Illustrated by Mary Beth Schwark. New York: Dutton, 1984 (80 pages). Warmly credible characterizations and a well-integrated plot distinguish this brief novel about shifting boy/girl friendships. Ages 9–11.

Hartling, Peter. *Crutches*. New York: Lothrop, Lee & Shepard Books, 1988 (163 pages). A man on crutches in postwar Vienna befriends a young boy who is searching for his mother. Together they find hope for the future. Ages 11 and up.

Havill, Juanita. *Jamaica tag-along*. Boston: Houghton Mifflin, 1989 (unpaged). Jamaica is told not to tag along when she follows her brother Ossie to the park and tries to join his game of basketball. Stung by rejection, she spurns little Berto's attempt to help her build a sand castle, then stops herself and teaches him how to help her. Ages 4–8.

Hest, Amy. *The best-ever good-bye party*. New York: Morrow Junior Books, 1989 (unpaged). Jessica tries to cheer herself up by throwing a going-away party for her best friend, who is moving to a new apartment. Ages 6–9.

Hines, Anna Grossnickle. *Cassie Bowen takes witch lessons*. Illustrated by Gail Owens. New York: Dutton, 1985 (124 pages). Cassie is hurt and confused when her best friend, Brenda, begins spending more and more time with Sylvia after a class project pairs the two together. Ages 8–11.

Honeycutt, Natalie. *The all new Jonah Twist*. New York: Bradbury Press; dist. by Macmillan, 1986 (110 pages). Jonah starts third grade determined to change his reputation for being slow and inattentive in class and to prove himself responsible enough to care for a pet at home. Ages 9–12.

Hopkins, Lee Bennett (Ed.). *Best friends: Poems*. Illustrated by James Watts. New York: Harper & Row, 1986 (48 pages). In this anthology of 18 short poems in picture-book format, Hopkins provides glimpses of many facets of youngsters' friendships: loving, playing, laughing, tussling, and missing other children. Ages 5–8.

Hurwitz, Johanna. *The cold and hot winter*. New York: Morrow Junior Books, 1988 (132 pages). Fifth-grader Derek and his best friend Rory are delighted when Bolivia, their neighbor's niece, comes for another visit. Derek begins to doubt Rory's honesty when a lot of objects are missing. Ages 9–12.

Hurwitz, Johanna. *Teacher's pet*. New York: Morrow Junior Books, 1988 (116 pages). When a new girl arrives in fourth grade, Cricket's expectations of being, as always, the teacher's favorite student are dashed. However, she begins to accept Zoe as a friend and realizes it is less important to be The Best than to do the best one can. Ages 7–10.

Iwamura, Kazuo. *Ton and Pon: Big and little*. Translated from Japanese. New York: Bradbury Press, 1984 (48 pages). Two friends discover that their friendship is more than the difference in their size. Ages 5–8.

Lowry, Lois. *Number the stars*. Boston: Houghton Mifflin, 1988 (137 pages). When Ellen's parents go into hiding to escape a Nazi roundup in wartime Copenhagen, best friends Annemarie and Ellen must pretend to be sisters. Ellen's parents are smuggled aboard Annemarie's uncle's fishing boat bound for freedom in Sweden. But it is Annemarie who actually saves all their lives by transporting a handkerchief coated with blood and cocaine to deaden the search dogs' sense of smell. Ages 10 and up.

Moore, Lilian. *I'll meet you at the cucumbers*. New York: Atheneum, 1988 (63 pages). Adam and Junius, two country mice, go for a visit to the city. Adam is upset when his dear friend admits he might like to stay. Ages 7–10.

Oppenheimer, Joan L. *A clown like me.* New York: Harper/Crowell, 1985 (171 pages). Fifteen-year-old Shelly Lucas hides behind her sense of humor. Becoming a 4-H clown shows her that facades are just that, proving her real personality is better than any she might hide behind. Ages 11–14.

Park, Barbara. *Buddies.* New York: Knopf, 1985 (116 pages). One reason 13-year-old Dinah Feeney wants to go to camp is to find out what it's like to be popular. Her experiences at camp are not quite up to her expectations, but she does learn some good lessons in life in this absolutely hysterical novel. Ages 11–14.

Pfeffer, Susan Beth. *Truth or dare.* New York: Four Winds Press, 1984 (131 pages). Eleven-year-old Cathy is obsessed with becoming friends with a popular classmate. Her attempts almost cause her to lose her old friends, until she begins to understand the meaning of true friendship. Ages 9–12.

Sachar, Louis. *Someday Angeline.* Illustrated by Barbara Samuels. New York: Avon/Camelot, 1983 (154 pages). A charming, offbeat story about an 8-year-old with a high IQ who has trouble fitting in with the rest of the world. Ages 9–11.

St. John, Charlotte. *Finding you.* New York: Ballantine/Fawcett Juniper, 1985 (170 pages). Though simplistic in its problem-solving and message, this book may appeal to the older junior-high reader because of its attack on the formulaic strong-but-silent hero and its frank treatment of the danger of pregnancy. Ages 12–15.

Tolles, Martha. *Darci and the dance con-*

test. New York: Dutton/Lodestar Books, 1985 (99 pages). Darci Daniels contends with settling into a new school. Now she must make new friends—a slow, sometimes stumbling process. Ages 10–13.

Wright, Betty Ren. *The summer of Mrs. MacGregor.* New York: Holiday House, 1986 (157 pages). Twelve-year-old Carolyn's elder sister Linda suffers from a serious heart ailment. Carolyn has ambivalent feelings toward her sister, who claims the lion's share of her parents' attention, leaving Carolyn to feel like a nobody. Then Carolyn finds a new friend. Ages 11–14.

Homeless

O'Connor, Karen. *Homeless children.* San Diego, CA: Lucent Books, 1989 (72 pages). Hundreds of thousands of children are homeless in America. O'Connor's book includes chapters that explore the causes and prevention of homelessness. Personal interviews with homeless children and with people involved in organizations that are working to solve the problem are interspersed throughout the book. Ages 10–12.

Relationships with Older Generations

Adkins, Jan. *A storm without rain: A novel in time.* Boston: Little, Brown, 1983 (192 pages). A young boy travels back in time to the days when his grandfather was young. Ages 9–11.

Blos, Joan W. *The Grandpa days.* New York: Simon & Schuster Books for Young Readers, 1989 (unpaged). Philip spends a week with his grandfather. He has a special project they will do together, but first he has to learn the difference between wishes and good planning. Ages 6–9.

Cameron, Ann. *The most beautiful place*

in the world. New York: Knopf, 1988 (57 pages). Seven-year-old Juan discovers the value of hard work, the joy of learning, and the location of the most beautiful place in the world as he grows up with his grandmother in a small Central American town. Ages 7–10.

Caseley, Judith. *Apple pie and onions.* New York: Greenwillow Books, 1987 (unpaged). Grandmother tells Rebecca many stories of "the old country." One day, when Grandma meets an old friend on the street and greets her loudly in Yiddish, Rebecca is mortified. Grandma tells her about an incident from her childhood in which she felt embarrassed by her father. Ages 6–9.

Fox, Mem. *Wilfrid Gordon McDonald Partridge.* Illustrated by Julie Vivas. Brooklyn, NY: Kane/Miller, 1985 (32 pages). A young boy named Wilfrid Gordon McDonald Partridge lives next door to an old people's home, where his favorite resident also has four names — Miss Nancy Alison Delacourt Cooper. One day he hears his parents discussing the fact that Miss Nancy is losing her memory. Wilfrid decides he will find out what a memory is, so he can help her get it back. Ages 5–7.

Gelfand, Marilyn. *My great-grandpa Joe.* Photographs by Rosmarie Hausherr. New York: Macmillan/Four Winds Press, 1986 (32 pages). With Americans living longer, four-generational families are becoming more common. This photographic essay takes a long, yet honest, look at the joys and problems of the elderly. Ages 3–12.

Greene, Jacqueline Dembar. *Nathan's Hanukkah bargain.* Illustrated by Steffi Karen Rubin. Rockville, MD: Kar-Ben Copies, 1986 (32 pages). Greene portrays a warm relationship between grandfather and grandson and at the same time shows Nathan's dedication to the spirit of the holiday. Ages 8–11.

Griffith, Helen V. *Grandaddy's place.* New York: Greenwillow Books, 1987 (unpaged). Janetta takes a vacation to the country with her mother to visit her grandfather for the first time. Her trip seems doomed until her grandfather tells of some incredible incidents that happened to him on that very farm. Ages 6–9.

Guthrie, Donna. *Grandpa doesn't know it's me.* Illustrated by Katy Keck Arnsteen. New York: Human Sciences Press, 1986 (30 pages). This story will be helpful to children with a family member who suffers from Alzheimer's disease. Lizzie is a young girl who loves her grandfather very much. But slowly her grandfather is becoming more forgetful. Finally, the most Lizzie can do is sit and hold his hand. Ages 5–8.

Guy, Rosa. *The ups and downs of Carl Davis III.* New York: Delacorte Press, 1989 (113 pages). Carl is sent to a small Southern town to live with his grandmother. In a series of letters to his parents and friends, he chronicles his initial anger, confusion and disdain, as well as his gradual change of heart about his new home. Ages 12 and up.

Landau, Elaine. *Alzheimer's disease.* New York: Watts, 1987 (67 pages). Many facts are discussed about this degenerative disease of the nervous system and its effects on the patient's family members. This book presents suggestions for coping and care. Ages 11 and up.

Levinson, Riki. *Watch the stars come out.* Illustrated by Diane Goode. New York: Dutton, 1985 (32 pages). A small red-haired girl curls up with her grandmother to hear a true story of yesterday, when another red-haired girl and her big brother traveled to America to join their parents and elder sister. Ages 6–8.

Moore, Elaine. *Grandma's house*. Pictures by Elise Primavera. New York: Lothrop, 1985 (32 pages). Kim spends her summers at her grandmother's country home, and these idyllic days are special for both of them. Ages 5–7.

Shyer, Marlene Fanta. *Grandpa Ritz and the luscious lovelies*. New York: Scribner's, 1985 (170 pages). Philip is not eager to visit his grandfather at New Paradise Valley, a retirement village. He perseveres and comes away with a new sensitivity toward older family members who may be experiencing a similar difficult time. Ages 10–13.

Smith, Robert Kimmel. *The war with Grandpa*. Illustrated by Richard Lauter. New York: Delacorte Press, 1984 (128 pages). Peter's grandfather comes to live with the family and occupies Peter's room. In spite of mixed emotions, Peter wages war but comes to realize that victory isn't what he expects. Ages 9–12.

Stevenson, James. *That dreadful day*. New York: Greenwillow Books, 1985 (32 pages). Grandpa relives the trials of his first day of school to help ease the frustrations of his grandchild's experience. Ages 4 and up.

Stock, Catherine. *Emma's dragon hunt*. New York: Lothrop, 1984 (32 pages). Grandfather Wong comes to visit from China. The book presents a warm intergenerational relationship bridging old and new cultures. Ages 6–8.

Winthrop, Elizabeth. *Belinda's hurricane*. Pictures by Wendy Watson. New York: Dutton, 1984 (54 pages). Visiting her grandmother in Fox Island, Belinda weathers a hurricane in the company of Granny May; her cantankerous old neighbor, Mr. Fletcher; and his growling bulldog, Fishface. Ages 7–11.

Sex Education

Cole, Joanna. *Asking about sex and growing up: A question-and-answer book for girls and boys*. New York: Morrow Junior Books, 1988 (90 pages). Cole has grouped the questions by subject: growing up, finding out about sex, differences in development of girls and boys, masturbation, crushes, intercourse, childbirth, preventing pregnancy, pregnancy, homosexuality, and protection from sexual abuse and disease. Answers are brief and to the point, ranging from a few sentences to a few paragraphs each. Ages 10–12.

Johnson, Eric W. *People, love, sex, and families: Answers to questions that preteens ask*. Illustrated by David Wool. New York: Walker, 1985 (122 pages). This book is the result of a survey conducted by Johnson, who polled 1000 young people on what they really wanted to know about people, love, sex, and families. Ages 10–14.

Kitzinger, Sheila. *Being born*. New York: Grosset & Dunlap, 1986 (64 pages). The author describes the nine months of gestation in terms of an experience every reader has had. "Once you were in a small dark place inside your mother's body," the book begins. Conception is accurately described, but the book focuses on changes that take place in the mother's body and on the recurrent miracle of the transformation in utero from a ball of cells to an infant ready to breathe independently. Ages 9–12.

Madaras, Lynda. *What's happening to my body? book for boys: A growing up guide for parents and sons*. New York: Newmarket Press, 1987 (251 pages). Frank, detailed information of the sexual and emotional changes that come with puberty are presented stage by stage. This book was first published in 1984; the 1987 edition contains expanded and updated information on AIDS, sexually transmitted diseases, and birth control. Ages 12 and up.

Madaras, Lynda. *What's happening to my body? book for girls: A growing up guide for parents and daughters.* New York: Newmarket Press, 1987 (269 pages). This guide discusses body changes, body image, menstruation, puberty, and sexuality and stresses the importance of liking and knowing one's own body. This book was first published in 1983; the 1987 edition contains updated and expanded sections on AIDS, sexually transmitted diseases, and birth control. Ages 12 and up.

Marzollo, Jean. *Getting your period: A book about menstruation.* New York: Dial Books for Young Readers, 1988 (99 pages). Information on menstruation is combined with quotations from girls who tell their own concerns and experiences. Subjects include getting your period for the first time, changes during puberty, the function and stages of the menstrual cycle, taking care of yourself during your period, a question-and-answer section, and other people and how they see you. Factual references are made to PMS, toxic shock syndrome, and sexually transmitted diseases. Ages 11 and up.

McCoy, Kathy, and Wibbelsman, Charles. *Growing and changing: A handbook for preteens.* New York: Putnam/Perigee, 1987 (159 pages). Aimed at youngsters on the verge of adolescence, this guide to the preteen and early teen years offers a wealth of information on physical development, health and hygiene, and the emotional changes that often accompany adolescence. The authors begin by defining puberty, then present a detailed look at its stages for each sex. Ages 11–14.

Pomeroy, Wardell B. *Boys and sex* (rev. ed.). New York: Delacorte Press, 1981 (192 pages). Dr. Pomeroy presents a straightforward attempt to clear up the misinformation, myths, fears, and inhibitions that plague the healthy sexual development of the average boy. Ages 8–12.

Pomeroy, Wardell B. *Girls and sex* (rev. ed.). New York: Delacorte Press, 1981 (192 pages). Dr. Pomeroy discusses the many areas of sexual development of the adolescent girl and attempts to dispel prevalent myths, fears, inhibitions, and misinformation. Ages 13 and up.

Sexual Abuse

Caines, Jeannette. *Chilly stomach.* Pictures by Pat Cummings. New York: Harper & Row, 1986 (32 pages). "When Uncle Jim tickles me, I don't like it. Sometimes he hugs me and kisses me on the lips and I get a chilly stomach," begins the brief but convincing narrative of Sandy, an 8- or 9-year-old girl. Wanting to tell her parents, yet afraid to, Sandy confides in Jill, a friend. Ages 4–8.

Girard, Linda Walvood. *My body is private.* Pictures by Rodney Pate. Niles, IL: Albert Whitman, 1984 (32 pages). A first-person narrative by a girl who looks to be about 7 or 8. Discussion of touching—good touching and unwanted touching—establishes the right of an individual to set limits on what's comfortable for one's own body and emotions. Ages 4–8.

Hall, Lynn. *The boy in the off-white hat.* New York: Scribner's, 1984 (87 pages). Skeeter Long, a live-in mother's helper, learns that Shane, the child in her care, is being molested by Burge Franklin. This book offers a good deal of information on sexual abuse and, implicitly, its prevention. Ages 11–14.

Hyde, Margaret Oldroyd. *Sexual abuse:*

Let's talk about it. Louisville, KY: Westminster/John Knox, 1987 (107 pages). This book was first published in 1984. The 1987 edition has been revised to include additional information about treatment and prevention, as well as new material on the sexual abuse of boys. Ages 11 and up.

Nathanson, Laura. *The trouble with Wednesdays*. New York: Putnam/Pacer, 1986 (176 pages). Becky Grant, whose family is on a shoestring budget, needs braces, but the relative her parents send her to for the work turns out to be a child molester. Ages 11–14.

Terkel, Susan N., and Rench, Janice E. *Feeling safe, feeling strong: How to avoid sexual abuse and what to do if it happens to you*. Minneapolis, MN: Lerner, 1984 (96 pages). This book relies on fictional vignettes to present various abuse situations. It stresses an important premise for developing a child's defensive psychology, dealing with child pornography, exhibitionism, incest, obscene phone calls, and rape. Ages 9–12.

Single Parents

Adler, C. S. *Good-bye, pink pig*. New York: Putnam, 1985 (176 pages). Amanda knows she reminds her mother of the colorless husband who deserted her soon after Amanda was born. The author evokes the loneliness of an imaginative girl retreating to a private world. Amanda is not openly abused by her mother, just disliked and overlooked; to keep the peace, the child learns to repress her own needs and to anticipate even the unspoken wishes of her mother. Ages 10–13.

Beatty, Patricia. *Behave yourself, Bethany Brant*. New York: Morrow, 1986 (192 pages). When her mother dies, Bethany's minister father uproots his family and resettles them with relatives while he rides a circuit ministry. Despite Bethany's genteel ways, she's no subservient wallflower, and she makes it clear that she is tired of the burden of being a preacher's daughter. Ages 10–13.

Brown, Anthony. *Gorilla*. New York: Knopf, 1985 (30 pages). Living in an apparently motherless household, Hannah patiently waits for her father to take her to the zoo, but he is always too busy. Ages 5–8.

Dolmetsch, Paul, and Shih, Alexa (Eds.). *The kids' book about single-parent families*. (By Kids for Everyone.) Garden City, NY: Doubleday/Dolphin Books, 1985 (193 pages). Defining single-parent families in a broad sense (including families separated by unusual work circumstances as well as by death or divorce), this is a firsthand look at growing up and coping in a one-parent household. Ages 11–15.

Fine, Anne. *My war with Goggle-eyes*. Boston: Little, Brown, 1989 (166 pages). Kitty is not pleased with her mother's boyfriend. However, unexpected events prompt her to help him find his place in the family. Ages 11 and up.

Fox, Paula. *The moonlight man*. New York: Bradbury Press, 1986 (179 pages). Fifteen-year-old Catherine Ames, the child of divorced parents, is looking forward to spending the summer with her father, who has moved into and out of—mostly out of—her life since she was 3. Ages 13 and up.

Orgel, Doris. *My war with Mrs. Galloway*. Illustrated by Carol Newsom. New York: Viking/Kestrel, 1985 (64 pages). Rebecca does not like being left with the strict babysitter

while her M.D. (Mom Doc) is out
working. Ages 8–10.

Roberts, Willo Davis. *Megan's island.*
New York: Atheneum, 1988 (187
pages). Megan and her younger
brother, Sandy, are secretly moved
to their grandfather's cabin in Lake-
wood, Minnesota. She learns that
her father, whom they had presumed dead for many years, recently died in prison. Her other
grandfather, who had earlier
tried to get custody of the children, has offered a reward to find
them. An attempt to kidnap the
children fails when the children
capture the kidnappers. Ages 11
and up.

Shura, Mary Frances. *The Josie gambit.*
New York: Putnam Publishing
Group, 1986 (160 pages). Josie becomes a pawn in a devious ploy by
a troubled girl named Tory, who
is scheming to leave her mother and
go live with her father. This well-
crafted novel is set against an
intriguing background of chess.
Ages 11–14.

Slote, Alfred. *Moving in.* Philadelphia:
Lippincott, 1988 (167 pages).
Eleven-year-old Robbie and
his 13-year-old sister, Peggy,
plan some elaborate schemes to
discourage their widowed father's
budding romance. They try to
persuade him to move back to
their old hometown. Ages
10–12.

Suicide

Hermes, Patricia. *A time to listen: Preventing youth suicide.* New York:
Harcourt Brace Jovanovich, 1987
(132 pages). A list of the warning
signs of suicide, guidelines for
when and how to intervene, instructions for getting help, and
ways to develop one's own listening

skills are included in this highly
significant, life-enhancing book.
Ages 12 and up.

Hughes, Dean. *Switching tracks.* New
York: Atheneum, 1982 (166 pages).
In this painful and gripping novel, a
boy is driven by guilt to the brink
of mental illness when he sup-
presses his memories of the day
his father killed himself. Ages
10–14.

Kolehmainen, Janet, and Handwerk,
Sandra. *Teen suicide: A book for
friends, family, and classmates.* Minneapolis, MN: Lerner, 1986 (70 pages).
This book alerts readers to the
symptoms of suicide and suggests
ways of getting help for someone
they fear may be suicidal. Ages
11–14.

Kunz, Roxane Brown, and Swenson,
Judy Harris. *Feeling down: The way
back up.* Illustrated by Mary McKeek.
Minneapolis, MN: Dillon Press, 1986
(47 pages). This first-person narrative is meant to educate children on
the subject of suicide. The story
makes the point that good family
communication is vital in trying to
ease the pressures and problems
that may lead a child or adolescent
to suicide. Ages 8–11.

Radley, Gail. *World turned inside out.*
New York: Crown, 1982 (116 pages).
Older readers will identify with
15-year-old Jeremy, who is trying to
cope with a beloved brother's suicide. Ages 10–15.

Stewart, Gail. *Teen suicide.* Mankato,
MN: Crestwood House, 1988 (47
pages). The author describes some
of the feelings experienced by teenagers thinking about suicide, reactions of family members, various
reasons for suicide, and seven warning signs to look for in a person
contemplating suicide. Ages 12
and up.

REFERENCES

Adams, C., & Fay, J. (1981). *No more secrets.* San Luis Obispo, CA: Impact.

Allen, L., & Majidi-Ahi, S. (1989). Black American children. In J. Gibbs & L. Huang (Eds.), *Children of color: Psychological interventions with minority youth.* San Francisco, CA: Jossey-Bass.

American School Counselors Association (1988). The school counselor and child abuse/neglect prevention. *Elementary School Guidance and Counseling, 22,* 261–263.

Arredondo, P. (1991). Counseling Latinas. In C. Lee & B. Richardson (Eds.), *Multicultural issues in counseling: New approaches to diversity.* Alexandria, VA: American Association for Counseling and Development.

Associated Press. (1985, September 2). Drug, alcohol use up in grammar schools. *The Knoxville Journal,* Section A-1.

Barney, J., & Koford, J. (1987). Schools and single parents. *Education Digest, 53*(2), 40–43.

Baron, A. (1991). Counseling Chicano college students. In C. Lee & B. Richardson (Eds.). *Multicultural issues in counseling: New approaches to diversity.* Alexandria, VA: American Association for Counseling and Development.

Bennett, W. (1987, Winter). AIDS and the education of our children. *Education, 108,* 135–137.

Bepko, C. (1985). *The responsibility trap: A blueprint for treating the alcoholic family.* New York: Free Press.

Bertoia, J., & Allan, J. (1988). School management of the bereaved child. *Elementary School Guidance and Counseling, 23,* 30–38.

Black, C. (1981). Innocent bystanders at risk: The children of alcoholics. *Alcoholism, 22–25.* In Lawson, G., Peterson, J., & Lawson, A. (Eds.), *Alcoholism and the family.* Rockville, MD: Aspen Publications.

Blanco, R. (1972). *Prescription for children with learning and adjustment problems.* Springfield, IL: Charles C. Thomas.

Blum, H., Boyle, M., & Offord, D. (1988). Single-parent families: Child psychiatric disorder and school performance. *Journal of the American Academy of Child and Adolescent Psychiatry, 27,* 214–219.

Brake, K. (1988). Counseling young children of alcoholics. *Elementary School Guidance and Counseling, 23,* 106–111.

Browne, A., & Finkelhor, D. (1986). Impact of child sexual abuse: A review of the research. *Psychological Bulletin, 99,* 66–77.

Bruhn, J. (1989). Counseling persons with a fear of AIDS. *Journal of Counseling and Development, 67,* 455–457.

Bryan, S. H., Ganong, L. H., Coleman, M., & Bryan, L. R. (1985). Counselors' perceptions of stepparents and stepchildren. *Journal of Counseling Psychology, 32,* 279–282.

Bundy, M., & Boser, J. (1987). Helping latchkey children: A group guidance approach. *The School Counselor, 35,* 58–66.

Buwick, A., Martin, D., & Martin, M. (1988). Helping children deal with alcoholism in their families. *Elementary School Guidance and Counseling, 23,* 112–117.

Carter, B. (1988). Counseling stepfamilies effectively: Stepfamily expert identifies major problems. *Children and Teens Today, 8*(8), 1.

Cork, M. (1969). *The forgotten children.* Toronto: Alcoholism and Drug Addiction Research Foundation.

Courtois, C. (1980). Studying and counseling women with past incest experience. *Victimology: An International Journal, 5,* 322–334.

Crosbie-Burnett, M., & Pulvino, C. (1990). Children in nontraditional families: A classroom guidance program. *The School Counselor, 37,* 286–293.

Cumberland Heights Alcohol and Drug Treatment Center (n.d.). *Facts.* Ashland City, TN: Cumberland Heights.

Cunningham, B., & Hare, J. (1989). Essential elements of a teacher in-service program on child bereavement. *Elementary School Guidance and Counseling, 23,* 175–182.

Dail, P. (1990). The psychosocial context of homeless mothers with young children: Program and policy implications. *Child Welfare League of America, 69*(4), 291–307.

Diamond, S. (1985). *Helping children of divorce.* New York: Schocken Books.

Eddowes, E., & Hranitz, J. (1989). Educating children of the homeless. *Childhood Education, 65,* 197–200.

Eisenberg, S., & O'Dell, F. (1988). Teaching children to trust in a nontrusting world. *Elementary School Guidance and Counseling, 22,* 264–267.

Elkind, D. (1980). Child development and counseling. *Personnel and Guidance Journal, 58,* 353–355.

England, L. W., & Thompson, C. L. (1988). Counseling child sexual abuse victims: Myths and realities. *Journal of Counseling and Development, 66,* 370–373.

Finkelhor, D. (1979). *Sexually victimized children.* New York: Free Press.

Finkelhor, D. (1984). *Child sexual abuse: New theory and research.* New York: Free Press.

Frears, L. H., & Schneider, J. M. (1981). Exploring loss and grief within a holistic framework. *Personnel and Guidance Journal, 22,* 341–345.

Fuller, M. (1988). Facts and fictions about stepfamilies. *Education Digest, 54*(2), 52–54.

Garbarino, J., Guttmann, E., & Seeley, J. (1986). *The psychologically battered child.* San Francisco, CA: Jossey-Bass.

Gardner, R. A. (1984). Counseling children in stepfamilies. *Elementary School Guidance and Counseling, 19,* 40–49.

Germain, R., Brassard, M., & Hart, S. (1985). Crisis intervention for maltreated children. *School Psychology Review, 14,* 291–299.

Gibbs, J. (1989). Biracial adolescents. In J. Gibbs & L. Huang (Eds.), *Children of color: Psychological interventions with minority youth* (pp. 322–350). San Francisco, CA: Jossey-Bass.

Gibbs, J., & Huang, L. (1989). *Children of color: Psychological interventions with minority youth.* San Francisco, CA: Jossey-Bass.

Glick, P. (1988). Fifty years of family demography: A record of social change. *Journal of Marriage and the Family, 50,* 861–873.

Goldman, R., & King, M. (1985). Counseling children of divorce. *School Psychology Review, 14,* 280–290.

Guidubaldi, J. (1984). Differences in children's divorce adjustment across grade level and gender: A report from the NASP–Kent State nationwide project. Kent, OH: Kent State University.

Guidubaldi, J. (1989). The poor achievement of children of divorce. *Children and Teens Today, 9*(5), 5–6.

Guidubaldi, J., Perry, J. D., Cleminshaw, H. K., & McLoughlin, C. S. (1983). The impact of parental divorce on children: Report of a nationwide NASP study. *School Psychology Review, 12,* 300–323.

Gunsberg, A. (1989). Empowering young abused and neglected children through contingency play. *Childhood Education,* 8–10.

Herring, R. (1990). Suicide in the middle school: Who said kids will not? *Elementary School Guidance and Counseling, 25,* 129–137.

Herring, R. (1991). Counseling Native American youth. In C. Lee & B. Richardson (Eds.), *Multicultural issues in counseling: New approaches to diversity* (pp. 37–47). Alexandria, VA: American Association for Counseling and Development.

Hetherington, E., Cox, M., & Cox, R. (1978). Play and social interaction in children following divorce. *Journal of Social Issues, 35,* 26–49.

Hill, M., & Peitzer, J. (1982). A report of thirteen groups for white parents of black children. *Family Relations, 31,* 557–565.

Holcomb, T. (1990). Fourth graders' attitudes toward AIDS issues: A concern for the elementary school counselor. *Elementary School Guidance and Counseling, 25,* 83–90.

Hollander, S. (1989). Coping with child sexual abuse through children's books. *Elementary School Guidance and Counseling, 23,* 183–193.

Holtgraves, M. (1986). Help the victims of sexual abuse help themselves. *Elementary School Guidance and Counseling, 21,* 155–159.

Hood, A., & Arceneaux, C. (1987). Multicultural counseling: Will what you don't know help you? *Counselor Education and Supervision, 26,* 173–175.

Huang, L., & Ying, Y. (1989). Chinese American children and adolescents. In J. Gibbs & L. Huang (Eds.), *Children of color: Psychological interventions with minority youth* (pp. 30–66). San Francisco, CA: Jossey-Bass.

Ivey, A. (1987). Cultural intentionality: The core of effective helping. *Counselor Education and Supervision, 26,* 168–171.

Kantrowitz, B., & Wingert, P. (1990 Winter–Spring). Step by step. *Newsweek Special Issue, 114,* pp. 24–28.

Kavanagh, C. (1982). Emotional abuse and mental injury: A critique of the concepts and a recommendation for practice. *Journal of the American Academy of Child Psychiatry, 21,* 171–177.

Kavanaugh, K., Youngblade, L., Reid, J., & Fagot, B. (1988). Interactions between children and abusive versus control parents. *Journal of Clinical Child Psychology, 17*(2), 137–142.

Kirp, D., & Epstein, S. (1989). AIDS in America's schoolhouses: Learning the hard lessons. *Phi Delta Kappan, 70,* 585–593.

Kohn, A. (1987, February). Shattered innocence. *Psychology Today, 21,* 54–58.

Kübler-Ross, E. (1969). *On death and dying.* New York: Macmillan.

Kupisch, S. (1984). Stepping in — to counseling with stepfamilies. *The Virginia Counselors Journal, 12,* 38–43.

Kupisch, S. (1987). Stepfamilies. In A. Thomas & J. Grimes (Eds.), *Children's needs: Psychological perspectives* (pp. 578–585). Washington, DC: National Association of School Psychologists.

Kupisch, S., Rudolph, L., & Weed, E. (1984). *The impact of the divorce process in the family,* March 1983, Southeastern Psychological Association. Presentation published in ERIC/CAPS. *Resources in Education,* January 1984 (ERIC Document Reproduction Service No. ED 233 277).

Kurdek, L. & Berg, B. (1983). Correlates of children's adjustment to their parents' divorce. In L. Kurdek (Ed.), *Children and divorce: New directions for child development series, 19* (pp. 47–60).

Kurdek, L., Blisk, D., & Siesky, A. (1981). Correlates of children's long-term adjustment to their parents' divorce. *Developmental Psychology, 17,* 565–579.

LaFromboise, T., & Low, K. (1989). American Indian children and adolescents. In J. Gibbs & L. Huang (Eds.), *Children of color: Psychological interventions with minority youth* (pp. 114–147). San Francisco, CA: Jossey-Bass.

Lawson, G., Peterson, J., & Lawson, A. (1983). *Alcoholism and the family.* Rockville, MD: Aspen Systems.

Lazarus, P. J. (1982). Counseling the Native American child: A question of values. *Elementary School Guidance and Counseling, 17,* 83–88.

Lee, C., & Richardson, B. (Eds.) (1991). *Multicultural issues in counseling: New approaches to diversity.* Alexandria, VA: American Association for Counseling and Development.

Lee, J., & Cynn, V. (1991). Issues in counseling 1.5 generation Korean Americans. In C. Lee & B. Richardson (Eds), *Multicultural issues in counseling: New approaches to diversity* (pp. 127–140). Alexandria, VA: American Association for Counseling and Development.

Lloyd, A. (1987). Multicultural counseling: Does it belong in a counselor education program? *Counselor Education and Supervision, 27,* 164–167.

Lovko, A., & Ullman, D. (1989). Research on the adjustment of latchkey children: Role of background/demographic and latchkey situation variables. *Journal of Clinical Child Psychology, 18,* 16–24.

Manning, D., & Wooten, M. (1987). What stepparents perceive schools should know about blended families. *The Clearing House,* 230–235.

Matter, D., & Matter, R. (1982). Developmental sequences in children's understanding of death with implications for counselors. *Elementary School Guidance and Counseling, 17,* 112–118.

Myer, R., James, D., & Street, T. (1987). Counseling internationally adopted children: A classroom meeting approach. *Elementary School Guidance and Counseling, 22,* 88–94.

Nagata, D. (1989). Japanese American children and adolescents. In J. Gibbs & L. Huang (Eds.), *Children of color: Psychological interventions with minority youth* (pp. 67–113). San Francisco, CA: Jossey-Bass.

Neese, L. (1989). Psychological maltreatment in schools: Emerging issues for counselors. *Elementary School Guidance and Counseling, 23,* 194–200.

Nelson, R., & Crawford, B. (1990). Suicide among elementary school-aged children. *Elementary School Guidance and Counseling, 25,* 123–128.

Newlon, B., & Furrow, W. (1986). Using the classroom to identify children from alcoholic homes. *The School Counselor, 33,* 286–291.

O'Brien, S. (1989, Summer). "Only the lonely": The latchkey child. *For Parents Particularly,* pp. 231–232.

Oehmen, S. (1985). Divorce and grief: Counseling and the child. *Elementary School Guidance and Counseling, 19,* 314–317.

Omizo, M., & Omizo, S. (1987). *Children and adults of divorce: Group intervention strategies.* Paper presented at the annual Hawaii Association for Counseling and Development Conference, Honolulu, HI.

O'Rourke, K. (1990). Recapturing hope: Elementary school support groups for children of alcoholics. *Elementary School Guidance and Counseling, 25,* 107–115.

Peterson, L. (1989). Latchkey children's preparation for self-care: Overestimated, underrehearsed, and unsafe. *Journal of Clinical Child Psychology, 18,* 36–43.

Peterson, L., & Magrab, P. (1989). Introduction to the special section: Children on their own. *Journal of Clinical Child Psychology, 18,* 2–7.

Ponterotto, J., & Benesch, K. (1988). An organizational framework for understanding the role of culture in counseling. *Journal of Counseling and Development, 66,* 237–241.

Prosen, S. S., & Farmer, J. H. (1982). Understanding stepfamilies: Issues and implications for counselors. *Personnel and Guidance Journal, 60,* 393–397.

Ramirez, O. (1989). Mexican American children and adolescents. In J. Gibbs & L. Huang (Eds.), *Children of color: Psychological interventions with minority youth* (pp. 224–250). San Francisco, CA: Jossey-Bass.

Reed, S. (1988). Children with AIDS: How schools are handling the crisis. *Phi Delta Kappan, 70,* 1–11.

Richardson, B. (1991). Utilizing the resources of the African American church: Strategies for counseling professionals. In C. Lee & B. Richardson (Eds.), *Multicultural issues in counseling: New approaches to diversity* (pp. 65–75). Alexandria, VA: American Association for Counseling and Development.

Roehl, J., & Burns, S. (1985). Talking to sexually abused children: A guide for teachers. *Childhood Education, 62,* 19–22.

Rudin, M. (1990). Cults and satanism: Threats to teens. *NASSP Bulletin, 74*(526), 46–52.

Sandberg, D., Crabbs, S., & Crabbs, M. (1988). Legal issues in child abuse: Questions and answers for counselors. *Elementary School Guidance and Counseling, 22,* 268–273.

Schaefer, C., Briesmeister, J., & Fitton, M. (1984). *Family therapy techniques for problem behaviors of children and teenagers.* San Francisco, CA: Jossey-Bass.

Seattle Institute for Child Advocacy, Committee for Children (1985). *Talking about touching: A personal safety curriculum.* Seattle, WA: Institute for Child Advocacy.

Sebring, D. L. (1985). Considerations in counseling interracial children. *Journal of Non-White Concerns in Personnel and Guidance, 13,* 3–9.

Segal, R. (1984). Helping children express grief through symbolic communication. *Social Casework: The Journal of Contemporary Social Work, 65,* 590–599.

Shaffer, C., Godwin, P., & Richmond, S. (1987, December). Talking to kids about AIDS. *Changing Times,* p. 23.

Shreeve, W., Goetter, W., Bunn, A., Norby, J., Stueckle, A., Midgley, T., & de Michele, B. (1986). Single parents and students' achievements—a national tragedy. *Early Child Development and Care, 23,* 175–184.

Siehl, P. (1990). Suicide postvention: A new disaster plan—what a school should do when faced with a suicide. *The School Counselor, 38,* 52–57.

Smith, E. (1982). Counseling psychology in the market place: The status of ethnic minorities. *The Counseling Psychologist, 10,* 61–68.

Spiegel, L. (1988). Child abuse hysteria and the elementary school counselor. *Elementary School Guidance and Counseling, 22,* 275–283.

Stefanowski-Harding, S. (1990). Suicide and the school counselor. *The School Counselor, 37,* 328–336.

Strangeland, C., Pellegreno, D., & Lundholm, C. (1989). Children of divorced parents: A perceptual comparison. *Elementary School Guidance and Counseling, 23,* 167–173.

Sue, D. (1977). Counseling the culturally different: A conceptual analysis. *Personnel and Guidance Journal, 55,* 422–425.

Sue, D., & Sue, D. W. (1990). *Counseling the culturally different: Theory and practice* (2nd ed.). New York: Wiley.

Sue, D. W. (1978). Counseling across cultures. *Personnel and Guidance Journal, 56,* 451.

Sue, D. W., & Sue, D. (1977). Barriers to effective cross-cultural counseling. *Journal of Counseling Psychology, 24,* 420–429.

Swander, K. (1987, January). *Death and dealing with children's grief.* Paper presented to the Smokey Mountain Association for Counseling and Development, University of Tennessee, Knoxville.

Tennant, C. (1988). Preventive sexual abuse programs: Problems and possibilities. *Elementary School Guidance and Counseling, 23,* 48–53.

Tomine, S. (1991). Counseling Japanese Americans: From internment to reparation. In C.

Lee & B. Richardson (Eds.), *Multicultural issues in counseling: New approaches to diversity* (pp. 91–105). Alexandria, VA: American Association for Counseling and Development.

U.S. Department of Health, Education, and Welfare. (1975). *Child abuse and neglect: A report on the status of research.* Washington, DC: U.S. Government Printing Office.

Vernon, A., & Hay, J. (1988). A preventative approach to child sexual abuse. *Elementary School Guidance and Counseling, 22,* 306–327.

Visher, E., & Visher, J. (1979). *Stepfamilies: A guide to working with stepparents and stepchildren.* New York: Brunner/Mazel.

Walker, D., & Hulecki, M. (1989). Is AIDS a biasing factor in teacher judgment? *Exceptional Children, 55*(4), 342–345.

Wallerstein, J. (1983). Children of divorce: The psychological tasks of the child. *American Journal of Orthopsychiatry, 53,* 230–243.

Wallerstein, J. (1984). Children of divorce: Ten-year follow-up of young children. *American Journal of Orthopsychiatry, 54,* 444–458.

Wallerstein, J., & Blakeslee, S. (1989). *Second chances.* New York: Ticknor & Fields.

Wallerstein, J., & Kelly, J. (1980). *Surviving the breakup: How children and parents cope with divorce.* New York: Basic Books.

Weddle, C., & Wishon, P. (1986, January/February). Children of alcoholics: What we should know; how we can help. *Children Today,* pp. 8–12.

Wegscheider, S. (1981). *Another chance: Hope and health for the alcoholic family.* Palo Alto, CA: Science and Behavior Books.

Welburn, B. (1989). Someone at school has AIDS: A guide to developing policies for students and staff members who are infected with HIV. In I. Rosofsky (Ed.), *Children and teens today, 9*(14), (p. 5). New York: ATCOM.

Werner, E. E., & Smith, R. S. (1982). *Vulnerable but invincible: A study of resilient children.* New York: McGraw-Hill.

Wheeler, B., Wood, S., & Hatch, R. (1988). Assessment and intervention with adolescents involved in satanism. *Social Work, 33,* 547–550.

Wilson, J., & Blocher, L. (1990). The counselor's role in assisting children of alcoholics. *Elementary School Guidance and Counseling, 25,* 98–106.

Wrenn, C. G. (1976). Values and counseling in different countries and cultures. *The School Counselor, 24,* 6–14.

CHAPTER 15

Counseling with Exceptional Children

THE SITUATION OF EXCEPTIONAL CHILDREN

Exceptional children are those children who are different in some way from their peers. They deviate from what is considered to be normal or average in physical appearance, learning abilities, or behavior. They may be exceptionally gifted, or they may be exceptionally limited in their abilities to learn or to function in life.

Unfortunately, many societies throughout history have not readily accepted people with disabilities but have viewed them as evil omens, demons, or even witches. At one point in history, people with disabilities were used as court jesters or placed on display in public streets or parks. In our not-too-distant history, people with disabilities were hidden in institutions that provided inadequate care for their needs. During the Middle Ages especially, a mentally or physically "defective" person was often considered possessed by evil spirits. Some have felt that children with disabilities were God's punishment for the sins of the parents. Many Native American tribes murdered children who had disabilities. Other tribes, however, worshipped them as gods, loving and protecting them. In recent years, the special needs of these children have been recognized, and people with disabilities have been treated more humanely. More emphasis has been placed on meeting these children's physical, psychological, and educational needs in a nonrestrictive environment (outside of an institution) and on providing support for the families through groups, associations, and legislation.

Though all of us deviate from the "average" to some degree—in height or weight, introversion or extroversion, the amount of happiness or sadness in our lives—myths concerning exceptional individuals still pervade our "enlightened" society today. These individuals continue to be stereotyped, shunned, rejected, pitied, "hidden in the closet," or wrongfully institutionalized. Much of our society still provides no medical, psychological, or educational help for exceptional children and continues to segregate them from the "normal" population. Buscaglia (1975) states:

> Though they may not be aware of it at the time, the infant born with a birth defect and the adult who is crippled later in life will be limited not so much by the actual disability as much as by society's attitude regarding the disability. It is society, for the most part, that will define the disability as a handicap and it is the individual who will suffer from this definition. [p. 11]

Too often, counseling with the exceptional child has been limited to assessment, assigning a vague diagnosis, and perhaps suggesting a prognosis. Parents and children have been left to cope with the developmental and adjustment problems as best they could. Usually, no thorough explanation of the condition has been given to the parents or children. They have not been told what to expect in terms of learning, social, or behavior problems. Nor have the parents and children been counseled to help them adjust to and cope with the handicapping condition. Doctors, nurses, teachers, and counselors have been inadequately prepared to work with the problems presented by being "different" in a society that has little tolerance for and understanding of the different.

Being a special child presents problems to both the parents and the special child. Parents are confused about the disability. They have fears concerning their child's present and future life. They may experience feelings of guilt ("Did I cause this?"), self-pity ("Why did it have to happen to me?"), or even self-hate. Having special children necessitates paying for medical specialists, diagnostic tests, special schools or teachers, and special therapies. Having special children causes a strain on personal resources and family relationships. Often the children must have extra attention and care. The time and energy required may take away the pleasure that could be derived from relationships with husband or wife, other children, or friends.

What will happen to the special child when he or she grows up? Will this child be self-supporting and able to find happiness; or will the child be rejected by the world, require institutionalization, or possibly become a criminal? These and many other worries, frustrations, fears, and questions plague the parent of the exceptional child.

What are the personal thoughts and concerns of the special child? From an early age, these children begin to realize they are different in some manner. This difference is often interpreted to mean "not as good as" other children. They cannot ride a bike like the kid next door; they look different from the child down the street; they do not understand jokes or what is going on in their surroundings; they are not accepted by the gang and are called *weirdo, dumb, retard,* or a multitude of other hurtful names. Even gifted children bear the burden of nicknames such as *weirdo* or *brain* and may feel rejection because of their exceptionality. The same messages are sometimes subtly conveyed to the children by parents and other significant adults. From verbal and nonverbal signals and interactions, the children are soon assured by the world that being different means being odd, inferior, or worthless.

Growth and maturity bring special problems to both child and parents. Upon entering school, some exceptional children have academic problems. The child may compensate for his or her problems by withdrawing from the school world physically or psychologically, or the child may become a behavior problem. After all, it is better that others think "I do not want to learn" than "I cannot learn." Social relationships may be a disaster; peers often do not understand the exceptionality. No one discusses exceptionalities with other children because society is uncomfortable with the idea of difference. This lack of understanding interferes with friendship, and classmates tend to isolate, reject, and taunt the special child. School can be a very painful place.

At home, things may not be much better, especially at report-card time and when notes come home from the teacher or principal: "Johnny is not doing well in school; he must study harder." or "Johnny is misbehaving in class; we simply cannot tolerate disruptive behavior." No one seems to understand that these learning and behavior problems may have underlying causes. Since most parents are ego-involved with their children's academic achievement, they may pressure the child to study harder or behave more appropriately. Perhaps Johnny has been working hard but still cannot meet the expectations of parents and school. He may decide "What is the use? I cannot please them no matter how hard I try." Unless someone intervenes, society may have lost the opportunity to help Johnny become a productive citizen and a happy adult.

Progress toward helping exceptional children become accepted members of society has been slow. In the 1880s, the first steps were taken toward recognizing the needs of persons with disabilities by the establishment of the first schools for the deaf and the blind. In the mid-1930s, the U.S. Congress passed the Crippled Children Act, authorizing financial aid to families of the orthopedically handicapped. President Franklin D. Roosevelt, a victim of polio and having a disability himself, undoubtedly gave impetus to this legislation. President John F. Kennedy, who had a mentally retarded sister, urged that attention be given to children's developmental disabilities, including mental retardation and learning disabilities. In 1961, a President's Panel on Mental Retardation was established, and in 1963 a National Institute of Child Health and Human Development was founded.

The "child advocacy" movement of the late 1960s and early 1970s resulted in the formation of the National Center for Child Advocacy. During the 1970s and 1980s, legislative appropriations and federal committees and agencies increased. In 1975, President Ford signed the Education for All Handicapped Children Act, Public Law 94–142. This law provides that all handicapped children shall receive free educational experiences designed to meet their particular needs. It describes specific procedures for identification and placement and for designing educational programs for children with certain disabling conditions. In 1977, the Education of the Handicapped Act was amended to define learning disabilities, and in 1978 the Gifted and Talented Children's Education Act was passed to provide money to states for planning, training, program development, and research. Amendments in 1983 extended the act to provide additional services to secondary school students and children from birth to 3 years (Wolf & Stephens, 1986).

Traditionally, exceptional children have been the responsibility of special educators. Only recently have counselors become more involved with these clients (Seligman, 1985). However, counselors purport to have a deep caring and respect for all individuals and their needs. They are committed to the idea that each person is a unique individual capable of reaching his or her potential. It seems inconsistent for counselors not to be involved in working with this large population of children.

The present authors have defined counseling as a therapeutic relationship, a problem-solving process, a reeducation, and a method for changing behavior. Counseling has also been discussed as a method for helping children cope with developmental problems and as a preventive process. Who more than exceptional children, constantly faced with rejection and failure, need an accepting relationship, someone to listen, assistance in setting present and future goals, guidance for improving interpersonal relationships, and perhaps most important, help in building a strong self-concept and confidence? Counseling with the exceptional child requires no magic formula; however, it does require counselor dedication to the philosophy that all individuals are unique and capable of growth to reach their potential.

Counseling literature suggests many ways of counseling with children's developmental and behavioral problems, but not enough research has been conducted in the area of counseling with the special problems of exceptional children. Seligman (1985) points out that even less research has been done with families of exceptional children. According to his review, other professionals, such as those in special education, pediatrics, and social work, have contributed to the literature, but articles written by counselors are just now beginning to appear. "Counselors have shown little concern for the families of handicapped children in regard to both research and practice endeavors; yet, the need for their involvement is considerable" (p. 274).

METHODS FOR COUNSELING WITH EXCEPTIONAL CHILDREN

Some recent literature has been devoted to the topic of counseling the exceptional child. However, the results of much of this research are inconclusive, many studies contain methodological problems, and many of the articles offer opinions or suggest methods of counseling without citing research to support their efficacy. A small number of articles focus on counseling with the families of exceptional children; others suggest methods for working with children who are gifted or who have learning disabilities or behavioral disorders. The suggestions for counseling exceptional children contained in this chapter combine the most helpful research and opinion published in the current literature. As is true with most counseling methods, the counseling strategies should be incorporated into a positive, accepting counseling relationship.

In order to understand the world of the exceptional child, counselors need to have a basic knowledge of the disabling condition. What are the symptoms and general characteristics of a child with this exceptionality? What are the child's limitations? What are the child's strengths and potentials? All children have some developmental and psychological needs in common, but are there other needs specific to the exceptional condition that must be considered? The counselor does not need to become an expert in the teaching techniques of special education, but knowledge of the needs and characteristics of these children is necessary for effective counseling.

Perhaps the primary concern of the counselor working with exceptional children should be the child's self-concept. Bailey and Winton (1986) write that the school-age years may be particularly difficult for the handicapped child because the self-concept may be eroded.

> It may be during this period that a younger sibling matches or exceeds the handicapped child's academic performance. Furthermore, it is during the school-age years, when children's peer relations are so critical, that handicapped children are more likely to experience rejection or overt teasing or hostility from their nonhandicapped peers. [pp. 89–90]

Although the authors were writing about the need for parents to help their child develop and maintain a positive self-concept, this task would certainly need to be addressed by counselors who work with children with disabilities.

A person's self-concept begins to form early in life and is determined by the feedback of significant persons in the child's world. In daily interactions, parents, friends, teachers, and peers send verbal and nonverbal messages to children about their worth and abilities. Exceptional children, even the gifted, often receive negative messages about their worth. Loeb and Jay (1987) found that gifted boys in the elementary grades have a more negative self-image than nongifted boys do because they do not conform to the stereotype of the traditional ideal male. Parents of children with disabilities may feel guilty or overprotective; friends and peers may pity these children or see them as a burden; teachers may resent having to work with them. "Normal" people feel uncomfortable with "different" children for a variety of reasons. Because most exceptional children experience some type of rejection and failure, it is not surprising that many have negative self-concepts.

In attempts to diagnose and find help for a child with special problems, the child as a person is sometimes forgotten in the proliferation of testing, diagnosing, and planning. Though these procedures are designed to aid the child, they may increase self-doubts and fears. Testing, diagnosing, and planning are necessary, but they cannot replace a good relationship—one in which the child feels free to express fears, anxieties, doubts, and insecurities. Being listened to is being respected. It may begin the process of developing or restoring a more positive self-evaluation. Building a better self-concept includes helping exceptional children see themselves as people who can and do perform and accomplish goals. Unfortunately, most people tend to focus on such children's limitations rather than emphasizing their strengths and what they can do, encouraging them to take responsibility for decisions about their own lives, and assisting them in finding ways to live productive lives.

CATEGORIES OF EXCEPTIONALITY

A controversy exists over the categorizing or labeling of children as *learning disabled, mentally retarded, deaf,* and so on. Hobbs (1975) points out that children who are so categorized may be permanently stigmatized, rejected, or prevented from developing in a healthy manner. There is the possibility that these children will be assigned to inferior educational programs, institutionalized, or sterilized because of poor diagnoses; this is especially true of minority children. Minority children, those most often categorized or labeled exceptional, are often the very children who need special attention or educational services to encourage their achievement. Furthermore, classification of a child can encourage the behaviors characteristic of the label.

Smith and Neisworth (1975) reviewed the literature on categorical special education and found that the most specific criticisms include the following.

1. The categories are educationally irrelevant.
2. Categorical groupings overlap.
3. Categories label children as "defective," implying that the cause of the educational or developmental deficiency lies only within the child.
4. Special educational instructional materials and strategies are not category-specific.
5. Preparation of teachers along traditional categorical lines results in redundancy of coursework and barriers within the profession.
6. Patterns of funding for special education have perpetuated the categorical approach. [p. 8–9]

Lerner (1989) cautions that labels may stigmatize but suggests they may help professionals communicate. She believes labels may be necessary because when one term is removed, a new categorical label appears to take its place. Hobbs (1975), too, agrees that classification is necessary to obtain services for exceptional children. Children who do not neatly fit categories may have trouble obtaining diagnostic services and treatment. Thus, in spite of its problems, classification and labeling are essential. Hobbs advocates better safeguards to decrease the detrimental effects of categorization. He concludes that exceptional children have the same needs as other children and should be treated no differently unless their behavior warrants such treatment.

Smith, Price, and Marsh (1986) argue, however, that there are many reasons to adopt a noncategorical or generic approach to serving children with disabilities. They believe that categorical descriptions are meaningless in a system that is moving to meet the needs of mildly disabling conditions, such as those of the educable mentally retarded, the learning-disabled, and the mildly emotionally disturbed/behavioral-disordered. The definitions and descriptions of these disorders are often similar and overlapping. In addition, the authors point out that these children are more likely to be educationally served in a school "resource room" that does not differentiate handicapping conditions. They conclude that the similarities among children with disabilities are greater than the differences are and contend that institutional methods do not differ significantly. Smith et al., therefore, seek ways to serve an inclusive category of "mildly handicapped" individuals rather than discretely labeled groups of children.

Haring (1986) is also encouraged by recent developments. He believes that educators have grown more sensitive to individual needs and rights and to the dangers of labeling—that they now focus on the exceptional individual's level of skill and the skills required to improve performance. It is Haring's belief that this shift in emphasis will mean greater acceptance for a wider range of individual differences and the realization that at some time in our lives all of us need special services.

Although differences in opinion continue to exist about categorization or noncategorization, the U.S. Department of Education reports the number of children receiving special education services for ten specific handicapping conditions each year: the learning-disabled, speech-impaired, mentally retarded, emotionally disturbed, deaf and hard of hearing, multihandicapped, orthopedically handicapped, other health-impaired, visually handicapped, and deaf-blind. Children with problems can be classified in many ways. It is beyond the scope of this chapter to discuss each exceptionality individually; therefore, what is included is a general discussion of gifted, mentally retarded, learning-disabled, and physically handicapped children and children categorized as having behavioral disorders. These conditions seem to be the most generally recognized exceptionalities and the conditions counselors are most apt to encounter daily. Although attention-deficit disorders are not among the exceptional conditions listed by the U.S. Department of Education as special education services provided, this condition is included here because of its increasing diagnosis.

The Gifted Child

Much of the discussion so far has focused on children who have disabilities or some handicapping condition. However, children who are gifted are also considered exceptional, and they, too, face unique problems related to their exceptionality. Hallahan and Kauffman (1986) point out that giftedness should be fostered but that the gifted child risks stigma and rejection if he or she appears to be too intellectually superior or achieving. They also believe that most of us feel a moral obligation to help disadvantaged or handicapped children but are unsure of our obligation to help those children who already have so much.

The definition of giftedness accepted by the U.S. Department of Education in 1978 is as follows:

> Gifted and talented children means children, and whenever applicable, youth, who are identified at the preschool, elementary, or secondary level as possessing demonstrated or potential abilities that give evidence of high performance capability in areas such as intellectual, creative, specific academic, or leadership ability, or in the performing and visual arts, and who by reason thereof require services or activities not ordinarily provided by the school. [Congressional Record, 1978, H-12179, cited in Wolf & Stephens, 1986, pp. 438–439]

Note that the definition includes not only intellectual ability, but also creative, leadership, and performing ability and other outstanding characteristics. Hallahan and Kauffman (1986) emphasize that many definitions of giftedness developed during the last two decades have included "exceptional academic ability, exceptional creativity, existence of special talents, superior achievement beyond peers in any value line of activity, [and] inclusion in the top x percent of children according to any criterion of giftedness" (p. 388). They feel that these definitions still include some children erroneously and exclude others who are gifted. The incidence of gifted and talented children is difficult to determine because of the variety of criteria various states have adopted, but most estimates range around 3 to 5 percent of the population; some estimates go as high as 20 percent.

It is difficult to describe all the characteristics of a person considered gifted. Terman and Oden (1947) attempted to describe the characteristics of the gifted in their studies during the early 1930s. They dispelled many of the myths concerning the gifted, but their studies focused primarily on the academically gifted. The characteristics identified do not seem adequate to describe the gifted or talented child of today. Because the definition of giftedness covers many different areas, it seems unfair to rely on a restrictive list of traits that could screen out a gifted student or talented child of today. Wolf and Stephens (1986) point out that it is difficult to identify gifted and talented children because they are an extremely heterogeneous group and certain kinds of giftedness are hard to identify. Intelligence and achievement tests; tests of creativity; teacher recommendations; and parent, peer, and self-referrals are often used. The authors state that none of these methods alone is adequate; however, used in combination, they contribute to the identification process.

Because gifted and talented children are seen as outstanding in many ways (especially academically), it has not been recognized that these children, too, may need the counselor's intervention to cope with social or emotional problems. Most people believe that the bright can solve almost any problem and find their way without help. Forgotten is the possibility that the bright child may have problems in relationships with friends because of advanced intellectual or creative interests. Some writers (Allen & Fox, 1979; Betts, 1986) have suggested that because of gifted children's potential, many talents, and the attention they receive because of their intellectual abilities, their emotional and social problems may be obscured. The writers point out that the gifted often feel isolated and alienated and experience low self-esteem and underachievement. Strong, Lynch, and Smith (1987) believe that school personnel should help parents find a range of programs, services, and financial resources needed to assist gifted children, especially those children from minority or other cultural groups. They also contend that career planning assistance is essential. Alexander and Muia (1982) suggest that gifted and talented youngsters need the counselor's help in recognizing the variety of career options open to them. Such children possess knowledge beyond their years but lack the physical and emotional ability to cope with this knowledge. The pressures parents, teachers, peers, and society place on gifted and talented children may be strong and overwhelming.

Wolf and Penrod (1980) believe that bibliotherapy is an effective counseling technique for gifted and talented children. They point out that these children are often avid readers and can be helped in solving problems in their lives through guided reading. As with other clients, the counselor should discuss the reading with the child and assist him or her in finding an appropriate solution for the situation.

Culross (1982) believes the guidance and counseling needs of the gifted include the need to recognize and accept one's own abilities, interests, and limitations; the need to recognize and accept the abilities, interests, and limitations of others; the need for adequate social relationships; the need to explore, discover, and create; the need for appropriate problem-solving skills; the need to develop one's abilities without regard to race, sex, or ethnic group; the need to work independently and to participate in decision-making; the need to understand the attitudes of parents or teachers; the need to set realistic goals and to evaluate realistically; and the need to be challenged (p. 25). She suggests a number of services to form a core of support for gifted and talented children.

The counselor may want to consider placing gifted or talented children in heterogeneous groups of peers to develop relationship skills or discuss concerns of mutual interest, or a homogeneous group of gifted and talented youngsters may want to meet to discuss their particular concerns. Before placing any child in a group, the purpose and composition of the group should be considered. Barnette (1989) found that a three-week group workshop for gifted and talented adolescents that included structured activities, community meetings, singing, meditating, poetry, and metaphorical readings "appeared to be successful in stimulating growth in personal worth and interpersonal relationships as well as growth of special gifts and talents" (p. 527).

Colangelo and Zaffrann (1979) suggest that behavioral techniques of counseling will help gifted individuals interested primarily in mastery and integration of new material and that a client-centered counseling approach will help the gifted who are more interested in exploration and creativity. According to Colangelo and Zaffrann, the primary tasks of the counselor are (1) to enhance learning opportunities; (2) to help children (and significant others) understand themselves, their potentials, and their limitations; and (3) to guide children in developing good social relationships.

Counseling with gifted and talented children will present a challenge to the counselor. These children are often very independent and want to solve their own problems. They are also bright enough to compensate or to disguise many of their concerns. They are perceptive and recognize insensitivity or inconsistencies immediately. However, because of their gifts and talents, they can be responsive clients.

Children with Emotional or Behavioral Disorders

Problems exist in defining an emotionally disturbed (ED) child or one considered to have a behavioral disorder (BD). Cullinan and Epstein (1986) write that one issue in attempting to define ED/BD is the subjectivity of standards that can vary by age, sex, subculture, community, politics, and economic conditions. They suggest that an additional problem lies in the fact that too few assessment tools are available to accurately measure the social, emotional, and behavioral problems of children. These writers summarize the definitions from federal guidelines and from others. The definition the Office of Special Education accepts includes symptoms such as an inability to learn that cannot be explained by intellectual, sensory, or health factors; difficulty developing and maintaining relationships; demonstrating inappropriate responses (behavior or feelings) to normal circumstances; pervasive unhappiness or depression; and physical symptoms, pains, fears, or reactions associated with personal or school problems. Other definitions focus on biological causes, behavior that deviates from some norm, personal disturbances, environmental conflicts, and educational or learning disorders (Cullinan & Epstein, 1986). Because of the lack of clarity in definitions, estimates of the prevalence of ED/BD vary widely; however, most estimate that approximately 2 percent of the population have some kind of ED/BD.

Emotional disturbances or behavioral disorders also may be classified according to degree. Severe disorders (psychoses) such as childhood schizophrenia and autism usually require treatment by psychiatrists and possibly institutionalization. Children with mild to moderate problems ordinarily function relatively well in the home environment and are educated in the public schools. This section discusses only mildly to moderately ED/BD conditions. Behaviors exhibited by these children may include, among others, cruelty, fighting, extreme tantrums, disobedience, hyperactivity, impulsivity, social maladjustment, anxiety, low self-confidence, withdrawal, and low intellectual performance and achievement (Cullinan & Epstein, 1986). Again, counselors are cautioned to note the frequency and intensity of such behaviors to make sure they are extreme and not a part of normal childhood development.

The possibility should be considered that the disturbance or behavior could be due to physiological causes or environmental factors. Children are expected to learn what is acceptable behavior and unacceptable behavior from socialization agents such as parents and schools. "Right" and "wrong" are taught through a system of rewards and punishments meted out by adults. Children depend less on these external reinforcements as the conscience, or internal control, develops. Because of individual differences, children vary in reaction to this training and their willingness to adapt to adult standards.

Cullinan and Epstein (1986) state that behavioral disorders are often discerned from observing and interpreting behaviors that indicate mental or emotional problems; from the frequency and/or intensity of behaviors that deviate from the "normal"; from impaired functioning that may include self-deprecating remarks, excessive anxiety, sadness or depression, a lack of academic skills, short attention span, or outwardly aggressive behaviors; and from other disorders such as hyperactivity, social problems, or other learning disorders. There can be biological or psychological causes for these symptoms.

ED/BD children need love and understanding, and they need a counselor who can provide security and stability. The counselor who is effective with ED/BD children can detect and reflect the feelings and frustrations of the children, discuss these feelings, and decide how to manage them effectively. Much of the success achieved from working with the emotionally disturbed has been due to the relationship between adult and child as well as to the technique used. These children have often experienced inconsistency in their relationships and may be suspicious of adults because of past experiences with hurtful people. The counselor needs to be strong enough to place consistent limits on the children, requiring them to assume responsibility for their behavior.

To bring consistency and stability to the life of the ED/BD child, the counselor can discuss expected and appropriate behaviors with the child.

At the time of the discussion, it is often helpful to write out what is considered inappropriate and the consequences of this behavior. Expected behaviors can be defined by such methods as contracting. The counselor, parents, teachers, and all significant people in the child's life must be willing to set limits and consistently maintain the rules. Behavior modification techniques emphasizing positive reinforcement have been found very effective. Relaxation exercises, talking therapy, physical activities, writing, drawing, or games may be scheduled into the child's day to provide outlets for tension and other emotions. Changes in the environment, expectations, stimulation, and conflicts should be reduced whenever and wherever possible. Peer groups can be used as effective reinforcers and to provide models for appropriate behavior.

Drug therapy was used widely in the mid-1900s to treat behavioral-disordered/emotionally disturbed children, especially those with acting-out behaviors or attention disorders. Smith, Price, and Marsh (1986) express reservations about this treatment, preferring behavioral techniques. They summarize the literature on the effectiveness of drug therapy by reporting that findings do not show learning and behavior are necessarily improved, and that drugs sometimes cause negative side effects. The researchers also found that while a variety of techniques for treating this disorder are available, drugs are often used as a first treatment rather than as a last resort.

The tasks of the counselor of an ED/BD child can be summarized as (1) forming a counseling relationship with the child that includes well-defined responsibilities and limits; (2) working to change the child's image and expectations through counseling and consultation with family and other significant people in the child's world; (3) conducting individual and group counseling to deal with feelings and behaviors, teach social skills, and improve academic performance; and (4) assisting parents and teachers in structuring the child's physical environment and schedule, establishing rules for behavior, and providing encouragement, reinforcement, and logical consequences for misbehavior.

The Learning-Disabled Child

According to Lerner (1989), the term *learning disabilities* was first introduced in 1963 by a group of parents of children with various disorders labeled as neurological. The various definitions of learning disabilities (LD) that have been proposed over the years have been ambiguous in many cases and quite controversial.

The Education for All Handicapped Children Act, Public Law 94-142, which was passed in 1975 and became effective in 1977, defined learning disabilities as follows:

> "Specific learning disability" means a disorder in one or more of the basic psychological processes involved in understanding or in using language,

spoken or written, which may manifest itself in an imperfect ability to listen, think, speak, read, write, spell, or to do mathematical calculations. The term includes such conditions as perceptual handicaps, brain injury, minimal brain dysfunction, dyslexia, and developmental aphasia. The term does not include children who have learning problems which are primarily the result of visual, hearing, or motor handicaps, or mental retardation, or emotional disturbance, or of environmental, cultural, or economic disadvantage. [U.S. Office of Education, 1977, p. 65083, cited in Mercer, 1986, p. 124]

This definition continues without change in the Reauthorization of the Education of the Handicapped Act of 1986, describing children with learning disabilities as having a severe discrepancy between "apparent potential for learning and low level of achievement" (Lerner, 1989). The National Joint Committee on Learning Disabilities and other groups have proposed similar definitions, but according to Lerner (1989) they all contain elements that refer to neurological dysfunctioning, uneven growth patterns, academic and learning difficulties, discrepancy between the child's potential and achievement, and exclusion of other causes.

Children who are achieving academically far below their estimated ability are suspect if the discrepancy is not due to a visual, hearing, or motor handicap; mental retardation; emotional disturbance; or environmental, cultural, or economic disadvantage. In general, the literature in the area includes such characteristics as hyperactivity, motor problems, perceptual impairments, specific learning problems related to reading, writing, or memory, short attention span, and social/emotional problems. A learning disability is primarily an academic problem and may not be detected and diagnosed until the child encounters problems in school (Mercer, 1986). Although the specific causes of learning disabilities are not known, researchers believe they include biological, genetic, and environmental factors. Biological factors include a variety of causes such as minimal brain dysfunction, biochemical disturbances (allergies to certain food, for instance), developmental delay of the nervous system, and nutrition. There is some evidence that heredity is a factor in the prevalence of LD, and some educators now feel that a poor or inadequate learning environment may contribute to LD problems (Mercer, 1986). The incidence of LD is estimated to be slightly over 4 percent of the school population, but some reported estimates have ranged from 1 to 30 percent.

As in counseling with other exceptional children, the counselor begins by recognizing and reflecting the feelings of the LD child. Because their characteristics tend to create an unstable world, these children have often experienced failure, rejection, isolation, and confusion. Perceptions of their world change; their visual perception plays tricks on them; their impulsivity causes them trouble with authority figures; they may have communication difficulties because of poor auditory or language skills; and they are often clumsy and awkward. These and the other behaviors that accompany their disability do not endear them to teachers, parents, or peers, and emotional problems often result.

Some LD children lack social perception and skills and perform poorly in social situations. They may lack good judgment and appear to be insensitive tattlers. They may have trouble making friends and forming good relationships in their families. Lerner (1989) presents numerous activities for building body image and self-perception, sensitivity to other people, social maturity and skills, self-esteem, and emotional well-being.

Rosen (1989) has produced a learning-disability workshop to help teachers, parents, and others understand the frustration, anxiety, and tension the LD child experiences. He states that these children experience frustration and anxiety when adults use sarcasm at their expense, move so rapidly that the children have trouble keeping up, or become intimidating and demanding in their communication with LD children. His suggestions for adults include the following:

- Move less rapidly in giving directions and information.
- Recognize that lack of participation in the group may be related to fear of risk taking.
- Avoid urging the child to "try harder"—he or she is already having trouble understanding the world.
- Be aware that visual or auditory misperceptions can lead the child to respond inappropriately.
- Reexamine what is "fair" to ensure that the child's needs are not being overlooked.

Counselors will find Rosen's videotaped workshop materials helpful in assisting others who live and work with LD children.

One of the tasks of a counselor working with an LD child may be to coordinate diagnostic services in order to pinpoint the child's specific strengths and weaknesses and plan an educational program based on these findings. A typical diagnostic evaluation will include physical, educational, and psychological assessments and perhaps the opinions of other specialists, such as speech pathologists or ophthalmologists. These data must be shared with all those working with the child to ensure development of a well-organized plan for remediation and to avoid overlap or omission of services.

Emotional problems, due primarily to feelings of failure and worthlessness, often compound the learning problems of LD children. Hawke and Lesser (1978) suggest that some children may respond to special teaching techniques, realistic expectations, and reduced pressures; others may need more specific help in dealing with the feelings of failure and discouragement. Individual or group counseling must be considered an essential part of any program planned for LD children. It may be necessary to involve the entire family in counseling in order to deal with the feelings and reactions of all family members. Behavior modification procedures, implemented both in the home and in school, have proven very effective in helping LD children because they provide structure and stability in a world of turmoil. Relaxation training can help LD children cope with tensions and anxieties. Talking therapy can provide an outlet for expression of pent-up feelings and exploration of doubts. The counselor's job is to build an improved self-concept, help the children to learn social skills, assist them in learning to cope with environmental demands, and guide them in planning ways to realize their potential.

In recent years, medical specialists have used drugs to control the attention, distractibility, and behavior of LD children. The use of drugs is extremely controversial, and the counselor is involved only in observing the effects of the drug and reporting these effects to the parents. Other therapies, such as diet control, megavitamins, and motor training, have been advocated by some professionals. These approaches, too, are still highly controversial. Most have little research support for their use in helping LD children.

Hallahan and Kauffman (1986) suggest that LD children need a structured learning program with clear instructions, directed primarily by the teacher until the children are educated to make effective decisions, as well as an environment in which stimuli have been reduced (perhaps a learning cubicle to reduce noise and light). Hallahan and Kauffman recommend cognitive behavior-modification techniques to teach self-initiative, problem solving, and reduction of inattention and impulsivity.

Rudolph (1978a) summarizes the tasks of counselors working with LD children:

1. Recognize the characteristics of learning disabilities, including those that may be masked by behaviors such as withdrawal or acting out.
2. Become familiar with the assessment instruments used to determine learning disabilities in order to be able to understand and communicate to others these children's learning problems.
3. Coordinate the activities of the professionals (resource teachers, school psychologists, medical doctors, special therapists) working with LD children.
4. Counsel and consult with parents in order to promote understanding and facilitate growth.
5. Counsel with LD children, who have their own unique learning, social, or emotional problems.
6. Counsel and consult with school personnel to promote their understanding of LD children's learning, social, and/or behavioral problems.

Attention-Deficit
Hyperactivity Disorder (ADHD)

The cluster of problems known as attention-deficit hyperactivity disorder (ADHD) form an extremely complex childhood problem and elicit the most frequent referrals for professional help, according to Goldstein and Goldstein (1990). They summarize the symptoms of this disorder as including inattention, overarousal, hyperactivity, impulsivity, and difficulty with delay of gratification. However, the American Psychiatric Association (1987) published 14 diagnostic criteria in the *Diagnostic and Statistical Manual of Mental Disorders* (third edition, revised) (DSM-III-R) that included other specific behaviors such as fidgeting, having difficulty remaining in a seat or awaiting a turn, blurting out, interrupting, losing things, and engaging in physically dangerous activities without awareness of the consequences. One should be aware when applying these criteria that the child should show at least 8 of 14 symptoms, the symptoms should have been present for at least six months, and symptoms should have appeared after the age of 7.

Lerner (1989) describes ADHD children as "impulsive; driven; and unable to stay on task, focus attention, and complete work. They give the impression that they are not listening. . . . They are easily distracted, racing from one idea or interest to another. Their work is sloppy and carelessly performed" (p. 210). Goldstein and Goldstein (1990) present a "common-sense definition" that includes four components: inattention and distractibility; overarousal; impulsivity; and difficulty with gratification.

Henker and Whalen (1989) report that learning disabilities often occur in conjunction with ADHD, as well as with two other conditions described by the DSM-III-R: conduct disorder and oppositional defiant disorder. Lerner (1989) quotes others in estimating that 33 to 80 percent of children with learning disabilities have symptoms of hyperactivity and/or attention-deficit disorders. Goldstein and Goldstein (1990) believe a reasonable incidence rate for attention deficit is only about 1 to 6 percent. They point out that the disorder occurs more frequently in lower socioeconomic areas (which may be a result rather than a cause of the disorder) and occurs five to nine times more often in males than females, although the latter finding is being questioned.

Goldstein and Goldstein (1990) argue that attention-deficit disorders with and without hyperactivity are different disorders. They cite research suggesting that children with attention deficits and hyperactivity generally are more aggressive, unpopular, and have greater trouble with their behavior. Other researchers have found attention-deficit children without hyperactivity to be shy, socially withdrawn, not very popular, and not adept in sports. Some have called the state of being attention-deficit without hyperactivity "undifferentiated attention-deficit disorder."

Goldstein and Goldstein (1990) contend that common sense dictates a multidisciplinary/multitreatment model. Usually, such teams will be composed of professionals such as physicians, psychologists, psychiatrists, counselors, and speech and other educational specialists.

A physical examination must be a part of the diagnostic process, then professionals must supervise medications as necessary. Medications such as Ritalin, Cylert, and Dexedrine continue to be the most common form of treatment. However, these drugs have unwanted side effects for small children, and the use of medication as a sole treatment is not recommended. Teachers, parents, and other adults who work with children on medication must be aware of the treatment in order to provide feedback about its effects.

As with other children's problems that involve hyperactivity, over-arousal, and inappropriate behaviors, behavioral techniques work well with children with attention-deficit disorders (ADD). They respond to a structured environment with limited stimuli and a consistent schedule. Counselors should work with parents and teachers to develop behavior modification programs and to apply rules at home and school. The children should know the rules and the consequences for not following them *before* infractions occur. All adults must remain patient, calm, and consistent while applying both positive and negative consequences. ADD children may need planned physical activities at intervals to help them deal with their activity level, although they may not be adept at sports and other games requiring coordination. Cognitive-restructuring techniques may teach the child more positive ways of thinking as well as self-monitoring of behavior. Group counseling to teach more effective social skills may be helpful at some point during treatment; however, counselors must be careful to assess the child's readiness to benefit from this interaction and to function as a group member.

For LD and ADD children, Ziegler and Holden (1988) propose a child and family model with three therapeutic objectives: (1) to increase behavioral controls and problem-solving abilities; (2) to define realistic but progressive behavioral and educational goals; and (3) to provide support and guidance for managing frustration. Levine (1987) states that both the children and parents will need information about ADD to "demystify" the problem. He suggests nontechnical, nonaccusatory discussions using concrete examples and analogies. Optimism, the attainment of short-term goals, and responsibility for self should be emphasized. Levine also believes the child needs an "advocate" to monitor treatment, resist irresponsible treatments, and provide advice and support.

The Mentally Retarded Child

The most commonly accepted definition of mental retardation is the one developed by the American Association on Mental Deficiency in 1973 and incorporated into Public Law 94-142. As revised by the American Association on Mental Deficiency in 1983, the definition is: "Mental retardation refers to significantly subaverage general intellectual functioning resulting in or associated with concurrent impairments in adaptive behavior and manifested during the developmental period" (Grossman, 1983, p. 11, cited in Patton & Payne, 1986, p. 237). Patton and Payne (1986) point out that this statement emphasizes three factors: intellectual functioning (*subaverage* usually refers to 2 standard deviations below the mean); adaptive behavior (maturation level compared to peers); and age of onset (between conception and 18 years). The writers believe the present trend is to define mental retardation more conservatively; thus the number of students classified as mildly retarded seems to be declining. Hallahan and Kauffman (1986) also point out that it appears fewer children are being identified as mentally retarded. According to these writers, the federal government for years has estimated the incidence of mental retardation to be 2.3 percent; however, the 1984 Annual Report to Congress identified only 1.92 percent of the school population as mentally retarded. They attribute this discrepancy to the fact that children must meet both criteria of low IQ and low adaptive behavior and to litigation over mislabeling.

Although Grossman (1983) classified anyone having an IQ of approximately 50–70 as mildly retarded, educators have labeled those with IQs of 50–70 as educable mentally retarded. Most children identified fall into this group. Trainable mentally retarded score about 25 to 50 on IQ tests, and the IQs of profoundly or severely mentally retarded people fall below 20 to 25 (Hallahan & Kauffman, 1986). It is suspected that when no brain damage exists and no single cause for the retardation can be determined, this group may be retarded because of poor socioeconomic conditions; therefore, they can benefit from academic support services and counseling (Hallahan & Kauffman, 1986). Biological causes usually relate to more severe forms of retardation. Characteristics of the retarded include personal-motivational factors such as expectancy of failure, dependence, external locus of control, and poor self-concept. The mentally retarded may exhibit poor social-behavioral skills and have learning problems related to attention, mediation, memory, generalization, and abstraction (Patton & Payne, 1986).

The behavior and potential of the mentally retarded will depend on the severity of the condition. A mildly retarded individual can be educated in the regular classroom with some special help. Vocational skills, independent living skills, and work/study programs are often a part of the educational plan. Mildly retarded individuals may be able to live independent lives and hold jobs, and some have satisfactory marriages and relationships with others.

The moderately retarded child is usually educated in a self-contained classroom, with instruction focused on taking care of personal needs, performing daily tasks, and getting along with others. Supervision in work or in the performance of other activities may be necessary.

Severely or profoundly retarded individuals usually are institutionalized and require constant care and supervision. Many are confined to bed and cannot care for even their most basic needs. Recent studies indicate that the severely or profoundly retarded respond to behavior modification techniques for learning and improving behavior.

The counseling techniques in this section are geared to mildly or moderately retarded children, the groups most likely to face societal problems and pressures. These children have physical and psychological needs similar to those of other children, but the added handicap of their exceptionality interferes with their adjustment. Hawke (1978) points out that

> the problems of mentally retarded children stem primarily from the deficits in intellectual and cognitive ability implicit in the diagnosis. In addition, these children are subject to stresses and emotional and social problems similar to, or even greater than, those experienced by children of normal and superior cognitive ability. The retardation, however, limits their ability to deal effectively with these problems. [p. 265]

Patton and Payne (1986) suggest that the areas most likely to be problematic for mildly retarded children are assuming self-direction and responsibility, developing social skills, and maintaining good interpersonal relationships. The counselor can concentrate efforts on promoting self-reliance and self-esteem and teaching appropriate standards, values, and behavior. Peer feedback and peer modeling can be highly effective counseling techniques. Group counseling can help the child learn and rehearse effective ways of behaving. Behavior modification techniques, such as the token system or contingency contracting, have been found to work effectively with the mentally retarded.

Counselors will need to work with the parents and other significant people in the child's life to help them understand and encourage the child's abilities. Special attention can be focused on teaching the child independent living skills as well as personal/social skills. The child and parents will also need guidance and assistance in planning for the child's educational and vocational future.

Studies about the value of counseling and psychotherapy for the mentally retarded are inconclusive; however, it seems obvious that the counselor can provide valuable services in the area of personal/social development and in helping the family deal effectively with adjustment and behavior problems.

The Child with a Physical Disability

Professionals, parents, and educators cannot agree on one definition to encompass the children with disabilities such as visual or hearing impairment, diabetes mellitus, epilepsy, muscular dystrophy, cerebral palsy, and other physical disabilities and health problems. Many children have more than one disability, and some conditions have overlapping symptoms. It would, of course, help counselors understand the child's world if they were aware of the characteristics, physical problems, symptoms, and prognosis of the child with a physical disability. Counselors will also want to know the child's strengths. Lack of knowledge and fear of the unknown can produce apprehension in the counselor, which can be sensed by the child.

The child may have anxiety, fears, shame, or other negative feelings because of his or her disability. These reactions usually reflect how the child has been treated by others, especially family. Family problems increase when a child has a disability; the demands for energy, time, and financial resources add a heavy burden of stress (Hallahan & Kauffman, 1986). The children's perceptions of self and their abilities are also determined by the child's age at the time the disabling condition occurred and the severity of the condition.

The counselor who works with children who have disabilities needs to be able to work with all agencies, professionals, parents, and other significant persons in the child's life. Coordinating services, rearranging physical environments, removing barriers and inconveniences, and securing special equipment and materials may be only the first step to meeting the needs of those with physical disabilities. The counselor should focus on building feelings of self-worth and healthy attitudes. The child may need to be encouraged to express and recognize his or her feelings toward the disability, helped to learn social/personal skills, counseled in the area of independent living, and assisted in making vocational plans for the future. More important than the physical limitation is the fact that each child is a unique individual and has capabilities and potential; it is the counselor's role to facilitate growth toward reaching this potential.

Summary

The tasks of the counselor working with any type of exceptional child might include the following:

1. Working toward an understanding of the child's specific exceptionality and the unique social, learning, or behavioral problems that may accompany this exceptionality;
2. Counseling to enhance self-concept;
3. Facilitating adjustment to exceptionality;
4. Coordinating the services of other professionals or agencies working with the exceptional child;
5. Helping the significant people in the child's life (parents and teachers especially) to understand the child's exceptionality, strengths and limitations, and special problems;
6. Assisting in the development of effective, independent living skills;
7. Encouraging recreational skills and hobbies;
8. Teaching personal and social skills;
9. Assisting in educational planning and possibly securing needed educational aids and equipment for the child;
10. Counseling with the parents; and
11. Acquiring a knowledge of and working relationship with professional and referral agencies.

Buscaglia (1975) best summarizes the ethical code and guidelines for the counselor working with an exceptional child. He reminds us that each child should be allowed to be his or her own person, unique and individual; that these children are *people* first; and that they have the same needs (love, self-actualization, and so on) and the same rights (even to fail) as other children. He suggests that it is our responsibility to listen, encourage, and facilitate their growth by supplying guidance and other resources. We must allow them to be themselves and to make choices about their lives without imposing our ideas, values, and attitudes on them. Buscaglia ends his summary by reminding us:

> And this above all — remember that the disabled need the best *you* possible. In order for them to be themselves, growing, free, learning, changing, developing, experiencing persons — *you* must be all of these things. You can only teach what you are. If you are growing, free to learn, change, develop and experience, you will allow *them* to be. [pp. 20–21]

COUNSELING WITH THE PARENTS OF EXCEPTIONAL CHILDREN

Seligman (1985) points out that parents need the help of a mental health professional to assist them with the problems they face:

> (a) the stress of having a handicapped child in the family, which may be more than the family can bear physically, financially, and psychologically; (b) siblings who may be at risk for psychological problems when there is a handicapped brother or sister in the family; (c) the differentiated roles and reactions of mothers and fathers to a handicapped child; (d) insensitive parent-professional encounters that leave long-term scars on the family; and (e) the reactions of extended family members, friends, and those in the immediate community, which affect family adaptation. [p. 274]

Seligman chides counselors for their lack of interest and research in the area of the problems children with disabilities and their families face, noting that with their sensitivity, skills, and knowledge, counselors are in an excellent position to assist these families.

Many parents are able to accept and adjust to their child's condition in a healthy manner, while others, even though they love their child, may have trouble dealing with their feelings and the situation. Parents may experience a range of emotions: grief, shock, and disbelief; fear and anxiety about the child's future; helplessness because they cannot change the condition; and disappointment because theirs is not the perfect child they expected. They may resent the child because of the burdens placed on the family by the disability. Whatever the feeling, the counselor needs to help the parents work through these feelings. Parents are the child's main support system, and they must be free to accept and support the child in his or her growth and development.

Parents of exceptional children who are gifted do not experience the shame, guilt, or helplessness that parents of other exceptional children may feel. However, they may find it difficult to cope with the creativity, advanced intellectual development, and precociousness of their child and wish their child were ordinary. Finding adequate, stimulating educational facilities may be frustrating and possibly financially draining.

Conroy (1987) points out that the parents of gifted children also are plagued by myths, stereotypes, and misunderstanding that cause them confusion about their role and responsibilities. She suggests a "partnership approach" to provide information to make decisions and deal with their feelings. Conroy has developed a three-session parent-education group to address definition and identification, needs and problems, and resources. She believes the sessions will give parents a better understanding of what it means to be gifted; a clear awareness of the needs and problems of their children, especially as they relate to being gifted; a realization that procedures for rearing gifted children are not very different from other child-rearing techniques; and finally, assistance with resources and referral services for the gifted.

West, Hosie, and Mathews (1989) state that the presence of a gifted child can be stressful to the family because "this situation (a) alters normal family roles, (b) affects parents' feelings about themselves, (c) requires the family to make several adaptations, and (d) often produces special family-neighborhood and family-school issues" (p. 121).

Switzer (1990) identified four family factors that affect the progress of learning-disabled children: level of acceptance of the problem, family engagement with achievement behavior, parental discipline method, and the role of the identified child. The family's reaction to the child's learning disability can affect appropriate identification of the problem and the child's expectations and achievement. Switzer describes a case in which the family was helped to change their perception of the learning-disabled child.

Lerner (1989) states that the first step in counseling parents of LD children is to help them get over their initial feelings about having a child with a disability. These may include mourning, misunderstanding, guilt, self-deprecation, and possibly shame. Parents may withdraw in confusion or aggressively try to "break down doors to get things done" (p. 155). Lerner recommends group counseling to help parents understand and accept their child's problem, share problems and solutions, and discuss issues of everyday living such as discipline, behavioral management, advocacy, legislation, and other relevant concerns (Lerner, 1989).

Goldstein and Goldstein (1990) recommend parent training for caretakers of ADD children. This training should be based on learning principles, especially methods for changing the environment to reduce the possibilities of inappropriate behavior. The writers contend that the child's activity negatively affects parental behavior, and effects to normalize relationships will benefit both the parent and child. They recommend that a variety of techniques be used to improve the parent/child interactional style and communication.

Parents may tend to overprotect children with disabilities from a world that is cold and hurtful. They may be overwhelmed with pity and express this feeling by becoming a servant to the child's needs. Some become martyrs, giving up their lives and their own needs to devote themselves totally to the child. The children of overprotective parents get the idea that they are not capable of doing anything for themselves because their parents have never allowed them the opportunity.

Parents often need to work through their own guilt feelings about the exceptionality. Mothers often feel that a handicap is the result of something they did while pregnant, such as horseback riding, tennis, or a fall. The parent may see the child's problem as a consequence or punishment for the parent's wrong behavior.

Shame concerning the exceptionality may be the parents' primary reaction: "What will other people think?" Parents are often afraid that other people will gossip, accuse, or ridicule. Parents continue to have vague uncertainties about the causes of disabilities and may suspect that neighbors are blaming them for "bad genes," poor health care, ignorance, or other shameful reasons for the disability.

Some controversy exists in the literature as to whether or not parents of children with disabilities go through a mourning process, similar to grieving after a loss, after diagnosis of the disabling condition. Fortier and Wanlass (1984) describe a stage model of families in crisis. They believe families initially react with anxiety and disorganization—the impact stage. The denial stage follows, with family members refusing to accept the diagnosis, shopping for cures, fictionalizing explanations, or engaging in wishful thinking. Grief is the third stage: family members express anger, blaming, questioning, sadness, helplessness, self-doubt, guilt, and aloneness. It is during the fourth stage, focusing outward, that coping begins. The family begins to accept the reality of the situation, seek information, evaluate alternatives, and plan for the future. Fortier and Wanlass suggest that what these families need first in the way of counseling is a good listener—a chance to verbalize their feelings. Later they will need information about how to work with their child's disability and plan for the future; they will need help in understanding the diagnosis and prognosis and in forming realistic expectations for the child's development.

McGown (1982) surveyed 260 families with children with disabilities to establish their needs. In summary, these needs were as follows:

1. A sympathetic and unhurried listener
2. Help with understanding the diagnosis and prognosis
3. Discussion of medical and ethical problems
4. Help with contacting professionals, disengaging from them, understanding them, and cooperating with them
5. Informational sources

6. Facilities and services available — schools, equipment, and so on
7. The rights of people with disabilities
8. Dealing with everyday routines affected by the person with a disability
9. Personal support

Counselors might want to review this list of needs in preparation for helping the parents of a handicapped child.

Widerstrom and Dudley-Marling (1986) have attempted to dispel some of the myths about living with a child with a disability. From their review of the literature, they conclude that although earlier studies indicated that families who have children with disabilities had more trouble coping with daily stresses, more recent research does not confirm this stereotype. Coping and adjustment depend on many factors — among them, the severity of the handicap, the support services received, and the family's adaptability and adjustment level. Although earlier studies indicated a higher rate of divorce in families with handicapped children, Widerstrom and Dudley-Marling conclude that some marriages may be negatively affected, but not all or even most. The marriage may be at greater risk because of the added stress, but the deciding factor seemed to be the stability of the marriage before the birth of the child. Widerstrom and Dudley-Marling also address the myth that fathers seem less able than mothers to cope with a child with a disability; they conclude that the father's involvement with the child's daily care and the support of family and friends contribute to acceptance by the father.

Counseling tasks for the counselor working with the parents of exceptional children might include the following:

1. Encouraging and helping parents to gain knowledge about their child's exceptionality, prognosis, strengths and limitations;
2. Assisting the parents in working through feelings and attitudes that may inhibit the child's progress;
3. Advising parents concerning state, federal, or community resources available for educational, medical, emotional, or financial assistance;
4. Assisting the parents in setting realistic expectations for their child; and
5. Encouraging the parents to view their child as a unique individual with rights and potentials and the ability to make choices about his or her own life.

A number of excellent books are available to help both children and parents understand the characteristics of an exceptionality and the future of children with a particular exceptionality. The books of R. A. Gardner contain a section written to the parents about the disability and a section written for children to explain the disability in terms they can understand. Some books to help children understand some of these exceptionalities (giftedness, learning disabilities, and physical, mental, and emotional handicaps) are listed at the end of this chapter.

Parent groups are probably one of the better ways of helping parents of exceptional youngsters. Through sharing, the parents learn that others have the feelings and problems they are experiencing. They realize they are not alone in their plight; many other parents have children who are different. Parents not only share their feelings in groups, they also share methods for problem solving. The particular crisis one set of parents is facing may have been experienced by others, and solutions can be discussed. Parent groups provide an atmosphere of understanding, acceptance, and support; they reassure troubled parents that they are not alone and that others care.

Counselors also may want to explore the possibilities of family therapy. It has been suggested previously that families of exceptional children often experience considerable financial, psychological, and physical stress. Family sessions could explore feelings of anger, frustration, and shame; tendencies to scapegoat, exclude, or overprotect; communication styles or blocks; and effective and ineffective interactions and other problems of families not functioning effectively.

COUNSELING WITH THE TEACHERS OF EXCEPTIONAL CHILDREN

It is interesting to note that although a limited amount of information exists recommending methods for working with parents of children with disabilities and gifted children, the literature contains almost nothing about counseling and consulting with the children's teachers, except for educational interventions. It is generally accepted that teaching is a stressful profession, and a few studies have reported the concerns of teachers of the exceptional.

Maes (1978) has pointed out that not only exceptional children and their families experience greater stress than typical children and their parents, but the teachers of exceptional children also experience stress beyond that of a typical teacher. In a survey of attitudes toward the exceptional student (Rudolph, 1978b), it was found that a high percentage of those school personnel questioned were concerned or apprehensive about having in their classrooms exceptional children or children with disabilities. Specific concerns of classroom teachers centered around their competence to meet the child's educational and personal needs and the teaching time exceptional children might require, limiting the teacher's ability to work with other children. Counselors can help the exceptional child indirectly by helping teachers and other school personnel relieve tensions and pressures. Listening and reflecting teachers' feelings and concerns, helping them understand the nature of the disability and the child's strengths and limitations, and assisting them in planning classroom-management procedures may be an important part of the counseling methods for helping the exceptional child. Strategies suggested in Chapter 12, "Consulting Techniques," may help refocus teachers' negative feelings toward these children.

Summary

The needs of special children and their families have been ignored for too many years. Stereotypes and societal attitudes must be changed. We need further research to help us counsel special children more effectively. We need money and resources to provide means for helping these children become productive citizens. Exceptional children can learn, enjoy life, be independent and productive, and fulfill their individual potential whether they are exceptionally gifted or have disabilities. Exceptional children are unique individuals just as "normal" children are unique. They have the same rights to respect and growth as other children and have the same needs. The challenge is there for counselors.

SUGGESTED READINGS
FOR EXCEPTIONAL CHILDREN*

Children with Emotional Disabilities

Levoy, Myron. *Pictures of Adam.* New York: Harper/Charlotte Zolotow Books, 1986 (190 pages). Adam has suffered heavy abuse at the hands of a long-departed father and now displays explosive behavior and suffers from emotional problems. Levoy creates memorable images and brings more depth to his story than is found in most first-person narratives. Ages 11–14.

Martin, Ann M. *Inside out.* New York: Holiday House, 1984 (152 pages). Eleven-year-old Jon and eight-year-old Lizzie have a younger brother, James, who is a real terror. When the family learns that James is autistic, they combine their efforts toward coping with the illness. Ages 9–12.

*Sincere appreciation and gratitude are given to Elinor Brown and Flo Plemmons, Linden Elementary School, Oak Ridge, TN; to Pamela Viator Strange and Beth Eades, Farragut Intermediate School, Knoxville, TN; to Katrina Cannon, Flenniken Elementary School, Knoxville, TN; to Harriet W. Thompson, Knoxville, TN, and to Margaret Sumner and Jan Walker, Austin Peay State University, Clarksville, TN, for their diligent efforts in compiling this list of suggested readings for children. Sincere appreciation and gratitude is also extended to Alicia Barber, librarian at Barksdale Elementary School, Clarksville, TN, for updating the suggested readings for this edition.
Annotations are derived from the following sources:
1. Booklist—including *Reference Books Bulletin.* Chicago: American Library Association, 1985, 1986, and 1987.
2. *The Elementary School Library Collection: A Guide to Books and Other Media.* Williamsport, PA: Brodart, 1984.
3. Dreyer, Sharon Spredemann. *The Bookfinder: When Kids Need Books.* Circle Pines, MN: American Guidance Service, 1985.
4. Yaakov, J. (1987). *Children's Catalog: 1987 Supplement to the Fifteenth Edition.* New York: H. W. Wilson.
5. Goldberg, J. (1988). *Children's Catalog: 1988 Supplement to the Fifteenth Edition.* New York: H. W. Wilson.
6. Goldberg, J. (1989). *Children's Catalog: 1989 Supplement to the Fifteenth Edition.* New York: H. W. Wilson.

Namovicz, Gene I. *To talk in time.* New York: Four Winds Press, 1987 (154 pages). Paralyzed into silence whenever he has to speak to anyone he doesn't know very well, 12-year-old Luke is forced to face his fears in order to protect a passing stranger from rabies. Ages 11 and up.

Paulson, Gary. *The crossing.* New York: Orchard Books, 1987 (114 pages). Fourteen-year-old Manny, a street kid fighting for survival in a Mexican border town, develops a strange friendship with an emotionally disturbed American soldier who decides to help him get across the border. Ages 12 and up.

Stern, Patti. *I was a 15-year-old blimp.* New York: Harper & Row, 1985 (184 pages). In a fast, first-person narration, Gabby Finklestein describes how it feels to be fat and the control she feels over her life when she "solves" her problem by becoming bulimic. Ages 11 and up.

Townsend, John. *Rob's place.* New York: Lothrop, Lee & Shepard Books, 1989 (201 pages). Eleven-year-old Rob is miserable because everyone is letting him down. His dad lives 50 miles away, his new stepfather is hard to warm up to, his baby half-sister is keeping everyone awake, and his best friend has moved. Rob finds a refuge when he discovers Pratt's Island. Ages 11 and up.

Children with Mental Disabilities

Bergman, Thomas. *We laugh, we love, we cry: Children living with mental retardation.* Milwaukee, WI: Gareth Stevens Children's Books, 1989 (48 pages). The home life, physiotherapy, and schooling of two mentally retarded sisters is described in this book. Ages 6–9.

Carrick, Carol. *Stay away from Simon!* Pictures by Donald Carrick. Boston: Clarion Books; dist. by Ticknor & Fields, 1985 (63 pages). Simon, a youth with a mental disability, is too slow to attend regular school, and the students alternately fear and make fun of the strange boy, who has the reputation of being dangerous. Ages 9–12.

Hamilton, Virginia. *Sweet whispers, Brother Rush.* New York: Putnam/Philomel Books, 1982 (224 pages). Teresa (Sweet Tree) is responsible for caring for her retarded elder brother in her mother's absence. Encounters with her uncle's ghost help her understand her family better. Ages 12 and up.

Laird, Elizabeth. *Loving Ben.* New York: Delacorte Press, 1988 (183 pages). Anna's teen years bring maturity and fulfillment as she experiences the birth and death of a loved and loving hydrocephalic brother, changing ideas about character in both boyfriends and girlfriends, and working with a child with Down's syndrome. Ages 11 and up.

Melton, David. *A boy called hopeless.* Independence, MO: Independence Press, 1976. Mary Jane tells the story of how her family loved and worked with her younger brother Jeremiah, who was declared mentally retarded by the doctors.

Sobol, Harriet Langsam. *My brother Steven is retarded.* Photographs by Patricia Agre. New York: Macmillan, 1977 (26 pages). An 11-year-old girl talks about the mixed feelings she has for her older, mentally retarded brother. Ages 6–12.

Children with Physical Disabilities

Aseltine, Lorraine, and others. *I'm deaf and it's okay.* Pictures by Helen Cogancherry. Niles, IL: Albert Whitman, 1986 (40 pages). A nameless narrator describes the frustrations caused by his deafness and explains how he copes. The authors portray the boy's dilemmas realistically, and readers will be both sympathetic and concerned. This book provides a good starting point for discussions of disabilities. Ages 8–11.

Baker, Pamela J. *My first book of sign.* Washington, DC: Gallaudet University Press, 1986 (76 pages). Children are pictured forming words in sign language. The 150 words used are alphabetically arranged and accompanied by illustrations of the words themselves. A discussion of fingerspelling and general rules for signing are also included. Ages 5–9.

Bergman, Thomas. *Finding a common language: Children living with deafness.* Milwaukee, WI: Gareth Stevens Children's Books, 1989 (48 pages). The activities of a 6-year-old Swedish girl are followed as she attends nursery school for the deaf. Ages 5–9.

Bergman, Thomas. *Seeing in special ways: Children living with blindness.* Milwaukee, WI: Gareth Stevens Children's Books, 1989 (54 pages). A group of blind and partially sighted children in Sweden reveal their feelings about their disability and the ways they use their other senses to help them see. Ages 6–9.

Brandenberg, Franz. *Otto is different.* Pictures by James Stevenson. New York: Greenwillow Books, 1985 (24 pages). Otto is an octopus who thinks he is different from his other animal friends because he has eight arms. However, he discovers that having eight arms can sometimes be a wonderful advantage! Ages 4–8.

Brown, Tricia. *Someone special, just like you.* Illustrated by Fran Ortiz. Bibliography by Effie Lee Morris. New York: Holt, Rinehart & Winston, 1984 (64 pages). Black-and-white photographs tell the story of disabled preschool children learning and playing together. Ages 5–8.

Butler, Beverly. *Maggie by my side.* New York: Dodd, Mead, 1987 (96 pages). Butler, who lost her sight at 14, is forced to find a new dog when her latest dog dies. She is introduced to a German shepherd, Maggie, at a guide-dog school in Ohio. Butler explains about guide dogs and the training that both they and their owners receive. Ages 10 and up.

Charlip, Remy. *Handtalk birthday: A number and story book in sign language.* New York: Four Winds Press, 1987 (unpaged). Mary Beth is celebrating a birthday. The sign-language vocabulary is introduced by Mary Beth guessing what is in her packages. Fingerspelling and signing on the double-page spreads tell the story. Ages 5–9.

Christian, Mary Blount. *Growin' pains.* New York: Macmillan, 1985 (179 pages). Someday Ginny Ruth plans to leave her tiny, poor Texas town. For the time being, though, she's stuck, and hoping for a brighter future. Ginny Ruth loves reading and is compelled to write poetry. She gets support from a neighbor with a disability who, though he can barely speak, communicates his approval of Ginny's literary bent. Ages 11–14.

Drimmer, Frederick. *The elephant man.* New York: Putnam, 1985 (143 pages). Merrick, who suffered from a disease now called neurofibromatosis, was so disfigured that he wound up in a freak show. It was impossible for him to walk down the street or have any semblance of a normal life. Ages 11–14.

First, Julia. *The absolute, ultimate end.* New York: Watts, 1985 (156 pages). Maggie Thayer is looking forward to junior high, but she is unhappy about one of her activities: she has been asked by the faculty to join a group that tutors students with disabilities. Maggie finds herself a reader for blind Doreen Marshall and eventually comes to appreciate both Doreen and the experience. Ages 11–14.

Gorman, Carol. *Chelsey and the green-haired kid.* Boston: Houghton Mifflin, 1987 (110 pages). Chelsey is a spunky 13-year-old girl who happens to be a paraplegic, and her friend Jack just happens to have green hair. When Chelsey witnesses a boy being pushed behind the bleachers during a basketball game, their lives become intertwined in a suspenseful mystery. Ages 11 and up.

Greenberg, Judith E. *What is the sign for friend?* Photographs by Gayle Rothschild. New York: Watts, 1985 (30 pages). Greenberg is smoothly effective at conveying information to hearing children as well as giving support for the hearing-disabled who are in the midst of mainstreaming programs. Ages 7–9.

Jensen, Virginia Allen. *Catching: A book for blind and sighted children with pictures to feel as well as to see.* New York: Philomel Books, 1984 (23 pages). When Little Rough and his friends play tag, they discover they can avoid being caught by changing into different shapes and colors. Visually impaired children can recognize the various characters by touching the assortment of textures. Ages 6–8.

Kaufman, Curt, and Kaufman, Gita. *Rajesh.* Photographs by Curt Kaufman. New York: Atheneum, 1985 (32 pages). A boy named Rajesh is the subject of this photo essay concerning a boy whose prostheses set him apart from his kindergarten classmates. Ages 7–9.

Kuklin, Susan. *Thinking big.* New York:

Lothrop, Lee & Shepard Books, 1986 (48 pages). Captivating photographs tell the story of Jaime Osborne, a dwarf, and describe the daily frustrations of being short and different. Ages 6–9.

Levinson, Marilyn. *And don't bring Jeremy.* Illustrated by Diane de Groat. New York: Holt, Rinehart & Winston, 1985 (128 pages). Adam is embarrassed by his brother, Jeremy, who has a neurological impairment. Ages 9–12.

Meltzer, Milton. *Dorothea Lange: Life through the camera.* Illustrated by Donna Diamond; photographs by Dorothea Lange. New York: Viking/Kestrel, 1985 (58 pages). As a result of childhood polio, Dorothea Lange walked with a limp, but this disability did not keep her from pursuing a rewarding career as a photographer. Ages 7–11.

Pollock, Penny. *Keeping it secret.* Illustrated by Donna Diamond. New York: Putnam, 1982 (110 pages). Mary Lou is embarrassed over being held back in school and having to wear a hearing aid. It takes a while, but she eventually sees the class's goodwill and starts several new friendships. Ages 9–12.

Powers, Mary Ellen. *Our teacher's in a wheelchair.* Pictures by the author. Niles, IL: Albert Whitman, 1986 (32 pages). This picture-book photo essay introduces a young man named Brian Hanson whose wheelchair doesn't stop him from teaching in a day-care center. Ages 4–6.

Roberts, Willo Davis. *Sugar isn't everything: A support book in fiction form, for the young diabetic.* New York: Atheneum, 1987 (190 pages). Eleven-year-old Amy manages to conceal her continual hunger, thirst, and need to use the bathroom until she collapses and is diagnosed as a diabetic. The subject of the novel focuses on Amy's acceptance of her disease. This involving novel provides a great deal of information about juvenile-onset diabetes. Ages 10 and up.

Rosenberg, Maxine B. *Finding a way: Living with exceptional brothers and sisters.* New York: Lothrop, Lee & Shepard Books, 1988 (48 pages). Rosenberg's book presents what it is like to be the brother or sister of a child with special physical problems. Subjects covered in the book include diabetes, asthma, and spina bifida. The author discusses the fact that the sibling who is not disabled also has problems of acceptance and adjustment. This book emphasizes the positive in its coverage of sibling relationships and in its demonstration that, disabled or not, children have similar needs and interests. Ages 7–10.

Rostkowski, Margaret I. *After the dancing days.* New York: Harper & Row, 1986 (221 pages). World War I is over, and Annie's father is coming home. At the train station, she is stunned at what she sees: not only happy, healthy soldiers spilling out of the train into the arms of loved ones, but also injured and horribly ailing ones returning home under the care of her doctor father. One of the young men in particular—a boy whose face has been terribly disfigured by mustard gas—indelibly marks Annie; she can't get him out of her mind. Ages 11–14.

Roy, Ron. *Move over, wheelchairs coming through!* Photographs by Rosmarie Hausherr. New York: Clarion Books, 1985 (83 pages). Lizzy, Jeff, Mark, and Jose are all confined to wheelchairs. Their joys and frustrations are shared in pictures and interviews. Ages 9–12.

Scott, Virginia M. *Belonging.* Washington, DC: Gallaudet University Press, 1986 (200 pages). Struck by meningitis at 15, popular Gustie Blaine is physically devastated by her illness. Though she slowly gets her strength back, her hearing is lost—at first minimally, then completely. Ages 12–14.

Southall, Ivan. *Let the balloon go.* New York: Bradbury Press, 1985 (136 pages). A sensitive story about a boy with cerebral palsy. Ages 10–13.

Walker, Lou Ann. *Amy: The story of a deaf child.* Photographs by Michael Abramson. New York: Dutton/Lodestar Books, 1985 (64 pages). Amy Rowley, a fifth-grader who is deaf, attends regular school and is the subject of this photo essay describing her everyday activities. Ages 7–10.

Windsor, M. A. *Pretty Saro.* New York: Atheneum, 1986 (200 pages). Fourteen-year-old Sarah Jean Banks has led a sheltered life, tucked away on a prosperous Kentucky horse farm run by her determined mother. Shyness, a sense of superiority encouraged by her mother, and an undiagnosed hearing problem have combined to keep Sarah apart from her classmates. Ages 11–14.

Gifted Children

Gilson, Jamie. *Double dog dare.* New York: Lothrop, Lee & Shepard Books, 1988 (126 pages). A new program for talented and gifted children, TAG, creates tension among classmates in Hobie's fifth-grade class. Molly, one TAG participant, is insufferable in her superiority. Nick, Hobie's best friend, has also been selected for the program; this causes a rift between the two boys. Hobie plays a clever trick on Nick and Molly that defuses the issue of what it means to be gifted and helps them all to see that there are many ways in which individuals are special. Ages 9–12.

Hurwitz, Johanna. *Class clown.* New York: Morrow, 1987 (98 pages). Though extremely bright, Lucas Cott is a problem child in class. He acts out involuntarily at the most inopportune moments. Things go wrong even when he is trying his best to do assignments properly. Ages 7–10.

Sebestyen, Ouida. *Words by heart.* Boston: Little, Brown, 1979 (144 pages). This is the story of a young African American girl who has a "magic mind" and her courage in trying to make a better life for her family and herself. Ages 9–13.

Learning-Disabled Children

Adams, Barbara. *Like it is: Facts and feelings about handicaps from kids who know.* Photographs by James Stanfield. New York: Walker, 1979 (96 pages). Children discuss their disabilities and the problems that often accompany them. The handicaps include a wide range of disabilities, from retardation to learning disabilities. Ages 9–12.

Cassedy, Sylvia. *M.E. and Morton.* New York: Thomas Y. Crowell, 1987 (312 pages). M.E. (short for Mary Ellen) is an excellent student at the private school she attends on scholarship. Because she is ashamed of her learning-disabled brother, she has few friends. A strange new girl named Polly moves into the neighborhood and becomes friends with M.E. and her brother. This new friendship brings a summer filled with imaginative games. Ages 12 and up.

Gilson, Jamie. *Do bananas chew gum?* New York: Lothrop, Lee & Shepard Books, 1980 (158 pages). Sam

thinks he is stupid because he reads and writes on the second-grade level. He is afraid for anyone to know about his problem but is elated to discover that something can be done to help him. Ages 9–12.

Hansen, Joyce. *Yellow Bird and me.* New York: Clarion Books, 1986 (155 pages). As Doris reluctantly helps Yellow Bird, the class clown, with his homework, she realizes his frustration with reading: he reverses words and letters. Ages 9–12.

Kamien, Janet. *What if you couldn't . . . ? A book about special needs.* Illustrated by Signe Hanson. New York: Scribner's, 1979 (83 pages). This book explains the causes and characteristics of deafness, dyslexia, blindness, impaired mobility, mental retardation, and emotional problems. Ages 9–12.

Morton, Jane. *Running scared.* Wheaton, IL: Elsevier/Nelson Books, 1979 (118 pages). This is a frank story of a learning-disabled boy's frustration and inability to communicate. An understanding counselor discovers and encourages Dave's running ability, engendering new feelings of pride and purpose in the underachieving teenager. Ages 10–14.

Osman, Betty B. *Learning disabilities: A family affair.* New York: Warner Books, 1980 (224 pages). Osman provides comforting advice, both wise and practical, for the parent whose child has a learning disability.

Pevsner, Stella. *Keep stompin' till the music stops.* New York: Clarion Books, 1977 (136 pages). Excellent character development provides a sympathetic picture of Richard's learning disabilities. Ages 10–13.

Savage, John F. *Dyslexia: Understanding reading problems.* New York: Messner, 1985 (90 pages). Savage offers a useful overall description of the learning disabilities that often come under the umbrella term *dyslexia.* He boils the disagreements down to some basic facts most people agree on: Dyslexia is a condition that causes problems in learning to read and write. It doesn't come from poor vision or hearing, and it doesn't come from an emotional block against learning. Ages 11–14.

Sullivan, Mary Beth, Brightman, Alan J., and Blatt, Joseph. *Feeling free.* Illustrated by Marci Davis and Linda Bourke. Reading, MA: Addison-Wesley, 1979 (192 pages). Written as a follow-up to the television series "Feeling Free," this book conveys the theme that "handicapped children are the same as everyone else." Ages 9–14.

Swenson, Judy Harris, and Kunz, Roxane Brown. *Learning my way: I'm a winner!* Illustrated by Lynne J. Kratoska. Minneapolis, MN: Dillon Press, 1986 (32 pages). In this piece of bibliotherapy, Dan, a fourth-grader, discusses his learning disability and the positive ways he is trying to deal with the situation. Ages 9–12; younger for reading aloud.

REFERENCES

Alexander, P. A., & Muia, J. A. (1982). *Gifted education: A comprehensive roadmap.* Rockville, MD: Aspen.

Allen, S. & Fox, D. (1979). Group counseling for the gifted. In E. Barnette (1989, May). A program to meet the emotional and social needs of gifted and talented adolescents, *Journal of Counseling and Development, 67.*

American Psychiatric Association. (1987). *Diagnostic and statistical manual of mental disorders* (3rd rev. ed.). Washington, DC: Author.

Bailey, D., & Winton, P. (1986). Families and exceptionality. In N. Haring & L. McCormick (Eds.), *Exceptional children and youth* (4th ed.) (pp. 71–93). Columbus, OH: Merrill.

Barnette, E. (1989). A program to meet the emotional and social needs of gifted and talented adolescents. *Journal of Counseling and Development, 67,* 525–528.

Betts, G. (1986). Development of the emotional and social needs of gifted individuals. In E. Barnette (1989, May). A program to meet the emotional and social needs of gifted and talented adolescents, *Journal of Counseling and Development, 67.*

Buscaglia, L. (1975). *The disabled and their parents: A counseling challenge.* Thorofare, NJ: Charles B. Slack.

Colangelo, N., & Zaffrann, R. T. (1979). Special issues in counseling the gifted. *Counseling and Human Development, 11,* 1–12.

Conroy, E. (1987). Primary prevention for gifted students: A parent education group. *Elementary School Guidance and Counseling, 12*(2), 110–116.

Cullinan, D., & Epstein, M. (1986). Behavior disorders. In N. Haring & L. McCormick (Eds.), *Exceptional children and youth* (4th ed.) (pp. 161–199). Columbus, OH: Merrill.

Culross, R. R. (1982). Developing the whole child: A developmental approach to guidance with the gifted. *Roeper Review, 5,* 24–26.

Fortier, J. M., & Wanlass, R. L. (1984). Family crisis following the diagnosis of a handicapped child. *Family Relations, 33,* 13–24.

Goldstein, S., & Goldstein, M. (1990). *Managing attention disorders in children: A guide for practitioners.* New York: Wiley.

Grossman, H. (1983). Classification in mental retardation. In N. Haring & L. McCormick (Eds.) *Exceptional children and youth* (4th ed.) (p. 237). Columbus, OH: Merrill.

Hallahan, D., & Kauffman, J. (1986). *Exceptional children: Introduction to special education* (3rd ed). Englewood Cliffs, NJ: Prentice-Hall.

Haring, N. (1986). Introduction. In N. Haring & L. McCormick (Eds.), *Exceptional children and youth* (4th ed.) (pp. 1–39). Columbus, OH: Merrill.

Hawke, W. (1978). Psychiatric aspects of mental retardation. In P. D. Steinhauer & Q. Rae-Grant (Eds.), *Psychological problems of the child and his family* (pp. 265–283). New York: Macmillan.

Hawke, W., & Lesser, S. P. (1978). The child with a learning disorder. In P. D. Steinhauer & Q. Rae-Grant (Eds.), *Psychological problems of the child and his family* (pp. 242–264). New York: Macmillan.

Henker, B., & Whalen, C. (1989). Hyperactivity and attention deficits. *American Psychologist, 44,* 216–223.

Hobbs, N. (1975). *The futures of children.* San Francisco, CA: Jossey-Bass.

Lerner, J. (1989). *Learning disabilities, theories, diagnosis, and teaching strategies* (5th ed.). Boston: Houghton Mifflin.

Levine, M. (1987). Attention deficits: The diverse effects of weak control systems in childhood. *Pediatric Annals, 16*(2), 117–130.

Loeb, R., & Jay, G. (1987). Self-concept in gifted children: Differential impact in boys and girls. *Gifted Child Quarterly, 31,* 9–14.

Maes, W. (1978). Counseling for exceptional children. *Counseling and Human Development, 10,* 1–11.

McGown, M. P. (1982). Guidance for parents of a handicapped child. *Child: Care, Health and Development, 8,* 295–302.

Mercer, C. D. (1986). Learning disabilities. In N. Haring & L. McCormick (Eds.), *Exceptional children and youth* (4th ed.) (pp. 119–159). Columbus, OH: Merrill.

Patton, J. R., & Payne, J. S. (1986). Mild mental retardation. In N. Haring & L. McCormick (Eds.), *Exceptional children and youth* (4th ed.) (pp. 233–269). Columbus, OH: Merrill.

Rosen, P. (Producer). (1989). How difficult can this be? Understanding learning disabilities. Frustration, anxiety, tension: The f.a.t. city workshop. Greenwich, CT: Kopel Films, Inc.

Rudolph, L. (1978a). The counselor's role with the learning disabled child. *Elementary School Guidance and Counseling, 12,* 162–169.

Rudolph, L. (1978b). *Perceptions of exceptional individuals: How are they viewed in the world?* Unpublished manuscript, Austin Peay State University, Clarksville, TN.

Seligman, M. (1985). Handicapped children and their families. *Journal of Counseling and Development, 64,* 274–277.

Smith, T. & Neisworth, J. (1975). In T. Smith, B. Price, and G. Marsh (1986). *Mildly handicapped children and adults,* St. Paul, MN: West Publishing Company.

Smith, T., Price, B., & Marsh, G. (1986). *Mildly handicapped children and adults.* St. Paul, MN: West.

Strong, J., Lynch, C., & Smith, C. (1987). Educating the culturally disadvantaged, gifted student. *The School Counselor, 34*(5), 336–344.

Switzer, L. (1990). Family factors associated with academic progress for children with learning disabilities. *Elementary School Guidance and Counseling, 24,* 200–206.

Terman, L. & Oden, M. (1947). *The gifted child grows up: Twenty-five years follow-up of a superior group.* Stanford, CA: Stanford University Press.

West, J., Hosie, T., & Mathews, N. (1989). Families of academically gifted children: Adaptability and cohesion. *The School Counselor, 37,* 121–127.

Widerstrom, A. H., & Dudley-Marling, C. (1986). Living with a handicapped child: Myth and reality. *Childhood Education, 62,* 359–367.

Wolf, J., & Penrod, D. (1980). Bibliotherapy: A classroom approach to sensitive problems. *Gifted/Creative/Talented, 15,* 52–54.

Wolf, J., & Stephens, T. (1986). Gifted and talented. In N. Haring & L. McCormick (Eds.), *Exceptional children and youth* (4th ed.) (pp. 431–473). Columbus, OH: Merrill.

Ziegler, R., & Holden, L. (1988). Family therapy for learning disabled and attention-deficit disordered children. *American Journal of Orthopsychiatry, 58,* 196–209.

CHAPTER 16

Legal and Ethical
Considerations for Counselors

INTRODUCTION

Schmidt and Meara (1984) have defined the differences among ethical, professional, and legal issues in counseling. They defined ethical issues as those that "arise from personal and professional standards of moral duty and obligation" (p. 56). Professional issues are technical, procedural, or cultural standards members of the profession are expected to accept; and legal issues are related to federal, state, and municipal standards of practice as regulated by law.

At this time, counseling is seeking to identify itself as a profession. One mark of a profession is its ability to set standards for the training and practice of its members. The American Association for Counseling and Development (AACD) is encouraging state organizations to seek licensure (or some type of credentialing) for counselors in private practice. The American Psychological Association (APA) has supported licensure for psychologists for many years, and most states have laws regulating the practice of psychology. The professional issues of training and credentialing professional counselors, psychologists, and other helping professionals are discussed in Chapter 1. Both AACD and APA have codes of ethics to guide and govern members (American Association for Counseling and Development, 1988; American Psychological Association, 1990). These codes have become a part of the counselor and/or psychologist licensure laws in various states. Unfortunately, unless these codes are a part of the law regulating the practicing psychologist or counselor, the provisions are unenforceable.

A code of ethics provides practitioners with a standard to assist in judging appropriate behavior in counseling situations. Ethical codes are only "statements of principles, which must be interpreted and applied to a particular context" (Stude & McKelvey, 1979, p. 453).

Talbutt (1981) summarizes the role of ethical standards in three ways: "(a) They are self-imposed regulations; (b) they prevent internal disagreement; and (c) they provide protection in case of litigation" (p. 110).

Talbutt believes that ethical standards are particularly important to the counselor today because of recent litigation; the standards may offer counselors some protection from litigation if the counselor's behavior was in line with the standards and if the counselor was acting in good faith.

Mappes, Robb, and Engels (1985) have reviewed the literature to determine the various functions of codes of ethics in the mental health profession. They found that the codes serve those in the helping professions by "(a) protecting clients, (b) providing guidance to professionals, (c) ensuring the autonomy of professionals, (d) increasing the prestige of the profession, (e) increasing clients' trust and faith in the members of the profession, and (f) specifying desirable conduct between professionals" (p. 246).

All the writers Mappes et al. reviewed maintained that a professional code of ethics is needed for a variety of reasons, but the various codes of the helping professions have problems. A code of ethics must be general; therefore, the standards or principles are open to interpretation. Addressing this issue, Mappes et al. (1985) cite Smotherman's observation that the "most important factor related to ethical behavior remains the integrity of the practitioner" (p. 251). Mappes et al. (1985) also point out that conflicts exist between codes of ethics and the law and among the codes of ethics of different professions in some instances—for example, on the questions of advertising, confidentiality, and the client's right to see his or her file.

PRIVACY, CONFIDENTIALITY, AND PRIVILEGED COMMUNICATION

Stadler (1990) believes confusion exists concerning the terms *privacy, confidentiality,* and *privileged communication.* She states that the right to privacy ensures that people may choose what others know about them. Confidentiality refers to the professional responsibility one has to respect and limit accessibility to clients' personal information. Privileged communication refers to the legal rights of professionals to protect clients' confidences. Stadler writes that issues of confidentiality are the ethical problems counselors most frequently encounter. She recommends that counselors be extremely careful to apprise their clients of their limits of confidentiality at the very beginning of counseling.

Confidentiality and privileged communication are areas of conflict and concern mentioned by a number of writers. Schmidt and Meara (1984) also point out that privileged communication is a right granted by law, protecting communication between therapist and client from disclosure; however, they emphasize that state laws vary widely in defining the extent to which professional relationships are privileged. Confidentiality is the responsibility of the counselor to protect information as dictated by that profession's code of ethics. Mappes et al. (1985) report that all professions have a code advocating that the helper maintain confidentiality, but there is a difference in laws and codes as to the circumstances that permit confidentiality to be broken. Failure to warn a person of a threat against his or her life in California may result in liability, as evidenced by the *Tarasoff* decision (*Tarasoff* vs. *Regents of the University of California*), whereas in Texas the counselor may be violating the law if he or she attempts to warn an intended victim. Warning a person of a threat against his or her life probably violates the professional's code of ethics, depending on the profession and the situation. The various laws and codes do not always agree, intensifying the problem of sorting out the ethical, professional, or legal behavior dictated by the situation.

Confidentiality is a special problem for counselors working with children. According to Huey (1986), parents are legally responsible for the child, but the counselor has an ethical responsibility to the child—and these two may conflict. His position is that

> Ethical codes do not supersede the law, and they should never be interpreted so as to encourage conduct that violates the law. Counselors must become familiar with local, state, and federal laws, but legal knowledge is not sufficient to determine the best course of action. Each case is unique, and laws are subject to interpretation; consequently, professional judgment will always play a role. [p. 321]

An issue of confidentiality particularly troubling to counselors is that of child abuse. State laws now require that child abuse or neglect be reported, and 45 states have included criminal penalties in their laws for failure to report. This obligation places the helping professional in a "double-agent" position, according to Stadler (1989). Briefly, she states that the duty to protect the child (beneficence) overrides the principles of autonomy.

Wagner (1981) conducted a survey of school counselors to determine the attitudes of elementary, middle, and secondary school counselors toward confidentiality. The counselors surveyed (347 elementary, 423 middle school, and 426 secondary school counselors) viewed the limits of confidentiality as being set by their counseling setting as well as by the age, maturity, and problem of the child. They agreed that informal discussion of a child's problem with a person not involved was a violation of confidentiality. Elementary counselors were the least stringent about maintaining confidentiality, followed by middle school counselors; secondary counselors were the most stringent. Counselors in elementary schools were more likely to inform parents and authorities about illegal behavior such as drug possession or sales; secondary counselors were least likely to inform. Wagner points out that these findings parallel the counselor's perceived responsibility to parents. They also seem to reflect the counselor's assessment of the child's age, cognitive level, and maturity level. The movement of a child toward adolescence and increasing independence from the family apparently encourages counselors to work with the individual rather than to bring in other individuals responsible for his or her care—parents or guardians.

The Rights of Minors and the Law

School counselors may be faced with legal questions concerning medical treatment of minors (for example, in cases of venereal disease), the rights of minors in abortion issues, drug counseling, and the rights of married or unmarried pregnant girls in school. Talbutt (1980) has published an enlightening article on these issues, citing court rulings, that may be of assistance to school counselors. His article addresses several issues related to the rights of minors, including the following important points:

1. U.S. Supreme Court decisions have favored the right of a minor to have an abortion without parental consent; however, some states have rejected this ruling. If state law is in conflict with a Supreme Court decision, the latter takes precedence. The issue of the right of a minor to have an abortion is extremely volatile. Counselors are urged to make themselves knowledgeable about state and federal laws concerning the issue and to follow closely changes in the law. Talbutt quotes Burgum and Anderson cautioning counselors that recent decisions do not "affect the civil liability of a counselor who may . . . have negligently interfered with parents' rights to advise a minor" (cited in Talbutt, 1980, p. 403). Talbutt (1983) believes counselors should urge minors to discuss abortion plans with their parents. He cautions counselors to be objective and aware of and accepting of differing attitudes, realizing that they may be legally liable if they impose their views on minors. Talbutt concludes that the decision for or against abortion is the client's; the counselor's role is to provide a nonthreatening atmosphere for exploration and problem solving.

2. Every state has a law dealing with child abuse. Some states levy fines for failure to report child abuse; in others, counselors could be found guilty of a misdemeanor (in addition to civil liability) if they fail to report child abuse. Because state laws vary, counselors have a responsibility to check legal regulations in their states.

3. Talbutt (1980) refers to the American School Counselors Association's position paper, published in 1976, on the counselor's responsibilities in drug counseling. The statement suggests that school counselors respect individuals' rights while helping them assume responsibility; focus their counseling on the individual's concerns rather than on the abuse of drugs; refer the client for appropriate services; and respect the parents' rights—all while abiding by ASCA professional ethics and staying within the limits of local, state, and federal laws. Following these guidelines may be difficult, however, because there are no clear-cut answers in every case; laws vary, and ethics and laws conflict at times.

Talbutt raises important questions about the legal responsibilities of counselors, pointing out that we have no well-defined answers. At this time, the best protection for counselors seems to be a thorough knowledge of local, state, and federal laws, trends, and court decisions.

Confidentiality of Files

Access to files presents another concern involving confidentiality. There appears to be a move toward allowing clients to see their own records. The federal Family Rights and Privacy Act gives parents and students of legal age the right to inspect their records (Burcky & Childers, 1976). Counselors need to be aware of the types of records kept in institutional files. They may not be able to maintain confidentiality if the parents of underage children request access to such files. A personal file may be kept for confidential notes because personal files do not fall under this law. However, files that have been seen by *anyone,* including office file clerks or secretaries, or have been discussed with anyone in the process of decision-making, are no longer considered personal notes. Van Hoose and Kottler (1977) write that

> counselors and psychotherapists have a right to collect information about a client in order to provide proper treatment, but they also have a responsibility to use this information wisely; if they do not, then they must be prepared to be held ethically and legally accountable for abuse of a privilege. [p. 85]

Remley (1990) points out that there is no legal or ethical requirement that counselors keep notes about their counseling sessions. He suggests that if notes are kept, factual information concerning actual occurrences in the session should be kept separate from the subjective section in which the counselor records diagnoses and develops future treatment plans. Remley also recommends that notes be carefully written with the thought in mind that they could become public one day and that counselors may want to document certain information that could be questionable or controversial.

Confidentiality in Groups

Davis (1980) is especially concerned about maintaining confidentiality in group counseling. She points out that leaders in the field of group counseling, such as Gazda, have asserted that confidentiality is essential to the development of trust within the group. Meyers and Smith (1977) found that, when confidentiality was not assured in a group situation, self-disclosure was reduced. Mappes et al. (1985) also believe the problems of confidentiality are exacerbated in group counseling. Davis (1980), however, found that group members discuss what occurs in the group process with others; "soliciting assurances of confidentiality may not be realistic"

(p. 201). She suggests that group leaders need to give accurate information about confidentiality in order that members may decide how much information they want to disclose during group counseling.

Breaching Confidentiality

In court cases in states where counselors and psychologists (or other helpers) are not protected by a licensure law providing for privileged communication, they have no recourse except to reveal the information if subpoenaed. Some courts, more tolerant than others, will allow the counselor to share the privileged information with the judge in private to determine if the information is necessary to the proceeding or if public disclosure would be too hurtful to those involved, such as children who are a part of the case.

Mappes et al. (1985) suggest that when it is necessary to breach confidentiality, the counselor should inform the client of his or her intention to do so and then invite the client to participate in the process. The counselor should explain the reasons why confidentiality must be broken, summarize what he or she must do and say, and then encourage the client to take responsibility for assisting in resolving the dilemma — perhaps by talking to the parents involved or calling the authority, whichever is appropriate. They point out that if the counselor has informed the client about the counseling process during the initial interview (as required by the AACD and APA codes of ethics), the process of breaching confidentiality will not be as easily misunderstood.

Denkowski and Denkowski (1982) believe that "the extent of confidentiality that can be assured under . . . legal limitations is not absolute and is declining" (p. 374). Mappes et al. (1985) contend that "it could be in the best interest of society and future mental health clients for the professional associations of the various mental health disciplines to join forces in lobbying for privileged communication at the state and federal level" (p. 249).

Summary

Much of the recent literature on ethical concerns has addressed specific issues such as child abuse, clients with AIDS, dual relationships, or sexual misconduct. Little has been written in recent years relative to the issues involved in working with children. With the number of children in counseling increasing and the recent focus on the rights of children as developed from international conferences, this area should be addressed promptly.

When counseling with children, special ethical and legal problems must be considered. AACD Ethical Standards, Section B, No. 8, cautions counselors that "when working with minors or persons who are unable to give consent, the member protects these clients' best interests" (AACD, 1988).

APA Ethical Principle 5d also cautions that "when working with minors or other persons who are unable to give voluntary, informed consent, psychologists take special care to protect these persons' best interests" (APA, 1990). For personal safety and ethical practice, counselors are encouraged to consult with supervisors, ethics committees, colleagues, or legal experts any time questions may arise.

TEST YOUR ETHICAL BEHAVIOR

Although an understanding of ethical and legal issues is of utmost importance to those who work in the helping professions, there seems to be a serious lack of training, research, and knowledge in the area. As a test of your general understanding of ethical and legal issues, we suggest you consider the following situations and describe methods and procedures you would use in handling the incident. For many situations, there will be no *right* solution; the final answer will depend on your counseling setting, the philosophy of your supervisor, the interpretation of the law by your local or state authorities, potential advantages or disadvantages of the solution, and the risks to the counselor and client. In these situations, *our comments are only our interpretation and not necessarily the right answer.*

The 1988 Ethical Standards of AACD, the Ethical Principles of Psychologists (APA, 1990), and the Code of Ethics for the National Association of Social Workers (1979) are referenced in the discussions of situations presented. Although we understand that other professionals bound by other professional codes will encounter these situations, we believe all codes have similarities, and the principles outlined here can be generalized to other professions.

Issues of Competence

Professional competence is a continuing concern for all helping professionals. Preparation standards are described for training individuals in the field, professionals are cautioned about not exceeding their limits of competence, and practicing professionals are urged to continue their education because of rapid changes in all fields. Professional codes of ethics, as well as many licensure laws, address these issues.

■ **Situation 1:**   You are introduced in a church meeting as Dr. _____, who specializes in working with children. You actually have a master's degree and all your coursework for the doctorate but have not completed the dissertation. Your presentation to the group is about parenting, but you do not specialize in working with children. Rather, most of your clients are adults. You agreed to speak on parenting because the program chair is your friend and needed a speaker on this subject. Because this is a small church meeting, you do not see a need to correct the introduction. It might embarrass your friend. Is this an ethical decision?

Response: AACD Ethical Standards, Section A, No. 4, states that "the member neither claims nor implies professional qualifications exceeding those possessed and is responsible for correcting any misrepresentations of these qualifications by others." APA Ethical Principle 2a states that "psychologists accurately represent their competence, education, training, and experience. They claim as evidence of educational qualifications only those degrees obtained. . . ." Likewise, NASW's Code of Ethics, I.B.2, warns that the "social worker should not misrepresent professional qualifications, education, experience, or affiliations." Even though the meeting is small and not one associated with a professional organization, the misrepresentation should be corrected.

■ **Situation 2:**   A local industry calls you to consult with them about the motivational and morale problems of their employees. You are trained and credentialed in school counseling but have a strong background in psychology. With your knowledge and training you believe you can help the organization. What would you do?

Response: AACD Ethical Standards, Section E, No. 3, states that "the member must be reasonably certain that she/he or the organization represented has the necessary competencies and resources for giving the kind of help that is needed." APA Ethical Principle 2, "Competence," advises that professionals should "recognize the boundaries of their competence and limitations of their techniques" and "only provide services and only use techniques for which they are qualified by training and experience." NASW I.B.1 also addresses the issue of accepting responsibility or employment based on competence. The counselor in this case must objectively consider his or her qualifications. It may be helpful to discuss the issue with a colleague or to consult a credentialing board.

■ **Situation 3:**   You have been counseling with a 10-year-old who has been setting small fires for the three months you have been working with him. As you evaluate your progress, you decide you have not accomplished the goals you established at the beginning of treatment. You decide that because this is a difficult case, it is not reasonable to expect improvement in the near future. Is there an ethical problem here?

Response: AACD, Section B, No. 12, suggests that "if the member determines an inability to be of professional assistance to the client, the member must either avoid initiating the counseling relationship or immediately terminate that relationship" and make a satisfactory referral. APA Principle 6e states that "psychologists terminate a clinical or consulting relationship when it is reasonably clear that the consumer is not benefiting from it. They offer to help the consumer locate alternative sources of assistance." NASW II.F.9 likewise states that social workers should terminate services when their services are no longer required or meet the clients' needs. It would seem that in three months of treatment, the client should show signs of progress. If the counselor has serious doubts about the reality of his or her goals, consultation with another professional is recommended.

■ **Situation 4:**   You have completed one course in projective techniques, which included the Children's Apperception Test (CAT), and are offered a job in the state children's home administering and interpreting this test. The results will be used to diagnose children's problems and develop treatment plans. What do you do?

Response: AACD, Section C, No. 4, reminds members to "recognize the limits of their competence and perform only those functions for which they are prepared." APA, Principle 8f, cautions that "psychologists do not encourage or promote the use of psychological assessment techniques by inappropriately trained or otherwise unqualified persons." NASW does not address assessment issues but cautions that social workers should "accept responsibility or employment only on the basis of existing competence or the intention to acquire the necessary competence" (I.B.1). The writers of this book believe that a person is not fully trained and prepared to administer and interpret a CAT after one course and recommend that the person decline the job unless he or she receives appropriate supervision.

Public Statements

Professionals in private practice and others must be aware of their professions' recommendations that guide their advertising, public statements, and presentations to the public. These statements were developed to maintain high standards for the professions and to ensure that the integrity of the helping relationship is protected.

■ **Situation 5:**   Your friend has just opened a private practice. She has included her membership in AACD, APA, or NASW on her business card. Is this ethical?

Response: AACD Ethical Standards, Section F, No. 4, states that "members do not present their affiliation with any organization in such a way that would imply inaccurate sponsorship or certification by that organization." APA Ethical Principle 4a allows members to list their APA membership status, but 4b cautions against presentation of an "affiliation with any organization in a manner that falsely implies sponsorship or certification by that organization. In particular and for example, psychologists do not state APA membership or fellow status in a way to suggest that such status implies specialized professional competence or qualifications." NASW cautions social workers to "make no misrepresentation in advertising as to qualifications, competence, service, or results to be achieved" (V.M.4). The friend, in this case, would probably be safer to omit any reference to affiliation with a professional organization on her business card to avoid even the appearance of misrepresentation.

■ **Situation 6:**   You are asked to appear on a local radio show to give general suggestions to parents going through a divorce about how they can tell their children about the breakup, what reactions to the divorce they can expect from their children, and to provide guidelines for good parenting after the divorce. Would you accept this request? Why or why not?

Response: AACD Section A, No. 6, allows members to provide general information to the public, subordinates, peers, or supervisors but states that members have a responsibility to ensure that "the content is general, unidentified client information that is accurate, unbiased, and consists of objective, factual data." APA Principle 4 cautions psychologists that "in public statements providing psychological information or professional opinions . . . psychologists base their statements on scientifically acceptable psychological findings and techniques with full recognition of the limits and uncertainties of such evidence." NASW does not address the issue directly.

Professional Relationships

Issues concerning respect for all persons, regardless of age, race, gender, culture, and so on, have been widely discussed in recent years. Most professions have written new guidelines emphasizing the need to avoid stereotyping and discriminatory practices and prohibiting dual relationships, especially sexual relationships. Sexual harassment has also been defined and condemned.

■ **Situation 7:**   A male colleague is conducting groups in a girls' home with 15-year-old girls that involves discussions of friendships, boy/girl relationships, and sexuality. The group has been working together for several months and has become very close. The counselor likes to hug and pat the girls because he feels they have not had good relationships in their past, and this lack of love is part of their problem. Recently, several of the girls have complained to you about the way he touches them. What would you do?

Response: Although AACD Ethical Standards, Section A, No. 9, states that "members do not condone or engage in sexual harassment which is

defined as deliberate or repeated comments, gestures, or physical contacts of a sexual nature," it is not clear that this is a case of sexual
harassment. APA Ethical Principle 7d also cautions that "psychologists do
not condone or engage in sexual harassment . . . comments, gestures, or
physical contacts of a sexual nature that are unwanted by the recipient."
NASW does not address the issue specifically but warns against sexual
relationships (II.F.5) and those that conflict with the interests of their
clients (II.F.4). The colleague's behaviors are certainly not professional,
but more evidence would be needed for a charge of sexual harassment.
It is also possible that the counselor is opening himself up to a charge of
child sexual abuse (fondling). As a colleague, it is suggested you first
approach the male counselor and discuss your concerns with him. It is
possible he has misperceived the situation. If this does not resolve the
issue, you may wish to speak with the administration of the home.

■ **Situation 8:**   Your friend and counseling colleague in a community
mental health center asks you to counsel her. She is new in the profession and looks to you as her mentor. You also supervise her work in the
unit. She needs assertiveness skills to overcome her shyness and dependency tendencies. You recognize these skills will be necessary for her
professional competence. Would you help her?

Response: AACD Ethical Standards, Section B, No. 13, clearly states
that "when the member has other relationships, particularly of an administrative, supervisory, and/or evaluative nature with an individual
seeking counseling services, the member must not serve as the counselor
but should refer the individual to another professional." APA Ethical
Principle 6a cautions that "psychologists make every effort to avoid dual
relationships that could impair their professional judgment or increase
the risk of exploitation. Examples of such dual relationships include, but
are not limited to, research with and treatment of employees, students,
supervisees, close friends, or relatives." NASW also cautions social workers to "avoid relationships or commitments that conflict with the interest
of clients" (II.F.4). As your friend's supervisor, assuming the role of
counselor to her would place you in a dual relationship. You should
refer her to another professional for help, explaining that ethical codes
prevent you from serving in dual roles.

Personal and Professional Roles and
Responsibilities: The Welfare of the Client

Counselors play many roles in their personal and professional lives. They
are owners of private practices, employees of organizations, individuals in
the community, volunteers, and members of a profession. Sometimes these
roles conflict, and questions about "to whom am I responsible" and "who
is my client" may arise.

■ **Situation 9:**   Mr. Smith brings his 14-year-old son to your office. He angrily tells you that he has caught the boy engaging in homosexual play with his friends, and he wants you to "straighten him out." He will not have a "queer" for a son! According to him, this would ruin his family name and reputation. What would you do?

Response: You may tell Mr. Smith that you will be glad to counsel with his son if the boy would like counseling; however, your primary obligation under the ethical code is to the young man and his choices. AACD Ethical Standards, Section B, states that the "member must recognize the need for client freedom of choice." Section B, No. 1, further advises the member that his or her "primary obligation is to respect the integrity and promote the welfare of the client(s)." APA Principle 6 also exhorts psychologists to "respect the integrity and protect the welfare of the people and groups with whom they work" and, further, to "freely acknowledge that clients, students, or participants in research have freedom of choice with regard to participation." NASW Standard II.G urges social workers to "foster maximum self-determination on the part of clients," and II.G.2 says that "when another individual has been legally authorized to act in behalf of a client, the social worker should deal with that person always with the client's best interest in mind." As a counselor, you can help the boy explore the advantages and disadvantages of homosexual and heterosexual lifestyles, but the choice is his. Perhaps Mr. Smith also needs to know that his son's behavior could be due to a curiosity about sex normal for the young man's developmental level.

■ **Situation 10:**   You have been offered a job working with institutionalized children. The institution has a severe discipline code and other regulations that put a great deal of pressure on the children. The job description requires the person in this position to be responsible for discipline. You have strong reservations about the policies and procedures of this institution. Should you accept the job?

Response: The philosophy of the counselor should be in agreement with that of the employing institution. AACD Ethical Standards, Section A, No. 2, states that

acceptance of employment in an institution implies that the member is in agreement with the general policies and principles of the institution. . . . If, despite concerted efforts, the member cannot reach agreement with the employer as to the acceptable standards of conduct that allow for changes in institutional policy conducive to the positive growth and development of clients, then terminating the affiliation should be seriously considered.

APA Principle 6 advises psychologists that "when conflicts of interest arise between clients and psychologists' employing institutions, psychologists clarify the nature and direction of their loyalties and re-

sponsibilities and keep all parties informed of their commitments."
NASW states that "the social worker should work to improve the
employing agency's policies and procedures, and the efficiency and
effectiveness of its services" (IV.L.1). The counselor has an obligation
to discuss honestly with the institution his or her philosophy before
reaching an agreement concerning employment. If no agreement can
be reached, the counselor may want to seriously consider not accepting the position. Working under the conditions described would
reduce the counselor's effectiveness and could place him or her in
ethical jeopardy.

■ **Situation 11:**   As a counselor in private practice, you have been identified as a resource person in times of crisis and called to a school after a
severe tornado did considerable damage in your area. The principal has
allowed you the 10:00–10:45 time period for this one day only to work
with a group of children extremely upset and frightened by this disaster.
At 10:45, the group has just begun to admit feelings of fear and terror
that continue to plague them, as well as anger, grief, and sadness. The
bell sounds for the next class. What do you do?

Response: AACD Ethical Standards, Section B, No. 1, indicates that
"the member's primary obligation is to respect the integrity and promote the welfare of the client(s)." Section B, No. 17 cautions that when
"the member is engaged in short-term group treatment . . . , the member
ensures that there is professional assistance available during and following the group experience." APA Principle 6 also states that "psychologists respect the integrity and protect the welfare of the people and
groups with whom they work." No mention is made of follow-up after
the group experience, but psychologists are urged to make use of other
professionals and secure for their clients the best possible professional
services (Principle 7a). NASW encourages social workers to "seek the
transfer, referral, or continuation of service" when the social worker
anticipates interruption or termination of services (II.F.11). The writers
of this book believe the counselor's primary responsibility is the client's
welfare and he or she should continue working with the children until
assurances are given that everyone was able to move to the next activity
without harm. Referrals for children needing additional counseling
should be arranged with the school counselor, parents, or school
personnel.

Legal and Ethical Conflicts/Issues
of Consent and Confidentiality

As discussed in the introductory portion of this chapter, counseling with
children can present ethical dilemmas because of the child's minor status
and the parents' rights to know confidential information about their child.

■ **Situation 12:**   A young male, age 14, asks your help to stay off drugs. He has "experimented" numerous times and found himself using drugs more frequently because he liked the feeling. After a frightening experience while "high," he turns to you for help.

Response: Several issues, both ethical and legal, are involved in this situation. A minor has asked for your assistance. Can you legally treat a minor without parental consent? AACD Ethical Standards, Section B, No. 8, states that "when working with minors or persons who are unable to give consent, the member protects these clients' best interests." APA Principle 5d states that "when working with minors or other persons who are unable to give voluntary, informed consent, psychologists take special care to protect these persons' best interests." NASW states only that "the social worker should make every effort to foster maximum self-determination on the part of clients" (II.G). What would happen if you provided counseling without parental knowledge? An illegal substance is involved. What are the legal ramifications of maintaining confidentiality? This young person needs treatment for drug abuse. Are you qualified to provide this assistance? *Before* encountering occurrences such as this, the counselor should be aware of state laws and local enforcement practices regarding drug use by young persons and of the feelings of law-enforcement officers about counseling for these children. Treating a minor for a drug problem that could have potentially harmful effects physically is also an issue that will require legal advice from someone in your area. If the drug could have lethal effects, the question of whether to break confidentiality because there is "clear and imminent danger to the client or others" (AACD, Section B, No. 4) must be resolved. APA Principle 5 states that confidentiality is broken only in "unusual circumstances in which not to do so would result in clear danger to the person or to others." NASW cautions that social workers "share with others confidences revealed by clients, without their consent, only for compelling professional reasons" (II.H.1). Does a compelling reason or clear danger exist? This is a situation about which both legal and other helping professionals should consult before its occurrence to ensure that all involved understand the parameters. The answer to the dilemma will depend on a variety of forces, including differing state and local laws.

■ **Situation 13:**   A counselor in private practice is interested in studying the effects of working mothers on their children. Because she wants to write a book describing her research findings on this topic, she tapes counseling interviews with these clients. She will not identify anyone by name in her book and will obscure any identifying information; therefore, she does not believe it is necessary to tell the children or their parents that she is taping interviews or to ask their permission to use the material. Is this ethical?

Response: AACD Ethical Standards, Section B, No. 8, states that all clients must be informed of the "purposes, goals, techniques, rules of procedure, and limitations that may affect the relationship at or before the time that the counseling relationship is entered." In addition, Section D, No. 5, advises counselors that "all research subjects must be informed of the purpose of the study except when withholding information or providing misinformation to them is essential to the investigation." Section B, No. 5, states that "revelation to others of counseling material must occur only upon the expressed consent of the client." APA Principle 9d also states that subjects must know about research procedures that "might reasonably be expected to influence willingness to participate." Principle 5a states that "information obtained in clinical or consulting relationships . . . is discussed only for professional purposes and only with persons clearly concerned with the case." NASW II.H.5 states that the professional must obtain permission from the client "before taping, recording, or permitting third party observation of their activities." Parents or children who recognize that their confidentiality has been broken and their confidences revealed in print (even though obscured) have every right to feel anger toward and distrust of this counselor.

■ **Situation 14:**   You are a school counselor. A family new in the area brings their child to school for admission and tells you he has AIDS that has developed from a blood transfusion. They want this fact to remain confidential, but you have already heard rumors about the child, and others are asking you who has AIDS. Some people are concerned about having their children in school with an AIDS student. What do you do?

Response: AACD allows counselors to break confidentiality only when "the client's condition indicates that there is clear and imminent danger to the client or others" (Section B, No. 4) and advises the counselor to consult with other professionals whenever possible. APA Principle 5 states that psychologists reveal confidential information "only with the consent of the person or the person's legal representative, except in those unusual circumstances in which not to do so would result in clear danger to the person or to others." NASW cautions social workers that they "should share with others confidences revealed by clients, without their consent, only for compelling professional reasons" (II.H.1). The research about AIDS children reviewed in Chapter 14 suggests that casual contact will not spread AIDS, and therefore there should be no "clear danger" to others in the school system. The most appropriate action would seem to be to request the parents' permission to talk with the child's physician to ascertain that there is no reason for alarm over the possibility of contact and to maintain the child's confidentiality. This is an area where the law is emerging and changes frequently. Counselors will want to stay current on new laws and court decisions concerning AIDS.

■ **Situation 15:**   Lynn, age 7, is upset over the death of her mother and tells you she plans to join her mother in heaven. She has found her mother's medicine and plans to take a large number of pills in order to die. You discuss the situation with her at length and try to convince her it is better to live, but you are not sure she agrees. When she leaves, you still fear she will try to "join her mother in heaven." What would you do?

Response: Because of the possible danger, the counselor should call Lynn's father or other responsible persons. The counselor should tell Lynn what action must be taken, and why, before making the call. If the counselor believes the threat is serious, Lynn should not be left alone at any time until the issue is resolved. Lynn should be invited to be present and even tell her father herself (in the presence of the counselor) if she wants to. AACD Ethical Standards, Section B, No. 4, allows counselors to inform "responsible authorities" when "there is clear and imminent danger to the client or others." APA Principle 5 states that psychologists "reveal such information to others only with the consent of the person or the person's legal representative, except in those unusual circumstances in which not to do so would result in clear danger to the person or others." NASW II.H.1 allows social workers to share confidences "only for compelling professional reasons."

Research

In recent years, the research of some professionals has been criticized publicly for dishonest practices. In addition, some people feel growing concern about the misuse of humans and animals for research purposes.

■ **Situation 16:**   A researcher is misleading children in a school classroom about the purpose of his experimental research. Because the subjects are children and "too young to really understand what is occurring," he sees no need to debrief them. React.

Response: AACD Ethical Standards, Section D, No. 5, states that *all* research subjects must be told the purpose of the study and that if the researcher is withholding information, corrective measures should be taken as soon as possible. APA Principle 9, Research with Human Participants, suggests the same procedures and states that research with children requires special safeguarding procedures. NASW I.E.2 requires social workers to obtain the voluntary, informed consent of research subjects and (in NASW II.G) to safeguard the rights of all clients.

■ **Situation 17:**   A researcher reports the results of a study on certain counseling techniques for improving children's behavior. One indication of the study is that corporal punishment contributed to withdrawal and depression in some children. The administration of the school that contracted for this study asks the researcher not to report that finding because the school favors a policy of allowing corporal punishment in schools and is concerned about parental response to the findings. The researcher decides it probably would not be wise to report this particular finding (the results were barely significant) because this school system is a good client. React.

Response: AACD Ethical Standards, Section D, No. 13, cautions that research "results reflecting unfavorably on institutions, programs, services, or vested interests must not be withheld," and APA Principle 1a states that "in publishing reports of their work, [psychologists] never suppress disconfirming data." NASW does not address this issue directly but states that research "should be guided by the conventions of scholarly inquiry" (I.E). To withhold this information is unethical.

Assessment

With the growing assessment movement, all professionals must become more concerned with administering instruments appropriately and reporting results accurately. Tests can be used in a beneficial manner for counseling, but persons untrained in assessment could use these data in detrimental ways to harm clients.

■ **Situation 18:**   You are administering a new instrument to a group of children to help in placement in a class for behavior disorders. Included in the group are children from other cultures (Japan, Korea, Italy, and Mexico) as well as several African American children. The manual states that norms were developed on a group of white middle-class children. Because you need a battery of tests to determine if these children are to be placed, you decide to include the results of this instrument in your report as another indicator. Is this ethical?

Response: AACD Ethical Standards, Section C, No. 12, states that members "must proceed with caution when attempting to evaluate and interpret the performance of minority group members or other persons who are not represented in the norm group on which the instrument was standardized." Further, Section C, No. 2, cautions that "general validity, reliability, and related issues may be questioned legally as well as ethically when tests are used for vocational and educational selection, placement, or counseling." APA Principle 8c maintains that "psychologists indicate any reservations that exist regarding validity or reliability because of the circumstances of the assessment or the inappropriateness of the norms for the person tested." NASW does not address assessment issues directly but cautions social workers to "prevent practices that are inhumane or discriminatory against any person or group of persons"

(I.B.2). This test should not for any reason be used on children who are not included in the norm group. The use of the instrument for placement could result in both legal and ethical ramifications.

■ **Situation 19:**   When children come to a children's center for assessment of their behavioral functioning, your colleague places them at a computer terminal with several computer counseling programs she has developed for assessment purposes. The children are free to come and go until they complete the program. Your colleague checks periodically to see how they are doing and mails her results to the school, doctor, or parent who referred the child. Is this ethical practice?

Response: It appears that this counselor is violating AACD Ethical Standards, Section B, No. 16, which states that the counselor must ensure that "the client understands the purpose and operation of the computer application; and . . . that a follow-up of client use of a computer application is provided to both correct possible problems (misconceptions or inappropriate use) and assess subsequent needs." Section C, No. 1, states that the member must "provide specific orientation or information to the examinee(s) prior to and following the test administration so that the results of testing may be placed in proper perspective." In the preamble to APA Principle 8, the code states that psychologists "guard against the misuse of assessment results." The APA ethical principles do not mention computer-assisted counseling. The counselor's lack of contact during the procedure and after completion of the program, and the lack of personal interpretation of the results does not show respect for the client's right to know as prescribed by all three codes of the helping professions. NASW does not address the ethics of assessment because most social workers are not involved in this area.

Professional Responsibility

As in all professions, some people in the field will knowingly or unknowingly violate ethical principles. Recognition of these violations presents colleagues with a dilemma concerning personal rights, legal possibilities, and friendship issues.

■ **Situation 20:**   You are aware of ethical violations in any one of the cases described above. You work with the person commiting the violations. What do you do?

Response: AACD Section A, No. 3, states that "when information is possessed that raises doubt as to the ethical behavior of professional colleagues, whether Association members or not, the member must take action to attempt to rectify such a condition. Such action shall use the institution's channels first and then use procedures established by the

Association." APA Principle 7g requires that when psychologists are aware of other psychologists' unethical behavior, "they informally attempt to resolve the issue by bringing the behavior to the attention of the psychologist." If this does not work or if the violation is serious, "psychologists bring it to the attention of the appropriate local, state, and/or national committee on professional ethics and conduct." NASW also states that the social worker "should take action through appropriate channels against unethical conduct by any other member of the profession" (V.M.2). It is preferable that the professional involved be contacted first and the matter discussed with him or her. If sufficient evidence indicates a violation is occurring, the professional may wish to pursue the matter with the offender's employing organization, contact the state or national ethics committee of the person's professional organization, or report the violation to the state board for credentialing.

Summary

It is difficult to recommend specific answers to the situations outlined in this chapter because situations, people, and laws vary. References are given to AACD, APA, and NASW codes of ethics to aid readers in formulating their own resolutions. It is hoped that readers will be stimulated to read the ethical standards thoroughly and to consider the issues in the light of presenting situations and regulations.

The foregoing situations are by no means all the ethical and legal situations encountered in counseling. Other situations and their resolutions for study appear in the casebooks prepared by AACD and APA. The situations in this chapter are intended only to give readers some indication of their own ethical knowledge and practices. Should uncertainty arise concerning interpretations of ethical practices, counselors have the option of consulting other professionals or local, state, or national professional ethics committees.

REFERENCES

American Association for Counseling and Development. (1988). *Ethical standards* (rev. ed.). Alexandria, VA: Author.

American Psychological Association. (1990). Ethical principles of psychologists (revised). *American Psychologist, 45,* 390–395.

Burcky, W. D., & Childers, J. H., Jr. (1976). Buckley amendment: Focus of a professional dilemma. *The School Counselor, 23,* 162–164.

Davis, K. (1980). Is confidentiality in group counseling realistic? *Personnel and Guidance Journal, 58,* 197–201.

Denkowski, K. M., & Denkowski, G. C. (1982). Client-counselor confidentiality: An update of rationale, legal status, and implications. *Personnel and Guidance Journal, 60,* 371–375.

Huey, W. (1986). Ethical concerns in school counseling. *Journal of Counseling and Development, 64,* 321–322.

Mappes, D., Robb, G., & Engels, D. (1985). Conflicts between ethics and law in counseling and psychotherapy. *Journal of Counseling and Development, 64,* 246–252.

Meyers, R., & Smith, S. (1977). A crisis in group therapy. *American Psychologist, 32,* 638–643.

National Association of Social Workers. (1979). *Code of ethics, adopted by the 1979 NASW Delegate Assembly and revised by the 1990 NASW Delegate Assembly.* Silver Spring, MD: NASW Press.

Remley, T. (1990). Counseling records: Legal and ethical issues. In B. Herlihy & L. Golden (Eds.), *Ethical standards casebook* (pp. 162–169). Alexandria, VA: American Association for Counseling and Development.

Schmidt, L., & Meara, N. (1984). Ethical, professional, and legal issues in counseling psychology. In S. Brown & R. Lent (Eds.), *Handbook of counseling psychology* (pp. 56–96). New York: Wiley.

Stadler, H. (1989). Balancing ethical responsibility: Reporting child abuse and neglect. *The Counseling Psychologist, 17,* 102–110.

Stadler, H. (1990). Confidentiality. In B. Herlihy & L. Golden (Eds.). *Ethical standards casebook* (pp. 102–110). Alexandria, VA: American Association for Counseling and Development.

Stude, E. W., & McKelvey, J. (1979). Ethics and the law: Friend or foe? *Personnel and Guidance Journal, 57,* 453–456.

Talbutt, L. (1980). Medical rights of minors: Some answered and unanswered legal questions. *The School Counselor, 27,* 403–406.

Talbutt, L. (1981). Ethical standards: Assets and limitations. *Personnel and Guidance Journal, 60,* 110–112.

Talbutt, L. (1983). Current legal trends regarding abortions for minors: A dilemma for counselors. *The School Counselor, 31,* 120–124.

Tarasoff vs. *Regents of University of California.* (1974). 13c. D177; 529 p. 2D553; 118 *California Reporter, 129.*

Van Hoose, W. H., & Kottler, J. A. (1977). *Ethical and legal issues in counseling and psychotherapy.* San Francisco, CA: Jossey-Bass.

Wagner, C. (1981). Confidentiality and the school counselor. *Personnel and Guidance Journal, 51,* 305–310.

APPENDIXES

Appendixes A and B suggest techniques for intervening with specific problem behaviors and are included to stimulate ideas. The lists, of course, are not exhaustive, but we hope they will be helpful to counselors attempting to develop treatment plans for children. Beside each heading are *suggested* DSM-III-R categories (American Psychiatric Association, 1987) to assist counselors in classifying client behaviors. Caution should be used in assigning classifications because the categories ordinarily describe mental disorders and are not appropriate for all problematic behaviors that are not a part of a pattern or syndrome of symptoms.

Appendixes C, D, and E present the ethical standards and guidelines for counselors as outlined by the American Association for Counseling and Development, the American Psychological Association, and the National Association of Social Workers.

Children's Conflicts with Others
Alternatives for Intervention

The suggestions in this appendix are techniques collected from a variety of resources on counseling children with learning and social problems. Some suggestions are to be used in working directly with the child; others are consultation techniques for use with parents and teachers. In each case, it is essential that the procedures be incorporated into a therapeutic counseling or consulting atmosphere that includes caring, respect, empathic understanding, and acceptance. The techniques presented can be preventive and developmental as well as remedial; it is nearly impossible to say that any given technique has one application to the exclusion of others. In any case, the techniques should be adapted to meet the unique needs of children and their behaviors.

V71.02
309.30
312.00
312.20
312.34

Fighting

Fighting is one of the most common behavioral problems of children today. Many children have not learned to settle their misunderstandings other than by physical means. Fighting may be a way of gaining attention; a learned behavior from parents, peers, or other significant people in the children's lives; or a way of striking back at a world perceived as cruel and hostile. Resolution of disagreements and conflicts by means other than fighting is a viable goal of school personnel and parents; however, fighting will occur despite the best efforts of adults. Following are various suggestions for working with fighting behavior. (See also "Destructiveness.")

1. Examine the situation that brought on the encounter. Determine the sequence of events and if there is a particular time, place, or situation in which fights are likely to occur. Become an environmental engineer; rear-

range the time schedule or the physical environment. Intervene in the sequence of events to prevent or circumvent fight-arousing conditions.

2. Fighting can be a compensation for feelings of inadequacy, ignorance of social skills, learned behavior from the home, or a means of covering up emotional or learning problems. Investigate these possibilities by becoming a "child watcher" and listening actively to the child (see Chapter 4).

3. Use group or family discussions to focus on how fighting helps or hurts the fighter, how others feel about fighting, the consequences of fighting, and ways in which the fighter could solve conflicts more effectively. Children should also be encouraged to practice new behaviors before the group and use their feedback to improve relationships.

4. Determine the goal of the fighter (see Chapter 10 regarding goals of misbehavior). Is the child seeking attention, power, revenge, or free time? Is the fighting a learned behavior? Could the fighting be due to a lack of social skills?

5. Contract with the fighter to not fight for a short period of time (two hours, four hours, one day). Continue to renegotiate the contract until the behavior decreases significantly. Rewards for not fighting and consequences for fighting behavior may be included (see Chapter 7 regarding contingency contracting).

6. Allow two evenly matched students to fight it out under supervision, using pillows, styrofoam bats, or socker-boppers. In an extreme case cited by Stradley and Aspinall (1975), a school administrator set aside one night a month for chronic fighters to meet, with parents required to be present.

7. Arrange with the physical-education teacher for students to work out their emotions with punching bags or other equipment, under supervision. Each time students are found fighting, encourage them to go to the gym and work out for a certain period of time (perhaps 15 minutes). After a cooling-off period, the fighters should be required to write a plan for avoiding future fighting. Nonwriters may dictate or tape their contracts.

8. Have the fighters write their side of the story or tell it to a tape recorder. Ask the children to read their stories to you, or listen to the tape with them. Discussion of the stories provides a release for emotion, as well as a stimulus for evaluating the behavior and its consequences and for planning other ways to resolve such situations in the future (Collins & Collins, 1975).

9. Films, television programs, or stories can stimulate children to think more objectively about fighting and its consequences. Follow the film or story with a family or group discussion examining the causes and consequences of fighting and other ways the situation could have been resolved.

10. Children and parents or teacher may cooperatively draw up a list of ground rules concerning fighting. Each time the adult notices the child about to become involved in a fight, the adult asks "What is the ground

rule?" Have the child repeat the rule. Early and consistent intervention is necessary. A variation of this technique is to clearly define the consequences of fighting and, when fighting is about to occur, ask "What happens when someone fights?"

11. Encouragement from friends or peers (or other kinds of peer pressure) can help the child control fighting behavior. Find the fighter a good model with whom to work or play. Ask the child to describe or list the model's behaviors. Rehearse and practice admired behaviors.

12. Have two fighting children clean a window, one on each side of the window, facing one another. Encourage them to look *really mean* and glare at each other. The first child to smile loses the game of "looking mean" but wins a hug or other reinforcement (Blanco, 1972).

13. Isolation techniques such as Seat 2, the quiet corner, and time-out rooms are effective for helping children cool off. When the children feel ready to return to the family group or classroom, they are allowed to do so without lectures or blame, provided they have a plan for staying out of fights (see Chapter 12 regarding isolation techniques).

14. The adult may quietly ask the fighters to leave the room and develop a plan for solving their conflict. Because the fighters are disturbing the other activities in the room, the adult may ask them to reschedule their fight for another time and place. Usually the children react in shock and quietly join in the group or family activities.

15. Three chairs are placed in a semicircle. The adult sits between the two fighters and asks them to describe what happened. The adult repeats verbatim to Child A what Child B says, and then to B what A says. This continues until usually everyone ends up laughing. The adults limit themselves to conveying messages between A and B, refraining from making judgments or placing blame (see Chapter 5). Discussion of a plan for avoiding future conflicts may follow.

16. Dreikurs, Grunwald, and Pepper (1971) suggest that parents who have trouble with their children fighting withdraw to the bedroom or bathroom until the fighting ceases. Precautions should be taken to prevent one child from harming the other.

17. Peer pressure, especially in small groups, is often effective in helping fighting children change their behavior. Carlin and Armstrong (1968) suggest a technique for reducing aggressiveness and rewarding cooperative group play. The adult may arrange rewards to be given to the group when they are playing or working cooperatively. The adult should present the reward to the group and tell the reason for it. Fines for the misbehavior of a member may also be levied on the group. The amount of the reward minus the fines is divided among group members at the end of the day. For the child who continually misbehaves and causes the group to be fined, isolation techniques are suggested. The misbehaving child would neither receive a portion of the reward for the time spent in isolation nor be the cause of excessive fining when in isolation.

18. Have the fighting children carry index cards and keep a record of the number of fights that occur each day. Have them role-play exactly what happened and the consequences. Discuss alternatives to fighting, rehearse how the situation could have been handled more appropriately, and develop a plan for not fighting in future situations.

19. Use methods for building self-esteem so fighting will not be necessary for the child to feel good about himself or herself. (see "Poor Self-Concept," Appendix B). Responsibility and praise for a job well done will add to a positive self-concept—for example, "I appreciate your helping put away the games we used during this activity."

20. If excessive punishment or brutality seems to be a factor, counsel with the parents to help them learn more effective ways of relating to the child. Books such as Ginott's *Between Parent and Child* (1965) or Gordon's *Parent Effectiveness Training* (1970) may be helpful.

21. Strongly confront older children with the reality questions (see Chapter 3), using these questions every time a fight occurs or is about to occur.

22. For very young children who have trouble with fighting, play therapy using puppets, art, or drawings to assess feelings that stimulate fighting may be helpful.

23. Relaxation techniques or music therapy may be helpful for angry or anxious children who fight often.

24. Boswell (1982) suggests helping children with their anger through a HELPING model: (1) educating the children for good *H*ealth; (2) assisting them to cope with *E*motions through play therapy, games, bibliotherapy, relaxation, and humor; (3) helping them *L*earn more about their angry feelings; (4) facilitating improvements in *P*ersonal relationships through counseling techniques such as assertiveness training, role-playing, and parent counseling; (5) using *I*magery; (6) teaching them improved cognitive control—the *N*eed to know; and (7) giving *G*uidance about actions, behaviors, and consequences.

25. Limit the student's independent movement, especially in areas where he or she might become more aggressive, and maintain constant supervision (Cummins, 1988).

26. Find a quiet place for the child to work or play away from peers. This procedure should not be used as punishment, but rather as an opportunity for productive work (Cummins, 1988).

V71.02
312.00
312.20
312.34

Verbal Abusiveness

Most verbal abusiveness, such as rudeness, sarcasm, impoliteness, and name-calling, is a cover for feelings of inadequacy, a learned behavior from adults or other models, a call for attention, or a way of striking back at an unfriendly world. In this instance, the child needs interactions with adults who are calm, rational, and consistent and who behave maturely. Adults need to be on guard and not allow the child's verbal abusiveness to provoke the same behavior from them. When adults resort to criticism, belittling, and name-calling, they have little chance of changing children's behaviors.

1. Determine the goal of the verbal abusiveness. Could it be that the child is seeking attention, revenge, or power? (See Chapter 10.) Become a "child watcher" and listen attentively to help determine these needs and goals. Once the goal has been defined, the adult can help the child find a more constructive means of meeting this need.

2. Meet privately with rude, sarcastic, impolite, or name-calling children. Interpret their behavior to them as a cry for help. Then discuss the reasons they feel it necessary to use verbal abusiveness. Plan with the children ways to avoid the behavior in the future.

3. Meet with the "victims" of the abuser. Explain to these victims that if they do not respond to the abuse, it is not as satisfying to the abuser and the behavior will decrease (Collins & Collins, 1975). Plan and rehearse their behavior when the abuser "attacks."

4. Contract with abusing children to reduce verbal abrasiveness. Clearly define unacceptable behaviors and their consequences. Rewards for appropriate responses may also be included in the contract (see Chapter 7).

5. Provide opportunities for success. Praise and reinforce nonabusive behavior. Example: "I noticed how understanding you were when Tom had his accident today. That was a nice thing to say to him."

6. Role-play or use films, filmstrips, or books to demonstrate and provide stimuli for group or family discussions. Examine what has occurred and the consequences. Discuss new and better methods of interacting. Behavior rehearsal may help children practice the new behaviors.

7. Call together the parties engaged in the verbal battle and have them write their story or tell it to a tape recorder. Read the story aloud with them, or play the tape, and allow the children to discuss and evaluate what has happened. Ask them to make a plan for avoiding future verbal battles.

8. Encourage the teacher, parents, or other children to learn to ignore the verbal abuser. If the behavior becomes so unacceptable that it cannot be ignored, use isolation techniques such as Seat 2, quiet corner, or the time-out room (see Chapter 12).

9. Use role reversal. Have someone else play the verbal abuser and the abuser play the recipient of the verbal attack. Discuss how it feels to be in each position. Plan for better ways of handling conflicts. Role-play the alternatives and the consequences of proposed new behaviors.

10. Use techniques for building self-esteem so the child will not have to resort to verbal abuse (see "Poor Self-Concept," Appendix B). Avoid

criticism, name-calling, and belittling remarks. Praise and reinforce cooperative behavior.

11. Give reprimands quietly, firmly, and calmly. Do not attack the child as a person. Focus on the behavior, and admit how the behavior makes you feel—for example, "I get really angry when I hear students talking like that, and I would like you to stop now." Avoid modeling the behaviors for which the reprimand is given.

12. Pair the child with good role models for work and other activities. Discuss with the child the behaviors he or she sees in the models and the positive and negative consequences of these behaviors. Encourage the child to rehearse and practice these behaviors.

13. Try the "satiation principle" (Krumboltz & Krumboltz, 1972). Every time children use abusive language, have them go into a room alone and practice being abusive. Ask them to talk to a tape recorder in an abusive manner for a specified period of time (perhaps 5 minutes). Children soon tire of this procedure and begin to speak more carefully.

14. Put up a "graffiti sheet" in the child's room or private area for writing out feelings. Emphasize to the child that if vulgar or derogatory language is to be used, it must be used in private (Stradley & Aspinall, 1975).

15. Every time a child is verbally abusive, quietly place a check on a chart or card. Contract with the child so that if a certain number of checks are accumulated, privileges will be lost or other consequences previously agreed on will be imposed. If there are fewer checks than the agreed number, the child is rewarded with special privileges chosen by the child. Avoid lecturing, reminding, scolding, or nagging when recording checks as this attention is reinforcing to the child.

16. Teach children new and acceptable ways of expressing feelings, and suggest words to say in situations in which they tend to be verbally abusive.

17. Help older children develop a self-management plan. Work with them using thought-stopping for irrational ideas and the techniques of cognitive restructuring to stop the feelings that accompany verbal abusiveness. Help them develop an alternative plan for expressing their feelings.

18. For older children, try confrontational techniques such as "Could it be?" questions ("Could it be you want to hurt me by calling me names?") or the reality questions described by Glasser (see Chapter 3).

19. Monitor the child's activities, especially in situations where verbal abusiveness is more likely to occur, and maintain constant supervision (Cummins, 1988).

20. Interact frequently with the child in order to monitor his or her language (Cummins, 1988).

21. Omizo, Hershberger, and Omizo (1988) present a guidance program for teaching children to cope with anger. They recommend activities for getting to know one another and for becoming aware of feelings. Specific incidents and feelings should then be discussed, relating the inci-

dent to a feeling represented on the Ferris color wheel. The next sessions involve making choices and finding alternative reactions to anger, modeling the behavior, role-playing, and summarizing.

V71.02
309.30
312.00
312.20
312.34

Physical Abusiveness

Physical abusiveness, or bullying, can be a compensation for a poor self-concept. Children often hide fears and feelings of inadequacy behind acts of bullying. Verville (1968) suggests that bullies generally feel inferior. Children may also be responding to or modeling adult behavior they have observed. Bullying may be an attempt to strike back at an unfriendly world or to seek power and attention the child cannot gain otherwise. Bullying children need calm, consistent adult/child interactions. However, because bullying behavior usually provokes anger in the adult, the child may receive only criticism and punishment—increasing feelings of worthlessness and hostility.

1. Give reprimands in a quiet, adult manner without devaluing the child as a person. Focus the reprimand on the behavior. Instead of calling the child a name such as *bully*, admit your feelings to the child: "I get angry when I see you hit other children like that, and I would like you to stop."

2. Sociograms are helpful in learning who the bully likes or dislikes. Activities may be grouped with liked children and appropriate role models. Discuss with children the behaviors they see in the models and the positive and negative consequences of these behaviors. Encourage children to rehearse and practice these behaviors.

3. Have a family or group discussion. Present to the group a hypothetical example similar to an actual incident. Films, filmstrips, or stories may be used to stimulate discussion. Guide the discussion to explore why children bully, how bullies feel about themselves, how other children feel about bullies, and more appropriate behaviors. Role-play and rehearse the new behaviors. Use feedback and group encouragement to promote changes in behavior.

4. Praise and reinforce friendly and cooperative behavior. For example, if the child helps another, verbally or physically, during play activities or during any social interaction, comment on the appropriate behavior. "Catching" children in good behavior is an effective intervention for most behavior problems.

5. Contract with the child to reduce specific acts of bullying. Clearly define unacceptable behaviors. Rewards for success may be included in the contract, along with negative consequences such as isolation for breaking the terms of the contract (see Chapters 7 and 12).

6. Provide outlets for the child's emotions in supervised activities such as running, hammering, writing out feelings, drawing, pictures, playing games, or talking out feelings.

7. Encourage responsibility by giving children responsible jobs at

which they can feel successful—for example, delivering materials or messages, watering plants, or feeding the fish. Avoid drudgery-job assignments.

8. Encourage cooperation by finding an interest or ability the bully has. Have the child pursue this interest or ability by helping others or sharing it with others (for instance, sharing a stamp or rock collection, building a science project).

9. Observe the child's environment to determine situations that provoke bullying behavior. Try to engineer the child's activities to reduce opportunities for bullying. Rearrange time schedules or the physical environment, if possible. Intervene before the opportunity for bullying occurs.

10. Determine the goal of the bullying behavior. Could the child be attempting to gain attention, power, or revenge, or to strike back at what he or she perceives to be a hostile world? (See Chapter 10.) Could the bullying be a learned behavior or the lack of social skills?

11. Use ideas for building a good self-concept (see "Poor Self-Concept," Appendix B) so the child will not have to resort to bullying to cover feelings of inadequacy. Reinforce and praise cooperative behaviors.

12. Use role reversal. Have someone else play the bully and the bully play the person being attacked. Discuss the feelings of each player. Allow the children to suggest more appropriate methods of behaving and to practice the new behaviors.

13. Find a quiet place for the child to work or play away from situations that may stimulate physical abusiveness. Monitor his or her behavior (Cummins, 1988).

14. Teach the child problem-solving skills so he or she can find better ways of reacting to frustrating situations (Cummins, 1988).

Cruelty to Peers, Animals, and Others

V71.02
312.00

Cruelty to people or animals is usually a sign of other problems. Extended counseling may be necessary to uncover the underlying reasons for the cruelty. Children who are cruel to peers or animals may be responding to punitive adults in their own life. Severe cases may require intensive psychotherapy or even residential treatment (see also suggestions under "Fighting" and "Destructiveness").

1. Closely supervise the children in all activities.

2. Give the children releases for emotional tension—for example, varying quiet activities with physical activities frequently. Encourage constructive physical releases such as running, playing ball, or cycling. Writing, music, art, and talking may also help. Schedule times for releases regularly throughout the day's activities.

3. Employ group or family discussions that emphasize cooperation with others. Discuss the feelings and events that provoked the cruel acts, and plan ways for coping with these feelings.

4. Encourage cooperation, responsibility, and pursuit of interests by

giving children responsible jobs in which they can feel success—for example, delivering messages or filing materials. Caution should be taken not to place more responsibility on the child than the child can tolerate. Find areas of interest, and structure activities and jobs around these interests.

5. Contracting and isolation techniques may be used to control behavior to some extent (see Chapter 12). Clearly define and explain acceptable and unacceptable behaviors and the rewards and penalties for each.

6. Carefully structure the child's environment and daily activities so there is little or no opportunity for unacceptable behavior. Plan each hour's activity in cooperation with the child, if possible. A daily schedule of work, play, study time, and planned leisure time can be posted in the child's room or school desk.

7. Avoid the use of physical punishment. Strong punishment produces further anger and the likelihood of aggression. It also provides a model for cruel, aggressive behavior. Limit TV viewing to nonaggressive programs. Remove as many models of aggression and cruelty as possible. Focus on strengths, and reinforce cooperative behaviors.

8. Determine the goal of the cruel behavior. Does the child see the world as cruel? Could the child be seeking revenge or power? What needs are not being met? (See Chapter 10.)

9. Diaries, play therapy, fantasy games, sentence completion, and active listening may be used as aids to understanding cruel children. Diaries and play therapy also allow children to vent their thoughts and feelings nondestructively.

10. Interpret the child's cruel behavior as a cry for help and an expression of loneliness and rejection. Ask the child to write out feelings of contempt and cruelty. Discuss the feelings, and make a plan for more constructive ways of handling them.

11. Ask the cruel child to find an admired model and to keep a list of the model's behaviors for a short time. Discuss the behaviors with the child, rehearse new behaviors, and encourage the child to try out new ways of behaving.

12. With the child, draw up a behavioral contract, setting out rewards for appropriate behaviors and the consequences of cruel behavior. Clearly define acceptable and unacceptable behaviors (see Chapter 7).

13. The child who has a tendency toward cruelty will need love, attention, acceptance, encouragement, patience, active listening, clearly defined limits, and structure in the environment (Dinkmeyer & McKay, 1973).

V71.02
309.30
312.00
312.20
312.34

Destructiveness

Destructiveness and vandalism are problems of increasing severity in our society (see also "Fighting"). One of the counselor's first concerns is to find what is happening in the child's environment to cause such intense feelings and behavior. Is the child so angry at someone or something (school, for instance) that there is an intense need to strike out and hurt that person or place? Could the destructiveness be caused by frustration, feelings of failure, or feelings of revenge because the child feels no one cares? A second concern is gaining the child's trust in order to change this self-defeating behavior—a task that requires time and patience.

1. Determine the goal of the child's destructiveness. Could the motive be attention, feelings of rejection, anger, a need for power, or revenge (see Chapter 10)?

2. Examine the situation that brought on the destructiveness or preceded the act. Is there a particular place, situation, or time in which destructiveness occurs most often? If so, become an environmental engineer, arranging the circumstances or schedule to avoid the situations.

3. Use logical consequences (see Dreikurs et al., 1971) as punishment or penalty for destructive behavior. Whatever the child destroys must be paid for or the cost worked off in some manner. Refrain from harsh punishments; they may reinforce the child's idea that the world is cruel and hostile and that destructiveness is the only way of getting back at this world.

4. Have the child write a description of the destructive act and a plan for avoiding such behavior in the future. If the act occurs in school, tell the child you will place the description in his or her school file and remove it at the end of a specified length of time if the act has not been repeated. If the destructiveness occurs in the home or some other environment, arrange to file the description of the act in a safe place with the understanding that it will be removed and destroyed at the end of a specified length of time if the act has not been repeated (Collins & Collins, 1975). A reward might be arranged to accompany the removal of the description from the file.

5. Confront the child nonjudgmentally by interpreting the destructive behavior as a distress signal. Offer to listen and to help. An attitude of genuine caring and interest is necessary to building a helping relationship (Collins & Collins, 1975). Help the child make a plan to avoid destructive behaviors in the future.

6. Start a campaign of "Keep our school (home) clean!" Working together to build pride in personal areas is often helpful in preventing vandalism or destructiveness, especially if the children are involved and consulted during the planning and are given some responsibilities (Collins & Collins, 1975). "We" feelings build cooperativeness and responsibility.

7. Determine the child's areas of interest and involve the destructive child in working with these interests—not busywork but productive tasks. Peer teaching, peer tutoring, or sharing the interest in another way may be helpful. Guiding the child in pursuing interests and special abilities may be a productive way of diverting the child's behavior toward more constructive actions and building feelings of success.

8. To handle the negative feelings that often accompany vandalism and destructiveness, many parents or teachers put up a large sheet of paper in the child's area or room—a "graffiti sheet." The child is allowed to write out feelings on the sheet (Stradley & Aspinall, 1975). Emphasize to the child that it is destructive to write out these feelings on other people's property.

9. Children can be encouraged to keep a diary of their feelings and thoughts or tell them to a tape recorder. Writing or talking provides a means of catharsis and gives the adult some insight into the child's world. The adult and child can then discuss these feelings and develop a plan for coping with them.

10. Play therapy with toys, Play-Doh, music, or drawing may be used in an effort to understand the feelings underlying the child's destructiveness and as a means of catharsis (see Chapter 8 regarding play therapy).

11. Hold group or family discussions focusing on the consequences of vandalism and destructiveness. Help the children look at what they are doing, the consequences, and alternative ways of behaving. Use behavior rehearsal to practice new methods of handling situations.

12. Help the destructive child find a friend and model. Encouragement and peer pressure are effective in helping vandalizing children redirect their behavior into more constructive paths. Pair destructive children with more mature role models to teach them effective ways of behaving. Discuss the behaviors of the model, and allow the children to practice and rehearse these behaviors.

13. Refrain from punishing, scolding, lecturing, moralizing, preaching, or degrading destructive children. These methods reinforce the children's thinking that the world and people are cruel and uncaring.

14. Use contracting with rewards to help the child change destructive behaviors (see Chapter 7). Be certain the child understands the rules. Define appropriate and inappropriate behaviors clearly, with the rewards and consequences of each.

15. A resource person from a local law-enforcement agency may be asked to discuss laws and penalties for destructiveness and vandalism with the children, but scare techniques and threats should be avoided.

16. Arrange the child's schedule so there is time during the day to work off energy. Vary the day's activities from quiet to physical. Encourage physical activities such as running, football or basketball, and bicycling, and quiet releases such as writing, music, art, or talking.

17. Work out a plan with the child and adult authority so that when the child's intense feelings are overwhelming, the child can signal the adult and report to some agreed-upon place to work out these feelings. For example, assisting the custodians with maintenance and cleaning might help in three ways: (1) to dissipate bad feelings, (2) to develop appreciation for the building, and (3) to create empathy for the custodian, who has to repair damage to the building.

18. Maintain supervision of all activities, and interact with the child often to monitor behaviors and discuss right and wrong methods for coping with situations (Cummins, 1988).

V61.20
V71.02
Tantrums
313.81

Temper tantrums may create feelings of anger, frustration, and helplessness in parents or other adults. Adults often feel they have completely lost control of the child and the situation when children throw temper tantrums. In some children, tantrums are a learned behavior for getting attention or getting their way. Some children have learned to manipulate adults by throwing tantrums; some seek revenge.

1. Determine the motive for the tantrum. Is the tantrum an effort to gain attention, to cover feelings of inadequacy, to manipulate, or to embarrass or strike out at adults (see Chapter 10)?

2. Children throw tantrums because it is a learned behavior that works for them. They get their way or what they want. The adult can stop the behavior by not allowing it to work. Ignore the behavior whenever possible; refuse to give in. The tantrum will thus become an unrewarding behavior.

3. If ignoring the tantrum becomes impossible, quietly ask the child to leave the room and write a plan for avoiding tantrums in the future. The child should have the option of returning and behaving appropriately after a cooling-off period. It may be necessary to physically remove the child from the room. It is not as much fun for the child to put on the act if there is no audience (see Chapter 12 regarding isolation techniques).

4. Alternative methods of venting feelings can be provided. Ask children to keep a diary of their feelings, write them out on paper, or talk to a tape recorder. Play therapy can be used, and fantasy games or storytelling may provide some catharsis and insight (see Chapter 8).

5. Use active listening to help understand the child's feelings and the motives behind the tantrums (see Chapter 4).

6. The possibility of the tantrums being related to a physical problem should be investigated if the behavior continues over a period of time. Refer the child to a pediatrician for examination.

7. Try to determine the sequence of events that brings on a tantrum or if there is a particular time, place, or situation in which tantrums are most likely to occur. Rearrange the environment or schedule to reduce the child's frustrations, if possible.

8. Avoid threats, lectures, scolding, and nagging. These can be reinforcing because they are forms of attention. Define the unacceptable behavior and the consequences for such behavior (see Chapter 7), and con-

sistently carry out the terms of the behavioral contract between the adult and the child.

9. Kaufman and Wagner (1972) describe a "barb" technique used to cope with tantrums in a male adolescent. They report a case study in which they (1) built rapport with the adolescent; (2) identified the situations provoking the tantrum; (3) defined the adolescent's actual behaviors; and (4) defined the consequences of those behaviors. Role reversal was used to demonstrate his behavior to him. The counselor then gave the adolescent a cue that a put-down or insult was coming, and he was rewarded for appropriate responses to the "barb." In later sessions, barbs were given by other people and became more subtle in order to help the adolescent generalize his newly learned responses. The authors caution that the technique must be used systematically; that unplanned barbs must never be used in anger; that when the tantrum is unrelated to a barb, nothing should be mentioned concerning the technique or its rewards; and that moving too slowly or too quickly through the program will hamper its effectiveness.

10. Severely disturbed children often have temper tantrums because they feel insecure. Using techniques of isolation and other forms of strictness may tend to intensify these feelings. In such cases, some tantrum-throwing children will become quiet when held affectionately and reassured.

11. Hare-Mustin (1975) found paradoxical intention an effective method for helping one 4-year-old boy. The child's tantrums were unpredictable and occurred anywhere. It was decided with the child that he should continue to have the tantrums, but only in a specified place. A room was selected, and each time the child began to have a tantrum he was immediately taken to this room. If he was not at home, he agreed to wait until he could return home and go to his "tantrum room." The next step was to decide on a time of day for tantrums to occur. The family selected a two-hour period. If the child started to have a tantrum at any other time, he was reminded to wait until the appropriate hour. The author reports a dramatic reduction in, and then disappearance of, the problem behavior.

12. Peer pressure can be an effective tool for modifying children's behaviors. Group or family discussions of temper tantrums and their effects on others may help the tantrum-throwing child understand how others react to the behavior.

13. Have another child role-play tantrum behavior. Discuss how the behavior helps or hurts the child and others, and make a plan for alternative ways of behaving. Rehearse and practice the new behaviors.

14. Help the child find a mature model. Ask the child to keep a list of the model's admired behaviors and ways in which the model handles frustrations. Rehearse and practice these ways of behaving.

15. Examine with children the self-messages that make them angry

enough to throw tantrums, and try to identify more rational and helpful self-messages (see Chapter 6).

16. Teach the child more appropriate ways for communicating his or her unhappiness through problem-solving techniques, role modeling, or other counseling strategies.

Chronic Complaining

V62.81
309.82
316.00

Chronic complaining about feeling ill is a method of gaining attention or sympathy and of avoiding unpleasant situations. This behavior can be manifested as an exaggeration of symptoms or fantasies of diseases: "I think I have cancer." Other kinds of hypochondria are consistent headaches, stomachaches, and muscle aches.

1. Recommend to the parents and child that the complaining child be examined by a pediatrician to rule out the possibility of an actual physical illness.

2. Try to determine the motive or goal of the chronic complainer. Are the complaints a result of feelings of inadequacy, fear of failure, a need for attention or sympathy, or an attempt to avoid an unpleasant task? Help the child find ways of meeting this need more effectively.

3. Enlist the cooperation of the pediatrician. Many pediatricians require the children to come straight to their office whenever they feel a pain. Children (and parents) soon tire of repeated trips to the pediatrician.

4. Actively listen to the child's complaints (see Chapter 4). Do not overly sympathize, but tell the child you will write a note or call the parents to suggest a trip to the doctor's office to check out the complaint.

5. Ask complaining children to write out their feelings or tell them to a tape recorder. A diary might be of help in determining the circumstances under which the feelings occur.

6. Excessive stress and tension can provoke chronic complaining. Check with parents, teachers, and other significant persons in the child's life. The child may be under pressure from schoolwork, from problems within the home, or from peers.

7. Precautions should be taken to ensure that the child is not ill when complaints occur; parents and other adults can then firmly insist that the complainer attend to the task or return to class. Reassure the child that should an illness occur, help will be provided (Blanco, 1972).

8. Chronic complaining may result from a lack of interest in the world around the child—school, friends, activities. Help these children to find an ability or activity in which they can feel successful. Encourage participation in groups, children's clubs or organizations, or neighborhood activities.

9. Enlist the aid of a "buddy" to encourage the complainer to become more involved in the world and to participate in friendships and activities.

10. Rutter (1975) suggests that "treatment consists of dealing with the

stresses which gave rise to the disorder and in helping the child find a better way of dealing with stress" (pp. 238–239). Actively listen for clues to what these stresses are, and plan with the child for more constructive means of coping with the tensions (relaxation techniques, physical activities, talking, writing, play therapy).

11. Have complaining children monitor their own behavior. Give these children an index card and ask them to check it every time they become aware that they are complaining. Catching oneself in the act often increases awareness of the behavior and reduces the incidence.

12. Try to find ways for complaining children to assume more responsibility in their lives. Feeling competent and worthwhile reduces the need to gain attention through sickness.

Tattling V62.81

The tattler, like a gossiper, is attempting to gain attention and favor, usually with an adult authority figure. It is difficult to ignore talebearers because many times they bring needed information to adults. However, the tattler is usually lonely and rejected by peers.

1. Determine the goal of tattling. Is the child attempting to gain attention or power or to seek revenge (see Chapter 10)? Confront the child with your hypothesis — for example, "Could it be that you are telling me this in order to get Warren in trouble?" (Dreikurs et al., 1971).

2. Meet privately with the tattler and interpret the behavior as a cry for help to gain acceptance and recognition in the group. Discuss the reasons the child may feel it necessary to tattle. Plan with the tattler for ways to avoid the behavior in the future and to gain attention and acceptance in other ways.

3. Help the tattler gain acceptance by capitalizing on special abilities and interests such as sports, hobbies, or special knowledge. Encourage the child to share these abilities and interests with others or to peer-teach or tutor another child.

4. The tattler may need help in learning social skills. Help the child find a model. Have the child list the model's admired behaviors and then rehearse and practice these new behaviors.

5. Turn your attention elsewhere when the tattler begins a tale. Say, "Rather than discussing that now, perhaps we should _____ ."

6. Use tattling as a topic for family or group discussions, guiding the group to look at motives for tattling and the reactions and feelings of others toward a tattler. Films, filmstrips, or stories may provide a stimulus for these discussions. List alternatives to tattling, and rehearse and practice them.

7. Use storytelling, choosing a hypothetical example similar to the child's problem, to show the consequences of tattling and the reactions of others to tattling (see Chapter 8). Ask the child questions about how the tattler must be feeling and how the child who is being tattled on must feel.

8. Instead of listening to the tattler, ask the child to write a brief note for you explaining what has happened.

9. Ignore the tattling behavior, but praise and reinforce appropriate behaviors. Give attention to the child for the cooperativeness.

10. When ignoring tattling becomes impossible, draw up a contract with the child with rewards for not tattling. Penalties and rewards for appropriate and inappropriate behavior may be included (see Chapter 7).

11. Use techniques for building self-esteem (see "Poor Self-Concept," Appendix B) so the child will not have to resort to tattling to gain attention and acceptance.

12. Pair tattlers with good role models for work and other activities. Discuss with the tattlers the behaviors they see in the model and the positive and negative consequences of these behaviors. Encourage the child to rehearse and practice these behaviors.

13. Krumboltz and Krumboltz (1972) suggest it is helpful to teach children the "discrimination principle"—identifying clues that will help them know when to report an incident to adults (such as danger to property or possible personal harm), as opposed to reports that are considered tattling.

14. Have tattling children monitor their own behavior. Ask them to check an index card each time they tattle or feel the urge to tattle. Increasing awareness of the behavior may decrease the frequency.

15. Encourage tattling children to problem-solve. Rather than having the adult take over the situation and seek a resolution, say to the child, "I wonder what could be done to straighten this out." Assist the child in seeking alternatives.

16. Teach the child what information is appropriate for reporting (emergencies, fighting, cheating, and so on) and what is inappropriate (Cummins, 1988).

V62.81
312.90
313.81

Swearing

Swearing may reflect a need for attention, an effort to shock others or prove to peers that the child is "big," or modeling behavior. Swearing can also be a release for pent-up aggression or tension or an expression of rebellion.

1. Determine the motive for the behavior (see Chapter 10). Is the goal a need for attention or power, an effort to cover feelings of inadequacy, or an emotional release? Or does the swearing reflect a lack of social skills?

2. Confront the child, interpreting the swearing behavior as a need to shock or gain attention—for example, "Could it be that you want to shock me by talking in that manner?" (Dreikurs et al., 1971). Work with the child to make a plan to avoid swearing in the future.

3. Examine the child's world. Is there a certain time of day, a partic-

ular situation, or a certain event that provokes the swearing? If so, attempt to reduce the frustrations by rescheduling or rearranging the environment.

4. Ignore the behavior, if possible. When this becomes impossible, contract with the child to decrease the swearing systematically (see Chapter 7). Build in rewards for success and consequences for unacceptable behavior. Isolation techniques (see Chapter 12) may or may not be used in the contract, depending on the severity of the problem.

5. Try a type of implosive counseling, or "flooding." Place the swearer in an isolated room, and ask the child to swear continually for a specified period of time, such as five minutes.

6. Small children may not be aware of the meaning of the words they use. Ask the child to define the word. Remind swearers that there are certain words that are acceptable in certain places and at particular times and others that are not appropriate.

7. Work with the swearer to draw up a list of acceptable words to express feelings. Write a contract with the child that states that, when frustrated, the child will use these words instead of the usual swearwords. The swearer might carry the list on an index card for easy reference.

8. Dreikurs et al. (1971) suggest inviting children to show how many bad words they know. The authors further suggest that the counselor help swearing children understand why they like to use these words and what they could do instead of swearing to feel important. Discuss alternative methods of for expressing emotions (physical activities, art, games, music, new verbal responses). Rehearse these alternatives, and contract with the child to try the new methods of responding to emotions.

9. Hold a family or group discussion focused on the motives for swearing and how others feel about the swearing person. Use role-playing and role rehearsal to help children see the behavior and its effects on others. Discuss alternatives to swearing, and role-play these alternatives.

10. Use storytelling (see Chapter 8) with a hypothetical example similar to the child's problem. Ask the child to react to the story.

11. If swearing seems to be a means of releasing tension or aggression, contract with the child to work off these emotions in more acceptable ways — running, writing, talking, physical exercises. Writing out feelings in a diary or talking into a tape recorder may also help the child vent feelings.

12. A type of aversive conditioning may be used with a child who wants to stop swearing. For example, every time the child says a swearword, the punishment might be for the child to snap a rubber band worn on his or her wrist.

13. Help the child find a model. Have the swearer watch the model for several days and list the ways the model reacts to frustrating situations. Rehearse and practice the new behaviors with the swearer.

14. Use cognitive restructuring to help angry children who use swearing as an outlet. They may be able to "reframe" the situation so it does not stimulate swearing.

15. Self-monitoring may help older children become aware of their behavior. Self-reward for *not* swearing should be included in the self-management program.

16. Teach children stress-management techniques, such as deep breathing, to help ward off the feelings that may stimulate swearing. When the child feels an urge to swear, he or she is encouraged to deep-breathe instead.

17. Use confrontational techniques such as the reality questions (Chapter 3) to encourage responsible behavior.

18. Fischer and Nehs (1978) successfully reduced swearing behavior in one 11-year-old boy by setting up a chore (a mildly aversive stimulus) as a consequence of the swearing behavior.

Lying

V68.81
309.00

As a part of their normal development, young children often lie because of their inability to distinguish fact from fantasy or because of fear of disapproval and punishment. Habitual lying may be due to feelings of inadequacy, insecurity, or pressure from parents or other significant persons in the child's life. It could also be a learned behavior to escape responsibility or punishment.

1. Determine what needs of the child are not being met (see Chapter 10). Is the child seeking attention or power? Is he or she attempting to evade reality or the consequences of misbehavior?

2. Arrange for successful experiences in learning and in daily interactions with peers. Use praise and other types of reinforcement for appropriate behaviors to build confidence and self-esteem. Lying may not be necessary if the child has confidence in himself or herself (see "Poor Self-Concept," Appendix B). Ignore the lying or fantasy behaviors while reinforcing positive behavior.

3. Avoid trying to trap the liar. If you have positive evidence that the child is lying, be quietly direct in your confrontation—for example, "Jeff, I know that you did not do your homework." If you do not have direct knowledge of the truth, admit to the child that you are having trouble understanding all of the story and ask for more details. This response lets the child know you do not believe all that is being said and gives the child a chance to tell the truth.

4. When the child continues to tell stories that are obviously fantasies, the adult may confront the fantasizer in a nonjudgmental manner, using statements such as "You know, I have never seen or heard anything like that, and I'm really having trouble understanding what you are telling me. Could we begin again?" With this technique, you do not call the child a liar, but you convey that you simply cannot accept all that is being said as the truth.

5. Note the areas in which lying seems to occur most often. Is the

child lying about schoolwork, parents, money, clothes, or aggressive abilities? If the lying occurs most frequently in one area, examine the possibilities of changing the circumstances in this area to decrease the temptation or pressure to lie.

6. Talk with parents, teachers, and others close to the child. Are the expectations and pressures placed on the child too great? Do parents expect perfect behavior and the highest school marks? Are teachers demanding too much work or work that is too difficult for the child? If so, consult with these adults concerning ways of reducing pressures on the child.

7. Ignore fantasy tales that are meaningless, or ask the child to write the story and give it to you. Caution should be exercised not to ignore the child altogether. Respond to positive behaviors.

8. If the problem seems to stem from excessive pressure, decrease the push toward competition with others and emphasize competition with self: "You did six math problems yesterday. Let's see if you can do eight today."

9. Use the technique of storytelling (see Chapter 8). Choose a hypothetical example involving behaviors similar to those exhibited by the lying child. Ask the child to react to the story, and discuss these reactions.

10. Review the child's academic progress. Is lying a way to compensate for a learning difficulty or a cover for some other real or imagined failure?

11. Films, filmstrips, stories, and other materials may provide stimuli for a good classroom or family discussion on lying and its consequences. Include in the discussion methods for avoiding lying and better ways of handling situations.

12. Dreikurs et al. (1971) suggest that adults not pay attention to or respond to lying behavior, fantastic stories, or something that seems exaggerated or incorrect.

13. A child who feels worthwhile, loved, and successful will not have to resort to lying (see also "Poor Self-Concept," Appendix B). Give the child responsible jobs such as carrying messages, watering plants, or feeding fish (not drudgery work) that will promote feelings of success. Use a sociogram to find admired classmates, and pair the child with these children for group activities.

14. Enlist the aid of a "buddy" to involve the child in activities. Ask the child to keep a record of a model's behaviors to aid in learning techniques for successful interpersonal relationships. Practice and rehearse these behaviors in a safe atmosphere. Encourage the child to try the new behaviors.

15. Contract with the child not to lie. The contract should include acceptable behaviors and their rewards and should clearly define unacceptable behaviors and their consequences (see Chapter 7).

16. Use self-monitoring to increase awareness of the behavior. Have children keep a record of each time they told the truth when they were tempted to lie. Build in self-reward for situations in which the child tells the truth.

17. Take no action unless there is conclusive evidence that the child is telling the truth (Cummins, 1988).

Teasing

Teasing is a form of attention-getting behavior with several possible motives. Children may get attention only when they misbehave; they may be showing friendship for another; or they may have a hostile motivation. Teasing is sometimes the result of a lack of knowledge about how to make friends, how to be a friend, or other social skills.

1. Determine the goal of the teasing (see Chapter 10). Is the motive attention-seeking, power, or revenge, or does the teasing come from a lack of social skills? Teasing can be a way of compensating for feelings of inadequacy or a means of covering up learning or emotional problems. Become a "child watcher," listening actively to investigate all possibilities (see Chapter 4).

2. Examine the circumstances under which the child engages in teasing. What is the sequence of events? Is there a particular time, place, or situation in which teasing occurs most frequently? If so, rearrange the environment or schedule to reduce provoking circumstances.

3. Group or family discussions may help the child see how teasing behavior affects others and can also produce suggestions and a plan for alternative ways of behaving. Peer pressure in group situations is an effective behavior modifier.

4. Ignore the teasing behavior as long as possible. When it is no longer possible to ignore the teasing, use an isolation technique such as Seat 2, quiet corner, or the time-out room (see Chapter 12). The teaser should be free to return to the group when the child has worked out a plan for behaving more acceptably.

5. Cooperatively draw up a contract to decrease teasing behaviors. Clearly define unacceptable behavior and the consequences (see Chapter 7). Rewards for appropriate behaviors may also be included.

6. Help the child find other ways to get the attention or acceptance desired. Encourage the child to pursue liked activities, interests, or hobbies and to share them with other children. Allow the child to peer-teach or tutor another child. Assign responsible tasks to the child; avoid meaningless work or drudgery jobs.

7. Teasing is often modeling behavior. Check the child's environment to determine if the teaser is modeling an admired person. Help the child find a more appropriate model, observe the model's behaviors, and rehearse new and more acceptable ways of interacting with peers.

8. Have another child role-play a teaser to allow the child to see the behavior more clearly and to observe how others respond to teasing. Use role reversal to allow the teaser to see how teasing helps or hurts personal

relationships. After the role playing, discuss the feelings of the person teasing and the person being teased.

9. Talk with the people being teased. Plan ways for these children not to reinforce the aggressor's teasing behavior. Explain to the victims of the teaser that the behavior is not as much fun if the person being teased does not respond. Explain to them that the motivation of the teaser is to get attention, even though it is negative attention. Role-play situations, teaching the victims new methods of responding using such techniques as cognitive restructuring or ignoring the teasers.

10. Albert Ellis's ideas of irrational thinking may be incorporated into counseling with the person being teased (see Chapter 6 for an explanation of cognitive restructuring). Teach the victim to change internal thinking from "It is terrible to be teased" to "I don't like to be teased, but it is not the end of the world, and I can just ignore the teasing."

11. Children will have little need to tease if they feel they are a part of their environment and successful in the world. Find ways of providing successful experiences. Capitalize on the child's interests and abilities. Encourage participation in activities at school, at home, or in the community.

Disobedience, Negativism, and Resistant Behavior V71.02 313.81

Disobedience, negativism, and resistant behavior are open displays of anger and antagonism toward authority figures. Children exhibiting these behaviors are often highly critical, easily irritated, and sometimes aggressive.

1. Determine the goals of the behavior (see Chapter 10). Actively listen to the child to learn about the child's feelings toward self, family interactions, and the school (see Chapter 4). Children tend to strike out when their needs for love and respect are not met. Recognize the child's feelings. Admit that the child has the power to disobey or resist. Avoid threatening the child. Refuse to become involved in a conflict; tell the child you will discuss the matter later (Dreikurs et al., 1971).

2. Dreikurs et al. (1971) suggest that adults interpret the goal of the misbehavior to the child with "Could it be?" questions, but not at the time of the conflict. Later the adult might ask, "Could it be that you would like to show me that you are boss?" The question opens the door for a non-judgmental discussion of the child's motives and for planning better ways of meeting these needs.

3. At a time when there is no conflict, discuss with the child the consequences of the negative behavior and plan alternative behaviors. Rehearse and practice alternative behaviors.

4. Avoid open confrontations with put-downs, threats, and name-calling. Try active listening in an attempt to learn the reason for the negativism or disobedience (see Chapter 4).

5. Assess the environment in which the child is disobedient, negative, or resistant. Is the child receiving some reinforcement from peers or other

significant persons? What are the circumstances provoking the behavior? Is there a time when negativism, resistance, and disobedience occur most often? Rearrangement of schedules or the environment may decrease the undesirable behavior.

6. Avoid possible conflict situations by allowing the child some choices—for example, "Do you want to complete the assignment now or after lunch?" Make a list of tasks to be done, and cooperatively plan the day's schedule with the child.

7. Specify in advance the consequences for disobedience, negativism, and resistant behavior. Hold a discussion with the child in which you draw up ground rules and the consequences for breaking the rules. Rules made in cooperation with children are carried out more readily.

8. When the child misbehaves, the inappropriate behavior should be clearly explained. Children often do not understand what they have done wrong. After defining the problem, work with the child to draw up a plan or contract to change behavior (see Chapter 7). The plan may include rewards for acceptable behavior and penalties for unacceptable behavior. Rehearse and practice new behaviors to help the child meet the terms of the contract.

9. Ignore the negativism, disobedience, and resistant behavior, if possible. When ignoring the behavior becomes impossible, isolation techniques such as Seat 2, quiet corner, or time-out room may be effective in changing the behavior (see Chapter 12). Avoid physical punishment; it only provides a model of aggression for the child.

10. Disobedience, negativism, and resistant behaviors are often attempts to cover up a lack of self-confidence, lack of social skills, or an inability to find success in school and other areas of life. Attempt to determine if the unacceptable behavior is compensatory behavior for a learning problem, a lack of self-esteem, or some other problem. Look over the child's academic progress to determine if the behavior could be related to a learning problem. Carefully watch the child's interactions with others to determine if the problem is related to difficulties with social relationships. Listen for clues that may help you understand the child's feelings about self and others (see the discussion of active listening in Chapter 4).

11. Praise, telephone calls, or notes to the child's home about good behavior, along with other positive reinforcers such as praise, privileges, or rewards, may be effective in decreasing negative behavior.

12. Barcai and Rabkin (1972) report they were successful in changing a 13-year-old girl's undesirable behavior by "excommunication." The girl had learned to control her family, behaving inappropriately to get their attention and manipulate their interactions. The family was instructed to define appropriate and inappropriate behaviors, to totally ignore her when she behaved in an unacceptable manner, and to talk with and respond to her when she was behaving appropriately.

13. Suggest that parents or teachers leave the room for a few moments

to remove themselves from the conflict. This arouses surprise and curiosity in the child about what the adult will do. The action also prevents the adult from entering into a conflict with the child (Dreikurs et al., 1971).

14. Encourage the child to use constructive methods for releasing negative feelings. Suggest techniques such as talking out or writing out feelings, drawing, music, or physical exercises. Arrange for periodic emotional outlets if necessary.

15. Find the negative, resistant, or disobedient child a model or friend. Ask the child to watch the model and record admired behaviors. Then rehearse and practice these behaviors with the child.

16. Encourage negative children to pursue interests, hobbies, and abilities and to become involved in activities, clubs, or other organizations in which they can feel successful. Enlist the aid of a friend or "buddy" to involve the child in activities.

17. Blumberg (1986) used a daily progress-report checksheet to change the disruptive classroom behavior of a 13-year-old boy. The inappropriate behaviors included constant talking, interrupting teachers, and daily altercations with peers. Each teacher rated the subject daily on positive and negative behaviors. Positive behaviors were reinforced with tangible rewards at first but increasingly with intangible rewards (praise, attention from special teachers) as time passed. Conferences were held with the parents to encourage their use of verbal praise.

V71.02
312.00
312.20
Stealing
312.32

Children may steal because of the high value society places on material wealth, because of ignorance of ownership rights, to impress others, or for the adventure of getting away with something. Although many children try stealing once or twice during their developmental years, persistent, repeated acts of stealing indicate other problems and require an understanding of the motives and needs behind the behavior.

1. Determine the motivation or goal of the behavior (see Chapter 10). Is the child seeking attention, power, or revenge; or is the behavior the result of a dare, an initiation, or peer pressure? Is this the first incidence of stealing, or is there a pattern of behavior? Actively listen to the child to try to understand the motive (see Chapter 4).

2. Temptation in all situations can be kept to a minimum to help the child control stealing. Adults can place too much temptation before even the most honest children.

3. Use logical consequences to cope with the stealing child. Have the child replace or make payment for stolen property, through work if possible.

4. Give the child an opportunity to return the stolen property anonymously to an unpoliced area at a certain time without accusing anyone.

5. Have group or family discussions about stealing, its consequences, and the rights of ownership. Films, filmstrips, books, and newspapers can stimulate such a discussion. Discuss alternatives to stealing. Plan and rehearse appropriate ways of handling situations that might be tempting to the child.

6. Make certain children are aware of ownership rights. Comments such as "This is school property, but it is our responsibility" remind the child of ownership rights.

7. If stealing occurs in a group, often the children can solve the problem themselves if allowed to do so. Present the situation to the group, ask them to draw up a plan for resolving the problem, and leave the room for a few moments. Upon returning, ask for a discussion of the plan, avoiding accusations and blame.

8. Avoid trying to trap the thief or making threats that cannot be carried out, such as "We are all going to stay here until the property is returned." Such threats inevitably end up with the adult having to withdraw the ultimatum.

9. If you have positive evidence that the child is stealing, be quietly direct in your confrontation. Ask the child for a plan to pay for the stolen item and for avoiding stealing in the future.

10. Use behavior rehearsal to practice situations in which the child could be tempted to steal. Include instances in which peer pressure might occur. Discuss ways to handle these situations, and practice the behaviors.

11. Adults can inform children when they are suspected of stealing. Discuss with the children the consequences should the behavior continue. Avoid scare tactics.

12. Use storytelling (see Chapter 8), posing a hypothetical example similar to the child's problem. Ask the child for a reaction to the story. Discuss what might happen to the story character involved in stealing.

13. Help the stealing child find a model. Have the child watch the model for several days and list admired behaviors. Rehearse and practice these behaviors with the child.

14. Children may be stealing to feel more accepted by their peers. Most children who find some success in their lives and feel they belong have no need to behave inappropriately. Find an interest, hobby, or ability (stamp or rock collection, knowledge on a subject of particular interest to children, sports ability) the child possesses. Use this strength to help the child become involved in activities and find friendships.

15. If stealing is a prevalent or persistent behavior, ask a local law-enforcement person to talk with the children about the legal consequences of stealing.

16. Encourage the child to focus on "reality, responsibility, right and wrong" through the techniques of reality therapy (see Chapter 3).

17. Azrin and Wesolowski (1974) suggest an "overcorrection proce-

dure" in which children are required to give back not only the stolen property but an additional item.

18. Miller and Klungness (1986) have reviewed behavioral literature on the various approaches to the treatment of stealing behavior. They suggest that aversive contingency-management techniques, including scolding, threatening, lecturing, and physical force, are ineffective because the punishment is usually delayed and because of legal constraints on school personnel. Positive contingency-management techniques (including group contingencies) — reinforcing the nonoccurrence of stealing and including consequences for stealing — combined with family intervention, seem to be preferred. They also recommend school prevention programs that promote prosocial alternative school activities.

19. Rosen and Rosen (1983) used a highly controlled and structured behavioral technique to eliminate stealing behavior in a 7-year-old boy. During the first phase of the study, all items in the subject's desk were marked with a green pen. His desk was checked at 15-minute intervals, and he earned points redeemable at the classroom store for having only items marked in green. Fines were levied for articles not marked. The check intervals were gradually lengthened, and the point-and-fine system phased out.

REFERENCES

American Psychiatric Association. (1987). *Diagnostic and statistical manual of mental disorders* (3rd rev. ed.). Washington, DC: Author.

Azrin, N., & Wesolowski, M. (1974). Theft reversal: An overcorrection procedure for eliminating stealing by retarded persons. *Journal of Applied Behavior Analysis, 7,* 577–581.

Barcai, A., & Rabkin, L. (1972). Excommunication as a family therapy technique. *Archives of General Psychiatry, 27,* 804–808. (Reprinted in C. Schaefer & H. Millman, Eds., *Therapies for children: A handbook of effective treatments for problem behaviors.* San Francisco, CA: Jossey-Bass, 1977.)

Blanco, R. (1972). *Prescription for children with learning and adjustment problems.* Springfield, IL: Charles C. Thomas.

Blumberg, T. (1986). Transforming low achieving and disruptive adolescents into model students. *The School Counselor, 34,* 67–72.

Boswell, J. (1982). HELPING children with their anger. *Elementary School Guidance and Counseling, 16,* 278–287.

Carlin, A., & Armstrong, H. (1968). Rewarding social responsibility in disturbed children: A group play technique. *Psychotherapy: Theory, Research and Practice, 5,* 169–174.

Collins, M., & Collins, D. (1975). *Survival kit for teachers (and parents).* Pacific Palisades, CA: Goodyear.

Cummins, K. (1988). *The teacher's guide to behavioral interventions: Intervention strategies for behavior problems in the educational environment.* Columbia, MO: Hawthorne Educational Services.

Dinkmeyer, D., & McKay, G. (1973). *Raising a responsible child.* New York: Simon & Schuster.

Dreikurs, R., Grunwald, B., & Pepper, F. (1971). *Maintaining sanity in the classroom.* New York: Harper & Row.

Fischer, J., & Nehs, R. (1978). Use of a commonly available chore to reduce a boy's rate of swearing. *Journal of Behavior Therapy and Experimental Psychiatry, 9,* 81–83. (Reprinted in C. Schaefer, H. Millman, S. Sichel, & J. Zwilling, (Eds.), *Advances in therapies for children.* San Francisco, CA: Jossey-Bass, 1986.)

Ginott, H. (1965). *Between parent and child.* New York: Macmillan.

Gordon, T. (1970). *Parent effectiveness training.* New York: Wyden.

Hare-Mustin, R. (1975). Treatment of temper tantrums by a paradoxical intention. *Family Processes, 14,* 481–485. (Reprinted in C. Schaefer & H. Millman, Eds., *Therapies for children: A handbook of effective treatments for problem behaviors.* San Francisco, CA: Jossey-Bass, 1977.)

Kaufman, L., & Wagner, B. (1972). Barb: A systematic treatment technology for temper control disorders. *Behavior Therapy, 3,* 84–90.

Krumboltz, J., & Krumboltz, H. (1972). *Changing children's behavior.* Englewood Cliffs, NJ: Prentice-Hall.

Miller, G., & Klungness, L. (1986). Treatment of non-confrontative stealing in school-age children. *School Psychology Review, 15,* 24–35.

Omizo, M., Hershberger, J., & Omizo, S. (1988). Teaching children to cope with anger. *Elementary School Guidance and Counseling,* 241–245.

Rosen, H., & Rosen, L. (1983). Eliminating stealing: Use of stimulus control with an elementary student. *Behavior Modification, 7,* 56–63.

Rutter, M. (1975). *Helping troubled children.* New York: Plenum.

Stradley, W., & Aspinall, R. (1975). *Discipline in the junior high/middle school.* New York: Center for Applied Research in Education.

Verville, E. (1968). *Behavior problems of children.* Philadelphia: Saunders.

APPENDIX B

Children's Conflicts with Self
Alternatives for Intervention

As in Appendix A, the following techniques have been derived from a variety of resources and methods for counseling with children. The reader is reminded that it is essential that the procedures be incorporated into a caring and accepting counseling or consulting atmosphere and that the techniques should be modified to meet the individual needs of children and their particular social, learning, or behavioral problems.

Self-Destructive or Suicidal Behaviors

296.2X
309.00
309.83

See Chapter 14 for information on suicidal behaviors and suggestions for counseling with children exhibiting these symptoms.

Poor Self-Concept

V62.81

Unfortunately, most of children's negative feelings about themselves are formed from evaluations placed on them by adults. Adults lecture, scold, moralize, nag, belittle, label, and criticize. Sometimes children decide they really are worthless, stupid, unlovable, and worthy of punishment because of the continued negative judgments adults place on them. Negative feelings about oneself can affect the child's motivation, work, interpersonal relationships, and future success. Once formed, a negative self-concept is difficult to reverse; however, these children can be helped.

1. Provide opportunities for success. Praise and reinforce the child's behavior whenever possible—for example, "You did a good job picking up the paper (straightening the books, throwing that ball, and so on)." Artificial and forced compliments are easily recognized by children and are ineffective.

2. Use strengths exercises with children in a group situation. Give each group member a list of the names of other group members. Each child

should write a positive adjective or statement beside each name. Have each child read his or her list aloud.

3. Discuss with the children what they would like to do or accomplish. Working with the children, set up realistic goals and a step-by-step program to guide the children toward achieving their goals. Continue this guidance until the children feel they can work toward their goals alone.

4. Allow children with poor self-concepts to help someone else; arrange peer teaching or tutoring. Doing something special for someone else helps the helper feel better about himself or herself.

5. Have the adult working with the children write a list of each child's strengths to help the adult form a more positive conception of the children. Encourage the adult to capitalize on these strengths whenever possible to promote success in each child's life.

6. Ask the children to write ten positive things about themselves—friendly, can play ball well, can repair a bicycle, can play the piano, and so on. Help the children find ways to use their positive attributes to increase positive feelings about themselves.

7. Supportive counseling with significant adults in the child's life can help these adults understand the child and the inappropriate behaviors that often result from a poor self-concept. Instruction in effective parenting may also be helpful. Books such as Ginott's *Between Parent and Child* (1965) and Gordon's *Parent Effectiveness Training* (1970), discussions, role-playing, and parent groups are effective in helping adults understand and relate to children.

8. Have the child list situations he or she finds uncomfortable or difficult. Discuss ways of behaving in these situations, and role-play new behaviors. Encourage the child to try the new behaviors in realistic situations and report the results to you.

9. Use active listening (see Chapter 4). Teach the child problem-solving skills; being able to solve one's own problems builds self-confidence.

10. Involve the child in group activities at home and at school. Encourage the child to join organizations such as Scouts, a church group, or a club in which he or she will feel accepted and achieve success. Adults should avoid encouraging participation in groups requiring skills the child does not possess. Give responsibilities or tasks in school and in the home at which the child can feel successful. Avoid drudgery jobs.

11. Use a contract with rewards for attempting new behaviors. Rehearse and practice the new behaviors in a safe atmosphere before they are tried in a real-life situation.

12. Help the child change thoughts of "I can't" to "I will try." Examine what would be the worst thing to happen if the child attempted the task (see Chapter 6 for a discussion of cognitive restructuring). Encourage positive thinking.

13. Accept no excuses for poor behavior. Avoid being judgmental and

criticizing. Ask the child what *can* be accomplished, and negotiate a contract or a new contract if the first one was not successful (see Chapter 7).

14. Children with poor self-concepts often benefit from assertiveness training (see Chapter 7).

15. Use diaries, drawings, incomplete sentences, fantasy games, storytelling, and play therapy as aids to understanding the child's feelings and thoughts (see Chapter 8).

16. Find an appropriate model or "buddy" for the child. Ask the child to describe admired behaviors of the model. Rehearse and practice these behaviors with the child.

17. Examine the family constellation (Dreikurs, Grunwald, & Pepper, 1971). Often poor self-concepts are formed when children are compared to elder or younger siblings and feel that they do not measure up.

18. *Guidance Activities for Counselors and Teachers* (Thompson & Poppen, 1987) offers two chapters on group techniques for improving self-concept, including several variations of strengths assessment. Also, *100 Ways to Enhance Self-Concept in the Classroom* (Canfield & Wells, 1976) is an excellent resource for helping counselors work with difficult children.

19. Oldfield (1986) found that children who practiced the relaxation response decreased their acting-out behaviors and improved their self-concepts more than those who only charted these behaviors.

20. Golub and Guerriero (1981) improved the self-esteem and peer acceptance of learning-disabled boys by teaching them the techniques of transactional analysis and asking them to read books such as *TA for Kids*. The program included demonstrations of stroking and role-playing.

21. Omizo, Cubberly, and Omizo (1985), after teaching learning-disabled children the principles of rational-emotive therapy, found improved scores on self-concept scales and locus-of-control measures. Specifically, the children learned the ABC format, acquired basic problem-solving skills, learned that feelings are influenced by thoughts and that feelings are not expressed in identical ways, transferred the learning to everyday life, and developed rational coping skills. They learned to express feelings and not generalities, to be empathic, and to dispute irrational thoughts.

22. Chirico (1985) describes three guidance programs that have helped children improve their self-image: (1) puppets with messages about rules and authority, social interactions, vandalism, divorce, and so on; (2) a student-of-the-week program that rewards a student who has tried hard both academically and behaviorally; and (3) a behavior-management program to provide constant positive reinforcement to children who need extra help.

Cheating

V71.02
V62.30
312.90

Our present school system and society strongly encourage competition and high grades — values that can contribute to cheating. Students cheat for a variety of reasons, the main one possibly being the pressure to achieve.

School personnel and parents can place less emphasis on competition and more on cooperation with others and competition with self. School personnel and parents can also let students know that they expect honesty.

1. Determine the type of pressures the child may be encountering. Talk with the child and significant adults about their expectations for the child. Often parents and teachers place unrealistic pressures on children to excel in school, sports, or other areas. If this is the problem, consult with the adults and cooperatively plan ways to reduce the stress.

2. Determine the goal of the cheater (see Chapter 10). Is the child trying to impress someone, earn recognition, please parents or teachers, or cover up a learning problem?

3. Talk with cheating children concerning their study habits and preparation for work. Building better study skills may increase self-confidence and reduce cheating.

4. Encourage teachers to hold class discussions with students on cheating, exploring ways to reduce cheating and drawing up guidelines for consequences should the problem occur. A film, story, or hypothetical example may stimulate a rewarding discussion. Combine your discussion with a sociodrama, role-play, or puppet play about cheating (see Thompson & Poppen, 1987, pp. 69–74, on role-playing).

5. Consult with teachers about reducing temptations to cheat by arranging classroom desks or tables to separate students.

6. Children are often asked by their friends to cheat, and many have trouble knowing how to handle the situation without losing the friend. A group or family discussion focusing on the problem with a question such as "What would you do if your best friend asked you for the answer to a question during a test?" may help children find an alternative to cheating or helping their friends to cheat.

7. Consult with the teacher about testing procedures. Could an open-book test be given? Could the teacher use alternative forms of the test? Is the teacher in the room monitoring the test at all times?

8. If a child is caught cheating, remove the child's paper quietly, and confront the child privately. Tell the child what you saw, and discuss what consequences should be imposed. Ask that a plan be made to solve the present cheating problem and to prevent cheating in the future.

9. Refrain from accusing a child of cheating unless there is proof. Do not attempt to force a confession. Avoid name-calling, scolding, lecturing, moralizing, and preaching.

10. Place more emphasis on cooperative behavior and less on competition in interactions with the child. Stress competing with self rather than competing with another person.

11. Dreikurs (1968) suggests that if two students are caught giving each other help on a test, each student should be given half the score. They will soon realize the effect of cheating on their grades.

12. Relaxation and systematic desensitization (see Chapter 7) may help a cheating child if the behavior is the result of anxiety or test phobia. Suspend competitive and punitive grading practices that create test anxiety.

13. Contract with the child to avoid cheating in the future. Clearly define cheating behavior and the consequences of the behavior (see Chapter 7).

14. Use the reality questions (Chapter 3) to encourage responsible behavior in the cheating situation.

15. Encourage children to ask for directions, explanations, or clarification of instructions for any communication they do not understand (Cummins, 1988).

Truancy

V62.81
V62.30
309.23
312.90

Truancy is defined as a deliberate absence from school without a valid reason. Truants are generally telling the school that they prefer to be elsewhere. Children who do not achieve well or who have other learning problems are often truant because they find school an unpleasant place. It is easier to avoid the situation than to face failure, rejection, or embarrassment.

1. The reasons for truancy may be difficult to pinpoint. Determine the motive for the behavior (see Chapter 10). Is the child experiencing learning problems, failure, or rejection? Does the child receive encouragement to attend school and find learning relevant? Determine the time sequence when truancy seems to occur most often. Is the truancy related to family problems or needs?

2. Personal interest from school personnel may be an effective reinforcer. Actively listen to the child for clues about what is happening in the child's life (see Chapter 4). Many students respond to special attention in the form of invitations from the teacher, other school personnel, or peers to come to school and participate in the activities.

3. Look over the truant's class schedule and academic progress. Determine if the classes are too difficult or the assignments beyond the child's capabilities. Are there other ways of learning in which the child might feel more success and find more relevance?

4. Check into the home situation. Could the truancy be the result of a lack of proper clothing or lunch money, or babysitting responsibilities or other job requirements? Enlist the parents' cooperation, and devise a system for keeping in touch with them concerning days present and absent.

5. Hold a group or family discussion about truancy. Discuss with truant children how their presence or absence in school is helping or hurting them in reaching their immediate or long-term goals. Work with them to make a plan to avoid truancy in the future.

6. Contract with the student to attend school the next day. Continue to renegotiate the contract, increasing days in attendance step by step. Include a clause in the contract making the child responsible for all work missed. Rewards and/or penalties for attendance and nonattendance may be worked out cooperatively with the child (see Chapter 7).

7. Older students serving as peer counselors may be helpful in devising ways to keep truant children in school. The attention of the older student will also serve as a reinforcer for attending school.

8. Involve the child in school activities that require his or her presence — for example, audiovisual or physical-education equipment handling, room responsibilities, or a responsibility in a group project of interest.

9. Refrain from using critical, sarcastic comments such as "Glad to see you made it today" or "If you had been here, you would have had the assignment." Avoid scolding, lecturing, punishing, and preaching. Concentrate on the child's positive behaviors. School must become a pleasant place for truant children if their behavior is to be changed.

10. Whenever possible, allow the children choices in arranging their daily school activities and learning. Adjustments might also be made in the curriculum to reflect the children's individual abilities and achievement levels.

11. For children who see little relevance in school life, hold a discussion of "What does it take to make it through life?" Ask the children to imagine themselves as adults in their jobs or daily activities. Discuss what abilities and skills they will need in order to make it in their imagined adult world.

12. Out-of-school suspension for truancy is seldom effective. The child who is consistently truant does not want to be in school, and suspension is no punishment. Seek ways to make school a pleasant, rewarding place.

13. Krumboltz and Thoresen (1976) report a case study in which an adolescent boy was encouraged to return to school and remain in attendance through the use of three techniques. First, he was asked to visualize his future and what he would like to be and do in the future if he did not go back to school. His future plans and the reasons that he should return to school were discussed with the counselor. Next, the counselor asked him to look at the self that tries to make us do what we really want to and the other self that interferes and keeps us from accomplishing those goals. Behavioral rehearsal was used to help the young person imagine going back to school and to practice coping with the problems that would arise. Finally, a behavioral contract was drawn up with his family and school authorities, placing responsibility for the boy's behavior on him and outlining contingencies and reinforcements.

14. Reframing or other cognitive-restructuring techniques may help the child see school in a different light.

15. Ask the truant to interview selected people who have dropped out of school to see how their lives are affected.

16. Allen and Gardner (1989) suggest a dropout prevention program entitled "Tender Loving Counseling," which involves individual and group counseling, resource speakers, tutoring, study skills development, and community involvement. Information about their program may be obtained from the National Dropout Prevention Center at Clemson University, Clemson, SC 29364.

17. Ruben (1989) used a Potential Dropout Profile to identify students at risk and presented ten guidance sessions to address success in school, being comfortable in school, being responsible in school, listening in school, improving in school, cooperating with teachers, the bright side of school, and the bright side of me.

Carelessness in Work and with Property

V62.30
V62.81
309.23

One of the more common complaints heard among teachers and parents is that children are careless with school property, books, the completion of assigned work, and personal property such as coats, sweaters, and other possessions. Lecturing, scolding, preaching, and nagging are seldom effective in changing their habits. Children need to learn responsibility for their own actions and possessions and that an adult will not always be present to assume responsibility for them. Dreikurs et al. (1971) emphasize that children should assume responsibility for property, for property rights, and for their actions to learn respect for property.

1. Determine the reason for the carelessness. Is the behavior due to a lack of interest or motivation? Could the carelessness be an attempt to cover up a learning or emotional problem or an attempt to get back at parents for some real or imagined wrong? Actively listen to the child for clues that may indicate the motivation for carelessness (see Chapter 4).

2. If the child is careless, the work can be redone until it is correct. Lost items or property can be paid for with time or work. Forgotten items such as lunches and tennis shoes should not be hurriedly brought by parents. The logical consequence of carelessness, forgetting, or losing is that the child must assume responsibility—redo the work, replace the property, or do without the forgotten items (see Chapter 10).

3. Praise and reinforce responsible behavior—for example, "That paper was well written," or "You did a good job cleaning out the basement." Consistently give attention to acceptable behavior.

4. Help the careless child find a model who behaves maturely and responsibly. Pair the child with the model for activities. Ask the child to observe the model's behaviors for several days. Discuss the behaviors of the model with the careless child. Role-play and rehearse these behaviors. Make a plan for the child to try the new learning.

5. Carelessness may be due to a lack of understanding. Give clear,

specific instructions to the child for proper preparation of work and other activities. Have the careless child write down the instructions to eliminate forgetting and mistakes.

6. If carelessness with homework assignments is a problem, ask the child to write down all assignments and take them home. Talk with parents to gain their cooperation in checking assigned work each night. Discontinue the procedure when the child begins to assume responsibility for homework. The parent should be available to assist the child but not do the homework for the child.

7. If the problem seems to stem from inability to cope with the amount of work or responsibility assigned, reduce the requirements for a time, requiring quality rather than quantity. Gradually work up to the point where the child meets the expected criteria (see Chapter 7).

8. Carelessness may reflect a difference in cultural values. The child's environment may not place a great value on achievement or the possession of property. Hold a group discussion focusing on the value of property and of assuming responsibility for oneself. Help the children to identify acts of carelessness and their consequences, and make a plan for avoiding careless acts.

9. Ask careless children to evaluate their work from your role or to assess consequences as they think you should. Discuss with them the reasons for their evaluations.

10. Encourage responsibility through the use of reality questions (see Chapter 3). Give small assignments designed for success. Focus on statements such as "I won't do my work correctly" rather than "I can't" statements (see Chapter 5).

Underachievement

V62.30
309.23

Underachievement is usually defined as a discrepancy between the child's ability and actual achievement. It may be related to a poor self-concept, cultural deprivation, lack of family involvement and encouragement, peer pressure, learning or emotional problems, physical illness, or a lack of interest in school subjects and content.

1. Try to determine the causes contributing to underachievement. Become a "child watcher," and use active listening to try to understand the child (see Chapter 4). Underachievement is often related to physical problems or other learning difficulties; therefore, a psychological evaluation and checkup with a physician may provide some insight into the problem.

2. Assess the academic level at which the child is performing, and help the teachers build learning and class assignments from this base. Much new learning is based on old learning; the child must be able to accomplish prerequisite skills before achieving success in new ones. Once the weak link in the chain of learning is identified—a past school experience, physical health, cultural background, or any other factor—

counseling can begin, and instructional materials can be designed to promote success.

3. Contract with the child to complete at least a small amount of work each day. Build in rewards for progress. The completion of two problems or questions is better than no progress. Renegotiate the contract periodically, increasing the amount of work expected (see Chapter 7).

4. Try peer teaching or peer tutoring. Students who are in an upper grade can tutor students in lower grades. They can also help peers who are having trouble in areas of their strengths. Both children will learn and benefit from the relationship.

5. Capitalize on an area of interest or ability by relating the assignment to that interest or ability. Situations in math, writing, spelling, and other subjects can often be related to the child's interests, hobbies, and skills.

6. Team teaching may be helpful. Two or more teachers are often able to generate more ideas to stimulate the child. The child may also be able to cooperate with one teacher more than with another.

7. Avoid lecturing, nagging, scolding, and threatening the child. Encouragement and a positive attitude will produce better results. See "Poor Self-Concept," earlier in this appendix, for additional ideas.

8. Vary school activities from physical to quiet to prevent fatigue and boredom. Involve the child in arranging the day's work. Children are likely to cooperate and complete assigned tasks if they have taken part in the planning.

9. Teachers can consult with underachieving children for alternative ideas for completing learning objectives. Since children learn in different ways, the child may be the best consultant for determining methods of achieving learning objectives.

10. Special arrangements can be made for testing or for completing other class assignments. For example, if the child has problems in reading or writing, oral testing, tape recorders, or typewriters can be used.

11. Help the child find an admired friend and model. Ask the child to talk with the model about study habits and to observe the model's methods of studying. Contract with the child to practice these procedures (see Chapter 7). Allow the two children to work and study together as much as possible.

12. Check on study skills, test-taking procedures, and place and time for studying. A contract incorporating a schedule for studying specific subjects at certain times and places will help the child plan study time more wisely and develop discipline for studying. Thompson and Poppen (1987) have suggested a study-habits survey.

13. If the underachievement is related to parental pressures, counsel with the parents about how to decrease this pressure. Plan with them for methods to reinforce studying without pressuring the child. Assist parents and the child in determining an appropriate place and time to study. Make a plan to avoid or cope with things that might interfere with study times (small siblings, telephone calls, peers).

14. When homework assignments are not completed at home, the logical consequence is for the child to complete the work during free time at school (see Chapter 12). Avoid nagging, scolding, or lecturing.

15. Focus on and reinforce improvements in work; past faults and failures should be forgotten. Emphasize the positive—for example: "Jimmy, you did a part of your homework assignment, and it was done very well. I wonder if you would be willing to work on these two additional questions."

16. It is better for the parent/child relationship if parents do not teach or tutor their own children. If the child asks for help, a parent may provide assistance; however, someone outside the family will be a more effective teacher or tutor.

17. For children with special learning problems, plan a consultation session with all resource persons and teachers involved. Cooperatively draw up a learning plan, with the role and objectives of each professional clearly defined.

18. Underachievers usually respond best to a structured environment for learning. Research by Laport and Nath (1976) indicates that underachievers need specific, hard goals. They found that children who were simply told to do their best set low goals and achieved below their maximum abilities. Give directions for assignments very clearly. A check or reward system may be used for completed work. Learning contracts may be helpful to the underachiever. Some underachievers will require additional time to complete all assignments; continue to encourage their completion.

19. Pecaut (1979) has described the underachieving personality as falling into one of four categories: trust-seeking, approval-seeking, dependence-seeking, and independence-seeking. He believes that approximately 75 percent of underachievers are dependence-seekers and exhibit such characteristics as vagueness, powerlessness, dependence on others to complete their work, and fear of success (they might have to assume responsibility). When working with dependence-seekers, Pecaut recommends that adults should never feel guilty when the child does not perform (guilt is a powerful tool!); adults should not accept excuses but should learn to see through the child's tendency to blame others for his or her mistakes or failures; adults should not make things easier for dependence-seekers by giving them options of easier courses or lowering expectations; adults should not fall into the trap of worrying about dependence-seekers and should resist the child's manipulative efforts for assistance; and adults should avoid giving dependence-seekers time extensions. These suggestions by Pecaut fit the model of reality therapy and Adlerian methods of counseling by encouraging children to accept responsibility for their behaviors.

Pecaut suggests that adults ask themselves four questions about children they are about to recommend for special classes because of poor academic work: (1) Does this student make a reasonable and consistent effort to learn?

(2) Has the student requested help when he or she has not understood the material? (3) Does the student complete homework? (4) Does the student pay attention and participate in class activities? Pecaut states that if the answer to any one of these questions is "no," the student may not be ready for a special class; he or she may be an underachiever.

20. Rimm and Lowe (1988) suggest methods for parents of gifted children to cope with underachievement, including cautions against too much praise and admiration, consistency in parenting, positive monitoring of homework and study habits, modeling the value of personal careers, and encouraging reasonable standards of organization.

Daydreaming V62.81

Daydreaming is not always bad; it sometimes clears confusion, solves problems, or is creative in other ways. However, excessive daydreaming or daydreaming at the wrong times—in school—can affect the child's academic progress. Adlerian theory suggests that daydreaming children are striving for superiority. These children have no faith in their abilities to achieve success in the real world; therefore, they create fantasies in which they are always great or superior.

1. Periodic eye contact between child and adult may help decrease daydreaming. If it is difficult to make eye contact with the child, a light touch on the shoulder should bring the child back to reality.

2. Interrupt children's fantasies by calling them by name. Avoid embarrassing children by asking them to answer a question they obviously have not heard.

3. Try incomplete sentences, storytelling, diary, or play therapy to learn more about the child and the possible reason for daydreaming.

4. Channel daydreaming into constructive channels by having the child write out the daydream. The writing could be incorporated into a learning exercise.

5. Write a contract with the daydreamer for completion of assigned work (see Chapter 7). Contract for only the amount of work the child feels he or she can accomplish. Renegotiate contracts for additional work in a step-by-step plan.

6. Tape an index card to the child's desk. When the child is working on a task, place a check on the card and give verbal reinforcement for the accomplishment. A contract may be made with the child to earn rewards or privileges for a certain number of checks. Ignore the daydreaming; reward on-task behavior.

7. Plan the child's environment and schedule, varying activities from quiet to physical. Assess the day's schedule to determine if activities are interesting, relevant, and appropriate for the child's level of maturity, interest, and ability.

8. Find the child a friend who will encourage participation in groups

and other activities. Encourage the teacher to include the daydreamer in group activities and projects. Counsel with the parents to plan for ways to reduce daydreaming at home and encourage participation in activities.

9. Often children retreat to a daydream world because the real one is too painful. Determine if the child is having learning, social, emotional, or physical problems. A psychological evaluation and physical examination may be helpful.

10. Daydreaming may be related to a poor self-concept. See "Poor Self-Concept," earlier in this appendix, for additional ideas for working with these children.

Shyness and Withdrawal

V62.81
309.83
313.21

Shyness and withdrawal are attempts to avoid participation in one's surroundings. The child may fear the situation, fear failure or criticism, lack self-confidence, or fear embarrassment or humiliation. It is also possible that the child is physically ill. Unfortunately, shy and withdrawn children are usually ignored because they cause little trouble compared to the attention-seeking child.

1. Try to determine the underlying cause for the reserved behavior. Use diaries, puppets, role-playing, incomplete sentences, drawing, storytelling, play therapy, or any similar technique to try to understand the child better. Children will often express their feelings through these means when they will not verbalize them.

2. Work on developing trust and good rapport with the child. Try active listening to increase understanding of the child (see Chapter 4).

3. Have the shy child help another student through peer teaching or peer tutoring. Capitalize on any interest or ability to promote sharing and participation.

4. Involve shy or withdrawn children in small-group activities or projects with other children they like. Often a shy child will talk in small groups. Encourage and reinforce these attempts to participate. Send them on errands with another child. A sociogram may help to determine other liked children.

5. Give the withdrawn child responsibilities such as carrying messages, feeding the fish, watering plants, handing out supplies, or helping the school secretary answer the phone and take messages. Avoid drudgery jobs, and do not ask the shy child to perform tasks that may be embarrassing (such as speaking in front of the class).

6. Make a list with the withdrawn child of things he or she would like to be able to do—for example, join a group of friends, speak to a particular person, or play a game. Have the child select one thing on the list and set a goal to accomplish this behavior. Use behavior rehearsal to help the child

practice certain responses or behaviors. Contract with the child to try these new behaviors (see Chapter 7).

7. Avoid embarrassing shy children by teasing them about their shyness or by calling on them to "perform" in front of a group without first discussing and arranging the activity with them. One technique for encouraging a child to participate in class is to plan a question and answer with the child. The teacher asks the question in class and the child agrees to answer with the response. When the child feels comfortable answering rehearsed questions, a contract is made with the child and teacher that the teacher will call on the child only when he or she volunteers to answer. Ask the child to volunteer at least a certain number of times per week. Renegotiate periodic contracts, encouraging participation in a step-by-step progression.

8. Find a model for the shy child. Ask the child to observe the model for several days and list admired behaviors. Role-play, rehearse, and contract with the child to try the new behaviors.

9. Withdrawn or shy children may benefit from assertiveness training (see Chapter 7). Have the children list situations in which they would like to be more assertive. Discuss possible ways of meeting each situation. Practice the new behaviors with the children, both individually and in small groups.

10. Keat (1972) suggests that a broad spectrum of techniques be used with the withdrawn child, including (1) building a relationship of trust, understanding, and confidence; (2) using the techniques of assertiveness training; (3) behavioral rehearsal, with the counselor role-playing the behavior and then the child rehearsing it; (4) relaxation exercises, such as breathing exercises, isometrics, and deep muscle-relaxation techniques; (5) motor-coordination training (if necessary); and (6) cognitive restructuring.

11. Zimbardo (1977) points out that shyness does have its advantages. The shy child can be selective in relationships, can observe situations cautiously, will never be considered obnoxious or overly aggressive, and may be considered a good listener. If the child decides to change the behavior, Zimbardo suggests five steps: (1) understand self; (2) understand the reason for the shyness; (3) build self-esteem; (4) develop social skills; and (5) help others overcome their shyness. Gestalt counseling techniques are often used to help a child look at weaknesses as secret strengths—for example, "Being shy helps me by _____." Behavioral counseling strategies are also designed to look at the payoffs of seemingly unhelpful behaviors.

12. Use a variety of play techniques, such as hand puppets, games, art, and music, to encourage expression. Pets may be a useful adjunct to therapy.

13. Franco, Christoff, Crimmins, and Kelly (1983) developed a program to teach extremely shy children social skills—specifically, conversational skills, including asking questions, making and responding to comments, improving eye contact, and displaying warmth. The training sessions in-

cluded a presentation of the skill, modeling, and then rehearsal using videotape. Reinforcement strategies and homework assignments were used to help children acquire and maintain the behaviors.

14. Matter and Matter (1985) suggest helping the lonely, shy child by teaching specific social skills similar to those of more aggressive children, combined with changing the environment to make it less conducive to isolation (for example, reducing class size and improving relationships through shared projects). The family/home environment may need to be assessed to determine if parents should be involved in the counseling process.

15. Allan and Clark (1984) describe a directed art technique in which they focus the next session or drawing on a particular portion of the previous drawing that seems to have been causing pain or a portion that required a considerable amount of time to draw. They believe these drawings tap the unconscious and that children work through the problems by expressing their feelings pictorially.

16. Sainato, Maheady, and Shook (1986) found that by appointing one child at a time as "classroom manager" for two weeks, they could increase the frequency of social interactions and improve social status. The "classroom manager" led the class in highly preferred activities and made assignments for "fun" chores. The results of the study indicated significant increases in positive social interactions; sociometric assessments showed improved social status; and parents reported that their children talked about school more often and were more eager to attend.

17. See "Poor Self-Concept," earlier in this appendix, for other ideas to encourage more participation in learning and interpersonal situations.

V62.81	309.21
309.24	313.21
300.00	313.00
300.29	

Excessive Tension and Anxiety

A little tension and anxiety may motivate a child, but excessive tension and anxiety interfere with learning and performance. Excessive tension and anxiety may be situational or a chronic condition. The symptoms include continued restlessness and movement, nail biting, tics, frequent blinking, rapid breathing, repeated throat clearing, and similar somatic complaints.

School-related tension and anxiety

1. Tell highly anxious children they have a right to fail. Take away the pressure to excel and to be perfect. This technique may ease the anxiety and allow further exploration of conditions causing the anxiety.

2. Highly anxious children function better with a teacher who is warm and understanding but also organized and structured. Suggest that teachers use teaching techniques such as behavioral objectives and learn-

ing contracts so highly anxious students will know exactly what is expected of them.

3. Consult with the child's parents and teachers. Determine if the anxiety is a result of pressures and perfectionistic expectations. If so, work with the child and the adults to encourage more realistic expectations.

4. Teachers and parents may help decrease tension and anxiety in children by talking quietly to them about relaxing—for example, "Relax your neck; relax your shoulders." Deep breathing exercises may also help the child relax (see Chapter 7).

5. Avoid overemphasizing the importance of success on a test or task. Many adults cause anxiety in their efforts to impress the child with the importance of doing well.

6. If the child is highly anxious about tests, use the "study buddy" system. Pair the child with a capable student who is willing to help. Developing better study skills may help reduce anxieties related to school.

7. Encourage teachers to deemphasize tests and to allow the child to demonstrate learning in other ways, such as oral tests, oral reports, projects, and papers.

8. Look over the child's schoolwork and academic progress. Anxiety is often related to learning disabilities.

9. Use cognitive-restructuring techniques to help children feel they can cope with situations. Discover the irrational, self-defeating, anxiety-provoking self-statements that the children are telling themselves and help them formulate more positive ones.

10. Use imagery techniques to help children see themselves coping with situations in a relaxed, positive manner.

11. Sycamore, Corey, and Coker (1990) outline general strategies, similar to a "game plan," for approaching test taking with confidence. They suggest that counselors advise students about good test taking procedures such as pacing responses according to the time allotted for the test, narrowing choices by eliminating obviously wrong answers, responding first to questions to which answers are known, giving last priority to questions not known, being aware of qualifiers such as "always" and "never," and marking your place with your hand or marker.

12. Wilkinson (1990) describes a guidance session with specific steps for overcoming test anxiety. The focus of the sessions is on students' feelings about tests, their preparation, finding the source of anxiety, and their responses to feelings of anxiety.

General anxiety

1. Some tension and anxiety may be related to fear of the unknown—for example, going to new places or being placed in new situations. A thorough explanation of the feared situation and/or a visit to a feared place with a trusted person may reduce situational anxiety.

2. Talk with anxious children and agree on methods, such as physical activity, talking, or writing, for release of these feelings. When children become highly anxious or tense, they could be allowed to signal the teacher or another adult and proceed to carry out the plan previously discussed. Counselors may suggest that anxious children come to their office when they experience intense feelings.

3. Diaries, autobiographies, drawing, puppets, and other forms of play therapy may assist in determining the causes for the anxious feelings (see Chapter 8).

4. Children will have less anxiety about situations if they feel competent. Discuss with the child the reasons for anxiety and ways of handling specific situations; rehearse the situations.

5. Relaxation methods and desensitization have been found to be effective methods of reducing tension and anxiety (see Chapter 7).

6. If the anxiety appears to be extremely debilitating, refer the child to a medical specialist for examination.

7. Peterson and Shigetomi (1981) successfully reduced children's anxiety about hospitalization by teaching them the techniques of muscle relaxation, imaginal distraction, and self-talk.

8. Kraft and McNeil (1985) point out that stress can be caused by a number of factors, such as separation and divorce, academic pressure, or parental influences, with the resulting disorders of fighting, restlessness, temper tantrums, destructiveness, inattention, bragging, and selfishness. They suggest that play, physical exercise, active relaxation procedures (such as yoga, progressive relaxation, or story plays), or passive relaxation techniques (deep breathing, imagery, autogenic training) be used to help children cope with their stresses.

9. Allan and Anderson (1986) suggest that for children going through a crisis and experiencing stress or anxiety, classroom discussion can help them talk about their problems and feelings, understand that others have similar feelings, and think about coping strategies. These meetings can help teachers recognize the personal concerns of students, decide who needs to be referred for counseling, and discover how discussion can facilitate the classroom climate.

10. Angus (1989) describes three approaches to stress management in children: guided fantasy, yoga and autogenic phrases, and thermal biofeedback.

V62.81
314.00
Distractibility/Short Attention Span
314.01

Being able to focus one's attention on the task to be done and ignore irrelevant stimuli in the environment is necessary for learning school material and new behaviors. Although attention span and the degree of distractibility vary with the child and the situation, these learning problems seem to be appearing with increasing frequency in today's classrooms.

1. Determine if the child is actually distracted easily and has a short attention span. The child's inattention may be the result of some other reason, such as the nature of the work the child is asked to do (boring or too difficult); noisy or more interesting surroundings (windows, TV, pictures, bulletin boards); or fatigue or physical illness.

2. Record the time when distractions and inattention seem most frequent. Rearrange the environment or schedule. Vary quiet activities with more physical ones. Limit overstimulation and distractors. Interesting bulletin boards, teachers' clothing and jewelry, mobiles, and brightly colored pictures can be distracting.

3. Use seating arrangements or some method of screening the distractible child from excessive stimuli. Consider small carrels or "offices." Bookcases, movable screens, or even large moving cartons that have been painted or decorated can be used to reduce distracting stimuli.

4. Contract for the completion of short assignments. Talk with distractible children about the amount of work they feel they can accomplish—two math problems, one paragraph of English. Write a realistic contract to ensure success. Continue to renegotiate the contract, increasing the assignments as the distractibility decreases.

5. Recommend that highly distractible children be checked by a medical specialist to determine if the behavior is a medical problem.

6. Shorten teaching time and study periods, and schedule the periods more frequently. Visual aids, games, and other teaching aids may add interest and maintain attention.

7. Acker, Oliver, Carmichael, and Ozerkevich (1975) report a case study of a 10-year-old boy whose attention span and on-task activity were increased by rewarding the whole class for the boy's on-task behavior. Periodic observations of behavior were made, and points were earned for appropriate behaviors. These points were exchanged for class privileges, such as trips to the museum. The decisions about how to "spend" the points were made by the boy and the whole class. The researchers suggest that the boy's peers tended to ignore off-task behavior, which resulted in an increase in on-task behavior.

8. Douglas (1972) contends that more time needs to be spent in teaching children to "stop, look, and listen." She thinks a short attention span is like impulsiveness; therefore, methods should be implemented to decrease impulsiveness and improve attentiveness and reflectiveness— for example, teaching reflective strategies and games requiring impulse control.

9. Use techniques such as raising or lowering your voice, placing your hand on the child's shoulder, or catching the child's eye to capture the distractible child's attention and direct it back to the task.

10. Encourage children to monitor their own behavior. Have them make a check mark on an index card when they catch themselves off-task and then immediately focus on the task. Increasing awareness of the

problem is often a productive technique in itself. Plan for self-reward when the child can refocus attention to the task. Christie, Hiss, and Lozanoff (1984) taught three third- and fourth-grade boys to self-record their identified inappropriate behavior. According to these researchers, self-recording behavior requires the child to become an active participant in the change plan and encourages decision-making about what is appropriate and inappropriate behavior.

The reader is encouraged to refer also to the section entitled "Attention-Deficit Hyperactivity Disorder" in Chapter 14.

Immaturity and Dependent Behavior   V62.81

Dependency may be the result of overprotective or critical parents who have told their children in many ways that they are not capable of functioning or thinking for themselves. Immature or dependent children usually do not achieve well in school because they are not ready to learn the subject matter presented. They may have trouble with interpersonal relationships because of their immature behavior and often become social isolates or discipline problems; alternatively, they may choose their friends from a younger group.

1. Work with the parents on strategies to help them trust the child's abilities and potentials. Suggest methods to develop independent behaviors. Books such as *Between Parent and Child* (Ginott, 1965) and *Parent Effectiveness Training* (Gordon, 1970) may help parents understand their children's development and abilities.

2. Have children identify areas in which they would like to be more independent or behaviors they would like to change. Discuss these situations and alternative ways of behaving with the child, and rehearse the situations until the child feels comfortable with the new behaviors.

3. Encourage and praise attempts to become more mature and independent. Ask the child to do jobs or assume responsibilities in the home and classroom to increase feelings of confidence. Avoid assigning drudgery jobs.

4. Have the child select a model and observe the model's behavior for several days. Pair children with mature models for group activities. Ask them to keep a list of the model's behaviors they particularly like. Rehearse the behaviors the children would like to acquire until they feel confident.

5. Encourage immature or dependent children to join groups such as Little League, Boy or Girl Scouts, clubs, or church groups. The children will need support and encouragement to take the first steps and continued counseling to learn social skills for good relationships in the groups.

6. Give children as many choices as possible—for example, whether to complete the reading or the math assignment first, or whether to wear a blue shirt or a red shirt.

7. Learn about the child's abilities, interests, and hobbies. Have the child peer-teach or tutor another student in one of these areas of expertise to build self-confidence. Both children will benefit from the teaching and the relationship.

8. Work with immature or dependent children to teach them problem-solving techniques. Counsel with parents and teachers to encourage these children to attempt to solve their own problems with adult guidance rather than to depend on others for solutions.

9. Avoid reinforcing dependent behaviors. Encourage immature children to make decisions and accept responsibilities within their capabilities. Reinforce efforts toward more mature behavior with praise and encouragement.

10. Use active listening to help immature and dependent children express their fears and other feelings (see Chapter 4). Help them develop realistic goals and make a systematic plan for attaining these goals.

Perfectionistic Behavior

V62.81
300.30

Compulsive and overly perfectionistic children usually perform their tasks and assignments well and therefore often "overachieve." This behavior can inhibit everyday functioning; for example, the child takes too much time to complete assignments and feels that everything must be absolutely perfect. Perfectionistic behavior is often accompanied by symptoms of anxiety.

1. Perfectionistic children usually perform best in a well-structured situation where rules and expectations are clearly defined. Clearly explain all instructions, and use teaching methods such as behavioral objectives and learning contracts to reduce anxiety concerning expectations.

2. Talk with parents and teachers to determine if pressures and expectations placed on the child are too great. Perfectionistic children often have perfectionistic adults for models. Counsel with adults about normal growth and development and the behaviors that can be expected of the child.

3. Involve the children in individual and group activities that do not require perfect performance. Techniques such as creative drawing or writing deemphasize perfection and also allow the child to express feelings.

4. Encourage the child to relax. Teach the child breathing exercises and other relaxation techniques (see Chapter 7). Encourage the child to change "internal self-talk" to recognize that perfection in all areas is not essential (see Chapter 6). "Shoulds" and "have-tos" can be changed to "It might be better ifs"–for example, "It might be better if I make all 'A's,' but that is not required for me to be a good person."

5. Use negative rehearsal to help perfectionistic children be less rigid. Observe a situation in which the child appears to be highly perfectionistic.

Role-play the same situation with the child, encouraging behavior that is less than perfect. Discuss with the child what would happen if the child were not 100-percent perfect in the situation. Make a plan with the child to decrease compulsiveness.

6. Allot an amount of time for the child to finish a task. Place a timer within the child's sight. When the timer rings, review the child's progress. If sufficient progress has not been made, contract with the child to set a new goal the next time.

7. The overly perfectionistic child may be compensating for feelings of inadequacy. See "Poor Self-Concept," earlier in this appendix, for further suggestions for working with these children.

8. Plan a self-management program with the child, encouraging him or her to monitor perfectionistic behavior and develop alternative ways of responding to situations. Build in self-reward for accomplishments.

9. Anxiety and tension may be related to perfectionistic behaviors. See "Excessive Tension and Anxiety," earlier in this appendix, for additional ideas.

School Phobia

V62.81
300.29
309.21

School phobia may grow out of unpleasant or embarrassing experiences in school, failure in school, fear of separation from the security of home and parents, fear of the unknown, or other experiences that may have associated bad feelings with school.

1. Actively listen to try to understand the phobic child's underlying feelings and to establish a feeling of trust and security (see Chapter 4).

2. The child can be desensitized by being brought to school by a parent and staying for a short time, such as 15 minutes the first day, 20 minutes the second day, 25 minutes the third day. Continue in this manner until the child can remain in school a full day.

3. The desensitization procedure may be used with rewards. Write a contract with the child to provide a reward for staying in school a certain amount of time—for example, 30 minutes (see Chapter 7). Renegotiate the contract for longer periods of time as the child is able to stay in school an increasing length of time.

4. If one parent is reinforcing the child's anxiety about school, suggest that the other parent or another adult bring the child to school. A parent may unconsciously be encouraging school phobia by conveying his or her own anxiety to the child, verbally or nonverbally (for example, "Now, you call me if you get afraid while you are in school" or becoming more nervous and irritable as they approach school).

5. Avoid placing the child in any situation that may increase fear or cause embarrassment. Explain all new situations and expectations clearly.

Role-playing expected behaviors may help the child feel more confident about meeting the new situation.

6. School phobia may be related to learning difficulties. Review the child's academic progress, and provide needed help. Children who find school an unpleasant place because they continually fail often become phobic.

7. Ask the teacher to involve phobic children in pleasant group projects and activities. The more pleasure the children derive from school, the more they will want to attend. Successful learning, good peer relationships, pleasant teachers and other school personnel, and enjoyable activities can be positive reinforcers.

8. Allow phobic children to phone home occasionally or at specific intervals if they feel fearful or insecure. Make arrangements with the parents so that they will be there to answer and to reassure the child.

9. Many parents include something from home in the child's lunch-box or with books—a picture or some favorite object, for instance.

10. Relaxation and desensitization procedures may be necessary for the extremely phobic child (see Chapter 7).

11. Blanco (1972) suggests that counselors work with parents, encouraging them to (1) make persistent and continued efforts to get the child to school daily, even for a short period; (2) seek family counseling if the child is extremely anxious and phobic; (3) have the child visit classes, playgrounds, and other areas before entering school; (4) get the child off to school in a natural way without tearful good-byes or overemphasis on parting; and (5) enlist the aid of a pediatrician if psychosomatic ailments occur. The pediatrician should be aware of the phobic problem if it occurs with any frequency.

12. Rutter (1975) outlines some areas of questioning that may help the counselor understand the phobic child: (1) What is the child like when not at school—temperamentally, socially, and so forth? (2) Does the child's refusal to go to school vary with the planned curriculum or activities for that day? (3) Does the child's refusal to go to school vary with what is occurring in the home—for example, when there is illness, unhappiness, or an argument, or the mother is beginning a new job or expecting a new baby?

13. Often school phobia is the result of family interactions in which children become overly dependent on parents. Consultation with the family may provide some insight into the family system and suggestions for treatment.

14. Barlow, Strother, and Landreth (1985) suggest play therapy for the child with school phobia in order to allow the child to feel less overwhelmed and provide support while returning to school.

15. See other ideas for working with the phobic child under "Excessive Tension and Anxiety," earlier in this appendix.

REFERENCES

Acker, L., Oliver, P., Carmichael, J., & Ozerkevich, M. (1975). Interpersonal attractiveness and peer interaction during behavioral treatment of the target child. *Canadian Journal of Behavioral Science, 7,* 262–273.

Allan, J., & Anderson, E. (1986). Children and crises: A classroom guidance approach. *Elementary School Guidance and Counseling, 21,* 143–149.

Allan, J., & Clark, M. (1984). Directed art counseling. *Elementary School Guidance and Counseling, 19,* 116–124.

Allen, K., & Gardner, N. (1989). Tender loving counseling: A dropout-prevention program. *The School Counselor, 36,* 389–392.

American Psychiatric Association. (1987). *Diagnostic and statistical manual of mental disorders* (3rd rev. ed.). Washington, DC: Author.

Angus, S. (1989). Three approaches to stress management for children. *Elementary School Guidance and Counseling, 23,* 228–233.

Barlow, K., Strother, J., & Landreth, G. (1985). Child-centered play therapy: Nancy from baldness to curls. *The School Counselor, 32,* 347–363.

Blanco, R. (1972). *Prescription for children with learning and adjustment problems.* Springfield, IL: Charles C Thomas.

Canfield, J., & Wells, H. C. (1976). *100 ways to enhance self-concept in the classroom.* Englewood Cliffs, NJ: Prentice-Hall.

Chirico, J. (1985). Three guidance programs in Providence, Rhode Island. *The School Counselor, 32,* 388–391.

Christie, D., Hiss, M., & Lozanoff, B. (1984). Modification of inattentive classroom behavior: Hyperactive children's use of self-recording with teacher guidance. *Behavior Modification, 8,* 391–406.

Cummins, K. (1988). *The teacher's guide to behavioral interventions: Intervention strategies for behavior problems in the educational environment.* Columbia, MO: Hawthorne Educational Services.

Douglas, V. (1972). Stop, look and listen: The problem of sustained attention and impulse control in hyperactive and normal children. *Canadian Journal of Behavioral Science, 4,* 259–282.

Dreikurs, R. (1968). *Psychology in the classroom* (2nd ed.). New York: Harper & Row.

Dreikurs, R., Grunwald, B., & Pepper, F. (1971). *Maintaining sanity in the classroom.* New York: Harper & Row.

Franco, D., Christoff, K., Crimmins, D., & Kelly, J. (1983). Social skills training for an extremely shy young adolescent: An empirical case study. *Behavior Therapy, 14,* 568–575. (Reprinted in C. Schaefer, H. Millman, S. Sichel, & J. Zwilling (Eds.), *Advances in therapies for children.* San Francisco, CA: Jossey-Bass, 1986.)

Ginott, H. (1965). *Between parent and child.* New York: Macmillan.

Golub, S., & Guerriero, L. (1981). The effects of a transactional analysis program on self-esteem in learning disabled boys. *Transactional Analysis Journal, 11,* 244–246.

Gordon, T. (1970). *Parent effectiveness training.* New York: Wyden.

Keat, D. (1972). Broad-spectrum behavior therapy with children: A case presentation. *Behavior Therapy, 3,* 454–459.

Kraft, R., & McNeil, A. (1985). Children and stress: Coping through physical activities. *The Physical Educator, 42,* 72–75.

Krumboltz, J., & Thoresen, C. (1976). *Counseling methods.* New York: Holt, Rinehart & Winston.

Laport, R., & Nath, R. (1976). Roles of performance goals in prose learning. *Journal of Educational Psychology, 3,* 260–264.

Matter, D., & Matter, R. (1985). Children who are lonely and shy: Action steps for the counselor. *Elementary School Guidance and Counseling, 20,* 129–135.

Oldfield, D. (1986). The effects of the relaxation response on self-concept and acting out behaviors. *Elementary School Guidance and Counseling, 20,* 255–260.

Omizo, M., Cubberly, W., & Omizo, S. (1985). The effects of rational emotive education groups on self-concept and locus of control among learning disabled children. *The Exceptional Child, 32,* 13–16.

Pecaut, L. (1979). *Understanding and influencing student motivation.* Lombard, IL: Institute for Motivational Development.

Peterson, L., & Shigetomi, C. (1981). The use of coping techniques to minimize anxiety in hospitalized children. *Behavior Therapy, 12,* 1–14.

Rimm, S., & Lowe, B. (1988). Family environments of underachieving gifted students. *Gifted Child Quarterly, 32,* 353–359.

Ruben, A. (1989). Preventing school dropouts through classroom guidance. *Elementary School Guidance and Counseling, 24,* 21–29.

Rutter, M. (1975). *Helping troubled children.* New York: Plenum.

Sainato, D., Maheady, L., & Shook, G. (1986). The effects of a classroom manager role on the social interaction patterns and social status of withdrawn kindergarten students. *Journal of Applied Behavior Analysis, 19,* 187–195.

Sycamore, J., Corey, A., & Coker, D. (1990). Reducing test anxiety. *Elementary School Guidance and Counseling, 24,* 231–233.

Thompson, C., & Poppen, W. (1987). *Guidance activities for counselors and teachers.* Knoxville, TN: Kinko's Copies.

Wilkinson, C. (1990). Techniques for overcoming test anxiety. *Elementary School Guidance and Counseling, 24,* 234–235.

Zimbardo, P. (1977). *Shyness.* Reading, MA: Addison-Wesley.

Ethical Standards
American Association for Counseling and Development
(Approved by AACD Governing Council, March 1988.)

PREAMBLE

The Association is an educational, scientific, and professional organization whose members are dedicated to the enhancement of the worth, dignity, potential, and uniqueness of each individual and thus to the service of society.

The Association recognizes that the role definitions and work settings of its members include a wide variety of academic disciplines, levels of academic preparation, and agency services. This diversity reflects the breadth of the Association's interest and influence. It also poses challenging complexities in efforts to set standards for the performance of members, desired requisite preparation or practice, and supporting social, legal, and ethical controls.

The specification of ethical standards enables the Association to clarify to present and future members and to those served by members the nature of ethical responsibilities held in common by its members.

The existence of such standards serves to stimulate greater concern by members for their own professional functioning and for the conduct of fellow professionals such as counselors, guidance and student personnel workers, and others in the helping professions. As the ethical code of the Association, this document establishes principles that define the ethical behavior of Association members. Additional ethical guidelines developed by the Association's Divisions for their specialty areas may further define a member's ethical behavior.

Section A: General

1. The member influences the development of the profession by continuous efforts to improve professional practices, teaching, services, and

research. Professional growth is continuous throughout the member's career and is exemplified by the development of a philosophy that explains why and how a member functions in the helping relationship. Members must gather data on their effectiveness and be guided by the findings. Members recognize the need for continuing education to ensure competent service.

2. The member has a responsibility both to the individual who is served and to the institution within which the service is performed to maintain high standards of professional conduct. The member strives to maintain the highest levels of professional services offered to the individuals to be served. The member also strives to assist the agency, organization, or institution in providing the highest caliber of professional services. The acceptance of employment in an institution implies that the member is in agreement with the general policies and principles of the institution. Therefore the professional activities of the member are also in accord with the objectives of the institution. If, despite concerted efforts, the member cannot reach agreement with the employer as to acceptable standards of conduct that allow for changes in institutional policy conducive to the positive growth and development of clients, then terminating the affiliation should be seriously considered.

3. Ethical behavior among professional associates, both members and nonmembers, must be expected at all times. When information is possessed that raises doubt as to the ethical behavior of professional colleagues, whether Association members or not, the member must take action to attempt to rectify such a condition. Such action shall use the institution's channels first and then use procedures established by the Association.

4. The member neither claims nor implies professional qualifications exceeding those possessed and is responsible for correcting any misrepresentations of these qualifications by others.

5. In establishing fees for professional counseling services, members must consider the financial status of clients and locality. In the event that the established fee structure is inappropriate for a client, assistance must be provided in finding comparable services of acceptable cost.

6. When members provide information to the public or to subordinates, peers, or supervisors, they have a responsibility to ensure that the content is general, unidentified client information that is accurate, unbiased, and consists of objective, factual data.

7. Members recognize their boundaries of competence and provide only those services and use only those techniques for which they are qualified by training or experience. Members should only accept those positions for which they are professionally qualified.

8. In the counseling relationship, the counselor is aware of the intimacy of the relationship and maintains respect for the client and avoids engaging in activities that seek to meet the counselor's personal needs at the expense of that client.

9. Members do not condone or engage in sexual harassment which is defined as deliberate or repeated comments, gestures, or physical contacts of a sexual nature.

10. The member avoids bringing personal issues into the counseling relationship, especially if the potential for harm is present. Through awareness of the negative impact of both racial and sexual stereotyping and discrimination, the counselor guards the individual rights and personal dignity of the client in the counseling relationship.

11. Products or services provided by the member by means of classroom instruction, public lectures, demonstrations, written articles, radio or television programs, or other types of media must meet the criteria cited in these Standards.

Section B: Counseling Relationship

This section refers to practices and procedures of individual and/or group counseling relationships.

The member must recognize the need for client freedom of choice. Under those circumstances where this is not possible, the member must apprise clients of restrictions that may limit their freedom of choice.

1. The member's primary obligation is to respect the integrity and promote the welfare of the client(s), whether the client(s) is (are) assisted individually or in a group relationship. In a group setting, the member is also responsible for taking reasonable precautions to protect individuals from physical and/or psychological trauma resulting from interaction within the group.

2. Members make provisions for maintaining confidentiality in the storage and disposal of records and follow an established record retention and disposition policy. The counseling relationship and information resulting therefrom must be kept confidential, consistent with the obligations of the member as a professional person. In a group counseling setting, the counselor must set a norm of confidentiality regarding all group participants' disclosures.

3. If an individual is already in a counseling relationship with another professional person, the member does not enter into a counseling relationship without first contacting and receiving the approval of that other professional. If the member discovers that the client is in another counseling relationship after the counseling relationship begins, the member must gain the consent of the other professional or terminate the relationship, unless the client elects to terminate the other relationship.

4. When the client's condition indicates that there is clear and imminent danger to the client or others, the member must take reasonable personal action or inform responsible authorities. Consultation with other professionals must be used where possible. The assumption of responsibility for the client's(s') behavior must be taken only after careful deliberation.

The client must be involved in the resumption of responsibility as quickly as possible.

5. Records of the counseling relationship, including interview notes, test data, correspondence, tape recordings, electronic data storage, and other documents are to be considered professional information for use in counseling, and they should not be considered a part of the records of the institution or agency in which the counselor is employed unless specified by state statute or regulation. Revelation to others of counseling material must occur only upon the expressed consent of the client.

6. In view of the extensive data storage and processing capacities of the computer, the member must ensure that data maintained on a computer is: (a) limited to information that is appropriate and necessary for the services being provided; (b) destroyed after it is determined that the information is no longer of any value in providing services; and (c) restricted in terms of access to appropriate staff members involved in the provision of services by using the best computer security methods available.

7. Use of data derived from a counseling relationship for purposes of counselor training or research shall be confined to content that can be disguised to ensure full protection of the identity of the subject client.

8. The member must inform the client of the purposes, goals, techniques, rules of procedure, and limitations that may affect the relationship at or before the time that the counseling relationship is entered. When working with minors or persons who are unable to give consent, the member protects these clients' best interests.

9. In view of common misconceptions related to the perceived inherent validity of computer generated data and narrative reports, the member must ensure that the client is provided with information as part of the counseling relationship that adequately explains the limitations of computer technology.

10. The member must screen prospective group participants, especially when the emphasis is on self-understanding and growth through self-disclosure. The member must maintain an awareness of the group participants' compatibility throughout the life of the group.

11. The member may choose to consult with any other professionally competent person about a client. In choosing a consultant, the member must avoid placing the consultant in a conflict of interest situation that would preclude the consultant's being a proper party to the member's efforts to help the client.

12. If the member determines an inability to be of professional assistance to the client, the member must either avoid initiating the counseling relationship or immediately terminate that relationship. In either event, the member must suggest appropriate alternatives. (The member must be knowledgeable about referral resources so that a satisfactory referral can be initiated.) In the event the client declines the suggested referral, the member is not obligated to continue the relationship.

13. When the member has other relationships, particularly of an administrative, supervisory, and/or evaluative nature with an individual seeking counseling services, the member must not serve as the counselor but should refer the individual to another professional. Only in instances where such an alternative is unavailable and where the individual's situation warrants counseling intervention should the member enter into and/or maintain a counseling relationship. Dual relationships with clients that might impair the member's objectivity and professional judgment (e.g., as with close friends or relatives) must be avoided and/or the counseling relationship terminated through referral to another competent professional.

14. The member will avoid any type of sexual intimacies with clients. Sexual relationships with clients are unethical.

15. All experimental methods of treatment must be clearly indicated to prospective recipients, and safety precautions are to be adhered to by the member.

16. When computer applications are used as a component of counseling services, the member must ensure that: (a) the client is intellectually, emotionally, and physically capable of using the computer application; (b) the computer application is appropriate for the needs of the client; (c) the client understands the purpose and operation of the computer application; and (d) that a follow-up of client use of a computer application is provided to both correct possible problems (misconceptions or inappropriate use) and assess subsequent needs.

17. When the member is engaged in short-term group treatment/ training programs (e.g., marathons and other encounter-type or growth groups), the member ensures that there is professional assistance available during and following the group experience.

18. Should the member be engaged in a work setting that calls for any variation from the above statements, the member is obligated to consult with other professionals whenever possible to consider justifiable alternatives.

19. The member must ensure that members of various ethnic, racial, religious, disability, and socioeconomic groups have equal access to computer applications used to support counseling services and that the content of available computer applications does not discriminate against the groups described above.

20. When computer applications are developed by the member for use by the general public as self-help/stand-alone computer software, the member must ensure that: (a) self-help computer applications are designed from the beginning to function in a stand-alone manner, as opposed to modifying software that was originally designed to require support from a counselor; (b) self-help computer applications will include within the program statements regarding intended user outcomes, suggestions for using the software, a description of the conditions under which self-help com-

puter applications might not be appropriate, and a description of when and how counseling services might be beneficial; and (c) the manual for such applications will include the qualifications of the developer, the development process, validation data, and operating procedures.

Section C: Measurement and Evaluation

The primary purpose of educational and psychological testing is to provide descriptive measures that are objective and interpretable in either comparable or absolute terms. The member must recognize the need to interpret the statements that follow as applying to the whole range of appraisal techniques including test and nontest data. Test results constitute only one of a variety of pertinent sources of information for personnel, guidance, and counseling decisions.

1. The member must provide specific orientation or information to the examinee(s) prior to and following the test administration so that the results of testing may be placed in proper perspective with other relevant factors. In so doing, the member must recognize the effects of socioeconomic, ethnic, and cultural factors on test scores. It is the member's professional responsibility to use additional unvalidated information carefully in modifying interpretation of the test results.

2. In selecting tests for use in a given situation or with a particular client, the member must consider carefully the specific validity, reliability, and appropriateness of the test(s). General validity, reliability, and related issues may be questioned legally as well as ethically when tests are used for vocational and educational selection, placement, or counseling.

3. When making any statements to the public about tests and testing, the member must give accurate information and avoid false claims or misconceptions. Special efforts are often required to avoid unwarranted connotations of such terms as IQ and grade equivalent scores.

4. Different tests demand different levels of competence for administration, scoring, and interpretation. Members must recognize the limits of their competence and perform only those functions for which they are prepared. In particular, members using computer-based test interpretations must be trained in the construct being measured and the specific instrument being used prior to using this type of computer application.

5. In situations where a computer is used for test administration and scoring, the member is responsible for ensuring that administration and scoring programs function properly to provide clients with accurate test results.

6. Tests must be administered under the same conditions that were established in their standardization. When tests are not administered under standard conditions or when unusual behavior or irregularities occur during the testing session, those conditions must be noted and the results designated as invalid or of questionable validity. Unsupervised or inade-

quately supervised test-taking, such as the use of tests through the mails, is considered unethical. On the other hand, the use of instruments that are so designed or standardized to be self-administered and self-scored, such as interest inventories, is to be encouraged.

7. The meaningfulness of test results used in personnel, guidance, and counseling functions generally depends on the examinee's unfamiliarity with the specific items on the test. Any prior coaching or dissemination of the test materials can invalidate test results. Therefore, test security is one of the professional obligations of the member. Conditions that produce most favorable test results must be made known to the examinee.

8. The purpose of testing and the explicit use of the results must be made known to the examinee prior to testing. The counselor must ensure that instrument limitations are not exceeded and that periodic review and/or retesting are made to prevent client stereotyping.

9. The examinee's welfare and explicit prior understanding must be the criteria for determining the recipients of the test results. The member must see that specific interpretation accompanies any release of individual or group test data. The interpretation of test data must be related to the examinee's particular concerns.

10. Members responsible for making decisions based on test results have an understanding of educational and psychological measurement, validation criteria, and test research.

11. The member must be cautious when interpreting the results of research instruments possessing insufficient technical data. The specific purposes for the use of such instruments must be stated explicitly to examinees.

12. The member must proceed with caution when attempting to evaluate and interpret the performance of minority group members or other persons who are not represented in the norm group on which the instrument was standardized.

13. When computer-based test interpretations are developed by the member to support the assessment process, the member must ensure that the validity of such interpretations is established prior to the commercial distribution of such a computer application.

14. The member recognizes that test results may become obsolete. The member will avoid and prevent the misuse of obsolete test results.

15. The member must guard against the appropriation, reproduction, or modification of published tests or parts thereof without acknowledgment and permission from the previous publisher.

Section D: Research and Publication

1. Guidelines on research with human subjects shall be adhered to, such as:

a. Ethical Principles in the Conduct of Research with Human Participants, Washington, DC: American Psychological Association, Inc., 1982.

b. Code of Federal Regulations, Title 45, Subtitle A, Part 46, as currently issued.

c. *Ethical Principles of Psychologists,* American Psychological Association, Principle #9: Research with Human Participants.

d. Family Educational Rights and Privacy Act (the "Buckley Amendment").

e. Current federal regulations and various state rights privacy acts.

2. In planning any research activity dealing with human subjects, the member must be aware of and responsive to all pertinent ethical principles and ensure that the research problem, design, and execution are in full compliance with them.

3. Responsibility for ethical research practice lies with the principal researcher, while others involved in the research activities share ethical obligation and full responsibility for their own actions.

4. In research with human subjects, researchers are responsible for the subjects' welfare throughout the experiment, and they must take all reasonable precautions to avoid causing injurious psychological, physical, or social effects on their subjects.

5. All research subjects must be informed of the purpose of the study except when withholding information or providing misinformation to them is essential to the investigation. In such research the member must be responsible for corrective action as soon as possible following completion of the research.

6. Participation in research must be voluntary. Involuntary participation is appropriate only when it can be demonstrated that participation will have no harmful effects on subjects and is essential to the investigation.

7. When reporting research results, explicit mention must be made of all variables and conditions known to the investigator that might affect the outcome of the investigation or the interpretation of the data.

8. The member must be responsible for conducting and reporting investigations in a manner that minimizes the possibility that results will be misleading.

9. The member has an obligation to make available sufficient original research data to qualified others who may wish to replicate the study.

10. When supplying data, aiding in the research of another person, reporting research results, or in making original data available, due care must be taken to disguise the identity of the subjects in the absence of specific authorization from such subjects to do otherwise.

11. When conducting and reporting research, the member must be familiar with and give recognition to previous work on the topic, as well as to observe all copyright laws and follow the principles of giving full credit to all to whom credit is due.

12. The member must give due credit through joint authorship, acknowledgment, footnote statements, or other appropriate means to those who have contributed significantly to the research and/or publication, in accordance with such contributions.

13. The member must communicate to other members the results of any research judged to be of professional or scientific value. Results reflecting unfavorably on institutions, programs, services, or vested interests must not be withheld for such reasons.

14. If members agree to cooperate with another individual in research and/or publication, they incur an obligation to cooperate as promised in terms of punctuality of performance and with full regard to the completeness and accuracy of the information required.

15. Ethical practice requires that authors not submit the same manuscript or one essentially similar in content for simultaneous publication consideration by two or more journals. In addition, manuscripts published in whole or in substantial part in another journal or published work should not be submitted for publication without acknowledgment and permission from the previous publication.

Section E: Consulting

Consultation refers to a voluntary relationship between a professional helper and help-needing individual, group, or social unit in which the consultant is providing help to the client(s) in defining and solving a work-related problem or potential problem with a client or client system.

1. The member acting as consultant must have a high degree of self-awareness of his/her own values, knowledge, skills, limitations, and needs in entering a helping relationship that involves human and/or organizational change and that the focus of the relationship be on the issues to be resolved and not on the person(s) presenting the problem.

2. There must be understanding and agreement between member and client for the problem definition, change of goals, and prediction of consequences of interventions selected.

3. The member must be reasonably certain that she/he or the organization represented has the necessary competencies and resources for giving the kind of help that is needed now or may be needed later and that appropriate referral resources are available to the consultant.

4. The consulting relationship must be one in which client adaptability and growth toward self-direction are encouraged and cultivated. The member must maintain this role consistently and not become a decision maker for the client or create a future dependency on the consultant.

5. When announcing consultant availability for services, the member conscientiously adheres to the Association's Ethical Standards.

6. The member must refuse a private fee or other remuneration for consultation with persons who are entitled to these services through the

member's employing institution or agency. The policies of a particular agency may make explicit provisions for private practice with agency clients by members of its staff. In such instances, the clients must be apprised of other options open to them should they seek private counseling services.

Section F: Private Practice

1. The member should assist the profession by facilitating the availability of counseling services in private as well as public settings.

2. In advertising services as a private practitioner, the member must advertise the services in a manner that accurately informs the public of professional services, expertise, and techniques of counseling available. A member who assumes an executive leadership role in the organization shall not permit his/her name to be used in professional notices during periods when he/she is not actively engaged in the private practice of counseling.

3. The member may list the following: highest relevant degree, type and level of certification and/or license, address, telephone number, office hours, type and/or description of services, and other relevant information. Such information must not contain false, inaccurate, misleading, partial, out-of-context, or deceptive material or statements.

4. Members do not present their affiliation with any organization in such a way that would imply inaccurate sponsorship or certification by that organization.

5. Members may join in partnership/corporation with other members and/or other professionals provided that each member of the partnership or corporation makes clear the separate specialties by name in compliance with the regulations of the locality.

6. A member has an obligation to withdraw from a counseling relationship if it is believed that employment will result in violation of the Ethical Standards. If the mental or physical condition of the member renders it difficult to carry out an effective professional relationship or if the member is discharged by the client because the counseling relationship is no longer productive for the client, then the member is obligated to terminate the counseling relationship.

7. A member must adhere to the regulations for private practice of the locality where the services are offered.

8. It is unethical to use one's institutional affiliation to recruit clients for one's private practice.

Section G: Personnel Administration

It is recognized that most members are employed in public or quasi-public institutions. The functioning of a member within an institution must contribute to the goals of the institution and vice versa if either is to accomplish their respective goals or objectives. It is therefore essential that the member and the institution function in ways to: (a) make the institution's goals explicit and public; (b) make the member's contribution to institutional goals specific; and (c) foster mutual accountability for goal achievement.

To accomplish these objectives, it is recognized that the member and the employer must share responsibilities in the formulation and implementation of personnel policies.

1. Members must define and describe the parameters and levels of their professional competency.

2. Members must establish interpersonal relations and working agreements with supervisors and subordinates regarding counseling or clinical relationships, confidentiality, distinction between public and private material, maintenance and dissemination of recorded information, work load, and accountability. Working agreements in each instance must be specified and made known to those concerned.

3. Members must alert their employers to conditions that may be potentially disruptive or damaging.

4. Members must inform employers of conditions that may limit their effectiveness.

5. Members must submit regularly to professional review and evaluation.

6. Members must be responsible for inservice development of self and/or staff.

7. Members must inform their staff of goals and programs.

8. Members must provide personnel practices that guarantee and enhance the rights and welfare of each recipient of their service.

9. Members must select competent persons and assign responsibilities compatible with their skills and experiences.

10. The member, at the onset of a counseling relationship, will inform the client of the member's intended use of supervisors regarding the disclosure of information concerning this case. The member will clearly inform the client of the limits of confidentiality in the relationship.

11. Members, as either employers or employees, do not engage in or condone practices that are inhumane, illegal, or unjustifiable (such as considerations based on sex, handicap, age, race) in hiring, promotion, or training.

Section H: Preparation Standards

Members who are responsible for training others must be guided by the preparation standards of the Association and relevant Division(s). The member who functions in the capacity of trainer assumes unique ethical responsibilities that frequently go beyond that of the member who does not function in a training capacity. These ethical responsibilities are outlined as follows:

1. Members must orient students to program expectations, basic skills development, and employment prospects prior to admission to the program.

2. Members in charge of learning experiences must establish programs that integrate academic study and supervised practice.

3. Members must establish a program directed toward developing students' skills, knowledge, and self-understanding, stated whenever possible in competency or performance terms.

4. Members must identify the levels of competencies of their students in compliance with relevant Division standards. These competencies must accommodate the paraprofessional as well as the professional.

5. Members, through continual student evaluation and appraisal, must be aware of the personal limitations of the learner that might impede future performance. The instructor must not only assist the learner in securing remedial assistance but also screen from the program those individuals who are unable to provide competent services.

6. Members must provide a program that includes training in research commensurate with levels of role functioning. Paraprofessional and technician-level personnel must be trained as consumers of research. In addition, personnel must learn how to evaluate their own and their program's effectiveness. Graduate training, especially at the doctoral level, would include preparation for original research by the member.

7. Members must make students aware of the ethical responsibilities and standards of the profession.

8. Preparatory programs must encourage students to value the ideals of service to individuals and to society. In this regard, direct financial remuneration or lack thereof must not influence the quality of service rendered. Monetary considerations must not be allowed to overshadow professional and humanitarian needs.

9. Members responsible for educational programs must be skilled as teachers and practitioners.

10. Members must present thoroughly varied theoretical positions so that students may make comparisons and have the opportunity to select a position.

11. Members must develop clear policies within their educational institutions regarding field placement and the roles of the student and the instructor in such placement.

12. Members must ensure that forms of learning focusing on self-understanding or growth are voluntary, or if required as part of the educational program, are made known to prospective students prior to entering the program. When the educational program offers a growth experience with an emphasis on self-disclosure or other relatively intimate or personal involvement, the member must have no administrative, supervisory, or evaluating authority regarding the participant.

13. The member will at all times provide students with clear and

equally acceptable alternatives for self-understanding or growth experiences. The member will assure students that they have a right to accept these alternatives without prejudice or penalty.

14. Members must conduct an educational program in keeping with the current relevant guidelines of the Association.

Ethical Principles of Psychologists
American Psychological Association
(Amended June 2, 1989)

PREAMBLE

Psychologists respect the dignity and worth of the individual and strive for the preservation and protection of fundamental human rights. They are committed to increasing knowledge of human behavior and of people's understanding of themselves and others and to the utilization of such knowledge for the promotion of human welfare. While pursuing these objectives, they make every effort to protect the welfare of those who seek their services and of the research participants that may be the object of study. They use their skills only for purposes consistent with these values and do not knowingly permit their misuse by others. While demanding for themselves freedom of inquiry and communication, psychologists accept the responsibility this freedom requires: competence, objectivity in the application of skills, and concern for the best interests of clients, colleagues, students, research participants, and society. In the pursuit of these ideals, psychologists subscribe to principles in the following areas: 1. Responsibility, 2. Competence, 3. Moral and Legal Standards, 4. Public Statements, 5. Confidentiality, 6. Welfare of the Consumer, 7. Professional Relationships, 8. Assessment Techniques, 9. Research with Human Participants, and 10. Care and Use of Animals.

Acceptance of membership in the American Psychological Association commits the member to adherence to these principles.

Psychologists cooperate with duly constituted committees of the American Psychological Association, in particular, the Committee on Scientific and Professional Ethics and Conduct, by responding to inquiries promptly and completely. Members also respond promptly and completely to inquiries from duly constituted state association ethics committees and professional standards review committees.

Principle 1: Responsibility

In providing services, psychologists maintain the highest standards of their profession. They accept responsibility for the consequences of their acts and make every effort to ensure that their services are used appropriately.

a. As scientists, psychologists accept responsibility for the selection of their research topics and the methods used in investigation, analysis, and reporting. They plan their research in ways to minimize the possibility that their findings will be misleading. They provide thorough discussion of the limitations of their data, especially where their work touches on social policy or might be construed to the detriment of persons in specific age, sex, ethnic, socioeconomic, or other social groups. In publishing reports of their work, they never suppress disconfirming data, and they acknowledge the existence of alternative hypotheses and explanations of their findings. Psychologists take credit only for work they have actually done.

b. Psychologists clarify in advance with all appropriate persons and agencies the expectations for sharing and utilizing research data. They avoid relationships that may limit their objectivity or create a conflict of interest. Interference with the milieu in which data are collected is kept to a minimum.

c. Psychologists have the responsibility to attempt to prevent distortion, misuse, or suppression of psychological findings by the institution or agency of which they are employees.

d. As members of governmental or other organizational bodies, psychologists remain accountable as individuals to the highest standards of their profession.

e. As teachers, psychologists recognize their primary obligation to help others acquire knowledge and skill. They maintain high standards of scholarship by presenting psychological information objectively, fully, and accurately.

f. As practitioners, psychologists know that they bear a heavy social responsibility because their recommendations and professional actions may alter the lives of others. They are alert to personal, social, organizational, financial, or political situations and pressures that might lead to misuse of their influence.

Principle 2: Competence

The maintenance of high standards of competence is a responsibility shared by all psychologists in the interest of the public and the profession as a whole. Psychologists recognize the boundaries of their competence and the limitations of their techniques. They only provide services and only use techniques for which they are qualified by training and experience. In those areas in which recognized standards do not yet exist, psychologists take whatever precautions are necessary to protect the welfare of their clients. They maintain knowledge of current scientific and professional information related to the services they render.

a. Psychologists accurately represent their competence, education, training, and experience. They claim as evidence of educational qualifications only those degrees obtained from institutions acceptable under the Bylaws and Rules of Council of the American Psychological Association.

b. As teachers, psychologists perform their duties on the basis of careful preparation so that their instruction is accurate, current, and scholarly.

c. Psychologists recognize the need for continuing education and are open to new procedures and changes in expectations and values over time.

d. Psychologists recognize differences among people, such as those that may be associated with age, sex, socioeconomic, and ethnic backgrounds. When necessary, they obtain training, experience, or counsel to assure competent service or research relating to such persons.

e. Psychologists responsible for decisions involving individuals or policies based on test results have an understanding of psychological or educational measurement, validation problems, and test research.

f. Psychologists recognize that personal problems and conflicts may interfere with professional effectiveness. Accordingly, they refrain from undertaking any activity in which their personal problems are likely to lead to inadequate performance or harm to a client, colleague, student, or research participant. If engaged in such activity when they become aware of their personal problems, they seek competent professional assistance to determine whether they should suspend, terminate, or limit the scope of their professional and/or scientific activities.

Principle 3: Moral and Legal Standards

Psychologists' moral and ethical standards of behavior are a personal matter to the same degree as they are for any other citizen, except as these may compromise the fulfillment of their professional responsibilities or reduce the public trust in psychology and psychologists. Regarding their own behavior, psychologists are sensitive to prevailing community standards and to the possible impact that conformity to or deviation from these standards may have upon the quality of their performance as psychologists. Psychologists are also aware of the possible impact of their public behavior upon the ability of colleagues to perform their professional duties.

a. As teachers, psychologists are aware of the fact that their personal values may affect the selection and presentation of instructional materials. When dealing with topics that may give offense, they recognize and respect the diverse attitudes that students may have toward such materials.

b. As employees or employers, psychologists do not engage in or condone practices that are inhumane or that result in illegal or unjustifiable actions. Such practices include, but are not limited to, those based on considerations of race, handicap, age, gender, sexual preference, religion, or national origin in hiring, promotion, or training.

c. In their professional roles, psychologists avoid any action that will violate or diminish the legal and civil rights of clients or of others who may be affected by their actions.

d. As practitioners and researchers, psychologists act in accord with Association standards and guidelines related to practice and to the conduct of research with human beings and animals. In the ordinary course of events, psychologists adhere to relevant governmental laws and institutional regulations. When federal, state, provincial, organizational, or institutional laws, regulations, or practices are in conflict with Association standards and guidelines, psychologists make known their commitment to Association standards and guidelines and, wherever possible, work toward a resolution of the conflict. Both practitioners and researchers are concerned with the development of such legal and quasi-legal regulations as best serve the public interest, and they work toward changing existing regulations that are not beneficial to the public interest.

Principle 4: Public Statements

Public statements, announcements of services, advertising, and promotional activities of psychologists serve the purpose of helping the public make informed judgments and choices. Psychologists represent accurately and objectively their professional qualifications, affiliations, and functions, as well as those of the institutions or organizations with which they or the statements may be associated. In public statements providing psychological information or professional opinions or providing information about the availability of psychological products, publications, and services, psychologists base their statements on scientifically acceptable psychological findings and techniques with full recognition of the limits and uncertainties of such evidence.

a. When announcing or advertising professional services, psychologists may list the following information to describe the provider and services provided: name, highest relevant academic degree earned from a regionally accredited institution, date, type, and level of certification or licensure, diplomate status, APA membership status, address, telephone number, office hours, a brief listing of the type of psychological services offered, an appropriate presentation of fee information, foreign languages spoken, and policy with regard to third-party payments. Additional relevant or important consumer information may be included if not prohibited by other sections of these Ethical Principles.

b. In announcing or advertising the availability of psychological products, publications, or services, psychologists do not present their affiliation with any organization in a manner that falsely implies sponsorship or certification by that organization. In particular and for example, psychologists do not state APA membership or fellow status in a way to suggest that such status implies specialized professional competence or qualifications. Public statements include, but are not limited to, communication by means of periodical, book, list, directory, television, radio, or motion picture. They do not contain (i) a false, fraudulent, misleading, deceptive, or unfair statement; (ii) a misinterpretation of fact or a statement likely to mislead or deceive because in context it makes only a partial disclosure of relevant facts; (iii) a statement intended or likely to create false or unjustified expectations of favorable results.

c. Psychologists do not compensate or give anything of value to a representative of the press, radio, television, or other communication medium in anticipation of or in return for professional publicity in a news item. A paid advertisement must be identified as such, unless it is apparent from the context that it is a paid advertisement. If communicated to the public by use of radio or television, an advertisement is prerecorded and approved for broadcast by the psychologist, and a recording of the actual transmission is retained by the psychologist.

d. Announcements or advertisements of "personal growth groups," clinics, and agencies give a clear statement of purpose and a clear description of the experiences to be provided. The education, training, and experience of the staff members are appropriately specified.

e. Psychologists associated with the development or promotion of psychological devices, books, or other products offered for commercial sale make reasonable efforts to ensure that announcements and advertisements are presented in a professional, scientifically acceptable, and factually informative manner.

f. Psychologists do not participate for personal gain in commercial announcements or advertisements recommending to the public the purchase or use of proprietary or single-source products or services when that participation is based solely upon their identification as psychologists.

g. Psychologists present the science of psychology and offer their services, products, and publications fairly and accurately, avoiding misrepresentation through sensationalism, exaggeration, or superficiality. Psychologists are guided by the primary obligation to aid the public in developing informed judgments, opinions, and choices.

h. As teachers, psychologists ensure that statements in catalogs and course outlines are accurate and not misleading, particularly in terms of subject matter to be covered, bases for evaluating progress, and the nature of course experiences. Announcements, brochures, or advertisements describing workshops, seminars, or other educational programs accurately describe the audience for which the program is intended as well as eligibility requirements, educational objectives, and nature of the materials to be covered. These announcements also accurately represent the education, training, and experience of the psychologists presenting the programs and any fees involved.

i. Public announcements or advertisements soliciting research participants in which clinical services or other professional services are offered as an inducement make clear the nature of the services as well as the costs and other obligations to be accepted by participants in the research.

j. A psychologist accepts the obligation to correct others who represent the psychologist's professional qualifications, or associations with products or services, in a manner incompatible with these guidelines.

k. Individual diagnostic and therapeutic services are provided only in the context of a professional psychological relationship. When personal advice is given by means of public lectures or demonstrations, newspaper or magazine articles, radio or television programs, mail, or similar media, the psychologist utilizes the most current relevant data and exercises the highest level of professional judgment.

l. Products that are described or presented by means of public lectures or demonstrations, newspaper or magazine articles, radio or television programs, or similar media meet the same recognized standards as exist for products used in the context of a professional relationship.

Principle 5: Confidentiality

Psychologists have a primary obligation to respect the confidentiality of information obtained from persons in the course of their work as psychologists. They reveal such information to others only with the consent of the person or the person's legal representative, except in those unusual circumstances in which not to do so would result in clear danger to the person or to others. Where appropriate, psychologists inform their clients of the legal limits of confidentiality.

a. Information obtained in clinical or consulting relationships, or evaluative data concerning children, students, employees, and others, is discussed only for professional purposes and only with persons clearly concerned with the case. Written and oral reports present only data germane to the purposes of the evaluation, and every effort is made to avoid undue invasion of privacy.

b. Psychologists who present personal information obtained during the course of professional work in writings, lectures, or other public forums either obtain adequate prior consent to do so or adequately disguise all identifying information.

c. Psychologists make provisions for maintaining confidentiality in the storage and disposal of records.

d. When working with minors or other persons who are unable to give voluntary, informed consent, psychologists take special care to protect these persons' best interests.

Principle 6: Welfare of the Consumer

Psychologists respect the integrity and protect the welfare of the people and groups with whom they work. When conflicts of interest arise between clients and psychologists' employing institutions, psychologists clarify the nature and direction of their loyalties and responsibilities and keep all parties informed of their commitments. Psychologists fully inform consumers as to the purpose and nature of an evaluative, treatment, educational, or training procedure, and they freely acknowledge that clients, students, or participants in research have freedom of choice with regard to participation.

a. Psychologists are continually cognizant of their own needs and of their potentially influential position vis-à-vis persons such as clients, students, and subordinates. They avoid exploiting the trust and dependency of such persons. Psychologists make every effort to avoid dual relationships that could impair their professional judgment or increase the risk of exploitation. Examples of such dual relationships include, but are not limited to, research with and treatment of employees, students, supervisees, close friends, or relatives. Sexual intimacies with clients are unethical.

b. When a psychologist agrees to provide services to a client at the request of a third party, the psychologist assumes the responsibility of clarifying the nature of the relationships to all parties concerned.

c. Where the demands of an organization require psychologists to violate these Ethical Principles, psychologists clarify the nature of the conflict between the demands and these principles. They inform all parties of psychologists' ethical responsibilities and take appropriate action.

d. Psychologists make advance financial arrangements that safeguard the best interests of and are clearly understood by their clients. They contribute a portion of their services to work for which they receive little or no financial return.

e. Psychologists terminate a clinical or consulting relationship when it is reasonably clear that the consumer is not benefiting from it. They offer to help the consumer locate alternative sources of assistance.

Principle 7: Professional Relationships

Psychologists act with due regard for the needs, special competencies, and obligations of their colleagues in psychology and other professions. They respect the prerogatives and obligations of the institutions or organizations with which these other colleagues are associated.

a. Psychologists understand the areas of competence of related professions. They make full use of all the professional, technical, and administrative resources that serve the best interests of consumers. The absence of formal relationships with other professional workers does not relieve psychologists of the responsibility of securing for their clients the best possible professional service, nor does it relieve them of the obligation to exercise foresight, diligence, and tact in obtaining the complementary or alternative assistance needed by clients.

b. Psychologists know and take into account the traditions and practices of other professional groups with whom they work and cooperate fully with such groups. If a psychologist is contacted by a person who is already receiving similar services from another professional, the psychologist carefully considers that professional relationship and proceeds with caution and sensitivity to the therapeutic issues as well as the client's welfare. The psychologist discusses these issues with the client so as to minimize the risk of confusion and conflict.

c. Psychologists who employ or supervise other professionals or professionals in training accept the obligation to facilitate the further professional development of these individuals. They provide appropriate working conditions, timely evaluations, constructive consultation, and experience opportunities.

d. Psychologists do not exploit their professional relationships with clients, supervisees, students, employees, or research participants sexually or otherwise. Psychologists do not condone or engage in sexual harassment. Sexual harassment is defined as deliberate or repeated comments, gestures, or physical contacts of a sexual nature that are unwanted by the recipient.

e. In conducting research in institutions or organizations, psychologists secure appropriate authorization to conduct such research. They are aware of their obligations to future research workers and ensure that host institutions receive adequate information about the research and proper acknowledgment of their contributions.

f. Publication credit is assigned to those who have contributed to a publication in proportion to their professional contributions. Major contributions of a professional character made by several persons to a common project are recognized by joint authorship, with the individual who made the principal contribution listed first. Minor contributions of a professional character and extensive clerical or similar nonprofessional assistance may be acknowledged in footnotes or in an introductory statement. Acknowledgment through specific citations is made for unpublished as well as published material that has directly influenced the research or writing. Psychologists who compile and edit material of others for publication publish the material in the name of the originating group, if appropriate, with their own name appearing as chairperson or editor. All contributors are to be acknowledged and named.

g. When psychologists know of an ethical violation by another psychologist, and it seems appropriate, they informally attempt to resolve the issue by bringing the behavior to the attention of the psychologist. If the misconduct is of a minor nature and/or appears to be due to lack of sensitivity, knowledge, or experience, such an informal solution is usually appropriate. Such informal corrective efforts are made with sensitivity to any rights to confidentiality involved. If the violation does not seem amenable to an informal solution, or is of a more serious nature, psychologists bring it to the attention of the appropriate local, state, and/or national committee on professional ethics and conduct.

Principle 8: Assessment Techniques

In the development, publication, and utilization of psychological assessment techniques, psychologists make every effort to promote the welfare and best interests of the client. They guard against the misuse of assessment results. They respect the client's right to know the results, the interpretations made, and the bases for their conclusions and recommendations. Psychologists make every effort to maintain the security of tests and other assessment techniques within limits of legal mandates. They strive to ensure the appropriate use of assessment techniques by others.

a. In using assessment techniques, psychologists respect the right of clients to have full explanations of the nature and purpose of the techniques in language the clients can understand, unless an explicit exception to this right has been agreed upon in advance. When the explanations are to be provided by others, psychologists establish procedures for ensuring the adequacy of these explanations.

b. Psychologists responsible for the development and standardization of psychological tests and other assessment techniques utilize established scientific procedures and observe the relevant APA standards.

c. In reporting assessment results, psychologists indicate any reservations that exist regarding validity or reliability because of the circumstances of the assessment or the inappropriateness of the norms for the person tested. Psychologists strive to ensure that the results of assessments and their interpretations are not misused by others.

d. Psychologists recognize that assessment results may become obsolete. They make every effort to avoid and prevent the misuse of obsolete measures.

e. Psychologists offering scoring and interpretation services are able to produce appropriate evidence for the validity of the programs and procedures used in arriving at interpretations. The public offering of an automated interpretation service is considered a professional-to-professional consultation. Psychologists make every effort to avoid misuse of assessment reports.

f. Psychologists do not encourage or promote the use of psychological assessment techniques by inappropriately trained or otherwise unqualified persons through teaching, sponsorship, or supervision.

Principle 9: Research with Human Participants

The decision to undertake research rests upon a considered judgment by the individual psychologist about how best to contribute to psychological science and human welfare. Having made the decision to conduct research, the psychologist considers alternative directions in which research energies and resources might be invested. On the basis of this consideration, the psychologist carries out the investigation with respect and concern for the dignity and welfare of the people who participate and with cognizance of federal and state regulations and professional standards governing the conduct of research with human participants.

a. In planning a study, the investigator has the responsibility to make a careful evaluation of its ethical acceptability. To the extent that the weighing of scientific and human values suggests a compromise of any principle, the investigator incurs a correspondingly serious obligation to seek ethical advice and to observe stringent safeguards to protect the rights of human participants.

b. Considering whether a participant in a planned study will be a "subject at risk" or a "subject at minimal risk," according to recognized standards, is of primary ethical concern to the investigator.

c. The investigator always retains the responsibility for ensuring ethical practice in research. The investigator is also responsible for the ethical treatment of research participants by collaborators, assistants, students, and employees, all of whom, however, incur similar obligations.

d. Except in minimal-risk research, the investigator establishes a clear and fair agreement with research participants, prior to their participation, that clarifies the obligations and responsibilities of each. The investigator has the obligation to honor all promises and commitments included in that agreement. The investigator informs the participants of all aspects of the research that might reasonably be expected to influence willingness to participate and explains all other aspects of the research about which the participants inquire. Failure to make full disclosure prior to obtaining informed consent requires additional safeguards to protect the welfare and dignity of the research participants. Research with children or with participants who have impairments that would limit understanding and/or communication requires special safeguarding procedures.

e. Methodological requirements of a study may make the use of concealment or deception necessary. Before conducting such a study, the investigator has a special responsibility to (i) determine whether the use of such techniques is justified by the study's prospective scientific, educational, or applied value; (ii) determine whether alternative procedures are available that do not use concealment or deception; and (iii) ensure that the participants are provided with sufficient explanation as soon as possible.

f. The investigator respects the individual's freedom to decline to participate in or to withdraw from the research at any time. The obligation to protect this freedom requires careful thought and consideration when the investigator is in a position of authority or influence over the participant. Such positions of authority include, but are not limited to, situations in which research participation is required as part of employment or in which the participant is a student, client, or employee of the investigator.

g. The investigator protects the participant from physical and mental discomfort, harm, and danger that may arise from research procedures. If risks of such consequences exist, the investigator informs the participant of that fact. Research procedures likely to cause serious or lasting harm to a participant are not used unless the failure to use these procedures might expose the participant to risk of greater harm, or unless the research has great potential benefit and fully informed and voluntary consent is obtained from each participant. The participant should be informed of procedures for contacting the investigator within a reasonable time period following participation should stress, potential harm, or related questions or concerns arise.

h. After the data are collected, the investigator provides the participant with information about the nature of the study and attempts to remove any misconceptions that may have arisen. Where scientific or humane values justify delaying or withholding this information, the investigator incurs a special responsibility to monitor the research and to ensure that there are no damaging consequences for the participant.

i. Where research procedures result in undesirable consequences for the individual participant, the investigator has the responsibility to detect and remove or correct these consequences, including long-term effects.

j. Information obtained about a research participant during the course of an investigation is confidential unless otherwise agreed upon in advance. When the possibility exists that others may obtain access to such information, this possibility, together with the plans for protecting confidentiality, is explained to the participant as part of the procedure for obtaining informed consent.

Principle 10: Care and Use of Animals

An investigator of animal behavior strives to advance understanding of basic behavioral principles and/or to contribute to the improvement of human health and welfare. In seeking these ends, the investigator ensures the welfare of animals and treats them humanely. Laws and regulations notwithstanding, an animal's immediate protection depends upon the scientist's own conscience.

a. The acquisition, care, use, and disposal of all animals are in compliance with current federal, state or provincial, and local laws and regulations.

b. A psychologist trained in research methods and experienced in the care of laboratory animals closely supervises all procedures involving animals and is responsible for ensuring appropriate consideration of their comfort, health, and humane treatment.

c. Psychologists ensure that all individuals using animals under their supervision have received explicit instruction in experimental methods and in the care, maintenance, and handling of the species being used. Responsibilities and activities of individuals participating in a research project are consistent with their respective competencies.

d. Psychologists make every effort to minimize discomfort, illness, and pain of animals. A procedure subjecting animals to pain, stress, or privation is used only when an alternative procedure is unavailable and the goal is justified by its prospective scientific, educational, or applied value. Surgical procedures are performed under appropriate anesthesia; techniques to avoid infection and minimize pain are followed during and after surgery.

e. When it is appropriate that the animal's life be terminated, it is done rapidly and painlessly.

This version of the *Ethical Principles of Psychologists* was adopted by the American Psychological Association's Board of Directors on June 2, 1989. On that date, the Board of Directors rescinded several sections of the Ethical Principles that had been adopted by the APA Council of Representatives on January 24, 1981. Inquiries concerning the substance or interpretation of the *Ethical Principles of Psychologists* should be addressed to the Administrative Director, Office of Ethics, American Psychological Association, 1200 Seventeenth Street, N.W., Washington, DC 20036.

These Ethical Principles apply to psychologists, to students of psychology, and to others who do work of a psychological nature under the supervision of a psychologist. They are intended for the guidance of nonmembers of the Association who are engaged in psychological research or practice.

The Ethical Principles have previously been published as follows:

American Psychological Association. (1953). *Ethical Standards of Psychologists*, Washington, DC.

American Psychological Association. (1958). Standards of ethical behavior for psychologists. *American Psychologist, 13*, 268–271.

American Psychological Association. (1959). Ethical standards of psychologists. *American Psychologist, 14*, 279–282.

American Psychological Association. (1963). Ethical standards of psychologists. *American Psychologist, 18*, 56–60.

American Psychological Association. (1968). Ethical standards of psychologists. *American Psychologist, 23*, 357–361.

American Psychological Association. (1977, March). Ethical standards of psychologists. *The APA Monitor*, pp. 22–23.

American Psychological Association. (1979). *Ethical Standards of Psychologists*, Washington, DC: Author.

American Psychological Association. (1981). Ethical principles of psychologists. *American Psychologist, 36*, 633–638.

Request copies of the *Ethical Principles of Psychologists* from the APA Order Department, P.O. Box 2710, Hyattsville, MD 20784; or phone (703) 247-7705.

APPENDIX E

Code of Ethics
National Association of Social Workers

I. The Social Worker's Conduct
and Comportment as a Social Worker

A. *Propriety.* The social worker should maintain high standards of personal conduct in the capacity or identity as social worker.
  1. The private conduct of the social worker is a personal matter to the same degree as is any other person's, except when such conduct compromises the fulfillment of professional responsibilities.
  2. The social worker should not participate in, condone, or be associated with dishonesty, fraud, deceit, or misrepresentation.
  3. The social worker should distinguish clearly between statements and actions made as a private individual and as a representative of the social work profession or an organization or group.
B. *Competence and professional development.* The social worker should strive to become and remain proficient in professional practice and the performance of professional functions.
  1. The social worker should accept responsibility or employment only on the basis of existing competence or the intention to acquire the necessary competence.
  2. The social worker should not misrepresent professional qualifications, education, experience, or affiliations.
C. *Service.* The social worker should regard as primary the service obligation of the social work profession.
  1. The social worker should retain ultimate responsibility for the quality and extent of the service that individual assumes, assigns, or performs.
  2. The social worker should act to prevent practices that are inhumane or discriminatory against any person or group of persons.

Code of Ethics of the National Association of Social Workers, as adopted by the 1979 NASW Delegate Assembly and revised by the 1990 NASW Delegate Assembly. Copyright 1990, National Association of Social Workers, Inc. Reprinted by permission.

D. *Integrity.* The social worker should act in accordance with the highest standards of professional integrity and impartiality.
  1. The social worker should be alert to and resist the influences and pressures that interfere with the exercise of professional discretion and impartial judgment required for the performance of professional functions.
  2. The social worker should not exploit professional relationships for personal gain.
E. *Scholarship and research.* The social worker engaged in study and research should be guided by the conventions of scholarly inquiry.
  1. The social worker engaged in research should consider carefully its possible consequences for human beings.
  2. The social worker engaged in research should ascertain that the consent of participants in the research is voluntary and informed, without any implied deprivation or penalty for refusal to participate, and with due regard for participants' privacy and dignity.
  3. The social worker engaged in research should protect participants from unwarranted physical or mental discomfort, distress, harm, danger, or deprivation.
  4. The social worker who engages in the evaluation of services or cases should discuss them only for the professional purposes and only with persons directly and professionally concerned with them.
  5. Information obtained about participants in research should be treated as confidential.
  6. The social worker should take credit only for work actually done in connection with scholarly and research endeavors and credit contributions made by others.

II. The Social Worker's Ethical Responsibility to Clients

F. *Primacy of clients' interests.* The social worker's primary responsibility is to clients.
  1. The social worker should serve clients with devotion, loyalty, determination, and the maximum application of professional skill and competence.
  2. The social worker should not exploit relationships with clients for personal advantage.
  3. The social worker should not practice, condone, facilitate, or collaborate with any form of discrimination on the basis of race, color, sex, sexual orientation, age, religion, national origin, marital status, political belief, mental or physical handicap, or any other preference or personal characteristic, condition or status.
  4. The social worker should avoid relationships or commitments that conflict with the interests of clients.
  5. The social worker should under no circumstances engage in sexual activities with clients.

6. The social worker should provide clients with accurate and complete information regarding the extent and nature of the services available to them.

7. The social worker should apprise clients of their risks, rights, opportunities, and obligations associated with social service to them.

8. The social worker should seek advice and counsel of colleagues and supervisors whenever such consultation is in the best interest of clients.

9. The social worker should terminate service to clients, and professional relationships with them, when such service and relationships are no longer required or no longer serve the clients' needs or interests.

10. The social worker should withdraw services precipitously only under unusual circumstances, giving careful consideration to all factors in the situation and taking care to minimize possible adverse effects.

11. The social worker who anticipates the termination or interruption of service to clients should notify clients promptly and seek the transfer, referral, or continuation of services in relation to the clients' needs and preferences.

G. *Rights and prerogatives of clients.* The social worker should make every effort to foster maximum self-determination on the part of clients.

1. When the social worker must act on behalf of a client who has been adjudged legally incompetent, the social worker should safeguard the interests and rights of that client.

2. When another individual has been legally authorized to act in behalf of a client, the social worker should deal with that person always with the client's best interest in mind.

3. The social worker should not engage in any action that violates or diminishes the civil or legal rights of clients.

H. *Confidentiality and privacy.* The social worker should respect the privacy of clients and hold in confidence all information obtained in the course of professional service.

1. The social worker should share with others confidences revealed by clients, without their consent, only for compelling professional reasons.

2. The social worker should inform clients fully about the limits of confidentiality in a given situation, the purposes for which information is obtained, and how it may be used.

3. The social worker should afford clients reasonable access to any official social work records concerning them.

4. When providing clients with access to records, the social worker should take due care to protect the confidences of others contained in those records.

5. The social worker should obtain informed consent of clients before

taping, recording, or permitting third party observation of their activities.

I. *Fees.* When setting fees, the social worker should ensure that they are fair, reasonable, considerate, and commensurate with the service performed and with due regard for the clients' ability to pay.

   1. The social worker should not accept anything of value for making a referral.

III. The Social Worker's
Ethical Responsibility to Colleagues

J. *Respect, fairness, and courtesy.* The social worker should treat colleagues with respect, courtesy, fairness, and good faith.

   1. The social worker should cooperate with colleagues to promote professional interests and concerns.
   2. The social worker should respect confidences shared by colleagues in the course of their professional relationships and transactions.
   3. The social worker should create and maintain conditions of practice that facilitate ethical and competent professional performance by colleagues.
   4. The social worker should treat with respect, and represent accurately and fairly, the qualifications, views, and findings of colleagues and use appropriate channels to express judgments on these matters.
   5. The social worker who replaces or is replaced by a colleague in professional practice should act with consideration for the interest, character, and reputation of that colleague.
   6. The social worker should not exploit a dispute between a colleague and employers to obtain a position or otherwise advance the social worker's interest.
   7. The social worker should seek arbitration or mediation when conflicts with colleagues require resolution for compelling professional reasons.
   8. The social worker should extend to colleagues of other professions the same respect and cooperation that is extended to social work colleagues.
   9. The social worker who serves as an employer, supervisor, or mentor to colleagues should make orderly and explicit arrangements regarding the conditions of their continuing professional relationship.
   10. The social worker who has the responsibility for employing and evaluating the performance of other staff members, should fulfill such responsibility in a fair, considerate, and equitable manner, on the basis of clearly enunciated criteria.
   11. The social worker who has the responsibility for evaluating the

performance of employees, supervisees, or students should share evaluations with them.

K. *Dealing with colleagues' clients.* The social worker has the responsibility to relate to the clients of colleagues with full professional consideration.

   1. The social worker should not assume professional responsibility for the clients of another agency or a colleague without appropriate communication with that agency or colleague.

   2. The social worker who serves the clients of colleagues, during a temporary absence or emergency, should serve those clients with the same consideration as that afforded any client.

IV. The Social Worker's Ethical Responsibility to Employers and Employing Organizations

L. *Commitments to employing organization.* The social worker should adhere to commitments made to the employing organization.

   1. The social worker should work to improve the employing agency's policies and procedures, and the efficiency and effectiveness of its services.

   2. The social worker should not accept employment or arrange student field placements in an organization which is currently under public sanction by NASW for violating personnel standards, or imposing limitations on or penalties for professional actions on behalf of clients.

   3. The social worker should act to prevent and eliminate discrimination in the employing organization's work assignments and in its employment policies and practices.

   4. The social worker should use with scrupulous regard, and only for the purpose for which they are intended, the resources of the employing organization.

V. The Social Worker's Ethical Responsibility to the Social Work Profession

M. *Maintaining the integrity of the profession.* The social worker should uphold and advance the values, ethics, knowledge, and mission of the profession.

   1. The social worker should protect and enhance the dignity and integrity of the profession and should be responsible and vigorous in discussion and criticism of the profession.

   2. The social worker should take action through appropriate channels against unethical conduct by any other member of the profession.

   3. The social worker should act to prevent the unauthorized and unqualified practice of social work.

   4. The social worker should make no misrepresentation in advertising as to qualifications, competence, service, or results to be achieved.

N. *Community service.* The social worker should assist the profession in making social services available to the general public.
1. The social worker should contribute time and professional expertise to activities that promote respect for the utility, the integrity, and the competence of the social work profession.
2. The social worker should support the formulation, development, enactment, and implementation of social policies of concern to the profession.
O. *Development of knowledge.* The social worker should take responsibility for identifying, developing, and fully utilizing knowledge for professional practice.
1. The social worker should base practice upon recognized knowledge relevant to social work.
2. The social worker should critically examine and keep current with emerging knowledge relevant to social work.
3. The social worker should contribute to the knowledge base of social work and share research knowledge and practice wisdom with colleagues.

VI. The Social Worker's Ethical Responsibility to Society

P. *Promoting the general welfare.* The social worker should promote the general welfare of society.
1. The social worker should act to prevent and eliminate discrimination against any person or group on the basis of race, color, sex, sexual orientation, age, religion, national origin, marital status, political belief, mental or physical handicap, or any other preference or personal characteristic, condition, or status.
2. The social worker should act to ensure that all persons have access to the resources, services, and opportunities which they require.
3. The social worker should act to expand choice and opportunity for all persons, with special regard for disadvantaged or oppressed groups and persons.
4. The social worker should promote conditions that encourage respect for the diversity of cultures which constitute American society.
5. The social worker should provide appropriate professional services in public emergencies.
6. The social worker should advocate changes in policy and legislation to improve social conditions and to promote social justice.
7. The social worker should encourage informed participation by the public in shaping social policies and institutions.

Name Index

Subject Index